ANNALS OF COMMUNISM

Each volume in the series Annals of Communism will publish selected and previously inaccessible documents from former Soviet state and party archives in a narrative that develops a particular topic in the history of Soviet and international communism. Separate English and Russian editions will be prepared. Russian and Western scholars work together to prepare the documents for each volume. Documents are chosen not for their support of any single interpretation but for their particular historical importance or their general value in deepening understanding and facilitating discussion. The volumes are designed to be useful to students, scholars, and interested general readers.

EXECUTIVE EDITOR OF THE ANNALS OF COMMUNISM SERIES

Jonathan Brent, Yale University Press

PROJECT MANAGER

Vadim A. Staklo

AMERICAN ADVISORY COMMITTEE

Ivo Banac, Yale University
Zbigniew Brzezinski, Center for Strategic and International Studies
William Chase, University of Pittsburgh
Victor Erlich, Yale University
Friedrich I. Firsov, former head of the Comintern research group at RGASPI
Sheila Fitzpatrick, University of Chicago
Gregory Freeze, Brandeis University
John L. Gaddis, Yale University
J. Arch Getty, University of California, Los Angeles
Jonathan Haslam, Cambridge University

Robert L. Jackson, Yale University
Czeslaw Milosz (deceased), University of California, Berkeley
Norman Naimark, Stanford University
Gen. William Odom, Hudson Institute and Yale University
Daniel Orlovsky, Southern Methodist University
Mark Steinberg, University of Illinois, Urbana-Champaign
Strobe Talbott, Brookings Institution
Mark Von Hagen, Columbia University
Piotr Wandycz, Yale University

RUSSIAN ADVISORY COMMITTEE

K. M. Anderson, director, Russian State Archive of Social and Political History (RGASPI)
N. N. Bolkhovitinov, Russian Academy of Sciences
A. O. Chubaryan, Russian Academy of Sciences
V. P. Danilov, Russian Academy of Sciences
A. A. Fursenko, secretary, Department of History, Russian Academy of Sciences (head of the Russian Editorial Committee)
V. P. Kozlov, director, Rosarkhiv

N. S. Lebedeva, Russian Academy of Sciences
S. V. Mironenko, director, State Archive of the Russian Federation (GARF)
O. V. Naumov, assistant director, RGASPI
E. O. Pivovar, Moscow State University
V. V. Shelokhaev, president, Association ROSSPEN
Ye. A. Tyurina, director, Russian State Archive of the Economy (RGAE)

Soviet Culture and Power
A History in Documents, 1917–1953

Katerina Clark and Evgeny Dobrenko

with Andrei Artizov and Oleg Naumov

*Narrative, Text Preparation, and Commentary
by Katerina Clark and Evgeny Dobrenko
Documents Compiled by Andrei Artizov and Oleg Naumov
Translated from the Russian by Marian Schwartz*

Yale University Press
New Haven & London

This book is based on selections from a book of documents compiled by Andrei Artizov and Oleg Naumov, published in Russian as *Vlast' i khudozhestvennaia intelligentsia: Dokumenty TsK RKP(b)-VKP(b), VChK–OGPU–NKVD o kul'turnoi politike, 1917– 1953 gg* (Power and the creative intelligentsia: Documents [of the Communist Party and the secret Police] on cultural policy, 1917–1953) by Mezhdunarodny fond Demokratia [International Democracy Foundation], Moscow, 1999.

Copyright © 2007 by Yale University.
All rights reserved.

This book may not be reproduced, in whole or in part, including illustrations, in any form (beyond that copying permitted by Sections 107 and 108 of the U.S. Copyright Law and except by reviewers for the public press), without written permission from the publishers.

Set in Sabon Roman type by The Composing Room of Michigan, Inc. Printed in the United States of America by Vail-Ballou Press.

Library of Congress Cataloging-in-Publication Data

Soviet culture and power : a history in documents : 1917–1953 / edited by Katerina Clark and Evgeny Dobrenko ; with Andrei Artizov and Oleg Naumov.
  p. cm. — (Annals of communism)
 "This book is based on selections from a book of documents compiled by Andrei Artizov and Oleg Naumov and published in Moscow (1999) as Vlast i khudozhestevennaia intelligentsiia : dokumenty TsK RKP(b)—VKP(b), VChK—OGPU—NKVD o kul turnoi politike : 1917–1953 gg."
  Includes bibliographical references and index.
  ISBN-13: 978-0-300-10646-6 (cloth : alk. paper)
  1. Soviet Union—Cultural policy—Sources. 2. Politics and culture—Soviet Union—Sources. 3. Power (Social sciences)—Soviet Union—Sources. 4. Communism and intellectuals—Soviet Union—Sources. 5. Communism and culture—Soviet Union—Sources. 6. Politics and literature—Soviet Union—Sources. I. Clark, Katerina. II. Dobrenko, E. A. (Evgenii Aleksandrovich) III. Artizov, Andrei. IV. Naumov, Oleg. V. Vlast, i khudozhestvennaia intelligentsiia.
  DK266.4.S678 2007
  947.084′2—dc22

2006029355

A catalogue record for this book is available from the British Library.

The paper in this book meets the guidelines for permanence and durability of the Committee on Production Guidelines for Book Longevity of the Council on Library Resources.

10 9 8 7 6 5 4 3 2 1

Yale University Press gratefully acknowledges the financial support given for this publication by the John M. Olin Foundation, the Lynde and Harry Bradley Foundation, the Historical Research Foundation, Roger Milliken, Lloyd H. Smith, Keith Young, the William H. Donner Foundation, Joseph W. Donner, Jeremiah Milbank, the David Woods Kemper Memorial Foundation, and the Milton V. Brown Foundation.

Contents

Introduction	ix
Note on Transliteration	xix
Note on the Documents	xxi
Soviet Organizational Acronyms and Abbreviations	xxiii

PART ONE. The Twenties — 1

INTRODUCTION. The Bolshevization of Culture, 1917–1932	3
CHAPTER 1. "Prohibit Travel . . ."	7
CHAPTER 2. "The Utterly Indecent Proposal to Preserve the Bolshoi Theater"	23
CHAPTER 3. Organizing the "Artistic Milieu": The Era of NEP	32
CHAPTER 4. The Organization of Proletarian Art: The Cultural Revolution	50
CHAPTER 5. "Gorky, Whom No One Takes Seriously in Politics"	76
CHAPTER 6. Work with the "Anti-Soviet Intelligentsia"	88

PART TWO. The Thirties — 137

INTRODUCTION. The Culture of High Stalinism, 1932–1941	139

CHAPTER 7. The Demise of RAPP	150
CHAPTER 8. The Writers' Congress	162
CHAPTER 9. The Gorky Factor	179
CHAPTER 10. The Union of Soviet Writers	194
CHAPTER 11. Stalin and the Moscow Art Theater	216
CHAPTER 12. The Anti-Formalist Campaign	229
CHAPTER 13. The Campaign for a Patriotic Culture	249
CHAPTER 14. The Censorship	261
CHAPTER 15. Presenting the Image of the Leader	276
CHAPTER 16. Stalin as Patron-Potentate	282
CHAPTER 17. Reports on Writers from the NKVD and Soviet Officials	302
CHAPTER 18. Petitions to Stalin	322
CHAPTER 19. The Stalin-Sholokhov Exchange	336
PART THREE. The Forties	345
INTRODUCTION. The Culture of Late Stalinism, 1941–1953	347
CHAPTER 20. The Literary Front: The War	352
CHAPTER 21. The Literary Front: "Zhdanovism" and Beyond	393
CHAPTER 22. "The Most Important Art"	432
CHAPTER 23. "Moments Musicaux"	459
CHAPTER 24. "The Revolution Has Ended at the Point Where It Began"	464
Notes	473
Glossary of Names	483
List of Documents	511
Index	520

Introduction

THE documents presented here cover the period from 1917 to 1953, the years when first Lenin and then Stalin ruled the Soviet Union. Lenin's rule lasted from the Bolshevik Revolution of 7 November 1917, through his death on 21 January 1924, and then Stalin progressively consolidated his power, winning out in a power struggle with rival Bolshevik leaders such as Bukharin and above all Trotsky. This process was more or less completed by 1929, and Stalin then ruled until his death in March 1953. The majority of documents in this volume come from the years when Stalin was head of the Soviet state, and provide case studies in the cultural history of Stalinism, including some of its prehistory.

This book is based on selections from a book of documents compiled by Andrei Artizov and Oleg Naumov and published in Moscow (1999) as *Vlast' i khudozhestvennaia intelligentsia: Dokumenty TsK RKP(b)-VKP(b), VChK–OGPU–NKVD o kul'turnoi politike, 1917–1953 gg.* (Power and the creative intelligentsia: Documents [of the Communist Party and the secret Police] on cultural policy, 1917–1953). Artizov and Naumov's pioneering collection presents documents that have become available to researchers only since the archives of the (former) Soviet Union became progressively more open to scholars in the years since Mikhail Gorbachev came to power in 1985 and instituted a new policy of *glasnost'* (openness). The kinds of documents Artizov and Naumov were able to publish include decisions and discussions of the Soviet Politburo and of the Secretariat of the Central Committee of the Soviet Communist Party, documents prepared by members of the Central Committee's departments responsible for making decisions on cultural matters, petitions and letters from intellectuals to Stalin and to other members of the leadership, and reports from the secret police (successively named the VChKA or Cheka, GPU, OGPU, and NKVD) detailing reactions among intellectuals to certain high-level decisions. They largely came from closed archives that even today remain inaccessible to most scholars, let alone the general public: the Archive of the President of the Russian Federation (AP RF), the Russian Archive of Contemporary Political History (RGASPI—the former Party archive and archive of the Comintern), the Central Archive of the Federal Security Service of the Russian Federation (i.e., the secret police—TsA FSB RF), the Russian State Archive of Literature and Art (RGALI), and the archive of the Gorky Institute of World Literature (IMLI).

Thus these documents provide the sort of information on which scholars writing on Soviet cultural history have until recently only been able to speculate. They not only fill in many lacunae in our knowledge of the dynamic of Soviet cultural history, of the workings of its institutions, and of the biographies of individual intellectuals and leaders, but also in many instances correct the standard accounts of how certain decisions were made in the cultural sphere, and of the mechanisms of decision making in general. They also bring to light the political underpinnings of particular events which scholars had previously been at a loss to explain.

Above all, the documents presented here on the activities of the Politburo oblige scholars to revise the standard accounts of "the Party's interference in the cultural sphere" and of the degree of its interference. One can even argue that to talk in terms of "interference" is to formulate the issue incorrectly. The Party leadership did not "interfere" inasmuch as it was the body charged with regulating all matters of the Soviet state, including cultural ones. Indeed, Soviet power could be described as a mechanism whereby nothing could function without decisions being made by Party bodies. In consequence, and as became evident during the Gorbachev era of *perestroika* (reform), the Soviet system turned out to be unreformable: it was simply unable to function without Party-cum-state regulation.

In these documents we come to appreciate the tremendous role that the highest Party bodies played in the cultural sphere. By these "highest Party bodies" we mean principally the Politburo (Political Bureau)—a select body comprising the Party's top leaders that occupied the highest level in the hierarchy of power other than that occupied by Stalin personally—and bodies of the Party's Central Committee: its Secretariat, its Orgburo (Organizational Bureau) and the apparatus of its various departments, such as Culture and Propaganda (Kultprop). Of these various bodies, however, the Politburo was the preeminent decision maker in the cultural sphere. These documents, then, disprove the claims that some scholars have made up to recent times that in reality only a small number of decisions were taken at the highest Party levels such as the Central Committee. As we see here, the opposite was the case: most cultural issues were decided at the highest levels and not principally on the level of the Central Committee, but actually on the higher level of the Politburo.

What is truly extraordinary is that the heads of state of a country that boasted being the largest in area ("one-sixth of the world"), and was for much of this period undergoing draconian modernization and a build-up of its military coupled with a protracted socio-politico-economic revolution, spent so much of its time on cultural matters. Culture was always in the purview of the Soviet leadership, and especially of Stalin. In the thirties, when the Politburo divided up stewardship of the various branches of government, that busy head of state took the area of culture for himself. Even in the most critical moments of inner-Party struggle, of terror or of war, the routine apparatus of control over cultural matters continued to function. Indeed, decisions were taken at the highest levels on issues of a fairly minor order, right down to who would be on the editorial board of a literary journal, who would run each of the journal's departments, and how much everyone would be paid. Decisions made by Stalin, the Politburo, and the Central Committee governed most cultural life in Moscow, Leningrad (Petersburg), and the Ukraine. In provincial areas, decisions on cultural matters tended to be made by the Party leadership of the given city or republic, but in making them they generally followed the line established by resolutions of the Politburo or the Central Committee. In effect, then, cultural policy in general, and in many of its specific details, was to an extraordinary degree the province of the leadership, especially during the 1930s and 1940s when the Stalin cult was most pronounced.

There are several reasons for this. An obvious one would be that these leaders were not just politicians, but as it were theocrats: they governed as the heads of a caste (the Party), that they saw as the designated representative of a belief system (Marxism-Leninism). This was also why, in the system of dual (Party/civil) government that operated in the Soviet Union, the Party assumed precedence and why, in consequence, though such civil service institutions as the Commissariat (later Ministry) of Culture played a significant role in the cultural history of the country, it was the higher Party bodies represented in these documents that were the ultimate arbiters in culture. Moreover, inasmuch as the state was organized as a quasi-theocracy, and consequently its government was dedicated to the implementation of the principal tenets of its belief system, the distinction between culture and ideology, never an absolute one, was all but obliterated to the extent that, for example, the choice of a Beethoven symphony for a concert performance or of a particular architectural style for a building were more often than not treated as ideological issues. At the same time, "aesthetic discourse," as the documents show, was by no means foreign to the Party elite.

Another reason that culture was of such constant concern to the leaders is because, in the last analysis, the sphere of culture and ideology was the sphere of legitimation of the state. One could argue that the greatest trauma for Stalinism was the trauma of its lack of legitimacy (a lack sensed by the Bolshevik leadership in general and by Stalin as leader in particular). The process of legitimation required using refined techniques for manipulating mass consciousness. It is hard to exaggerate the role of culture in this process.

The Bolshevik leaders had assumed power in an armed uprising that had deposed a state structure that had stood for centuries. They had never been elected by democratic process. Hence the regime's claims to legitimacy were largely grounded in a claim to cherishing and realizing more closely than might any rival the principles of the belief system—a secondary justificatory line of argument being improvements in the national economy and the material well-being of the citizens as indicators that they were progressing along the "road to Communism". As a consequence, written texts assumed enormous importance in the political life of the country. In the Soviet Union writing had such an authoritative status because it was felt it would establish the truth of the order to be found in Bolshevik experience. Writing was a means for promulgating the Party's ultimate authorship of Soviet reality.

The thirties were a decade framed and punctuated by authoritative texts. The decade opened with a flurry of publishing Marxist texts, many of which were previously unknown and which came from archives in Germany but had been worked over in the late twenties by scholars in Soviet institutes. But even as these texts were being published they were also being interpreted. The Bolshevik position was marked off from false readings and false appropriations made by, in particular, German Marxists and rival factions within Russia. A deviation from the correct political line (*zagib, peregib*) was effectively a deviation from the canonical texts. The Stalin era was consequently a time of textual anxiety, one when institutions and individuals were obsessed with slippage, with measuring the gap between text and reality and especially between the most canonical texts and any individual text generated.

Throughout the period represented in this volume a major preoccupation was also how to shape subjects for the nation. Those in power had to rationalize the Revolution, the change from one world order to another. All states have to manufacture subjects, but what is peculiar about the Soviet example is the need to create new subjects out of the old. As it were, they needed to put new software into the old machine. Writing was, in effect, seen as a means of producing that software. Hence literature became in the thirties the flagship of Soviet culture, but even nonverbal texts were ascribed a narrative function.

Thus writing was both to systematize reality—Bolshevik experience—and also to manufacture subjects. The two purposes were to be met by giving the Bolshevik regime a new narrative of identity. The leadership looked to their army of cultural producers to present them with an exemplary representation of the nation, whether in literature, film, or art. In the 1930s this task was approached more systematically. After the Writers Union was founded in April 1932, "Socialist Realism" was pronounced *the* method for all of Soviet literature and the arts; in practice, what Socialist Realism entailed was an increasingly standardized version of this narrative of identity.

In effect, there was operating in the society a hierarchy in anthropology based on the individual's relationship to texts (with Stalin at the apex). There were essentially three overlapping but not synchronized hierarchies: firstly, one structured in terms of who had access to which texts, so many of which were proscribed for all but a few and kept behind closed doors; secondly, a hierarchy in terms of authorship ranging from those whose function was to replicate texts in both their lives and on paper (the bulk of the population), through those whose function it was to flesh out Party policies and holy writ (writers), to those who could generate new authoritative texts (essentially only Stalin or someone privileged to be delegated by him to perform that function). The third and arguably most important hierarchy in this era of anxiety about textual purity was that of guardian of the texts—the censor. In this collection we sense the enormous amount of time Stalin—the head of state!—spent reviewing and editing books, film scripts, and plays. In terms of the Soviet system Stalin was not "interfering" in requiring changes to these texts but conscientiously fulfilling his role as guardian of the purity of the texts. When he reviewed a film script he particularly looked at the representation of individual historical figures or of sociological types to ensure that it conformed to a model that was implicitly textual.

In terms of these hierarchies, then, the intelligentsia occupied a sort of intermediate—or, more accurately, intermediary—role between those with textual authority (the leadership) and the populace at large. Whether painting a picture, making a film, or composing a poem, creative intellectuals were to function as explicators of the texts. Western historiography has tended to divide them into "true" intellectuals and Stalinist "hacks," and to represent the "true" intellectuals as victims or opponents of Stalinism. Traditionally, the intelligentsia had seen themselves as independent of the state—critics trying to keep the state honest—or even as in opposition to it. This was a role they had inherited from the tsarist era and to some extent that continued to be their identity in Soviet Russia. In historical reality, however, for every "dissident" intellectual in tsarist Russia there was another in some way implicated in the apparatus of the state; several quite prominent writers served as censors. A similar ambiguity in the Soviet intelligentsia emerges in this volume.

The documents presented here provide a more reliable account of instances of resistance and independence among Soviet intellectuals than we have had before. Examples include the dissident broadsheet distributed at the First Congress of the Writers Union in August 1934 (doc. 71); the underground society of Ukrainian writers (doc. 134); and signs of independence among writers' groups in Leningrad (doc. 133) and in their village of Peredelkino outside Moscow (doc. 140). But, at the same time, the intelligentsia should not be idealized, as they so often are in Western historiography, nor should they be seen as an extrasystemic category. Intellectuals were implicated in the workings of the state, which not only "repressed" them but also rewarded them with one of the most privileged existences available in Soviet Russia.

Several leading writers, including Isaac Babel, were close to the heads of the secret police, as these documents show. The documents also show the extent to which the intelligentsia assimilated the habits of mind, discourse, and practices of Soviet society, including in particular the proclivity for factional squabbles and for mutual denunciation. In some instances leading intellectuals, far from closing ranks when one of their number was attacked or purged, or from being outraged or dismayed, expressed approval and even exulted in the demise of a rival. Conversely, we see how intellectuals coveted the baubles (state prizes and orders) that the regime meted out to them and were offended when they did not receive them.

As these documents show, central to the lives of Soviet intellectuals was a hierarchical system of patronage and arbitration that was centered in the Party. In the absence of a pluralism of opinion and of a genuine court of appeal the Politburo performed the function of a court in general and an arbitration court in particular. Moreover, it performed that function not only in culture but also in such other areas as the economy. In these documents we can see many examples of the dynamic whereby aggrieved intellectuals appealed to Gorky (who would in turn appeal on their behalf to Stalin or to a member of the Politburo), or to some figure on the Party hierarchy, often to Stalin himself. Similarly, favors (positions, trips abroad) were dispensed by these powerful patrons to client intellectuals.

As the documents also reveal, Stalin was himself not an entirely extrasystemic figure. Rather as in the doctrine of the "king's two bodies" (the king's actual, physical body and his divinely anointed self), Stalin was both an actual individual historical actor and someone who occupied the structural slot at the pinnacle of a centralized and hierarchical state. We see here that it was not only the state but also Stalin himself who became progressively "Stalinized." A striking confirmation of this would be Stalin's note of 3 July 1922 (doc. 20) in which, in advocating the formation of a single body for poets who were pro-Soviet under a rubric such as "The Society for the Development of Russian Culture," he insists that no attempt should be made to involve this group in any official body because the group should be "independent" and ideally headed by a non-Party writer. By the mid-thirties any notion of "independence" was completely absent from the programmatic discourse of the leadership, and of Stalin most particularly.

This document also contains other material which marks the earlier off from the later Stalin. For example, he implicitly endorses the Trotsky position in that he is skeptical and dismissive about demands for a "proletarian" literature (as Trotsky had been in his *Literature and Revolution* [Literatura i revoliutsia] of 1923, a book based on articles he published over the previous two years). Not only would Trotsky and "Trotskyism" become anathema to Stalin by the mid twenties, but during the "cultural revolution" that took place during the years of the First Five Year Plan (starting in approximately 1928) "proletarianization" of all areas of cultural life became central to the leadership's platform. By "proletarianization" was meant instituting a culture of, for, and by the proletariat, a category that was itself ambiguous and interpreted by some as meaning actual workers but by others as meaning the Party, "vanguard of the proletariat." This policy of "proletarianization" was, however, effectively dropped around 1931.

Thus Stalin did not "create" (legislate) Soviet culture by an act of parthenogenesis but was himself participating in a culture system, a milieu from which he derived many of the ideas underpinning his policies. "Stalinism" evolved gradually and the years of Stalin's rule were punctuated by subperiods each of which had its own distinctive cultural program and also its own distinctive bureaucratic procedures. We have organized this book into sections which take into account the major subperiods.

This volume, then, provides previously unknown documentary material that elucidates many of the landmark moments in Soviet cultural history. But it does not, and cannot, provide a complete picture of culture under Lenin and Stalin. Rather, it frees the picture we have formed to date from many blank or murky spots. In order to provide a more comprehensive account of the dynamic of Soviet cultural history one would have to supplement these documents with material from government (as distinct from Party) bodies such as the Ministry of Culture, the publishing houses, the creative unions, creative intellectuals, and even from the actual works themselves. Then one might more fully appreciate the dynamic of their interaction, an interaction that generated Soviet culture. However, this volume illuminates that most crucial and even mysterious factor in the evolution of Soviet culture, the role of the state's leadership. Inasmuch as culture and Soviet power were so closely linked, the collection also sheds light on the general functioning of the Soviet state.

Due to space limitations, our collection comprises approximately only one-third of the documents published in *Vlast' i khudozhestven-*

naia intelligentsia. Thus we have been obliged to select rather ruthlessly from among the documents provided there. Since we assume that specialists in Soviet culture will be able to read the full collection in its Russian version we used the following criteria in our selection that would make the present volume most suitable for the nonspecialist reader or for the classroom: (1) keeping every document written by or to Stalin or in which his vote on a particular issue is recorded, and to a large extent doing the same for Maxim Gorky who was the first head of the Writers Union (though in some instances we were obliged to abridge documents by him); (2) publishing all documents concerning Soviet intellectuals and cultural events well-known in the West such as Babel, Bulgakov, Eisenstein, Meyerhold, Pasternak, and Shostakovich; (3) publishing primarily documents concerning the most prominent Soviet intellectuals and cultural bureaucrats. Exceptions were made for the secret police reports on intellectuals, many of which recount the opinions of minor figures but are intrinsically interesting for the light they throw on intelligentsia attitudes; and also for cases when the content of the document is particularly revealing, or essential for providing the widest possible spectrum of leadership involvement in culture. In the interests of accessibility for the nonspecialist we have also provided notes for some of the texts to identify the subjects mentioned, and an index which gives brief biographical information on each name mentioned in the documents.

These documents, which have been languishing in archives, dictate the themes of our narrative. But the historical and cultural commentary we provide aims not just at helping readers get their bearings in the profusion of documents but also at introducing the documents to history, which is itself the product of a narrative.

Katerina Clark
Evgeny Dobrenko

Note on Transliteration

In transliterating from Russian to English we have used a modified version of the standard Library of Congress system in the text and documents. The following changes have been imposed for proper names.

In the final position:
    ii in the LOC system becomes y (Trotsky, not Trotskii)
    iia = ia (Izvestia, not Izvestiia)
In the initial position:
    E = Ye (Yezhov, not Ezhov)
    Ia = Ya (Yaroslavsky, not Iaroslavsky)
    Iu = Yu (Yudin, not Iudin)

Strict Library of Congress transliteration is used in source notes and for Russian words or phrases other than proper names that appear in the text.

Note on the Documents

The overwhelming majority of documents used or cited here are from Russian archives listed below. Russian archival documents are cited and numbered by collection (*fond* or f.), inventory (*opis'* or op.) or preservation unit (*yedinitsa khranenia* or ed. khr.), file (*delo* or d.), and folio (*list* or l., or in the plural ll.). The verso side of a folio is indicated with "v." Thus, for example, RGALI, f. 99, op. 66, d. 73, ll. 45–46.

Some of the documents were too long to be reproduced in full in this volume, and some excisions were made by the Russian authorities in the process of declassification. Our editorial excisions are indicated by ellipsis dots within square brackets [. . .]. Excisions in the original published version of these documents (i.e., in Andrei Artizov and Oleg Naumov, comps., *Vlast' i khudozhestvennaia intelligentsia: Dokumenty TsK RKP(b)-VKP(b), VChK–OGPU–NKVD o kul'turnoi politike, 1917–1953 gg.* [Moscow, 1999]) are indicated by dots within angle brackets < . . . >. Excisions during declassification are indicated by dots within curly brackets { . . . }. Ellipses not in brackets indicate omissions in the original documents.

All documents cited here exist in the indicated archive either as original typescripts or as manuscripts, or, in the case of many of the letters and summary reports, as typed copies. The status of each document is indicated immediately following the archival citation. Except where otherwise indicated, we have tried to render in the English translation the original punctuation and syntax of the Russian.

In this volume documents from the following archives are used:

AP RF   Arkhiv prezidenta Rossiiskoi federatsii (Presidential Archive of the Russian Federation)

GARF   Gosudarstvennyi arkhiv Rossiiskoi federatsii (State Archive of the Russian Federation)

IMLI   Institut mirovoi literatury imeni Gor'kogo (Gorky Institute of World Literature)

OR GPB Otdel rukopisei gosudarstyvennoi publichnoi biblioteki (Manuscript Department of the State Public Library)

RGALI   Rossiisky gosudarstvennyi arkhiv literatury i iskusstva (Russian State Archive of Literature and Art)

RGASPI Rossiisky gosudarstvennyi arkhiv sotsial'noi i politicheskoi istorii (Russian State Archive of Social and Political History), formerly known as RTsKhIDNI—Rossiisky tsentr khraneniia i izucheniia dokumentov noveishei istorii (Russian Center for Preservation and Study of Documents of Modern History)

TsA FSB Tsentral'nyi arkhiv Federal'nogo soveta bezopasnosti (Central Archive of the Federal Committee for State Security)

TsAOD   Tsentral'nyi arkhiv obshchestvennykh dvizhenii goroda Moskvy (Central Archive of Public Movements of the City of Moscow)

Soviet Organizational Acronyms and Abbreviations

Agitmass	*[Otdel] agitatsionno-massovoi raboty* (Department of Agitational and Mass Work)
Agitpropotdel	See Agitprop
Agitprop	*Agitatsia i propaganda* (Agitation and Propaganda; Department of Agitation and Propaganda of the Central Committee)
AKhRR	*Assotsiatsia khudozhnikov revoliutsionnoi Rossii* (Association of Artists of Revolutionary Russia)
AP	*Assotsiatsia pisatelei* (Association of Writers)
APPO TsK	*Agitatsionno-propagandistsky podotdel TsK* (Agitation and Propaganda Subsection of the Central Committee)
ASM	*Assotsiatsia sovremennoi muzyki* (Association of Contemporary Music)
ASNOVA	*Assotsiatsia novykh arkhitektorov* (Association of New Architects; a Constructivist group)
Cheka	*Chrezvychainaia komissia* ([All-Russian] Extraordinary Commission [for Combating Counterrevolution, Sabotage, and Speculation], 1918–22, succeeded by GPU)
Comintern	Communist International

Detgiz	*Gosudarstvennoe izdatel'stvo detskoi literatury* (State Publishing House of Children's Literature)
FOSP	*Federatsia Ob"edineny sovetskikh pisatelei* (Federation of Unions of Soviet Writers)
GABT	*Gosudarstvennyi akademichesky Bol'shoi teatr* (State Academic Bolshoi Theater)
GIKhL	*Gosudarstvennoe izdatel'stvo khudozhestvennoi literatury* (State Publishing House for Literature)
GIZ	See Gosizdat
Glaviskusstvo	*Glavnoe upravlenie iskusstva* (Chief Directorate of Art)
Glavlit	*Glavnoe upravlenie literatury* (Chief Directorate of Literature; organ of literary censorship)
Glavpolitprosvet	*Glavnoe upravlenie politicheskogo prosveshchenia* (Chief Directorate of Political Education)
Glavrepertkom	*Glavnyi repertuarnyi komitet* (Main Repertoire Committee; organ of theater censorship)
gorkom	*gorodskoi komitet* (city committee of the Communist Party)
Gosizdat	*Gosudarstvennoe izdatel'stvo* (State Publishing House)
Goslitizdat	*Gosudarstvennoe izdatel'stvo khudozhestvennoi literatury* (State Publishing House for Literature)
Gosplan	*Gosudarstvennyi komitet po planirovaniiu* (State Planning Committee)
GOSTIM	*Gosudarstvennyi teatr imeni Meierkhol'da* (Vs. Meyerhold State Theater)
GPU	*Gosudarstvennoe politicheskoe upravlenie* (State Political Administration; the secret police [1922–32], successor to the Cheka)
GRK	See Glavrepertkom
GUGB	*Glavnoe upravlenie gosudarstvennoi bezopasnosti* (Central Directorate of State Security)
GUK	*Gosudarstvennoe upravlenie kinematografii* (State Administration of Cinematography)
GULAG	*Gosudarstvennoe upravlenie lagerei* (State Administration of Camps; the labor camp system)
IKP	*Institut krasnoi professury* (Institute of Red Professors)

IMLI	*Institut mirovoi literatury imeni Gor'kogo* (Gorky Institute of World Literature)
Informburo	*See* Sovinformburo
INO	*Inostrannyi otdel* (Foreign Department)
ispolkom	*ispolnitel'nyi komitet* (executive committee of a soviet)
Kogiz	*Kooperativnaia organizatsia gosudarstvennykh izdatel'stv* (Cooperative Organization of State Publishing Houses)
kolkhoz	*kollektivnoe khoziaistvo* (collective farm)
Komakademia	*Kommunisticheskaia akademia* (the Communist academy)
Komsomol	*Kommunistichesky soiuz molodezhi* (Communist Union of Youth)
KPK	*Komitet partiinogo kontrolia* (Party Control Commission)
KPSS	*Kommunistichskaia partia Sovetskogo Soiuza* (Communist Party of the Soviet Union)
krai	administrative territory roughly equivalent to oblast
kraiobllit	krai branch of Glavlit
KUBU	*Komitet po uluchsheniu byta uchenykh* (Committee to Improve Scholars' Living Conditions)
Kultprop	*Kul'turno-propagandistsky otdel* (Department for Culture and Propaganda)
Kultpropotdel	*See* Kultprop
Kultprosvet	*Kul'turno-prosvetitel'nyi otdel* (Department for Cultural-Educational Work)
Kultprosvetotdel	*See* Kultprosvet
LEF	*Levyi front iskusstva* (Left Front in the Arts)
Lengorlit	Leningrad city branch of Glavlit
Lengublit	Leningrad province branch of Glavlit
Litfond	*Literaturnyi fond* (Literary Fund, for assistance to writers)
Litfront	*Literaturnyi front* (Literary Front)
LOKAF	*Literaturnoe ob"edinenie Krasnoi Armii i Flota* (Literary Association of the Red Army and Navy)
MGSPSRT	*Moskovsky gorodskoi sovet professional'nykh soiuzov rabotnikov teatra* (Moscow City Committee of Theater Workers Trade Unions)

MK	*Moskovsky komitet* (Moscow Party Committee)
MKhAT	*Moskovsky khudozhestvennyi teatr* (Moscow Art Theater)
MOPR	*Mezhdunarodnaia organizatsia pomoshchi bortsam revoliutsii* (International Organization for Assistance to Revolutionary Fighters, founded in 1922 by the Comintern)
MORP	*Mezhdunarodnoe ob"edinenie revoliutsionnykh pisatelei* (International Union of Revolutionary Writers)
Mosfilm	Moscow Film Studio
Mosgorlit	a *Moskovskoe gorodskoe upravelenie literatury* (Moscow city branch of Glavlit)
Mosgubispolkom	*See* Mosoblispolkom
Mosgublit	*Moskovskoe gubernskoe upravlenie literatury* (Moscow province branch of Glavlit)
MOSKh	*Moskovskoe ob"edinenie sovetskikh khudozhnikov* (Moscow Association of Soviet Artists)
Mosoblispolkom	*Moskovskii oblastnoi ispolnitel'nyi komitet* (Moscow Regional Executive Committee)
MTS	*Mashino-traktornaia stantsia* (machine tractor station)
Narkomat	*Narodnyi komissariat* (People's Commissariat)
Narkomindel	*See* NKID
Narkomfin	*Narodnyi komissariat finansov* (People's Commissariat of Finance)
Narkomprod	*Narodnyi komissariat prodovol'stvia* (People's Commissariat of Production)
Narkompros	*Narodnyi komissariat prosveshchenia* (People's Commissariat of Enlightenment, i.e., of culture and education)
NEP	*Novaia Ekonomicheskaia Politika* (the New Economic Policy), instituted in 1921
NKGB	*Narodnyi komissariat gosudarstvennoi bezopasnosti* (People's Commissariat for State Security)
NKID	*Narodnyi komissariat inostrannykh del* (People's Commissariat of Foreign Affairs)
NKP	*See* Narkompros
NKRK	*Narodnyi komissariat raboche-krestianskoi inspektsii* (People's Commissariat of Workers' and Peasants' Inspection)

NKVD	*Narodnyi komissariat vnutrennykh del* (People's Commissariat for Internal Affairs; from 1934 the successor to the OGPU)
NKVDNudel	*See* NKVD
NKVT	*Narodnyi komissariat vneshnei torgovli* (People's Commissariat of Foreign Trade)
nomenklatura	people chosen by the Party apparatus to serve in various responsible positions
OB	acronym for Orgburo
Oberiu	*Ob"edinenie real'nogo iskusstva* (Association for Real Art)
obkom	*oblastnoi komitet* (oblast committee of the Communist Party)
oblast	administrative unit, region
oblit	an oblast administration for Glavlit
Ogiz	*Ob"edinennoe gosudarstvennoe izdatel'stvo* (Amalgamated State Publishing House)
OGPU	*Ob"edinennoe gosudarstvennoe politicheskoe upravlenie* (Unified State Political Administration; the secret police [1932–34], successor to the GPU)
okrug	an administrative unit between the raion and the oblast
Orgburo	*Organizatsionnoe biuro* (Organizational Bureau)
Orgkom	*Organizatsionnyi komitet* (Organizational Committee)
Osobotdel VChK	*Osobyi otdel VChK* (Special Department of the Cheka)
OST	*Obshchestvo stankovistov* (Society of Easel Painters)
Partkollegia	*Partiinaia kollegia* (Collegium of the Party)
PB	acronym for Politburo
Politburo	Political Bureau of the Central Committee
Politotdel	Political Department
Proletkult	Proletarian Culture, a cultural organization
Rabis	*Profsoiuz rabotnikov iskusstva* (Union of Arts Workers)
Rabkor	*Rabochy korrespondent* (worker correspondent)
raion	administrative unit, between okrug and oblast in size
Raispolkom	*Raionny ispolnitel'nyi komitet* (District Executive Committee)

RAPM	*Rossiiskaia Assotsiatsia Proletarskikh Muzykantov* (Russian Association of Proletarian Musicians)
RAPP	*Rossiiskaia Assotsiatsia Proletarskikh Pisatelei* (Russian Association of Proletarian Writers)
Repertkom	See Glavrepertkom
RK	*Raionnyi komitet* (District Committee)
RKI	*Raboche-krestianskaia inspektsia* (Worker-Peasant Inspection)
RKKA	*Raboche-krestianskaia krasnaia armia* (Worker-Peasant Red Army)
RKP	*Rossiiskaia kommunisticheskaia partia* (Russian Communist Party)
ROPKP	*Rossiiskaia assotsiatsia proletarsko-kolkhoznykh pisatelei* (Russian Association of Proletarian Kolkhoz Writers)
ROSTA	*Rossiiskoe telegrafnoe agentstvo* (Russian Telegraph Agency)
RSDRP(b)	*Rossiiskaia sotsial-demokraticheskaia partia (bol'shevikov)* (Russian Social Democratic Workers Party [Bolsheviks])
RSFSR	*Rossiiskaia Sovetskaia Federativnaia Sotsialisticheskaia Respublika* (Russian Soviet Federative Socialist Republic)
Sanprosvet	*Sanitarnoe prosveshchenie* (Sanitary Enlightenment)
SNK SSSR	*Sovet narodnykh komissarov SSSR* (Council of People's Commissars of the USSR)
Sovinformburo	*Sovetskoe informatsionnoe biuro* (Soviet Information Bureau)
sovkhoz	*sovetskoe khoziaistvo* (state farm employing wage labor)
Sovnarkom	See SNK SSSR
SPO	*Spetsial'nyi politichesky Otdel* (Special Political Department of the secret police)
SR	Socialist Revolutionaries
SSP SSSR	*Soiuz sovetskikh pisatelei SSSR* (Union of Soviet Writers of the USSR)
TASS	*Telegrafnoe agentstvo Sovetskogo Soiuza* (Telegraph Agency of the Soviet Union)

Torgprom	*Torgovaia promyshlennost'* (retail industry)
TRAM	*Teatr rabochei molodezhi* (Theater of Worker Youth)
TsDKA	*Tsentral'nyi dom Krasnoi armii* (M. V. Frunze Central House of the Red Army)
TsIK	See VTsIK
TsKK	*Tsentral'naia kontrol'naia komissia* (Central Control Commission of the Party)
TsK RKP(b)	*Tsentral'nyi komitet Rossiiskoi kommunisticheskoi partii (bol'shevikov)* (Central Committee of the Russian Communist Party [Bolsheviks])
TsK VKP(b)	*Tsentral'nyi komitet Vsesoiuznoi kommunisticheskoi partii (bol'shevikov)* (Central Committee of the All-Union Communist Party [Bolsheviks])
UNKVD	*Upravlenie Narodnogo komissariata vnutrennikh del* (People's Commissariat of Internal Affairs Administration)
VAPP	*Vsesoiuznaia Assotsiatsia Proletarskikh Pisatelei* (All-Union Association of Proletarian Writers)
VChK	*Vsesoiuznaia chrezvychainaia komissia* (All-Union Extraordinary Commission; see Cheka)
VLKSM	See Komsomol
VOAPP	*Vsesoiuznoe Ob"edinenie Assotsiatsii Proletarskikh Pisatelei* (All-Union Alliance of Proletarian Writers Associations)
VOKP	*Vserossiiskoe ob"edinenie krest'ianskikh pisatelei* (All-Russian Union of Peasant Writers)
VOKS	*Vsesoiuznoe obshchestvo kul'turnykh sviazei s zagranitsei* (All-Union Society for Cultural Relations with Abroad)
VSNKh	*Vsesoiuznyi sovet narodnogo khoziaistva* (All-Union Council of the National Economy)
VSP	*Vserossiisky soiuz pisatelei* (All-Russian Union of Writers)
VSSP	*Vserossiisky soiuz sovetskikh pisatelei* (All-Russian Union of Soviet Writers)
VTsIK	*Vsesoiuznyi tsentral'nyi ispolnitel'nyi komitet* (All-Union Central Executive Committee [of soviets])

VTsSPS	*Vsesoiuznyi tsentral'nyi sovet professional'nykh soiuzov* (All-Union Central Board of Trade Unions)
VUSPP	*Vseukrainsky soiuz proletarskikh pisatelei* (All-Ukrainian Association of Proletarian Writers)
Zhurgaz	*Zhurnal'no-gazetnoe ob"edinenie* (journal and newspaper conglomerate)

I
The Twenties

Introduction: The Bolshevization of Culture, 1917–1932

IN the late 1920s, Anatoly Lunacharsky observed in an address to young people on the subject of the revolutionary era: "Old people lived so slowly it didn't matter if they fell asleep. In the old days, you could drift off, sleep two years away, wake up, and pick up your life as if nothing had happened. Life moved along like a cart, but now it speeds by madly. Event after event, crisis after crisis. And our emotional life, indisputably, is livelier, more colorful and varied."[1] It would be hard to disagree with this description of racing time. That is exactly what the revolutionary era, which in Soviet cultural history came to be called the Twenties, was like. It was drastically different not only from the prerevolutionary era but also from the 1930s—in its political climate, its cultural development, and its aesthetic uniqueness. However, it was itself far from homogeneous internally, combining as it did at least three highly specific periods: the Civil War, NEP (New Economic Policy), and the cultural revolution. The boundaries of this cultural period are marked by two dates, 1917 and 1932. Between these two years, a culture was created in Soviet Russia that was fundamentally new—in its social functions, its system of cultural institutions, the social structure of its producers and consumers of cultural values, and their aesthetic demands.

The civil war and the resulting era of War Communism (1917–1921) that broke out after the Revolution had the gravest of consequences for culture. The abrupt and radical change in the country's political and ideological situation led not simply to a crisis but to the collapse of the entire cultural infrastructure. In the forefront of the country's cultural life was the "problem of the intelligentsia": during the few years of the revolution, Russia lost almost all of its former cultural elite, some of whom succumbed to hunger or disease in this chaotic time, while some were killed, some emigrated, and others simply fell silent. This process went very quickly. During the course of it, a system of relationships formed between Soviet power and the intelligentsia. As the Politburo archives show, at center stage at this moment was the issue of the intelligentsia leaving the country. This issue was distinctly political from the very beginning and in the hands of the state became a reliable instrument of control over the cultural elites for many long years (Chapter 1).

Another high priority was the issue of the "cultural legacy." The first revolutionary years were marked by the cultural domination of the leftist avant-garde, the Proletkult and the Futurists, whose aesthetic programs were uniformly negative when it came to the cultural tradition and entailed the creation of a completely new culture. The official attitude toward these trends was not, as has been traditionally asserted, unambiguously positive. On the contrary, it was ambivalent. Naturally, ideological closeness was prized in figures of the new culture, but it was Lenin, the leader of the "proletarian state," who applied all his efforts to destroying the bulwark of the new culture, the Proletkult, and to minimizing the influence of so-called "left artists" (avant-gardists) on the country's cultural life. The further matters went, the further "to the right" (i.e., towards conserving the old culture) the state veered toward the end of the civil war. Illustrative in this sense is the episode involving the Politburo's receipt of materials connected with the fate of the Bolshoi Theater (Chapter 2).

The culmination of this turnabout was the introduction of the New Economic Policy, known as NEP (1921–1928), which revitalized the country's cultural as well as economic life. A defining moment for Party cultural policy was the maneuvering during this period between the "fellow travelers" (intellectuals who were generally in favor of the Bolshevik revolution but not committed politically), whose art was seen to lack ideological restraint and optimism, and the "proletarian writers," who were seen as possessing greater political virtue but not "artistic mastery." The fellow travelers' domination in the cultural sphere provoked constant attacks by the proletarian writers and pressure from them on the Party leadership to "defend" them from the "fellow travelers' sway." As Politburo documents here attest, the Party leadership tried to jockey between the two sides in an attempt to bring fellow travelers into collaboration with the state while maintaining as much influence as possible among the "proletarian men of letters" (Chapter 3). The culmination of this struggle was a Central Committee (TsK) resolution of 1925, "On Party policy in the sphere of literature." This resolution reinforced the relatively "liberal" course and aesthetic "tolerance," strengthening the position of the fellow travelers in literature and weakening that of radical supporters of the "hegemony of proletarian literature."

The late 1920s saw a shift in the upper echelons of power, which was connected with the 1927 defeat of the "left opposition" (Leon Trotsky, Grigory Zinoviev, Lev Kamenev). This defeat (paradoxically) heralded the end of NEP, and led not only to a change in the political atmosphere within the Party and the country but also to a "straightening out of the literary front." The sharp turn "to the left" brought about by Joseph Stalin (the First Five Year Plan, rapid industrialization, collectivization) meant that those cultural groups which espoused "pure proletarian culture" gained the ascendant. The "cultural revolution" (1928–1932) and "class war" declared in the country led to the creation of a "cultural front" that rested on completely new foundations.

First to change was the Party's policy toward proletarian writers. RAPP (Russian Association of Proletarian Writers) became the bulwark of the Party in the "Bolshevization of literature," and the 1925 resolution's idea of combining smaller writers' groups into a federation on an equal footing turned into the virtual monopolization of the cultural field by RAPP (Chapter 4). Parallel to this was the process of drawing Maxim Gorky into Soviet cultural life, which, although concealed, found reflection in Politburo materials (Chapter 5). Stalin was grooming Gorky to be the "leader of Soviet literature" and "consolidator of literary forces"—functions he was fated to carry out in the 1930s. The culture of the future, which was seen as "consolidated on a unified base," required ceaseless efforts by the Party to "cut off" "unhealthy forces" and combat the "anti-Soviet intelligentsia" (Chapter 6).

The culmination of the struggle of the cultural revolution, which abruptly altered the entire course of previous cultural development while being simultaneously its logical result, was the Central Committee's 1932 resolution "On restructuring literary and artistic organizations," which created an institutional framework for literature to carry out its new functions. This resolution was a milestone in the history of Soviet culture and closed the period when there were "alternative" possibilities for its future development. If before 1932 the state had to take the various positions espoused by the cultural elites into account when making policy, after the formation of a unified institution (the Writers Union) and the proclamation of a unified artistic method (Socialist Realism), this type of consideration was no longer necessary (and the alternative positions vanished with it). Ahead lay a new, "alternative-free" period of development for Soviet culture.

CHAPTER ONE

"Prohibit Travel . . ."

The Civil War era was characterized by sharp conflict between the new state and the prerevolutionary cultural elites. The intensity of this conflict is well known from emigré memoir literature. Central Committee documents presented here finally allow us to see the situation from the other side of the "cultural front." Out of the total body of documents, we have selected only those which bring out a few themes that are critical for understanding this process. We are intentionally not going to touch here upon the problem of the state's attitude toward the emigration, which has been illuminated fairly well in the literature; rather we will focus on its confrontation with the intelligentsia inside the country.

The new authorities were undoubtedly trying to halt uncontrolled emigration and take charge of the situation—both with respect to the ban on leaving and to the obverse, the deportations (among which one of the best known is the "deportation of philosophers" of 1922 when at Vladimir Lenin's insistence the most prominent philosophers of prerevolutionary Russia were deported to the West). One reason why so many intellectuals wanted to leave during the initial years of Soviet power was because of the harsh conditions. A Politburo resolution dated 16 August 1919, concerning food rations for writers, which had been preceded by numerous appeals from writers and cultural figures as well as efforts by Gorky, was aimed at stabilizing the situation. The Politburo resolved "to satisfy the request of the Mos[cow] Tr[ade] Union of Writers to transfer them to the first category [for rations], seeing that [their] labor is socially essential and beneficial."[1] Thanks to this, many figures in culture and art managed to survive the Civil War in hungry Russia, albeit on very meager rations.

The main factor in the initial emigration, however, was not just the food situation but also the Terror. In this connection not only Gorky, who was influential and authoritative in the country and the world, and the intelligentsia itself, with its appeals to the authorities, but also some Party leaders themselves, were troubled. One sign of this was an appeal by Kamenev, Lunacharsky, and Gorky to the Central Committee against the mass arrests of professors, scholars, and cultural figures who had previously belonged to the Kadet Party (the Constitutional Democratic Party, one of the liberal bourgeois parties of prerevolutionary Russia). A Politburo resolution dated 11 September 1919 demanded that "the dispute on the matter of releasing various arrested individuals be brought before the Central Committee" and created a commission to oversee this that included, in particular, Felix Dzerzhinsky, Nikolai Bukharin, and Lev Kamenev.[2] Meanwhile, arrests were being made on a mass scale and included several leading intellectuals. For example, the arrests undertaken under the rubric "Kadet Party Central Committee" and made by the VChK (All-Russian Extraordinary Commission for Combating Counterrevolution, Sabotage, and Speculation, the "Cheka") included the founders of the Moscow Art Theater, K. S. Stanislavsky and V. I. Nemirovich-Danchenko, together with that theater's leading actor, I. M. Moskvin. Gorky sent Lenin harsh letters on the subject of these repressions. Agreeing that "mistakes had been made," Lenin continued to insist in a letter to Gorky that "on the whole, the measure to arrest the Kadet (and quasi-Kadet) public was essential and correct."[3] Against this background, the intelligentsia's desire to leave the country is perfectly understandable.

The documents selected here from the Politburo archives are connected primarily with this conflict, but before we proceed to examine them, it should be pointed out that the decision-making mechanism during the Civil War—paradoxical though it may seem—was fairly democratic. On many issues, various Politburo members did not share the same opinion; also decisions were often shaped (or altered) as a particular issue passed through different bodies—sometimes several times—on its way to the Politburo. The materials here also demonstrate not simply the presence of a "hard" or "soft" line in the Party leadership but also the fact that these "lines" not only did not reflect ideological differences but also were virtually de-ideologized in that the different sides represented different bureaucratic bodies. At the base of the "soft line" lay primarily the departmental interests of the People's Commissariat of Education (Narkompros); at the base of the "hard line," the departmental interests of the VChK. How Politburo rejections were decided is evident from the situation that arose around a foreign tour by the Moscow Art Theater in 1921. The following document preceded the decision on this matter:

· 1 ·

Memorandum from VChK Chairman F. E. Dzerzhinsky to the
TsK RKP(b) with objections to the intercessions of RSFSR people's
commissar of education on behalf of art figures going abroad.
AP RF, f. 3, op. 35, d. 35, l. 3. Original. Typewritten.
19 April 1921.

Esteemed Comrades:

Of late there have again been frequent instances of intercession by various artistic circles—individuals and entire theaters—concerning permission to travel abroad. These intercessions have been systematically supported by Com. Lunacharsky.

Based on its prior experience, the VChK categorically protests this. So far, not a single released individual (for instance, Kusevitsky, Gzovskaia, Gaidarov, Balmont) has come back, and some—Balmont in particular—are waging a malicious campaign against us.

This show of weakness on our part represents a thoroughly unjustified misappropriation of our cultural treasures and only strengthens our enemies' ranks.

Now Com. Lunacharsky is attempting to submit a petition to allow the First Studio of the Art Theater to travel abroad. Meanwhile, according to very reliable information, a group of artists from this theater is in close contact with American circles very closely connected to intelligence agencies. The theater has been promised material assistance abroad. The artist Sukhacheva has been in close contact with a number of these individuals.

Before this, the Chamber Theater submitted a petition as well.

Allusions to rest and treatment are by no means convincing, since the artists could easily use their vacations for trips to the provinces.

Firmly opposed to such petitions, the VChK asks the Central Committee to treat this matter with all seriousness.

With Com[munist] greetings,
VChK Chair[man] Dzerzhinsky

P.S. I am addressing the Central Committee because in his appeal Com. Lunacharsky mistakenly says that he will be addressing the Central Committee on this matter.

A few weeks later, on 7 May 1921, the Politburo resolved: "Defer decision on the matter, instructing Com. Lunacharsky to present an exact list of those who have been permitted to go abroad and a report on how many of those individuals from the scholarly and artistic worlds who were permitted to go abroad have returned, sending all information to the VChK Special Section for an additional review."[4] It is worth pointing out that as it made its decisions the Politburo was anxious to cover its own rear; the expert in such matters was, naturally, the VChK. Three days later, on 10 May 1921, a decision was reached on a trip abroad by the premier Russian singer, Fyodor Chaliapin. The minutes of the Politburo session recorded: "Allow Chaliapin to go abroad on condition of a guarantee from the VChK that Chaliapin will return. If the VChK objects, the matter must be reconsidered."[5] In point of fact, Chaliapin never did return.

A few days later, Lunacharsky, who always acted as intercessor for art world figures, proposed a palliative to the problem:

· 2 ·

Memorandum from RSFSR People's Commissar of Education A. V. Lunacharsky to the Politburo of the TsK RKP(b) on the procedure for allowing art world figures to travel abroad. [Not before 12 May 1921]. AP RF, f. 3, op. 35, d. 35, l. 11. Original. Typewritten.

To the Politburo of the TsK RKP(b)
Dear Comrades:

In accordance with the resolution of the Politburo of the TsK, I have compiled a list of the individuals who have been sent abroad. Now the Politburo must make a final decision on the matter of sending several artists abroad, specifically, the First Studio troupe and the Stradivarius Quartet along with the pianist Orlov, and also give Narkompros the right to permit several other individuals to travel. Comrade Oleynikov, who is a consultant in Narkompros, has proposed an extremely clever method: draw up a list at the Main Arts Committee for all artists wishing to travel abroad and let them out three or five at a time with the admonition that the next will be allowed to leave only after the return of those who have already left. In this way, we establish a natural mutual guarantee. We will send them off only at the petition of the artists, perhaps through the trade union or through the loc[al] commune, so that they themselves will be to blame if someone in the first group of five stays abroad and in this way automatically blocks travel for others. It occurs to me that we could set these same conditions for troupes, i.e., let the First Studio go now on condition that the Art Theater's trip will be possible only if the Studio returns. Simultaneously with this I am appending an extremely important letter to me from Com. Krasin with a note from Deputy People's Commissar Karakhan, and I would ask you not to delay examining this matter and appointing him as quickly as possible.

People's Commissar of Education A. Lunacharsky
Secretary A. Flakserman

Meanwhile, wholly in the spirit of the time, the VChK could not agree to such a proposal, which in fact legitimized a unique kind of "hostage taking". A few days later, a letter signed by I. Unshlikht arrived at the Central Committee:

· 3 ·

Letter from Deputy VChK Chairman I. S. Unshlikht and VChK Foreign Department (INO) Head L. Davydov to the TsK RKP(b). AP RF, f. 3, op. 35, d. 35, l. 8. Original. Typewritten.
18 May 1921.

To the TsK RKP, Com. Molotov.
On the Politburo resolution dated 7 May 1921, no. 23, p. 16.

By confirming its first statement, the VChK has once again drawn the Central Committee's attention to Narkompros's utterly impermissible attitude toward foreign travel by our artistic forces. There is not the slightest doubt that a large majority of the artists and painters who travel abroad will be lost to Soviet Russia, at least for the next few years.

In addition, many of them are waging an overt or covert campaign against us abroad.

Of those who have gone abroad with the permission of Narkompros, only five have returned; the remaining nineteen have not, and one (Balmont) is waging the vilest of campaigns against Soviet Russia.

As for the First Studio of the Art Theater, the VChK can say with confidence that it will not return. All the artists in the Art Theater who are abroad at the present time are enjoying tremendous success and living magnificently in the material respect.

In addition, a number of famous artists (in particular Sukhacheva) have close ties with foreign missions in Moscow, and there is reason to believe that their dealings with them are not merely of a personal nature.

    VChK Deputy Chair[man] Unshlikht
    INO Head Davydov

The departmental correspondence ends with a final Politburo decision of 28 May 1921: "Reject the First Art Studio's request for permission to travel abroad."[6] Lunacharsky, however, would not accept this personal defeat and demanded that the Politburo resolve the problem "in principle."

The best illustration of how spontaneous Politburo decisions were—although they often by no means strengthened the new state's authority—might be the fate of one of the most popular prerevolutionary writers, Fyodor Sologub, and the foremost poet of prerevolutionary Russia, Aleksandr Blok. On 20 December 1919, the Politburo resolved in response to Sologub's petition to go abroad which had been referred to them by Trotsky: "Reject. Instruct Commission for the Improvement of Scholars' Living Conditions to add fifty major poets and writers, including Sologub and Balmont, to its list of those served."[7] Later, Lunacharsky revisited the problem:

· 4 ·

Letter from A. V. Lunacharsky to the TsK RKP(b). RGASPI, f. 17,
op. 84, d. 228, l. 40–40v. Original. Typewritten.
7 June 1921

To the TsK RKP, Com. Molotov:

I am turning to you concerning two matters. The first is personal; the second is general and recurrent. The personal matter you will understand immediately when you read the letter from Gorky attached hereto; the general one is that I am insisting with all the means at my disposal that the TsK consider my more than modest proposal, which consists of the following points:

    1. That the People's Commissar of Education be allowed to permit temporary foreign travel for artists of all types, for a period of time not to exceed four months, for five individuals.

    Comment 1. The For[eign] Section of the Spec[ial] Department may detain such individuals only for strictly political motives, which must be reported in secret to the People's Commissar for Education and the TsK Secretariat.

Comment 2. In the event that the individuals being sent abroad wish to travel with their families, the issue of allowing entire families shall remain within the competence of the Special Department.

2. After the return of each of these five individuals, the People's Commissar for Education shall have the right to send abroad the next individual on the list of candidates. If they break their word and remain abroad permanently, they will automatically block whoever is next in line.

Under this procedure, we can count on a certain mutual guarantee and can even inquire of the collectives, which have, accordingly, a special interest in this kind of travel, whether or not they want to risk, say, sending so-and-so or so-and-so abroad. It is in their own interests to send only loyal people, so as not to rob others of the opportunity for foreign travel.

I insist that this matter be raised with the Orgburo or the Politburo and that it be considered only in my presence. The torrent of negative decisions just now passed by the TsK on the issue of foreign travel can yield only one result—mass flight abroad. Naturally, the Cheka does this lightly—it's easy to do lightly—and refuses to issue the papers, but realistically it cannot detain the artists, and as a result such individuals as Boleslavsky, Smirnov, Romanov, Gzovskaia, Evelinov, and a number of others have crossed the border without the slightest hitch, thereby showing others the way as well. I wholly support the sole sensible point of view of People's Commissar for Foreign Trade Krasin, who says that the scandalous flights abroad will cease only when we allow artists, in a careful way, to travel abroad for a period of time. I sent Krasin's handwritten letter about this to the TsK a long time ago.

Although an issue already examined by the Politburo must be considered final, as I have been informed, I nonetheless protest in advance any consideration of matters concerning Narkompros made in my absence.

People's Commissar of Education A. Lunacharsky
Secretary A. Flakserman

The attached letter from Gorky, dated 3 May 1921, to People's Commissar for Education Lunacharsky, in which he referred to a letter he had received from Blok, said, "Aleksandr Alexandrovich Blok has scurvy, moreover lately he has been in such a heightened nervous state that his doctors and friends fear the onset of serious psychiatric illness." In this letter, Gorky asked the People's Commissar of Education to do everything possible, leaving no stone unturned, "so that Blok, with all due speed, may travel to Finland, where I could help him get settled in one of the best sanatoria."⁸ The VChK did not delay its response to Lunacharsky's letter:

· 5 ·

Letter from INO VChK Head L. Davydov to the TsK RKP(b).
RGASPI, f. 17, op. 84, d. 175, l. 48. Original. Typewritten.
28 June 1921

Top secret. Ex[tremely] urgent. To TsK RKP, Com. Molotov

At the present time the INO VChK has applications from several writers—in particular Vengerova, Blok, and Sologub—for permission to travel abroad.

Bearing in mind that the writers who have gone abroad are waging the most active campaign against Soviet Russia and that some of them, such as Balmont, Kuprin, and Bunin, are not stopping at the vilest fabrications, the VChK deems it impossible to grant similar petitions.

Unless the TsK RKP has specific reasons for considering it more desirable for a given writer to be abroad than in Soviet Russia, then the VChK for its part sees no grounds for allowing them to leave in the near future.

In any case, we would consider it desirable to refer such matters to the Orgburo.

To illustrate the above, attached herewith is a copy of a letter from Com. Vorovsky in Rome.

> INO VChK H[ead] L. Davydov
> Personal Secretary Rudnikov

Lunacharsky continued to insist:

· 6 ·

Letter from A. V. Lunacharsky to RSFSR Narkomindel. AP RF, f. 3, op. 34,
d. 206, l. 5. Verified copy. Typewritten.
8 July 1921

To Narkomindel Com. Chicherin
Copy to Osobotdel [of the VChK] Com. Menzhinsky
Copy to Sovnarkom Administration Com. Gorbunov

The general situation for writers in Russia is difficult in the extreme. You must be familiar with the case of Sologub being granted permission to go abroad and the request for the same from Remizov and Bely; but the case of Aleksandr Blok, undoubtedly the poet most talented and most sympathetic to us of all the best-known Russian poets, has taken an especially tragic turn. I endeavored to take every step in my power, both in the sense of permitting Blok to go abroad and in the sense of arranging relatively satisfactory conditions for him here. As a result, Blok is now seriously ill with scurvy and in grave psychic distress, so that there is fear of serious psychological illness.

By not releasing the poet and at the same time not giving him the necessary decent conditions, we have tortured him in the literal sense of the word. It goes without saying that this will be exploited accordingly by our enemies. I am not to blame for this because I never refused a single request from Blok or other writers of that sort, I did everything I could to support their requests, but I constantly encountered either outright refusal or else systematic failure to meet the obligations undertaken (for example, with the academic food ration) on the part of both the Petrograd food and Soviet institutions and the Spec[ial] Department. Meanwhile, public opinion in Russia and Europe holds me above all accountable for such incidents. Therefore I once again, and in the most energetic way, protest the department's lackadaisical attitude toward the needs of the foremost Russian writers and with the same energy petition for immediate permission for Blok to go to Finland for treatment.

People's Commissar of Education A. Lunacharsky
Secretary A. Flakserman

"Immediate permission" did not follow. Lunacharsky wrote another letter to the TsK with a copy to Lenin:

· 7 ·

Letter from A. V. Lunacharsky to the TsK RKP(b). [11 July 1921]. RGASPI, f. 2, op. 1, d. 19699, l. 1. Dispatch. Typewritten.

To the TsK RKP
Copy to Com. Lenin

The poet Aleksandr Blok, who throughout these four years has remained completely loyal to Soviet power and who has written several compositions considered abroad to be obviously sympathetic to the October revolution, has at the present time suffered a serious nervous breakdown. In the opinion of his doctors and friends, the only possibility of helping him is a temporary release to Finland. I personally and Com. Gorky are petitioning for this. The papers are in the Special Department, and we ask the TsK to exert its influence over Com. Menzhinsky in a sense favorable for Blok.

People's Commissar of Education A. Lunacharsky

On the letter is Lenin's note to his colleague in the VChK: "Com. Menzhinsky! Your response? Come back, please, with a response. Com[munist] gr[eetings]! Lenin." A "response" from the VChK followed that same day:

· 8 ·

Note from V. R. Menzhinsky to V. I. Lenin. RGASPI, f. 2, op. 1, d. 19699, l. 2.
Handwritten.
11 July 1921

Esteemed comrade!
Not only Lunacharsky, but Bukharin as well vouched for Balmont. Blok is a poetic nature; some story will produce a bad impression on him, and before you know it, quite naturally, he'll be writing against us. I don't think there's any point letting him out. Instead, we should set Blok up in good conditions somewhere in a sanatorium.

With com[munist] gr[eetings]
V. Menzhinsky

The next day, 12 July 1921, a decision followed from the Politburo: "Reject the petition from Comrades Lunacharsky and Gorky to let A. Blok go to Finland. Instruct Narkomprod to improve Blok's food situation."[9] The next point of the same decision: "Allow F. Sologub to go abroad."[10] A letter from Gorky to Lenin is dated the same day, 12 July:

· 9 ·

Letter from A. M. Gorky to V. I. Lenin. [Not before 12 July 1921]. IMLI. A. M. Gorky Archive. Handwritten draft.

Vladimir Ilich!

"Ignore the little things"—that's a very good rule, especially for someone—like you—who must deal and is used to dealing with masses, states, and nations. I'm not one of those people who consider that kind of behavior the behavior of an "ostrich in danger," since I know very well how terribly and vilely those damnable little things can get in the way of a peaceful life and doing what you want.

But I, a man who never forgets that the tuberculosis, cholera, and syphilis bacilli are little things, I don't forget, and I see how those little things can wreck extremely valuable and complex organisms. Therefore I cannot ignore the tremendous importance of little things in life and have decided to write to you about those "little things."

In a social organism, scoundrels and swindlers play the disastrous role of pathogenic bacilli. You know that in any case we have our own swindlers and that there were a particularly large number of them in the grand cause of our revolution—the perfectly natural legacy of the "old world," which is, in essence, one big swindle.

For some time now I have been convinced that here, in Soviet Russia, the black but invisible hand of a swindler is doing its sly but clever work. That work is felt everywhere anything serious begins to develop successfully, no matter how small. I have been observing the work of this hand—for over two years—in the work of the Expert Commission.

By a resolution of the Sovnarkom it was decided to accelerate this commission's work, increase the number of its workers to two hundred, and give them a good ration. The resolution was passed in October 1920, but despite my persistent efforts, it has yet to be implemented, and a few days ago the Commission for Provisioning the Workforce firmly refused to issue rations. The commission's work has been delayed, the employees are scattering, and the swindlers are triumphing, stealing and stealing.

In another sphere. An honest writer incapable of abuse or slander against the Soviet government, A. A. Blok, is dying of scurvy and asthma. He must be allowed to go to Finland, to a sanatorium. He is not being let out, while at the same time three writers were allowed to go abroad who are going to abuse and slander—they will. I know Soviet power will not suffer from this, and I would like to let everyone go abroad who wants to, however, I don't understand this bizarre policy. It seems suspicious, deliberate. It makes me think of the incident with Shpitsberg, the "Communist" and VChK investigator on matters of the clergy. During the times of the tsarist regime, this Shpitsberg was a petty, nasty lawyer for divorce cases. A shady character, he even raised suspicions in the Spiritual Consistories. After October he declared himself a "theomachist," spoke at meetings with A. V. Lunacharsky, edited the journal *Church and Revolution* [*Tserkov' i revoliutsia*] with Krasikov, and finally penetrated into the VChK. Working there as an investigator he has committed innumerable vile acts of all kinds that have been extremely injurious to the prestige of the Soviet government. I heard he was finally driven out of the VChK, and yes, out of the Party, by the way. This is good, but isn't there more than one Shpitsberg left there?

The "Commission to Improve Scholars' Living Conditions" managed to purchase 30,000 cans of tinned goods in Lithuania for Soviet banknotes and very cheaply. Five months ago, I sent a petition to the VChK about allowing a certain Adolia Rode to travel to Lithuania to examine, test, and receive the purchased tinned goods. They promised to let Rode out, and I gave permission to give the sellers an advance. A few days ago, however, I was informed that they aren't letting Rode go to Lithuania. Why? "Politically unreliable." Excuse me, but that is nonsense. In October, when Rode was arrested along with other bourgeois, Uritsky himself went to the prison and got him out of there. He, Rode, is well known to Badaev, Bakaev, and Pakhiev. He was an innkeeper in the past, but now he is a superb and selfless worker for KUBU [the Commission to Improve Scholars' Living Conditions], a man who is extremely flattered by the fact that he left the innkeepers only to land in the midst of scholars and that they value highly his intelligent work. A Lithuanian by birth, he could have chosen to leave—had he wanted that. But, if he does choose to do that, they won't let him back into Russia and he will lose a good situation. And the Commission will lose a marvelous worker. Why was this done? This prohibition greatly irritates people who have nothing to eat and who, at this difficult moment, nonetheless are able to work marvelously.

Furthermore, the Grzhebin affair is gradually taking on the quality of a minor Beilis affair. They are persecuting Grzhebin like a dog or—even worse—like a Jew. You well know that I organized Grzhebin's publishing house with your permission. I spent two years working to organize that publishing house, commissioned dozens of new popular books on the natural sciences by our most prominent scholars, and achieved rare success. Through persistent work we liberated the Russian scholarly book market from the sway of the German publishers and publications. However, Gosizdat [the State Publishing House] keeps rejecting the manuscripts I offer from our best scholars and itself is publishing old translations of books that have already lost their scientific importance, for ex[ample], *Chemistry* by Rosko and Geiki's *Physics*. These books were published in Russian in the 1870s. Gosizdat rejected Zlatogorov's *What Is Cholera* for publication, nor did it accept the *Manual for Hospital Orderlies and Disinfectors* and several very necessary textbooks.

Despite the fact that on 26 April a commission of the TsK RKP(b) approved the agreement between Grzhebin and Gosizdat obligating the latter to come up with a list of books, print runs, and prices in one week's time, Gosizdat dragged the matter out for several months, and now it has refused to carry out the resolution of the TsK Plenum. The resolution itself was not given to me and has been lost by both Gosizdat and the TsK.

All this is odd, you'll agree. Gosizdat is the talk of the town, everyone is shouting that the institution must be reformed, that Veis should be fired, that the board, which is made up of people who understand nothing about the business and whom Veis leads around by the nose, should be removed. Despite the general protests, though, Gosizdat continues to follow its own line. I consider this line not only clumsy but nasty and harmful. No paper? The attached clipping from *Pravda* attests to where the paper is going. And there are dozens of testimonies like it.

A few days later, Lunacharsky joined in again:

· 10 ·

Letter from A. V. Lunacharsky to TsK RKP(b). AP RF, f. 3, op. 34, d. 206, l. 6–6v. Original. Typewritten.
16 July 1921

To the TsK RKP

The TsK RKP resolutions reported to me on the subject of Blok and Sologub seem to me the fruit of an obvious misunderstanding. It is hard to imagine a decision whose irrationality could be more tremendously startling. Who is Sologub? An old writer who inspires no more hopes, is inclined in the most malicious and poisonous way against Soviet Russia, and is taking abroad with him a spiteful satire entitled *The Chinese Republic of Equals* [*Kitaiskaia respublika ravnykh*]. And this person, concerning whom I have never insisted, for whom I, as People's Commissar of Education, have never once vouched (and it would be unconscionable to do so), about whom I have only said that I have been put in a difficult position because the VChK won't let him go and Narkomprod and Narkomfin won't give me the means to support him, this man you are letting out. Who is Blok? A young poet who inspires tremendous hopes, who along with

Briusov and Gorky is the principal adornment of our entire literature of yesterday, so to speak. A man about whom the *Times* newspaper recently wrote a major article, calling him the most outstanding poet of Russia and pointing out that he recognizes and praises the October revolution.

While Sologub is simply a little bit hungry, having, actually, a large salary, Blok is suffering from grave hypochondriasis and his travel abroad has been recognized by the doctors as the only way to save him from death. But you won't let him go. Meanwhile, on the eve of receiving your decision, I was discussing this fact with V. I. Lenin, who asked me to send a corresponding request to the TsK, with a copy to him, promising to support Blok's release to Finland in every way.

However, the TsK by no means considers it necessary to ask the People's Commissar of Education his motives, examines these issues behind my back, and, of course, commits a crude mistake. I can tell you in advance what will come as a consequence of your decision. The highly gifted Blok will die in a couple of weeks, and Fyodor Kuzmich Sologub will write an essay of despair full of cursing and oaths on this subject, against which we will be defenseless, since the basis for this article, i.e., the fact that we destroyed Russia's most talented poet, will not be subject to the slightest doubt or refutation.

I am sending a copy of this letter to V. I. Lenin, who took an interest in Blok's fate, and to Com. Gorky, so that Russia's best writers know that I am not to blame for this foolhardy (the TsK will forgive me this expression) decision.

      People's Commissar of Enlightenment A. Lunacharsky
      Secretary A. Flakserman

It is difficult to say what actually influenced Lenin's decision to reconsider his position—Gorky's emotions or Lunacharsky's arguments—but the following note is in the archive:

· 11 ·

Note from L. B. Kamenev to V. M. Molotov. [No later than 23 July 1921]. AP RF, f. 3, op. 1, d. 175, ll. 7–7v. Handwritten.

To Com. Molotov
Lenin and I propose:
1. Reconsidering the matter of foreign travel by A. A. Blok. At the last PB Tr[otsky] and I voted in favor, and Len[in], Zin[oviev], and Mol[otov] voted against. Now Len[in] is joining us. . . .

>L. Kamenev
>1 ab[stention] Com. Molotov,
>Com. Kamenev—in favor,
>Com. Lenin—in favor.

Lenin's position proved decisive. That same day the Politburo approved a new decision:

· 12 ·

Resolution of the Politburo of the TsK RKP(b) on L. B. Kamenev's proposal to reconsider the previous resolution banning A. A. Blok from foreign travel. RGASPI, f. 17, op. 3, d. 192, l. 2. Authenticated copy. Typewritten.
23 July 1921

No. 53-a. n. 5—Proposal of Com. Kamenev—to reconsider the Politburo's resolution on allowing A. A. Blok to travel abroad.
Allow A. A. Blok to travel abroad.

Aleksandr Blok passed away in Petrograd two weeks later, on 7 August 1921.

The death of Blok, the premier poet of Russian Symbolism—like the execution that followed a few days later of Nikolai Gumilyov, one of the founders and premier poets of Russian Acmeism—is traditionally regarded not simply as a milestone in relations between the intelligentsia and Soviet power but as a turning point, the end of an entire era; nine years later, the suicide of Vladimir Mayakovsky would be perceived in a similar way. No matter how Blok's death is interpreted, it became a symbol long ago, the Politburo materials now available allow us to see that for the Party leadership the problem of Blok's departure, which was discussed a great deal in the cultural elites, was considered routine. It took the usual bureaucratic route and reached its resolution too late for Blok. It did not save the poet's life, but it did quite a bit to add to his immortality. Lunacharsky was right even in the fine points; the "cursing and oaths" that came crashing down on the Bolsheviks were well deserved. The fact that they had persecuted Russia's most talented poet was indeed "not subject to the slightest doubt or refutation." The Politburo documents do not refute any myths but merely demonstrate that any political mythology (including the demonization of the Bolsheviks) and the reality of how specific political decisions are made lie on completely different planes.

CHAPTER TWO

"The Utterly Indecent Proposal to Preserve the Bolshoi Theater"

Being a radical type of revolutionary, Lenin was by no means always anxious to appease the intelligentsia. When it came to steps that were unpopular among the cultural elites but in keeping with Bolshevist programmatic aims, he was quite open to confrontation. Moreover, he sometimes obtained what he thought were the right solutions by applying direct pressure. This was the situation that arose around the Bolshoi Opera Theater. After the Revolution, the theater, which stood for the "old culture," not only in the eyes of the "Party rank and file" but also among that other category of the population known as "the top ten thousand stuffed bellies," found itself in an extremely difficult position. Previously one of several court theaters directly supported by and under the control of the tsar's administration, the Imperial Chamber, it now lost not only its state subsidies but also private donations and was literally on the brink of shutting down. The issue of closing the Bolshoi Theater was discussed several times in the government. The theater in point of fact was barely functioning. Lenin, who often had to interrupt his work due to illness, found out that during one of these interludes, when he had been absent due to illness, the Sovnarkom had passed a resolution to preserve the Bolshoi Theater. He sent a memo to Molotov:

· 13 ·

Memo from V. I. Lenin to V. M. Molotov. AP RF, f. 3, op. 35, d. 4, l. 7. Copy. Typewritten.
12 January 1922

To Com. Molotov.

Having learned from Kamenev that the SNK has unanimously approved Lunacharsky's utterly indecent proposal to preserve the Bolshoi Opera and Ballet, I propose that the Politburo resolve:

1. To instruct the VTsIK [All-Russian Central Executive Committee] Presidium to rescind the SNK resolution.

2. To leave just a few dozen artists from the opera and ballet for Moscow and Petersburg so that their performances (both operas and dancing) can pay for themselves,[1] i.e., eliminate any major expenses for sets and such.

3. From the billions saved in th[is] way, to spend at least half to wipe out illiteracy and for reading rooms.

4. To call Lunacharsky in for five minutes to hear the defendant's last word and to make it clear to him and to all the people's commissars that introducing and voting on a resolution like that now being rescinded by the TsK henceforth will entail stricter measures on the part of the TsK.

Lenin

In the Politburo, Lenin's opinion was, as we have already seen, final. The very same day, the Politburo took a decision "to instruct the VTsIK Presidium to rescind the SNK resolution on preserving the Bolshoi Opera and Ballet."[2] The decision-making procedure was typical. It included all three "branches" of power—the Party, the legislature, and the executive, that is, the Politburo, which "instructed" the Soviet organ to rescind the government's decision. All the structures were directed by the same individuals, and all the decisions were taken in the Politburo. The next day, though, Lunacharsky sent a letter to Lenin:

· 14 ·

Letter from A. V. Lunacharsky to V. I. Lenin. AP RF, f. 3, op. 35, d. 4, ll. 12–13v.
Original. Typewritten.
13 January 1922

Very urgent. Personal.
To Com. Vladimir Ilich Lenin.
Dear Vladimir Ilich,

Yesterday, Com. Yenukidze told me that at the last meeting of the Politburo it was once again decided to close the Bolshoi Theater and an instruction was given to the VTsIK Presidium to reexamine this matter and decide it in the previously indicated vein. I am taking the liberty of splitting this matter into two parts, its formal aspect and its substance. Formally, I protest in the most categorical way such an examination of any matter of no matter what kind. In point of fact, the matter has been taken up by Com. Larin's commission, in the Small and Large Soviet [of People's Commissars], as well as in the VTsIK Presidium more than once, with an extremely attentive hearing of all the pros and cons. As a result, both the Large Sovnarkom and the VTsIK Presidium resolved to let the Bolshoi Theater remain open. Then the Central Committee suddenly plans, without a single word to me or listening to a single competent individual, to make a gesture which, as I am about to prove to you, is compromisingly absurd. No matter how wise the Central Committee is, in deciding among great affairs of state relatively trifling details such as the matter of the Bolshoi Theater, it is certainly taking the risk of committing these kind of absurd lapses if it not only does not hear any specialists but does not even listen to the person it itself assigned to this matter, in this case me, who for the last four years must have acquired some experience in matters of this sort. Working from these notions, I formally protest the decision of the Central Committee taken without me and categorically demand that this decision be reconsidered after my arguments against it are heard.

I am sending a statement to this effect to the TsK secretary.

Now a few words about substance. You will immediately realize from these few lines that you have been misled.

Under the tsarist regime, the Bolshoi Theater's deficit was as much as a million rubles a year, which is at least 100 billion in our money. Next year, in 1922, the state is supposed to pay the Bolshoi Theater 144[,000] gold rubles in all, i.e., less than one-sixth of the previous expenditures. At the same time, under the tsar, the best seat in the Bolshoi Theater cost 5 rubles, while at the present time in gold money it costs 30 kopeks. Twenty-five percent of all the seats, including the most expensive, are given to VTsSPS [All-Union Central Board of Trade Unions] organs for free. After this, you will of course ask by what miracle can we maintain this theater? Indeed, it is a genuine miracle in both the administrative respect and with respect to the sacrifices all the artists make for this cause, for not one of them receives more than 20 percent of his former salary, and some significantly less. At the same time, the multibillion theater property is being kept in remarkable condition with which even the best storehouse of the VSNKh [All-Union Council of the National Economy] scarcely compares. For all this, Com. Malinovskaia should be awarded the Order of the Red Banner, instead of which she is being awarded with loss of health as a consequence of all the slander, in which not only the acting rabble and the swindlers who dart in and out around the theater but also several Soviet high officials are taking part.

Say, now, that we shut down the Bolshoi Theater. What will come of this? Here's what. Even Com. Larin's commission, which resolved to shut down the Bolshoi Theater, felt it necessary to keep its orchestra as the top European entity of European importance in Russia. In addition, we need to maintain the enormous building, which we need for the sessions of the Soviet, and finally, we need to preserve the entire multibillion theater property. As a result, we are going to be spending on all this the same paltry 12,000 gold rubles a month that the state is paying now. The performances will stop, but so will the income from them, and it's the performances that pay for the troupe and themselves; the subsidy in fact goes to pay for maintenance and equipment, and if we add to this the orchestra, then there might not even be enough for expenses. So that with your measure you are not giving Narkompros a single ruble, unless you want all this demagoguery to strip the theater clean of your property or the Bolshoi Theater itself to collapse as a European way of demonstrating our lack of culture. Add to this the fact that those one and a half thousand people who feed themselves from the theater are going to be thrown out on the street in the middle of winter though you have already signed a contract with them for the season. In any country where labor is the least bit protected (and it seems to me that the workers' and peasants' Republic ought to resemble such a country), they could sue for breach of contract in court, and, of course, any court would recognize their perfect right to receive such a forfeit, and if the theater is shut down this would mean a tremendous expense for the state. If we as "dictators" do not take on this tremendous expense, then that will simply mean that without deriving any benefit ourselves we will have taken a crust of bread away from one and a half thousand people and their families, and several dozen children might die of hunger. That is what shutting down the Bolshoi Theater actually means.

The continuation of its existence would mean that we, without spending a single kopek over and above those 12,000 rubles a month needed to maintain the building, preserve the materials, and support the orchestra, at the same time have a theater about which laudatory reviews are still coming in from representatives of foreign powers and the foreign press, and every evening we are allowing 2,000 people, including 500 workers, to spend their time in a well-lit, warm building listening to good music and allowing as many laborers as would make up a small district town to exist quite decently by their special labor.

Those are the circumstances.

Because I am still of sound mind and strong memory, I cannot in any way allow you to continue insisting on shutting down the Bolshoi Theater now that you have learned these circumstances. We may commit unconscious mistakes and stupidities, but consciously, of course, we don't. I am almost ready to agree with Com. Yenukidze that those who frivolously led the Central Committee into error—and such individuals doubtless exist—should be submitted to a Party trial.

Now one more point for my conclusion. You voted in the Politburo to reprimand me for not safeguarding my department's interests properly, because I did not keep an eye on how Osinsky, without warning me, decided a matter affecting Narkompros. You said I have to keep an eye on everything. Maybe the TsK as well? Maybe I should ask some member of the TsK who is more amicably inclined toward me to take on such oversight? The TsK is constantly raising Narkompros issues without calling in any of my colleagues. Then Com. Sosnovsky was barred from chairing all commissions because in discussing a matter concerning Narkompros he did not warn it. I think that this is not a matter of the constitution but of recognizing the complete unreasonableness of such conduct. If the laws of the constitution do not apply to the TsK, then the laws of reason certainly do. What can we do and who can we complain to?

I am confident that you, Vladimir Ilich, will not be angry at my letter but on the contrary will correct the mistake that has been made, and I firmly shake your hand.

People's Commissar of Education Lunacharsky

Nonetheless, this time the arguments, appeals to the law, and simple practical considerations had no effect. The next day Lunacharsky made a new appeal to the TsK:

· 15 ·

Letter from A. V. Lunacharsky to V. M. Molotov. AP RF, f. 3, op. 35, d. 4, l. 11. Original. Typewritten.

14 January 1922

To TsK Secretary Com. Molotov

Com. Yenukidze has informed me that the TsK Politburo has taken a decision to shut down the Bolshoi Theater. I categorically protest the passage of such a decision without warning me or hearing my arguments. I categorically demand a reexamination of this matter in my presence. I have sent a detailed letter about this to Vladimir Ilich.

>With Communist greetings,
>Lunacharsky

The TsK apparatus sent copies of Lunacharsky's appeal to all the members of the Politburo. But help for Lunacharsky came from the official head of the Soviet state, TsK member and VTsIK chairman M. I. Kalinin. In his letter, he protested the Politburo's decision of 12 January (as we recall, it was the VTsIK that ordered "Kalinin's department" to shut down the theater) and requested that the TsK explain the motives for its decision: "It seems to me," wrote Kalinin,

> that before destroying an immense cultural asset in the persons of the opera and ballet artists and their professional cohesion, which has been building up for generations, we must first decide who is to take their place, i.e., what type of fine art is going to take the place of the destroyed opera and ballet.
>
> The next question is why, out of nowhere, did the persecution of the opera and ballet suddenly coalesce? Is this type of art really incompatible with the Soviet order? Or are the auditoriums ever empty? . . . If it is a matter of closing the theater for purposes of economy, then this consideration . . . does not hold up under criticism either. For who would ever think, for example, to shut down or destroy the Rumiantsev Museum or the public library for the purposes of economy merely on the grounds that few workers go there? The Bolshoi Theater without a doubt plays no less of an educative role for its visitors than the public library does. It's not true that only speculators attend the Bolshoi Theater. I think it was the king of Persia or some other country who burned down a Greek temple of art in order to win his fame in history. I think that the TsK RKP has enough positive work to its credit

not to have to resort to such dubious means, and I hope that the Politburo will reconsider and rescind its decision.[3]

Kalinin's letter was also distributed to the members of the Politburo.

This time, after just five days, on 17 January, the Politburo was no longer "instructing" but "requesting the VTsIK to consider the substance of Com. Lunacharsky's statement,"[4] and in another three weeks, on 9 February, it approved a resolution not on "closing the Bolshoi Theater" but on "the possibility of preserving" it. This time, economic rather than political and ideological motives show up: "Instruct the RKI [Worker-Peasant Inspection] to submit a precise inventory of the contents of the Bolshoi Theater in its current form and the cuts in expenditures that could be gained if it were closed down."[5] The head of the RKI was Stalin. It came to be that the Bolshoi Theater was fated to play an important role in Soviet political history. But it was no secret to anyone (as has been mentioned many times in the literature) that those involved in its destiny—Lunacharsky, Kalinin, Yenukidze, and later Voroshilov—were great admirers of the Bolshoi Theater ballerinas. Stalin took full advantage of this circumstance, blackmailing his comrades-in-arms with the threat of publicity and of being compromised.

A threat to the academic theaters[6] broke out less than a year later. On 26 October, the Politburo approved a resolution to cut financing for theaters. Having created a commission that included Kamenev and Lunacharsky in particular, the Politburo decided to "elaborate measures to make maximum cuts in state subsidies for any and all theaters and to close the Mariinsky and Bolshoi theaters in the event that these two, given a minimal subsidy from the state, find themselves in the course of half a year to be incapable of becoming self-supporting. The commission has one week to complete its work."[7] And indeed, exactly a week later, the Politburo issued a resolution that apparently put an end to the exhausting battle over the Bolshoi Theater:

· 16 ·

Resolution of the Politburo of the TsK RKP(b) on the closure of the Bolshoi and Mariinsky theaters. RGASPI, f. 17, op. 3, d. 320, ll. 2–3. Authenticated copy. Typewritten.
2 November 1922

No. 34, n. 4—On the academic theaters (Com. Kamenev).

1. Deem it impossible for the Bolshoi Theater and the former Mariinsky to make the transition to the principles of self-support.

2. As a result of this, for the purpose of reducing the government subsidy for state and academic theaters by 395 million a year (calculated from 1922 data), close down the Bolshoi Theater and the former Mariinsky, ceasing to issue them a subsidy, starting with the current budget quarter, and allocating the necessary funds to preserve the theater property and theater buildings.

3. Assign the 395 million rubles freed up to the needs of popular education (support first-level teachers and students [of primary schools], eliminate illiteracy, and help libraries).

Assign the distribution to a commission made up of Comrades Yakovlev, Bem, and Krupskaia.

4. Form a special commission to implement the resolution set forth in the second point, giving this commission the right to discuss other measures that could lead to cuts in government subsidies for the theaters of the sum indicated above so that the Bolshoi Theater and former Mariinsky would not have to be shut down.

Appoint Com. Kolegaev one of the members of the commission and assign him to find his bearings, make a report to Comrades Stalin and Kamenev, and reach an agreement with them on other members of the commission.

The fourth point, as one can see, implied the possibility of reconsidering this resolution. There is no trace of Lenin's ideological maximalism; the ideological motivation has been wholly replaced by the economic. However, economic considerations never predominated over political ones in Politburo decisions. Here is what happened two and a half years later:

· 17 ·

Resolution of the Politburo of the TsK RKP(b) on the academic theaters.
RGASPI, f. 17, op. 3, d. 509, ll. 4–5. Authenticated copy. Typewritten.

2 July 1925

No. 69, p. 16—Report of the Politburo commission on theaters (PB, 25 June 1925, pr. no. 68, p. 7) (Comrades Rykov, Kalinin, Sokolnikov, Lunacharsky).

a. In light of the major expenditures incurred in transferring the ac[ademic] theaters to conservation status, consider their further functioning expedient even on condition of state subsidy, but in such a way that this subsidy does not exceed the funds that might be needed to preserve less profitable theaters. Instruct the SNK RSFSR to achieve the least loss, even if it means reducing the troupes of the academic theaters.

b. Close down the ballet theater in Leningrad before the upcoming season.

c. Destroy the "workers' strip,"[8] in line with the proposals of the VTsSPS. The SNK shall provide workers with benefits in the form of a discount at the discretion of the administration of the state academic theaters.

Two months later the matter of the Leningrad ballet was decided as well. A Politburo resolution dated 3 September on preserving the Leningrad ballet proclaimed: "In view of the finding that disbanding the ballet troupe will not yield an economy, rescind the Politburo decision of 2 July of this year (pr. N 69, p. 16-b) on closing down the ballet theater in Leningrad."[9] The happy ending to this story came on 10 May 1930, when, based on a report by K. E. Voroshilov, a Politburo resolution was approved "on the curatorship of the Bolshoi Theater." It proclaimed: "The Bolshoi Theater, along with its branch, the Experimental Theater, and all their enterprises, shall be transferred to the control of the TsIK of the USSR."[10] Thus Stalin's favorite, the Bolshoi Theater, was elevated once again to a rank comparable with the old court theater. It was taken out of the competence of Narkompros and made directly subordinate to the TsIK. The story of how the academic theaters were not shut down is an example of the political as well as ideological "Great Retreat."[11] This was the opening of the era of the "classics," the "grand style," the Soviet epos—the flowering of the Bolshoi Theater.

CHAPTER THREE

Organizing the "Artistic Milieu": The Era of NEP

The era of NEP did more than just set new goals for the Party leadership in the sphere of ideology; it also created new forms of leadership in the cultural sphere. Meanwhile, two fundamental problems remained: the attitude toward the old cultural elites and that toward the new, proletarian culture. According to Western Sovietology, the Party worked consistently to destroy the former and support the latter. As we have already seen, though, the attitude toward the "legacy of the past" was ambivalent both in the practice of permission to travel and in the specific case of the Bolshoi Theater. The determining factor was not any "political line" but actual political interests. Just as it is incorrect to think, however, that the Party leadership came out unambiguously in the first postrevolutionary years against the prerevolutionary intelligentsia, so too it is incorrect to think that the Party unambiguously supported "their own," proletarian culture. On the contrary, it was the Party that proved the most powerful brake on the development of proletarian culture, having wrecked Proletkult (Proletarian Culture, a cultural organization) in the years 1920–1922. This policy was continued later as well, during NEP and the cultural revolution, when the Party leadership would support first one and then another faction, stimulating their struggle and in this way maintaining control over the situation.

Trotsky's *Literature and Revolution* (*Literatura i revoliutsia*, 1923) could be called one of the initial cultural milestones during NEP (several of its sections had appeared previously in print). Trotsky formulated here the following guidelines for the Party's policy in the area of cultural administration: "The Party guides the proletariat, not the historical process. There are spheres where the Party guides directly and imperiously. There are spheres where it monitors and assists. There are spheres where it only assists. And there are, finally, spheres where it is simply trying to find its bearings. The sphere of art is not one where the Party is called upon to command. It can and must safeguard, assist, and only indirectly—guide." Naturally, this is a revealing statement, since "indirectly guide" meant to define the "political course" in the cultural sphere.

Two factors were decisive here: the situation in the cultural elites, which dictated the necessity of supporting first some, then other groups; and the situation at the top of the Party, which had determined a need to eliminate various opposition groups. One must not conclude from this, however (and this view is widespread to this day), that "in the liberal 1920s" the Party had no "concept of cultural policy." The Party leadership (which, as we know, at this time was itself changing constantly) maintained unified goals (the reinforcement and support of power and control over the sphere of "cultural production") and the methods for achieving these goals. As for formulating some "concept" for culture to give it a kind of "aesthetic integrity," then it is worth recalling that even under Stalin's unified leadership, the line in culture changed several times. Suffice it to say that in aesthetic and ideological respects the late 1920s and early 1930s (the "shift to the left" with the policy of "proletarianization" and cultural revolution during the First Five Year Plan) and the second half of the 1930s (the "shift to the right" to be seen in the "struggle against formalism" and the increasing demand that culture embody the "national character") look like two different cultures.

The Party's main efforts during NEP were aimed at creating alternative organizations to both Proletkult and the fellow traveler organizations, ones that would be controlled by the Party apparatus. The first document in the Politburo archives that concerns these issues is a memo from Trotsky on young writers and artists:

· 18 ·

Memo from L. D. Trotsky to the Politburo of the TsK RKP(b) on young writers and artists. AP RF, f. 3, op. 34, d. 185, ll. 8–10. Original. Typewritten.
30 June 1922

To the Politburo
On young writers, artists, and oth[ers].

Without a doubt, we are risking losing the young poets, artists, and others who are drawn to us. There is no or almost no attention being paid to them, or more precisely, attention to individuals is manifested occasionally by individual Soviet workers or in strictly amateurish ways. In the material sense we are pushing even the most gifted and revolutionary toward the bourgeois publishing houses or others hostile to us, where these young poets are forced to fall into line, i.e., hide their sympathies for us.

We must set as our goal the careful, fully individualized treatment of representatives of young Soviet art. For these purposes we must:

1. Keep a serious and carefully drawn up register of poets, writers, artists, and others. This register should be concentrated under the Main Censorship Administration in Moscow and Petrograd. Each poet should have his own dossier, in which biographical information about him, his current connections, literary, political, and otherwise, are gathered. The data should be such that:

   a. they can orient the censor in letting the appropriate works through,

   b. they can orient Party literary critics with regard to suitable poets, and

   c. on the basis of this data we can undertake various measures of material support for young writers and others.

2. Single out right now a short list of undoubtedly gifted writers who are undoubtedly sympathetic to us and who are being pushed toward the bourgeoisie by the struggle to earn a living and who may tomorrow end up in a hostile or semihostile camp, like Pilnyak (as Com. Ionov has informed me). Assign the compilation of the list of such writers and artists to Comrades Meshcheriakov, Voronsky, and Lebedev-Poliansky in Moscow for three signatures, and to Comrades Ionov and Bystriansky (and maybe Com. Zinoviev will name someone else) in Petrograd.

3. Issue an instruction to the editorial offices of the most important Party publications (newspapers, journals) that reviews of these young writers should be written more "utilitarianly," i.e., with the aim of winning definite influence over the given young writer. With this aim, the critic should first familiarize himself with all the facts about the writer, in order to get a clearer picture of the line of his development. It is also very important to establish (through the editorial offices or by other means) the

personal connections between individual Party comrades interested in matters of literature and these young poets and others.

4. Our censorship must also have the above-indicated pedagogical direction. We can and must manifest strictness with respect to publications whose writers have fully formed bourgeois artistic tendencies. We must show no mercy toward those artistic and literary factions that are in fact the center of concentration for Menshevik-SR elements. At the same time, an attentive, cautious, and gentle attitude is essential toward those works and authors who, although they carry an abyss of all kinds of prejudices inside them, are clearly developing in a revolutionary direction.

Insofar as we are talking about works of the third category, only in an extreme case would their publication be subject to prohibition. First, we must try to bring the author together with a comrade who can truly explain to him, competently and convincingly, the reactionary elements in his work so that if the author is not convinced then his work will be published (if there are no serious arguments against publication) but at the same time there will be a critical article written from a pedagogical point of view.

5. The question of the form of support for young poets is subject to special consideration. It would be best, of course, if this support were expressed in the form of an honorarium (individualized), but this would require that the young authors have somewhere to publish. Due to its purely Party character, *Red Virgin Soil* [*Krasnaia nov'*] is an inadequate field of activity for them. Perhaps we will have to create a purely literary, non-Party journal under general firm guidance but with sufficient room for individual "deviations."

6. In any event, a certain sum of money will obviously have to be allocated for this.

7. The same measures should be applied to young artists, too. Here, though, we need to discuss specially the matter of which institution the above-indicated dossiers are to be kept in and whom to entrust personally with this work.

L. Trotsky

Trotsky's initiative (like all his initiatives during the intense intra-Party struggle) was met with cautious attention. Evidently on instructions from Stalin, the deputy head of the TsK's Agitprop (Agitation and Propaganda Department), Ya. Yakovlev, prepared information for the General Secretary about the situation among writers:

· 19 ·

Report from TsK RKP(b) Agitation and Propaganda Department Deputy Head Ya. A. Yakovlev to I. V. Stalin on the situation among writers. [No later than 3 July 1922]. AP RF, f. 3, op. 34, d. 185, ll. 6–7. Original. Typewritten.

To Comrade Stalin

In response to your inquiry, I can report the following:

1. At the present time a number of writers *of all groups and literary persuasions* that stand precisely and definitely on our position *have already set themselves apart.* 1921 was a year of stormy literary flowering that brought forth dozens of major new literary names from among our young people. At the present time, there is a struggle going on between us and the counterrevolution to win over a significant portion of these literary forces. (The whole émigré press is trying to "buy" our literary young; *Morning Frosts* [*Utrenniki*], the journal of the Petersburg House of Writers, an organ of blatant counterrevolution, has been compelled to use the same literary names as we do.) The main literary organizational centers are in the hands of the Whites (covert or open)—the Petersburg House of Writers, the All-Russian Union of Writers. Our organizational centers are ineffective and impotent and don't know how to attract the new revolutionary writer, a Soviet who is nevertheless not a member of the RKP. (In this sense, the Moscow Press House is moribund, and the Petrograd Association of Proletarian Writers excluded Vsevolod Ivanov for reasons of an objectively harmful, "Puritan" nature).

2. The main groups close to us politically at the present time:

a. old writers who joined us during the first period of revolution—Valery Briusov, Sergei Gorodetsky, Gorky, and so on;

b. proletarian writers, the Proletkult (in Petersburg and Moscow), which counts a number of unquestionably talented people;

c. Futurists—Mayakovsky, Aseev, Bobrov, and so on;

d. Imaginists—Mariengof, Yesenin, Shershenevich, Kusikov, and so on;

e. Serapion Brothers—Vsevolod Ivanov, Shaginyan, N. Nikitin, N. Tikhonov, Polonskaia, and so on; a number of wavering, politically unformed writers for whose souls a real war is being waged between the camps of the emigration and us (Boris Pilnyak, Zoshchenko, and so on);

f. those leaning our way after a change of orientation—Aleksei Tolstoi, Ehrenburg, Drozdov, and so on.

3. Create sympathy for us and attract those leaning to our side by creating a unified center combining these groups of writers. This association must definitely be non-Party. The Communist minority must reject impermissible, unjustifiable Communist arrogance, which hampers Communist

influence over writers who do not belong to the Party but are politically and socially close to us, especially among the young.

4. The All-Russian Union of Writers, which has a certain material base and which with a little work (fairly tactical and cautious) could be won over, could become this organizational center. If it were reorganized, the Moscow Press House could become the Moscow base for such an all-Russian union.

We could also take another path—organizing a "Society for the Development of Russian Culture"—as a non-Party society uniting especially young writers and having a certain material base.

We could take a combined path—creating a "Society" with a more severely limited makeup and simultaneously winning over the All-Russian Union of Writers, whose framework could in this case be broader.

5. Both organizations must be given significant publishing opportunities.

Ya. Yakovlev

That same day, Stalin sent a memorandum in support of Trotsky's proposals to the members of the Politburo:

· 20 ·

Memorandum from I. V. Stalin to the Politburo of the TsK RKP(b) on the subject of L. D. Trotsky's proposals on young writers and artists. AP RF, f. 3, op. 34, d. 185, l. 5. Original. Typewritten.

3 July 1922

To all members of the Politburo

The issue raised by Com. Trotsky on winning over young poets sympathetic to us by means of material and moral support for them is, in my view, very timely. I think that the formation of Soviet culture (in the narrow sense of the word) that so much was written and talked about at one time by various "proletarian ideologues" (Bogdanov and others), has only now begun. This culture, evidently, must grow up in the course of struggle between young poets and writers drawn to the Soviets and the various counterrevolutionary tendencies and groups in the new arena. Joining Soviet-inclined poets into a single core and doing everything possible to support them in their struggle—this is our task. I think that the most expedient form for this joining together of young writers would be the organization of an independent society, say, "The Society for the Development of Russian Culture," or something of that kind. Trying to pin young writers to a censorship committee or any other "bureaucratic" institution would be pushing young poets away and upsetting matters. It would be good to put definitely a non-Party member but someone Soviet-inclined at the head of this society, someone like Vsevolod Ivanov. Material support up to and including subsidies couched in some acceptable form is absolutely essential.

For your information I'm attaching Agitprop Deputy Head Com. Yakovlev's reply to my inquiry in this matter.

I. Stalin

The result was the Politburo resolution supporting artistic youth. The political goal of the triumvirate's support for Trotsky's initiative was to keep the latter from occupying the position of "defender" of youth. It should be recalled that with the departure from the Party of many radically inclined figures in the art world during the era when NEP was being introduced, and as time went on, Trotsky became the symbol and defender of the left-radical utopias "betrayed" by NEP. He had broad support not only inside the Party but also among the young—among the Komsomol and student population. This is why it was so important to "recover the initiative" from Trotsky.

The Politburo resolution of 6 July 1922 is wholly based on Trotsky's memorandum, with only a few changes. Instead of a journal it deems essential "the creation of a literary publishing house (with a state subsidy) that would be under the general and overall control of Gosizdat."[1] Two weeks later, on 20 July, a Politburo commission under Kamenev made refinements to this Politburo resolution: "Include the following in the publishing house initiative group: Aseev, Vs. Ivanov, Pilnyak, Liashko, Semyonov, Briusov, Voronsky, and one of the Serapion Brothers agreed upon with Shaginyan. Instruct Com. Voronsky to communicate with the more reliable ones from this group." In this way, the main emphasis was put on fellow traveler writers: "Make the main form of subsidy a subsidy for the publishing house to raise the honorarium and lower the cost of publication; the publishing house (company) must be given a building where a club as well as a dormitory could be set up for about forty and where an assistance fund could be organized for writers. Instruct Com. Voronsky to identify from the list of writers those in need of an immediate subsidy."[2]

Less than a month later, on 17 August 1922, a new publishing house of this kind was authorized and Trotsky's proposal was implemented, "in spades." According to Kamenev's report, the Politburo decided "to approve the proposal for Gosizdat to invest 150 billion 1921 rubles in Circle [Krug], a mixed publishing company, on condition that this company be organized on shareholding principles and that the controlling packet of shares be held by Gosizdat, Narkomfin will issue Gosizdat 150 billion rubles, assign the definition of the structure, the company, and its administration and expenses to Kamenev, Shmidt, and Voronsky, and start publishing books within a month from now."[3] Given the shortage of paper and funds for publishing fine literature, this was an impressive demonstration of the advantages of "constructive collaboration" with the state. A month later, on 14 September 1922, according to Voronsky's report, the Politburo decided to give material support to the opposing wing—a group of proletarian poets called Smithy (Kuznitsa), allocating 80 million rubles for the proletarian writers.[4] During both NEP and the Civil War, the state retained its role as principal (and now sole) patron.

Party support for proletarian culture would seem to have gone without saying, but that was not the case. In 1923–24, the struggle between proletarian writers and fellow travelers reached its peak with proletarian writers doggedly attacking the fellow travelers for their lack of ideological commitment. The most radically and militantly inclined figures of proletarian literature, who rallied around the group October (*Oktiabr'*) and the journal *On Guard* (*Na postu*), the nucleus of what later came to be known as the Russian Association of Proletarian Writers (RAPP), demanded "the hegemony of proletarian literature." Their leverage would be a congress of proletarian writers, on which the more radical supporters of the "Bolshevization of literature" placed high hopes, seeing in it a weapon for consolidating all anti-fellow traveler forces in literature and creating a unified "cultural front" to oppose the fellow travelers. It was at this moment that the Party leadership, which had previously supported the On Guard group, began slowing the "assault on bourgeois culture." Indicative in this sense is the resolution of the TsK Orgburo, dated 3 November 1924, on the inexpedience of holding a congress of proletarian writers, but conceding that they had "No objection to holding a small conference of proletarian writers belonging to the October group."[5]

All these were steps toward the TsK (actually, the Politburo) resolution of 18 June 1925. This resolution—which, for opposite motives, was sought by both the On Guard group and the fellow travelers (each was counting on support)—became the chief official Party document, defining its course for the immediate future, until the 1932 resolution "On restructuring literary and artistic organizations." At first, the 1925 resolution was called, "On proletarian writers." The commission working on it included Bukharin, Kamenev, Tomsky, Frunze, Kuibyshev, Andreev, Lunacharsky, and Vareikis (Politburo resolution of 5 February 1925).[6] Taking part in the Politburo commission's work were representatives from a broad spectrum of Soviet culture, from the directors of VAPP (All-Union Association of Proletarian Writers, the broader body of which RAPP was part), i.e., Vardin, Rodov, Raskolnikov and Lelevich, Smithy (Yakubovsky), and Proletkult (Pletnev) to representatives from Crossing (Pereval—Artem Vesely), LEF (Left Front in the Arts—Mayakovsky), and Voronsky, the editor-in-chief of *Red Virgin Soil,* who patronized the fellow travelers (Minutes of a meeting of the Politburo Commission, 13 February 1925).[7]

The TsK archives finally lift the veil of mystery from the question of "who was behind the resolution," whose political line ("soft" or "hard") won out; largely speaking, it was the "soft." The Politburo commission instructed Bukharin to compose a text for the resolution on the basis of Vareikis's theses. Then the draft resolution was supposed to be considered by a Politburo commission made up of Vareikis, Bukharin, Frunze, and Lunacharsky, which discussed it once again "in the presence of representatives of the literary organizations."[8] The final text of the resolution was signed by Bukharin, Lunacharsky, and Lelevich, and then, after its publication in *Pravda* on 1 July 1925, it was approved retroactively by the Politburo on 2 July 1925 (prot. no. 69, p. 13). Here is the original text of the Politburo resolution:

· 21 ·

Resolution of the Politburo of the TsK RKP(b) "On Party policy in the sphere of literature." RGASPI, f. 17, op. 3, d. 506, ll. 4, 31–37. Authenticated copy. Typewritten. Published in its final version in *Pravda*, 1 July 1925, and *Izvestia TsK RKP(b)*, no. 25–26 (1925): 8–9.
18 June 1925

No. 67, p. 13—*Report of the Politburo commission on proletarian writers (Politburo, 5 May 1925, pr. 62, p. 33) (Comrades Vareikis, Bukharin, Lunacharsky, Raskolnikov, Lelevich).*

a. Approve the draft resolution of the TsK literature commission (see attachment).

b. Assign a commission made up of Comrades Bukharin, Lelevich, and Lunacharsky to compose a final version of it; assign Com. Lunacharsky to convene the commission.

c. Suggest to Com. Trotsky that he submit his corrections to the commission in written form.

Attachment to p. 13, Politburo pr. no. 67, 18 June 1925

1. The rise in the material well-being of the masses of late in connection with the turnabout produced in people's minds by the Revolution, the increase in mass activity, the tremendous expansion of their world view, and so forth, is creating tremendous growth in cultural needs and demands. We have, thus, entered the zone of cultural revolution, which is a prerequisite for any further advance toward a Communist society.

2. A part of this mass cultural growth is the growth in the new literature—proletarian and peasant above all, starting from its embryonic forms, which are at the same time unprecedentedly broad in scope (rabkor [worker correspondents], selkor [peasant correspondents], wall newspapers, and so forth), and ending with the ideologically conscious output of fine literature.

3. On the other hand, the complexity of the economic process, the simultaneous growth in contradictory and even directly hostile economic forms caused by this development of the processes of engendering and strengthening the new bourgeoisie; the inevitable, albeit in the beginning not always conscious, attraction to it among some of the old and new intelligentsia, the chemical extraction from the depths of society of more and more new ideological agents of this bourgeoisie—all this must inevitably have an effect on the literary surface of public life.

4. Thus, just as class struggle has not ceased among us in general, so it has definitely not ceased on the literary front. In a class society there is not nor can there be neutral art, although the forms of the class significance of art in general, and of literature in particular, are infinitely more diverse than, for example, the forms of the class significance of politics.

5. However, it would be absolutely incorrect to lose sight of the basic fact of our public life, and in particular the fact of the seizure of power by the working class and the presence of a proletarian dictatorship in the country. If before the seizure of power the proletarian Party ignited the class struggle and followed a line that led to an explosion of the entire society, then in the period of the proletarian dictatorship, the Party of the proletariat faces the issue of coming to terms with the peasantry and slowly remaking it, the issue of allowing some collaboration with the bourgeoisie while slowly pushing it out, the issue of putting the technical and other intelligentsias into the service of the revolution and winning them away from the bourgeoisie ideologically.

Thus, although the class struggle has not ended, it is changing form, for its goal for the proletariat is different than it was before the seizure of power and different in the conventional sense that instead of its destructive task it now has the task of positive construction, which must encompass broader and broader strata of society under the guidance of the proletariat.

6. While preserving, strengthening, and constantly expanding its leadership, the proletariat must occupy a corresponding position in a great number of new segments along the ideological front. The penetration of dialectical materialism into completely new spheres (biology, psychology, the natural sciences in general) has already begun. Winning positions in the literary sphere definitely must sooner or later become fact.

7. We must remember, however, that this task is infinitely more complex than the other tasks being resolved by the proletariat, for within the limits of capitalist society the working class could ready itself for a victorious revolution, build for itself cadres of fighters and leaders, and elaborate a magnificent ideological weapon of political struggle for itself. However, it could not sort out issues of either the natural sciences or technology, just as it, as a culturally oppressed class, could not develop its own literature, its own particular artistic form, its own style. If now the proletariat has in its hands unerring criteria for the social and political content of any literary work, it does not have the same kind of precise answers to all questions regarding artistic form.

8. The above must determine the policy of the proletariat's guiding Party in the sphere of literature. This involves, above all, the following issues: correlation between proletarian writers, peasant writers, so-called fellow travelers, and others; the Party's policy with respect to the most proletarian writers; issues of criticism; issues of the style and form of artistic works and methods for elaborating new artistic forms; and finally, issues of an organizational nature.

9. Correlation between various groupings of writers on the basis of their social class or social group content is defined by our general policy. However, here we must bear in mind that leadership in the sphere of literature belongs to the working class as a whole, with all its material and ideological resources. The hegemony of *proletarian writers* has not yet come to pass, and the Party must help these writers *earn* for themselves their historic right to this hegemony. Peasant writers must meet with a friendly reception and enjoy our unconditional support. The task is to switch their growing cadres onto the rails of proletarian ideology and certainly not, however, to try to exterminate from their art the peasant literary and artistic images that are an essential prerequisite for influencing the peasantry.

10. With regard to fellow travelers, we must bear in mind: (1) their differentiation; (2) the significance of many of them as highly qualified "specialists" in literary technique; (3) the reluctance present among this stratum of writers. The general directive here must be a directive of a tactical

and cautious attitude toward them, i.e., an approach that will ensure all the conditions for their speediest possible switch to the side of Communist ideology. By sifting out the antiproletarian and antirevolutionary elements (now extremely insignificant) and by fighting the ideology of the new bourgeoisie now forming among some of the fellow travelers of the changing-landmarks bent, the Party must be tolerant toward intermediate ideological forms, patiently helping these inevitably numerous forms become obsolete in the process of increasingly close comradely collaboration with the cultural forces of communism.

11. With regard to proletarian writers, the Party must take the following position: while doing everything it can to foster their growth and supporting them in every way possible, the Party must use every means to prevent the manifestation of Communist conceit among them as a most ruinous phenomenon. Because it sees in them the future intellectual leaders of Soviet literature, the Party must do everything it can to fight against this frivolous and careless attitude toward the old cultural legacy, as well as toward specialists of the artistic word. Against capitulation, on one hand, and against Communist conceit, on the other—that is what the Party's slogan should be. The Party should also fight attempts at purely hothouse "proletarian" literature; writers should present a broad scope of phenomena in all their complexity; not get stuck inside the framework of a single factory; let literature be not of the workshop but of the great fighting class leading behind it millions of peasants—that should be the framework for the content of proletarian literature.

12. In general and overall, the above defines the task of *criticism,* which is one of the chief educational weapons in the hands of the Party. Without yielding communism's position for a minute, without retreating one iota from proletarian ideology, and while revealing the objective class meaning of various literary works, Communist criticism must mercilessly fight counterrevolutionary manifestations in literature, expose changing-landmarks liberalism, etc., and at the same time display the utmost tact, caution, and tolerance with regard to all those literary strata which may join and are joining the proletariat. Communist criticism must drive out of its usage the tone of literary command. This criticism will only have a profound educative significance when it bases itself on its *ideological* superiority. Marxist criticism must decisively drive out of its midst any pretentious, semiliterate, and self-satisfied Communist conceit. Marxist criticism must set a slogan for itself—to learn—and must resist any pulp literature or self-important writing in its own midst.

13. While identifying unerringly the social and class content of literary trends, the Party as a whole can by no means limit itself to an attachment to any one tendency in *literary form.* While guiding literature as a whole, the Party can do just as little to support any *one* faction of literature (clas-

sifying these factions according to the difference of their views on form and style) as it can resolve with resolutions matters of the form of the family, although in general it undoubtedly guides *and must guide* the construction of the new daily life. A style that corresponds to its era will be created, but it will be created by other methods, and the solution to this issue has yet to be outlined. Any attempts to tie the Party in this direction in the given phase of the country's cultural development must be rejected.

14. Therefore, the Party must speak out in favor of free competition among the various groups and trends in this sphere. Any other solution of the issue would be a bureaucratic pseudosolution. Just as inadmissible would be *legitimizing a monopoly* on the literary and publishing business by any group or literary organization by a decree or resolution of the Party. While supporting proletarian and proletarian-peasant literature materially and morally, and while helping the fellow travelers, etc., the Party cannot grant a monopoly to any of the groups, even the most proletarian in its intellectual content. That would mean wrecking proletarian literature above all.

15. The Party must take every measure to eradicate attempts at improvised and incompetent administrative interference into literary affairs; the Party must concern itself with the painstaking selection of individuals in those institutions which deal with press affairs in order to ensure truly correct, beneficial, and tactical guidance for our literature.

16. The Party must point out to all workers in literature the need to correctly delimit functions between critics and writers-artists. The latter must shift the center of gravity in its work to literary output in the literal sense of this word, utilizing in the process the tremendous material of modernity. Increased attention, too, must be paid to the development of national literature in the numerous republics and oblasts of our Union.

The Party must emphasize the need to create literature intended for the truly mass reader, the worker and peasant; we have to break more boldly and decisively with the *prejudices* of the gentry in literature and, taking advantage of all the technical achievements of the old artistry, elaborate our own form comprehensible to the *millions*. Only when it resolves this great task will Soviet literature and its future proletarian avant-garde be able to carry out their cultural-historic mission.

The 1925 resolution was decisive for the development of Soviet literature in the NEP era. Without a doubt it was provoked by left-radical adepts of "proletarian literature" (which is why it was initially called "On proletarian writers"; it was they who were the real problem for the Party, consistently burning the "bridges" the new Party was trying to build for "constructive collaboration with the fellow travelers"). The fact that it helped not the proletarian writers but the fellow travelers (since despite the words about ideological support for proletarian writers, in reality it preserved the book market for fellow travelers) was not the consequence of anyone's machinations or influences (Gorky's, for example) or the result of any alleged "soft line" in the Party leadership, as the traditional history of literature has explained—above all because there was no "soft line" in the Party leadership such as they surprisingly link to the allegedly "anti-Stalinist" Frunze (for the reason, previously not entirely clear, that Frunze perished during an operation that Stalin had insisted on). As the Politburo materials show, at the base of the 1925 resolution lay a document composed by Vareikis, who was in fact the main literary censor in the TsK, a loyal Stalinist, who never had any part in any "soft lines" (which did not save him, of course, from later repressions), and the editing of the "soft" Bukharin changed neither the orientation nor the tone of the resolution. Moreover, virtually every literary grouping took part in the discussion of the resolution during its preparation (from February to July 1925).

Therefore there is no reason to think, in particular, that the turns in culture's "general line" were the product of a struggle inside just the political elites. The cultural elites played a definite role in working out solutions. Every "turn" in the Party line was accompanied by broad campaigns in support of or against the different decisions. Inasmuch as the situation was approximately identical in all spheres of culture, decisions in one sphere (most often, the sphere of literature) were mandated for all other branches of culture, triggering new skirmishes "on the cultural front." These skirmishes were accompanied by complaints and denunciations to the TsK against opponents in art. For example, the 1925 resolution on literature triggered a wave in the fine arts. Half a year later, figures in several artistic groups which were not in the proletarian camp, and including several from the leftist avant-garde, addressed a letter to Stalin:

· 22 ·

From a letter from a group of artists to I. V. Stalin. [No later than 3 February 1926]. RGASPI, f. 17, op. 60, d. 805, ll. 56–66. Original. Typewritten.

[. . .] In Moscow there are several artistic groups consisting of a fairly uneven composition of artists, such as AKhRR [Association of Artists of Revolutionary Russia], OST [Society of Easel Painters], Makovets, 4 Arts [4 iskusstva], Being [Bytie], ASNOVA (Assoc[iation] of New Archi[tects]),

Society of Young People [Obshchestvo molodykh], and several others. Each of these artistic societies has artists who have received a greater or lesser degree of recognition and who have had a notable influence on the condition and development of Soviet fine arts. All of them feel called upon to advance that cultural superstructure of our new social-political and social-economic structure which is still searching for its own vivid and fruitful revelation and which will appear in the forms and models of the new style, the new art of the Soviet era. *As in literature, those inquiries, those efforts, and that ferment of cultural development which in the future should yield the ripe fruits of genuinely Soviet art are only beginning to take shape here.*

From the standpoint of this process, *the objective role of all these groups is identically valuable and essential.* The seeds of future expressive artistic forms, which cannot be obtained through circulated directives, have been placed in their mutually intersecting development.

For the interests of the normal and uninhibited development of this art, *it would be disastrous and culturally shortsighted to proclaim one of these factions as embodying the politically and socially recognized and officially recommended course of development for Soviet fine art.*

Meanwhile, though, the conditions for the existence of modern art groups reveal an advantage for one of them, due not so much to objective causes as to the direct action and exceptional moral and material support of the government, in contrast and counterbalance to all the other art factions. *This major group, which has been marked by extremely tangible marks of favor, is the Association of Artists of Revolutionary Russia (AKhRR). This support is not only creating a solid material base for AKhRR but (what is much more important) is giving it a priori moral credit in the eyes of broad circles of Soviet society,* which cannot in any way be justified by the cultural-artistic level and achievements of this group in comparison with others.

A very impressive act of exceptional attention on the part of the government was manifested toward AKhRR, though: a major subsidy of 75,000 rubles from the central government. AKhRR receives the same exceptional acknowledgment for support in all instances when state sums are distributed, the lion's share usually goes to AKhRR compared with other groups. Alongside the extraordinary material need, alongside the glaring poverty of the other artistic societies, AKhRR is easily acquiring the economic base other artists lack in their struggle for fruitful labor, for the right to create, for the right to carry out *a real search for a genuine revolutionary art.* The objective significance of this kind of example of an exceptionally attentive attitude toward AKhRR on the part of the government cannot be viewed as a manifestation of simple goodwill toward this association of artists. The significance of these kinds of acts goes beyond their direct purpose, intensifying the unfavorable conditions of existence for the other groups and for all non-AKhRR artists.

What can justify the support rendered to and the advancement of this one artistic group in the eyes of the leading state organs and the monopoly on official recognition that seems bound up with it? After all, this justification essentially ought to rest solely on considerations of the exceptional value of the art personified by this group, the superior significance of its ideological or formal virtues. But *a serious, unbiased analysis in this regard does not let us find anything in the composition or the achievements or the ideology of the AKhRR group that might serve as grounds for indisputably distinguishing it from the other groups.* From the standpoint of such an analysis, neither the name "revolutionary artists" itself nor the formal revolutionary phraseology nor the bald proclamation of a revolutionary ideology in the form of a declaration can, of course, have any defining significance. A proper assessment here must inevitably be based on the facts that lie on the plane of practice, art, or the individual artists representing it. In and of itself, the personal makeup of the Association of "revolutionary artists" does not in any way point to any "revolutionary quality" in them that is greater than in any of the other groups. [. . .]

To an even lesser degree has AKhRR's "revolutionary" label manifested itself in specific artistic achievements. AKhRR's seven consecutive exhibits have shown that if this association is destined to enrich our art with new, revolutionary forms, then this is merely the conjectured future; there has as yet been no call to remark on any notable conquests. Apart from philistine, petty bourgeois assessments, *adapting ingrained old forms to the demand for portraits of prominent contemporaries or for popular themes cannot in fact be considered revolutionary art.* It must be stated with all the decisiveness and directness of the artistic conscience that *drawing the portraits of Party and Soviet leaders in the manner and style of the old portraits of generals not only does not coincide with genuine revolutionary art but actually lies off its anticipated paths.* [. . .]

Finally, from the standpoint of artistic mastery, the proportionate weight of it in AKhRR as a whole is significantly lower than in several other groups, not only objectively but also, if you like, at the admission of the Association itself. Only now the AKhRR, as a circulated appeal to members of the Association makes clear, is setting out to master 100 percent of the prewar level, in the sense of craft.

All the considerations set forth here are by no means aimed at belittling the Association's significance. It may, of course, lay claim to the same respect as other artistic groups, however *its claims to a monopoly on revolutionary art must be decisively rejected.* [. . .] At the same time, we cannot forget that AKhRR, like other artistic groupings, is under the jurisdiction of Narkompros and, moreover, is an organization under the State Academy of Artistic Sciences, thanks to which the Association's official "title" therefore has a deceptive outward credibility. The revolutionary tag seems to come equipped with a state guarantee. As a result, AKhRR's label objectively implies one group's unique and highly tangible privilege. Not only that, but it tacitly encourages the false conviction among broad circles of consumers that artists of other groups are supposedly "nonrevolutionary" artists, and maybe even counterrevolutionary. [. . .]

The practical consequences of the position set forth here are enormous. Artists of other groups, with the exception of personally well-known, major masters, are losing more and more ground in that social milieu which consumes the artist's art. Despite equal or even greater artistic and cultural attributes, they are spontaneously being crowded out of production and are materially withering. [. . .] *The general feeling of being "Soviet stepchildren" creates in artists of these groups, on one hand, a psychology of oppression and, on the other, an artistic instability and suspicious flexibility that pushes them to join AKhRR by way of dubious accommodation and hack-work temptations.* The totality of these phenomena creates vividly abnormal conditions for the development of our fine art.

The well-known resolution of the Party's TsK on the issue of fine literature provides by analogy grounds for thinking (1) that in the sphere of fine art as well the time has not yet come for an open proclamation or other form of bestowing on any faction the role of bearer of genuine revolutionary, genuine proletarian art, (2) that in art as well the substantive and essential prerequisite for its fruitful development is a fair and tolerant if not equally attentive attitude by the Party and state toward all those groups working for Soviet social and state interests, and (3) that here, too, the interests of genuine artistic culture advanced by facts of a creative order ought not and cannot be sacrificed to revolutionary phraseology until it goes beyond the framework of verbal declarations. [. . .]

> OST D. Shterenberg, L. Vainer
> Makovets M. Rodchenko, Lev Bruni, D. Gero
> 4 Arts Istomin, Pavel Kuznetsov
> Being A. Osmerkin
> Soc[iety] of Youth Feldman

In his letter to Stalin, Lunacharsky supported the signatories and spoke in favor of the Party taking a decision on policy in the fine arts, "by analogy with its directive in matters of literature."[9] No such resolution followed, but the TsK's 1925 resolution continued to play a decisive role in the literary battle in the 1920s. It did not obligate the TsK in any way to either the fellow travelers or the proletarian writers; on the contrary, it created opportunity for political maneuvering. A direct result of the 1925 resolution was the collapse of the On Guard group, which had sought a monopoly in literature (in which the Party had no interest at that moment), and the formation of FOSP, the Federation of Unions of Soviet Writers, which was founded in 1927 as a response to the Party resolution on literature of 1925—the first attempt to bring writers together into a single organization. The literary struggle took a completely new turn: the Party refused direct support from any group, and by retaining its freedom of action, preserved its role as arbiter. The resolution turned out to be another blow to its "own," proletarian literature. However, a few years later, during the cultural revolution, it would be the proletarian writers who had been "torn away" in 1925 who would become the TsK's main instrument in the struggle for the "Bolshevization of literature."

CHAPTER FOUR

The Organization of Proletarian Art: The Cultural Revolution

The turn toward a harsher line in the cultural sphere began not in 1929, as is usually thought, but at least as early as 1927. Based on the two foundations of party cultural policy cited above, there were two reasons for this shift. One was the rout of the Left Opposition in the Politburo (above all of Lev Trotsky, who had broad support in the revolutionary artistic milieu). The second was the uncontrollability of the "literary front" across the board: from the fellow travelers, who on the whole sympathized with the Revolution, to the routed Proletkult, which found itself at the time in a crisis between RAPP and LEF (the Left Front in the Arts, a body comprising erstwhile Futurists and Constructivists). The rout of the "left artists" and the driving out of "Trotsky supporters" everywhere abruptly altered the situation in cultural administration. Walter Benjamin, who found himself in Moscow at the beginning of 1927, recorded in his *Moscow Diary* a vivid picture of the "rout of the leftists": the "literary milieu" was demoralized, many active and high-level "workers of the cultural front" were sent into exile, accused of "Trotskyism" and "leftism."[1]

Although the Politburo continued to support the idea of creating some type of writers' association (with the aim of controlling them better), FOSP (the Federation of Unions of Soviet Writers) did not coalesce, and the "literary front" remained split and, most important, poorly controlled. At this time, the party leadership was still hoping that a different, more cohesive and more controllable federation might materialize. One of the last attempts to breathe life into this idea was the Politburo's resolution of 5 May 1927.

· 23 ·

Resolution of the Politburo of the TsK VKP(b) "On writers' organizations."
RGASPI, f. 17, op. 3, d. 633, ll. 3–4. Authenticated copy. Typewritten.

5 May 1927

No. 100 p. 3—On writers' organizations (Politburo, 28 April 1927, pr. no. 98, p. 3) (Comrades Lunacharsky, Gusev, Broido).

a. Approve the basic principles worked out by Com. Krzhizhanovsky's commission on the following issues: (1) the legal status of writers, with the exception of the point about extending to literary workers the Code of Labor Laws, having instructed according to procedure that the need be established to make literary labor equivalent to the labor of workers and employees in individual instances; (2) copyright; and (3) the labor contract between writers and publishing houses.

b. Instruct Narkompros, together with the writers' trade union section bureau, to implement the above principles according to Soviet legislative procedure.

c. Transfer the issue of fee standards for authorial labor of various types to consideration according to Soviet procedure in conjunction with the VTsSPS.

d. Deem expedient the organization of a federation of writers based on the principles elaborated by Com. Krzhizhanovsky's commission. Send the federation's draft charter to be examined according to Soviet procedure.

e. Assign the commission made up of Comrades Gusev, Lunacharsky, and Knorin (with the right of substitution) to further assist in the organization of a federation of writers.

f. Assign the same commission to examine the issue of transforming this federation into an all-union one, bringing representatives of the union republics into the discussion of this matter.

g. Deem expedient the organization of a special publishing house under the federation, meaning the transformation of Circle pub[lishers] into just such a publishing house, with its corresponding radical reorganization. Consider it possible to allocate up to 200,000 rubles for federation publishing activities.

h. Deem expedient the creation of a mutual assistance fund for writers and allocate to it a subsidy of 100,000 rubles.

i. Assign the detailed elaboration of an organization plan and the actual creation of the fund to the federation after it arises.

j. Propose to the TsK press division shared oversight to ensure that the indicated fund is used both to help particularly needy writers and to cultivate young emerging literary forces.

Presumably, the party's disappointment with the federation, which was potentially the prototype for the future Writers Union, proved the necessity for uniting writers on a completely different basis. The organizational structures for the future "restructuring of literary-artistic organizations" was worked out specifically at this time—both the system of administration for the "cultural front" and the record of mistakes that were not repeated in 1932 during the organization of the now genuine and effective new Writers Union.

The Politburo resolution of 10 October 1927, "On releasing Com. A. Voronsky from his responsibilities as a member of the editorial board of *Red Virgin Soil*,"[2] can be viewed as a report on the new stage in the management of literature. The removal of Voronsky, who had held back the press of "proletarian writers" and who had supported Trotsky and become the chief defender of fellow travelers in literature, meant a turn away from the 1925 resolution. Notably, a month later, on 11 November 1927, the TsK Secretariat decided to "satisfy the request of the VAPP party faction for permission for an All-Union Congress of Proletarian Writers": "Deem expedient the convocation of an All-Union Congress of Proletarian Writers in March 1928."[3] As we recall, three years before, to the VAPP request to convoke a congress, the Orgburo had replied with a refusal and what seemed like a joke with its decision "not to oppose the convocation of a small conference of proletarian writers belonging to the group October."

The attitude toward the parent body VAPP was changing abruptly. The new party leadership had begun to put emphasis on its more activist unit, RAPP (and, in particular, on RAPP's new, "non-Trotskyite" leadership), which was supposed to subordinate FOSP to itself. Based on this, on 26 July 1928, the Politburo approved a decision "to permit the publication of a weekly literary newspaper of the Federation of Soviet Writers, and, moreover, with its appearance, to cease publication of the Gosizdat newspaper, *Reader and Writer (Chitatel' i pisatel')*."[4] Instead of this pluralist "nonparty" newspaper, a year later *Literaturnaia gazeta*, which was in fact subordinated to RAPP, would start coming out. A similar and characteristic development was the "proletarianization" of *Red Virgin Soil,* a journal previously considered the bulwark of fellow traveler literature. By its special decisions, the Politburo was not only changing editors-in-chief, appointing increasingly orthodox RAPP-connected officials, but was also entering upon an examination of the makeup of the journal's editorial board.

Sensing a change in their position and how needed they now were, figures of "proletarian culture" began to work actively to Bolshevize literary (and more broadly, cultural) organizations. Their tone of address to the higher party leadership changed, too. An example of this type is the letter from the Proletarian Theater association to Stalin (it might be noted that one of the signatories is Asja Lacis—here spelled Latsis—Walter Benjamin's love interest in *Moscow Diary*).

· 24 ·

Letter from the Proletarian Theater Association to I. V. Stalin. [December 1928].
Original. Typewritten.
Moscow, December 1928

Esteemed Comrade Stalin!

While wholly confident in you as the expresser of a definite political line, we, the undersigned members of the Proletarian Theater creative association, would like to know your opinion on the following issues, which concern not only special circles but also, indisputably, have general cultural and general political significance:

1. Do you think that the right-wing danger in politics established by the party, while feeding off the same roots, is also seeping into various ideological productions, in particular, literature and theater? Are such facts as the sensational conflict at MKhAT-2 (Moscow Art Theater-2) (where the Soviet public has thus far been victorious), the "Golovanovism" (which before it was completely eliminated at the Bolshoi Theater reared its head in the conservatory, where the party cell took its side!), and Glaviskusstvo's [Main Committee on Art] encouragement of the shift to the right by MKhAT-1 (where the Soviet and party constituencies are as yet without power) some of the manifestations of the right-wing danger?

Do you think that the statement by Com. Svidersky (published in *Workers Newspaper* [*Rabochaia gazeta*]) about how "any (?) artistic work is by its very essence revolutionary" is Marxist and Bolshevist? Do you think an arts policy constructed on such an assertion is Marxist and Bolshevist?

2. Do you find it opportune, in the given political conditions, instead of pushing such a major artistic force as MKhAT-1 toward revolutionary themes, or at least a revolutionary interpretation of the classics, to do everything possible to make it easier for this theater to slip to the right, to disorganize intellectually that part of young MKhAT that already can and wants to work with us, to knock them off track, to push back that portion of theater specialists who are staging a play like Bulgakov's *Flight* [*Beg*]— which according to the unanimous response of Glavrepertkom's [Main

Repertoire Committee] arts and politics council and a meeting at the MK [Moscow Committee] RKP(b) is a weakly masked apology for White heroics—a much more blatant justification for the White movement than *Days of the Turbins* [*Dni Turbinykh*] (by the same author)? Are there any political considerations dictating the necessity of showing the White emigration as a victim crucified on Golgotha on Moscow's premier stage?

3. Why, when we are dealing with the dry and schematic propaganda of the White newspapers, do we not rely on the "immunity" of the broad reader and instead confiscate the random copies of this newspaper that reach us, by no means thinking about restoring freedom of the press for the bourgeoisie; whereas dealing with essentially the same propaganda but artificially masked by the high artistic craft of the "artists," and thus a hundred times more intensified in its power to impress, a hundred times more subtle, effective, and dangerous—we are equally confident of the . . . audience's "immunity" and generously spend the people's money on these kinds of productions?

Would it be possible in any bourgeois country (England, for example) that was not in a socialist milieu for the bourgeois dictatorship not only to turn a blind eye to analogous manifestations of proletarian ideology but also to generously subsidize them out of the state budget?

In this case, are we dealing with the manifestation of a type of Soviet democracy that is higher in principle or simply with an inappropriate starry-eyed idealism?

4. How are we to assess the actual "greatest good will" toward the most reactionary authors (like Bulgakov, who has gotten four blatantly anti-Soviet plays staged in the three premier theaters of Moscow; moreover, plays that are by no means outstanding for their artistic qualities but that are, at best, on an average level)? We can speak about the "greatest good will" because the organs of proletarian oversight for the theater are virtually powerless when it comes to authors like Bulgakov. For example: *Flight,* which was forbidden by our censor but still broke through that prohibition! while all the other authors (including the Communists) are subject to the repertory commission's oversight.

How are we to look on this real division of authors into the dregs and the cream, when the cream of the Whites enjoys better conditions?

What is the meaning of the existence of Glavrepertkom, the organ of proletarian dictatorship in the theater, if it cannot carry out its purpose properly (not, we repeat, due to any fault of its own)?

5. If everything cited above allows us to say that "all is not well" in arts policy, then, in your opinion, is the struggle being waged against this "not-wellness," in the development of which we have had to listen to references from the more consistent representatives of the right-wing "liberal" course to your sympathy, sufficiently intensive and effective?

Do these kinds of references, which we cannot in any way identify with the well-known political course you have presented, correspond to the truth?

All these questions (particularly the last), as you know, cannot help but disturb the broad party and Soviet public interested in matters of the cultural revolution, and we would ask you to give them the same kind of direct and pointed reply we have been accustomed to hearing from you on other issues.

Members of the Proletarian Theater Association

> V. Bill-Belotserkovsky (playwright),
> E. Liubimov-Lanskoy (director, MGSPS Theater director),
> A. Glebov (playwright),
> B. Reich (director),
> F. Vagramov (playwright),
> B. Vaks (playwright and critic),
> A. Lacis (theater worker and critic),
> Es-Khabib Vafa (playwright),
> N. Semyonova (theater worker and critic),
> E. Beskin (critic),
> P. Arsky (playwright).

On instruction from the group's members: V. Bill-Belotserkovsky, A. Glebov, B. Reikh.

This letter, which was primarily aimed, as we can see, at Bulgakov, whom the RAPPites considered a "right-wing fellow traveler," is astonishing for its tone, almost an ultimatum. As we know, Stalin's attitude toward Bulgakov was complicated. More than once he came forward as virtually his sole protector, inasmuch as ideologically Bulgakov was totally unacceptable, especially to the RAPPites, on whom Stalin put the emphasis during the cultural revolution and who thought of themselves as radical ideological puritans. What followed shows how pragmatic and flexible Stalin was in matters of culture. After a few months filled in particular with the struggle over M. Bulgakov's play *Flight*, Stalin responded to the left-radical playwright V. Bill-Belotserkovsky as if he hadn't noticed the "tone" of the Proletarian Theater's letter, having decided to use the letter for his own purposes. By defending Bulgakov, he demonstrated an unexpected "breadth," rejecting the primitive system of classifying writers into "left-wing" and "right-wing."

· 25 ·

Letter from I. V. Stalin to playwright V. N. Bill-Belotserkovsky. Original. Published with editorial corrections in I. V. Stalin, *Sobranie sochineny* (Collected works), vol. 11 (Moscow, 1949), pp. 326–329.

1 February 1929

Com. Bill-Belotserkovsky!

I am writing with great delay. Better late than never, though.

1. I consider the very formulation of the question about "right-wing" and "left-wing" in literature (which means the theater, too) incorrect. The concept of "right-wing" or "left-wing" at present in our country is a party concept, specifically—intraparty. "Right-wing" and "left-wing" refer to people who deviate in one direction or the other from the purely party line. Therefore it would be strange to apply these concepts to such a nonparty and incomparably broader sphere as literature, theater, etc. These concepts could also be applied to one party (Communist) circle or another in literature. Inside such a circle there could be a "right wing" and "left wing." However, applying them to literature in general, where there are all kinds of tendencies, including anti-Soviet and frankly counterrevolutionary ones, means turning all concepts upside down. It would be most correct to operate in literature with concepts of a class nature, or even the concepts "Soviet," "anti-Soviet," "revolutionary," "antirevolutionary," etc.

2. From what has been said it follows that I cannot consider "Golovanovism" a "right-wing" or "left-wing" danger. It lies outside of party considerations. Golovanovism is a phenomenon of an anti-Soviet order. This does not imply, of course, that Golovanov himself cannot turn over a new leaf, that he cannot free himself from his mistakes, that he should be persecuted and badgered even when he is prepared to bid farewell to his mistakes, that he must be forced in this way to go abroad.

Or, for example, Bulgakov's *Flight*, which cannot be considered a manifestation of a "left-wing" or "right-wing" danger, either. *Flight* is a manifestation of the attempt to evoke pity, if not sympathy, for certain strata of pathetic émigrés, probably an attempt to justify or semijustify the White cause. *Flight* in its present form is an anti-Soviet phenomenon. Actually, I would have nothing against staging *Flight* if Bulgakov were to add to his eight dreams one or two more dreams depicting the internal social springs of the Civil War in the USSR so that the spectator could understand that all these, in their own way "honest" Serafimas and various university lecturers were chucked out of Russia not due to the Bolsheviks' caprice but because they were living off the people (despite their "honesty"), that in driving out these "honest" exploiters, the Bolsheviks were carrying out the will of the workers and peasants and therefore acting perfectly correctly.

3. Why are Bulgakov's plays produced so often? Probably because we don't have enough of our own plays good enough for staging. In a land without fish, even *Days of the Turbins* is a fish. It is easy to "criticize" and demand a ban on nonproletarian literature. But easiest is not always best. It's not a matter of a ban but of driving old and new nonproletarian pulp off the stage step by step by way of competition and by creating realistic, interesting, artistic plays of a proletarian nature to replace it. Competition is a major and serious matter, for only in a situation of competition can we achieve the formation and crystallization of our proletarian literature. As for *Days of the Turbins* itself, it's not all that bad, it yields more good than harm. Don't forget that the main impression the viewer takes away from this play is an impression favorable for the Bolsheviks: "If even people like the Turbins are forced to put down their weapons and submit to the will of the people, admitting their cause finally lost, that means the Bolsheviks are invincible and there's nothing you can do about the Bolsheviks." *Days of the Turbins* is a demonstration of the crushing force of Bolshevism. Of course, the author is not at all "guilty" of this demonstration, but what do we care about that?

4. It is correct that Com. Sviderksy is constantly committing the most incredible mistakes and distortions. But it is also correct that in its work the repertory commission commits just as many mistakes, albeit in the other direction.

Recall *Crimson Island* [*Bagrovyi ostrov*], *A Conspiracy of Equals* [*Zagovor ravnykh*], and other pulp like that, which for some reason they willingly passed for the truly bourgeois Chamber Theater.

5. As for "rumors" of "liberalism," better not to talk about that. Let the Moscow merchant wives engage in their "rumors."

I. Stalin

Stalin supported Bill-Belotserkovsky in his struggle against RAPP. The reason for the conflict was Bill-Belotserkovsky's statement of 23 September 1928, in which he welcomed the departure from the USSR of MKhAT-2 director and actor Mikhail Chekhov and Vsevolod Meyerhold's request to leave his theater, which in the summer of 1928 was on tour in Paris, and at the time remained abroad. Bill-Belotserkovsky stated that "the working class loses nothing from this trip. One can even say with confidence that it's not Chekhov and Meyerhold who are leaving but, on the contrary, Soviet society that is making them go." The RAPPites accused the playwright of leaning to the left and of contempt for the cultural legacy. As a sign of protest, Bill-Belotserkovsky and his friends quit RAPP and organized their own group, Proletarian Theater.⁵ Such is the backdrop for Stalin's letter published below:

· 26 ·

Letter from I. V. Stalin to the Communist writers of RAPP. IMLI, f. 40, op. 1, d. 1153. Copy. Typewritten.
28 February 1929

Esteemed com[rades]!

1. You are dissatisfied that in a conversation with Com. Averbakh I defended Com. B[ill]-Belotserkovsky from the attacks by *On Literary Guard* [*Na Litpostu*]. Yes, I did indeed defend Com. B-Belotserkovsky. I defended him since the attacks on Com. B-Belotserkovsky set forth in *On Literary Guard* are fundamentally unfair and impermissible. Let *On Literary Guard* find itself some naïve people wherever they like; the serious reader will never believe that Com. B-Belotserkovsky, the author of *Storm* and *Voices of the Depths* [*Golosa nedr*] is a "déclassé lumpen," or that Com. B-Belotserkovsky's statement about Meyerhold and Chekhov is "a repetition of statements from the émigré press," or that Com. B-Belotserkovsky is an "objective (?!) class enemy" (see *On Literary Guard,* no. 20–21). Criticism has to be true above all. The whole problem is that the criticism in *On Literary Guard* is fundamentally untrue and unfair.

2. Did Com. B-Belotserkovsky make a mistake in his statement about Meyerhold and Chekhov? Yes, he did make a small mistake. With respect to Meyerhold, he was more or less wrong—not because Meyerhold is a Communist (there are plenty of good-for-nothing people among the Communists) but because he, i.e., Meyerhold, as a theater figure, in spite of certain negative features (posing, affectations, sudden and harmful leaps from living life toward the "classical" past), is unquestionably connected with our Soviet society and, of course, cannot be counted a "stranger." Actually, as we can see from the materials attached to your letter, Com. B-Belotserkovsky himself, it turns out, recognized his mistake concerning Meyerhold two months before the criticism appeared in *On Literary Guard.* . . . As for Chekhov, I have to admit that Com. B-Belotserkovsky is largely right nonetheless, despite the fact that he overdoes it a little. There cannot be any doubt that Chekhov went abroad not out of love for Soviet society and in general behaved swinishly, from which, however, it does not follow, of course, that we have to throw all the Chekhovs out on their ear.

But can we, on the basis of those excesses committed by Com. B-Belotserkovsky and for the most part already corrected by him, qualify B-Belotserkovsky as a "class enemy"? Clearly, we can't. Moreover, qualifying B-Belotserkovsky *that way* means committing the worst of all possible excesses. People don't gather in the Soviet camp *that way*. You only scatter and confuse them to please the "class enemy" *that way*.

3. "But maybe you (i.e., I) object to the harshness of tone?" you ask. No, it's not a matter of harshness of tone here, although tone also has more than a little significance. The problem is, first of all, that *On Literary Guard's* criticism against B-Belotserkovsky is unjust and incorrect for the most part (it is only partially correct). The problem is, secondly, that RAPP obviously doesn't know how to build a literary front properly and to array its forces on this front *in such a way* that a victory comes naturally from a defeat, and this means a victory in the war against the "class enemy" as well. It is a poor military leader who doesn't know how to find a suitable place on his front for both shock troops and weaker divisions, cavalry and artillery, and regular units, and partisan brigades. A military leader who doesn't know how to take into consideration the characteristics of all these diverse parts and utilize them *variously* in the interests of a *unified and indivisible* front—forgive me, Lord, but what kind of military leader is that? I'm afraid that sometimes RAPP resembles just that kind of military leader.

Judge for yourselves: the general line we have is correct for the most part, and we have enough forces, for you possess many apparatuses and press organs; as workers you are unquestionably capable and exceptional people; the desire to lead—you have more than enough—and still your forces are arrayed on the front; yes and your front itself is constructed in such a way that you often get cacophony instead of harmony, breaches instead of successes.

You talk about a "protective attitude toward fellow travelers," about "their Communist reeducation in a comradely environment." And at the same time you're prepared to *destroy* B-Belotserkovsky and an entire group of revolutionary writers over a trifle! Where is the logic, the consistency, the proportion here? Do you have many revolutionary playwrights like Com. B-Belotserkovsky?

Take a fellow traveler like Pilnyak, for example. We know that this fellow traveler knows how to perceive and depict only the rear end of our revolution. Isn't it odd that for fellow travelers like that you have found words about a "protective" attitude whereas for B-Belotserkovsky you didn't? Isn't it odd that while cursing B-Belotserkovsky as a "class enemy" and defending Meyerhold and Chekhov from him, *On Literary Guard* did not find a single word in its arsenal to criticize Meyerhold (and he needs criticism!) or, especially, Chekhov? Can you really construct a front *like that?* Can you really array your forces on the front *like that?* Can you really fight the "class enemy" in literature *like that?*

It's obviously a matter not of harshness of tone but of the leadership of the very complicated front of Soviet literature. And it is you and only you who have been called upon to lead this front, for you are the Russian Association of Proletarian Writers. You've forgotten that so much has been given you. You've forgotten that much is asked of whoever is given much. It's ridiculous to complain and whine: "They're criticizing us," "They're slandering us." Who else would they criticize and "curse" if not you?

4. Did Com. Kerzhentsev act correctly when he spoke in defense of B-Belotserkovsky against the attacks of *On Literary Guard?* I think that Com. Kerzhentsev did act correctly. You emphasize the formal point: "The TsK still doesn't have a formal decision." But do you really doubt that the TsK won't support the policy of destroying B-Belotserkovsky conducted by *On Literary Guard?* Who do you take the TsK for? Maybe the issue should in fact be raised for TsK consideration? I'll give you some friendly advice: don't insist on it; it's not to your advantage and you're sure to fail.

5. Among the many questions raised in your letter, there is one question which for some reason you didn't want to formulate and raise clearly but runs through every line of the letter. I have in mind the question of my correspondence with B-Belotserkovsky. You think, it seems to me, that my correspondence with B-Belotserkovsky is not a coincidence, that it, this correspondence, is a sign of some change in my attitude toward RAPP. This is wrong. I sent Com. B-Belotserkovsky my letter in reply to a collective statement from a number of revolutionary writers led by Com. B-Belotserkovsky. I don't know B-Belotserkovsky himself personally—unfortunately, I've never had occasion to meet him. At the moment when I was writing my reply, I had no idea of the disagreement between RAPP and Proletarian Theater. Nor did I know about the separate existence of Prol[etarian] Theater. I will continue in the future to respond (if I have time) to any comrade who has a direct or indirect relationship to our revolutionary literature. This is necessary. This is useful. This is, finally, my duty.

It occurs to me that your disagreements with proletarian writers like B-Belotserkovsky are not and cannot be substantive in nature. You can and must find a common language with them, even in the presence of a certain organizational "misunderstanding." You can and must do this, for the disagreements among you, ultimately, are microscopic. Who now needs a "polemic" that reminds them basically of an empty squabble: "Oh, you bastard!" "I'm listening to the bastard"? Clearly, no one needs that kind of "polemic."

As for my attitude toward RAPP, it remains just as close and friendly as

it has always been. This doesn't mean that I refuse to criticize its mistakes as I see them.
With Com[munist] greeting.

I. Stalin

P.S. Your question about Com. Lebedev-Poliansky and his "theory" is now moot. You can't demand that the TsK "react" to anything and everything in the world.

I. Stalin

Stalin's letter inflamed rather than cooled those fighting for the "purity of proletarian culture," who were bigger Stalinists than Stalin himself. During a meeting with Ukrainian writers, the leader entered into an explanation of his attitude toward Bulgakov. An uncorrected shorthand report of Stalin's speech preserved the marginal notes of the author, which he made in the latter half of the 1940s, when he was thinking about including the speech in his collected works, although he later rejected this idea.

· 27 ·

Excerpt from an uncorrected shorthand report of I. V. Stalin's speech at a meeting with Ukrainian writers. RGASPI, f. 558, op. 1, d. 4490, ll. 3–17. Copy.
Typewritten.
12 February 1929

<...> The same must be said about national culture. Uniting national culture on the basis of a shared socialist content by strengthening the development of national cultures. That is how the question stands. This is what people don't understand. Do you Marxists really think that a common language will ever be created (and it will, and it won't be Russian or French; the national question cannot be solved in a single state, the national question has been separate from the state for a long time) if a common language is ever created—and it unquestionably will be created—then this will be after the world dictatorship of the proletariat is won, and only after that, as long as it takes for socialism to be asserted not in one country but in all countries. So you see, the development of national cultures during the era of the dictatorship of the proletariat, maximum development, and guardianship of national cultures, this is why we are shelter-

ing these cultures so that when they have exhausted themselves entirely, they will create the ground for the development of a worldwide language, not Russian but an international language. When will this be? Too long from now. Lenin is right in saying that it will be a long time until the international dictatorship of the proletariat is established worldwide. That is how to put the question. People, Marxists, who think too simply, who oversimplify very complicated questions of national development, people who don't understand certain interpretations when the whole point is in these interpretations, also don't understand that we want to prepare the elements. . . . they cannot digest the fact that we want to prepare the elements of an international socialist culture by means of maximum development of national culture, just as they don't understand that we want to arrive at the destruction of classes by strengthening the class struggle, or that we want to arrive at a withering away of the state through an unprecedented expansion of the functions of this state, or that we want to unify the nations of various countries by dividing them, by freeing them from any yoke, by offering them the right to form a nation-state. Whoever doesn't understand this vital formulation of the question doesn't understand that we are conducting a policy of maximum development of national culture so that it can exhaust itself completely and then a base can be created for organizing an international socialist culture in form as well as content.

It would be a mistake for anyone to think that central workers could maintain a policy of neutrality when it comes to the development of the national cultures of backward nationalities: Well, they say, a national culture is developing, so be it, the best of luck developing, that's none of our affair. That kind of viewpoint would be wrong. We are in favor of a protective policy toward the development of national culture among backward nationalities. I emphasize this so that those simplifications that there are in this matter realize that it is our affair and we are active figures protecting the development of national culture. We are in favor of making culture, the spiritual baggage a given nationality possesses, the legacy of the entire nation.

In what language, for example, can we raise the culture of Ukraine? Only Ukrainian. We are facing a primitive problem whose solution will cost us dearly and that has already been solved in many states: the problem of universal and compulsory elementary education. We have to make it so that the worker or peasant comes to the factory and plant, or to the agricultural enterprise, literate, with at least a fourth-grade education. This degree was achieved a long time ago by such states as Germany, England, France, Switzerland, etc. In what language can we achieve this? Russian? Only the native language. If we want the broad masses of the people to rise to the highest degree of culture, or not the highest but just an average or even a low degree of culture, we have to develop the native language of every nationality to the maximum because only in the native language can we achieve this. There are no other means for raising the culture of the masses besides the native language.

This is why it would be absolutely incorrect and mistaken to take a position of neutrality with regard to the development of national culture. Then we would have to admit that we aren't going to raise any kind of industry or create any kind of defense. For what does a country's defense depend upon? The cultural level of the population, what our soldier is going to be like, whether he is comfortable with the elementary concepts of culture, whether he can use a compass, for example, whether he is comfortable with maps, whether he has at least a primitive literacy and culture so that he can understand orders, etc. If these elementary conditions are absent, we cannot create a real defense for the country. Just as we are absolutely not indifferent to the condition in which our workers enter our plants and factories. After all, we are now reequipping our industry and starting to reequip agriculture as well, because with his old tools the peasant could not cope with the tasks and demands made by a newly grown industry and the entire economy. I repeat, we are far from indifferent to the form in which workers enter our factories and plants, to whether or not they are cultured. This is a very serious matter. We are not going to be able to develop any serious industry without making the entire population literate.

It's all nonsense if they think you can make completely uncultured, illiterate people develop their labor and also use machines the way this is done by nations where the cultural level is high. So you see, even to carry out the most elementary propaganda for improving literacy, even for this, national culture is the very air we need if we are to take a step forward. This is why any neutrality, even indirect, is criminal; it goes against the interests of the proletariat, against the party, and against the people.

You ask what the prospects are for national culture. Clearly, it is going to develop. Of course, coming to a country we might say, "Well, we're going to wait a little while to see how the party apparatus is nationalized in the Ukraine, literature, the professional apparatus, the state apparatus, and so forth." We can't look on it this way, we have to move this matter forward actively. So when it comes to the rate—herein lies the protective policy of Soviet power toward the development of national cultures, i.e., what makes Soviet power differ fundamentally from any other power. Any other power would be afraid to develop national culture because, according to the bourgeois, the development of other nationalities is a decision in the direction of (inaudible).

What are the prospects? The prospects are that the national cultures of even the very smallest nations of the USSR are going to develop, and we are going to help them. Without this we are not going to be able to move forward, raise millions of the masses to a higher degree of culture, and thereby prepare our industry and our agriculture for defense. Without this we won't be able.

The peasant—it's one thing if he has completed four grades, acquired a little elementary agronomic knowledge, and he can orient himself—that kind of peasant is improving agriculture; it's another thing if he is absolutely illiterate and has no elementary knowledge. What language can he be educated in? Only his native language because he doesn't know any other languages.

Prospects are such that national cultures are going to develop and Soviet power must assist the development of national cultures. Com. Kaganovich has spoken with you about this, so I will not dwell on it, but I will say a few words, that you have to distinguish two aspects in a national culture: form and content.

When people say form doesn't mean anything—that's nonsense. An awful lot depends on form, without which there can't be any content. The form is national; the content socialist. This doesn't mean that every writer has to become a socialist, a Marxist, and so on. That isn't essential. This means that in literature, since we're talking about literature, new heroes have to appear. Before, other kinds of heroes were usually put forward; now there have to be heroes from the people, from the peasants, from the bourgeoisie—in the light which they deserve.

Take fellow travelers, for example—I don't know whether these writers can strictly be called fellow travelers—writers like Vsevolod Ivanov and Lavrenev. Maybe you've read Vsevolod Ivanov's *Armored Train 14-69* [*Bronepoezd 14-69*], maybe many of you have seen it, maybe you've read or seen Lavrenev's *Break* [*Razlom*]. Lavrenev is not a Communist, but I assure you that these writers have done much more good with their *Armored Train* and *Break* than 10–20 or 100 Communist writers who cram and cram and not a damn thing comes of it: they don't know how to write, it's not artistic.

Or take, for example, someone everyone knows, Bulgakov. If you take his *Days of the Turbins,* he's a foreigner to us, unquestionably. He's hardly Soviet in his way of thinking. However, with his *Turbins* he has nonetheless brought great benefit, unquestionably.

Kaganovich: The Ukrainians don't agree (noise, conversations).

Stalin: And I'm telling you, I'm judging from the standpoint of the viewer. Take *Days of the Turbins*—what kind of impression is the audience left with? In spite of its negative aspects—I'll tell you what they are, too—the impression that the audience is left with when they leave the theater is an impression of the invincible might of the Bolsheviks. Even strong, steadfast, and in their own way honest people, in quotes, like

Turbin and the people around him, even people like that who are irreproachable in their own way and honest in their own way, in quotes, have to admit in the end that you can't do anything about these Bolsheviks. I don't think the author wanted that, of course, in that he's innocent, but that's not the point, of course. *Days of the Turbins* is a magnificent demonstration in favor of the all-crushing force of Bolshevism.

Voice: And Changing Landmarks.

Stalin: Excuse me. I cannot demand that a writer be a Communist and follow the party point of view. Literature needs other measures—nonrevolutionary and revolutionary, Soviet and non-Soviet, proletarian and nonproletarian. But you cannot demand that literature be Communist. Often people say: whether it's a right-wing or left-wing play, it depicts the right-wing danger. For instance, the *Turbins* is the right-wing danger in literature. Or, for example, they banned his *Flight*—it's a right-wing danger. This is wrong, comrades. Right-wing and left-wing danger—that's purely a party concept. A right-wing danger means that people are deviating somewhat from the party line, a right-wing danger inside the party. A left-wing danger is a deviation from the party line to the left. Does literature have anything to do with the party? It doesn't, of course, it's much broader, literature is, than the party, and there the measures have to be different, more general. There you can talk about the proletarian character of literature, about its antiproletarian or worker-peasant character, about its anti—worker-peasant character, about its revolutionary, nonrevolutionary, Soviet, anti-Soviet character. If you demand that literature and the author follow the party point of view, then you have to drive out all the nonparty members. Is that the truth or not?

Take Lavrenev, just try to drive that man out, he's capable, and he's captured something out of proletarian life, and fairly accurately. Workers will tell you flat out, to hell with your right-wing and left-wing, I like going to see *Break,* and I'm going to go see it—and the worker is right. Or take Vsevolod Ivanov's *Armored Train.* He's not a Communist, Vsevolod Ivanov. Maybe he considers himself a Communist (noise, conversations). Well, he's a sham Communist (laughter). But that hasn't kept him from writing a good piece that has great revolutionary significance, its educational significance is indisputable. What would you say—is he right-wing or left-wing? He's not right-wing or left-wing because he's not a Communist. You can't apply purely party measures mechanically to the writers' sphere.

I believe that the com[rade] in glasses sitting there doesn't want to understand me. From this standpoint, from the standpoint of the larger scale, and from the standpoint of other methods of approaching literature, I'm saying that even *Days of the Turbins* has played a major role. Workers go to see this play and they see: Aha, no force can take the Bolsheviks!

There you have the general impression left from this play, which can't in any way be called Soviet. There are negative features in this play. These Turbins in their own way are honest people, they're shown as individuals torn away from their milieu. But Bulgakov doesn't want to sketch out the genuine state of affairs, he doesn't want to sketch out the fact that even though they may be honest people in their own way, they're living off someone else. They're drummed out of the country because the people don't want people like that living off them.

This same Bulgakov has a play *Flight*. That play shows the type of a certain woman—Serafima—and a certain lecturer. These people are drawn as honest, and so forth. You just can't figure out what the Bolsheviks are actually persecuting them for. After all, both Serafima and the lecturer are refugees and in their own way are honest, incorruptible people, but Bulgakov—and this is what makes him Bulgakov—didn't depict these people as living off anyone else. They're driven out of the country because the people don't want people like that living off them. Here's the underpinning of why such people, honest in their own way, are being drummed out of our country. Intentionally or unintentionally, Bulgakov is not depicting this.

But even people like Bulgakov have something useful to offer. I'm talking in this instance about *Days of the Turbins*. Even in a play like that, even a man like that, still has something useful to offer. Why am I saying all this? Because you need to apply broader scales in assessing literature. Right-wing and left-wing aren't appropriate. You can say proletarian or antiproletarian, Soviet or anti-Soviet.

Take *Ingots* [*Bruski*] by Panfyorov, for example. Right now what is most characteristic for the village is the fact that there isn't just one village. There are two villages. The new village, which is turning toward the city, awaiting tractors, agronomic knowledge, etc., wants to live in a new way, work in a new way, make contact with the city. That's the new village. And there's the old village, which wants to scorn everything new, the tractor, agronomic knowledge, etc. The old village wants to live in the old-fashioned way—and will perish. In *Ingots* Panfyorov does a marvelous job of sketching these two villages and the struggle between them.

Does the literature that draws the village have to be peasant literature? Here we have Panfyorov's *Ingots*. Panfyorov can't be called a peasant writer, though in his composition he writes only about the peasantry and there's not a word in him about the city. Or take another less well-known work, *Katya Dolga,* by Korobov. Korobov marvelously depicts here the kulaks' cheating and all their various tricks. It's wonderfully shown how the new village is growing and how the new types of peasants have come to be. This isn't the kind of peasant who lives in a slovenly, necessarily filthy way, no, he may have spent time with the Red Army, he may have been in the factories and plants, he may have picked up some knowledge, he's reading a book, he wants to run agriculture in a new way, the peasants are still waiting to get a tractor, they're organizing a collective farm and running it so that the land yields two or three times more. Here the new village is depicted magnificently.

Of course, it's wrong when they say that in the Ukraine literature has to be purely peasant. That's wrong. It's quite correct that before the workers in the Ukraine were Russians, but now they're Ukrainians. The makeup of the working class, of course, is going to change, filled out by newcomers from the surrounding villages. That's the universal law of national development all over the world. If you take the Hungarian towns forty years ago, they were German, but now they're Hungarian. Take the Latvian towns—before they were Estonian, and now they're Latvian. The working class has to be filled in from the surrounding villages. You can't drag the nationalities out by their hair, that's hard and could provoke resistance among the Russian elements and even give rise to Russian chauvinists; however, if you take the natural process—and not lag behind this process—the nationalization of the proletariat must happen and must follow step by step. This is a general law, and the national linking, the union between the city and the village, will follow.

Ukrainian workers are going to be appearing as heroes in works; there are a lot of them now. Even native Russian workers who used to brush it aside and didn't want to learn the Ukrainian language—and I know many like that who have complained to me, "I can't learn the Ukrainian language, Com. Stalin, my tongue won't turn that way"—now they're talking differently, they've learned Ukrainian. I'm not talking about the new workers who are going to fill out the working class. You're going to have the same kind of literature as here, as the Russians have. It will depict workers and peasants and the bourgeoisie, negatively or positively—it's just a matter of taste. They're going to be depicted just as they are in other Soviet countries. And discussions about how among you there can only be peasant literature, in the sense of heroes, conceal a certain chauvinism with respect to the fact that things have started badly, so they say; even the workers of the Ukraine seem to have slowed things down and feel that the literature should be Russian for their workers and Ukrainian for the peasants. This is the conscious or unconscious machination of people who don't want to understand that the working class is going to be constantly filling out with newcomers from the surrounding villages. There you have the matter of perspectives.

So I've said something about the fates of national cultures during the transition to socialism, during the dictatorship of the proletariat, and on the character of Ukrainian literature. < . . . >

Another important topic involves Stalin's attitude toward the "main proletarian poet," Demian Bedny, whose popularity during the days of the Revolution and the Civil War was tremendous (as the author of thousands of propaganda poems, Demian Bedny was on close personal terms with virtually all the leaders of the party, from Lenin and Trotsky to Stalin and Bukharin back from prerevolutionary times). Raised on Bolshevik rhetoric, during the cultural revolution Demian Bedny continued to reject "patriotic values." This made him a convenient target for criticism in the early 1930s. The correspondence between Stalin and Bedny allows us to take a new look at Stalin's "left leanings" and "right leanings." According to established opinion, there was a turn "to the left" during the cultural revolution, collectivization, and the First Five Year Plan, but beginning in 1936 movement starts in the opposite direction (assertion of patriotic values, the struggle against Formalism, and other avant-gardist tendencies). Meanwhile, as can be seen, in 1930 Stalin's position was already far from simple but rather pragmatically flexible. Reproduced below are three documents that illuminate this episode.

· 28 ·

Resolution of the TsK VKP(b) Secretariat "On the feuilletons of Com. Demian Bedny, 'Climb Down off the Stove' ["Slezai s pechki"] and 'Without Mercy' ["Bez poshchady"]." RGASPI, f. 17, op. 114, d. 201, l. 13. Original. Typewritten.
6 December 1930

No. 26, p. 74 g—*On the feuilletons of Com. Demian Bedny, "Climb Down off the Stove" and "Without Mercy."*

a. The TsK draws the attention of the editors of *Pravda* and *Izvestia* to the fact that recently in the feuilletons of Demian Bedny there have begun to appear false notes expressed in the indiscriminate censuring of "Russia" and "Russian" (the articles "Climb Down off the Stove" and "Without Mercy"); in the declaration of "laziness" and "sitting on the stove" as practically the national trait of Russians ("Climb Down off the Stove"); in the failure to understand the fact that in the past there were two Russias, revolutionary Russia and antirevolutionary Russia, and moreover what was right for the latter could not be right for the former; in the failure to understand that present-day Russia is represented by its reigning class, the working class, and above all the Russian working class, the most active and most revolutionary brigade of the worldwide working class, moreover the attempt to indiscriminately apply to it the epithets "lazybones" and "lover of stove sitting" cannot help but be a crude sham.

The TsK hopes that the editors of *Pravda* and *Izvestia* will in the future bear in mind these defects in the writings of Com. Demian Bedny.

b. The TsK believes that *Pravda* acted rashly in printing a certain part in Com. D. Bedny's feuilleton "Without Mercy" concerning false rumors about uprisings in the USSR, the murder of Com. Stalin, etc., for it could not have helped knowing about the ban on printing reports of such rumors.

Note the use of the ecclesiastical language, Old Church Slavic, in the second to last sentence of Bedny's following letter:

· 29 ·

Letter from D. Bedny to I. V. Stalin. RGASPI, f. 558, op. 1, d. 2939, ll. 7–9.
Notarized copy. Typewritten.
8 December 1930

Iosif Vissarionovich!

I am literate, too, you see. And you will become literate as well, "as the matter approaches the noose." I want to introduce clarity into the matter so that there won't be any reprimands later on about why I didn't say something.

The hour of my catastrophe has arrived. Not for being too "right" or too "left" but for being too "curved." How great the arc of this curve is, i.e., at what distance its and my second and final point lie, I still don't know. But here's what I do know and what you should know, too.

There was an appeal from the TsK published—without you—that has upset me. I immediately supported it with my feuilleton "Climb Down off the Stove." The feuilleton had an astounding resonance: *On Literary Guard* printed it as a model of heroic propaganda, Molotov praised it to excess and ordered that it be immediately included in a series of literature "for shock workers," and it came out under just this heading in a separate brochure. Even Yaroslavsky, who has never done this, sent me a letter that touched me (see enclosure). Poets are a special people: don't feed them bread, praise them. I was waiting for praise from the man for whom my relationship has always been colored with biographical tenderness. Joyfully I hurried to see this man at his first call. I opened wide my ears, which you tenderly scratched behind. You pulled me hard by these ears: "Climb

Down off the Stove" isn't any damn good!! I started mumbling that I had another curious topic published. The topic isn't any damn good!

I returned home, trembling. I'd been doused with a tub of cold water. Worse: I'd been thoroughly unsettled. I was paralyzed. I couldn't write. I just barely squeaked through to 7 November.

On 7 November you and I met. Joking with you in conversation, I thought: I'm a fool! Why am I clumsily setting out to him in prose the plan of the feuilleton when I can write this feuilleton cleverly and convince him with the very quality of the feuilleton.

I sat down to work. I worked like a slave. It was hard to write given my dubious mood, as well as having influenza. I wrote it. I handed it in to be typeset. At about twelve o'clock at night there was a hitch in the editorial offices: Yaroslavsky felt that the introductory part, being too historical, weakened the second, propaganda part, so shouldn't we toss out this introductory part? I did not object. But seeing probably from my disappointed face that this was causing me pain, Yaroslavsky said: Oh, let it go, since it's already typeset and in pages. Yaroslavsky departed. I was left with my thoughts. I knew something Yaroslavsky didn't: I would have a captious reader in you. What if suddenly I couldn't win over this reader?

After giving it some thought, I categorically stated to Mekhlis and Savelyev, I'm removing the first part! There was a commotion, since the hour was late, and now we had a resetting. I let Yaroslavsky know. He called me on the telephone and insisted that I "stop acting capriciously," as it seemed to him. Let the whole feuilleton go through. It wasn't hard to convince me.

And that's all!

A live voice either should have praised my work or else amiably and in fairly convincing form pointed out my "curve." Instead of this I received a discharge from the Secretariat. This discharge shone a Bengal light on my isolation and my doom. I have been crossed off at *Pravda* and also at *Izvestia*. Things are not going well for me. They are not going to read me after this not just in these two newspapers, everyone has put up their guard. The well-informed Averbakhs have already put up their guard. No one was eager to praise me. There will be no end to those eager to spit in my tracks. The titles of my feuilletons, "Climb Down off the Stove" and "Without Mercy," are becoming symbolic. For twenty years I have been the cricket on the Bolshevik stove. I'm climbing down off it. The time has come, you see. There was a time when even Ilich corrected me and allowed me to respond in *Pravda* with a poem, "How Poets Should Be Read" ["Kak nado chitat' poetov"] (see the sev[enth] vol[ume] of my works, p. 22, if you're interested). Now I have also sat down to write a reply, but while I was writing I came to the firm conviction that they won't print it or, if they do, they'll start continuing a policy toward me that will only bend my curve even more and bring my fateful, catastrophically final point closer. Maybe it's true, you can't be a major Russian poet without cutting your path catastrophically short. But what voice would my army shout in after this, after it has been abandoned by its commander, my eighteen regiments (volumes), my hundred thousand fighters (lines). That would be something unimaginable. Here you can't help but pray: "My Father, if it is still possible, may this ordeal pass me by!"

But with this letter I will finish the question I began above: "Nevertheless, not as I will, but as Thou wilt"!

I decline any responsibility for what happens next.

Demian Bedny

· 30 ·

Letter from I. V. Stalin to D. Bedny. RGASPI, f. 558, op. 1, d. 2939, ll. 1–6.
Copy. Typewritten.
12 December 1930

To Com. Demian Bedny.

I received your letter of 8 December. Evidently you need my reply. All right then, you shall have it.

First of all, about a few of your minor and petty phrases and insinuations. If they, these ugly "pettinesses," were a chance element, one could overlook them. But there are so many of them and they gush so spiritedly that they set the tone of your whole letter. And the tone, as we know, makes the music.

You judge the decision of the TsK [Secretariat] a "noose," a sign that "my (i.e., your) hour has come." Why, on what grounds? How can you call someone a Communist who instead of giving close thought to the essence of a decision of [the executive organ of] the TsK and correcting his mistakes interprets this decision as a "noose"?

Dozens of times the TsK has praised you when they needed to. Dozens of times the TsK has protected you (not without considerable effort!) from attacks by individual groups and comrades from our party. The TsK has called dozens of poets and writers to order when they made individual mistakes. You considered all this normal and understandable. Now that the TsK has had to subject your mistakes to criticism, though, suddenly you're grousing and shouting about the "noose." [Why], on what grounds? Doesn't the TsK have the right to criticize your mistakes? Doesn't the TsK decision apply to you? Is your poem above all criticism?

Don't you find that you have been infected by that unpleasant disease called conceit? A little more modesty, Com. Demian.

You contrast Com. Yaroslavsky to me (why me and not the TsK Secretariat?), though it's clear from your letter that Yaroslavsky doubted the need to print the first part of "Without Mercy" and had only been swayed by your "dismayed face" when he gave his approval to publish. But that's not all. You go on to contrast Com. Molotov to me, assuring me that he found nothing wrong in your "Climb Down off the Stove" and even "praised it in the extreme." First of all, allow me to have my doubts about the truthfulness of your report concerning Com. Molotov. I have every reason to believe Com. Molotov more than you. Secondly, isn't it odd that you don't say anything in your letter about Com. Molotov's attitude toward your "Without Mercy"? But then, what meaning could your attempt to contrast Com. Molotov to me have? It could only have one meaning: to imply that the decision of the TsK Secretariat is in fact not a decision of this latter but the personal opinion of Stalin, who, obviously, is passing off his own personal opinion as a decision of the TsK Secretariat. But that is going too far, Com. Demian. That is simply unscrupulous. Must you really make the special qualification that the resolution of the TsK Secretariat "On the Errors in D. Bedny's feuilletons 'Climb Down off the Stove' and 'Without Mercy'" was passed by all the votes of the members of the Secretariat present (Stalin, Molotov, Kaganovich), i.e., unanimously? Could it really be otherwise? I recall now how a few months ago you told me over the telephone: "It turns out there are disagreements between Stalin and Molotov. Molotov is intriguing against Stalin," etc. You must remember that I cut you off rudely then and asked you not to trade in gossip. At the time I took this lapse of yours as an unpleasant episode. Now I see that you had an ulterior motive—to gain from momentary disagreements and profit thereby. A few more scruples, Com. Demian . . .

"Now I have sat down to write," you write, also a reply, but while you were writing you came to the firm conviction that they would not publish it or, having published it, *they will continue a policy toward me* that will only bend my curve even more and bring my fateful catastrophically final point closer. Maybe it's true, *you can't be a major Russian poet without cutting one's path catastrophically short.*"

And so, this means there is some special policy toward Demian Bedny. What kind of policy is this and what does it consist of? It, this policy, turns out to consist of forcing "major Russian poets" to "cut their path catastrophically short." There is, as we know, a "new" (entirely "new") Trotskyite "theory" which asserts that in Soviet Russia only the dirt is real, only "Pererva" is real. Evidently you are trying to apply this "theory" now to TsK policy toward "major Russian poets." Such is the measure of your "trust" in the TsK. I don't think that you are capable, even in a state of hysterics, of agreeing to such vile antiparty actions. Not for nothing when reading your letter was I reminded of Sosnovsky. . . .

But enough about "pettinesses" and petty "outbursts." There is such a pile of these "pettinesses" in your letter ("captious reader," "informed Averbakh," and other charms), and they are so similar to each other, that there is no point going on about them any more. Let's move on to the essence of the matter.

Wherein lies the essence of your mistakes? In the fact that the compulsory and necessary criticism you develop fairly accurately and competently in the beginning eventually carried you away, and once it had, it started mounting in your works into slander against the USSR, against its past, against its present. Such are your "Climb Down off the Stove" and "Without Mercy." Such is your "Pererva," which I read today on the advice of Com. Molotov.

You say that Com. Molotov praised "Climb Down off the Stove." That may very well be. I may have praised this feuilleton no less than Com. Molotov, since in it (as in other feuilletons) there are many magnificent parts that go straight to their mark. But there is also a fly in the ointment that spoils the whole picture and transforms it into nothing but another "Pererva." This is the problem and this is what sets the tone in these feuilletons.

Judge for yourself.

The whole world now recognizes that the center of the revolutionary movement has moved from Western Europe to Russia. Revolutionaries of all countries are looking hopefully to the USSR as the seat of the liberation struggle for the workers of the whole world, recognizing in it their sole fatherland. Revolutionary workers of all countries unanimously applaud the Soviet working class and, above all, the Russian working class, the avant-garde of Soviet workers, as its recognized leader, which is carrying out a more revolutionary and more active policy than the proletariats of other countries ever dreamed of conducting. The leaders of revolutionary workers of all countries are greedily studying the instructive history of Russia's working class, its past, Russia's past. They know that besides reactionary Russia there also existed revolutionary Russia, the Russia of the Radishchevs and Chernyshevskys, the Zhelyabovs and Ulianovs, the Khalturins and Alekseevs. All of this plants (cannot fail to plant!) in the hearts of Russian workers a feeling of revolutionary national pride that can move mountains and work wonders.

And you? Instead of comprehending this greatest of all revolutionary processes in history and making the work of the bard of the advanced proletariat soar, you've slipped into a depression and become tangled up in very boring quotations from the works of Karamzin and equally boring sayings from *Homemaking* [*Domostroi*], proclaiming to the whole world that Russia in the past was a vessel of abominations and desolations, that present-day Russia is one big "Pererva," that "laziness" and the urge to "sit on the stove" are practically a national trait of Russians in general, and that means Russian workers as well, who, having made the October Revolution have, of course, not ceased to be Russians. And you call this Bolshevik criticism! No, my highly respected Com. Demian, this is not Bolshevik criticism but slander against our people, the *dethronement* of the USSR, the *dethronement* of the proletariat of the USSR, the *dethronement* of the Russian proletariat.

And after all this you expect the TsK to keep quiet! What do you take our TsK for?

You want me to be quiet, too, because, it turns out, you feel a "biographical tenderness" for me! How naïve you are and how very little you know Bolsheviks.

Maybe you, as a "literate" man, will not refuse to listen to the following words of Lenin:

"Is a feeling of national pride alien to us, the conscious Great Russian proletariat? Of course not! We love our language and our homeland, we are working most of all so that its laboring masses (i.e., nine-tenths of its population) can rise to the conscious life of democrats and socialists. What pains us most is to see and feel the violence, oppression, and humiliation our marvelous homeland was subjected to by the tsarist executioners, noblemen, and capitalists. We take pride in the fact that this violence evoked resistance from us, the Great Russians, that we produced Radishchev, the Decembrists, the nonnoble revolutionary intellectuals of the 1870s, that in 1905 the Great Russian working class created a mighty revolutionary party of the masses, that the Great Russian muzhik started at that time to become a democrat, started to overthrow the priest and landowner. We remember how half a century ago the Great Russian democrat Chernyshevsky, in giving his life to the cause of revolution, said: 'A pitiful nation, a nation of slaves, from top to bottom—slaves all.' Overt and covert slaves—the Great Russians (slaves of the tsarist monarchy) do not like to recall these words. But in our opinion these were words of genuine love for the homeland, a love that languished due to the lack of revolutionariness among the Great Russian masses. At the time there was none. Now there is very little, but there is some. We are filled with national pride for the Great Russian nation has also created a revolutionary class and also proven that it is capable of giving humanity great models of the struggle for freedom and socialism and not just great pogroms, rows of gallows, torture chambers, great famines, and great servility before the priests, the tsars, the landowners, and the capitalists" (see Lenin, "On the National Pride of the Great Russians" [*O natsional'n(oi) gordosti velikorossov*]).

This is how Lenin, the greatest internationalist in the world, could speak about the Great Russians' national pride. And he spoke that way because he knew: "The interest (not in the servile sense) of the Great Russians' national pride coincides with the socialist interest of the Great Russian (and all other) proletarians" (see ibid.).

Here it is, Lenin's clear and bold "program." This "program" is perfectly understandable and natural for revolutionaries deeply connected to the working class and the popular masses.

It is incomprehensible and unnatural for degenerates like Lelevich, who are not and cannot be connected to the working class and the popular masses.

Can this revolutionary "program" of Lenin's be reconciled with the unhealthy tendency that runs through your latest feuilletons?

Clearly it cannot. It cannot because they have nothing in common.

Here is the problem, and here is what you don't want to understand. This means you need to be turned onto the old Leninist road, no matter what. There aren't any other roads.

Herein lies the essence. Not in the empty lamentations of the frightened intellectual who rambles on out of fright about how they supposedly want to "isolate" Demian and how Demian "won't be published anymore," etc. Understood?

You asked me for clarity. I hope I've given you a clear enough reply.

I. Stalin

The episode with Demian Bedny characterizes not only the Stalinist style of personal relations (as has already been stated, Stalin knew Demian Bedny long before the Revolution) but also the leader's pragmatism (naturally, at bottom too lay the personal conflict between Stalin and Demian Bedny). When we talk about cultural policy in the Stalinist era, we must remember that Stalin was a politician not burdened by principle. Manipulation and exploitation of different allies to resolve different current problems were characteristic of his entire political career. This is why his attitude to the same individuals and groups at different times is so variable. Highly indicative in this regard is the relationship between the state and Gorky.

CHAPTER FIVE

"Gorky, Whom No One Takes Seriously in Politics"

Gorky played an utterly singular role in the history of Soviet culture. A man of letters with radical views who was close to the Bolsheviks and a personal friend of Lenin, Gorky received the revolution hostilely, seeing in it the "raging of the bestial instincts of the mob." He accused the Bolsheviks of betraying the idea of the socialist proletariat and relying on a pack of drunken soldiers for the sake of seizing power. He also stood up in defense of the intelligentsia. The period during which he wrote a number of essays later collected in the book *Untimely Thoughts* (*Nesvoevremennye mysli*), 1917–1918, a book of essays by Gorky harshly criticizing the revolution, ended in his nearly open opposition to the state. Gorky's authority was so great, however, that the Bolshevik leaders had to contend with his position. The "Gorky factor" first shows up in Politburo materials fairly early on. The Politburo passed resolutions many times on his endless applications and petitions even before his actual emigration from Soviet Russia. Gorky's views on the revolution were so unorthodox that the TsK had to distance itself several times from the writer, whose earlier collaboration with the Party was widely known. Here is the decision on Gorky's essays:

· 31 ·

Resolution of the TsK RKP(b) Politburo on the essays of A. M. Gorky.
RGASPI, f. 17, op. 3, d. 99, l. 1. Authenticated copy. Typewritten.
31 July 1920

No. 32, p. 9—Lenin's statement on the essays of Com. Gorky in issue 12 of *III International* [*III Internatsional*].

Approve the following resolution:

"The TsK deems highly inappropriate the placement of Gorky's essays in issue no. 12 of *Com[munist] Int[ernational]* [*Kommunistichesky Internatsional*], especially the lead essay, for there is nothing Communist about these essays, but there is a great deal that is anti-Communist. Henceforth by no means place similar essays in *Com[munist] Int[ernational]*."

However, Gorky not only published essays in Communist publications, he also, as we have seen, addressed harsh personal letters to Lenin and sharp political statements to the Politburo:

· 32 ·

Letter from A. M. Gorky to A. I. Rykov. Published in *Izvestia TsK KPSS*, no. 1
(1989), p. 243.
1 July 1922

Aleksei Ivanovich!

If the trial of the Socialist Revolutionaries is going to end in murder, it's going to be an intentional murder—a vile murder.

I beg you to inform L. D. Trotsky and the others of this my opinion. I hope it will not surprise you, for you well know that throughout the Revolution I pointed out to Soviet power a thousand times the senselessness and criminality of exterminating the intelligentsia in our illiterate and uncultured country.

Currently I am convinced that if the SRs are murdered this crime will provoke a moral blockade against Russia on the part of socialist Europe.

M. Gorky

The letter bears Rykov's instruction of 19 July 1922, "Disseminate through the Secretariat to all Politburo members"; an attached note by L. D. Trotsky: "I propose instructing the *Pravda* editors to do a *soft* article on the artist Gorky, whom no one takes seriously in politics, and publishing the article in foreign languages"; and two signatures: "In favor—Tomsky, Rykov." Despite the protests from Gorky and leftwing European figures, twelve of the thirty-four SR defendants were sentenced to death. On 20 July 1922, at Trotsky's suggestion, the Politburo approved the following resolution: "(a) Instruct the troika on the SR case to order a number of essays written and see that they get published to the effect that the petitions of Gorky and Anatole France have no significance for Soviet Russia, (b) inform Com. Piatakov that the Politburo feels it is absolutely essential to end the trial on 1 August."[1] Even earlier, on 18 July 1922, *Pravda* published a harsh article by O. Zorin, "Nearly at the Bottom (On the Recent Speeches of M. Gorky)" ("*Pochti na dne [O poslednikh vystupleniakh M. Gor'kogo]*"—a title that parodies the title of Gorky's well-known play, *The Lower Depths* [*Na dne*]). The essay mentioned the writer's letter to A. I. Rykov and emphasized that "Maxim Gorky is harming our revolution with his foreign political speeches. And harming it powerfully."

Even during the gravest disputes with Gorky, Party policy under both Lenin and Stalin consisted of cajoling Gorky, in hopes of exploiting his authority. Politburo documents bristle with decisions such as this one: "With regard to releasing money to Com. Gorky for medical treatment abroad (Com. Lenin's proposal). Add Com. Gorky to the list of comrades being treated abroad, and instruct Com. Krestinsky to ensure that he is provided in full with the amount he needs for treatment" (pr. 243, p. 8, 21 December 1921);[2] "(a) Instruct Narkompros to acquire the copyright for his works from M. Gorky. (b) Instruct the Berlin office of NKVT [People's Commissariat of Foreign Trade], together with Com. Krestinsky, to write up this arrangement and immediately begin financing Gorky" (pr. 103, p. 10, 25 February 1922).[3] What kind of agreement this was and what sums they were talking about is clear from the documents attached to the Politburo materials: copies of a letter from the RSFSR Trade Office in Germany, dated 21 June 1922, reporting on the agreement reached and the need to allocate for its implementation in the current year 17.5 million German marks, or 150,000 gold rubles (including payment of an advance on the author's fee amounting to 800,000 German marks and subsequent monthly payments of 100,000 marks, until the publication was complete), as well as the agreement itself, dated 13 June 1922, and estimates for the publication of Gorky's complete collected works.[4]

On 17 November 1927 (pr. 136, p. 13), the Politburo formed a commission to organize the celebration of the fortieth anniversary of Gorky's literary career. The commission consisted of high-level Party ideological workers—Lunacharsky, Khalatov, Skvortsov-Stepanov, Bukharin, Tomsky, Smidovich, Pokrovsky, and Ganetsky.[5] On 17 May 1928 (pr. 25, p. 2), the Politburo considered the issues involved in organizing a meeting with Gorky on the report of the special commission.[6] A ceremonial meeting was held with Gorky, who was arriving from Italy, at the Belorussian train station in Moscow on 28 May 1928. He was met by N. Bukharin, K. Voroshilov, G. Ordzhonikidze, M. Litvinov, A. Lunacharsky, and A. Bubnov.

Gorky was in continuous correspondence with Stalin. Stalin's letters show how hard the General Secretary worked to draw Gorky into the cultural and political life of the country, supplying him "at first hand" with various materials (mainly about so-called wreckers) and his responses to current cultural and political events, informing him of news, which undoubtedly flattered Gorky's vanity. These letters are rather bizarre if one considers that Stalin was writing them at the very peak of the intra-Party struggle. Stalin's letters to Gorky are interesting in the context of Stalin's correspondence with Molotov and with his (Stalin's) family. In the letters to Molotov we see a careful politician admonishing, guiding "behind people's back," and calculating the possible moves of his political rivals—a daring, sly, and enthusiastic gambler. In his letters to his family there is a tension and unnaturalness to his tone; he is fulfilling an obligation that is obviously a burden to him. Behind the letters' cheerful tone one senses a total disinterest in family affairs. Stalin's letters to Gorky are another matter. In them, Stalin is in his role as Stalin: the fair-minded historical judge, the high-principled Party leader fully immersed in the cares of state and pulling the wagon of his historical mission, the solicitous leader.

· 33 ·

Letter from I. V. Stalin to A. M. Gorky. AP RF, f. 45, op. 1, d. 718, ll. 3–4.
Handwritten.
11 June 1929

Aleksei Maxim[ovich]!

1. I'm sending the two letters I promised yesterday. They give a reply to a number of questions posed to me by B[ill]-Belotserkovsky and RAPP by way of our personal correspondence.

2. I did read Spiridonov's play, 26 *Communards* [26 *kommunarov*]. I think the play is weak. It is a story, from time to time a messy story, about events of tremendous importance whose internal connection the author has failed to grasp.

You can't understand from the play *why* and *how* the Baku Bolsheviks *abandoned* power (and I mean abandoned, not just surrendered). This is the main issue in the Baku events, though. Either spare the memory of Shaumian and other comrades and don't write a play about the twenty-six Communards, or if you do write it don't skirt this main issue and let all kinds of trivial matters overshadow it. The author has committed a great sin against histor[ical] truth here, and not only histor[ical] truth but also against the younger generation, which wants to learn from the mistakes and failures (as well as the successes and achievements) of their older com[rades].

I can't condone the author's attempt to depict *Caspian* sailors as *nothing but* a band of mercenary drunks. This is inaccurate from the standpoint of histor[ical] truth. It doesn't happen during civil war, which brings differentiation and schism to even the most closed institutions and organizations. This could not have been then given the presence of such a fact as the existence of Soviet Russia.

I don't understand the absence in the play of the working class as *subject*. The case occurs in an oil kingdom, in a city of workers, in Baku, but the workers are nowhere, or almost nowhere, to be seen as a functioning and struggling class. This is incredible. But it is a fact. There are eight or ten magnificent, juicy pages in the play that speak to the author's talent. The figure of Petrov came out very well. Sandro and MacDonald didn't come out badly either. The other characters are vague and lackluster. The play's few merits don't (and can't) compensate for its great deficiencies.

Generally speaking, the play is weak.

Well, that's enough.

Greetings!
I. Stalin

· 34 ·

Letter from I. V. Stalin to A. M. Gorky. AP RF, f. 45, op. 1, d. 718, ll. 80–81.
Handwritten.
24 October 1930

Esteemed Aleksei Maximovich!

I have recently returned from a rest. Previously, during the congress, because of the press of work, I didn't write to you. This is not good, of course. But you must forgive me. Now is another matter; now I can write. I probably have a chance to repair my sin. Actually, "if you don't sin, you can't repent; if you don't repent, you can't be saved."

Things here are not going badly. We're moving the wagon along; it's creaking, of course, but we're moving forward. That's the whole point.

People say you're writing a play about wreckers and wouldn't mind receiving relevant material. I've collected new material on wreckers and will be sending it to you any day now. You'll receive it soon.

How is your health?

When are you thinking of coming to the USSR?

I am well.

I firmly shake your hand.

I. Stalin

· 35 ·

Letter from A. M. Gorky to I. V. Stalin. AP RF, f. 45, op. 1, d. 718, ll. 82–82v.
Handwritten.
2 November 1930

Dear Iosif Vissarionovich,

Kriuchkov brought me your note, thank you for the greeting. I was very happy to learn that you had a rest over the summer.

I was utterly shaken by the new acts of wrecking, so deftly organized, and by the role of right-wing tendencies in these acts. At the same time, however, I was encouraged by the work of the GPU [State Political Administration; the secret police], the truly indefatigable and vigilant guardian of the working class and Party. Well, I'm not going to write about these moods of mine. You will understand without me saying anything, I know that among you there has grown up a hatred of enemies and a pride in the power of our comrades. Here is what, dear I[osif] V[issarionovich]—if the writers Artem Vesely and Sholokhov petition for a trip abroad, you must allow them to go. Both of them, like Vsevolod Ivanov, are involved in the work on the "History of the Civil War"—working up the raw material. Their work will be edited by historians under the supervision of M. N. Pokrovsky. It would be useful for me, as well as for them, to talk over the methods of this work now, before spring, when I will be coming.

In a few days' time 200 "shock workers" will be arriving in Naples, and I will go to meet them. I'm very happy to be having a chat with these fine fellows.

I've abandoned writing my play about "wreckers." It wasn't working out. There wasn't enough material. It's extremely fine that you are sending me "new"! It would be even better, though, of course, if there were nothing new in this regard.

Today I read an article by Poincaré in *Excelsior*. In my view, with this article he has acknowledged that he was quite familiar with the affairs of the "industrial" and "peasant" party and that the Kondratievs and K. were men not unknown to him. Evidently, even the issue of intervention is making some little progress. However, I still can't believe in its feasibility; the "setting" for this doesn't seem suitable. But you know better, of course.

I feel the time has come to cart my old bones home. My health improved over the summer. I'm maintaining a strict regime. I'll arrive before the First of May.

I firmly shake your hand, dear comrade.

A. Peshkov

· 36 ·

Letter from I. V. Stalin to A. M. Gorky. [No later than 15 December 1930]. AP RF, f. 45, op. 1, d. 718, ll. 100–101v. Handwritten.

Greetings Aleksei Maximovich!

I am writing with some delay, since the diplomatic post only goes to you in Italy at certain times, once in twenty days, I believe.

Sholokhov and the others have already left to see you. They were given everything required for the trip.

I'm not sending Osadchy's testimony, since he repeated it at the trial, and you can familiarize yourself with it from our newspapers.

I saw Com. Peshkova. Dr. Levin will be visiting you in a few days. Whether a month and a half or more remains—you'll tell me.

The Ramzin group's trial is over. We decided to substitute ten or fewer years' imprisonment for execution. By doing this we were trying to emphasize three things: (a) the main people to blame aren't the Ramzin people but their bosses in Paris—the French interventionists and their Torgprom rabble; (b) Soviet power is not opposed to sparing people who have repented and disarmed, for the Soviet Party is guided not by a sense of vengeance but by the interests of the Soviet state; (c) Soviet power is not afraid of enemies abroad or their agents in the USSR.

Things aren't going badly here. In industry and in agriculture the successes are undeniable. Let them, each and every medieval fossil, caterwaul there in Europe, at the tops of their voices, about the "downfall" of the USSR. They aren't going to change our plans or our affairs one iota that way. The USSR is going to be a first-rate country with the biggest technically equipped industrial and agricultural production. Socialism is invincible. There's not going to be any more *"beggarly"* Russia. That's over! There's going to be a mighty and plentiful *vanguard* Russia.

On the 15th we're calling a plenum of the TsK. We're thinking of replacing Com. Rykov. A nasty business, but there's nothing you can do: he can't keep up with progress, he lags devilishly behind (despite his desire to keep up), and he trips on his own feet. We're thinking of replacing him with Com. Molotov. A bold, smart, very modern leader. His real name is Skriabin, not Molotov. He's from Viatka. The TsK is wholly behind him.

Well, I guess that's all.

I shake your hand.

    I. Stalin

P.S. If you really have decided to come by spring, it would be good to get here by 1 May, in time for the parade.

· 37 ·

Letter from I. V. Stalin to A. M. Gorky. AP RF, f. 45, op. 1, d. 718, l. 103.
Handwritten.
10 January 1931

Dear Aleksei Maximovich!

I am sending you documents about (1) the Kondratiev group and (2) about the Mensheviks. A request—don't take the content of these documents too much to heart and don't worry. The heroes of the documents aren't worth that. Also, there are worse scoundrels in the world than these wretches.

Things are going well here. Transportation matters aren't so good (they've had too great a burden dumped on them), but we'll set things right in the near future.

Guard your health.

Greetings!

I. Stalin

The tension in the relationship between Gorky and Stalin gave rise to an episode in late 1929, when at Stalin's insistence the Politburo approved an unprecedented proposal:

· 38 ·

Resolution of the TsK VKP(b) Politburo "On the speeches against Maxim Gorky by certain Siberian writers and literary organizations." RGASPI, f. 17, op. 3, d. 768, l. 2. Authenticated copy. Typewritten. Attachment published in *Pravda*, 26 December 1929; *Spravochnik partiinogo rabotnika* [Party worker guidebook], no. 7, pt. 2, 1930, p. 272.
15 December 1929

No. 109, p. 5—On Gorky (Com. Stalin).

Instruct a commission made up of Comrades Kaganovich, Stetsky, and Syrtsov to write up within one week's time a draft Politburo resolution in connection with the campaign against Gorky in the Siberian newspapers and magazines.

Com. Kaganovich should convene the commission.

Attachment to p. 5, pr. PB no. 109, 15 December 1929

On the speeches against Maxim Gorky by certain Siberian writers and literary organizations.

Without going into an examination of the substance of the argument on literary matters, and while believing that a number of the matters touched upon in these arguments will find their resolution in a special TsK instruction on literary matters, the TsK VKP(b) feels it is crudely mistaken and bordering on hooliganism to characterize M. Gorky's speech as "the speech of a wily masquerading enemy" (resolution of the Siberian Proletkult, *The Present* [*Nastoiashchee*], no. 8–9, 1929), as are the allegations that M. Gorky "more and more often is becoming a mouthpiece and shield for the entire reactionary portion of Soviet literature" (resolution of the Communist associates of the krai newspaper of Siberia, *The Present*, nos. 5, 6, 7), and alleging that M. Gorky is defending "the whole Soviet 'Pilnyakian trend' in all its manifestations, i.e., not only on the literary front" (*Soviet Siberia* [*Sovetskaia Sibir'*], no. 218).

Such speeches by certain Siberian writers are connected with crude distortions of the Party's literary-political line in certain Siberian organizations (the *Present* group, Proletkult, the Siberian AP [Association of Writers]) and diverge at root from the attitude of the Party and the working class toward the great revolutionary writer Com. M. Gorky.

The TsK VKP(b) resolves:

1. To announce a harsh reprimand against the VKP(b) faction of Siberian Proletkult for its part in issuing a resolution containing irresponsible attacks against Gorky.

2. To reprimand the editors of *The Present* [for] running in the magazine materials with impermissible attacks against M. Gorky.

3. To remove Com. Kurs as effective editor of *The Present* and from his duties as editor of *Soviet Siberia,* recalling him to the disposition of the TsK VKP(b).

The TsK VKP(b) suggests that the Siberian Krai Executive Committee strengthen its supervision of the literary organizations of Siberia (The Siberian Union of Writers, *The Present,* et al.) and ensure, along with a decisive struggle against bourgeois trends in literature, the correction of "left-wing" deviations in the line and activity of its literary organizations.

The publication of this resolution put Gorky in a false position. He hastened to distance himself from this way of resolving literary disputes, appealing to Stalin:

· 39 ·

Letter from A. M. Gorky to I. V. Stalin. IMLI, A. M. Gorky Archive.
Handwritten.
8 January 1930

Dear Iosif Vissarionovich!

Rudder [*Rul'*] reports that in Chita some magazine failed to praise me and that it was punished for this. If you count the TsK's rebuke of the people in Novosibirsk, then this is the second instance. I am quite sure that there will be a third, a tenth, etc. I consider this phenomenon perfectly natural and inevitable, and I don't think there is any need to punish those who write unflattering and hostile things about me.

Like you, like all of us "old men," I receive a lot of hostile letters. The leaps and swoops of the letters' authors convince me that after the Party puts the countryside decisively on the tracks of collectivism, the social revolution will take on a genuinely socialist character. This is a nearly geological turnaround. It is bigger, immeasurably bigger and deeper, than everything the Party has done so far. A way of life is being destroyed that has existed for millennia, a way of life that created a man who is most misshapenly unique and capable of horrifying with his animal conservatism and his private property instinct. There are twenty million people like that. The task of reeducating them in a short period of time is the insanest of problems. Nonetheless, here it has practically been solved.

It is perfectly natural that many of the millions become very genuinely and furiously insane. They don't even realize the full depth of the turnabout that is occurring, but they feel instinctively, down to their bones, that the destruction of the deepest foundation of their centuries-old life is beginning. You can rebuild a destroyed church and set any god you like in it, but when the earth slips out from under your feet, that is irrevocable and forever. And so here people who have mechanically mastered the revolutionary phrase, the revolutionary lexicon, curse wildly, very often concealing beneath this phrase the vengeful feeling of the ancient man whose "end has come." Notice that those from Siberia and the Far East, where the muzhik is stronger, curse the strongest of all.

"Words will never hurt me," though, and they don't bother me, and in my work, they encourage me. I'm not a Party man, as you know, and this means that nothing aimed against me can hurt the Party or its guiding members. Let them curse. Especially since some, even many, are cursing out of misunderstanding, and ignorance, and when you explain to them the essence of the matter, they'll stop. Many are in a hurry to declare their own orthodoxy, hoping to gain something thereby—and they are.

But generally speaking everything is going excellently. Much better than one could have expected. So don't punish the cursers, Iosif Vissarionovich, I beg of you. Those of them who are incurable aren't worth thinking about, and those who have fallen only mildly ill will recuperate. This life of ours is the most talented of doctors.

Taking advantage of the occasion, I congratulate you once again on your half-century of service to life. A fine service. To your health!

A. Peshkov

Will you write for *Literary Studies* [*Literaturnaia ucheba*]? You ought to. This would be useful for beginning writers. Very. Write! A. P[eshkov].

Naturally, Stalin realized the position he was putting Gorky into with his "concern." But this was Stalin's style of "tending" and "protecting" necessary people. Ivan Gronsky, who was close to Stalin in the early 1930s as editor-in-chief of *Izvestia* and the virtual director of the Organizing Committee of the USSR Writers Union in the years 1932–1934, recalled the work of this Politburo commission during preparations for the celebration of the fortieth anniversary of Gorky's literary activity:

> At one of the sessions, Stalin made a proposal: "Give Nizhnii Novgorod and the oblast Gorky's name. Rename Tverskaia Street in Moscow after him. Give Aleksei Maximovich the Order of Lenin. Name the [Moscow] Art Theater after Gorky. . . ."
> "But Comrade Stalin, that is more Chekhov's theater," I pointed out. "And anyway, you've already piled it on pretty damn thick, so to speak."
> "That doesn't matter. That doesn't matter." Leaning over, very quietly, he said to me: "He's an ambitious man. We have to bind him to the Party."
> Once again at Stalin's suggestion, a decision was taken to give Gorky Riabushinsky's private home on Malaia Nikitskaia Street and a palace on the bank of the river with a huge park. . . .
> Stalin was a brilliant artist. He had a talent for instantaneous transformation that was truly of Chaliapinesque proportions. . . . He played out his friendship with Gorky just as artistically while in actual fact not trusting him. This was a very subtle game. Surprisingly, Gorky was a writer, an "engineer of human souls," whose very profession, seemingly, presumes knowledge of human nature, but in my opinion, Gorky never was able to penetrate to Stalin's core. . . . Stalin realized full well that Gorky, just like Barbusse, like a lot of other prominent cultural figures, was "political capital."[7]

It must be admitted that Stalin dealt with him to maximum advantage when the time came to "restructure the literary arts organizations" and centralize culture.

CHAPTER SIX

Work with the "Anti-Soviet Intelligentsia"

One of the most persistent myths of Soviet cultural history is the myth of the "liberal 1920s," which declares NEP, with its relatively free trade and entrepreneurship, a golden age. The newly opened archives, however, allow us to say that NEP was an era of ideological clamping down, not liberalism, and the Politburo documents from this period allow us to consider this organ the country's supreme censor. There is no doubt whatsoever that the main censorship decisions went through the Politburo, and that they were almost always (not counting complicated cases, such as that of M. Bulgakov, when the decisions were bound up with Stalin's personal biases) extremely harsh.

Sometimes these decisions were all bark and no bite: "Reprimand the editors of *Red Field* [*Krasnaia niva*] [for] impermissibly running stories in the Soviet press like "Lel" (*Red Field,* no. 30), which discredits the RKP and is cheap and vulgar in content" (pr. 29, p. 9, 21 August 1923);[1] "Deem it a mistake to run the story "Grigory Pugachev" in *Red Virgin Soil* [*Krasnaia nov'*]; recommend that the editors of R[ed] V[irgin] S[oil] take a more cautious attitude toward plots touching upon the work of the GPU" (pr. 74, p. 17, 7 August 1925).[2] In these instances the motives for taking one decision or another lay in the sphere of departmental interests. Thus, the resolution about "Grigory Pugachev" was approved on the basis of a letter from G. Yagoda of the secret police, who was displeased with his department's image in the story.

Sometimes decisions were accompanied by fairly harsh "organizational conclusions" (exemplary punishment for the guilty, removal from office, disbandment of the editorial board, repressions). Such was the episode involving the publication in *Young Guard (Molodaia gvardiia)* of a story by Artem Vesely, "The Barefoot Truth" ("Bosaia Pravda"]. We have the resolution from the TsK Secretariat, dated 8 May 1929, "on the punishment for the editorial board of *Young Guard.*" The text of the resolution is written in Stalin's hand and signed by Molotov and Kaganovich.³ The resolution proclaimed: "Announce a harsh reprimand for the editors of *Young Guard* for placing in issue no. 5 of *Young Guard* Artem Vesely's 'quasi-story' 'The Barefoot Truth,' which (the 'quasi-story') presents a one-sided, tendentious, and basically caricaturish depiction of Soviet reality that is objectively beneficial only to our class enemies. . . . The TsK Secretariat, in conjunction with the TsK Youth Bureau, shall review the makeup of the *Young Guard* editorial board with a view to guaranteeing the Party and Komsomol [Communist Union of Youth] against such undesirable incidents."⁴ The materials from the interrogation of the writer himself help us to understand the reasons for such concerted interest in the story on the part of Stalin, for the harshness of the formulations, for the severity of the reprisal, and for the demonstrative publication of usually carefully concealed decisions. As the arrested Artem Vesely reported at his first interrogation on 28 November 1937, the issue of *Young Guard* with his story was confiscated by OGPU (Unified State Political Directorate; the secret police), he read this story in the apartment of Lev Kamenev, formerly an all-powerful protector of Stalin in the Politburo, and subsequently Stalin's victim in the presence of the boss and people close to him.

Even more severe measures were taken in instances that affected Stalin personally. In this case, the matter would grow into broad-scale political action. Such was the situation that came about around Boris Pilnyak's long story, "The Tale of the Unextinguished Moon" ("Povest' nepogashennoi luny"}, which was based on an infamous incident when the army commander Mikhail Frunze was forced to agree to an operation at the General Secretary's insistence and then died on the operating table.

· 40 ·

Resolution of the Politburo TsK VKP(b) on B. A. Pilnyak's "Tale of the Unextinguished Moon." RGASPI, f. 17, op. 3, d. 560, ll. 5–6. Authenticated copy. Typewritten.
13 May 1926

No. 25, p. 22—On *Novy mir* [*New World*], no. 5 (Comrades Molotov, Skvortsov-Stepanov, Polonsky, Voronsky, Lebedev-Poliansky).

a. Recognizing that Pilnyak's "The Tale of the Unextinguished Moon" is a malicious, counterrevolutionary, and slanderous attack on the TsK and the Party, confirm the seizure of the fifth volume of *Novy mir*.

b. Reprimand the members of the *Novy mir* editorial board, Lunacharsky, and Stepanov-Skvortsov [for] placing this story by Pilnyak in *Novy mir*, and give the most severe reprimand against Comrade Polonsky, as the member of the editorial board in charge of the literary department.

c. Propose to Com. Voronsky that he write a letter to the editors of *Novy mir* rejecting Pilnyak's dedication with the appropriate motivation, which must be agreed upon by the Secretariat TsK.

d. The editorial board of *Novy mir* must publish simultaneously with Com. Voronsky's letter its own statement concurring in Com. Voronsky's opinion and deeming the printing of this story a gross and crude error.

e. Take Pilnyak off the list of associates of *Red Virgin Soil*, *Novy mir*, and *Star* [*Zvezda*] (Leningrad).

f. Prohibit any reprinting or republication of Pilnyak's "Tale of the Unextinguished Moon."

g. Instruct Com. Broido to review the agreement made between GIZ [State Publishing House] and Pilnyak for the purpose of eliminating from publication those works of Pilnyak which are unacceptable in the political respect.

h. Instruct the TsK press department to disseminate the same to the other Soviet publishing houses.[5]

i. Suggest that the TsK press department print a confidential directive on issues connected with the closing of *New Russia* [*Novaia Rossia*] and the seizure of the fifth volume of *Novy mir*, especially emphasizing in it the need to observe strictly the distinction between criticism aimed at strengthening Soviet power and criticism having as its purpose its discrediting.

j. State that the entire plot and individual elements of Pilnyak's "Tale of the Unextinguished Moon" could not have been created by Pilnyak otherwise than on the basis of slanderous conversations held by certain Communists around the death of Com. Frunze and that some of the responsibility for this rests with Com. Voronsky. Announce punishment against Com. Voronsky for this.[6]

Sometimes, on the contrary, the trial was not quick but dragged on—when that was what Stalin wanted. Such was the case with M. Bulgakov's play *Days of the Turbins*, Stalin's favorite production at the Art Theater. This play concerns an intelligentsia family during the Civil War with ties to the White Army. Given the problematic class status of its protagonists this "anti-Soviet work"—even though it enjoyed the leader's personal favor—was initially banned from production by Narkompros everywhere except—by way of exception—the Moscow Art Theater, and then for just one season. The GPU, however, resolved the matter its own way, as Lunacharsky reported to the head of the government, Rykov:

· 41 ·

Postal telegram from A. V. Lunacharsky to A. I. Rykov on the GPU prohibition of M. A. Bulgakov's *Days of the Turbins*. AP RF, f. 3, op. 34, d. 240, l. 2. Original.
27 September 1926

Dear Aleksei Ivanovich.
  At a meeting of the Narkompros board, with the participation of Repertkom, and including the GPU, it was decided to permit Bulgakov's play just for the Art Theater and just for this season. At Glavrepertkom's insistence, the board allowed it to make a few cuts. On Saturday evening, the GPU informed Narkompros that it was banning the play. This matter must be considered at the highest level, or else the Narkompros board's decision, which is already known, must be confirmed. Rescission of the Narkompros decision by the GPU is highly undesirable and even scandalous.

  In view of the special importance of the matter, three days later, on 30 September, the Politburo once again approved a resolution "not to rescind the resolution of the Narkompros board concerning Bulgakov's play."[7] The Narkompros board's resolution of 24 September 1926 was confirmed a year later, on 15 September 1927. This time the production was allowed for one more year, with its exclusion from the Art Theater's repertoire beginning with the 1927–1928 season. However, instead of confirming this resolution, "incredible events," as Bulgakov himself might have put it, occurred in the Politburo.

· 42 ·

Memorandum from TsK VKP(b) Orgburo member and RSFSR People's Commissar for Agriculture A. P. Smirnov to the TsK VKP(b) Politburo concerning lifting the ban on *Days of the Turbins*. AP RF, f. 3, op. 34, d. 239, l. 21. Original. Typewritten.
8 October 1927

To the TsK VKP(b) Politburo

We ask that the PB change its decision on the matter of the Moscow Art Theater's production of *Days of the Turbins*.

Experience has shown that (1) this is one of the few theatrical productions providing an opportunity for young artistic forces to develop; (2) the piece is artistically restrained and useful. Talk of any counterrevolutionariness it might contain is absolutely wrong.

We ask that the decision to extend the production of *Days of the Turbins* in the future be made by surveying the members of the PB.
With Communist greetings

    A. Smirnov

Below the memorandum from the people's commissar of agriculture (!) is a handwritten note: "I concur in the main with Com. Smirnov on his proposal. 8 October 1927. Voroshilov." Two days later the Politburo reached a decision: "Repeal immediately the ban on the production of *Days of the Turbins* at the Art Theater" (pr. 129, p. 22, 10 October 1927).[8] Standing behind the unexpected and full rehabilitation was the all-powerful General Secretary, proof of which is Lunacharsky's letter to Stalin, in which the people's commissar of education asks him to defend Lunacharsky's department from attacks by orthodox Party critics, inasmuch as Narkompros (whose competence included Glavrepertkom), as became clear, had only been officially carrying out Stalin's will:

· 43 ·

Letter from A. V. Lunacharsky to I. V. Stalin. RGASPI, f. 142, op. 1, d. 461, ll. 8–8v. Copy. Typewritten.

12 February 1929

To Com. Stalin.
Copy: A. P. Smirnov
Dear Iosif Vissarionovich.

You well remember that the matter of the production of *Days of the Turbins* was decided in a positive sense by the Politburo three years ago. The Politburo's resolution said that *Days of the Turbins* was permitted only for production in Moscow and only for one year. At the end of the year, Narkompros, mechanically implementing this resolution, banned any further production of *Days of the Turbins*.

A few days after this, I received an instruction from the Politburo permitting *Days of the Turbins* for one more year, which was done. At the beginning of the current season, at the suggestion of Repertkom, the Narkompros board once again resolved to halt any further performances of *Days of the Turbins*, but you, Iosif Vissarionovich, telephoned me personally, suggesting to me that we lift this ban and even reproaching me (gently, it's true), saying that Narkompros ought to have checked with the Politburo beforehand.

If various irresponsible journalists and demagogic young people are trying to pin the blame on Narkomp[ros] for permissiveness with regard to *Days of the Turbins*, then Narkompros responds to this with silence and willingly bears full responsibility for implementing the Politburo's instruction, but when Agitprop, taking advantage of these circumstances, on the pages of the Party's central organ, and therefore before the entire Party—the entire country, you might say—starts to aim bitter reproaches at Narkompros for this same permissiveness, then you have something utterly impermissible. Agitprop must know about the Politburo's decision. In this way, by coming down hard on NKP [People's Commissariat of Enlightenment], it is indirectly, but consciously, disavowing the Politburo's instruction.

You will agree, Iosif Vissarionovich, we absolutely cannot put up with a situation whereby the Politburo prescribes a certain act that is later condemned by lower-ranking organs, and, moreover, the censure for its implementation is delivered publicly. In issue no. 33 of *Pravda*, dated Saturday, 9 February, in an article entitled "Toward the Arrival of the Ukrainian Writers," signed by the head of the political department of the Agitprop press, Com. Kerzhentsev, there is the following paragraph:

"Some people have still not freed themselves from great power chauvinism and look down on the culture of the Ukraine, Belorussia, Georgia, et al. Nor are we doing everything we can to put an end to mistakes already made. Our largest theater (MKhAT I) continues to produce a play that distorts the Ukrainian revolutionary movement and insults Ukrainians. Neither the theater's director nor RSFSR Narkompros is sensitive to the kind of harm this inflicts on our relationship with the Ukraine."

Further commentary on this disgraceful attack against NKP is unnecessary. I would add only that we are constantly experiencing this kind of effort by individual workers in Agitprop TsK to ascribe right-wing bias and inadequate social sensitivity to us—an effort that hinders our work and that is as little justified in other instances as it is in this, when Kerzhentsev reproaches NKP for not realizing the harm inflicted on our nationalities policy, while knowing full well that through NKP he is striking directly at the guiding organ of our Party.

If the TsK Politburo has changed its attitude toward *Days of the Turbins* and maintains Agitprop's point of view, then I request we be given the appropriate instruction, which we will implement immediately. If not, then I request that Agitprop be instructed not to put us and themselves in a difficult and false position.

Of course, very few in the Party know about the relevant Politburo instruction, but how must those who do know about it react when they read lines such as those written by Com. Kerzhentsev?

Lunacharsky

Bulgakov's case was exceptional, however. More typical was the situation that arose around *Conspiracy of Equals* (*Zagovor ravnykh*), a play written by Mikhail Levidov, a playwright and journalist popular in the 1920s. This example allows us to trace the complete cycle of censorship decisions made by the Politburo and to see the mechanism in action. The impetus was a letter of denunciation:

· 44 ·

Letter from Deputy Chief of Agitpropotdel TsK VKP(b) S. N. Krylov to V. M. Molotov. AP RF, f. 3, op. 34, d. 221, ll. 1–2. Copy. Typewritten.
16 November 1927

Viacheslav Mikhailovich!

The Chamber Theater has produced as its jubilee play *Conspiracy of Equals* by the vulgar pamphleteer Mikh[ail] Levidov.

The author gives a squib directed at the Party under the guise of a "historical" depiction of the Directory and the conspiracy of Babeuf.

The play bristles with words like "gravediggers of the Revolution," "those who were set up, fed, and reared by the Revolution," "traitors to the Revolution," "the people are weary," "under Robespierre life was better," "the Revolution is over," "I'm an old hand at politics (Barras)," and little expressions like that taken wholesale from the platform and speeches of the opposition.

Levidov read the play this summer to a group of oppositionists in Kislovodsk and received approval there. Then A. V. Lunacharsky read and also approved it. Then Glavrepertkom approved it (under letter A, i.e., in the first category, beyond all doubt), moreover Glavrepertkom member Popov-Dubovsky did not familiarize himself with the piece, but Pikel did go through it, and Com. Mordvinkin sanctioned it.

At a viewing of the play in the theater on 5 November, I told Glavrepertkom that a big mistake had been made allowing this decadent squib on stage, that I personally was in favor of withdrawing it but had to confer on the matter with Com. Krinitsky. That same evening, I informed Krinitsky of my conclusion. Krinitsky wanted to familiarize himself with the play. After reading the play, on the day of his departure for Viatka, he left a letter, which I attach and ask you to read. Krinitsky's opinion coincides with mine.

At Com. Krinitsky's suggestion, I scheduled one more viewing of the performance on the evening of the 15th. Also invited to the viewing were responsible worker Communists—thirty to thirty-five people. From the exchange of opinions after the viewing the following was clear:

1. total unanimity (with the exception of Pikel and Lunacharsky) in their assessment of the play as a bad play that should not have been allowed to be produced and

2. disagreement over whether the play should be withdrawn from the repertoire. Most of the comrades expressing an opinion (Lunacharsky, Pikel, Mordvinkin, Polonsky, Lebedev-Poliansky, Kerzhentsev, Raskolnikov, Sapozhnikov, et al.) consider it impossible to withdraw the play for various reasons, primarily political. A minority (Popov-Dubovinsky, Krylov, Cherniavsky, Volin, et al.) expressed themselves in favor of immediate withdrawal.

There have been rumors going around about the play since the summer, put out, evidently, by the opposition. The play obviously intended to lead the viewer to think of analogies: Directory—Politburo, Babeuf—Trotsky, Thermidor and Fructidor—our era, bread store lines—our lines, etc.

The public was already intrigued by the performance even before the premiere: all the tickets for the four performances announced were snapped up.

During the performances, there may be demonstrative outbursts.

Given the current political situation, there would be less harm from the play's immediate withdrawal from the repertoire than from leaving the squib on the stage.

I ask that you issue me a directive immediately, bearing in mind that tomorrow, the 17th, is the premiere, and then the performance of *Conspiracy* three days in a row.

    S. Krylov

P.S. I'm attaching a copy of Com. Krinitsky's letter and a copy of *Conspiracy of Equals*.

The next day (inasmuch as the matter was urgent), an "information-gathering commission" was formed (and the play was banned even before any information was gathered!). There followed requests from interested individuals:

· 45 ·

Letter from A. Ya. Tairov to M. P. Tomsky. AP RF, f. 3, op. 34, d. 221, l. 8.
Authenticated copy. Typewritten.
19 November 1927

Deeply esteemed Mikhail Pavlovich.

Allow me to inform you that the viewing of our last performance of *Conspiracy of Equals* by the special commission of which you are a part is scheduled for Monday, 21 November, at nine o'clock in the evening. This is, so to speak, an official announcement. Apart from this, allow me with all fervor and persuasiveness to ask you to be sure to keep this time free and attend the viewing. You realize, of course, without any explanation from me, the moral importance of this matter of survival for our theater, and I deeply believe that you will come to the viewing and then be convinced personally of the immense and honest work we have done, which has every right to take its place among the October performances for the tenth anniversary [of the October Revolution].
With sincere respect for you,

    A. Tairov

Tairov's letter infuriated Tomsky, who was the leader of the trade unions and a member of the Politburo, inasmuch as what was most important in all the Politburo's work was its confidentiality: Politburo decisions were secret and anonymous. An infuriated Tomsky sent a memorandum to Molotov:

· 46 ·

Memorandum from M. P. Tomsky to V. M. Molotov. AP RF, f. 3, op. 34, d. 221, l. 7. Authenticated copy. Typewritten.
21 November 1927

Dear Viacheslav!
I am attaching to this a copy of Tairov's letter to me of the 19th of th[is] m[onth]. Isn't it time we put an end to the shameless chatter about the Politburo and its resolutions? How did Tairov find out about the PB resolution? Why does he need to know this? Can't you instruct someone to investigate?

With Communist greeting,
M. Tomsky

The finale to this story was the usual one: a ban and punishment of the guilty parties.

· 47 ·

Resolution of the Politburo TsK VKP(b) on banning M. Yu. Levidov's play *Conspiracy of Equals*. RGASPI, f. 17, op. 3, d. 661, l. 2. Authenticated copy. Typewritten.
24 November 1927

No. 137, p. 13—On *Conspiracy of Equals* (Comrades Voroshilov, Tomsky, Skvortsov-Stepanov).
a. Take under advisement the report from the Politburo commission deeming it unnecessary to permit the performance of *Conspiracy of Equals* in the theaters.
b. Deem the commission's work finished.
c. Ask the TsKK [Central Control Commission of the Party] within one week's time to investigate those guilty of disclosing the Politburo resolution on *Conspiracy of Equals*.[9]
d. Instruct the Orgburo to examine, within two weeks' time, the makeup

of Glavrepertkom with a view to changing it and selecting individuals who can ensure the proper work of Glavrepertkom, and to submit to the Politburo its proposal on this matter.[10]

This is how a case of an "anti-Stalinist play" was resolved. An "anti-Bolshevik" play was another matter. The incident around Bulgakov's play *Flight* (*Beg*), on the life of the White Russian emigration, ended in the same ban but was accompanied by enormous efforts on Stalin's part to "preserve Bulgakov." The case began, to judge from Politburo materials, with a letter of denunciation from a high Party functionary—the deputy head of TsK Agitprop, Platon Kerzhentsev. We reproduce this document, which is a model of apparatchik "literary criticism," in full.

· 48 ·

Report from P. M. Kerzhentsev, Deputy Head of Agitprop TsK VKP(b), to the Politburo of the TsK VKP(b) on M. A. Bulgakov's *Flight*. [No later than 6 January 1929]. AP RF, f. 63, op. 1, d. 241, ll. 69–80. Original. Typewritten.

Bulgakov's *Flight*
Bulgakov's new play describes the White Guard world at the moment of the Crimea's fall and during its emigration. As in *Days of the Turbins*, the author idealizes the White Guard leaders and attempts to evoke the viewers' sympathy for them. In doing so, *Flight*'s author first and foremost tries to vindicate and ennoble those White leaders whom he himself condemned in *Days of the Turbins*. *Flight* is the apotheosis of Wrangel and his closest aides.
Description of the play's characters.
The main hero is front commander General Khludov. He's sick. But this sickness is not physical in nature. He is dissatisfied with the decay, treachery, self-seeking, greed, and corruption of the rear, with the "Sevastopol swine" who are destroying the White Guard movement. He is courageously shouldering the heavy burden of their mistakes. "You realize," he tells Wrangel, "how a man can hate who knows nothing will ever come of it and who has to persevere anyway."
He is disenchanted not with the idea of the White movement but with those on top who plan its political and tactical execution.
Khludov is a brilliant military leader. His staff works up until the very last minute, the troops in his charge fight like lions, even though they're naked, barefoot, and hungry. His orders are precise, his military decrees

speak to his profound operational mind and outstanding capabilities as a commander. Khludov is by no means a limp rag or a bundle of tense nerves but rather an extremely tough individual.

This tough purposefulness comes out very distinctly in Khludov's decision to return to his homeland as well: "It's all clear to me now. I'm not going to swim in buckets; I'm no cockroach, I don't run." Khludov goes home.

Charnota is a "typical soldier," an upstart, the regimental swashbuckler, a madly courageous commander, with great natural wit. By nature he is an Epicurean and a daredevil. For him the war is above all a risky and entertaining adventure in which he might be staking his life at any moment, just as he would his entire fortune at chemin de fer. He is generous, good, and direct and will always help a comrade in misfortune. In short, a stand-up kind of fellow.

In the first part of the play, the author envelops him in a halo of heroic romanticism. Charnota is miraculously saved in the guise of Madame Barabanchikova from the onslaught of the Reds. Just as miraculously, he breaks through Budenny's cavalry. Charnota smashes counterintelligence, for which he is demoted to private. In emigration, Charnota goes to pieces. But his moral identity is unshakeable. He travels to Paris with Golubkov, to help him get money for Serafima, joins a card game to save her, and is prepared to give them both (Serafima and Golubkov) all his winnings and categorically refuses to return to the Bolsheviks.

From the stage, this colorful image of a White Guard, a lovable upstart, wins over every viewer and puts him wholly on his side.

Wrangel, according to the author, is brave and cunning. He knows how to look danger frankly in the eyes. When an ominous situation developed on the front, he brought all his aides together at front headquarters and honestly warned each and every one of them that "we have no land but the Crimea." He fights the deterioration of the rear. He blasts Korzukhin for the yellow lying tones of the newspaper articles the latter edits.

Wrangel is characterized as a great patriot and fine politician.

Korzukhin. The typical melodramatic villain. The author has allotted him all the vices a negative character could have. Korzukhin is the representative of Russian bourgeois finance and industry. This is the typical self-seeking low-life of the postwar years. It is characteristic that out of the entire crowd of White Guard heroes in the play, the author found negative colors only for Korzukhin, whom Charnota is ready to shoot, Khludov to hang, and Wrangel to put on trial.

Thus, according to the play, the White movement has absolutely no connection to Korzukhin, as a representative of his class. The typical caste-class antagonism toward representatives of the financial and industrial bourgeoisie that ran the provisional government has taken its toll in the author's characterization of Korzukhin, on the one hand, and of the top brass, on the other.

The former squandered their homeland; the latter, each in his own way, tried to save and fight for a single, indivisible Russia. This kind of formulation, of course, absolutely distorts the entire class essence of the White Guard movement.

Golubkov. In his remarks the author indicates that he is the son of an idealist professor. This remark should be expanded upon: he himself is an idealist of the very first water. Helpless in everyday matters, extremely unpractical, he is entirely consumed by one single thought—being Serafima Korzukhina's guardian angel. He loves Serafima with the pure and unstained love of a Werther, and he is prepared to share all life's burdens with his beloved without a murmur. He returns to Russia exclusively under her influence. Throughout the play he is awarded many times, frequently ironically, the epithets "intellectual," "intelligentsia," etc. The author has consciously generalized in Golubkov's image all the features of our intelligentsia as it appears to him: pure, crystalline in its decency, bright of spirit, but utterly detached from life and helpless in struggle.

Serafima. A Petersburg lady. Married Korzukhin because he was rich, perhaps at her parents' insistence. She has a sensitive, responsive heart. But she is just like Golubkov, only in a skirt. She is capable of self-sacrifice. This is a type of woman, maybe not deep or far-sighted, but passionate, who courageously travels the entire path of the émigré Golgotha.

Lius'ka. In no instance can she be described as a negative character. This is a unique kind of canteen-woman in the Civil War. She has fallen physically, but not morally. She is deeply human, sensitive, and even at times tragic in her split character. She has a vast emotional emptiness. For her, Serafima is like a glimmer of her pure and innocent past. Throughout the play, Lius'ka takes special care of Serafima. And her final words are: "Look after her."

Such in the author's depiction are all the main heroes of the play and this is how the viewer will see them from the theater's stage.

Analysis of the play.

The author has veiled the play's political tendentiousness carefully in its psychological point of view. According to multiple statements by Bulgakov, and in particular the directors of MKhAT, the main thing in the play is the problem of crime and punishment.

In the name of his idea, Khludov has committed a number of crimes. He has lynched, executed, and fought, aware that his struggle is futile and being waged by unworthy means. And here is the failure. Externally, there is the rout of the front and the capture of the Crimea by the Reds; internally, there is Krapivin's [sic] hanging. The result of this is a crisis. Khludov, like Nekhludov in Tolstoi's novel *Resurrection* [*Voskresen'e*], arranges a "reading of the soul." According to the author, he examines himself and reaches the conclusion that for the crimes he has committed he must take his punishment there, in his homeland. He must redeem them, no matter what it costs, even if, upon his return to Russia, he is immediately stood against the wall [shot].

Of course, it would be awkward to demand that the author characterize the representatives of the White movement as a degenerate, drunken band of crude, robbing, raping officers. We need to show the enemy on stage as a strong opponent, and we have little interest in seeing him as a colossus with feet of clay. However, we must always demand a correct political criterion for the facts set forth.

If in *Days of the Turbins* Bulgakov showed a particular episode from the Civil War, and an invented one at that, then in *Flight* he chooses an entire historical period of it and consciously distorts it.

After all, what is the one contrast between Korzukhin and all the other White Guard characters in the play worth? Korzukhin is a "swine," and the generals are all heroes, each in his own way. Korzukhin is the representative of the financial-industrial bourgeoisie, i.e., that which made policy in the Civil War, sold out to interventionists of various stripes in turn, gave birth to Kornilov's movement, and held in its hands the armed forces of counterrevolution. The author is contrasting Korzukhin to the White Guard movement. One of the main class stimuli for reaction in the Civil War turns out to be simply the scum, the swine, the mud in the White camp. According to the author, the financiers and industrialists betrayed Russia, whereas the officers and generals were true sons and patriots of a Russia united and indivisible.

Given this kind of approach, the entire class substance of the White Guard movement is emasculated. It turns out that the armed struggle against the Bolsheviks at a specific historical stage was not the common political task of the domestic and international bourgeoisie but a feat of a certain group of knights without fear or reproach who may have erred but who were honest, intelligent opponents.

And so, in the play the White movement is presented in an absolute distortion of its class nature. It should be noted that the author did this very cautiously and subtly.

He manifests his political concept through the conflict between Khludov and Wrangel, through the legendary adventures of Charnota, in occasional retorts, in the psychological sufferings of General Khludov, [in] the symbolic likening of the entire White Guard movement to fleeing cockroaches.

A few words about Khludov's psychological conflict. Khludov's crime is social, not criminal in nature. If he had been drawn from crime to repentance, then the process would be natural for him only as the result of a crisis of world view, specifically in the social context. But there's not a word of this in the play. Only someone who has recognized his historical mistakes, who has understood and realized the historical correctness of our revolutionary movement, can redeem his guilt before the working class. That is what Slashchev did. But Khludov? Not a bit. He returns to Russia for emotional redemption. He does not consider his idea disgraced and discredited. His soul demands judgment upon itself, and that is why he goes home. This action bears a certain heroism and self-sacrifice, but there is no crisis of world view. Like Nekhludov in *Resurrection,* who remained a gentleman and did not reject his views but is drawn to Siberia to follow Katiusha Maslova in order to redeem his old sin, so Khludov, too, is drawn to the RSFSR.

This kind of psychological formulation, of course, is absolutely alien and unacceptable for us. It is in just the same totally unmotivated and unjustified context that the fact of Golubkov's and Serafima's return to the homeland is offered up. (One felt like strolling along the banks of the Karavannaia; the other wanted to see snow.)

What is extremely dangerous in this play is its general tone. The whole play is structured on the moods of compromise and compassion that the author tries to and indisputably does evoke for his heroes among the audience.

Charnota will suborn the viewers with his immediacy, Khludov with his Hamletesque torments and "redemption of original sin," Serafima and Golubkov with their moral purity and decency, Lius'ka with her self-sacrifice, and even Wrangel will impress viewers.

The author draws the horrors of their material and moral life in emigration. Bulgakov does not stint on the colors to show how this group of people, among whom each is in his own way quite fine, has been tormented, suffering and tortured, frequently undeservedly and unfairly.

The totality of these circumstances, one can be sure in advance, will dispose the audience toward a generous assessment of the heroes' conduct.

The author's tendency is perfectly clear: he is not accusing his heroes but vindicating them. The viewer will do the same thing. He is vindicating those who were our class enemies (both intentional and unintentional). For the three or four hours the performance lasts, the class consciousness of the proletarian viewer will be dulled, unbalanced, and enslaved by an element alien to us.

At a moment when petty bourgeois ideology is attempting—and not always unsuccessfully—to exert its influence in all spheres of art, the appearance of *Flight* would be an unjustified, unprincipled concession to the more conservative and reactionary factions in the theater and would only make it harder to bring Soviet theater closer to the worker-audience.

In addition, the staging of *Flight* at MKhAT would throw this theater back again to the positions of 1922–23, and would be a substantial loss for its new repertory policy, which is bringing the theater closer to the worker-spectator. After *Armored Train 14-69* [*Bronepoezd 14-69*] and *Blockade* [*Blokada*], *Flight* at MKhAT would be a victory for the most reactionary and right-wing factions inside Soviet theater. The worker-spectator rejects this play as absolutely alien to him ideologically and in the political context altogether unacceptable.

The play's political significance

1. In describing the central phase in the White Guard movement, Bulgakov distorts the class essence of the White Guard movement and the entire meaning of the Civil War. The battle between the volunteer army and the Bolsheviks is depicted as the chivalrous deed of valorous generals and officers; moreover, it completely ignores the social roots of the White Guards and its class slogans.

2. The play sets out, using the artistic devices and methods of the theater, to rehabilitate and aggrandize the leaders and participants in the White movement and to evoke the viewers' sympathy and compassion for them. Bulgakov does not provide material for understanding our class enemies; on the contrary, he has drawn a veil over their class essence and attempted to evoke the viewer's sincere sympathies for the play's heroes.

3. In this connection, the author depicts the Reds as wild animals and does not stint on the most vivid colors in extolling Wrangel and the oth[er] generals. All the leaders of the White movement are presented as great heroes, talented strategists, noble and daring men capable of self-sacrifice, heroism, etc.

4. The staging of *Flight* in a theater where *Days of the Turbins* is already playing (at the same time as the similar *Crimson Island* [*Bagrovyy ostrov*]) means strengthening at the Art Theater the group that is fighting the revolutionary repertoire. It also means surrendering positions won by the theater with the staging of *Armored Train 14-69* (and, probably, *Blockade*). This would be a step backward for all of theatrical policy and grounds for wresting one of our strongest theaters away from the worker-spectator. As you know, the trade unions have refused to buy the performances of *Crimson Island*, as a play alien to the proletariat. A production of *Flight* would create the same kind of break with the worker-spectator for the Art Theater as well. Such isolation of the best theaters from the worker-spectator is extremely harmful politically and undermines our entire theatrical line.

The artistic council of Glavrepertkom (made up of several dozen people) has come out unanimously against this play.

We must ban the performance of *Flight* and suggest to the theater that it cease any preparatory work on it (discussions, readings, studying of roles, etc.).

Attachment
Content of Bulgakov's *Flight*.

Kerzhentsev

The matter took the usual turn. The Politburo created a "commission to examine M. Bulgakov's play *Flight*," made up of Voroshilov, Kaganovich, and A. P. Smirnov, for a "final decision" (pr. 60, p. 21, 14 January 1929). Three days later, at the suggestion of Voroshilov, M. Tomsky was added to the commission (pr. 60, p. 41, 17 January 1929), and another two weeks later the commission finished its work, as Voroshilov reported in his note of 29 January to the Politburo (the note was addressed to Stalin): "In the matter of Bulgakov's *Flight*, I can report that the members of the commission have familiarized themselves with its content and have deemed it politically inexpedient to stage the play in the theater."[11] The very next day the Politburo resolved: "To approve the proposal of the Politburo commission on the inexpedience of staging the play in the theater."[12] After this, as we recall, there followed the correspondence between Stalin and Bill-Belotserkovsky and the leader's explanations at his meeting with Ukrainian writers and in his letter to the Communist writers of RAPP. The result of this was Bulgakov's petition to the Soviet government asking it either to give him work or to allow him and his wife to leave the USSR. The request was passed on to A. I. Sviderky, the head of RSFSR Glaviskusstvo, after a meeting with him. Sviderky reported on this meeting to the Central Committee:

· 49 ·

Note from RSFSR Glaviskusstvo Head A. I. Sviderky to TsK VKP(b) Secretary
A. P. Smirnov on his meeting with M. A. Bulgakov. AP RF, f. 3, op. 34, d. 239,
l. 8. Copy. Typewritten.
30 July 1929

I have had an extended conversation with Bulgakov. He makes the impression of a persecuted and doomed man. I'm not even certain his nerves are in order. His situation is truly desperate. Judging from my general impression, he wants to work with us, but they aren't letting him or helping him in this. Under these conditions, satisfaction of his request is fair.

A. Sviderky

In sending Sviderky's letter out, TsK Secretary Smirnov wrote:

· 50 ·

Note from TsK VKP(b) Secretary A. P. Smirnov to the TsK VKP(b) Politburo concerning M. A. Bulgakov's petition. AP RF, f. 3, op. 34, d. 239, l. 6. Original. Typewritten.
3 August 1929

To the TsK VKP(b) Politburo—to Com. V. M. Molotov.

I am sending you copies of the petition from the writer Bulgakov and the letter from Svidersky—I ask you to distribute it to all members and candidate members of the Politburo.

For my part, I think that with respect to Bulgakov our press has taken the wrong stand. Instead of trying to draw him in and correct him, they have practiced only persecution, but judging from Com. Svidersky's letter, we could pull him back to our side.

As for Bulgakov's request for permission to go abroad, I think it should be denied. Letting him go abroad with those moods means increasing the number of our enemies. It would be better to keep him here, while giving the APPO TsK instructions about the need to work to draw him over to our side. He's a talented writer, and it's worth taking the trouble with him.

We cannot overlook OGPU's wrongful actions in confiscating Bulgakov's diaries. We should suggest that OGPU return the diaries.

A. Smirnov

The issue of Bulgakov was raised several times in the Politburo (5 and 12 September 1929), but no decisions were made. The persecution in the press continued, and the diaries that the OGPU confiscated from Bulgakov during the raid back on 7 May 1926 never were returned. In late March 1930, Bulgakov wrote his famous appeal "To the Government of the USSR," and only after this, on 18 April, did a phone call to Bulgakov follow from Stalin promising to arrange a job for the writer at the Art Theater. In this way the conflict was settled. But only temporarily. A year later Bulgakov would write to Stalin requesting permission to go abroad for medical treatment and to work.

· 51 ·

Letter from M. A. Bulgakov to I. V. Stalin. OR GPB, f. 562, k. 19, ed. khr. 30.
Draft manuscript.
Moscow, 30 May 1931

Esteemed Iosif Vissarionovich!
"The more time passes, the more the desire has strengthened in me to be a modern writer. However, at the same time I have seen that, while depicting modern times, one cannot be in that elevated and tranquil condition essential for carrying out a great and harmonious labor.

"The present is too lively, it rustles too much, it irritates too much, the writer's pen unwittingly turns to satire.

". . . It has always seemed to me that in my life I would face some great sacrifice and that for the service of my native land I would have to take my education somewhere far away from it.

". . . I knew only that I was going not in order to take pleasure in foreign lands but rather in order to endure much, exactly as if I had a presentiment that I would learn Russia's worth only outside Russia and I would gain a love for her far away from her."

   N. Gogol

I fervently ask that you petition for me before the Government of the USSR in regard to sending me on foreign leave for the period from 1 July to 1 October 1931.

I report that after a year and a half of my silence, new creative plans have ignited with a force that cannot be curbed, and that these plans are broad and powerful, and I ask the Government to give me the opportunity to carry them out.

Since late 1930 I have been ill with a serious form of neurasthenia, with attacks of terror and precardiac pain, and at the present time I am simply spent.

I have plans, but I do not have the physical strength or the conditions I need to carry out the work, none at all.

I know precisely the cause of my illness:

In the wide field of Russian letters in the USSR, I was the one sole literary wolf. I was advised to dye my pelt. Stupid advice. A wolf may be dyed, a wolf may be shorn, but a wolf will still never look like a poodle.

They have treated me like a wolf. And for several years they have chased me through the rules of the literary garden in a fenced yard.

I bear no malice, but it wore me out, and in late 1929 I collapsed. After all, even a wild animal gets weary.

The wild animal stated that he was no longer a wolf or a writer. He denied his profession. He fell silent. This, let us be blunt, is pusillanimity.

There is no such thing as a writer who can fall silent. If he has fallen silent, that means he wasn't a real writer.

But if a real writer falls silent—he perishes.

The cause of my illness is the years and years of persecution, followed by the silence.

In the last year I have done the following:

despite very great difficulties, I have turned N. Gogol's *Dead Souls* [Mertvye dushi] into a play,

worked as a director at MKhAT in rehearsals of this play,

worked as an actor, substituting for actors who were ill at these rehearsals,

was appointed a director at MKhAT for all the campaigns and revolutionary celebrations this year,

served in Moscow's TRAM [Theater of Worker Youth], going from daytime MKhAT work to nighttime TRAM work,

left TRAM on 15 March 1931, when I felt my brain refusing to work, so that I was of no use to TRAM,

started a production at the Sanprosvet [Sanitary Enlightenment] theater (which I will finish by July).

Nights, I began writing.

But I overstrained myself.

Right now all my impressions are monotonous, my plans are laced with black, I am poisoned by my melancholy and habitual irony.

Throughout my writing career, all citizens, Party and non-Party alike, from the very moment I wrote and published my first line, instilled in me the idea that to the end of my days I would never see other countries.

If this is so, then the horizon has been closed to me, the highest school of writing has been taken away from me, and I am deprived of the chance to resolve the big questions for myself. The psychology of the prisoner is now ingrained.

How can I sing the praises of my country—the USSR?

Before writing you, I weighed everything. I need to see the light and, once I have, return. This is the key.

I am informing you, Iosif Vissarionovich, that I have been very seriously warned by major figures in the world of art who have traveled abroad that I cannot remain there.

They have warned me that if the Government opens the door for me, I must be deeply cautious to be sure I don't unwittingly slam this door shut behind myself and cut off my way back, don't suffer a misfortune even worse than the ban on my plays.

According to the general opinion of everyone seriously interested in my work, I am impossible in any other land but my own, the USSR, because I have been drawing upon it for eleven years.

I am sensitive to these warnings, but the weightiest of them was from my wife, who has been abroad and who informed me when I asked to be expelled that she has no wish to remain abroad and that I would die from sadness there within a year.

(I myself have never been abroad. The information in the *Great Soviet Encyclopedia* that I was abroad is incorrect.)

"Soviet theater doesn't need that kind of Bulgakov," wrote one of the critics moralistically when I was banned.

I don't know whether or not Soviet theater needs me, but I need Soviet theater as I do air.

I ask that the Government of the USSR let me go until the autumn and allow my wife, Liubov Evgenievna Bulgakova, to accompany me. I request this latter because I am seriously ill. The person closest to me must accompany me. I suffer from attacks of terror when I am alone.

If any explanations additional to this letter are needed, I will give them to whoever calls me in.

However, in closing my letter, I want to tell you, Iosif Vissarionovich, that my dream as a writer is to be called in personally to see you.

Believe me, not only because I see in this the most advantageous opportunity but because your conversation with me over the telephone in April 1930 left a keen trace in my memory.

You said, "Maybe you really do need to travel abroad . . ."

I was not spoiled by that conversation. Touched by that phrase, I worked for a year not out of fear as a director in the theaters of the USSR.

M. Bulgakov

Permission did not follow, evidently because Stalin, who valued Bulgakov highly as a writer, was worried he might remain abroad. Be that as it may, Stalin never did let Bulgakov go abroad, but the story did have a continuation (see doc. 122).

The Bulgakov episode sheds light on Stalin's role in decision making. What is most striking is the attention Stalin paid to these seemingly personal questions at a moment of tense intra-Party struggle. Virtually all these events were unfolding at the very height of the "great turning point," at the moment when the peasantry was under attack, at the very height of collectivization and intense struggle with the Right Opposition (Bukharin et al.) which resulted in Stalin's final usurpation of power. Indeed, the leader would still have to resort to various tricks and maneuvers in order to defend—let us at last call things by their names—his favorite Soviet-anti-Soviet playwright. Noteworthy is the persistence with which Stalin decided issues "behind the scenes of events" however he wanted, combining personal interest with the "general line." The "line" was aimed at frightening and disorganizing the fellow traveler writers. Selected as objects of the persecution waged by RAPP members in 1929 and 1930 under the leadership of Agitprop TsK were the most "odious" of them, whom RAPP refused to consider even fellow travelers but rather termed "anti-Soviet writers": Zamyatin, Pilnyak, and Bulgakov. Zamyatin and Pilnyak led the VSP (All-Russian Union of Writers) in Leningrad and Moscow, respectively. The campaign against them had as its purpose breaking fellow travelers' resistance to "the proletarianization of literature" that RAPP was carrying out with the TsK's support.[13]

The Zamyatin case was probably the simplest. At the height of the persecution he sent a letter to Stalin:

· 52 ·

Letter from E. I. Zamyatin to I. V. Stalin. Published in Evgenii Zamyatin, *Sochinenia* [Works] (Moscow, 1988), pp. 490–493.
June 1931

Respected Iosif Vissarionovich,

The author of this letter—who has been sentenced to the supreme punishment—turns to you with a request for another measure for this.

You probably know my name. For me as a writer, being deprived of the opportunity to write is a death sentence, and circumstances have coalesced in such a way that I cannot continue my work because no art is conceivable if one has to work in an atmosphere of systematic persecution that only gets worse by the year.

By no means do I want to make myself out to be an injured innocent. I know that for the first three or four years after the Revolution, besides everything else I wrote, there were pieces that might serve as grounds for attack. I know I have the inconvenient habit of saying what I think is the truth instead of what would be to my advantage at any given moment. In particular, I have never tried to hide my attitude toward literary servility, fawning, and repainting. I have always believed that these demean both the writer and the revolution equally. At one time it was this issue, in a blunt form, which offended many people and appeared in one of my articles (*House of Arts* [*Dom iskusstv*], no. 1 [1920]), that signaled the beginning of the campaign against me in the newspapers and magazines.

This campaign has continued ever since, on various pretexts, to this very day, and in the end it has led to what I would call fetishism: as once the Christians, for a more convenient embodiment of all kinds of evil, created the devil, so the critics have made of me the devil of Soviet literature. Spitting at the devil is considered a good deed, and everyone has been spitting as best he can. In each piece I have published, they have invariably sought out some diabolical intention. In order to find it they have not hesitated to reward me even with the gift of prophecy. Thus, in one of my tales ("God" ["Bog"]), published in the magazine *Chronicle* [*Letopis*] back in 1916, one critic was clever enough to find "a mockery of the revolution in connection with the transition to NEP." In a story ("Inok Erazm" ["The Monk Erasmus"]) written in 1920, another critic (Mashbits-Verov) espied "a parable about leaders who wised up after NEP." Regardless of the content of any of my pieces, my signature alone has become enough to declare the piece criminal. Recently, in March of this year, Leningrad's Oblit [local administration of Glavlit (Chief Directorate of Literature; organ of literary censorship)] took measures to make sure no doubt remained about this. I had edited Sheridan's comedy *School of Scandal* for the Akademia publishing house and had written an essay on his life and work. Naturally there was not nor could there have been any scandal in this essay—and nonetheless Oblit not only prohibited the essay but prohibited the publishing house from even mentioning my name as the translation's editor. Only after I appealed to Moscow, after Glavlit evidently suggested that you really couldn't behave with such naive frankness, was permission granted to publish both the essay and even my criminal name.

I cite this fact here because it shows the attitude toward me in its perfectly naked, so to speak chemically pure form. Out of an extensive collection, I will cite here one more fact connected with an occasional essay and with a major play which I worked on for nearly three years. I was certain that my play—the tragedy *Attila*—would silence, at last, those who liked to make me out to be some kind of obscurantist. I thought I had every reason for that certainty. The play had been read at a session of the Arts Council of the Leningrad Bolshoi Dramatic Theater, and attending the session were representatives from eighteen Leningrad factories—and here are excerpts from their responses (quoted from the minutes of the meeting of 15 May 1928):

Representative of the Volodarsky Factory: "This is a play by a contemporary author who treats the theme of class struggle in ancient times that is in keeping with modern times. . . . Ideologically it is perfectly acceptable. . . . The play makes a strong impression and demolishes the reproach flung at modern playwriting that it is not giving us good plays." The representative from the Lenin Factory, noting the revolutionary character of the play, found that "the play reminds me in its artistic value of a Shakespearean work. . . . The play is tragic and extremely full of action and it will entertain the viewer greatly."

The representative of the Hydromechanical Factory felt "all aspects in the play are very strong and engrossing" and recommended timing its performance for the theater's anniversary.

Perhaps the comrade workers overdid it about Shakespeare, but at least M. Gorky wrote about this play that he considered it "very valuable both literarily and socially" and that "the play's heroic tone and its heroic subject are extremely useful for these times." The play was approved for performance by the theater, permitted by Glavrepertkom, and then . . . shown to the worker-spectator who gave it this evaluation? No, then the play, which had already been half rehearsed by the theater and was already announced on posters, was prohibited at the insistence of Leningrad Oblit.

The death of my tragedy *Attila* was truly a tragedy for me. After this, the futility of any attempts to alter my position became perfectly clear to me, especially since soon after there was the famous story with my novel *We* [*My*] and Pilnyak's *Mahogany*. In order to exterminate the devil, naturally, any garbling is permissible—so a novel written nine years before, in 1920, was put side by side with *Mahogany* as my latest, newest work. Persecution the likes of which was unprecedented in Soviet literature was organized and noted even in the foreign press: everything was done to bar me from any opportunity for further work. My comrades, publishing houses, and the theaters of yesterday began to fear me. My books were banned for lending from libraries. My play *The Flea* [*Blokha*], which ran with invariable success at MKhAT-2 for four seasons, has been removed from the repertoire. Printing of my collected works at Federatsia pub[lishers] was halted. Any publishing house that has tried to publish my works has been subjected for this to immediate bombardment, which both Federatsia and Zemlia i fabrika, and especially the Writers' Publishing House in Leningrad, have experienced. For an entire year this last publishing house risked having me among its board members. It has had the courage to make use of my literary experience, assigning me to make stylistic corrections in the works of young writers, including Communists. This spring the Lenin[grad] off[ice] of RAPP got me removed from the board and put a halt to this work of mine. *Literaturnaia gazeta* [*Literary Gazette*] announced this with ceremony, adding quite unambiguously: "The publishing house must be preserved, but not for the Zamyatins." The last door to the reader was shut for Zamyatin: the death sentence for this author had been pronounced.

In the Soviet code, the next step after the death sentence is deportation of the criminal outside the country's borders. If I am truly a criminal and deserve punishment, then I don't think it is one as heavy as literary death, and so I ask that this sentence be replaced with deportation outside the borders of the USSR—with the right to have my wife accompany me. If I am not a criminal, then I ask that I and my wife be allowed, temporarily, if only for a year, to travel abroad—so that I can come back as soon as it becomes possible here to serve great ideas in literature without fawning over little men, and as soon as the view of the artist of the word changes at least somewhat. And that time, I am certain, is near, because immediately following the successful creation of a material base, the issue of creating the superstructure will inevitably arise—art and literature that would truly be worthy of the Revolution.

I know it will be very hard for me abroad because I cannot be there in the reactionary camp—my past speaks sufficiently to this (my membership in the RSDRP(b) [Russian Social Democratic Workers Party (Bolshevik)] in tsarist times, then prison, deportation twice, brought to trial during the war for an antimilitarist story). I know that if here, by force of my habit of writing according to my conscience and not on command, I was declared right-wing, then there, sooner or later, for the same reason, they would probably declare me a Bolshevik. Even under the harshest conditions there, though, I would not be sentenced to silence; there I would be able to write and publish—even if not in Russian. If circumstances lead me to the impossibility (temporary, I hope) of being a Russian writer, maybe I, like the Pole Joseph Conrad, will be able to be an English one for a while, especially since I have already written about England in Russian (the satirical story "Island Dwellers" ["Ostrovitiane"], etc.), but it's a little harder for me to write in English than in Russian. Ilya Ehrenburg, while remaining a Soviet writer, has long since worked, primarily, for European literature—for translations into foreign languages. Why is it that what Ehrenburg is allowed cannot be allowed for me as well? And at the same time another name comes to mind: B. Pilnyak. Like me, he has fully partaken of the role of devil, he was the main target of criticism, and for a respite from this persecution he was allowed a trip abroad. Why is it that what Pilnyak was allowed cannot be allowed for me as well?

I could also ground my request to travel abroad in more ordinary, though no less serious, motives. In order to rid myself of this old chronic illness (colitis), I need to be treated abroad; in order to put my two plays translated into English and Italian on the stage (*The Flea* and *Society of Honorary Bell Ringers* [*Obshchestvo pochetnykh zvonarei*], which have already been performed in Soviet theaters), once again I myself need to be abroad. The proposed performance of these plays, in addition, gives me the opportunity not to burden Narkomfin with a request to issue me foreign currency. All these motives are plain, but I do not want to hide the fact that the main reason for my request for permission to go abroad with my wife is my desperate situation as a writer, here, the death sentence issued against me, as a writer, here.

The exceptional attention that other writers who have appealed to you have met with on your part allows me to hope that my request, too, will be honored.

    E. Zamyatin

Stalin did not deny him, and permission to travel abroad followed even without a formal resolution of the Politburo.

Unlike Zamyatin, Pilnyak never did ask to emigrate. As a fully Soviet writer, he asked to go abroad "on a creative business trip." In a letter to Stalin, Pilnyak wrote:

· 53 ·

Letter from B. A. Pilnyak to I. V. Stalin. AP RF, f. 45, op. 1, d. 786, ll. 47–48.
Original. Typewritten.
4 January 1931

---

14 2nd Yamskoe Pole Street, apt. 21, Moscow 40.
Deeply esteemed Comrade Stalin,

I am turning to you with a request for assistance. If you could find time to receive me, I would be happy to tell you much more convincingly about my purpose in writing to you.

Allow me to say in the first place that definitely, I have always linked my life and my work with our Revolution, considering myself a revolutionary writer and believing that even my bricks are in our construction. I do not see my fate outside the Revolution.

There have been so many mistakes in my writer's fate. I know them better than anyone. I can vindicate myself for them only through deeds. I must say nevertheless that, paradoxical though it might seem, in thinking over my mistakes, very often, alone by myself, I have seen that many of my mistakes stemmed from my conviction that a writer of the Revolution can only be someone who is sincere and righteous in the Revolution. It has seemed to me that if I was given the right to bear the great honor of being a Soviet writer, then there must also be trust in me.

My latest mistake (mine and VOKS's [All-Union Society for Cultural Relations with Abroad]) was publishing *Mahogany* [*Krasnoe derevo*]. Our press came crashing down on me with indignation. I suffered punishments. I did not deny my mistake and felt that the correction of my mistakes should be not only declarative letters to the editors but also deeds: with the greatest difficulty (they were probably afraid of me), I found a publisher and printed my novel, *The Volga Runs into the Caspian Sea* [*Volga vpadaet v Kaspiiskoe more*] (which is now translated and being translated into eight foreign languages and the German translation of which I am now sending you), I went to Central Asia and published sketches about Tadzhikistan in *Izvestia of the TsIK*; the last one I published, in connection with the trial against the wreckers, I am attaching to this letter and ask that you read at least what is underlined in red pencil. I considered the content of these pieces a correction of my writing mistakes; with these pieces I hoped to dispel the distrust that has arisen toward my name since the press campaign against *Mahogany*.

My books are being translated from Japan to America, and my name is well known there. The mistake of *Mahogany* has been commented upon not only by the Russian-language press but also by the Western European, American, and even Japanese press. The bourgeois press has attempted to depict me as a martyr; I responded to this "martyrdom" with a letter in the European press and with the pieces indicated above. It seemed to me, though, that this martyrdom could be used politically as well, which would not be a bad effect, if this "martyred" writer in sound body and mind, not badly dressed and no less literate than any European writer, appeared on the literary streets of Europe and the USNA [United States of North America] (I have had an invitation to come to the USNA from American writers for three years, and in Europe I would be received as an equal by writers, apart from proletarian writers, like Stefan Zweig, Romain Rolland, and Shaw), if this writer stated just that he was proud of his country's history of recent years and was convinced that the laws of this history would be and are already rebuilding the world. That would be politically significant. It seemed to me that specifically in order to finally correct my mistakes and use my position for the Revolution I would have to go abroad—all the worse that this used to be my habit, since beginning in 1921, when I was first abroad, I have crossed the Soviet border fourteen times, but now I haven't been there since 1928.

In addition, I have other reasons for needing to travel abroad.

One half-reason I think, is the fact that if I don't go to a place, I can't seem to settle my translation and literary affairs there, and translators godlessly rob me—although this half-reason would yield the State Bank a thousand or fifteen hundred foreign currency rubles a year if I could arrange for the receipt of my royalties.

My chief reason is the following. The years are passing and time does not wait—and since the tenth anniversary of October I have thought I would write a novel, which I am approaching as my first great and authentic work. My writer's age and my feelings tell me that it is time for me to start a large canvas and that I will find the strength for this in myself. This novel is devoted to the last fifteen years in the history of the globe, and I want to contrast the history we are making, building, and creating to all the rest of the history of the globe, current, passing, passed, dying. After all, in fact the overlayering of the recent years of history is huge—and in actual fact we are rebuilding history. The plot aspect of this novel has already been worked out and I have it in my head. The place of action of this novel is the USSR and USNA, Asia and Europe—Asia and Europe I can imagine, but I've never been in the USNA—I don't have enough knowledge, and I have to make the novel with every intensity.

I set forth these notions of mine to a number of my comrade Party members, and on their advice I submitted a petition for permission to travel abroad for three to six months. I did not ask for foreign currency, since some of my translations have been paid for.

I was refused permission to travel abroad.

Why—I don't know. Must I really assume that people think I'll run away? But that is nonsense, really! How can I run away from myself or my writer's fate, from the Revolution, from my country, from my language, my wife and children!?

I have to assume that this is more of the same mistrust for me—or are they punishing me? I find myself in the position of a little boy because, after my discussions with comrades, I was convinced I would receive a passport. In connection with this I attended to the foreign visas involved, negotiated with the press department of the NKID [People's Commissariat of Foreign Affairs] and with VOKS about my routes and proposed affairs and speeches abroad. If this is punishment, then it is very cruel.

Iosif Vissarionovich, I give you my word of honor on my entire fate as a writer that if you help me go abroad and work, I will earn your trust a hundred times over. I can go abroad only as a revolutionary writer. I will write the necessary piece.

Allow me in conclusion to speak about my current condition. I have spoken about my mistakes and about the method I have chosen to correct them. With all my heart and all my intentions I want to be with the Revolution, but very often this last year I have had the feeling that someone is pushing me away from it. I am surrounded by mistrust, and I cannot work in this atmosphere. If you only knew how I have left no stone unturned at *Izvestia* to publish the article I am sending you, and I am still doing so, in order to finish publishing my Tadzhik sketches, which were accepted but for which there is a catastrophic lack of space in the newspaper.

I can't go to everyone and say: trust me.

But I can ask you—and I am asking you to help me.
I look forward to your reply with the greatest impatience.
Allow me to wish you all the best.

Bor. Pilnyak

Two columns of resolutions have been preserved on the letter: first, "Read this. St[alin]" and the signatures of Politburo members—"Read. Molotov," "Voroshilov," "V. Kuibyshev," "Kirov," "Kalinin," "Ia. Rudzutak"; and second, "I suggest allowing him to go. I. Stalin," "Ia. Rudzutak," "Molotov," "Kaganovich," "Voroshilov," "M. Kalinin," "Kirov." Stalin's answer followed three days later:

· 54 ·

Letter from I. V. Stalin to B. A. Pilnyak. AP RF, f. 45, op. 1, d. 786, ll. 51–51v. Handwritten.
7 January 1931

Esteemed Com. Pilnyak!
I received your letter of 4 January. A check has shown that the organs of oversight have no objections to you traveling abroad. They did have hesitations, it turns out, but those have fallen by the way. In this respect your departure abroad can probably be considered assured.
All the best.

I. Stalin

Pilnyak was one of "their own." There was no call to worry about his dissidence; it was always for show, as Stalin probably well understood, offering him his "trust" in the future as well—right up until his arrest in 1937.

A very different model of behavior was shown toward "reconstructed fellow travelers" like Marietta Shaginyan. After writing a model "production novel," *Hydrocentral* [*Gidrotsentral*], which glorified the heroic labor of the participants in the First Five Year Plan, Shaginyan wrote Stalin asking him to write a foreword for it and defend her from critics' attacks. Stalin replied:

· 55 ·

Note from I. V. Stalin to M. S. Shaginyan concerning her novel *Hydrocentral*.
RGASPI, f. 558, op. 1, d. 2968, l. 1. Photocopy of handwritten text.
20 May 1931

Est[eemed] Com. Shaginyan!

I must apologize to you that at the present time I do not have an opportunity to read your work and provide a foreword. About three months ago I still might have been able to grant your request (and would have with pleasure), but now—believe me—I have lost any opportunity to grant it due to the unexpectedly excessive burden of current practical work.

With regard to hastening the appearance of *Hydrocentral* in the world and defending you from immoderately "critical" criticism, then I most certainly will do that. Just tell me specifically who I should pressure to set this matter in motion.

  I. Stalin

It is unlikely Shaginyan caught the irony at the end of the letter. People say that in the 1930s she always carried Stalin's note wrapped in cellophane in the handbag she kept with her—like a safe conduct; Pilnyak kept his letter from Stalin under glass in a frame hanging on the wall.[14] Stalin occupied a unique position in the country's cultural life. He was in fact the country's principal censor and simultaneously its principal patron and writers' friend. Nearly everyone who was "refused" turned to him with requests for permission. In these instances, by giving his permission, Stalin gained the greatest political capital, acting as an individual much broader than the local censors. Just one episode concerns the staging of a play, *The Suicide* (Samoubiitsa), by one of the most talented satirical playwrights of the 1920s, Nikolai Erdman, at the Art Theater. The play was banned by Glavrepertkom on 25 September 1930, and a month later Stanislavsky sent a letter to Stalin:

· 56 ·

Letter from K. S. Stanislavsky to I. V. Stalin. RGALI, f. 2570, op. 1, d. 140. Copy. Typewritten.
29 October 1931

Deeply respected Iosif Vissarionovich!

Knowing your constant attention to the Art Theater, I am turning to you with the following request:

You already know from Aleksei Maximovich Gorky that the Art Theater is deeply interested in Erdman's play *The Suicide,* in which the theater sees one of the most significant works of our day. In our opinion, Nikolai Erdman has succeeded in revealing the diverse manifestations and inner roots of the philistinism that resists the country's construction. The device with which the author has shown the real live philistines and their ugliness is something genuinely new, which, however, is wholly in keeping with Russian realism in its best representatives, such as Gogol and Shchedrin, and is close to the traditions of our theater.

Therefore, after the author completed the play, the Art Theater felt it was important to apply its artistry to revealing the comedy's social meaning and artistic righteousness. However, at the present time this play is under the censor's ban.

I would also like to ask your permission to begin work on the comedy *The Suicide,* in the hope that you will not refuse to view it before it is performed by our actors.

After such a viewing, the fate of this comedy might be decided. Of course, the Art Theater will not make any expenditures on staging it before you view it.

Stanislavsky

Stalin's reply followed ten days later.

· 57 ·

Letter from I. V. Stalin to K. S. Stanislavsky. RGALI, f. 2570, op. 1, d. 141. Copy. Typewritten.
9 November 1931

Most esteemed Konstantin Sergeevich!

I am not of a very high opinion of *Suicide* [*Samoubiistvo*]. My closest comrades think it is rather empty and even harmful. You can learn Repertkom's opinion and motives from the document attached. Repertkom's response does not seem far from the truth. Nonetheless, I have no objection to allowing the theater to try an experiment and demonstrate its artistry. The theater may well achieve its goal. The Kultprop [Department of Culture and Propaganda] of our Party's TsK (Com. Stetsky) will assist you in this matter. The supers will be comrades who know their craft. I am a dilettante in these matters.

Greeting
I. Stalin

In that time, Stalin managed not only to read the play (not very closely, evidently, judging by his garbling of the title—*Suicide* rather than *The Suicide*—but also to put a decision through the Politburo: "Approve the proposal of Comrades Stalin and Molotov to transfer the 1st Art Theater to the charge of the TsIK SSSR" (pr. 73, p. 24/1, 2 November 1931).[15] Thus, the Art Theater, like the Bolshoi, was transformed into a court theater with consequent high status within culture. News of these "boons" spread quickly through the art world, creating a thoroughly munificent image of the leader's unfailing personal involvement in artistic affairs.

This is how Stalin behaved toward the "non-Party intelligentsia." He had a completely different model of behavior, as we have seen, for members of RAPP. With them, the leader used Party jargon. They were accomplices and for that reason were supposed to be of like mind. Stalin treated voices and opinions from the other—fellow traveler—writers with demonstrative tolerance, but he brooked no criticism from those who were supposedly of like mind. As a "proletarian writer," Andrei Platonov nominally belonged to this second category of writers, although by the latter half of the 1920s he was moving farther and farther away from orthodox Bolshevism and proletarian radicalism and becoming more and more disenchanted with what was happening in the country. Here we will dwell on an episode involving the publication of his story "To Advantage" ("Vprok"), in which he describes the collectivization process then under way in satirical tones. The story was noticed by Stalin and became the pretext for a broad campaign against Platonov, after which his way into print was virtually barred. In order to see the mechanism of the persecution campaign's unfolding, we will cite excerpts from the 1970 reminiscences of a prominent RAPP member, Vladimir Sutyrin:

One evening, a courier from the Kremlin came to my apartment (out of old habit we called them "cyclists") and said that a car was waiting downstairs to take me to the Kremlin. I was not supposed to ask where I was going or whom I was going to see. I was driven to the Kremlin, and I realized I was being taken to see Stalin. In Poskrebyshev's waiting room was a rather pale Fadeev. A little while later, Poskrebyshev, evidently having received a signal, stood up and suggested that we go into Stalin's office. In a large room behind a long table sat—see in what order!—the members of the Politburo. Here was Kalinin, next to him Voroshilov, and here were Molotov and all the rest. Somehow I couldn't bring myself to examine them all, but I did look at Stalin, who was pacing around the table, puffing away at his pipe. He was holding a magazine that was easy to recognize—*Red Virgin Soil*. Fadeev and I exchanged looks. We realized this was going to be about Andrei Platonov's story.

Without inviting us to sit down, Stalin, turning to Fadeev, asked:

"Are you the editor of this magazine? Is it you who published Platonov's kulakish, anti-Soviet story?"

White as a sheet, Fadeev said:

"Comrade Stalin! I did indeed sign off on that issue, but it was compiled and sent to press by the previous editor. Not that this absolves my guilt, I am still the editor-in-chief, and that is my signature on the magazine."

"Who did compile the issue?"

Fadeev replied < . . . >

Stalin called in Poskrebyshev.

"Bring so-and-so here." And turning to us he said: "You may sit down."

We sat down. And started waiting. Five, ten, twenty minutes passed. . . . Everyone in the room was silent. . . . Twenty or thirty minutes must have passed in that way. The door opened and into the room, pushed by Poskrebyshev, walked the former editor (I. M. Bespalov). He didn't walk in, he crawled, terrified, he couldn't stand up, sweat was pouring down his face. Stalin looked at him with satisfaction and asked:

"So it was you who decided to publish this swinish kulakish story?"

The editor could not answer. He started not talking but babbling, you couldn't make out anything from those incoherent noises.

Turning to Poskrebyshev, who had not left but was standing in the doorway, Stalin said with contempt:

"Take him away . . . And this is what's running Soviet literature . . ." And turning to us: "Comrade Sutyrin and Comrade Fadeev! Take this magazine, in it are my comments, and tomorrow you will write an article for the newspaper in which you will expose the anti-Soviet significance of the story and its author. You may leave."

We left. The car was waiting for us and we went over to my place. We did not wait for the next day. We sat right down to write the article. Stalin's comments determined not only the sense but also the character of the article. These comments were of the most abusive quality. We sat there all night writing that article. In the morning Fadeev took it away to rewrite it in final form and send it to the editors.[16]

Now we have the opportunity to read both the "comments" and Stalin's actual note to the editors of *Red Virgin Soil*—models of Stalinist literary criticism:

· 58 ·

Note from I. V. Stalin to the editors of *Red Virgin Soil* concerning A. P. Platonov's "To Advantage" ("Vprok") [May 1931]. AP RF, f. 45, op. 1, d. 201, l. 5. Handwritten.

For the information of the editors of *Red Virgin Soil*.

A story by an agent of our enemies, written for the purpose of debunking the kolkhoz movement and published by Communist bunglers for the purpose of demonstrating their own unsurpassed blindness.

    I. Stalin

P.S. The author and the bunglers should both be punished so that the punishment works for them "to advantage."

The note was originally written on the title page of "To Advantage" right in the journal (*Red Virgin Soil*, no. 3, 1932), but then it was typed out for the editors' information. Through the text of the story itself, which Stalin read closely, there are numerous underscores accompanied by the following epithets addressed to the author: "Fool," "Vulgarian," "Joker," "Toothless wit," "This isn't Russian, it's some sort of gibberish," "Dolt," "Scoundrel," "Yes, the fool and vulgarian of the new life," "Blackguard; so these are the direct leaders of the kolkhoz movement, the cadres of the kolkhozes?! Scoundrel," etc. In Stalin's personal archive there is a letter to him from A. Platonov in which Platonov apologizes for the ideological mistakes committed in the story, recognizing it as "vile" and "delirious."[17] This episode gives a fairly complete notion both of Stalin's political and aesthetic preferences and of the mechanisms for taking various decisions in the sphere of culture and Stalin's role in them.

Stalin and the Politburo intervened only when the matter concerned well-known figures in art and culture and might have great resonance or yield political dividends. The routine censoring process was left to Glavlit, but the Politburo fully monitored the censorship agencies' strategy and work methods. Formed in 1922, at the very beginning of "liberal NEP," Glavlit reported frequently on its work to the Orgburo, Politburo, and special commissions of the TsK. A 1927 report preserved in the archives gives some notion of the scale of the censorship department's activities:

· 59 ·

From a report by Glavlit Chief P. I. Lebedev-Poliansky to the Orgburo TsK VKP(b) "On the activities of Glavlit." [No later than 7 March 1927]. RGASPI, f. 17, op. 113, d. 271, ll. 129–143. Original. Typewritten.

1. Considering the reasons and circumstances calling for the report, and in order to concentrate on the issues of the moment, I am going to talk exclusively about the press, setting aside for now the theater, cinema, and radio broadcasting. These issues will arise only in passing in the discussion of Glavlit's structure.

2. Glavlit's tasks over its five-year existence have taken the form of:

A. ideological-political monitoring and regulating of the book market, brought about by means of:

  a. a statistical account of the literature coming out,

  b. ideological-political analysis of individual types of literature,

  c. permitting and shutting down publishing houses and periodical publications,

  d. approving the programs of publishing houses and publications,

  e. approving publishers and editors,

  f. regulating print runs;

B. a preliminary and subsequent survey of literature that takes the following lines

  a. ideological-political,

  b. keeping economic and military secrets;

C. removing from the book market and from libraries any harmful literature that was published either in the prerevolutionary years or during the years of the Revolution.

< ... >

5. Glavlit is guided in its work by the general principles found in the SNK decree dated 6 June 1922. They are the following:

Publication and distribution is forbidden of works:

a. containing propaganda against Soviet power,

b. spreading the republic's military secrets,

c. inciting public opinion by means of reporting false information,

d. inciting nationalist and religious fanaticism,

e. of a pornographic nature.

Inasmuch as for various reasons, including some of a political nature, these principles in the decree have not been developed, and practice has demanded more detailed directives, instructions "On measures for influencing the book market" have been worked out according to Party procedure as a Politburo plan. Examined in a number of different commissions, it was sent via Agitprop TsK VKP(b) to Glavlit and lay at the base of its practical activities. It boils down to the following positions:

1. In issuing permissions to book publishers and magazines, Glavlit must be guided by economic and pedagogical as well as political considerations, adapting private publishing houses to the needs of the state and not allowing publishing houses to pursue profit alone, moreover, in the development of the decree of 6 June of this year to be guided by the following:

a. in the sphere of literature, on issues of art, theater, and music, to eliminate literature aimed against Soviet construction and the flow of vulgar literature, while permitting in individual instances those publications of a light genre which help spread Soviet influence to the broad philistine masses,

b. literature on problems of philosophy and sociology of a vividly idealistic tendency and intended for a broad audience must not be allowed, permitting, in limited print runs only, classical and scientific literature, if they cannot be replaced by textbooks and supplementary texts or serve for self-education,

c. literature on natural science that is obviously not of a materialist tendency must not be allowed, permitting, in limited print runs only, narrow scientific literature and literature especially intended for a restricted circle of individuals or useful in practical work,

d. economic literature of anti-Marxist content must not be allowed, permitting, in limited print runs only, economic literature of a non-Marxist tendency and that which has scientific interest or practical importance,

e. of children's and young adult literature, allow publication only of literature that promotes a Communist upbringing,

f. of religious literature, allow publication only of literature of a liturgical nature. These principles apply to all dogmas, sects, and tendencies.

Moreover, at various times individual directives have been issued by the

Orgburo and Politburo TsK VKP(b). Their essence boils down to the following:

1. In permitting belles-lettres for publication, do not consider as an impediment description of the dark aspects of modern Soviet life if these works on the whole are not hostile to Soviet power (p. 29, pr. 147 of the Orgburo TsK session of 27 February 1922).

2. Our censorship also must have the above-indicated pedagogical bias. We can and must demonstrate strictness with respect to publications whose writers have fully formed bourgeois artistic tendencies. We must show no mercy for those artistic-literary groupings which are actually the center of concentration of Menshevik-SR elements. At the same time, an attentive, cautious, and gentle attitude is essential toward those works and authors which, although they bear an abyss of all kinds of prejudices, are obviously developing in a revolutionary direction.

Inasmuch as it is a matter of works of the third category, their publication should be subject to prohibition only in the extreme case. Preliminarily we need to attempt to bring the author together with a comrade who can truly clarify for him competently and convincingly the reactionary elements of his work so that if the author is not convinced, then his work is published (if there are no truly serious arguments against publication), but at the same time a critical article written from a pedagogical point of view will appear (p. 4 att[achment] to Politburo TsK VKP(b) resolution no. 16, p. 5, 6 June 1923).

< ... >

The number of prohibited manuscripts that have passed through Glavlit and Mosgublit [Moscow province branch of Glavlit], for all private publishing houses is forty-seven, which is 3.4 percent of all prohibited manuscripts for all publishing houses together. Lengublit [Leningrad province branch of Glavlit] has prohibited sixty-eight manuscripts of private publishing houses, which is 4.1 percent of all manuscripts prohibited by Lengublit.

However, the increase in the output of private publishing houses is not dangerous, even if it is noteworthy. For Moscow it is expressed in 2 percent of the output of all soviet-Party publishing houses for numbers of published titles and 3 percent of this output for numbers of published pages. In Leningrad the proportion of private publishing houses is more significant: 7 percent of the total output of all publishing houses. After Glavlit divides the private publishing houses into different categories, the influence of private publishing houses will drop even more. Generally speaking, it should be noted that with the strengthening of soviet-Party publishing houses, private publishing houses will markedly wither and become more submissive, pursuing commercial rather than ideological goals. The exceptions are Kolos [Ear of Grain], a purely populist publishing house, Kniga [Book], a Menshevik-oriented publishing house, Golos Truda [Voice of Labor], the anarchists' publishing house, and a few, three to five, other publishing houses.

Glavlit's specific and firm approach to writers naturally arouses a spiteful attitude among writers toward Glavlit. In V. Veresaev it has taken the form of the following lines:

"A general moan has gone up nearly all along the front of modern Russian literature. We cannot be ourselves, they are constantly violating our artistic conscience, our art is becoming increasingly two-tiered; one we write for ourselves, the other for publication.

"Herein lies the most tremendous misfortune for literature, and it could become irreparable: this kind of systematic violation of the artistic conscience cannot leave the writer unscathed. This kind of systematic leveling of writers to a single range cannot leave literature unscathed.

"What is there to say about artists who are ideologically alien to the ruling Party? In spite of this alienness, is it all right for them to be silent? And silent are such major artists of the word as F. Sologub, Max. Voloshin, and A. Akhmatova. It is awful to say, but if Dostoevsky were to appear among us now, so alien to modern aspirations and at the same time so necessary in his incinerating fieriness, he would have to file away in his desk one manuscript of his novels after another bearing Glavlit's stamp of prohibition."

< ... >

12. In assessing literature for its worth, we must indicate the following:

< ... >

e. Fine literature. Glavlit must battle brutally in original literature and literature in translation against:

a. pornography,

b. unhealthy eroticism,

c. obscenities,

d. hack work and pulp novels,

e. the depiction of OGPU as a torture chamber,

f. sometimes against blatant counterrevolution.

Some works, to be sure, are published anonymously abroad, some of the manuscripts go from hand to hand, some are kept, as some put it, "until better times." Much literature is crudely time-serving, published exclusively for purposes of earning a living. Individual works occasionally slip through when Glavlit doesn't look closely enough, some are consciously let through by editors who are responsible Communists. Kallinikov's pornographic novel *Relics* [*Moshchi*], in three volumes, came out in *Circle* [*Krug*]. *Red Virgin Soil*, no. 5, 1925, ran A. Yavich's impermissible story "Grigory Pugachev." Everyone knows the story with the fifth volume of *Novy mir*. V. Bulgakov's [sic] *Fatal Eggs* [*Rokovye yaitsa*], a work of a highly dubious nature, came out in *Depths* [*Nedry*], and the same publishing house attempted, though Glavlit did not allow it, to publish *Notes on Cuffs* [*Zapiski na manzhetakh*] and *Heart of a Dog* [*Sobach'e serdtse*] by the same Bulgakov, blatantly counterrevolutionary pieces. It put out a number of vividly erotic novels by Margueritte under the guise of criticism of bourgeois society, not taking into account the mass composition of our readership. There is pornography and obscenity at GIZ and Young Guard. Dubious literature has appeared in *Surf* [*Priboi*], *New Moscow* [*Novaia Moskva*], and others. Commercial considerations have played a major role in the publication of the indicated literature.

In order to offer these tendencies, which grow out of the contradictions of our life, organized and steady resistance, we must:

a. reexamine reactionary apparatuses and the body of senior editors at major and influential publishing houses and magazines,

b. destroy fictitious editors who never read any material, do not examine it, and do not familiarize themselves with the books published,

c. adopt a steady course toward strong editors who are responsible for their publications,

d. give our support to worker and peasant writers organizations that stand wholly on the Soviet platform.

< . . . >

17. Glavlit's work is exceptionally difficult. You must constantly walk the razor's edge. Trying to maintain your balance, you lean first to one side, then to the other, and naturally you are struck from both sides. You are constantly being reproached in the press and orally for unreasonable cruelty, and this circumstance has forced Glavlit sometimes to be softer than it finds necessary. In general, however, it has maintained its position without violating the country's cultural interests and without adopting an outwardly fierce appearance or allowing anything that might hinder Soviet and Party construction. In the practical conduct of this line, Glavlit has believed it better to hold something excessive or dubious than to allow any unforeseen breakthrough on the part of a hostile element.

< . . . >

Glavlit Chief Lebedev-Poliansky

Scholars of Soviet administrative structures have traditionally noted the doubling of functions in the bureaucratic apparatus (Soviet state organs were doubled and monitored by Party organs), but nowhere did this doubling reach such a degree, probably, as in the organization of the censorship agencies. Active here were not only Glavlit but also the organs of oversight inside editorial offices, publishing houses, film studios, theatrical literary departments, the TsK press departments of the republics and Party obkoms (oblast [regional] committees), which were subordinated in turn to the Department of Propaganda and Agitation and to the Secretariat. Censorship and self-censorship were probably the most finely tuned mechanisms in Soviet culture. Periodically, the Politburo attempted to systematize all this and to regulate or specify responsibilities, to reorganize:

· 60 ·

Resolution of the Politburo TsK VKP(b) on the reorganization of Glavlit.
RGASPI, f. 17, op. 3, d. 794, ll. 11–12. Original. Typewritten.
3 September 1930

No. 6, p. 41/41—*On Glavlit (OB [Orgburo], 3 September 1930, pr. 11, p. 3 gs).*
a. In connection with the restructuring of the publishing business in the center, and the rise of the local press and radio broadcasting, and for the purposes of improving the monitoring of literature, radio broadcasting, lectures, exhibits, etc., instruct Narkompros to reorganize Glavlit on the following bases:
I. Release Glavlit's central apparatus from any operative work in the preliminary review of printed material from both the political-ideological and the military-economic standpoint. Preserve for the Glavlit apparatus the following functions:
1. overall unification of all types of censorship;
2. overall leadership and inspection of subordinate agencies and agents;
3. subsequent monitoring of published literature from both the political-ideological and the military-economic standpoint;
4. permission and prohibition of publications and publishing houses;
5. publication of rules and instructions for implementing the requirements of the Party and government in the area of censorship;
6. examination of appeals of decisions made by Glavlit's agencies and agents;
7. elaboration in conjunction with other departments and implementation of lists of information involving top state secrets;
8. compilation of surveys of literature and the phenomena occurring in it;
9. calling to account those guilty of violating the requirements of Glavlit and its organs in the area of censorship;
10. presentation of representatives and directors of kraiobllit [krai (regional) branch of Glavlit] to NKP for approval and dismissal;

11. presentation of editors and editorial boards to NKP for approval.

II. Recognize the institution of agents as the main link in the preliminary oversight over literature, radio broadcasting, and so forth. Perform the entire preliminary review of all printed material in the publishing houses themselves, obligating the latter to maintain the necessary staff of Glavlit agents. In district newspapers, newspaper editors may appoint agents who also hold other positions.

b. Require NKP to carry out the reorganization of Glavlit within twenty days' time.

No matter what these reorganizations, though, they always had the same purpose: tightening censorship:

· 61 ·

Resolution of the Politburo of the TsK VKP(b) "On strengthening political oversight over the output of the periodical and nonperiodical press." RGASPI, f. 17, op. 3, d. 818, ll. 19, 33–34. Original. Typewritten.

5 April 1931

No. 31, p. 52/52—*On strengthening political oversight over the output of the periodical and nonperiodical press (PB, 11 March 1931, pr. 29, p. 14/33).*

Approve the draft resolution (see attachment) proposed by the Politburo commission.

Attachment to p. 52/52, pr. PB no. 31, 5 April 1931

Resolution on the question of strengthening political oversight over the output of the periodical and nonperiodical press.

1. Introduce preliminary oversight by Glavlit for the following sets of issues:

a. materials concerning the country's defense;

b. materials bearing the nature of official government documents, as well as materials of separate economic organizations whose publication could directly or indirectly affect economic-political relations between the Sov[iet] Union and the outside foreign capitalist world, statistical information of an export-import nature, transportation, etc.

In this regard, all the listed materials may be accepted for publication if they have the official stamp of the director of Narkomat or one of the various economic institutions and the official stamp of Glavlit.

In the event of a violation of the established rules for the publication of materials, Glavlit and the director of the institution that allowed the material to be published shall be responsible before a Soviet court and the appropriate Party oversight agencies.

2. For publications on political-economic and general economic issues and artistic and technical literature, maintain the oversight procedure established by the PB decision of 3 September 1930 (pr. 6, p. 41/41), requiring directors of st[ate] publishing houses to assign and be personally responsible for reliable political editors approved by Glavlit and Kultprop TsK.

Political editors shall be accountable to a Soviet court and the appropriate Party oversight organs if they allow the publication of anti-Soviet publications or materials that distort Soviet reality or publish information of a confidential nature.

Require publishing houses to create for political editors an appropriate situation that allows them to fully exercise this preliminary oversight (appropriate staff, appropriate apparatus, timely information, etc.).

3. decision—OP.[18]

4. Introduce the institution of political editors into all editorial offices of all magazines.

5. Instruct typographer cells to perform social-Party oversight through Communist typesetters, who, when a question arises, without delaying the typesetting, must warn the institution's director.

6. Suggest to republic and krai (oblast) Party organizations that they organize in their republic or krai (oblast) the same procedure for oversight over the periodical and nonperiodical press.

7. Department directors must submit to Glavlit monthly a list of confidential state information, in particular, matters concerning defense, export and import, and transportation, as well as a list of the type of information whose publication at the given moment could be used abroad to harm the Soviet Union.

8. Require Glavlit to strengthen its operative leadership of its local agencies; in especially important instances Glavlit directives must be transmitted not only down the Soviet line but also down the Party line, through Kultprop TsK VKP(b).

9. Kultprop TsK VKP(b), in conjunction with Glavlit, Ogiz [Amalgamated State Publishing House], and OGPU, must within one month's time review the corps of political editors in publishing houses and newspapers, assigning to this work qualified and ideologically seasoned comrades.

Suggest to the republic and krai (oblast) Party organizations that they conduct the same review of the political editors of Glavlit agencies locally within the same time period.

10. Instruct NKP, in conjunction with Kultprop TsK VKP(b), within twenty days' time, to reinforce the central apparatus of Glavlit with an additional number of highly qualified political editors.

11. Require Ogiz to contact scientific research institutes and organize there a review and assessment of the literature being published in a procedure of ex post facto and, in especially important instances, preventive recall.

Was there any need for such a thorough reinforcement of censorship? OGPU compiled annual reports based on "agent information" for the top Party leadership on the mood of the creative and scientific intelligentsia. Below is its report for 1931. Such is the picture of the moods of the "anti-Soviet intelligentsia" on the eve of Stalin's "restructuring of literary-artistic organizations"—the disbanding of all literary groupings and the creation of a single Union of Soviet Writers.

· 62 ·

From a report by the OGPU Secret Political Department "On anti-Soviet activity among the intelligentsia in 1931." [No earlier than 10 December 1931]. TsA FSB RF, f. 2, op. 9, d. 518, ll. 1–25. Notarized copy. Typewritten.

The year 1931 was characterized, primarily, by the rout of counterrevolutionary organizations of the intelligentsia that had taken shape in the early reconstructive period (c[ounter]r[evolutionary] groups in USSR publishing, in the film industry, in local history and economic research, in museum and archeological societies) and by the exposure of a new type of c[ounter]r[evolutionary] formation among the intelligentsia characterized, primarily, by not only a deeply conspiratorial method of anti-Soviet activity but also a conscious, deep encoding of a[nti]-S[oviet] activity under the guise of "ideological irreconcilability," "high public activism," and "unqualified devotion to the Party."

< ... >

Creative positions of the anti-Soviet intelligentsia
In their creative practice, anti-Soviet elements among the intelligentsia (literature, cinematography) have taken up the position of crude timeserving and political hypocrisy—in the name of social masking and, in a number of instances, material prosperity. At the same time, there is an underground literature "for oneself," for the true "appreciative reader" of capitalist society (more rarely, works come out in print with a consciously encoded c[ounter]r[evolutionary] meaning).

Characteristic of this creative formulation is an appeal by a member of an anti-Soviet group of literary scholars to the young writers they are working on: "My ideological speeches are prostitution. You have to work and work. You need to write and put what you've written in your briefcase; you cannot forget about yourself, that *tomorrow the situation will be different*. You need to look to tomorrow. You have to accumulate values. When tomorrow decent people ask you, What have you done? you will be able to say: If you please, here is this and here is that. You need to create a tight, closed working environment. You need to meet, to check on one another, support one another, force your mood. We will fight for our ideology."

This is how the writer M. Savichev depicts his own work on material collected during a trip through the provinces: "What I saw was terrible, with famine and suffering, and tormenting. I'll write about this for myself, it will never see the light of day. To publish you need rosy syrup, I'll try proposing that to a publishing house."

Illegal literature has been created by the Leningrad anti-Soviet lit[erary] group known as Shakespeare-Bandzho, and a number of Muscovite writers and anti-Soviet writers' groups possess illegal anti-Soviet works, which are read "in their own circle." The Konstromoltsy group (Sniping) had illegal literature. The Konstromoltsy clearly hid a system of literary double dealing, a combination of time-serving "for sale" and counterrevolutionary art "in earnest" (underground or with encoded c[ounter]r[evolutionary] content) in their testimony on the cases of the illegal literary group (Sniping) they created. Interesting is the underground poem by a member of the Assanov group, Scapegoat, dedicated to the justification of literary time-serving.

< . . . >

Characteristic of the creative moods of right-wing film directors are the following statements.

Director Gavronsky (Leningrad):

"The reasons for the failures and idle mood of artistic cadres in cinematography lie wholly in the dreadful condition in which the country finds itself. Just think what pictures they are producing—class struggle again, elevating Party organs to the heavens again. This is why all the directors are hungry for foreign material. Recently I produced *Dark Kingdom* [*Temnoe tsarstvo*]—a pessimistic picture that, indisputably, disarms. This picture, of course, is non-Soviet and counterrevolutionary. It was only allowed in Moscow and Leningrad. *One can and must make only these kinds of pictures using Soviet material.*"

Director Beresnev (Leningrad):

"Well, there are the themes and there are the times. I don't understand politics in art, I hate all that. Just think what themes we have in cinema and art—tractor building, diesel building, and muck like that."

Director Krol:

"You have to run away from cinema. You don't feel like working and can't. Neither I nor any single director is fired up with this enthusiasm—there isn't any, all this is repugnant. We're all sick and tired of class struggle."

The bearers of these kinds of moods either are waging "creative sabotage" or else have started down the road of political hypocrisy, producing creatively untalented, false pieces that repel the Soviet spectator.

At the Belgoskino film studio, there is a group of obviously anti-Soviet-inclined directors who are politically illiterate, untalented craftsmen. They have achieved "outward prosperity" by declaring their devotion to Soviet power and producing pseudorevolutionary, "polished" pictures that are inwardly devastated and castrated.

Veinshtok, a member of the group, characterizes his artistic activities like this:

"Here I do a production. Politically 'for hurrah' (how it turns out, I don't know—I'm not heartened in the least). The GRK [Glavrepertkom, Main Repertoire Committee; censorship organ] is satisfied. The public doesn't go to see it. I'm working for the GRK. My estimates and deadlines are in order, in all that I'm the number one shock worker and social activist. What fun."

Director Kresin:

"Generally speaking it would be good to run away from all this, but for now it's not so bad being a director. Making cultural films that have a lot of slogans and people shouting: 'Hurray, hurray, long live!' I can do that as well as anyone else. This way the sheep will be whole and the wolves will be sated. I will be a revolutionary director and I will not have the trouble I used to have. My advice to you is to become a director, right now it's a marvelous, cushy business."

Organized c[ounter]r[evolutionary] activity among the intelligentsia (based on materials on group[s] and org[anizations] eliminated in [19]31)

Characteristic of the extreme right wing of reactionary circles of the intelligentsia are the mystical religious moods that have gripped a significant portion of it and that in content and organization are linked to the philosophical mysticism of the bourgeois West.

In Moscow, an underground organization of Anthroposophists was uncovered that consisted chiefly of teachers from secondary and lower schools and several lib[rary] workers. The intellectual inspiration and director of the organization was the writer and mystic A. Bely.[19]

The political face of the organization and its leadership are characterized well enough by the following entries in A. Bely's diary:

"*The ideas of social rhythm should not be applied in practice to gorillas.* Reality shows us that the concepts of community, collective, and individual in our day and age are 'spectacles in the hands of a marmoset.' It 'sniffs at them and then puts them on its tail.' . . . *The East will perish from the chaos of its ignorance.* The West will perish from the tumors of its 'belly,' but it is not for the ignorant East to operate on that tumor. . . . Only someone who knows how to operate can operate. Someone who doesn't know how to just murders, *and we are murdering ourselves and the West.*

". . . Everything has acquired a dull-senseless tinge. Your interests in science, the world, art, man—who needs them in the 'USSR'? . . .

"What the world was interested in for millennia . . . has collapsed in the last five years here. We have canceled out the accomplishments of millennia by decrees, for we are living through an 'unprecedented surge.'

"But is it joy that is glinting in the eyes of those we pass on the street? Overexhaustion, malice, fear, and mistrust for one another are harbored in these gray, gaunt, and in part already deformed, beast-like faces. The faces of slaughtered animals, not of men.

"Closer to suffering, grieving, burdened friends. A huge fingernail is crushing us like bugs, snapping our lives with pleasure, with the one distinction that we are not bugs, *we are the true salt of the earth without which a people is not a people.* People have taken pride in us in all ages and among all nations, and people will take pride in us in the future as well. . . .

"We are men of a new consciousness. Like Noah, we must build an ark, and if it tries it can soar into outer space. Even the ruin of the earth is not the ruin of the universe, and we are men of the universe, for we are universal."

The organization was created by several underground children's circles, where the children are educated in the spirit of mysticism. The organization had ties abroad and throughout the [Soviet] Union.

In Leningrad, an anti-Soviet group of children's writers has been discovered that had seized a children's literature publication and under the screen of "trans-sense" worked toward mystical-idealistic goals.

Vvedensky:

"Our political trans-sense, i.e., the special form of poetic art adopted in our anti-Soviet group of children's writers, derives wholly from mystical-idealistic philosophy, and we use it to actively resist the sway of materialism in the USSR. Our trans-sense has as its goal the diversion of specifically inclined circles from concrete Soviet reality; it gives them an opportunity to form a circle that maintains positions hostile to the contemporary order."

Tufanov:

"I have used poetic trans-sense as a form to help me set forth my counterrevolutionary, nationalistic ideas."[20]

< . . . >

SPO OGPU Chief G. Molchanov
4th Division Chief Gerasimov

The OGPU's "special memorandum" "On writers' responses to the assistance rendered by the government to the son of the writer M. E. Saltykov-Shchedrin" which was sent to Stalin may help complete this picture:

· 63 ·

OGPU special memorandum "On writers' responses to the assistance rendered by the government to the son of writer M. E. Saltykov-Shchedrin." March 1932.
AP RF, f. 3, op. 34, d. 186, ll. 213–215. Original. Typewritten.
March 1932

In Leningrad writer circles, the news about the assistance rendered by the Soviet government to the son of the writer Saltykov-Shchedrin has spread with unusual speed and has been discussed and commented upon at length. The story of this assistance so interested writer circles that for a time it pushed aside all other urgent matters for the literary world, becoming in the full sense of the word the sensation of the day. The story of the assistance was transmitted each time in one version or another, with only insignificant variations in the details, moreover individual writers, desiring to clarify the circumstances of the matter more precisely, have checked the report they were given with Saltykov himself.

The fact of assistance to Saltykov-Shchedrin's son has been commented upon among the mass of fellow traveler writers highly sympathetically; moreover, this fact is invariably linked with the Party's attitude toward the intelligentsia. This fact in and of itself showed yet again the change in policy toward the intelligentsia in the direction of increased softening.

Fellow traveler Kozakov said the following on this topic:

"Now it is becoming generally known that such stories as this Saltykov one and the somewhat earlier Bulgakov one are far from chance facts and have occurred in connection with Stalin's recognition of the old intelligentsia's great significance in the country's cultural life. And although Stalin must overcome the hostility toward the intelligentsia among many members of the TsK who have kept their old leaven still, Stalin is maintaining his line stubbornly and decisively."

The writer A. N. Tolstoy says:

"I admire Stalin and find myself more and more feeling enormous respect for him. My personal conversations with Stalin have convinced me that this is an exceptionally straightforward man. Other mistrustful smart alecs try to present the Saltykov story as another dirty trick by the Bolsheviks. But after all, this simply cannot raise any question of some specially conceived bribe to someone. Saltykov is a useless wreck, and help for him can only be explained by the fact that Soviet Russia cares about the memory and services of its great men."

The literary critic Medvedev:

"Stories like this Saltykov one betray facts, however strange it might seem at first glance, of a second defining feature of Stalin, who is above all a most decisive and stern politician: his essence as a great liberal and patron in the best sense of that word. Every day we hear about a conversation between Stalin and some writers, or about some assistance rendered at his instruction to one among many writers. In Stalin, literature and writers have a great friend."

Simultaneously with the revelation of the character of the broad exchange of opinions on the assistance to Saltykov it emerged that individual writers, noting the unusual effect of various writers' appeals to Com. Stalin (Zamyatin's trip abroad, the Bulgakov story, etc.) themselves decided to make a few requests to him. The writers Eikhenbaum, N. Radlov, and Zoshchenko suggested appealing personally to Com. Stalin for permission to travel abroad. The children's writer K. Chukovsky, who, in connection with Krupskaia's article, was no longer being published, for permission to publish, the writer Tynianov with a request to sway the critics so that the latter would stop persecuting him, etc.

In connection with the conversations noted, a story was conveyed, meanwhile, about the writer Pilnyak using a letter to Com. Stalin to get a halt to the persecution started against him and the publication in the c[entral] o[rgan] *Pravda* of a letter of apology, as well as permission for another trip abroad.

Among right-wing writers in the salon of Ivanov-Razumnik in particular, the news of the assistance rendered to the son of the writer Saltykov-Shchedrin was met with great mistrust and commented upon quite maliciously.

Ivanov-Razumnik, Shishkov, and Petrov-Vodkin expressed the following point of view on this topic:

"In all these stories one hears the motifs of an oriental despotism. All these stories have to be compared to the terrible importance and power every word Stalin utters has, which makes his power significantly mightier than the power of even the most unlimited oriental despot, for there power is material, physical, whereas here on top of this is power over minds, over the slightest manifestation of free thought. In connection with this all these conversations about fairytale transformations in the fates of individual people at a single word from the leader take on a special characteristic historical meaning."

Detective Officer of the 4th Division SPO [Special Political Department (of the secret police)] Kogan

It was March 1932. A month later, at a single word from the leader about "restructuring literary-artistic organizations," there would be "miraculous transformations" in the fates not only of "individual men" but of all Soviet culture. The process of its final—this time institutional—"statization" would begin. The "centralization" and "statization" of culture were not Stalin's invention, but they were a radical solution to the problems that had accumulated in the revolutionary culture itself. The Party's "cultural leadership" had no legitimate place in the cultural process of the 1920s. During those years, the authorities, as we have seen, truly did "meddle" in cultural matters, whereas a system was needed that possessed a built-in authority. Apart from the problem of the legitimacy of the Party leadership (which, functioning behind closed doors, acquired a precise vertical structure of subordination and accountability), the problem of that leadership's effectiveness was also acute in the 1920s. All the vagaries in the Party's guidance of culture (now dispersing proletarian culture, now supporting fellow travelers, now strengthening proletarian culture and, by contrast, the persecution of fellow travelers, etc.) undoubtedly had but one goal: effective administration of cultural and ideological production. Over and over, this policy failed. By supporting the fellow travelers, the state made the "proletarian wing" line up in opposition to it, and vice versa. Control over the cultural sphere in its entirety could only be the result of total centralization. That was the outcome of the fifteen-year history of incessant struggle between culture and the state.

II
The Thirties

Introduction: The Culture of High Stalinism, 1932–1941

The 1930s were a turbulent time, especially during the years 1936 to 1938 which were marked by three show trials of leading Bolsheviks, and by the Great Purge. It was also the decade when a distinctive Soviet culture was canonized, one that was to define it for the rest of the Stalin period. This culture was of course Socialist Realism. However, Socialist Realism did not exist before the term was coined in May 1932 and declared the mandatory "method" for every branch of Soviet culture. Slightly earlier, on 23 April 1932, the Politburo passed a resolution (doc. 64) that abolished all independent writers' organizations and founded the single Union of Writers, stipulating that analogous measures should be taken in all other branches of the arts. Thus in effect Socialist Realism was to be a "method" not just for literature but for an entire bureaucratically centralized culture. Culture and Soviet power were finally hitched together.

Having promulgated the term "Socialist Realism" Soviet officialdom had to define what it actually meant. Critics scurried around trying to do that from the day the term was promulgated until August 1934 when the First Congress of the Writers Union was held and Socialist Realism was given its authoritative definition in the two official speeches, one by Gorky, and the other by A. A. Zhdanov, representing the Central Committee. Most canonically, then, Socialist Realism was defined in terms of literature. Indeed, for most of the thirties literature was the flagship of Soviet culture and the other branches of the arts were expected to follow its models. This is no accident. In a decade when the Soviet leadership sought to legitimize and codify its regime, written texts assumed enormous significance. One can sense this in the fact that in the early years (1932–1934) all the energy in Central Committee bodies with oversight on cultural matters such as the Orgburo and Kultprop went into literature. Moreover, around the time of the Writers Union Congress the NKVD [People's Commissariat for Internal Affairs; the secret police] prepared reports on the mood of writers every two or three days. And most matters having to do with this congress such as the dates when it would be held, its speaker's topics, and even their reports (doc. 69) had to be approved by the Central Committee and Politburo. When, starting around late 1935 or early 1936, other branches of the arts such as film, opera, and ballet began to receive more attention from the leadership, most often it was the verbal text of a given work that was given most scrutiny. Of course it was also hard to see what "Socialist Realism" could possibly mean in such fields as music (except perhaps giving a composition a politically correct title) or architecture, but in this decade in all artistic fields particular styles assumed symbolic, and hence in some senses textual, importance.

With all aspects of art so heavily politicized it is hardly surprising that it was essentially in practice rather than in theoretical pronouncements that the tradition of Socialist Realism was established. It evolved as authoritative spokesmen cited positive models to be emulated and condemned negative models. Their injunctions more often than not proved persuasive, thanks to a system of positive inducements to conform (such as handsome royalties, state honors, and access to the new good life of fine apartments, dachas, cars, etc. [see doc. 75]) and to negative inducements (such as the danger that one's work would be banned, or actual repression).

Inevitably, then, relations of power and patronage, and the dynamic interplay between the Party, state bodies, and intellectuals played a crucial role in the formation of Socialist Realism, and in cultural life of the thirties generally.

As these documents demonstrate, the role of Stalin, and of the Politburo, was decisive. It is a staggering fact that from the beginning of the thirties the Politburo, the Orgburo, and to some extent the Party Secretariat took an active role in making most decisions in the sphere of culture, including quite minor ones. Stalin's involvement is particularly striking. From 1930 until his death in 1953 there was virtually not a single ideological (and therefore cultural) question before the Politburo in which the decision was not made by him, or was made without his knowledge (and therefore assent). Yet over the same period some questions having to do with industry, agriculture, transport, defense, and even state security were sometimes examined by the Politburo in his absence. Moreover, in the division of oversight responsibilities among secretaries of the Central Committee from at least mid 1934 Stalin was assigned Kultprop, the special sector, and the Politburo. Only on 27 November 1938, after the appearance of the *Short Course* (of Party history), did he delegate to Zhdanov some of his oversight in the cultural sphere (for the press and directives to publishing houses). As is amply demonstrated in the documents here, in the thirties, and especially in the decade's second half, Stalin played an active role in censoring the *content* of individual works of literature, drama, and film, though largely in terms of political content, the representation of Bolsheviks, etc., rather than because of aesthetic concerns.

One should not conclude from this, as have many, that Soviet culture was forged as "Stalin and his henchmen" coerced the unsuspecting intellectuals into following their dictates. The Party was itself divided on many cultural issues and the dividing line between intellectuals and the Party was murky because so many leading figures in the cultural sphere, especially in literature, were also Party members. It was not even the case that, technically, Stalin dictated cultural policy in the Politburo. Several of the documents presented here indicate a vote among Politburo members and though, admittedly, Stalin never lost the votes recorded here, still there are often votes cast for the opposing position. Moreover, occasionally he solicited responses from his colleagues on a particular issue.

Actually, in some senses the 1932 resolution forming the Writers Union weakened the Party's dominance in literature in that it specifically abolished RAPP. Since RAPP, an overwhelmingly powerful and militantly "proletarian" literary organization, pushed for a purely Party literature under its hegemony, it might be assumed, as many did *initially*, that although there would now be a single writers union which might seem to constrain diversity, henceforth there would nevertheless be greater tolerance for non-Party writers (compare the mood in doc. 68 with that in doc. 72). And there was. In other respects, however, after 1932 the Party enjoyed greater and more direct control in literature than before inasmuch as the most powerful group within the Writers Union was its "Party faction." Moreover, in the 1930s the leadership of the Writers Union was closely linked to the Party's highest bodies, and to its Party faction. The first secretary of the Organizational Committee of the Writers Union, I. M. Gronsky, was simultaneously the secretary of the Communist faction of the Union. The secretary of the Organizational Committee, V. Ya. Kirpotin, was at the same time an official of the Central Committee as head of the Literature Section of its Culture and Propaganda Department (Kultprop). Later, A. S. Shcherbakov was to combine his post as general secretary of the Board of the Writers Union with director of the Department of Cultural-Educational Work of the Central Committee (Kultprosvet). Moreover, in practice the RAPP leadership did not fall from power in the aftermath of the April 1932 resolution. Rather, the former RAPP leadership became divided, with some members, and especially those who declared their support for the 1932 resolution, given powerful positions on Writers Union bodies. For example, V. P. Stavsky was made secretary of the Writers Union after Gorky's death in 1936, and A. A. Fadeev occupied a series of leadership positions in the union, culminating, in 1939, in secretary, while others, such as L. Averbakh (shot in 1937 as a Trotskyite) and Yu. Libedinsky were soon struggling to keep their literary careers. However, the Party faction itself did not represent a united front but had significant divisions, as we can sense in these documents.

Indeed, these documents reveal that the deep divisions among intellectuals in the cultural sphere persisted despite official attempts at unification. Essentially, in mandating Socialist Realism for all, the Party was finally acceding to the demands of a wide spectrum of factions in the twenties that a single approach be canonized for Soviet culture. In many respects, the battles of that earlier decade over what form a truly Soviet culture should take continued into the thirties, if conducted at times in more oblique ways. Many of those who participated were advancing or defending positions they had championed in the debates of the twenties. But now the stakes were higher and the Party hierarchy was a more active player.

Despite Party supervision, and despite the increasingly dire potential consequences of dissent, as these documents reveal, dissenters were more vocal and activist than many have assumed. There was a top-down chain of power and patronage, to be sure, but there were also competing lobbies in the cultural world, many of which had their own periodical outlets or Party patrons, and they were prepared to fight the good fight. This dynamic is vividly illustrated in the case of Eisenstein's film *Bezhin Meadow* (*Bezhin lug*) which several powerful cultural bureaucrats wanted banned in 1937, as they succeeded in doing. But documents published here show that, even in 1937, the worst year of the

Great Purge, an entire range of Soviet intellectuals joined forces and, using institutions like the premier film studio Mosfilm (Moscow Film Studio) and prominent periodicals (*Izvestia, Sovetskoe iskusstvo* [Soviet Art]), conducted a campaign to avert this.

These documents also reveal more widespread dissatisfaction among intellectuals than scholars have been able to establish before, the most striking example being the dissident leaflet distributed at the First Writers' Congress (see doc. 71). The NKVD reports published here on the reactions of various figures to cultural events provide more reliable evidence and specificity about the attitudes of intellectuals than can be found in sources used earlier such as memoirs, diary entries, and oral narratives. It must be cautioned, however, that even these reports cannot be assumed to be completely accurate inasmuch as it was the function of the NKVD informant to provide evidence of dissent. Nevertheless, they show a range of opinions among intellectuals, some of whom wholeheartedly endorse repressive actions of the Soviet leadership or official cultural policies. They also show how individuals were particularly anxious to receive recognition from the state and discontented if they did not get it (docs. 72, 80, 97).

We also see in these documents pockets of independence among intellectuals, as distinct from dissent (e.g., doc. 133 on the Leningrad writers). In particular, the writers' settlement of Peredelkino, a place where selected writers lived in magnificent dachas set in the woods a short train ride from Moscow, emerges as a center where to some extent writers formed a community with its own intellectual life centered around discussion groups and networks that were relatively independent of the programmed supervision of Moscow. Neither Stalin nor Gorky (it is to be noted in docs. 78 and 79) had been in favor of setting up such a separate writers' settlement, but it was built anyway.

The power of Gorky in Soviet literature of the thirties, and in culture generally, and his relationship to Stalin, are key issues in the period's cultural history which have been debated for decades. Scholars have argued over whether, for example, the founding of the Writers Union in 1932 was a gesture for Gorky (it was done on the eve of his return to the Soviet Union from Italy); an attempt to liberalize the literary world by liberating writers from the hated RAPP, thereby improving the situation of so-called fellow travelers for many of whom Gorky had played mentor over the twenties; or whether it was a gesture to "totalitarianize" literature by putting it under central control, in which case perhaps it fed some megalomaniacal tendencies in Gorky who became head of the Writers Union. Or was he Stalin's unwitting stooge? As the following documents demonstrate, not one of these accounts is really true. Gorky appears in them as essentially one of several powerful players determining the fate of Soviet culture. Far from being gratified with the 1932 resolution, he was opposed to it because he believed it was too harsh on the RAPP leadership and he lobbied to have certain of them included in the Writers Union committees. But within RAPP he favored writers like Averbakh (some allege because of family connections) and Afinogenov, both of whom became progressively less powerful in the literary sphere. His support of Averbakh was one of many instances where Gorky was essentially in opposition to the Party faction and to the Party-appointed literary and cultural bureaucrats. But Averbakh was also a Party member.

Many have assumed that Gorky had a special relationship to Stalin, which made his position stronger. In the correspondence with Stalin published here we see how he used his access to Stalin, and even blackmail (the threat of withdrawing from his office in the Writers Union, doc. 74), to push for his own candidates for various offices and to have opponents replaced. Stalin appears to have supported Gorky in many of his battles (e.g., the debate on language in which he was opposed to Panfyorov and Serafimovich, see doc. 77). Gorky was also accorded many privileges and gestures were made to flatter his ego, such as grand housing, a generous allowance in precious foreign currency for his trip abroad in 1932, and naming many places and institutions after him (ranging from the central artery of Moscow to the Literary Institute), but Gorky and Stalin do not appear particularly close in the correspondence published here, and Gorky did not always succeed with his petitions.

In these documents Gorky appears less as some all-powerful figure in the arena of culture than as yet another principal player who, no less than the others, has his lists of people he wants demoted or promoted and lobbies for this. In doc. 81, for example, he claims not to know the lists of those proposed for the various governing committees of the Writers Union. Gorky also does not emerge, as some have portrayed him, as an extrasystemic figure, who fought for intellectual values. Often in these documents his stated criterion in evaluating who should be appointed and who fired is the individual's cultural level and mastery of the craft of literature, yet, against the background of the other documents published here, he appears as less than entirely high-minded and disinterested and more caught up in the climate of denunciation and jockeying for power that characterized this decade; his journalism is frequently inflected with expressions symptomatic of the purge mentality, such as "predators," "wreckers," and "petty-bourgeois contagion." Moreover, Gorky's power to effect policy in literature waned over the course of the thirties (one factor being his closeness to Bukharin) and many of his projects and protégés fared badly after his death in June 1936.

As these varying fortunes over the course of the decade suggest, in terms of cultural politics the thirties do not represent a seamless period but tend to fall into *at least* two if not three parts with the dividing line coming in approximately late 1935 or early 1936 (in other words before Gorky died). The shift more or less coincides with the establishment of the Committee on Arts Affairs (*Komitet po delam iskusstv*) in December 1935, which progressively centralized virtually every aspect of cultural life under this one body. Whether as cause or effect, the dominance of literature over all other aspects of the arts which had characterized the years since at least 1932 was lessened at this time and all branches of the arts came under scrutiny, resulting in for example the campaign against formalism and naturalism in the arts that was initiated with an attack on Shostakovich's opera *Lady Macbeth of Mtsensk District* [*Ledi Makbet Mtsenskogo uezda*] (see Chapter 12). This campaign ushered in a period of mutual denunciation and recrimination among intellectuals, which only intensified as the country moved toward the Great Purge of 1937–1938.

The resolution of 16 December 1935 founding the Committee on Arts Affairs was a landmark event in the history of cultural life under Stalin. In effect, the Committee overshadowed the Writers Union in terms of power (especially given that Gorky was in failing health and in fact died on 18 June the following year), and even to a large extent the Ideological Department of the Central Committee. The 1932 resolution which founded the Writers Union had provided for parallel organizations in the other fields of the arts. Thus between 1932 and the founding of the Committee each field had been centralized but there had not been any overall centralizing body that oversaw all the arts (other than the Central Committee and the Politburo). With the setting up of the Committee, however, all the arts were administered by the one body. Even all the theaters were incorporated; they had previously been under the oversight of various bodies but by December 1936 were all under the oversight of the Committee. Its head, appointed in January 1936, was Platon Kerzhentsev who had formerly held a variety of jobs including head of *Izvestia* in Petersburg, head of ROSTA (the Russian Telegraph Agency, a predecessor of TASS), Soviet diplomat, and deputy head of Agitprop and the Communist Academy; he had most recently headed the Radio Committee.

After the Committee on Arts Affairs was formed there was a marked shift in cultural policy that was most apparent with the publication on 20 January 1936 of the *Pravda* article "Muddle Instead of Music" attacking a production of Dmitry Shostakovich's opera *Lady Macbeth of Mtsensk Region*. The *Pravda* article condemned the opera as "leftist art"—this is not a political label but a reference to those Constructivists and other avant-gardists of the twenties who had proclaimed their work "left art"—"which, with its deliberately dissonant, confused stream of sound . . . denies for the theater simplicity, realism, comprehensibility of imagery, and the natural sounds of words" and is ridden with "rotten naturalism." "Leftist distortion in opera," the article continues, "stems from the same source as leftist distortion in painting, poetry, education, and science." It also concludes that *Lady Macbeth* represents a translation into opera and music of "the most negative features" of what it terms 'Meyerholdism.'"

After publication of this article and several subsequent ones of similar import an intense campaign was launched against "formalism" and "naturalism" in all branches of the arts. One after the other articles appeared in the press attacking "formalism" in this or that field, often naming alleged perpetrators, and throughout the country meetings were organized at the local branches of the various creative unions at which writers, composers, filmmakers, and so forth were expected to denounce "formalism" and recant their sins in this area. In effect, this was a campaign against modernist tendencies in the arts. However, it should be noted that, despite the pressures, many individuals were unrepentant at these meetings, defending those individuals or trends being attacked, and that though the denunciations led to the withdrawal of some material from circulation and made it impossible for many to publish their work, they were largely about a given individual's creative approach rather than his or her alleged political connections and allegiances to "enemies," as became the case later.

By late August 1936, however, in the wake of the first show trial (held earlier that month) of Kamenev, Zinoviev, and other members of an alleged "Trotskyite-Zinovievite Center," the mutual denunciations began in earnest and gathered steam, reaching their height in March 1938 after the third and most publicized of the show trials, that of

Nikolai Bukharin and other members of the Party elite. As we will note in the following documents, however, those purged were far from being exclusively modernists; for example, many RAPP leaders and Marxist critics were purged as Trotskyites.

Dating from about this time, Soviet culture was expected to exemplify *narodnost'*, a broad term which signified that works should be accessible to the masses, imbued with the national (and sometimes folk) tradition, and patriotic (or even statist). The attack in doc. 107 on the opera *Bogatyri* (that is, medieval knights extolled in folk ballads) by the writer and long-standing contributor to *Pravda* Demian Bedny, is symptomatic of this. An implicit corollary to the demand for *narodnost'* was a drawing away from closeness to Western cultural life (generally referred to here as "Western-bourgeois"). This was problematical in the era when the Soviet Union was involved in the antifascist cultural alliance of the Popular Front. Moreover, as is clear in the opinions expressed by creative workers that are reported by NKVD informers in doc. 108 presented below, most intellectuals were particularly concerned about what their counterparts in Europe might think about measures taken by their leadership. There were also frequent visits by prominent Western antifascist intellectuals, one of the most famous being that of André Gide in 1936 (mentioned in doc. 135) where he met with the writer Isaac Babel and the filmmaker Sergei Eisenstein. When, following this visit, and as Babel anticipated, Gide wrote *Back from the USSR*, which was seen as a scurrilous attack on the country, the German antifascist writer Lion Feuchtwanger produced his travel memoir *Moscow 1937* as a semiofficial rejoinder.

What we also see in these documents (especially in the NKVD reports) is the alacrity with which cultural figures denounced their rivals, and exulted when they came under attack (as in the case of Stanislavsky and Meyerhold's comments on the predicament of the rival theatrical director Tairov in doc. 108). Rather than finding in these documents signs of solidarity among intellectuals we more often sense a meanness abroad in the intellectual community that was probably exacerbated by the tight reins held on power and privilege and by the climate of fear. These documents also indicate the broad range of cultural figures purged that includes not just the more dissident or "modernist" among them; close association with the NKVD leadership or high officer class in the military, two categories decimated by the purges, could prove more fatal (as in the cases of Babel and Averbakh, representatives of opposed cultural tendencies).

The Great Purge is generally considered to have ended in early March 1938, or at any rate to have been drastically reduced in intensity. There ensued a period of stocktaking and backpedaling when many of those in leading roles within culture were fired and replaced. For example, on 25 January 1939 Aleksandr Fadeev was appointed secretary of the Presidium of the Writers Union (that is, head), replacing Stavsky who had acted in close consultation with the secret police and under whose leadership the Writers Union had seen a virtual orgy of denunciations, many of them leading to arrests. As docs. 86 and 88 reveal, during the Great Purge the business of actually producing literature had virtually ground to a halt as writers had been expected to attend the endless meetings where they or their fellows were attacked and expected to recant. Furthermore, so many writers had been compromised by the denunciatory material generated in the climate of the purge that, had it all been acted upon, the membership of the union would be even further decimated (the ranks of the Party faction had been particularly—dangerously—depleted).

From January 1936 until January 1938, the Committee for Arts Affairs had held sway, but on 21 January 1938 Kerzhentsev was dismissed as its head, and although the Committee continued to exist its power was reduced. In September 1938 a decision was taken to make Zhdanov the head of a reorganized Central Committee Directorate for Propaganda and Agitation (*Upravlenie propagandy i agitatsii Tsk VKP[b]*), after which all the branches of the arts came under Party leadership. Around this time changes were made in the leadership of various other branches of the arts. For example, Boris Shumiatsky was dismissed as head of cinema on 7 January 1938—Eisenstein, whom he had particularly oppressed, toasted his demise with champagne. Thus we see here yet another example of political changes within culture that meant, paradoxically, *both* greater centralization and Party control, *and* relatively reduced repression. But these years also represent the prelude to Soviet involvement in World War II (Czechoslovakia was invaded by the Nazis in 1938). Apprehension about impending war colored much cultural activity in these years and they saw an intensification of the nationalistic trend that had been marked since 1936. Increasingly, films, literature, and art depicted models from the tsarist past associated with defending or expanding Russian territory, such as Aleksandr Nevsky or the military commander Suvorov.

We have organized our documents below thematically as in Part One rather than in strict chronological order, but it should be noted that according to the overall trajectory of cultural politics over the course of the decade it can be divided into three periods: 1932–1935, the period of reaction against the extremes of the preceding cultural revolution and also the time when Socialist Realism was instituted; 1936–1938, the time of the Great Purge and also of the campaign against "formalism" and "naturalism" in the arts; and 1938–1941, a possible third would be the post-purge phase when the country was in the shadow of the anticipated war.

CHAPTER SEVEN

The Demise of RAPP

As we saw in Part One, during the period of the cultural revolution RAPP had become the main implementer of Party policy in literature. Precisely in this period RAPP succeeded in eliminating practically all literary groupings from contention. Under pressure from RAPP, LEF "disbanded" in 1929 and in the same year, as the result of a campaign against Evgeny Zamyatin and Mikhail Bulgakov led by RAPP, they succeeded in completely subordinating FOSP to their organization and in gaining power in the VSP, previously a center-right group. The next year RAPP "completed" its rout of the independent writers' group Crossing, gained influence over the rival proletarian group Smithy, centralized minor independent writers' groups from VAPP (such as Smena [changeover], Vagrianka [furnace top], and Zakal [temper]), split the Constructivists, part of whom joined RAPP, to be followed later by the other half, and in the same year Mayakovsky joined RAPP (shortly before his suicide). In 1931 there was a "revolution" in the All-Russian Union of Peasant Writers (VOKP), which was converted into the Russian Union of Proletarian-Kolkhoz Writers (ROPKP)—a kind of "kolkhoz branch" of RAPP. By this time almost all literary publications were in RAPP's hands, ranging from the "thick journals" and *Literaturnaia gazeta* in Moscow to provincial journals. By 1931 RAPP was getting the public support of the Central Committee: one might just cite here two editorials in *Pravda*, "For Proletarian Literature" of 18 April 1931 and, on 31 August of the same year, "For the Hegemony of Proletarian Literature," where it was stated that "RAPP is the principal and leading organization in proletarian literature, one that represents the Party line on literary issues."[1]

The Demise of RAPP

Yet, at the very height of its influence and success, in April 1932, came the totally unexpected and unforeseen end not only to the all-powerful RAPP but also to the entire system of control in culture as it had operated thus far.

There was no press coverage of the TsK resolution of 23 April 1932, "On restructuring literary and arts organizations," either before it was passed or immediately after. This was in part because the resolution itself was prepared in deep secrecy, and an unprepared RAPP was tremendously displeased with it (something which was understandably not made public). On 8 March 1932 a special resolution of the Politburo set up a "Commission to Examine Questions Concerning the Activities of RAPP" which comprised members of the Politburo—Stalin, Molotov, Kaganovich, and Postyshev—plus A. I. Stetsky, the head of Department for Culture and Propaganda (Kultprop) of the Central Committee.[2]

The following resolution was to have a very profound effect on Soviet cultural life, ushering in a new era.

· 64 ·

Resolution of the TsK VKP(b) Politburo "On restructuring literary and arts organizations." RGASPI, f. 17, op. 3, d. 881, ll. 6, 22; op. 163, d. 938, ll. 37–38.
Original. Typewritten.
23 April 1932

No. 97, p. 21—*Organizational issues in literature and art (PB dated 8 March 1932, pr. no. 91, p. 50/18) (Comrades Kaganovich, Averbakh, Panfyorov).*

Approve the draft of proposals submitted by Com. Kaganovich (see attachment) and publish it in the press.

Attachment to p. 21, pr. no. 97, dated 23 April 1932
On restructuring literary and arts organizations

1. The TsK confirms that in recent years, on the basis of significant successes in socialist construction, major quantitative and qualitative growth has been achieved in literature and art.

A few years ago, when the significant influence of alien elements was still apparent in literature, especially those which had emerged in the first years of NEP when the cadres of proletarian literature were still weak, the Party did everything possible to help create and strengthen particular proletarian organizations in the sphere of literature and [other types of] art for the purpose of strengthening the position of proletarian *writers and workers* in art [and facilitating the growth of the cadres of proletarian writers and artists].[3]

At the present time, when the cadres of proletarian literature and art have managed to grow up and new writers and artists have come forth from the plants, factories, and kolkhozes, the framework of existing proletarian literary and arts organizations (VOAPP [All-Union Association of Proletarian Writers Associations], RAPP, RAMP [sic],[4] et al.) has become too narrow and is slowing the serious sweep of [literary and] artistic creativity. This circumstance is creating the danger that these organizations will transform *from being a means* of the greatest possible mobilization of [truly] Soviet writers and artists around the tasks of socialist construction into a means for cultivating exclusive circles, for detachment [sometimes] from the political tasks of the modern day and from significant groups of writers and artists who sympathize with socialist construction [and are ready to support it].

Hence the necessity for an appropriate restructuring of literary and arts organizations and for expanding the base of their operation.

On this basis, the TsK VKP(b) resolves:

1. to eliminate the Association of Proletarian Writers (VOAPP, RAPP);
2. to unite all writers *who support the platform of Soviet* [who support the policy of Soviet] power and are striving to participate in socialist construction into a single Union of Soviet Writers that includes a Communist faction inside it;
3. to carry out an analogous *change along this line in the other types of art* [an association of musicians, composers, artists, architects, and other such organizations];
4. to instruct the Orgburo to elaborate practical measures for implementing this decision.

In this TsK resolution the restructuring of literature is the main aim. All other branches of the arts (originally named in point 3, but then crossed out by Stalin) were to form parallel organizations. This did not in fact occur overnight. In music, for example, embryonic versions of the Composers Union formed in Moscow and Leningrad but the overall Composers Union was not set up until a Politburo resolution of 3 May 1939, and even then the union was not really formed completely until 1948. Single unions were formed initially in literature and architecture, then the two leading branches of the arts—architecture because of the ambitious program launched in June 1931 to rebuild Moscow as emblem of the new socialist society. One should also note that an explicit reason why RAPP was being disbanded was because of its negative attitude towards "significant groups of writers and artists who sympathize with socialist construction," by which was meant the fellow travelers so reviled by RAPP.

As the following document shows, although RAPP as an organization had been disbanded in the TsK resolution of April 23, this did not mean a lessening of Party dominance in literature or of all leading figures from RAPP. Those listed here as responsible in the formation of the Organizational Committee (no. 107, p. 3) comprise Stetsky, head of Kultprop; Bubnov, head of the Commissariat of Enlightenment and Culture; Volin, the head of Glavlit; an editor of *Pravda*, Rabichev, deputy head of Kultprop; and Party writers, primarily from RAPP. The Writers Union was to have, besides Gorky as honorary chairman, Gronsky as its chairman who was simultaneously head of the Party faction within the union, and as its secretary Kirpotin, the head of the Literary Department of the Central Committee from 1932 to 1934. The membership of the Organizational Committee comprised primarily writers who were Party members, most of whom were also former members of RAPP, plus Pavlenko, a Party member in the former literary group Crossing; Bakhmetiev, a Party member who had been active in the rival proletarian literary organization Smithy; Zamoisky, formerly from VOKP; and some fellow travelers (from Fedin through Slonimsky in the list of committee members below).

· 65 ·

Resolution of the TsK VKP(b) Orgburo on measures to implement the resolution of the TsK VKP(b) Politburo "On restructuring literary and arts organizations."
RGASPI, f. 17, op. 114, d. 295, ll. 1–3; AP RF, f. 3, op. 35, d. 32, ll. 24–24v.
Original. Typewritten.
7 May 1932

No. 107, p. 2—Practical measures to implement the PB decision on restructuring: (a) music organizations, (b) organizations of artists, (c) organizations of architects (PB res. dated 23 April 1932, pr. no. 97, p. 21) (Comrades Stetsky, Rabichev, Dinamov, Bubnov, Viazmensky, Verkhotursky, Pshebyshevsky, Shatsky, Zaslavsky, Osipov, Kozelkov, Cherkassky, Fridman, Bekker).

A. On music organizations:
1. Eliminate RAMP [sic][5];
2. Begin organizing a single union of Soviet composers so that the most

authoritative individual figures in musical art (conductors, prominent performers) join the union;

3. Instruct a commission made up of Comrades Stetsky (chairman), Bubnov, Yenukidze, and Kosarev to present for approval at the next session of the OB:

a. the personnel composition of the organizing committee and proposals on organizational issues (date for convening a congress, etc.) and a draft resolution for publication in the name of the organizations;

b. a conclusion about those revolutionary-popular songs which, as a result of the campaign being waged against them, have stopped being performed at the district level;

c. proposals on the creation of mass songs and military marches.

4. Instruct the same commission (Com. Stetsky's) to plan and submit for approval by the next session of the OB the personnel composition of the organizing committees for the Union of Artists and the Union of Architects, bearing in mind the exchange of opinions that took place at the OB meeting.

Consider possible the inclusion in the Union of Architects of art figures working in the field of architecture.

No. 107, p. 3—Practical measures to implement the PB decision on restructuring the organizations of writers. (PB res. dated 23 April 1932, pr. no. 97, p. 21) (Comrades Stetsky, Rabichev, Kirpotin, Bubnov, Averbakh, Ilyenkov, Chumandrin, Fadeev, Panfyorov, Pavlenko, Volin).

a. Approve an organizing committee for a union of Soviet writers (for the RSFSR) composed of Comrades (1) M. Gorky (honorary chairman), (2) Gronsky (chairman of the union and faction secretary), (3) Kirpotin (secretary of the union), (4) Fadeev, (5) Panfyorov, (6) Kirshon, (7) Pavlenko, (8) Serafimovich, (9) Zamoisky, (10) Stavsky, (11) Berezovsky, (12) Zhiga, (13) Bill-Belotserkovsky, (14) Chumandrin, (15) Bakhmetiev, (16) Bezymensky, (17) Fedin, (18) Tikhonov, (19) Malyshkin, (20) Aseev, (21) Vs. Ivanov, (22) Seifullina, (23) Leonov, and (24) Slonimsky.

Register the creation of the organizing committee in the name of the corresponding literary organizations (the former RAPP, ROPKP, Union of Soviet Writers, etc.).

b. Create analogous organizing committees in the national republics (Ukraine, Belorussia, Trans-Caucasus, Tadzhikistan, Uzbekistan, Turkmenistan).

c. Form an organizing committee for an all-union federation of Soviet writers consisting of the RSFSR Organizing Committee and representatives of the organizing committees of the national republics.

d. The All-Russian Organizing Committee shall receive all the files and property of RAPP and before the convocation of the RSFSR congress of writers shall bring about the supervision of all existing writers' organizations, as well as the entire network of existing literary circles.

e. The All-Union Organizing Committee shall receive all files of the organizations and the journals and property of VOAPP.

f. The issue of the deadline and procedure for eliminating all other literary organizations (VSSP [All-Russian Union of Soviet Writers], ROPKP, Crossing, LOKAF [Literary Association of the Red Army and Navy]) shall not be predetermined at the present time, having suggested that the faction in the RSFSR Organizing Committee discuss this issue.

g. Instruct the RSFSR Organizing Committee to submit for approval to the Orgburo its proposals on the literary journals that have been published up until now by the various literary associations.

Among writers negative reactions to the TsK resolution were to be found only within that minority group most rebuffed by it, the RAPP leadership. The absolute majority of writers and cultural workers not only did not pick up the negative implications in the formation of a single writers union and the new "creative method" of Socialist Realism (promulgated in May 1932), but saw these measures as a long-awaited liberation to be celebrated as a feast day (the resolution was announced on the eve of the Orthodox Easter).

The following document shows the initial outrage at the resolution on the part of A. A. Fadeev, a former member of the RAPP leadership and its most successful author. It is to be noted, however, that he soon reversed this position and went on to enjoy considerable power in the Writers Union, heading it after Stavsky was ousted in 1939.

· 66 ·

Letter from A. A. Fadeev to TsK VKP(b) Secretary L. M. Kaganovich. RGASPI, f. 17, op. 163, d. 941, ll. 68–69. Original. Typewritten.

10 May 1932

Dear Lazar Moiseevich!

Com. Kirpotin has informed me that the text of the announcement from the literary organizations about the elimination of RAPP and the creation of an organizing committee has been approved by you. Although it pains me very much to write you this letter, I think that in political matters truthfulness is deeply necessary in relations between Communists and leading comrades. Therefore I must tell you that the text of this announcement is undeservedly insulting to me, someone who has been in the Party for more than a little while and who served it with faith and truth in the most difficult moments of the revolution. You see, by signing this text, I, among other comrades, must admit that at least eight years of my mature Party life were spent not fighting for socialism, on the literary front of this struggle, were spent not fighting the class enemy for the Party and its TsK but on a cliquishness and exclusivism which I—along with other comrades who have fought beside me shoulder to shoulder—must now acknowledge to the entire nation and so become the laughing-stock of all enemies of proletarian literature.

Therefore, with great bitterness I must ask you to bring up this text with the TsK, so that I can see that such is the will of the Party, which for me is indisputable, of which you can be assured.

With Com[munist] greeting
A. Fadeev

In the following document another leader of RAPP, V. Kirshon, in trying to defend the RAPP faction, accuses their enemies of then recognized "deviations": "Pereverzevism," a deviation associated with V. F. Pereverzev, a Marxist literary historian discredited from 1929 who had advocated a class-based account of literary evolution; "Voronskyism," associated with A. Voronsky, a leading Party-appointed literary editor for much of the twenties and patron of fellow-traveler writers who was dismissed in 1927 as a "Trotskyite"; and "Deborinism," named after the prominent Marxist philosopher A. M. Deborin.

· 67 ·

Letter from V. M. Kirshon to I. V. Stalin and L. M. Kaganovich. [No earlier than 26 May 1932]. RGASPI, f. 17, op. 114, d. 305, ll. 118–119. Original. Typewritten.

Dear comrades!

I could not convey the content of this letter to you orally. However I feel it absolutely essential that I familiarize you with the decisions that have been taken in the last few days by the Organizing Committee's Presidium.

It has been resolved to change the editorial staffs of all the literary newspapers and journals. This change, as is evident from the attached minutes, has as its goal the *complete elimination* of the former leadership of RAPP and the writers and critics who shared its positions. Not only have editors Averbakh, Fadeev, Selivanovsky, and Kirshon been removed, but the editorial boards have been composed in such a way that only Comrades Fadeev and Afinogenov have been brought into the editorial offices, where besides them there are 8–10 people, Comrade Averbakh was kept a member of the editorial board of *Literary Heritage* [*Literaturnoe nasledstvo*], but the other comrades—Makariev, Karavaeva, Yermilov, Sutyrin, Buachidze, Shushkanov, Libedinsky, Gorbunov, Serebriansky, Illés, Selivanovsky, Troshchenko, Hidas, Luzgin, Yasensky, Mikitenko, Kirshon, and others, have been removed from everywhere and according to this resolution are not joining a single editorial staff.

I felt that this kind of mass removal from everywhere of a group of Communist writers who for several years have defended, albeit with errors, the Party's line on the literary front cannot achieve consolidation of Communists into a single union. It seems to me that this is not consolidation but elimination. In a conversation with me, Lazar Moiseevich said, "We want to keep all of you on the literary front." The resolution of the Organizing Committee's Presidium runs decidedly counter to this statement.

In the situation of the campaign that is being waged against us, our literary opponents, who are shouting that RAPP has been eliminated because of the mistakes of the RAPP leadership, the act of removing us completely from the editing of literary journals cannot help but be perceived as a reluctance to have us participate in carrying out the Party line on the literary front.

Com. Stalin has spoken of the need to put us in "equal conditions." In this situation, though, we might end up not with "equal conditions" but a rout.

The Organizing Committee's resolution does not leave us a single journal. Approved as editors-in-chief by the Organizing Committee are comrades from the philosophical leadership that fought us bitterly and supported Panfyorov's group. Com. Raltsevich [the future editor of *Literaturnaia gazeta*] also has a long history of fighting us and at one time was an ardent Pereverzevite.

Here, of course, there is no question of "equal conditions." I don't think this is the only point, however. I did not feel that the Communist writers had so discredited themselves before the Party that they could not be entrusted with editing a single literary journal or that comrades had to be invited in from another segment of the ideological front—philosophers—to supervise literature.

It seems to me that the comrades who have been appointed, who have never done any literary work and are unfamiliar with its practice, are going to run the magazines worse in the new and complicated conditions than the Communist writers would.

I could not express my ideas to the Organizing Committee faction. The decision was made in the following way: the faction's office (Comrades Gronsky, Kirpotin, and Panfyorov) approved all these decisions without any discussion whatsoever with the Communist writers, *not even with the members of the Organizing Committee,* and then it was taken to the Presidium with *fellow-traveler* writers, where it was approved.

I could not even express my ideas on the reorganization of the mass workers magazine *Rost* [*Growth*], which I edited. Com. Stetsky told me that I would continue editing it, but the com[rades] from the Organizing Committee approved the reorganization plan and removed me without even informing me that such an operation was going to be carried out.

Working in an atmosphere of mistrust is hard and onerous. We want to fight actively and energetically for the implementation of the TsK decision. We want to put out Bolshevist works. We ask you to give us an opportunity to do work on the literary front, to correct the mistakes we have made, and to adapt to the new conditions.

In particular, we are asking the TsK to leave us *On Literary Guard*. In 1926, under the Party's leadership, we created this magazine, which has fought mostly correctly for the Party line for six years. It was *On Literary Guard* that repulsed the ideologues of bourgeois, kulak literature, the Trotskyites, Voronskyism, Pereverzevism, ultra-left vulgar-obstructionism, and so on.

By no means do we deny that during the magazine's existence a number of errors and blunders were committed involving elements of cliquishness, abusive criticism, the influence of Deborinism, deficient struggle to implement TsK instructions in our work. There is also no doubt that we failed to take up energetically and actively enough the implementation of the TsK's last decision. We passed a special resolution on the occasion of the eleventh and twelfth issues of *On Lit[erary] Guard,* condemning this mistake.

However, we are asking the TsK to keep *On Literary Guard* the organ of our creative movement. We did have elements of cliquishness; however, our movement did not take shape over several years on the basis of cliquishness. While defending for several years our principles in literature and criticism, we set ourselves no other task than implementing most correctly the Party line both in art and in literary policy. We set ourselves no other task even now.

We want our creative movement to have its own organ for the elaboration of problems of creativity and Marxist criticism. We want to have an organ that would help writers create Bolshevist works. We pledge to put a decisive and merciless stop to any manifestation of cliquishness in our ranks. We shall apply all our efforts to implementing the historic decision of our TsK as successfully as possible.

With Communist greeting
V. Kirshon

The first plenum of the Organizational Committee of the Writers Union, which took place six months after the resolution, demonstrated the optimism felt by many non-Party writers after the TsK resolution disbanded RAPP. However, despite the relative unanimity (as seen in the following document) among writers representing a range of literary positions, one can also sense some of the major ongoing divisions among factions seen in, for example, the clash between Averbakh (backed by Gorky) and Gronsky (Gorky's opponent), and the clear division among the former RAPP leadership (Averbakh, Libedinsky, Fadeev). Rabichev refers here to a "Magnitostroi of cliquishness" by which he means cliquishness taken to an extreme by analogy with Magnitostroi, the name for a new, major industrial complex beyond the Urals that was now also a term frequently used in Party rhetoric for something truly monumental and astounding.

· 68 ·

Memorandum from TsK VKP(b) Kultpropotdel Deputy Head N. N. Rabichev to the TsK VKP(b) secretaries "On the progress of the plenum of the writers' organizing committee." AP RF, f. 3, op. 34, d. 186, ll. 298–299. Original.
Typewritten.
1 November 1932

To TsK VKP(b) Secretaries Com. Stalin
Com. Kaganovich
Com. Postyshev

As of the evening of the 31st [October], the nature of the plenum was fairly well set. First of all, I should note its composition: major writer delegations convened from the republics, and prominent Moscow and Leningrad writers were constantly present in the hall.

This plenum is now an authentic plenum of a *unified* union. For the first time, all the wings of literature are speaking out in a single discussion: Communist writers, writers like Ivanov and Nikulin, right-wing writers from the old literary intelligentsia (Prishvin, Bely), writers from the union and nat[ional] republics.

Bely spoke about interactions among writers, Communist scholars, and non-Party writers: he asked to be taught Marxism-Leninism, and he would teach artistry.

Prishvin noted that he had been given a situation in which he could speak. He spoke about writers' "mutual delight" in one another.

Prishvin thinks that cooperation between Communists and the non-

Party writers should take place on an *equal* footing in the sense, obviously, that Communists should not fill a special supervisory role in the journals and literature.

V. Ivanov spoke out against Efros, speaking about the fact that the writer in essence does not need criticism.

Nikulin in his speech made it clear that for him the issue has become the Party membership card.

Oreshin said that for the first time he was hearing reports without a stick.

Chumandrin spoke out decisively and harshly criticizing cliquishness. He stated that in the last six months the On Guard people had slowed the implementation of the TsK resolution, that On Guard-ism is the Magnitostroi of cliquishness. He did not criticize individual comrades from the On Guard group.

Libedinsky relinquished his turn to speak, joining with Chumandrin.

Averbakh made a major speech in which he pointed out RAPP's mistakes with respect to the intelligentsia and also pointed out its cliquishness and the fact that the merit of the Organizing Committee that has already been set is its creation of conditions for collaboration for all writers, and he underscored his readiness to collaborate with the Organizing Committee's leadership.

During Averbakh's speech the following incident occurred. Averbakh said: "This doesn't mean that there were no stupidities, no outright loutishness, as in *Litgazeta*, in what RAPP and individual RAPPites did in that time. That all happened, but those are production costs" (Gronsky: "This is an answer to a speech"). Averbakh: "You don't have to answer a failed speech like a lout." Gronsky: "But you don't have to answer the Organizing Committee's speech like a lout." The hall reacted with long applause for Com. Gronsky.

This portion was deleted from the transcript (with the agreement of Gronsky and Averbakh).

The overall tone of the speech was Averbakh's characteristic "highhanded" tone.

Fadeev made a good speech when he remarked on some less than correct notes struck in Averbakh's speech.

Libedinsky, responding to Averbakh's idea that others are doing a good thing when they criticize him, tossed out a slogan about the need for self-criticism of one's own mistakes.

TsK VKP(b) Kultprop Dep[uty] Head Rabichev

As is evident here, when RAPP was disbanded the "literary struggle" did not come to an end. It just took new forms conditioned by the new institution in which writers were operating, the Union of Soviet Writers. As with all elite Soviet institutions under Stalin the Writers Union offered its members a high social status and a slew of privileges and perquisites, but the Union was totally dependent on the Party leadership—initially the Writers Union answered directly to the TsK. In consequence, the decade of the 1930s was marked by tussles among writers over power and privilege.

CHAPTER EIGHT

The Writers' Congress

The Writers' Congress was the first large public event in Stalinist culture, the culmination of a period of relative thaw before the purge time. The congress was prepared over more than two years and almost all the members of the Party leadership were involved in some way (some of them directly). In these years Stalin's right-hand man in literature was Ivan Mikhailovich Gronsky, a Party journalist and administrator, chief editor of *Izvestia,* head of the Organizational Committee of the Writers Union and of the union's "Party faction." Subsequently condemned to the Gulag which he survived, Gronsky later in his memoirs recalled the time when both the Writers Union and the new "method" of Socialist Realism were established.

The question of how this new literary "method" came to be formulated has long been debated. Until Stalin's death it was maintained that the term "Socialist Realism" was "created by our leader," as was also often speculated in the West, but after Khrushchev denounced Stalin in his secret speech to the Twentieth Party Congress in 1956 and all public references to him were banned, Socialist Realism was alleged to be a product of the development of Soviet literature itself. Gronsky's recently published memoirs throw light on this issue. In 1972 Gronsky wrote a series of letters (not published until perestroika) in which he recalled those days. Of greatest interest in these letters are the parts where he describes his role in a Politburo commission comprising Stalin, Kaganovich, Postyshev, Stetsky, and himself which had been set up to review the petitions sent by RAPP members after it was disbanded. This commission met from April to May 1932 and according to Gronsky's account, at one of these meetings, which took place in Stalin's study, the term "Socialist Realism" was invented. As Gronsky recalls:

> On the eve of the commission's meeting Stalin telephoned me and asked me to come to see him. I found him reading petitions of the RAPP leaders. When he asked me if I had read these petitions and what was my attitude to them I replied that RAPP members are opposing the TsK resolution "On restructuring literary and arts organizations" and hence their demands must be condemned and rejected.
> "Organizational issues having to do with the restructuring of literary and arts organizations," Stalin said, "have been decided by the Central Committee and there is absolutely no basis for reviewing them. But issues having to do with creative [methods] have not been resolved, and the main one of these is the issue of RAPP's dialectical materialist creative method. Tomorrow at the Commission members of RAPP are sure to raise this issue. Consequently we must beforehand, before the session, work out our position on it: are we going to adopt it or, on the contrary, reject it. Do you have any suggestions in this regard?"
> I had no suggestions prepared. One had to come up with them and formulate them. Consequently, in responding to Stalin, I *firstly,* came out most decisively against accepting the RAPP creative method, pointing out, in particular, that there were no grounds for *mechanically* transferring the philosophy of Marxism—Leninism (dialectical materialism) into the sphere of literature and art; *secondly,* I talked about the creative method of prerevolutionary progressive literature—*critical realism*—which had arisen in Russia during the period of *the bourgeois-democratic social movement* and, as is known, did not take literature beyond capitalist society; thirdly, I pointed out that our literature, which represents a continuation and further development of the literature of critical realism, has been formed in totally different historical conditions—in the stage of the proletarian *socialist* movement. It takes all aspects of social life into account but not from a general democratic position, rather from the positions of the working class, its struggle for power, for the dictatorship of the proletariat, for the socialist reconstruction of society. This is a completely new literature, new in terms of its societal, and in terms of its aesthetic ideals. These are its special features which in my view should be reflected in the creative method of Soviet literature, a method which I propose to call *proletarian socialist,* or *even better communist realism.* In this definition of the creative method, I said, we are emphasizing two aspects: *firstly,* the class and proletarian nature of Soviet literature; *secondly,* we will indicate to literature the aim of the entire movement, of the entire struggle of the working class—communism.

"You are right in pointing to the class, proletarian character of Soviet literature," noted Stalin in responding to me, "and you have named the aim of our struggle correctly. But should we in defining our creative method, a method which is to unite all those working in literature and the arts, stipulate specially, and even emphasize, the proletarian character of Soviet literature and art? I think there is no special need for that. It would also be wrong to indicate the ultimate aim of the working class—communism. After all for the time being we aren't even proposing the issue of going from socialism to communism as a *practical* task. The time will undoubtedly come when the Party will confront this issue, confront it as a *practical* task, but this will not happen soon. In pointing to communism as a practical aim you are running a little ahead. You have found the right way of resolving the issue but haven't found a very good formulation for it. What would you think if we were to call the creative method of Soviet literature and art *Socialist Realism?* The virtue of that definition consists, firstly, in its brevity (just two words), secondly in its ready comprehensibility and, thirdly, in the way it indicates a continuity in the development of literature (the literature of critical realism which arose in the period of the bourgeois-democratic social movement, changes over, develops beyond that during the period of the proletarian socialist movement to a literature of Socialist Realism).

I did not insist on my formulation which I. V. Stalin had shortened so well, reducing it to a mere two words.

I. V. Stalin proposed that I present at the Commission a critique of the RAPP dialectical-materialist creative method and announce that the Party does not support this method and is replacing it with another method—the method of Socialist Realism which it is proposing as a *Party-oriented* [partiiny] method, a method that will define the position of the Party on questions of literature and the arts.

I said that it would be better, more authoritative, if he, Stalin, were to address the Commission with this announcement. [. . .]

The session took place in the Kremlin, in Stalin's study, and lasted 6 or 7 hours.

The members of RAPP understood that they were mistaken in the position they took about issues to do with the restructuring of literary and art organizations, they renounced their dialectical-materialist creative method, and accepted the *Party-oriented* creative method proposed by the Commission—*Socialist Realism*. At the session all the members of the Commission who spoke and P. P. Postyshev who presided declared that *Socialist Realism* as a creative method for literature and art, had in effect emerged long ago, well before the October Revolution, principally in the work of A. M. Gorky, and now we only gave it a name (formulated it). [. . .]"[1]

That was how Socialist Realism came about. However, its inauguration occurred only two years later. During this time Gronsky played a key role in the creation of the Writers Union and the organization of the 1934 Writers' Congress. The atmosphere in which the congress was conducted is indicated in the following document. Here one should note the major role played by the TsK in oversight of the Writers Union, including vetting the content of speeches to be delivered at its first congress.

· 69 ·

Memorandum from I. M. Gronsky to the TsK VKP(b) secretaries on preparations for the All-Union Writers' Congress. RGASPI, f. 17, op. 114, d. 341, ll. 22–23.
Original. Typewritten.
16 March 1933

To the TsK VKP(b) secretaries
Comrades I. V. Stalin and L. M. Kaganovich

By decision of the TsK VKP(b), the Writers' Congress was postponed until the middle of May 1933. Based on this decision, we have developed the work of the Organizing Committee of the Union of Soviet Writers: we have held two plenums of the All-Union Organizing Committee, fostered the discussion of creative issues at them and in the press, sounded out writers' moods, and finally, overcome cliquishness (mostly). A few organizational issues have not been fully worked out (the acceptance of members into the Union of Soviet Writers), but in the second half of March and April we will be able to do this work and before the republic congresses (late April—early May) we will finish it entirely.

If the date for convening the writers' congress remains unchanged (and there is no reason to reconsider it), we must approve right now:

1. the agenda and speakers and
2. the standard for representation to the congress.

The *agenda* has been worked out, approximately, as follows:

1. Opening words by A. M. Gorky on the tasks facing the Union of Soviet Writers;
2. A political report (speaker assigned by the TsK VKP(b))
3. Report from the Organizing Committee of the USSR Union of Soviet Writers (speaker Com. Gronsky);
4. The tasks of Soviet dramaturgy (it would be good to approve as speaker Com. Stetsky, who would speak simultaneously as chairman of the jury for the best play competition);

5. The charter of the Union of Soviet Writers (speaker Com. Subotsky);
6. Report of the mandate commission;
7. Elections for the union's board and review commission.

We propose setting the *standard for representation to the congress,* based on the total number of delegates to the congress, at 500–600 people, i.e., *one delegate for every ten members of the union* (according to preliminary calculations, the union may have 5,000 members).

The theses of the reports and the resolutions should preferably be approved beforehand by the TsK VKP(b). In connection with this, the TsK's decision on convening the Writers' Congress should include a special point requiring speakers to present the theses of their reports to the TsK for approval no later than 10 April.

> Faction secretary of the VKP(b) Organizing Committee
> I. Gronsky

Party organs intervened in the running of the congress, even when it was in session, as is evident in the following letter written by Andrei A. Zhdanov, the Central Committee's representative to the Writers Union Congress who gave a keynote address (as did Gorky). Gorky's address was somewhat rambling, and the more concise formulation made in Zhdanov's speech became the classic formulation of the nature of Socialist Realism.

· 70 ·

Letter from A. A. Zhdanov to I. V. Stalin. [28 August 1934]. RGASPI, f. 77, op. 3, d. 112, ll. 2–8. Handwritten draft.

Dear Com. Stalin!

At the writers' congress right now there are debates under way concerning the reports on dramaturgy. In the evening is Bukharin's report on poetry. We're thinking of ending the congress on the 31st. People are already wearying of it. The delegates' mood is very good. The congress is being praised by everyone up to and including the incorrigible skeptics and ironists, of whom there are quite a few among the writers.

For the first two days there were serious concerns for the congress. This was when the reports were being delivered on the first item. As long as they were being read, people wandered through the corridors. The congress couldn't seem to find itself. But then the debates on Gorky's report and on Radek's report were very lively.[2] The Hall of Columns was bursting with listeners. The enthusiasm was such that they sat without a break for four hours at a time and the delegates scarcely walked around at all. The auditorium was packed, the side halls were overflowing, the colorful greetings, especially from the Pioneers and the collective farmer Smirnova from Moscow Region had a wonderful effect on the writers. The overall unanimous impression is that *the congress has been a success.*

The writer saw the country's attitude toward literature, he saw himself, he felt tremendous responsibility for his activity. Therefore all the speeches bore the stamp of serious preparation. The overall tone set at the congress immediately excluded the possibility of the congress being transformed into an arena for intergroup struggle. Everyone tried as best they could to outdo one another with the *ideological content* of their speeches, the depth of their statement of creative questions, and the outward polish of their speech.

A major role in this matter was played by the warning we issued at the two meetings of Communists before the congress—the Party groups of the Orgkom [Organizational Committee] and the congress—where we warned of the danger of RAPPite attitudes and that the TsK would strike hard at cliquish attitudes if they came out at the congress.

Yesterday we issued one more warning in connection with Bukharin's upcoming report. A group of Communist poets (Bezymensky and others) were planning to give Bukharin a working over at the congress, exploiting his usual sins against dialectics, planning to rout him and connect him to past mistakes.

We stated at the Presidium's Communist group that (1) we condemn advance meetings of groups, (2) while criticizing individual points with respect to poetry, we will not allow criticism to be carried over into the sphere of political generalizations. In doing so we emphasized that the strategy adopted before the congress had wholly justified itself during the course of the congress. The Communists promised to make every effort not to spoil anything.

The TsK warnings and the atmosphere at, and around, the congress forced the RAPPites and their "sympathizers" to change their position and instead of taking others down to show their own wares and come out with their creative baggage. As for their speeches, those of the Communists were paler, grayer, than those of the fellow travelers. From this, however, it seems to me unfair to draw the kinds of conclusions Gorky did when before the congress he said and wrote that Communists enjoy no authority whatsoever among writers. The speeches of non-Party members . . .[3]

Despite such care and despite the various precautionary measures taken (such as vetting speeches in advance) to avert undesirable incidents at the congress, a scandal was caused when an "underground leaflet" was discovered among the participants. As is evident in the following document, during the course of the congress the secret police made an analysis of the handwriting in an effort to find the culprits.

· 71 ·

Note from GUGB (Central Directorate of State Security) NKVD SSSR Secret Political Department Deputy Head G. Liushkov to USSR People's Commissar of Internal Affairs G. G. Yagoda on the discovery of an underground leaflet at the All-Union Writers' Congress. TsA FSB RF, f. 3, op. 1, d. 56, l. 150. Handwritten.
20 August 1934

Genrikh Grigorievich.

I am attaching a copy of a leaflet distributed among congress participants through the post. So far 9 cop[ies] have been discovered. The leaflet was written in block letters in pencil with carbon copies.

It is entirely possible that this was done by one of the congress's participants. We are checking the handwriting against the delegates' questionnaires. I have taken every operational measure to uncover the authors.

Liushkov

During the course of the congress the secret police also performed more routine functions. The "Reports on the Mood among the Writers" which were regularly submitted to the Politburo by the NKVD not only attest to a network of informers set up among the participants at the congress, but also provide some insight into the moods of the writers themselves at this critical moment in Soviet cultural history.

· 72 ·

Special report from GUGB NKVD SSSR Secret Political Department "On the progress of the All-Union Congress of Soviet Writers." [No later than 31 August 1934]. TsA FSB RF, f. 3, op. 1, d. 56, ll. 185–189. Original. Typewritten.

Writers' responses to the congress's work.
Quoted below are statements by a number of writers giving their assessment of the congress's organization and work. { . . . }
M. M. Prishvin: I keep thinking, how can I get out of here faster. The tedium is unbearable, but there are problems with leaving. I am getting to be

on full display. They gave a portrait in *Vecherka* [Evening Moscow], they are doing an interview, and there are dozens of admirers—Dinamov, Stavsky.

Stavsky even asked me persistently to speak: "You must," he says, "Mikh[ail] Mikh[ailovich], you need to shake the congress up a little." I told him this in reply: "Whether or not I need to, it's insulting that here, among 52 writers, they still could not find a seat for me on the presidium."

I constantly feel a bad bitterness over this.

Valerian Pravdukhin: Nonetheless I'm attending and I myself don't know why. After all, I am distinctly aware that there's no place for me in this servile gathering. I can't and I won't bow, I won't play the part of an obsequious waiter.

Everything that's happening right now in literature is shameless demagoguery and publishing terror, publishing houses have become utterly boorish, which is possible only in our country, where there is neither respect for people nor elementary decency. It's embarrassing to speak in earnest about the congress: if anything did present itself that was more or less lively—the reports by Radek and Bukharin—then even that withered before it managed to blossom fully: people say the two reports were substantially cut by TsK officials.

A. Novikov-Priboy: I sit and listen in pain: according to the speeches and reports, everything's fine, but for anyone, like me, who knows the present literary situation, it's a real impasse. The period of literature's total bureaucratization is upon us. A few days ago, for example, I was at the new publishing house, Sovetsky Pisatel' [Soviet Writer], and I left there with the bitterest feeling. I had made an attempt to plead for the scattered books of my friends Pravdukhin and Zinger, and in reply I got: "I have an order that I need to print the best of the best." Among this "best" they are printing a book by Shildkret, whom they're printing only because he's "from over there." Orders in literature are the end.

[. . .]

Babel: We have to demonstrate to the world the unanimity of the Union's literary forces. But seeing as how all this is being done artificially, under the stick, the congress feels dead, like a tsarist parade, and naturally no one abroad believes this parade. Let our press go ahead and overinflate the stupid fabrications about the delegates' colossal enthusiasm. After all, there are also correspondents from foreign newspapers who will shed true light on this literary requiem. Look at Gorky and Demian Bedny. They hate each other, but at the congress they're sitting side by side like lovebirds. I can imagine how gratified they'd each be to lead their own group into battle at this congress.

Semenko: Everything's going so smoothly, I'm overcome by a simply maniacal urge to take a piece of sh[it] or rotten fish and throw it at the congress presidium. Maybe that would liven things up a little.

Can you really call all this mendacious ceremony anything other than a mockery? A good half of the people sitting in the hall, especially the delegates from the na[tional] republics, are dying to scream about the mass of injustices, to protest, demand, speak in a human, not a lackeyish language, but they're forced to listen submissively to the leaders' totally mendacious reports about how fine everything is. And we sit and applaud like wind-up soldiers, while the true artists of the word, the fighters for our national culture, rot somewhere in the swamps of Karelia and the torture chambers of the GPU.

[. . .]

Dep[uty] Head of the Fourth Division
V. Petrovsky

· 73 ·

Special report from GUGB NKVD SSSR Secret Political Department "On the progress of the All-Union Congress of Soviet Writers."4 TsA FSB RF, F. 3, op. 1, d. 56, ll. 272–277. Original. Typewritten.
31 August 1934

In circles close to the Organizing Committee leadership, they are expressing confidence that at the meeting being held today in V. M. Molotov's office they will find a modus for further joint work between Gorky and former Organizing Committee Presidium members Yudin and Stavsky, Panfyorov and others on the future board of the Union of Sov[iet] Writers.

About the foreign delegates

Malraux said that a certain person in authority whose name he doesn't mention suggested that he show leadership initiative in creating a united antifascist bloc of literary forces. This suggestion was made in very confidential form, and commenting on the fact itself and the form of its proposal, Malraux states: "The aim of this suggestion is the same as the aim of the demonstration Radek organized at the congress. In point of fact, the matter is clear—they're offering a bribe, but how crudely they have done so."

Jean Richard Bloch: "Radek spoke with me about creating a united antifascist front. In our conversation he insistently emphasized that he is showing me the kind of trust he could not show Malraux. Can't he see that I understand his game? You see, it's clear to me that he's saying the same thing to Malraux. It's perfectly obvious."

O. Shvartsbakh: Among the foreigners who have come to the congress, a young woman by the name of Shvartsbakh has attracted attention. In conversation the foreigners jokingly call her their "chaperone."

Shvartsbakh came to the USSR with the German writer Klaus Mann.

On the debates over Bukharin's report

Com. Bukharin's report and his closing words on it continue to receive lively comments from writers' groups.

{ ... }

Pyotr Oreshin: All the speeches at the congress deserve one another. Ridiculous speeches that subsequent generations are going to mock. Bukharin's speech, which everyone liked, is nothing remarkable. What can you expect from Bukharin if he proclaims the senseless and vacuous Pasternak our number one poet? You have to lose your last shreds of reason to proclaim formalist trinkets the foundation of poetry. As to the fact that there is struggle brewing all around, that the revolution continues—they forgot all about that. You can't approach poetry the way Bukharin does. That plays right into the hands of those who want poetry here to be a "refined dish" for the few.

[...]

Brodsky: Someone should draw organizational conclusions from this. But if Bukharin is going to be on the Union's board, this isn't going to change very much. Despite his mind's considerable sharpness, this man is good only in the formal stylistic aspect.

[...]

Borisov: Bukharin's closing word was a slap in the face of the entire congress. The fact that he called poets, no matter who they were, illiterate and worthy of being sent to the OGPU Bolshevo Commune[5]—that's boorishness. It means that all of us are nothing and that the congress was organized just for the sake of political window-dressing.

Smelyakov: Actually, they organized a banquet here so that the poets could agree on vengeance against "Nikolai the Saint Bukharin."

Zharov read the following epigram aloud:

> Joyous and bright was our congress,
> Terrifically sweet was this day—
> Old man Bukharin paid us notice,
> And with a blessing swept us into our grave.

On Kliuev.

The poet Nikolai Aseev received a letter addressed to him through the congress's presidium from Pyotr Kliuev, the brother of the admin[istratively] exiled poet Nikolai Kliuev, in which the former asks him to help ameliorate Nikolai Kliuev's situation.

Judging from the letter's content, Aseev was not the only addressee.

Dep[uty] Head of the SPO GUGB 4th Div[ision] V. Petrovsky

The real power struggle broke out back stage at the congress when there was a discussion about who would be included in the leadership of the new union. The main players included the many fellow-traveler writers, Gorky and his protégés, and a group of Party writers headed by Gronsky. Ironically, however, it was the former members of RAPP, seemingly so recently routed, who were the main beneficiaries of this struggle. It was decided to make Gorky an "honorary chairman," thereby depriving him of real power while at the same time conferring authority on him. This decision was partly the result of pressure Gorky exerted on the TsK. In the following letter Gorky says he wants to resign as chairman of the union's board, a threat which undoubtedly strengthened his position. He was appointed Chairman by a Central Committee resolution of 1 September 1934.

· 74 ·

Letter from A. M. Gorky to the TsK VKP(b). [30 August–1 September 1934]. Draft written in the author's hand. Published in *Izvestia TsK KPSS*, 1990, no. 5, pp. 217–218.

To the Party TsK.
Respected comrades,
The congress of writers of the Union of S[oviet] S[ocialist] Republics revealed nearly unanimous awareness on the part of writers of the need to improve the quality of their work and, in this way, admitted the need to improve their professional technical qualifications.

Writers who cannot or do not want to study but are used to playing the part of administrators and are trying to secure managerial posts for themselves are now an insignificant minority. They are Party men, but their speeches at the congress were ideologically lackluster and revealed their professional ignorance. This ignorance allows them not only not to understand the need to improve their output but also inclines them against admitting this need—as was evident from the speeches of Panfyorov, Yermilov, Fadeev, Stavsky, and two or three others.

However, Com. Zhdanov has informed me that these men will be put on the Union's Board. In this way, ignorant people will be directing people who are significantly more literate than they are. It goes without saying that this will not create the atmosphere on the Board that is essential for amicable and unanimous work. Personally I know these men as quite clever and experienced in the "creation" of all kinds of internecine strife, but I absolutely do not feel them to be Communists and I do not believe in their sincerity. Therefore I refuse to work with them, for I prize my time and do not feel I have the right to waste it on fighting the trivial "squabbles" that will inevitably and immediately arise.

And they already have: in the seventh issue of *October* [*Oktiabr'*], which was edited by Panfyorov's group, there is a speech by Com. Vareikis which I consider harmful and which is aimed against the slogan of struggle for literary quality and which is illiterate in general.

This circumstance makes my position even harder and more complicated and forces me even more insistently to ask you, comrades, to release me from my responsibility as chairman of the Writers Union's Board.

NKVD documents now make it possible to see the reaction of the literary rank and file to the election of the new leadership of the Writers Union.

· 75 ·

Report from the GUGB NKVD SSSR Secret Political Department "On writers' attitude toward the recent writers' congress and toward the new leadership of the Union of Soviet Writers." [No earlier than 9 September 1934]. TsA FSB RF, f. 3, op. 1, d. 56, ll. 70–93. Original. Typewritten.

According to information { . . . } immediately after the congress, writers began to arrange their own personal affairs: purchasing cars, building dachas, many before or immediately after the congress was over went on creative trips or on vacation, and so forth. Therefore, in anticipation that by winter, when everyone returns, the situation will come clear, writers are reacting listlessly to the social-literary situation that has taken shape since the congress.

What is most surprising is that after the Writers' Congress very little was said about it. As if they had all agreed to maintain silence.

[. . .]

Al. Mitrofanov only said that young but qualified writers had virtually dropped out of the Organizing Committee's field of vision from the very beginning.

[. . .]

We will cite the most characteristic statements by writers recorded in the first few days after the congress.

L. Leonov: "We are all too experienced and tested for anyone to expect any sudden turns in literature, you need to live and act within the limits of what's real. The congress gave us nothing new besides Bukharin's report, which stirred up the swamp and provoked such harsh opposition on the part of the Fadeevs and Bezymenskys.

You can't expect anything in particular from the new leadership, which is going to take its lead from the two laureate apparatchiks Shcherbakov and Stavsky (Stavsky is an official person, too, after all). Inasmuch as Shcherbakov is inexperienced when it comes to literature, Stavsky will be doing the instructing, and we are all familiar with Stavsky's literary policy. Consequently, all remains in order in the union—a typically bureaucratic department."

M. Shaginyan: They're going to be attacking Gorky now. His report at the congress is wrong, incorrect, anything but Marxist, more like Bogdanovist,[6] it's Gorky's same old mistakes. Gorky is an anarchist, a *raznochinets* [intellectual not of noble birth], a populist, a petty bourgeois populist moreover, he doesn't come from the peasants, he's a populist from the petty bourgeoisie. And that showed in his report. Everyone was displeased with the report, even the foreigners. I know they're going to be attacking him, that the German Communist Party is going to pick apart and go through his report. The report is going to be disavowed by Stalin as well. Stalin didn't read the report because Gorky finished it just before the congress itself.

[. . .]

Once again there's going to be diarchy in the Union, because Gorky wants a monopoly, but the Party won't give him a monopoly, and once again there are going to be two trends, which, of course, will reflect above all on us, i.e., we writers are going to keep suffering.

Shcherbakov is a very fine man, cultured, he knows us writers, but he's too soft by nature. In this respect he's going to be weaker than Yudin. Yudin may be fairly stupid, crude, and dense, but as a Party man he's the stronger. Shcherbakov is softer, and for us that's worse.

Novikov-Priboy: The slogan for this congress was "Long live Gorky." That's really all the congress yielded: "Long live Gorky."

Bor. Pilnyak: I'm no politician, but I will say that there has to be moderation in everything. Even when it comes to praise. Conditions for me in the writer's world are such that I can't even speak. At the congress, many people were afraid to greet me. I'm going to write Stalin a letter. He tells everyone: "Writers should write the truth." I want to work on the union's board. I am going to work, I am going to work honestly, but I'm afraid that they aren't going to create the proper situation. At the plenum of the board, they applauded Gorky twice. The matter evidently is going to be such that when someone is left standing alone with Gorky, he'll be applauded as well. Do you think Fadeev and Panfyorov have become reconciled to the situation and love Gorky? I can't allow even that thought.

They saw that they weren't strong enough and quickly shifted gears. Vsevolod Ivanov doesn't like anyone. He's gambled on Aleksei Maximovich and he thinks he'll be his heir, but that's never going to happen.

L. Seifullina: It's a complicated situation, predators all around, traitors. I can work only if I divorce myself from the situation. In the union there are bureaucrats, bosses, who despise writers.

[...]

Many people are offended. A few days ago there was a drinking Party at Lev Gumilevsky's. Pilnyak brought me. I thought they were just going to chatter, but it turns out a faction of the offended had gathered and arranged a drinking party. There are all kinds of ways of correcting one's affairs, but I find this way repugnant. How dare they think I would ever stand up for "Dog's Lane" ["Sobachii pereulok"]?[7] I gave Pilnyak a good dressing down, too. Why does he have to poke his nose into those affairs? What does he have to be offended about? He got moral satisfaction. I didn't like his new story[8]—there's something like a parody of the writers' congress in it, although Pilnyak denies that. And the story has already been accepted at *Novy mir,* and naturally it will go through, while good authors like Pravdukhin are kept down.

[...]

P. Sletov: I've never been one of the optimists, but right now, since the congress, I have to say that it looks like our brother is going to breathe a little easier. True, 90 percent of what was said at the congress is the usual bureaucratic drivel: the half-empty hall speaks very well to that. All this is redeemed, though, by the truly historic significance of Bukharin's stunning report. No one can diminish the significance of this report: neither his "apology," nor its partial disavowal on the part of Stetsky. This is a matter of tremendous principle: the question has been posed point-blank about the two forces fighting it out in literature—the official "lack of talent raised on the shield" (the Bezymenskys, Zharovs, and, the logical continuation, the Stavsky-Panfyorovs), and the free and independent masters (Pasternak, Vasiliev, Olesha, et al.). Nothing you do could burn the descriptions given for Bezymensky and Demian [Bedny] from the consciousness of millions of readers, just as nothing you do could drown out the ovations addressed to the same Pasternak and Olesha.

This is the only valuable result of the congress. Herein lies our right as writers to continued work.

Ilia Selvinsky: At the congress, in the speeches of the same orators, there was an odd mixture of sincerity and officialese.

Radek was afraid in his report of the witticisms and liberties that we expect from him, so that they wouldn't be taken for oppositionism, and he spoke in lackluster fashion, without his usual brilliance. And Bukharin decided you could speak the way you thought—so he was forced to apologize and wasn't chosen for anything, although he himself told me he had been offered something before.

What will happen now, while Gorky is in power, is hard to say. After all, the whole trouble lies in the fact that they are trying not to do what's best for literature but to please their superiors. Dinamov doesn't do what he should but what, in his opinion, Stetsky would like. Stetsky does the same with respect to Zhdanov. It's political maneuvering. Fadeev is squeezed because Averbakh doesn't like him, whereas Averbakh does like Gorky.

Gorky is the breeder of worse cliquism than under RAPP because bad taste plays an even greater role. Favoritism of the worst kind is developing. Vs. Vishnevsky was at a banquet at Gorky's and he tells how important it was there, even, who sat closer to or farther away from Gorky. He says the spectacle was so repulsive that Pasternak couldn't take it and got out in the middle of the banquet. (Here it should be noted that Selvinsky feels Gorky is to blame for all the bad things that have happened to him).

[...]

Boris Lapin: It's going to be harder now for Gorky to be the boss in literature, especially if Shcherbakov remains working at the TsK. Yudin could be at someone's beck and call and evoke Gorky's displeasure, but Shcherbakov's hardly going to be his little boy.

S. Budantsev: [. . .] You can't count on anything now—everything will have to take its course. But the literary atmosphere is stifling. The sole consolation is that just as 23 April [1932] eventually came, when for the first time Stalin personally tackled the solution of literary problems, the moment will again come when literature demands authoritative intervention. Novich was telling me that right now Stalin is refraining from radical intervention in literature, allowing discussion there, and as a result there is a battle going on constantly in literature between the two lines—Fadeev and Stavsky, and Gorky, who just can't stomach them. The Shcherbakov-Ivanov-Stavsky triumvirate is obviously a compromise between the two lines. But insofar as Gorky is just an "icon," and Ivanov is a man without any talent for organization, we are once again under the "aegis" of Stavsky, the worst of all RAPPites.

[...]

L. Kassil: The constant "office switching" at the Orgkom has yielded no creative results of any kind. Now a more or less "firm" authority has been organized. What will come of it, we shall see, not laboring under any especial delusions, of course. It's hard in general to labor under any delusions with Gorky presiding. If he does have his own policy, then it is determined by personal considerations exclusively. What a petty and vindictive old man he is after all. He will never forgive the deceased V. V. Mayakovsky, for example, for his poems about him. We heard how he attempted to "lower" him in his closing word: "the influential and original poet." He never forgives anyone anything as a general rule. All Prokofiev had to do was come out one time with a critical review of him, and, if you please, in that same closing word he stupidly, without any pretext, came crashing down on Prokofiev.

N. Shkliar: No matter what they said there, the main business was taken care of because such marvelous speeches came thundering out to the whole world from the congress tribune, such as the speeches by Ehrenburg, Olesha, and Pasternak, proving that genuine literature, in defiance of the forces [assailing it], is alive, so in the future this stream of the living, unofficial word is going to get through, countering more and more steadfastly the numbing cliché of what is called "proletarian literature." The only regret is that Gorky did not find in himself the same courage as Bukharin did to snatch the bedaubed masks off pompous celebrities. Let us hope that the process will take its course: that the emphasis on artistry, on genuine writers, takes the upper hand. Let us hope in general that a literature not made to order will eventually revive here.

[. . .]

Yury Nikulin: "I look on things like this, that we should be competing not with corpses like Fadeev, Stavsky, and others, but with living people, with Pushkin and Tolstoy, so what does the congress mean to me? It was a congress of people already brushed by decay. Are we really supposed to expect any good to come of it? Talk with the whole mass of writers. Did even one of them really expect anything to come of the congress, and did anyone really get anything out of it? All it did was tickle the vanity of the people sitting on the presidium."

[. . .]

Let us cite a report < . . . > that indicates the manifestation of hostile, great power—chauvinistic moods among the group of poet-translators from the national languages. "The attention paid by the congress to the national literatures evoked unique, chauvinistically colored moods among translators. The general tone was this: nat[ional] writers are bad. It's we who actually make them into writers, sacrificing our own creativity. For this, not only do we not see any gratitude, but we encounter perpetual dissatisfaction, behind-the-scenes accusations, and so on. These writers are widely published here and surrounded with esteem, chosen for central organs of the union and so forth, whereas we always take a back seat."

[. . .]

Gusev said also that having worked with Uzbeks he was convinced of their work's profound lack of talent, the insincerity of their attitudes, and the rottenness of their literary milieu, where everyone hates everyone and informs on everyone, and that he is not going to engage in translation anymore.

N. Ushakov said with bitterness that the nationals demand translations, but they themselves have no desire to translate anyone and behave "as in a conquered country." He will finish the translations he has taken on, but after that "he will starve, but he will write his own things."

[. . .]

All these individuals, as well as Zenkevich and Narbut, were saying that the congress yielded nothing, that they had no occasion for "genuine" discussion about genuine tasks, that "there" (at the TsK—Zenkevich) they couldn't possibly understand that you can't command literary work, that you can't create anything to order, and that you have to give up on the union and work "for the drawer."

In particular, Narbut stated that writers who were not allowed into the hall and were slighted will never forget this ridicule; then he expressed his indignation at the disavowal of Bukharin, who had "dared to have his own opinion." He told how D. Bedny, after Bukharin's letter, told Bezymensky and Zharov: "Don't be afraid, boys, you'll never be lost with me around."

> Ch[ief] of the GUGB Sec[ret] Polit[ical] Department
> *Molchanov*
> Dep[uty] ch[ief] SPO GUGB 4-th div[ision]
> *Petrovsky*

As we see from these remarks by writers representing very different positions, the key role played by Gorky was for many a guarantee not only of continuity of literary traditions but also of the balance of power in the new union. The "special relationship" formed between Gorky and Stalin in the late 1920s (see Chapter 5) was seen by many as ensuring that they would be protected. Many myths were generated around this relationship, but the documents from the archive of the Politburo throw light on the character of their relationship and demythologize it.

CHAPTER NINE

The Gorky Factor

The correspondence of Gorky and Stalin, examples of which are presented here, was one between two public figures who had need of each other and hence needed to compromise. At the same time we see here how, behind the façade of the much-advertised closeness between the nation's leader and its principal writer, they were not close and there was no trust between them. Gorky emerges in the correspondence as a highly placed supplicant who uses the leader's predisposition towards him to his advantage. Nevertheless, he tries to address Stalin as an equal; by contrast, his letters to writers have a somewhat patronizing tone.

The following letter provides a good example of the nature of their relationship. It should be noted that it was written before the Party decree abolishing all independent writers' organizations including RAPP, and founding the single Union of Soviet Writers. Most of this letter comprises a shopping list of requests to which he wants Stalin to accede. Essentially, Gorky, as a patron of certain writers and editors, appeals on behalf of some of his protégés to Stalin as his own patron in the chain of patronage (e.g., to reinstate Zazubrin, a minor writer). In this letter, as in other sources, he acts as advocate for Averbakh, the RAPP leader, and also for Mikhail Slonimsky, a fellow-traveler writer who had worked as his secretary in postrevolutionary Petrograd (Leningrad). In other words, so often his pleading is for figures with personal connections to himself. We also see how, and characteristically, Gorky attempts to have certain officials dismissed on the basis of lack of cultural competence and also alleged character defects, but to some degree he is settling old scores and batting for his own team against another side. For example, Ionov had earlier, in 1925, thwarted several of Gorky's journal publishing schemes; Gorky also believed Ionov was behind the arrest that year of A. N. Tikhonov who had edited the banned journal *Russky sovremennik* (Russian Contemporary) with which Gorky had been associated. The writers he advocates—Sholokhov, Fadeev, Stavsky, and Gorbunov—were officially favored and all but Gorbunov had some connection to the RAPP leadership (Fadeev and Stavsky were secretaries of RAPP).

We will also note Gorky's proclivity for encyclopedism, for putting out series of books that were intended to provide a comprehensive history of some sociological category or event. Gorky instituted and headed a number of such ventures after his return to Soviet Russia, *History of the Civil War* being, predictably, the most important (together with another such Gorky-sponsored series, *History of the Factories*). Funding for such expensive pet projects was among the favors extended to him by the leadership.

· 76 ·

Letter from A. M. Gorky to I. V. Stalin. On the letter there is a comment by A. N. Poskrebyshev dated 3 February 1932: "For the information of TsK VKP(b) secretaries L. M. Kaganovich and P. P. Postyshev." AP RF, f. 45, op. 1, d. 718, ll. 134–135. Original. Typewritten.

25 January 1932

Dear Iosif Vissarionovich,

I am attaching a copy of my letter to Ilya Ionov, I beg of you to note the very unhealthy squabble this abnormal person has started, which could completely destroy Akademia Publishers. Ionov likes books, and this, in my view, is his sole virtue, but he is not literate enough to run that kind of cultural business. I have known him since 1918 and observed him for three years, and even then he gave me the impression of someone psychically unbalanced and extremely—"lordly"—rude with people and incapable of work involving major responsibility. Later it seemed to me that his trip to America healed him somewhat, but I was wrong. America only developed the arrogance, conceit, and philistine—"proprietary"—rudeness in him. He absolutely cannot stand people who are smarter and more literate than he is and by his very nature he is an incurable individualist in the worst sense of the word.

It seems to me that he should be replaced at Akademia by someone else—and not just one person even. Wouldn't Lev Kamenev, Sutyrin, P. S. Kogan, or someone else be suited to that work? It's a very important matter and requires great knowledge.

Tikhonov and Vinogradov are being defended by me not on the basis of personal sympathies, not at all, but specifically because these are knowledgeable men. Right now I am compiling plans for young people's editions—*History of Woman from Primeval Times to Our Day, History of the Worldwide Merchant, History of Russian Daily Life,* i.e., the history of the middle bourgeoisie—the lower middle classes. Work on these editions requires serious cultural efforts.

I am also attaching a letter from someone named Irinin. I don't know who he is, but I've heard he works in one of our Berlin institutions. The letter is confused, as you can see.

In the three weeks Averbakh spent with me, I got a good look at him and I think that this is a highly intelligent, finely gifted person who has not yet developed as he should and who needs to study. He should be looked after. He is overburdened with work, he has neurosis of the heart and desperate neurasthenia by reason of overexhaustion. He's been treated a little here, but that's not enough. Can't he be given a couple of months' leave, until May? In May he has a major job beginning, a major job for the congress of writers and preparations for the celebration of the 15th [anniversary of the] October Revolutionary.

I beg of you: issue an instruction allowing the writer Mikh[ail] Slonimsky to come here, he is traveling for work on a new novel. I've heard much that is gratifying about the works of Sholokhov, Fadeev, Stavsky, and Gorbunov. It looks like '32 will see a bumper crop for literature.

Tomorrow in Naples they are launching a second trawler, the *Amurets;* the *Ussirets* was launched recently and has left for the Far East. Our boys—the officers—on these vessels are very fine. The third vessel will be launched in February.

I am distressed that the plan I worked out for the *History of the Civ[il] War* has yet to be checked. I am anxious to put out the first volume of it for the 15th year!

I'm not going to write about the Italians' intentions, you probably know this better than I.

I have a request for you: isn't it time to reinstate Vladimir Zazubrin, the Siberian writer, in the Party? He's a wonderfully well-disposed man, he wrote a very fine novel, *Mountains* [*Gory*], and he's been punished hard enough. And it was scarcely deserved to that extent. A very valuable person.

Be well, I firmly shake your hand.
A. Peshkov

Undoubtedly Gorky's direct access to Stalin made it possible to resolve many literary issues behind the scenes. Several times Stalin publicly supported Gorky's initiatives and he most demonstratively took Gorky's side in various arguments (through resolutions and actions by the TsK). Within the intelligentsia this support enhanced Stalin's authority, which was high in any case but at the same time it made Gorky more dependent on Stalin's support.

Gorky's following letter to Stalin was written before the April resolution and before Gorky's return to the Soviet Union. Gorky had been embroiled since at least 1931 in a bitter debate with the Panfyorov-Serafimovich group. Both these writers had produced officially acclaimed novels (Panfyorov's *Ingots* [*Bruski*] on collectivization [1928–1937], and Serafimovich's *The Iron Flood* [1923] on the Civil War), but Gorky in his campaign to institute a standardized language for Socialist Realism attacked their works repeatedly as negative examples that used too many subliterary constructions and dialecticisms. Despite strong Party support for these two writers (both were leading members of the Party faction in the Writers Union) in this power struggle Gorky's position was endorsed at the Writers Union plenum of March 1934 and the matter was laid to rest. However, it should be noted that Stavsky, whom he also attacks here, was to head the Writers Union after Gorky's death in 1936.

· 77 ·

Letter from A. M. Gorky to I. V. Stalin. AP RF, f. 45, op. 1, d. 719, ll. 38–38v.
Original. Typewritten.
24 March 1932

Dear Iosif Vissarionovich—

I received your telegram and took the appropriate measures. I regret that R. Long's lack of tact ruined a serious matter, but I think that in a while this matter should be revived, not at our initiative naturally, and in a somewhat different form.

Taking advantage of the occasion, I am allowing myself to share with you the impression I received from the polemic between the Panfyorov-Serafimovich group and the leading RAPP group. The former group's ideological motives are not entirely clear for me, but as far as I understand, they are striving for a primitivism and simplification in the sphere of literature, they want to narrow the framework of themes, however they do not indicate with sufficient clarity the reason or purpose that makes this necessary. If I'm not mistaken, then—this desire is harmful and in it one senses the presence of an element of servility toward beginning writers and a desire on the part of the Panfyorov group to occupy a commanding position.

Beginning writers have to be convinced to study! It is not right to indulge their careless attitude toward literary work. This polemic introduces confusion and discord among the mass of RAPP members and causes them to waste time on investigating the question not of "who is right" but of "whom should we follow?" This is exactly how young writers formulate their mood in their letters to me. As you see, it's not a formulation you can praise.

The endless group disputes and squabbles in RAPP, in my view, are extremely harmful, especially since it seems to me that at their base lie not ideological but primarily personal motives. That's what I think. But then it seems to me that replacing the leading RAPP group—which brings together the most literate and cultured of our Party writers—with the Serafimovich-Stavsky-Panfyorov group, will not benefit RAPP's further growth.

Here, in Naples and Venice, trawlers are being built for Murmansk and Vladivostok. When they finish building a trawler, it waits there a month and a half for the crew to arrive from the Union.

I'm attaching a translation of a short article from the *Roma* newspaper, perhaps it slipped past comrades for whom such remarks are not without interest.

I wait impatiently for when I can travel to Moscow. I'm well.

> I firmly shake your hand.
> A. Peshkov

Afinogenov just arrived.

In the following two documents we sense the flavor of Gorky's (somewhat formal) exchange with Stalin. It is to be noted that Gorky's suggestion of a "Club for Masters of Culture" was realized. However, so was the writers' village to which in these documents both he and Stalin were opposed.

· 78 ·

Letter from A. M. Gorky to I. V. Stalin. AP RF, f. 45, op. 1, d. 719, l. 104. Handwritten. In AP RF there is also a typewritten copy of this letter with Stalin's underscoring and his instructions: "To Kaganovich, Stetsky (for raising the issue in the TsK Sec[retariat]). I. Stalin" and "To my archive. I. St[alin]."

28 February 1933

Dear Iosif Vissarionovich—

Allow me to acquaint you with my letter to I. M. Gronsky.

The very serious matter of organizing a literary institute requires your participation, for this issue is entirely new, and it must be posed in exemplary fashion, without excessive word play, based on a rigorous study of the material of history.

Then I would earnestly ask you to think about the idea of organizing a "Club for Masters of Culture." It seems to me that an institution of this type might play a highly significant role in the development of our culture.

The "writers village"—as you see—makes me skeptical.

I have been reading reports on the congress of kolkhoz shockworkers with the deepest pleasure. A most excellent idea that should yield excellent results.

I firmly shake your hand. Be well, dear and mighty man.

A. Peshkov

· 79 ·

Letter from I. V. Stalin to A. M. Gorky. [No earlier than 1 March 1933]. AP RF f. 45, op. 1, d. 719, l. 112. Handwritten.

Greetings, dear Aleksei Maximovich!

I received your (second) letter.

1. Regarding the "writers village." I agree with you entirely. This is a far-fetched business that could also remove writers from the real world and develop their conceit.

2. A *club for writers* (who are already trained and writing) is a necessary and useful business. It would be good to have a specific plan for the club's organization. When you arrive we will definitely move this matter forward.

3. What do you think, shouldn't we organize a *literary institute* named after you either attached to or associated with the writers' club?

Things aren't going badly here.

    Greetings!
    I. Stalin

One measure of how important Gorky was to Stalin as a public figure was the fact that the organs of the NKVD regularly reported on intellectuals' responses to this or that speech by Gorky. The following document concerns an article by Gorky which occasioned a strong reaction among many writers. Though Gorky's authority was exceptionally high, he was not, as we see here, beyond criticism. The creation of a new system for organizing literature did not only mean strengthening Gorky's authority but also creating an entire new bureaucratic system within literature with its rigid (and harsh) system of subordination, often resented by the literary rank and file.

On 14 June 1934 Gorky published in *Literaturnaia gazeta* an article "Literary Amusements" in which, inter alia, he attacked the poet Pavel Vasiliev (who often wrote about the Cossacks and was roughly speaking a figure in the mold of Sergei Yesenin). Gorky saw Vasiliev as too much of a "hooligan" in his conduct, but also as too Russian nationalist in his work, to Gorky's mind veering in the direction of fascism. Many consider that this attack was connected to Gorky's conflict with Gronsky in that Vasiliev was married to the sister of Gronsky's wife, and lived in Gronsky's apartment. In any event in January the following year Vasiliev was excluded from the Writers Union, which meant in effect that he could not be published, and on July 15 he was sentenced to a labor colony. The appeal he sent to Gorky from there seems to have been effective because he was released early, in the spring of 1936, but after a further arrest in February 1937 he was shot. As is evident in the following exchange, Vasiliev had defenders.

· 80 ·

Special Report from GUGB NKVD SSSR Secret Political Department "On progress in the preparations for the First Congress of the Union of Soviet Writers."¹ [No earlier than 10 July 1934]. TsA FSB RF, f. 3, op. 1, d. 54, ll. 231–233. Original. Typewritten.

Responses to Gorky's "Literary Amusements"
*1. Article in defense of Usievich.*²
{ . . . }

The *Literary Gazette*'s editorial office has received an article by Rozental (from *Literary Critic*) which is evidently an attempt to whitewash E. Usievich in connection with the reproaches cast against her in Gorky's article concerning her patronage of P. Vasiliev, Ya. Smelyakov, and others. This article was obviously written by Rozental under pressure from Usievich herself.

Usievich and P. Vasiliev himself have shown great impatience and personal interest in the publication of this article in *L[iterary] G[azette]*.

Usievich has made several calls to Sen[ior] Secretary Tseitlin and his dep[uty] Berkovich in the editorial office on this subject, however Tseitlin and Bolotnikov are still holding the article back, trying to come to an agreement on it with Yudin and demanding, at Yudin's insistence evidently, that Rozental make several corrections.

In connection with the publication of this article, P. Vasiliev himself came to the offices of *Lit[erary] Gazette* to inquire as to when the article would be released and discussed this with Tseitlin.

2. Pasternak on Gorky's article.

Boris Pasternak, when he met Pavel Vasiliev at the Herzen House, shook his hand and said demonstratively loudly: "How do you do, enemy of the fatherland," and laughing, he walked on. Later he said the following on the subject of Gorky's article:

"You get the feeling that Gorky harbors a bitterness toward everyone. He doesn't understand, or pretends not to understand, the significance each word of his has, the resonance that any given speech of his has. Gorky's nuances turn into the rumbling of a truck.

"As for Pavel Vasiliev, Gorky's article is no reflection on him. He will also be published and also accepted among the public.

"With regard to Aleksandr Prokofiev, Gorky was too harsh ('A poet, I guess'), and moreover the 'I guess' was in quotes. This is all too petty for Gorky."

Moving on to the matter of acceptance into the union and Shaginyan's letter, in which she declines the title of union member, Pasternak said:

"It turns out that heroic gestures are now in fashion. I didn't make myself Soviet in time. I should have stayed the way I was two years ago. At the time I was seething and raging, I was capable of all kinds of gestures. Then I started to think that this was the wrong position, that I was a rotten intellectual, that everything around me was reforming itself and that I should, too. And I sincerely did, and so now it turns out that I could have gotten along without it. I missed the mark again. I say all this laughing, but seriously, there is a certain truth in it. One conversation with someone who stands at the apex—I'm not going to name him—has convinced me that now, as I said, the fashion is for another type of writer. When I spoke with this person in the usual Soviet tone, he suddenly told me that one shouldn't speak in that way, that this was time-serving. I get the feeling that many at the top would like it better now if I was the way I was before I reformed myself."

{ . . . }

Assis[tant] to the Head of SPO OGPU Gorb

In the opening of the following letter to Stalin Gorky mentions that he is sending him his "speech" for Stalin to make corrections. Presumably Gorky is referring to the keynote address on Socialist Realism that he was to give to the First Congress of the Writers Union on August 17, a fact which provides further evidence of Stalin's major role in literature. We will also note here how Gorky is essentially petitioning Stalin as he attacks many highly placed Party people who are playing major roles in literature and whom he would like to see removed from their posts: Pavel Yudin was deputy head of the Central Committee's Section for Culture and Propaganda of Leninism, Mekhlis was the editor of *Pravda* from 1930 to 1937, and Vareikis was a member of the Central Committee from 1930 to 1939. Here Gorky also continues his campaign against Panfyorov, contrasting *Ingots* with two other books about collectivization, M. Sholokhov's *Virgin Soil Upturned* (*Podniataia tselina*) (1932–60) and I. Shukhov's *Hatred* (*Nenavist'*) (1931). Also significant is the attack on Fadeev, the former RAPP leader and a rising power in literature, and his comments regarding Mirsky's attack on Fadeev's novel *The Last of the Udegs* (*Posledny iz Udege*) (about a tribe in the Soviet Far East during the Civil War). (Prince Sviatopolk-) Mirsky, a Russian, returned to the Soviet Union in 1932 from emigration in London, after joining the Communist Party in 1931. He survived under Gorky's patronage and some have suggested that the attack on Fadeev's novel was actually written at Gorky's bidding (Mirsky attacked it as unworthy of a Soviet writer). Following Gorky's death in 1936 Mirsky's position became precarious; he was arrested in 1937 and perished in 1939.

· 81 ·

Letter from A. M. Gorky to I. V. Stalin. IMLI, A. M. Gorky Archive. Copy.
Typewritten.
2 August 1934

I am sending you my "speech" and beg of you to acquaint yourself with it as quickly as possible so that I can enter any corrections in it that you might make.

I am attaching a letter to me from Comrades Mirsky and Yasensky, as well as a copy of the latter's article, which was sent to *Pravda* and has not yet been printed. It probably will not be printed, either, for Yudin and Mekhlis are men of the same line. The ideology of this line is unknown to me, but its practice comes down to organizing a group that wants to run the Writers Union. This group, which has the "will to power" and leans on the Party's central organ, is capable, of course, of running it, but in my opinion it does not have the right to the actual and necessary ideological leadership of literature, does not as a result of the weak intellectual power of this group, as well as a result of its extreme ignorance with respect to the past and present of literature.

The Union's board is being appointed from the individuals listed in Yudin's article, which I have also attached. Serafimovich, Bakhmetiev, and Gladkov—who is spent, in my opinion—are intellectually feeble men. The last two are hostile toward Fadeev, whereas he, arrested in his development, is evidently suffering this as a drama, which, by the way, is not hindering his aspiration to play the role of lit[erary] leader, although for him and literature it would be better if he studied. I consider Mirsky's assessment of *The Last of the Udege* absolutely correct, but judging from Yudin, Fadeev just took it as an insult. My attitude toward Yudin is becoming more and more negative. I'm offended by his peasant cunning, his lack of principle, his duplicity, and the cowardice of someone who, while aware of his own personal impotence, attempts to surround himself with people even more insignificant and to hide among them.

I don't believe the sincerity of Panfyorov's communism. He is another ignorant peasant, also cunning, painfully ambitious, but a fellow of great will. He has fought very effectively against the critical attitude toward *Ingots* and has attracted as his protector Vareikis. Someone named Grechishnikov put out a book praising him in which it says that the "cognitive significance of *Ingots* is, without the slightest exaggeration, tremendous." He repeats a sentence from Vasilkovsky's article: "*Ingots* has not been and cannot be replaced by any research on collectivization, no matter how specialized." Naturally, this book doesn't say a word about Sholokhov's *Virgin Soil Upturned* or Shukhov's *Hatred*. It is perfectly natural that immoderate praise for Panfyorov has a painful and harmful effect on these authors.

For me personally, Panfyorov, Molchanov, and the others of this group are bringing into the milieu of the literati and literature the [mentality of] the peasant, with all his individualistic and "proprietal" [*edinolichny*] baggage. For them, literature is "seasonal labor" and a springboard for jumping to higher positions. My mistrustful and even hostile attitude toward the peasant is not diminished by the fact that the peasant sometimes speaks in the language of the Communist. Literature by peasants and literature about peasants demands especially close reading and especially pointed criticism. More and more often one is forced to comment that the peasant is not studying as avidly as the proletarian. Here is the latest instance: Molchanov was offered funds in order to travel to one of the large construction sites, live there a while, and look at how the proletariat is working to revive the countryside. He refused, citing the fact that he was writing a new book. The criticism of his *Peasant* [*Krest'ianin*] slid off him like water off a duck's back.

Vishnevsky, Libedinsky, and Chumandrin cannot be directors over the non-Party writers, who are more literate than those three. The Communist faction in the Orgkom enjoys no authority among writers, in front of whom a struggle among cliques has developed openly. And I have to say that these cliques are created among us as a fact of patronage: some of our country's com[rades] are men of letters whom the "grandees" particularly patronize and who are especially and recklessly praised. Around each of their writers who are marked by the sympathy of the "bosses" a small group has been organized of writers even less talented than they but organized not as around a 'teacher" but for ordinary, narrowly personal motives: someone in turn, too, playing the role of patron, produces in the publishing house the unripe "fruits of creativity" of young perches, pikes, and other fish of the predator variety. Someone fusses about getting a ration allocation and an apartment for his admirer, whom he calls a "pupil," but he doesn't teach him his job, nor can he, for he himself is an ignoramus. To this I must add that we are dealing primarily with people of about age thirty, i.e., those who experienced the "hard times" in their adolescence and young adulthood, and these times are reflected in the psyches of many thirty-year-olds very badly: they are too greedy for the pleasures of life, in too much of a hurry to enjoy, and don't like to work conscientiously. And some are in such a "hurry to live" that their haste creates the impression that they are not confident that the reality being created by the Party has strengthened sufficiently and is going to develop exactly the way it has been doing, they think that the peasant is only pretending to be a collectivist and that we have all the prerequisites for fascism and that "war could set us farther back than NEP." If it was only the philistine, the petty bourgeois, who thought this it wouldn't matter, but this is how some "Party men" think, and this to me is alarming, although, as you know, I'm an "optimist."

To this I should add as well the activities of the wreckers among the school-age youth, which Ivan Makar'ev has told me about and which, according to him, he has told you about as well. I was told by com[rades] from the GPU about another form of wrecking among children in the Crimea. I have been taking a very close look at children and in a few days will keep my promise to write about them—it is not my fault that I am late doing this.

Children must be protected from petty bourgeois contagion—that's the whole point.

Everything stated above—albeit very incompletely—convinces me of the necessity for the most serious attention to literature—"the bearer of ideas into life"—and, I add, not just ideas but attitudes. Dear, sincerely respected, and beloved comrade, the Writers Union must have very solid ideological leadership. Right now there is a selection of individuals going on that suits the interests of ambitious people and predicts the inevitability of a petty, personal struggle among cliques in the Union, a struggle along anything but the line of organizing literature as a force acting in an ideologically unified way. Few understand literature's cultural-revolutionary significance. I know you will be presented with lists of people who are being recommended for the Board and Presidium of the Writers Union. I don't know who they are, but I can guess.

It seems to me personally that the individuals named in the attached list would give the Union the strongest leadership. But even if the makeup of the Board of the Writers Union is approved, I sincerely beg you to release me from the chairmanship in the Union due to my weak health and extreme lit[erary] work load. I don't know how to be a chairman, and I'm even less capable of sorting out the Jesuitical cunning of these cliques' politics. I will be much more useful as a worker in literature. I've accumulated so many themes on which I don't have the time to work.

I sincerely shake your hand and wish you a good rest.[3]

M. Gorky

Cultural life of the mid-thirties was colored not only by the purges and the increasing centralization of the arts but also by the Soviet

Union's joining the Popular Front. This international alliance, centered in France, was intended to unite all parties and individuals genuinely committed to the antifascist cause. In the area of culture, the Soviet Union had been particularly active in attempting to attract antifascist intellectuals from throughout the world to their side. To that end, they (de facto) organized and bankrolled a Congress for the Defense of Culture held in Paris in June 1935 and attended by writers, including a delegation from the Soviet Union that included Pasternak. In the aftermath of the Congress the International Society of Revolutionary Writers (somewhat under the wing of the Comintern) was abolished and replaced by an organization centered in Paris with Soviet operations recentered in the Foreign Commission of the Writers Union, headed by Mikhail Koltsov (referred to in the following document). Particular efforts were made to attract antifascist French intellectuals to declare themselves for the Soviet Union, and hence a number of leading figures were invited to the country, where they were feted, such as Malraux as in this letter. In the letter Gorky also seems to be trying to lessen the severity of the "anti-Formalist" campaign which was launched after a *Pravda* attack on Shostakovich (see Chapter 12).

· 82 ·

Letter from A. M. Gorky to I. V. Stalin. [No earlier than 7–10 March 1936]. Handwritten draft. Published in *Literaturnaia gazeta,* 10 March 1993.

Dear Iosif Vissarionovich,

I am reporting to you the impressions I gained from my direct acquaintance with Malraux.

I had heard much praise and many solidly grounded responses from Babel, whom I consider someone who has an excellent understanding of people and the smartest of our writers. Babel has known Malraux for some time, living in Paris as he did, and has steadily followed the rise in Malraux's significance in France. Babel says that ministers reckon with Malraux and that among the contemporary intelligentsia of the countries speaking Romance languages this man is the most prominent, talented, and influential figure, and in addition he possesses talent as an organizer. Babel's opinion is confirmed by my other informer, Maria Budberg, whom you saw at my place; she has been circulating among Europe's writers for a long time and knows all the attitudes and all the assessments. In her opinion, Malraux is truly a man of exceptional abilities.

From direct acquaintance with him, I got approximately the same impression: a very talented man who deeply understands the world significance of the Union of Soviets' work, who understands that fascism and nationalistic wars are an inevitable consequence of the capitalist system, that while organizing Europe's intelligentsia against Hitler and his philosophy and against Japanese warmongering, one has to convince Europe of the inevitability of a worldwide social revolution. Com. Koltsov will inform you about the practical decisions we took.

I see Malraux's deficiencies in his tendency to go into too much detail, to talk too much about trifles, in a way that they do not merit. A more substantial deficiency is his stance, typical for all of Europe's intelligentsia, "for man, for the independence of his creative work, for the freedom of his internal growth," etc.

Com. Koltsov has informed me that Malraux's first questions were questions about Shaginyan and Shostakovich. The main purpose of this letter of mine is also to tell you candidly about my attitude toward these issues. On this score I have not yet worn your patience out, but now, when we need to be occupied with broadly uniting the European intelligentsia, these issues must be raised and clarified. In the course of your speeches, as well as in your articles in *Pravda* last year, you spoke more than once about the need for a "protective attitude toward man." In the West, they heard this and it lifted and broadened their sympathies for us.

But now there is this story with Shostakovich. Rave reviews were printed about his opera both in organs of the central press and in many regional newspapers. The opera ran with success in theaters in Leningrad and Moscow and received excellent reviews abroad. Shostakovich is a young man, about twenty-five, an indisputably talented man, but very self-assured and quite high-strung. The article in *Pravda* hit him over the head like a brick, and the lad is completely crushed. It goes without saying that, in speaking about a brick, I meant not the criticism but the tone of the criticism. And even the criticism itself is not conclusive. "Muddle"— but why? In what and how is it expressed, this "muddle"? Here the critics must provide a technical assessment of Shostakovich's music. But what the *Pravda* article gave permitted a herd of untalented people, hacks, to persecute Shostakovich any way they liked. And they're still doing it. Shostakovich lives by what he hears, he lives in a world of sounds, he wants to be their organizer, to create a melody out of chaos. The attitude expressed toward him by *Pravda* cannot be termed "protective," and he fully deserves just as protective treatment as one of the most gifted of all contemporary Soviet musicians.

[...]

There are few theaters in Moscow and a children's theater is essential, but where is the repertoire for such a theater? And why, for whom, do the theaters of the brilliant Meyerhold and no less brilliant Tairov exist? Some think that one of these theaters is necessary for the actress Raikh, and the other for the actress Koonen.

This letter was written by Gorky several months before his death. "The smartest of our writers" whom he refers to here—Isaak Babel, Mikhail Kol'tsov and the "brillant" Meyerhold will soon be shot, Meyerhold's wife Zinaida Raikh will be brutally murdered in her own apartment and in mysterious circumstances. Meyerhold and Tairov's theaters will be closed. Attacks on Shostakovich will continue after the war (see Chapter 23). In mid 1936, at the beginning of the Great Terror Stalin was not particularly inclined to listen to the advice of Gorky who had by now lost his usefulness.

CHAPTER TEN

The Union of Soviet Writers

In the initial years after Gorky's return his and Stalin's ties to each other were mutually advantageous. Stalin particularly needed Gorky in the years 1932–1934 because Gorky's international stature helped legitimize Stalin's project for restructuring literature and the arts and for making Socialist Realism mandatory for all Soviet culture. Gorky for his part took advantage of the fact that Stalin was all-powerful to push through his many pet projects and to expand his tremendous influence in the cultural sphere. The aging Gorky was given the role of father figure in Soviet literature, but he had to pay for it with endless editing and supervising of unskilled writers. However, Gorky soon became disillusioned with the new literary order and though he continued to play a role as titular head of literature he effectively had little power in what had become a huge bureaucratic institution. This disappointment can be sensed in many of Gorky's letters to Party bodies where he complains about unprincipled fights over privileges, a lack of responsibility, unjust distribution of material resources, patronage, and so forth. At the same time, and as can be seen in the following example of such letters, he had little or no power to change anything:

· 83 ·

Letter from A. M. Gorky to TsK VKP(b) Secretary A. A. Andreev. RGASPI, f. 73, op. 2, d. 44, ll. 17–20. Original. Typewritten.
8 December 1935

Dear Andrei Andreevich,

[. . .]

The second matter is much more complicated. Under discussion is the Union of Soviet Writers. The situation there, it seems to me, is impermissible. It is characterized by an almost total lack among the writers of an awareness by them of their corporate, collective responsibility for their work, for their social behavior in front of the Soviet reader, as well as in front of the international reader. Rooted in this lack of awareness of their responsibility, in my view, is the cause of all the sins of our literature, the cause of the political ignorance and cultural poverty of its members, the cause of their reluctance to study, to teach young people, the cause of their reluctance to fight mercilessly against any petty bourgeois manifestation among them—the bases of fascism.

I realize, naturally, that the fault for all these sins rests with the Union's chairman, however I am compelled to live far from Moscow, immersed in work that I must finish before I turn up my toes, and I worry I won't finish in time. To a certain extent the fault for writers' lack of supervision and their shakiness may also lie with the Party's TsK. The Party has put the workforce of the entire land of the Soviets ahead of mankind, and by wisely strengthening, developing, and cultivating this force is decisively leading it toward a great goal, toward the reorganization of the entire world's social structure. The Party gives quite a lot of attention and assistance to the workers in science and technology, less to doctors, and even less to teachers, and very little to writers, the "engineers of souls." Creating the Union and awarding it a budget of 10 million rubles is, of course, generous assistance for literature. So generous that it may even be harmful. Literature's "head" is rich. Litfond assistance is astonishing and at times storied. They often give out money without an attentive approach, without taking into consideration the real needs of Union members. Frequently the needy writer is refused assistance but the writer's sister is given 5,000 rubles. The government gave money to build a dacha settlement, and 700,000 of this money has vanished like smoke in the wind. The instances of such generosity are many.

Alongside these, a writer may live at the seashore but not swim, which would be healthy for him. Why doesn't he swim? He doesn't have the 3 rubles to buy a bathing suit. And he's a highly valued worker in the provinces, he's been working there for over twenty years, and in a worker center like Voznesensk. There are dozens of young writers without rooms —they live in cellars, in "corners"—there are even rumors that they live in cemeteries and crypts. Is such a sharp distinction between the sheep and the goats really all right? The goats are our young people.

The attitude toward writers is quite varied. There is "patronage," and very often a writer is valued not on his merits but on his sympathies. [Pilnyak has been forgiven his story about the death of Com. Frunze, a story which asserts that the operation was unnecessary and done at the insistence of the TsK. Pilnyak has been forgiven "Mahogany" and much else that is scandalous as well. Instances of this type are many, of course.][1] This, naturally, creates rotten moods and discussions among writers.

[. . .]

I have issued specific practical instructions several times. It has been said that we have no criticism. People have talked and talked, but there's still no criticism. We ought to get twenty or thirty critics together, organize an ongoing seminar around, say, some extremely necessary topic, like "The History of Literature." This kind of seminar is doubly necessary: we'll end up with critics, for one, and secondly, the most important issues in the history of literature will be worked out. Given the Writers Union's multimillion budget, it costs nothing to spend a few hundred thousand rubles on training critics. I will put together a plan for this seminar and the leaders for it if the Writers Union decides to implement this idea in earnest.

Training for young writers is on an extremely weak footing in the Union. Sometimes it seems that the decisive slogans of the Party go right by the Writers Union. What has been done to implement Stalin's slogan, "Cadres decide all"? Where are the young people educated by the Writers Union? And here we cannot limit ourselves to amateurish attempts, rather we must centralize the matter of training literary cadres.

I have asked strenuously to arrange lectures for writers on the philosophy of Marxism and the history of literature, reports on current work in Soviet scholarship, on the situation in the West, and so on. Nothing has been done. Is this really so difficult?

As a rule, writers don't read one another's books. We should arrange lectures with evaluations of book output at least twice a year. We must follow regional literature keenly and do surveys of this literature in one of our moribund journals.

It occurs to me that we need to reorganize the Union's secretariat, transforming it into a regularly functioning institute. We could bring in Comrades Eideman, Luppol, Lakhuti, and one or two other writers. Moreover, we need two more: one who is a good manager; and another as a lecture organizer and, so to speak, "Head of Improving Writers' Qualifications." The main thing, though, is for the secretariat to be a working institution within which there is an efficient division of labor and strict accountability for assigned work.

I entreat you to help us all!

> A firm greeting
> M. Gorky

It is instructive to compare Gorky's above letter to Andreev with the following letter sent to Stalin by Shcherbakov, a very different figure. Shcherbakov had been "assigned" by the Party to work in the Writers Union and in the following document he deals with very similar problems to those touched on by Gorky above but, in contrast to Gorky, analyzes them not in terms of structural problems but in terms of intrabureaucracy conflict (such as Stavsky's being a poor administrator).

· 84 ·

Memorandum from SSP SSSR (Union of Soviet Writers of the USSR) Secretary A. S. Shcherbakov to I. V. Stalin on the situation in literature. RGASPI, f. 88, op. 1, d. 474, ll. 1–8. Copy. Typewritten.

2 January 1936

Com. Stalin!

I have been working as secretary of the Writers Union board for fifteen months. Now, in the interests of the cause, I am compelled to disturb you and ask for assistance and instructions.

Based on the directives I received when I was sent to work at the Writers Union board, I first kept trying to provide in the Union a situation in which writers could work well. The secretariat tried to wipe out meeting fuss and stir, ceremonial show, and tried to provide more perhaps not immediately obvious but genuine practical assistance for writers. There are grounds for saying that for the most part a situation was created that was conducive to work, and this could not help but have a positive effect on writers' creativity.

Right now the literary movement has entered a new stage, which I ask you to sort out.

I.

Literature has always grown and strengthened on criticism. At the given moment, when after a fairly lengthy period in which there have been few new works, new works are beginning to appear—the literary movement has an especially acute need of criticism. This matter was raised in a timely fashion by *Pravda* in its literary pages.

However, in order for criticism to orient writers correctly, we need to correctly define the condition of the literary movement. Disagreement begins above all with this question. There are assessments such as these: literature is going through a general troubled period (Lezhnev, an article in *Pravda*), literature's lag is becoming ominous (Stavsky). Voices are being heard about a crisis in Soviet literature. Quite a few have been found who are willing to express themselves more strongly. If we take these assessments as the point of departure for criticism, then it seems to me we are disorienting the writers.

What is the true situation?

In 1933 and 1934, there were few new works (meaning those worthy of attention). In 1935, especially the latter half of the year, new works began appearing, and their flow has been intensifying in 1936.

[. . .]

However, here it must be said with all harshness that literature's lag has not been eliminated, that there are few good books, that in the light of the unprecedented upsurge in the country, literature's successes are unsatisfactory. If eight to ten months ago we were concerned about the question, *Why are there no new works?*, then now we cannot help but be alarmed by the question, *Why are there no genuinely good works worthy of our great age?*

II.

This is how matters stand with the first question.

Another important question is the sense of measure in criticism. Criticism's greatest faults are either vague opinions ("I read your book, which is good, they say") or else indiscriminate praising of some works and equally indiscriminate censuring of others. I felt the correct line was the one aimed at what was honest that excluded the factional approach and a preconceived attitude toward a work and [fostered] a protective attitude toward people. . . .

[. . .]

A few days ago, there was a meeting of the Party group of the SSP board. At this meeting, one comrade raised the question of the difficult situation of the so-called "middle of the road" group of writers, whose works, in connection with the rising demands for quality, are finding the going hard getting through at the publishing houses. In speaking about this group, then, one comrade added: "one of these writers, Anatoly Vinogradov, has been bringing up suicide and even made an attempt to poison himself." In reply to this, the critic Yermilov stated: *"Let those kind poison themselves, they won't be missed."*

In this instance, Yermilov's anti-Party and ugly behavior was repulsed.

However, this statement, which testifies to the frivolous, unprotective, unsolicitous attitude of some critics toward writer cadres, finds expression in the daily work of these people. ...

[...]

The issue of the proper assessment of the contemporary condition of literature and the issue of the proper organization of critics seem to me fundamental issues. In a month, the III plenum of the Writers Union board is gathering. In the next few days, the Party group and presidium are going to be examining their theses for the plenum.

Right now literature needs a specific battle slogan that can mobilize writers. Help us Com. Stalin, put forward this slogan.

III.

When I was sent to work with the writers, I was given an instruction not to let loose and to resist any manifestation of sectarianism. I cannot remain silent before you about the crudest sectarian recidivism that has manifested itself in Com. Stavsky.

Since the very first days of our joint work, Com. Stavsky has undertaken a series of steps in order to tie me more closely with *Pravda*. I considered such contact beneficial and maintained it. However, then Com. Stavsky's desire to bring our work into contact with *Pravda* began to spill over into forms that affected the independence of the secretariat's line. In this, I could not agree with Com. Stavsky.

Com. Stavsky has taken it as a rule to keep a number of comrades from *Pravda* informed constantly and in full detail about everything that is going on at the Writers Union, about all our undertakings, intentions, and proposals. Naturally, I had nothing against this until his information became specific. On 31 December, there was an incident that fully revealed these "specifics."

On 30 December, there was a meeting of the Board's Party group where a number of issues were discussed on the work of the Union. The Party group instructed me, Stavsky, and one more comrade to write about this meeting for *Pravda* and the other newspapers. On 31 December, having met with Com. Stavsky, I proposed a draft. Com. Stavsky suggested that I rework it more for form than content. I agreed, Com. Stavsky personally wrote it, and we both approved it. In the middle of the day, Com. Stavsky called and reported that he had changed his mind and he had a different text. In the evening he brought this new text. I said that I was not used to deciding matters in such an off-handed way, I'd read it over, think about it, tell him my opinion, but we were not going to send the item to the newspaper today. In the evening, when I was through receiving writers, Com. Stavsky and I sat down to edit the text of the item together. And suddenly I happened to find out (not from Stavsky) that Com. Stavsky had already sent the text to *Pravda*. I demanded he have it held up.

This act by Stavsky involved one of two things: (a) sending an unapproved text, presenting it as approved, printing it, and in this way presenting the Party group and myself with a fait accompli and thereby predetermining any discussion of the matter: (b) sending his own text, later worked out by us together, indicating the difference, and then saying: "Here's my position, and here's someone else's position."

I must add that I have had no differences of principle with Com. Stavsky and in all the time working, Com. Stavsky has never stated his disagreement with my line or his disagreement with any undertaking of mine.

IV.

At the meeting of the Party group on 30 December, the organizational issue was also touched upon. Some comrades indicated that of late in connection with my joint appointment, the hard, organizational work at the SSP has slacked off and the secretariat's leadership has deteriorated.

I have to agree with this. During my two-month trip to Eastern Siberia, the Party group and presidium never met once. This is my fault, despite all the circumstances I was obliged to ensure normal work.

The following two documents illustrate the extent to which the Party leadership was involved in literary matters, not just in pronouncing on general or ideological questions, but also in deciding or approving issues concerning specific writers. The first of them is a curious document. Its subject, Yevgeny Zamyatin, best known as the author of the dystopian novel *We* [*My*] of 1920 which was banned from publication until Gorbachev's perestroika because it was considered an attack on the Soviet order, had emigrated from the Soviet Union in 1930, having petitioned Stalin for permission to do so (see Document 52). Here he is being recommended for membership in the Soviet Writers Union by writers who were formerly his associates in the Leningrad branch of the All-Russian Union of Writers (VSP), a right of center body which he formerly headed, and also by Pasternak who was at this time favored by Stalin.

· 85 ·

Report from the SSP SSSR Organizing Committee Secretary P. F. Yudin to I. V. Stalin on the request of writer Ye. I. Zamyatin to be accepted as a member of the Union of Soviet Writers. AP RF, f. 3, op. 34, d. 187, l. 62. Original. Typewritten. On the report are these instructions: "I suggest granting Zamyatin's request. I. Stalin" and "Reported to Com. Yudin 21 June 1934. B. Dvinsky."

14 June 1934

To Com. Stalin.

The writer Zamyatin has sent the Leningrad Organizing Committee a statement (telegram) from Paris requesting that he be made a member of the Union of Soviet Writers.

Zamyatin's statement evoked strong support and satisfaction with this act among fellow-traveler writers Konst. Fedin, Al. Tolstoy, N. Tikhonov, M. Slonimsky, B. Pasternak, and others. Inasmuch as Zamyatin's acceptance as a member of the Union is connected to issues that go beyond the bounds of the Writers Union, I request your instructions.

    Secretary of the Writers' Organizing Committee
    P. Yudin

It will be noted in this second document, from the late 1930s, that the list of those to receive state awards had, before being approved by the Presidium of the Supreme Soviet, to be approved by Stalin, but even before that by the NKVD (here in the person of Beria).

· 86 ·

Memorandum from TsK VKP(b) Secretary A. A. Andreev to I. V. Stalin on Soviet writers' awards. [July 1938]. RGASPI, f. 17, op. 121, d. 1, ll. 39–40. Draft. Typewritten.

To the TsK VKP(b)—Comrade Stalin.

I am sending you the draft edict of the USSR Supreme Soviet Presidium on awards for Soviet writers that was submitted to the TsK by Comrades Fadeev and Pavlenko. The list of writers proposed for an award has been reviewed by Com. Beria.

[. . .]

With respect to the remaining candidates for an award who have been compromised to some degree or another by NKVD materials, I feel that they can be awarded, bearing in mind their significance and work in Soviet literature.

In the historiography on Soviet Russia, March 1938 is generally taken as the end of the Great Purge of 1936–1938 (arrests continued, of course, but on a very reduced scale). As the Great Purge was winding down there began a period when officials started to attack some of the excesses of the previous years (rather as, in the early thirties, some of the excesses of the cultural revolution had been attacked). In particular, in early 1938 complaints were aired about the crippling bureaucratization of the Writers Union for which its head Vladimir Stavsky was held particularly responsible. The attack on Stavsky also reflects a reversal of the tide of terror which had seen many writers shot or sent to the camps; the Great Purge of 1936–1938 coincided more or less exactly with Stavsky's stewardship of the Writers Union and he was consequently a signatory of the arrest orders. Thus these documents are also interesting as, effectively, denunciations to the TsK. It is well known that writers wrote denunciations, but it has often been assumed that in culture denunciations produced "innocent victims" of the terror. These documents attest to the general climate of denunciation and the way denunciations could also turn against those in power.

· 87 ·

Memorandum from TsK VKP(b) Press and Publishing Department Head A. E. Nikitin to the TsK VKP(b) secretaries "On the situation in the Union of Soviet Writers." RGASPI, f. 17, op. 114, d. 955, ll. 286–292. Original. Typewritten.
28 February 1938

To the TsK VKP(b) secretaries—Comrades Stalin, Kaganovich, Andreev, Zhdanov, and Yezhov

The current state of the Union of Soviet Writers is alarming in the extreme. The creative association of writers called upon politically and organizationally to *rally* the writing masses and fight for the lofty ideological and artistic quality of Soviet literature, through the efforts of its present leaders is more and more turning into a unique bureaucratic department of literary affairs.

The TsK VKP(b) resolution dated 23 April 1932 has been ignored by the Union leadership for the last two years. The Union is not doing any serious work with writers. At the center of its attention is not the writer and his activity but primarily only various management issues and quasi-literary squabbles.

The Union has been transformed into a huge chancellery in the bowels of which endless meetings go on. Writers who do not want to break away from the Union essentially have no time to write because of the incessant bustle of meetings. It has reached the point, for example, where at one of the meetings of the Secretariat Com. Stavsky offered the writer Vishnevsky creative leave. Vishnevsky, as we know, does not work in any institution, and consequently, "creative leave" for him means leave from endless meetings at the Union.

As a consequence of this state of affairs in the Union, writers face a dilemma: they must either "work" in the Union, i.e., attend meetings, or else write.

This situation has come about as a result of the unacceptable, un-Bolshevik organization in the Writers Union. The Union's Board, and in particular its Presidium and Secretariat, in practice proved weak in both the political and the practical respects. Of the 101 members of the administration elected at the First Congress of Writers, only 58 people remain at the present time. The rest left for different reasons, moreover 33 people have been exposed as enemies of the people. In the Board's Presidium, of its 37 members, 21 remain, and of the 5 elected by the congress in the Secretariat, 3. The Board's Presidium, which includes a number of prominent writers, has been idle and practically never meets. In effect all affairs are taken care of by the Secretariat, most of them by Com. Stavsky alone.

On the Secretariat's board, which is headed by Com. Stavsky, not only is there no unanimity, there is not even elementary harmony. Sometimes it simply reaches the point of scandalous incidents. On 25 February, for example, at an expanded session of the Presidium at which local representatives participated, Com. Stavsky, in the name of the Secretariat, submitted a plan for discussion. The Writers Union's other secretary, Vs. Ivanov, who spoke at this session, stated to the general bewilderment that this plan had not been approved by the Secretariat and that he, as one of the Union's secretaries, protested Stavsky's proposals. As a result, the plan was rejected.

[. . .]

Seeing that the situation in the Union is deteriorating with each passing day and that the current leadership is bankrupt, a few days ago a group of non-Party writers decided to write a letter to Com. Stalin on this matter. At the session of the Union's Party group that took place on 26 February, Com. Vishnevsky for some reason characterized this attempt by the writers as a manifestation of hostile attitudes.

All this is just playing into the hands of anti-Soviet elements. Taking advantage of the absence of any productive creative work in the Union, individual "venerables" are attempting, not without success, to unite around them a number of writers. Right now, for example, in Peredelkino, in the writers' rest house, there is a sort of second "parallel" literary center whose magnetic force is K. Fedin. There is a hidden danger here of a certain portion of writers becoming enveloped with political attitudes hostile to us.

Having lost all authority among writers, Com. Stavsky is attempting to improve his status by various demagogical and essentially provocational maneuvers. Thus, blatantly playing up to the unhealthy, dependent moods of individual writers, he has decided without preliminary approval from the TsK to bring forward at the expanded session of the Union's board on 26 February, K. Fedin's report on writers' material situation. The main thesis of this report by Fedin is that the material situation of our writers has deteriorated as a result of such measures as the closure of several theaters and the elimination of Akademia publishing house; Soviet writers are worse off now than ever before.

[. . .]

The role of the "thick" journals in the formation of a writer and the organization of the literary community is potentially huge. Given the correct formulation of the issue and a firm editorial board with a good Bolshevik backbone, every journal, by uniting around it a group of "major," as well as capable young writers who are creatively connected, forms a kind of primary creative cell of the Union. Writer collectives grouped around one journal or another are easier for both the Union's board and the TsK to monitor. Here people will be connected not by formal meetings but by creative activity. The activism of many writers is now being wasted on useless meetings at the Union and could find successful application at creative meetings in the editorial offices of journals, in the discussion of manuscripts, and so on.

The editorial boards of most literary journals today enjoy little authority among writers; they are usually constructed in such a way that a cluster of flatterers and toadies forms around the editor-in-chief. As a result, the following situation comes about: the Union holds meetings, and in the journals' editorial boards, which are constructed through friendship ties, i.e., through networks, clusters of untalented spongers accumulate who "exploit" the name of their boss and the state purse.

We must create strong editorial boards that include the most prominent writers and young people who have recommended themselves with their works. These editorial offices can broadly unite writers around themselves and use their creative and public activism.

A decision of the TsK Orgburo has formed the editorial board of *Novy mir*. This decision instructed the TsK press office to construct editorial boards in all the other literary journals. We will submit corresponding practical proposals on the makeup of the editorial boards of these journals to the Orgburo simultaneously.

The current situation in the Writers Union can be explained to a significant degree as well by the weak work of the Union's Party organization. We think that the TsK O[rganizational-]d[is]t[ribution] Section or the Moscow Committee should send a strong Party committee secretary to the Union's Party organization.

In informing the Central Committee about all this, we ask to be given appropriate instructions.

> Head of the TsK VKP(b) Department of the Press
> and Publishing Houses
> A. Nikitin

· 88 ·

Statement from *Literary Gazette* editor O. S. Voitinskaia to A. A. Zhdanov on the situation in the SSP SSSR. [Before 15 March 1938]. RGASPI, f. 17, op. 120, d. 304, ll. 146–150. Original. Typewritten. On the first page of the statement is the following instruction: "To Comrades Molotov, Andreev, Kaganovich. Please familiarize yourself with Voitinskaia's letter on the situation in the Writers Union. The letter is of undoubted interest. A. Zhdanov."

Com. Zhdanov!

I consider it my Party duty to tell you about the situation that has come about in the Writers Union, a situation that is the result of the fact that the TsK resolution of 23 April 1932 has not been implemented.

The Writers Union has been transformed into a department on literary affairs that is constantly in session and has no relationship to literary-creative matters.

The matter has reached the point where Com. Stavsky has proposed giving Vishnevsky creative leave so that Vishnevsky can write. We know that Vishnevsky does not work in state institutions and, consequently, "creative leave" means leave from the endless sessions in the union that nobody needs.

Consequently, a writer must either "work" in the union, i.e., go to meetings, or write. Such a situation was able to come about thanks to the incorrect, un-Bolshevik organization of the Writers Union.

Meanwhile, the processes going on among writers demand serious work of the Union. A number of writers who a few years ago were still politically inert have now been drawn to the Party and have taken a vital interest in the struggle for the Party line.

By way of example, I will cite the attitudes of several major writers.

1. *Leonov*—I've realized there are only two paths: communism and fascism. And therefore I am going with the Communist Party. There is still a lot I don't understand. I can't limit myself to the illustration of newspaper articles. In order for me to write a full-fledged artistic work about socialism, I need help.

2. *Pogodin*—I am deeply offended by Feuchtwanger's book[2] and therefore I wrote an essay, "Comrade Stalin." Stalin is the pride of our era.

3. *Selvinsky*—At one time I used to visit Trotsky. Bukharin might have attracted me. And so now I'm happy that I exposed the spy, informing on him to the NKVD organs. I am in favor of the Party because otherwise fascism would triumph.

4. In Kiev I spoke at length with *Tychina*. Tychina, a former nationalist, is a poet who has great influence in Western Ukraine. The Ukrainian Writers Union, busy with its squabbles, "doesn't have time" to take an interest in Tychina.

I went to see him to talk about the condition of Ukrainian literature. Tychina told me: "Enemies have tried to make us quarrel with Soviet power" (he spoke to me at length about the provocations of Khvylevy, Senchenko, et al.), "but I wrote a book of poems, *The Party Leads* [*Partia vede*], true the Party has no time for us." I told him about Comrade Stalin's letter to Sobolev, a letter from which the Union's leadership was unable to draw the appropriate conclusions for itself. Tychina was stunned: "If a man as great as Stalin has time for us, that means we're needed."

[. . .]

At the same time, there is an obviously incorrect understanding of freedom of the press as the bourgeois freedom of the press, of a bloc, as concessions. The same Pogodin said: "We need our own non-Party newspaper headed by Fedin" (Fedin is someone who has right-wing attitudes and is politically very slippery).

[. . .]

On the editorial board itself, it will be necessary to keep the fight going against non-Party members of the editorial board, people who are indisputably with us but who still don't understand a lot.

For example, Petrov seriously tried to prove to me that *Literary Gazette* shouldn't print the resolutions of the TsK plenum and Comrade Molotov's speech since it had nothing to do with literature.

Feuchtwanger's book met with great sympathy among a certain group of writers. "Feuchtwanger was able to say what we have been forbidden to say."

All these facts attest to the tremendous responsibility that rests on Communists working in literature.

We are talking about political responsibility to the Party's TsK for genuine Bolshevik influence on non-Party writers.

[. . .]

We at *Literary Gazette* have spoken out with an editorial against unprincipled cliquishness.

I asked the secretary of the Party Committee: "Here you are engaged in a war of the sections, but does the Party committee know how Feuchtwanger's book was received?" "We haven't had time to get to that." "Well then, what are writers' moods before the elections? Can we say what the moods are of Leonov or Ivanov?" "We haven't looked into that."

That fact is very characteristic and attests to their style of work.

Party organizations in writers' organizations do not work with non-Party members. We know that most Communist writers have serious political grounds for punishment (at one time the Party organization elected B. Yasensky to the Party committee by secret ballot, knowing about his ties to spies). Meanwhile nothing is being done to increase and strengthen the Party core of the Writers Union. In the last few years, not one writer has joined the Party. Even A. Korneichuk isn't a member of the Party. Meanwhile, in Kiev, there are 14 Communist writers, of whom several do not inspire political confidence, it would seem that the most natural way to strengthen the Party core is with honest people devoted to the Party. The lack of growth is explained by the absence of work with the non-Party members. It is characteristic that when the Party committee of the Writers Union in Moscow invited non-Party members to the Party committee no one showed up.

[. . .]

In quite a few republics there are no Communists since the exposure of enemies in the writers organization (in Leningrad there isn't a single Communist critic). Instead of struggling for the consolidation of forces, Communists from the Union board are busy with their own squabbles.

[. . .]

The Union's board has supported and promoted several people who turned out to be enemies of the people. [. . .] In *Georgia*, everything was entrusted to Pasternak and Mirsky, who are closely tied to the group of the spy Yashvili.

[. . .]

In the presidium there has never been a report given on the art of writers from the ethnic minorities, there has been no fond concern for writers' fates. This explains the impermissible indifference of the Union board to the radical shift in the work of Tychina (Tychina could have played a huge role in the struggle with Ukrainian nationalists that would have resonance in Western Ukraine), the absolute indifference to the fate of Korneichuk's creative work.

[. . .]

[. . .] in the Union there are no discussions of manuscripts, that is, the Union is not doing what it is supposed to do. *Writers gather in apartments, and enemies frequently take advantage of this.* The current condition of work aids wrecking. It is not for nothing that the Writers Union is so politically compromised. The situation in the Writers Union is made even worse by the fear of self-criticism, a fear, I would say, that has grown out of the political activism of non-Party members. Writers are extremely dissatisfied with the existing situation and are talking about this openly. It would be very good if the TsK called a group of Communists and non-Party writers in for a discussion.

  O. Voitinskaia
  Editorial Board of *Literary Gazette*

 One should note that these documents are from late February–early March, 1938. As we see in the following document, by mid-March the campaign was joined by the TsK secretary Andreev, who oversaw cultural questions until Zhdanov took it over that year. His conclusion in the following letter is clear: Stavsky must be removed.

· 89 ·

Memorandum from TsK VKP(b) Secretary A. A. Andreev to I. V. Stalin on the conference with writers. [No earlier than 27 March 1938]. RGASPI, f. 73, op. 2, d. 17, l. 105. Copy. Typewritten.

To Comrade Stalin.
 I am sending you an example of Com. Stavsky's leadership in the Writers Union—his circular, where he gives out his assessments to writers, moreover it's odd that the most flattering responses he gives to works by exposed enemies of the people.
 Com. Zhdanov and I have called on the TsK of the Union's presidium and about twenty Party and non-Party writers to clarify the situation in the Union and among writers. We listened to them for two evenings. Upon Com. Zhdanov's arrival in Moscow we want to continue the discussion with them, but I can already say that the situation in the Writers Union is grave. It is evident from everything that intentional wrecking has gone on there to disorganize the writers' milieu. Stavsky looks very bad in all this, and his conduct has been blatantly suspicious and provocational with respect to writers. It is evident he was tightly connected to Kirshon, Yasensky, and other wreckers.
 In the Writers Union, everything was done to split up Party and non-Party writers, to support the split and fighting along the line of old writer factions, and to keep writers out of Union affairs, while many idlers have been living off the apparatus and around the Union.

Stavsky has virtually replaced the Presidium and secretariat of the Writers Union and by his entire conduct has created great dissatisfaction among writers against the Union.

Stavsky should be removed, but in addition it is obvious that a decision is needed from the TsK on the essence of the work of the Writers Union.

If you are interested in the writers' speeches at the meeting, I am sending Com. Poskrebyshev excerpts from their speeches.

Emboldened by Andreev's position, at a meeting of writers with the TsK that took place on 25 and 27 March 1938, the writers said bluntly that Stavsky should be sent on a long vacation and the leadership of the Writers Union should be put in the hands of a group of five comprising Pyotr Pavlenko, Leonid Sobolev, Valentin Kataev, Anna Karavaeva, and Valeria Gerasimova. However, it was reported that Stavsky would not give in and continued to oppress writers. During 1938 Fadeev put himself forward for the position of head of the Writers Union (secretary of the Presidium of the Writers Union) and was confirmed in that position by the Politburo of TsK on 25 January 1939, a post to which he was elected by the TsK secretariat three days later.

In the historiography Fadeev's headship of the Writers Union from 1939 to 1954 has received diametrically opposed evaluations (partly as a result of his suicide in 1956). His defenders cite his interventions in defense of colleagues who were repressed, and examples of his help to writers out of favor. His detractors, in whose eyes he was the embodiment of the Stalin regime in literature, cite examples of terrible betrayals, of his persecuting former friends, instances when he was settling scores, and so forth. There is no shortage of material in support of both positions. Fadeev undoubtedly helped Anna Akhmatova, Nikolai Zabolotsky, Olga Forsh, and many others, but it was also Fadeev who after the war led an anti-Semitic campaign against figures in literature and the arts and gave support in the Writers Union to a group of mediocre writers who were anti-Semitic.

Fadeev should also be held responsible for disbanding the most intellectual of all the literary journals, *Literary Critic* (*Literaturnyi kritik*), the only one in the 1930s devoted to literary theory. One of the editors of the journal, which was founded in 1933, was Elena Usievich, the daughter of the prominent Polish Communist Feliks Kon (both had returned with Lenin from Zurich in 1917 in the armored train); its leading contributor was the Hungarian Communist Gyorgy Lukács who lived in the Soviet Union from 1929 to 1931 and 1933 to 1945.

The journal and its regular contributors had enjoyed favor in the thirties; making it possible to, for example, publish fiction by Andrei Platonov, widely regarded as one of the greatest prose writers of the Soviet era but whom it was virtually impossible to publish at this time. In the early thirties members of the Lukács group (Lukács, Mikhail Lifshits, Ernst Fischer) produced several scholarly anthologies of documents and monographs about the utterances of Marx, Engels, and Lenin on literature which helped make particularly authoritative the group's attacks on "vulgar sociology" (analyzing literature purely in terms of its socio-economic underpinnings) and their support of a select canon of literary masterpieces from the past as signposts in the evolution from "realism" to Socialist Realism. In the late thirties, however, the attitude to the journal shifted radically and it was closed down in 1940. It will be noted, however, in the following document from that year, how the new line on the journal was justified by pointing out that its position on the heritage of the past rationalized the fact that most writers included in their canon were far from lower-class.

· 90 ·

Excerpt from a memorandum from SSP SSSR Secretaries A. A. Fadeev and V. Ya. Kirpotin to the TsK VKP(b) secretaries "On the Anti-Party Faction in Soviet Criticism." AP RF, f. 3. op. 34. d. 209. ll. 51–69.
10 February 1940

To the TsK VKP(b)—Com. Stalin
  Com. Molotov
  Com. Zhdanov
  Com. Andreev
  Com. Malenkov

The working conditions for Soviet criticism cannot be considered wholly normal. Some people who have organized as a group comprising a minority of critics have wound up in an exceptionally privileged position in the sphere of criticism. They have entirely in their hands *Literary Critic,* the sole scholarly literary journal in Russian in the USSR especially for criticism, and *Literary Review* [*Literaturnoe obozrenie*], the sole bibliographical literary journal. The group is supported by the newspaper *Soviet Art* [*Sovetskoe iskusstvo*]. The group is under the patronage of Tregub, a worker in the literary section of *Pravda,* which is reflected in the choice of persons invited to collaborate in *Pravda's* lit[erary] section, which uses the group to whip up rumors about the Party support allegedly rendered to them. The guiding individuals in the group are G. Lukács, Mikh. Lifshits, Ye. Usievich. G. Lukács is a man with a very confused biography, at the beginning of his career an unconcealed bourgeois idealist who subsequently joined the Hungarian Communist Party, a leftist about whom Lenin wrote back in 1920: "The article by G. L. is very left-wing and very bad. The Marxism in it is purely verbal" and so forth ([*Sobranie sochineny*], vol. 25, p. 291).

G. Lukács's political and philosophical works have been subjected to criticism several times in the Soviet press for his revision of Marxism. Com. Lifshits is a candidate for VKP(b) membership, and Ye. Usievich is a Party member.

The group includes V. Kemenov, Grib, Sats, M. Rozental (editor of *Lit[erary] Critic*), F. Levin (deputy editor of *Lit. Critic* and editor of *Lit. Review*), V. Aleksandrov, Andrei Platonov, the author of *Benefit* [*Vprok*], a literary lampoon of the kolkhoz movement. Close to the group are the recently arrested critics Malakhov and Ragozin. F. Levin, the dep[uty] editor of *Lit. Critic* and editor of *Lit. Review,* himself stated at a public meeting that the journals in which he works represent an "ideological tendency." Just the fact that two state journals have become organs of cliques, organs of some "[wrong] tendency," is an absolute outrage. However, the matter does not end with this. According to the logic of group existence, the group's members have accumulated many mistakes and harmful theories on which they insist, which they actively defend, and which have become their line. Here are the principal points of their views, which are a bourgeois-liberal revision of Marxism.

Rejection of the theory of class struggle in the assessment of literary phenomena

After the publication of the well-known "Comments on the synopsis of the textbook on *The History of the USSR* [*Istoria SSSR*] and *Modern History* [*Novaia istoriia*]" [sic][3] over the signature of I. Stalin, S. Kirov, and A. Zhdanov, a battle began in Soviet criticism and Soviet literary scholarship against vulgar sociological distortions. Participating in the criticism of vulgar sociology were also M. Lifshits, V. Kemenov, V. Grib, and M. Rozental, who, however, were working from false non-Marxist premises. In their speeches the general, abstract concept of "national character" supplants the issue of classes and class struggle. In their characterizations of Balzac, Shakespeare, Tolstoy, and other writers any element of class characterization is lost.

It is hard to grasp the opportunistic theory from excerpts, however it is enough to read any work by any of the members of this group in order to see their fundamental "divergence." The concept of "the people" has lost any specific historical and class content among this group. Lenin, in characterizing the contradictions in the world view and art of Tolstoy, sees in them a reflection of the strength and weakness of the peasant movement during a specific historical period. The clique's ideologues, Lifshits and Kemenov, replace the specific concept of the peasantry, in specific historical conditions, with the general concept of "the people." As a consequence of this they emasculate the Leninist class characterization of Tolstoy.

"Nowhere in Lenin will we find," writes Lifshits, "those allegedly precise but in fact vulgar definitions of the class nature of Tolstoy that our sociologists have such a penchant for" ("Critical Comments" ["Kriticheskie zametki"], *Lit. Gazette*, 24 May 1936). Simultaneously, the clique's ideologues make specific prejudices and the reactionary aspects of the peasant movement a feature of national character in general:

"Lenin demonstrated the dual nature of a national character. *National character in the art of great writers reflects not only the common sense of the masses but also their prejudices*" (V. Kemenov, "Lenin and Issues of National Character in Art" ["Lenin i voprosy narodnosti v iskusstve"], *Soviet Art*, 21 January 1940).

For Marxism-Leninism, what is national in a writer is that which serves the interests of the workers and moves them ahead. Whereas this clique, by revising Marxism-Leninism and backpedaling from Belinsky and Chernyshevsky, uses the writers' concept of national character in a "tailist," pseudo-worker way, blindly bowing to the prejudices and backwardness of the masses.[4]

Their extra-class attitude toward literature leads clique members to a noncritical, apologist attitude toward decadent writers.

[. . .]

Rejection of the theory of class struggle leads to replacing specific historical research with abstract, a priori schemes. Thus, in *Toward a History of Realism* [*K istorii realizma*] (Goslitizdat, 1939, ed. M. Lifshits, all the main essays of this book were first printed in *Lit. Critic*), G. Lukács shows that Russia in the second half of the nineteenth century was a mature capitalist country, in line with the Western European type, and that tsarism was a capitalist authority. "And so," writes G. Lukács, "Tolstoy depicts a world in which relations between people and people's relations with society are very close to the type of relations depicted by Western realist writers after the 1848 revolution" (p. 289).

This sentence is an explanation for the social formation discovered by Lukács anew: "Capitalism in its specifically tsarist form" (p. 286), whereas autocracy is transformed into "an apparatus of the capitalist state" (p. 287).

What kind of "Marxist" G. Lukács is we know, but the editor of this book, M. Lifshits, is a candidate for the Party, and the editors of *Lit. Critic* are Communists. We have the right to demand that the Communist editors at least not mislead writers studying history by foisting on them non-Marxist, non-Leninist views of the Russian historical process.

< ... >

The desire to tear Soviet literature away from politics

The rotten theoretical positions of the *Lit. Critic* clique lead them naturally to the conclusion that politics is harmful to art.

Ye. Usievich writes: "It must be said that the works of Western revolutionary writers *groping their way toward communism frequently possess to a much greater degree the specific traits* of artistic creativity and act in a much more revolutionary way *than do the works of many of our writers who approach art with readymade Communist conclusions*" ("On the Laws of Development by N. Virta" ["O 'Zakonomernosti' N. Virta"], *Lit. Critic*, no. 7, 1937).

[...]

Lit. Critic considers all of Soviet literature illustrative (i.e., didactic, second-rate) on the basis of the fact that it is permeated with political tendentiousness. "*So far our literature has primarily illustrated the Marxist understanding of reality*" (the lead article in *Lit. Critic*, no. 9–10 [1938]: 9).

In the sphere of poetry, Ye. Usievich cites the false and harmful idea that political poetry as a separate genre has never existed in great literature and should not exist in Soviet poetry. Political poetry, in Ye. Usievich's opinion, is the result of artistic decline: "Only in this era of *artistic decline,* conditioned by the specific characteristics of bourgeois development, does 'apolitical' or 'antipolitical' poetry arise. Contrasted to it is poetry having a clearly expressed political content, that sets itself directly political tasks, and wholly limits itself to praise or censure of political figures, facts, and slogans" (Ye. Usievich, *Paths of artistic truth* [Puti khudozhestvennoi pravdy], 1939, p. 106).

"... In other words, *attempts to return to poetry its lost organic social content have poured over into a one-sided, deliberate form: political verse,* where a directly political theme was expressed rationally, detached from all life's richness: it simplified the theme, became illustrative and lost, as a consequence of this, both its poetic power and its political acuity" (ibid., pp. 109–110).

Usievich has calumniated the history of literature. Pushkin wrote "For the shores of a distant fatherland" [Dlia beregov otchizny dal'nei], but also "Village" ["Derevnia"] and "Liberty" ["Vol'nost'"], Lermontov not only "Branch of Palestine" ["Vetka Palestiny"] but also "Death of a Poet" ["Smert' poeta"]. Both are brilliant but relate to different genres of lyricism. "Village," "Liberty," and "Death of a Poet" are examples of the political lyric. In modern Soviet literature, Ye. Usievich supports trends that express the defeated bourgeois resistance to socialism. Therefore, for her Andrei Platonov, the author of *Benefit,* is the most talented Soviet writer: "*the most talented of the writers* who are not satisfied with merely humanistic generalizations but seek vital, specific, and difficult, often tragic forms of development *among us is Andrei Platonov*" (*Lit. Critic,* no. 9–10 [1938]: 171).

Lit. Critic made Platonov its emblem. He is contrasted to other writers. He is pointed to as an example. V. Aleksandrov in his article "Private Life" ["Chastnaia zhizn'"] suggests to Pasternak that he cure himself . . . with Platonov (*Lit. Critic,* no. 3 [1937]). Even Platonov's short stories, which were rejected by other journals, have been printed in *Lit. Critic.*

Platonov has become the clique's political writer and critic. In *Lit. Critic* he tries to prove that all of Russian literature since Pushkin is pure decline, and that Gorky has absorbed . . . a little fascism: "Russian literature was compelled (after Pushkin) to agree to a certain *impoverishment.*" In *Dead Souls* [Mertvye dushi] and *Inspector General,* Gogol is an "*approximate imitation*" of Pushkin (p. 72). "Pushkin himself *appeared after all not out of abundance or excess of the powers of the people, but out of its need,* out of extreme necessity, virtually as a self-defense or a sacrifice" (p. 68). "Gorky was always on the front line of the battle for the future proletarian destiny, he was one of the first to take on all the attacks of the bourgeois and later the *fascist opponent.* And, naturally, Gorky's consciousness was "distorted" in a way because in battle even the winner receives wounds. Here the fighting went on inside the man, since he had to destroy the enemy in his very spirit and reason, and for this *you need to let him get extremely close*—to yourself" ("Pushkin and Gorky" ["Pushkin i Gor'kii"], *Lit. Critic,* no. 6 [1937]: 80).

Further commentaries are superfluous!

A volume of similar essays by Platonov and edited by Ye. Usievich has been withdrawn as an anti-Soviet book.

<. . .>

Conclusions

The *Lit. Critic* group has degenerated into a handful of people who represent a modern revision of Marxism-Leninism, who represent the bourgeois-liberal resistance to Marxism-Leninism in literature. As it happens, the *Lit. Critic* clique pays special attention to young people. It groups graduate students by type of "school." One sees its influence in teachers' colleges, and its destructive influence is especially strong in the Chernyshevsky Institute of History, Philosophy, and Literature.

Following all the rules of group tactics, this clique covers each other's mistakes, coordinates their essays and speeches, and treats all those who disagree with them as "non-Marxists." Over a number of years, no matter who has stood at the head of the Writers Union, this clique has functioned as a unique "opposition" and kindled strife between writers and critics.

In the system of their views and the methods of their work, the Literary Critic clique is an anti-Party *faction in literature.*

Lit. Critic and Lit. Review must be taken out of the faction's hands and made into organs of the Union of Soviet Writers, and the editorial boards of these journals wholly and fully replaced.

The views of the Lit. Critic clique must be exposed in order to put a halt to its destructive influence on literature and young students.

Pravda must come out with a condemnation of the Lit. Critic line.

Conditions that facilitated the formation of the Lit. Critic group

The people who gathered at Lit. Critic were able to form into a group as a result of an incorrect attitude toward criticism in certain circles of the Soviet public, including among writers. There are people and even organizations that look on criticism with contempt, as a second- or third-rate literary activity. *Pravda, Izvestia,* and *Komsomolskaia Pravda* never review critical books and essays. Literary criticism has fallen outside the field of attention of the Party and Soviet public and until recently was outside the field of vision of the Writers Union. The positive results achieved by Soviet criticism have not been supported, which has led to an underestimated picture of the achievements of Soviet criticism. After all, despite its privileged position, the Lit. Critic group is a minority. On the other hand, negative phenomena have not received a timely rebuff. Despite the signals, the central Party press did not attempt to sort out the mistakes in criticism as they appeared. Criticism, they said, is something unimportant, of minor relevance! As a result, the processes going on in criticism were not studied or placed under Party control. And the Lit. Critic group that run several organs of the press got the opportunity to freely propagandize their books and their views, to actively inculcate their erroneous and harmful theories.

>With Communist greeting,
>A. Fadeev
>V. Kirpotin

Half a year after this denunciation, on 26 November 1940, the TsK Orgburo took a special resolution "On literary criticism and bibliography," the first article of which stipulates that "Publication should be stopped of the journal Literary Critic which is isolated from writers and the literary world."[5]

CHAPTER ELEVEN

Stalin and the Moscow Art Theater

During the 1930s a system of state patronage became very entrenched. Earlier, during the 1920s, the prerevolutionary system of support in the arts was destroyed, as we saw in Part One. Initially, the premier institutions of the old culture such as the Bolshoi were imperiled as representing the aesthetic of the old regime, though the danger that they might be closed never existed for long because Party tastes in culture were fairly conservative. That conservatism was ever more in evidence as the thirties progressed and Party control increased. The history of Stalin's relations with the Moscow Art Theater provides an interesting case study of this.

Konstantin Stanislavsky and Vladimir Nemirovich-Danchenko founded the Moscow Art Theater (MKhAT) together in 1898. Best known in the early years for its productions of Chekhov (his widow, the renowned actress Olga Knipper-Chekhova, appears in the documents below), MKhAT was generally enormously popular both in Russia and abroad where the acting theories of Stanislavsky have had a widespread influence, most notably as the basis of "method" acting which has been the dominant school in the American theater and cinema. The theater's original aim to provide a more authentic re-creation of actuality on stage (what is often called "psychological realism"), and especially its fame overseas, were critical factors in MKhAT's, and Stanislavsky's theories on actor training method progressively becoming the dominant model for Soviet theater and the principal bête noire of would-be avant-gardists. Even before Stanislavsky's theories were effectively canonized in the mid-thirties, the two directors received many official favors and were able to travel overseas extensively, with generous provision of foreign currency, doctors to accompany Stanislavsky, and so forth.[1] However, relations between Stanislavsky and Nemirovich-Danchenko had become estranged in the prerevolutionary period and for much of the Soviet period they operated separately, rarely meeting, each with his own coterie of actors and administrators in the theater, and periodically clashing by proxy or via correspondence. The clash was exacerbated by the history of the production of Bulgakov's *Molière*. The play had been passed by Glavrepertkom (the Central Repertoire Commission) in 1931 and rehearsals had begun the following year. However, its direction had to be taken away from Stanislavsky in 1935 because his constant interference with the text dragged out the production and angered Bulgakov. The several documents on MKhAT presented below attest to the acrid atmosphere in the theater, typical of the mid 1930s. The TsK paid close attention to this situation, as is evident in the following document:

· 91 ·

Memorandum from TsK VKP(b) Department of Cultural Educational Work Head A. S. Shcherbakov to the TsK VKP(b) secretaries on the situation at MKhAT. AP RF, f. 3, op. 35, d. 24, ll. 10–11. Original. Typewritten.

3 August 1935

To TsK VKP(b) Secretary Com. I. V. Stalin
Com. A. A. Andreev
Com. N. I. Yezhov

At the instruction of the secretaries of the TsK VKP(b), the TsK Department of Cultural Educational Work has familiarized itself with the situation at the Gorky MKhAT.

Lately relations between individual groups of workers have been greatly exacerbated. In connection with this, the mood of a number of MKhAT artists is depressed. This has taken its toll, particularly in the discussion of Comrade Stalin's speech at the Military Academy's graduation ceremony. The discussion lasted for two days (2 and 3 June). At this meeting, People's and Honored Artists, art world figures, and several prominent actors in the theater frankly raised painful questions from the life of MKhAT.

[. . .]

Honored Artist Koreneva, Honored Artist Stanitsyn, and the director Gorchakov spoke about the ordeals of the actors involved in the play

Molière (the first rehearsal of this play began while the first metro tunnel was being built, but the production is still not ready). People's Artist Tarkhanov, comparing the old and new MKhAT, drew the conclusion that the theater is getting progressively sicker and that it is being sucked dry by formalities and red tape. "Yesterday," he said, "we opened our mouths because Comrade Stalin's speech had had such a powerful effect on us. There they're calling us to love, but here they're calling us to dry formalism and red tape paper work." People's Artist Knipper-Chekhova in her speech pointed to the theater's detachment from life and also stated that the atmosphere of joy, love, and respect for one another had disappeared from the theater.

With the animated support of the audience, Honored Artist director Sakhnovsky underscored that the basic misfortune lies in the absence of a unified leadership: the theater's two leaders, Stanislavsky and Nemirovich-Danchenko, never say anything clear (from his seat Com. Tarasov's comment—"a madhouse"). People's Artist Leonidov, who was greeted with an ovation, also declared: "The main thing is that we have two directors. Usually there's one director, but we have two. Also, in their thirty-six years of work they could never agree on their views. And therefore both these directors each have a theater to which they give more than they are capable of."

As a result of the two-day debates, the meeting passed a resolution signed at the instruction of the meeting by Kachalov, Leonidov, Knipper-Chekhova, Tarkhanov, Sakhnovsky, Tarasova, Sudakov, Stanitsyn, and Markov. Pointing to the exceptional attention of the Party and government to the theater, the meeting notes the theater's lag behind life, the absence of a definite artistic line and the necessary tempos. The meeting feels that Stanislavsky and Nemirovich-Danchenko need to be unburdened of administrative-organizational work and a director put at the theater's head.

These events at MKhAT are of course no accident. They are the result of that internal struggle being waged between Stanislavsky and Nemirovich-Danchenko. The theater is going through a difficult crisis. It must be helped immediately.

The TsK VKP(b) Department of Cultural-Educational Work feels that it is essential to eliminate the diarchy at MKhAT-1 as quickly as possible and appoint a director there—a member of the VKP(b). Stanislavsky and Nemirovich-Danchenko need to be left as artistic directors and "honorary directors" (Yuzhin was that kind of "honorary director" at the Maly Theater). In conversations with a number of individuals, Nemirovich-Danchenko has expressed his willingness to be appointed director. Stanislavsky will certainly be opposed.

    H[ead] of the TsK VKP(b) Department of Cultural-
    Educational Work
    A. Shcherbakov

As is clear in the following memorandum, the problem of governance in the theater worried the TsK because a power vacuum threatened to split up the troupe and jeopardize the repertoire program. Just as in the case of literature, in the theater an "honorary director" had been set up (in literature Gorky, in this theater its two founders) who for assorted reasons did not run the theater, and a Party bureaucrat was proposed to replace them. One and a half months after Shcherbakov sent the above letter, he followed up with a memorandum declaring a crisis in MKhAT and suggesting getting it out of its impasse by appointing someone who would really manage the theater.

· 92 ·

Memorandum from TsK VKP(b) Department of Cultural-Educational Work Head A. S. Shcherbakov to the TsK VKP(b) secretaries on the situation at MKhAT. AP RF, f. 3, op. 35, d. 24, ll. 18–21. Original. Typewritten. On the document is the instruction: "Discuss. St[alin]."

17 September 1935

To TsK VKP(b) Secretaries Com. I. V. Stalin
Com. L. M. Kaganovich
Com. N. I. Yezhov

At the instruction of the TsK VKP(b) secretaries, the Department of Cultural-Educational Work has familiarized itself with the situation at the Gorky MKhAT for a second time.

The theater's situation is no better and no worse. The MKhAT leadership, K. S. Stanislavsky and V. I. Nemirovich-Danchenko, take no interest in the theater whatsoever. They are more involved with their opera theaters. The mutual squabbling between them, which gets increasingly intense, has completely destroyed any unified leadership at MKhAT. The theater now has two lines, two camps recruiting their own supporters, drawing actors and directors into petty intrigues and quarreling. Two secretariats have been created which are energetically fanning the disputatious atmosphere.

There is no firm repertoire plan, the theater lives on a day-to-day basis. The theater's work is not planned, and right now no one knows what the theater will be doing in a year or two. The directors are not doing any creative work and have no line of principle. The actor corps, with rare exceptions, is in a depressed state. The theater has eight staff directors and the same number of assistants, but they are staging only a few performances, and the others, while receiving a salary at the Art Theater, are working only on the side (Sakhnovsky, Litovtseva, Mordvinov, Teleshova, etc.).

There have been very few new productions, and most of even the most prominent actors have had no new roles. [. . .] V. Ya. Stanitsyn has been rehearsing the role of Molière for four years, and no one knows when the performance will be.

No creative work is being done with the actors, who are left to their own devices. The situation is particularly bad with the so-called young actors (with ten years' seniority at MKhAT): they are completely at a loose end, don't get new roles for years, no one is teaching them, no one is interested in their needs and requests.

[. . .]

The general state of dissatisfaction found especially vivid expression in a discussion of Com. Stalin's speech at a general meeting of artists at the graduation of students from the Military Academies. The meeting went on for two days, and at it the theater's principal leading directors and artists spoke.

[. . .]

After this meeting the mood deteriorated even more, for no changes occurred, and K. S. Stanislavsky's circle (deputy managing director Egorov and others) started behaving provocatively, slipping into counterrevolutionary speeches. [. . .]

The Department of Cultural-Educational Work feels it is essential that urgent measures be taken to bring MKhAT back to health and that, after eliminating the diarchy, a director be appointed there who is a member of the VKP(b) and has the necessary experience and authority among the artistic intelligentsia.

Stanislavsky and Nemirovich-Danchenko should be kept on as artistic directors and honorary directors.

One of the following candidates could be nominated for the position of director:

1. Boiarsky—VKP(b) member since 1919, VTsIK member, now chairman of the Rabis [Union of Arts Workers] TsK.

2. Cherniavsky—VKP(b) member since 1919, VOKS [All-Union Society for Cultural Relations with Foreign Countries] second deputy chairman.

3. Litovsky—VKP(b) member since 1918, head of Glavrepertkom.

4. Apletin—VKP(b) member since 1919 (form[er] Left SR, 1905–1918), was VOKS deputy chairman. Now secretary of the International Organization of Revolutionary Writers (MORP).

5. Imas—VKP(b) member since 1920, deputy head of the administration of theatrical performance enterprises of RSFSR Narkompros.

> Head of the TsK VKP(b) Department of Cultural-
> Educational Work
> A. Shcherbakov

· 93 ·

Letter from K. S. Stanislavsky to Stalin. AP RF, f. 3, op. 35, d. 24, ll. 29–32.
Original. Typewritten.
1 January 1936

Dear, deeply esteemed Iosif Vissarionovich.

I received your greetings, conveyed to me by Com. Zhivotova (the assis[tant] to the MKhAT director) and am deeply touched by your attention and your concern. From her I learned that you are interested in the situation at the Art Theater, and this obliges me to tell you the whole truth about it. I realize that I must do this very briefly, keeping in mind your heavy burden of matters of global importance.

The tremendous advances that are going on in all spheres of construction in our homeland, the new men, the new daily life, the new human civilization being conceived, compel me, one of the oldest representatives of the theater, seriously devoted to art as I am, to be alarmed over its fate. Our Theater can and must become our country's most vanguard theater in its reflection on stage of all the fullness of the inner spiritual life of the working man, who has become the master of our land.

Theater is in a state of stagnation all over the world. Ages-old traditions are dying out.

Fortunately, however, the USSR is at the present time the genuine heir to the best traditions of both the European theater and everything good there was in the old traditions of the Russian theater. We have to succeed at conveying what is most valuable to the young up-and-coming generation and together with them not only hold on to it but also strengthen it for further development. We, the representatives of contemporary theater, must be most concerned about preserving these seeds of age-old achievements in the theater and the development from them of a splendid new art. They can only be preserved in a theater of the very highest culture and the very highest artistry. This theater must be the epitome to which all other theaters aspire. At one time, the Maly Theater was that epitome, and later the Art [Theater]. Now there is no such true epitome. The Art Theater has plunged from its heights and been transformed at best into a decent production theater, but the audience's demands are growing and could outstrip it.

I would like to give all my experience, all my knowledge, all my time and health, all my last years to the creation of a genuine creative theater. In search of ways to create such a theater I have turned to the young people, having organized several months ago the Opera-Drama Studio, and with this same goal I am working on my second book, in which I want to pass on all my experience and all my knowledge. However, one of the most important ways is the preservation and development of the creative riches accumulated by the Art Theater. A certain section of the troupe treats these riches carelessly; they find unnecessary and inconvenient any creativity which makes great demands on the human artist.

It is this struggle between high aspirations and petty ephemeral interests that is going on at the present time at the Moscow Art Theater and that is tearing it to pieces. Creative experience and the aspiration to great art are on the side of the few remaining "old men" and some of the up-and-coming young people. On the other side is great energy directed at small, achievable tasks.

It is a difficult struggle, and timely assistance is needed in order, given the advanced age of both of us directors and the difference in our creative principles and the relations between us, which have become tangled in their forty years, to be able to pull the Theater out of the state in which it now finds itself. An experienced, cultured Communist director is essential, someone who could help V. I. Nemirovich-Danchenko and me settle our mutual differences for the Theater's cultural guidance. The most suitable candidate for this complex and difficult job seems to me to be Com. M. P. Arkadiev, head of the Theatrical Administration of the RSFSR NKP [People's Commissariat of Enlightenment], as someone with theatrical experience, tact, and great energy.

Along with this, the Theater's Party organization must be strengthened with a cultured and qualified director.

Essential too is a painstaking and strict review and reassessment of the Theater's entire creative collective in order to determine who is capable of great creative experimental work and of creating a genuine theater. We need to require Theater workers to improve their qualifications with all speed to reach the level of true masters of the art, establishing for this purpose a bonus reward.

We in the theater must fling out the slogan, "tempos to improve acting mastery," and then the rates of theatrical production, naturally, will rise on their own.

Persons who cannot join the collective of qualified masters must continue to work under the former conditions in the theater's Branch under MKhAT direction, filling their ranks with new actors to create a production theater.

MKhAT must be transformed into the epitome of the theatrical art. Knowing your love for the theater, I am counting on your help.

    Your devoted
    K. Stanislavsky

Stalin wrote on Stanislavsky's letter the instruction: "To Comrades Molotov, Akulov, Kerzhentsev, Bubnov, Shcherbakov. What should we do? I. Stalin." A reply came in just one week:

· 94 ·

Memorandum from TsK VKP(b) Department of Cultural-Educational Work (Kultprosvetotdel) Head A. S. Shcherbakov to I. V. Stalin on the situation at MKhAT. AP RF, f. 3, op. 35, d. 24, ll. 33–34. Original. Typewritten.
8 January 1936

To Com. I. V. Stalin

Regarding the essence of Com. Stanislavsky's letter, I report the following: The TsK VKP(b) Kultprosvetotdel, in its two memoranda addressed in your name, shed light on the difficult situation at the Gorky Moscow Academic Theater (the absence of unified leadership, the poverty of the repertoire and small number of new productions, the idleness of the artists who are therefore working on the side, the hopelessness and sadness among the artists, etc.). In reporting on this situation at the Gorky MKhAT, the department posed the question of appointing a Communist director to the theater who has the necessary authority and knowledge. All the actors are demanding leadership and strong authority.

A while ago, Stanislavsky was opposed to the appointment of a Communist director.

Now Com. Stanislavsky, striving to restore the position MKhAT has lost as the "epitome of the theatrical art," himself is requesting the appointment of a Communist director to the theater. I consider this proposal correct.

Besides the candidacy of Com. Arkadiev—for the post of theater director—we can nominate Com. Litovsky, the ch[ief] of Glavrepertkom.

A review and reassessment of the theater's creative collective are without question needed, but this undertaking must be carried out very cautiously and in any event after the theater's new leadership can familiarize itself with the actual state of affairs at the theater.

As concerns the remaining questions (training for actors, rates of work, expansion of the repertoire) posed by Com. Stanislavsky, they will be resolved together with the general recuperation of the situation at the theater.

Com. Stanislavsky and Com. Nemirovich-Danchenko should be left as honorary directors of MKhAT.

> H[ead] of the TsK VKP(b)Department of Cultural-
> Educational Work
> A. Shcherbakov

Arkadiev was appointed to direct MKhAT. Since his appointment was opposed by Nemirovich-Danchenko this fact probably attests to

Stanislavsky's enjoying greater favor with the Politburo. In this letter to Stalin Arkadiev mentions the fact that MKhAT was sent to Paris in 1937 to perform in conjunction with the famous exposition held there that year, an important moment in Soviet-Nazi Germany rivalry in that the exhibition pavilions of the two countries were placed across from each other so that they rivaled each other architecturally. However, in June 1937 Arkadiev was dismissed as director on the grounds that on several occasions, while in Paris for the 1937 Exposition, he had given interviews in which he gave details of MKhAT's future repertoire, though it had not yet been approved by the government.

· 95 ·

Excerpt from a letter from MKhAT director M. P. Arkadiev to I. V. Stalin.
RGASPI, f. 17, op. 163, d. 1147, ll. 88–90. Original. Typewritten.
26 April 1937

Dear Com. Stalin,
 I am writing this letter not because with its recent work MKhAT has proved that it is the leading theater of our Union and I want in any way to take advantage of this success for the theater.
[. . .]
 The most terrible disease for the theater, which threatened it with catastrophe, was creative inertia.
 MKhAT's creative work has manifested itself only in the fact that it has prepared a play once every two years. This was too little, and it was extremely dangerous for the normal, full-blooded life of the theater.
 The theater was growing sickly and decrepit, as were its actors, who had sat without work for years.
 I can say with full responsibility that now this disease has been eliminated and the entire collective is immersed in creative work to the maximum. This season MKhAT has already put on two major works: *Liubov Yarovaia* and *Anna Karenina*.
 But this is only half of the matter. I have set myself the task of putting on two more plays before the end of the season: Korneichuk's *Banker* [*Bankir*] and Pushkin's *Boris Godunov*.
[. . .]
 Even this would not be enough and I would consider my task unfinished if the repertoire [and] the timely output of plays next year were not provided for.
 Next year is a special year. It is an anniversary year, a year of triumph for our Party, Soviet power, and the workers.

Therefore I am proposing next year to put on at least three plays by Soviet playwrights and one classic play.

Work has already begun on two plays—Virta's play *Earth* [*Zemlia*] from his novel *Solitude* [*Odinochestvo*], and L. Leonov's play *Polovchan Gardens* [Polovchanskie *sady*]. I am trying to talk M. Sholokhov into writing the third play, but so far without success.

[. . .]

I am writing you this letter because, despite everything, I cannot conceal from you a mood of some offense that the theater's actors harbor and those abnormalities which from my point of view are hindering the theater's work.

The main thing the theater's collective talks about, anticipates, and worries about is the matter of an award for the theater.

As you know, four theaters already have the Order of Lenin. Not one of the Russian theaters has received an order.

The theater dreams of going to the Paris Exposition under the title—Order of Lenin Theater. It seems to me that these are worthy sentiments and good dreams.

I don't think I would be being overly subjective if I said that the theater has earned this award.

The second matter is more minor. But I am powerless to do anything more. Therefore, forgive me, I am writing to you.

[. . .]

How anyone can survive on this salary, I can't imagine. I know that from time to time I am forced to sew a suit or pants, to buy boots, to borrow small sums of money, and so forth.

One needs to have a great love for the theater and tremendous persistence in order to withstand these conditions.

But even the middle category of actors is not in terrific material condition. Their average salary is 600 rubles a month.

[. . .]

Forgive me for bothering you about these matters.

This is a very simple and at the same time a very complicated matter which I have been struggling with in vain for half a year.

Therefore I decided to write to you.

    With Communist greetings
    M. Arkadiev

On the letter are the following instructions: "To Molotov. I think we can approve both of Arkadiev's proposals with a correction, i.e., (a) give MKhAT the Order of Lenin, and (2) [*sic*] set the salary for MKhAT actors at from 400 rubles (minimum) to 3000 rubles (maximum). I. Stalin" and "To Com. Kerzhentsev. Please submit a draft on this basis. V. Molotov." Thus though the director was changed the crisis was also—and this was typical—resolved by compensating the potentially aggrieved in some positive way such as handing out material benefits or honors. In this case, more was also done and Stanislavsky was effectively canonized in his lifetime.

· 96 ·

Resolution of the TsK VKP(b) Politburo "On undertakings to mark the seventy-fifth anniversary of K. S. Stanislavsky's birth." RGASPI, f. 17, op. 3, d. 994, l. 66.
Original. Typewritten.
19 January 1938

No. 56, p. 307g—*On undertakings to mark the seventy-fifth anniversary of K. S. Stanislavsky's birth.*
Approve the following draft resolution of the Presidium of the USSR Supreme Soviet:
"Marking the exceptional services of People's Artist of the USSR Konstantin Sergeevich Stanislavsky in the development of the Soviet theatrical art, the Presidium of the USSR Supreme Soviet, in connection with the seventy-fifth anniversary of the birth of K. S. Stanislavsky, resolves:
1. To rename Leontiev Lane in Moscow, where K. S. Stanislavsky lives and works, K. S. Stanislavsky Street.
2. To establish five stipends in Stanislavsky's name at the A. V. Lunacharsky State Theatrical Institute.
3. To include in the plan for capital construction of the All-Union Committee on Arts Affairs under the USSR Sovnarkom for 1938 the construction of a new building for the Stanislavsky Studio at the USSR Order of Lenin Moscow Art Academic Theater named for M. Gorky.
4. To propose that the All-Union Committee on Arts Affairs under the USSR Sovnarkom publish the literary and scholarly works of K. S. Stanislavsky."

In the following document we see the impact of handing out honors to members of the Art Theater troupe. The document is also revealing of the mentality of Soviet cultural elite in 1937, the worst year of the purges, and the way they craved recognition from on high (coveted privileges also came with such awards).

· 97 ·

Special Report from the GUGB NKVD SSSR Secret Political Department on the reaction of the artists of the Bolshoi Theater to the awarding of orders and the bestowing of honorary titles. RGASPI, f. 17, op. 163, d. 1151, ll. 110–115. Original. Typewritten.

3 June 1937

The government's published resolution on the awarding of the Order of Lenin to the USSR State Academic Theater as well as orders and titles to many workers has evoked general enthusiasm.

The following statements have been recorded:

Ozerov, People's Artist of the RSFSR:

"Lately, they have not been giving me work. I'm thrilled at this attitude of the government toward me. They have given my spirits a terrific boost. I now have fresh new strength for further fruitful work."

Golovanov, Honored Figure of the Arts:

"I'm amazed at receiving the Order of the Red Banner of Labor. I'm afraid it was a mistake, that they confused me with Golovin, who is not on the list of recipients. If no mistake was made, then I look on this award as the very highest of the whole collective, for I had been feeling out of favor."

[. . .]

Melik-Pashaev, a conductor at GABT [*the State Academic Bolshoi Theater*], Honored Figure of the Arts:

"There are no bounds to my happiness. I cannot convey my delight. I am also happy because Nebolsin (a conductor at GABT) received a lesser one than mine."

[. . .]

Lepeshinskaia, ballet soloist of the Bolshoi Theater:

"I'm very happy. I'm only twenty-one and I've already received such a high award. This could only happen in the USSR."

Gabovich, ballet soloist of the Bolshoi Theater, Honored Artist of the Republic:

"I'm having the happiest day. Today I received an order, the title of Honored Artist, and today I was promoted from candidate to member of the VKP(b)."

Zlatogorova, Honored Artist:

"Rumors have been flying for months about the upcoming awards. I didn't believe this. Today's resolution is almost a complete surprise for me. I'm endlessly happy."

Politkovsky, Honored Figure of the Arts:

"I never expected such a high award. I'm very pleased. I hope that for the twentieth anniversary of the October Revolution I'll receive the title of People's Artist. Then I'll be completely content."

Maksakova, Honored Artist:

"I'm deeply touched at receiving the Order of the Red Banner of Labor, but at the same time I'm amazed at why they didn't award me the title of People's Artist, as they did Khanaev, who has only been on stage for ten years, while I've been on it seventeen."

[. . .]

Golovin, Honored Artist of the Republic:

"They didn't give me anything. I'm absolutely dead. Evidently they don't trust me politically. I'm afraid that repressive measures are going to be taken against me for statements that have been interpreted as praise of Trotsky. Despite the insult, I'm going to try to work wonderfully and show what I'm capable of. I'm going to get myself an order."[2]

Sulamith Messerer, ballet soloist of the Bolshoi Theater:

"I've spent eleven years working in the theater. The whole time I've been playing leading roles. When the rumors went around about the upcoming awards, I didn't have the slightest doubt that I'd be awarded somehow. What a bitter disappointment. Lepeshinskaia, who has only been working a few years, got an order, but I didn't. I can't show my face at the theater. I'm so ashamed."

[. . .]

Head of the GUGB NKVD Fourth Department
Sen[ior] Major of State Security
Litvin

CHAPTER TWELVE

The Anti-Formalist Campaign

On 16 December 1935 the Politburo passed a resolution "On the Organization of an All-Union Committee on Arts Affairs" (Komitet po delam iskusstv) which stipulated that it be organized "under the USSR Sovnarkom, investing it with the leadership of all arts affairs and subordinating to it the theaters, film organizations, and music, painting, sculpture, and other institutions," including "the main administration of the film and photography industry."[1] Now a single body ran not just a particular branch of the arts, but all the arts.

Shortly thereafter, in early 1936, a series of articles was published in *Pravda* that attacked the remnants of modernism in Soviet art. The first of these was "Muddle Instead of Music," published on 20 January 1936, which attacked Shostakovich's opera *Lady Macbeth of Mtsensk District* [*Ledi Makbet Mtsenskogo uezda*]. The criticisms were directed not just against this opera, but also against all "antipopular tendencies in music," as exemplified in the atonal music of the Shostakovich opera and its lack of melody. The critic was particularly exercised by the fact that the opera was, allegedly, hard for the broad masses to comprehend. In effect, the anti-Formalist campaign launched by this series of articles was conducted under the sign of an art that should be "simple," accessible to the broad masses.

The *Pravda* article attacking Shostakovich's opera was unsigned, making it all the more authoritative, and speculation continues to this day as to who actually wrote it. On 6 February 1936 a second article attacking Shostakovich appeared in *Pravda*, "Balletic Falsity" [Baletnaia fal'sh], which attacked the ballet *Limpid Stream (Svetlyi ruchei)*, a flawed attempt at a contemporary Soviet ballet set among kolkhoz workers in the Kuban region for which Shostakovich had written the music, some of it recycled sections of an earlier industrial ballet *Bolt*. During the ensuing months a large number of creative intellectuals were attacked as "Formalists" and a general campaign was launched against Formalism with meetings organized at every branch of the various creative unions at which individuals were denounced as "Formalists" and expected to recant. The principal targets of the "anti-Formalist campaign"—Shostakovich, Eisenstein, and Meyerhold—were all cult figures of the leftist avant-garde from the 1920s. All three were now labeled "Formalists," a label that had also been used against them in earlier attacks of 1930–1931. Those forces within Soviet culture that were opposed to modernism were now much more powerful, however. Already the day after "Balletic Falsity" appeared, a deeply shaken Shostakovich had the following audience with Kerzhentsev:

· 98 ·

Memorandum from P. M. Kerzhentsev, chairman of the Committee on Arts Affairs under the SNK SSSR, to I. V. Stalin and V. M. Molotov on his conversation with D. D. Shostakovich. AP RF, f. 3, op. 35, d. 32, l. 42.
Original. Typewritten.
7 February 1936

To Com. Stalin
To Com. Molotov

Today the composer Shostakovich came to see me (at his own initiative).

To my question about what conclusions he had drawn for himself from the article in *Pravda,* he replied that he wants to show by his creative work that he has accepted *Pravda*'s instructions for himself.

To my question about whether he acknowledges the criticism of his art in full, he said that he acknowledges most of it but has not fully comprehended it all. He asked me whether I felt it was necessary for him to write some letter. I said that for us the most important thing was that he reform himself, reject Formalist errors, and in his art attain something that could be understood by the broad masses, that his letter with an overview of his creative past and with some new obligations would have political significance, but only if it isn't a purely formal reply but is dictated by a genuine awareness of the fact that he must follow a different path.

I indicated to him that he should free himself from the influence of certain obliging critics, like Sollertinsky, who encourage the worst aspects in his art, which came about under the influence of Western Expressionists. I advised him, following the example of Rimsky-Korsakov, to travel through the villages of the Soviet Union and record the folk songs of Russia, the Ukraine, Belorussia, and Georgia and from them select and harmonize the hundred best songs. This suggestion piqued his interest, and he said he would follow up on it.

I suggested to him that before writing any opera or ballet, he should send us the libretto and during the process of working try out separate finished parts in front of an audience of workers and peasants.

He asked me to pass on the message that Soviet composers would like very much to meet with Com. Stalin for a discussion.

Kerzhentsev

From the very beginning the anti-Formalist campaign was recognized by those involved in the arts as relevant not just in terms of controversies in music or the ballet but much more broadly, for all of Soviet culture. One indicator of this is the fact that the NKVD followed reactions to these articles among intellectuals in all branches of culture—writers, poets, critics, theater directors, film directors—and of course composers as well.

· 99 ·

Report from the GUGB NKVD SSSR Secret Political Department on responses from writers and arts workers to articles in *Pravda* about the composer D. D. Shostakovich. [No later than 11 February 1936]. TsA FSB RF, f. 3, op. 3, d. 121, ll. 31–38. Original. Typewritten.

The publication in *Pravda* of "Muddle Instead of Music" was greeted positively by the majority of Moscow's writers and arts workers.

But along with this we have identified negative and anti-Soviet statements by individual writers and composers.

Below are cited the most characteristic of the negative responses.

Iu. Olesha (prose writer): In connection with the article in *Pravda* against Shostakovich, I am very concerned about the fate of my picture, which is supposed to come out on the screen any day now. My picture is many times more left-art than Shostakovich. What if they open fire on me with all their weapons? I don't understand the two contradictory acts: the adulation of Mayakovsky and the humiliation of Shostakovich. Shostakovich is Mayakovsky in music, he is the plenipotentiary for Soviet music abroad, he is a brilliant man, and a blow against Shostakovich is a calamity for art. If this is the new course, then it will lead to nothing except the authors of this article discrediting themselves. Great art will live despite everything.[2]

I. Babel: There's no need to make so much fuss over nothing at all. After all, no one took this seriously. The people are holding their tongue, but deep down they're having a good chuckle. Budenny cursed me even worse, and we got through it.[3] I'm certain the same will happen with Shostakovich.

L. Slavin (prose writer and playwright): I don't like Shostakovich, and I don't understand anything about music, but I'm afraid that a blow to Shostakovich is a blow to everyone who is trying to work along other than conventional lines. Even if *Pravda* was not contemplating such a blow, nonetheless literary bureaucrats, who are "happy to oblige," will immediately draw the appropriate organizational conclusions in literature. [. . .]

It's getting harder and harder to work.

I. Selvinsky (poet): In the West, Shostakovich's opera has been running with great success for three years. This kind of crude article, which thoroughly discredits Shostakovich, will be judged in the West as a blow to Soviet music.

[. . .]

Grigory Sannikov (prose writer): This careless treatment of a great gift is shocking. The force of the blow should be commensurate. They praised and praised him, and now, all of a sudden, Bang on the head! And all because at a viewing of *Quiet Flows The Don* [*Tikhy Don*],[4] the VKP(b) leadership happened to comment that Shostakovich was a lousy composer. Immediately, an article was readied for *Pravda*.

Viktor Shklovsky (writer): After Stalin's resolution on Mayakovsky came out, there was an instant effort to give it a limited interpretation. As if to say, this doesn't apply to Aseev. Now they've swept Shostakovich away without failing to give Meyerhold a swift kick. And what does it mean when it says that we have absolutely no need of "petty bourgeois innovation"? It's very carelessly written.

Vissarion Sayanov (writer): Here in Leningrad we greeted the Shostakovich story very gloomily. How easily it's all done: they went and took away a man's opportunity to work. The second article was written more gently, but still, the phrase concerning "unceremonious and clever people" is very reckless. Shostakovich should have been criticized a long time ago. I personally don't like him. But they should not have behaved this way.

[. . .]

A. Lezhnev (prose writer): "The horror of any dictatorship consists in the fact that the dictator does what his left foot wants. Like Don Quixotes, we are constantly dreaming, but reality simply teaches us the truth. I look on the Shostakovich incident as a phenomenon of like category to the book burning in Germany. What makes it any better? This fact has confirmed once again what I said previously, that we have much in common with the Germans, although we are ashamed of this kinship.[5]

S. Gorodetsky (poet): Although they did write that Shostakovich had created nonsense, I will tell one and all that *Lady Macbeth* is the best work of Soviet music; it's ridiculous to write as law what someone's left foot wants. And then it's terribly sad that they can make short shrift of people that way.

P. Zenkevich (poet and translator): This is a simple matter. The VKP(b) leadership didn't like Shostakovich's opera. Obsequious scribblers immediately latched on to the occasion and wrote that article.

But the article goes beyond insolence, it's false through and through, it ascribes qualities to Shostakovich that he doesn't have at all. Moreover, it's obvious that the article was written by someone who doesn't understand anything about music. And what is all this anyway: today they make short work of Shostakovich, and tomorrow they could do the same to Babel, Pasternak, and Meyerhold. Ultimately, you see, no one actually thinks there are music connoisseurs sitting on the TsK, and if the occasional opinion of one leader or another is going to be canonized right away, then the devil only knows what depths we'll sink to. If this had been published somewhere other than *Pravda,* you could make some objection, but now you can't. And what's most comical of all is that in this instance the leadership's point of view coincided with the point of view of all the counterrevolutionaries in art, who have rejected Shostakovich.

A. Shteinberg (poet): You can't call this anything but a sneak attack by hooligans. It's horrible that you can't even defend yourself. Here it is, our celebrated freedom: they spat in the face of all the honest arts workers, and we're supposed to keep quiet.

V. Kantorovich (prose writer): I think that the article about Shostakovich is a very ominous sign. And since there are allusions in it to "Meyerholdism" as well, and Left Art devices in poetry, I think that this is a signal for a return to the RAPP era. Under the flag of struggling for simplicity, a tacit censorship will be created that's even worse than RAPP.

If criticism here was in constant terror in general, then now people will be even more afraid to praise anything. The fear will be great. This article has done a great deal of harm.

A. Gatov (poet and translator): When there's a horde of hacks and when untalented people who are beneath Shostakovich's notice get the Order of Lenin, I consider this action against Shostakovich like a pogrom. And the fact that the documents were published simultaneously—the dethronement of the brilliant master Shostakovich and the awarding of medals to blockheads like Vurgun and Lakhuti—this testifies to the sad state of affairs here.

Lakhuti got a medal because he's a court poet, but he's got a lot less talent than the court poets of old.

Now the editors will start seeing dangerous innovation in everything. Naturalism and bad Panfyorovism are going to flourish in literature and art. RAPPites of all stripes are rubbing their hands with glee now that the end has come to freedom for writers and artists.

Andrei Platonov (prose writer): In the sphere of art, everything here is being built haphazardly, sometimes on personal grounds. An example is the review in *Pravda* of Shostakovich's opera *Lady Macbeth*. The play has been running for more than a year, after all, everyone has been praising it to the skies, and suddenly this anonymous sabotage. It's clear that someone very high and mighty happened to stop by the theater, listened without understanding anything about music, and sabotaged it. It really is wild. Shostakovich has been writing for a long time, he's an acknowledged master, he's been praised and lifted up to the heavens, and only just now has he suddenly tripped up. We are seeing a general decline in art here. And in vain do people think that if our writers are translated and read abroad then it is due to their talent or for some other reason. No, it's just that they like to read something exotic from time to time. They translate and publish Hindu writers, Chinese, Japanese, and ours, too, for the sake of the exotic. Whereas here they have triumphed.

[. . .]

G. Munblit (critic): The article may well be correct in its essence. Many musicians have said the same thing about Shostakovich before. But I very much dislike the fact that zealous people are drawing organizational conclusions from this article. Shostakovich's works are being removed from all concert programs. I don't think the TsK was looking for "those kinds of conclusions." Soon they'll start taking the furniture out of Shostakovich's apartment, but this is a man with European fame. Especially distasteful in the article is the reference to the fact that the foreign bourgeoisie likes Shostakovich. This is not an argument.

V. Grossman (prose writer): In my opinion, you should not write articles like that. According to my information, Shostakovich is still going strong, and in addition Europe is for him. Nonetheless, they have given him an undeservedly stiff sentence.

[. . .]

K. Dobronitsky (VKP(b) member, writer): The article was placed by Mekhlis after a phone call from the TsK. This is a direct order: struggle with formal experimentation. I'm not an admirer of Shostakovich, but he is searching for something new. And now all the composers are going to be writing tunes for the people. Here, if the higher-ups say "a," then down below they recite the entire alphabet.

Goffenshefer (critic): ... It's hard to think that all this was undertaken with the knowledge of the higher Party leadership. This is the deed of overzealous *Pravda* workers who will get a slap on the wrist for it.

[...]

Vs. Meyerhold: Pasternak is not going to attend the SSP [Writers Union] plenum, despite the fact that he was invited. He was very upset by the appearance of the article on Shostakovich, since he took the admonition about comprehensibility to apply to him. His verse, of course, is incomprehensible, and he knows it.

Shostakovich needs to be hit to make him get down to business and not write whatever comes to mind. But they hit him too hard. Now he's not going to know how to write. What would Mayakovsky have done if they'd told him: write this way, well, say, like Turgenev.

The article "Balletic Falsity" is incorrectly titled; it should be called "Ballet as Falsity." It's false art, on the stage both the kolkhoz farmers in *Limpid Stream* and the sailors from *Red Poppy* [*Krasnyi mak*] look identically false. We should be putting homegrown art on the stage, not showing a kolkhoz farm woman wearing a tutu and little wings.

Right now Shostakovich is in a very bad way. He received a call from my theater for him to write new music for *The Bedbug* [*Klop*], but he said he couldn't do anything.

It's hard for me as well. Right now I'm working on a production of *The Bedbug* and several times during work I've caught myself thinking—no, this would be Meyerholdism, it needs to be different.

[...]

The composer Derzhanovsky: The people are in tears laughing since it's turned out that the Party men don't know what to say about composers. It's a wonder after this outrageous incident we don't strike off for the remote provinces, into the lap of the nineteenth century.

The composer Shaporin: This article is worse than RAMP criticism. If during the RAMP era you could complain to the Party's TsK, for example, then now there's nowhere to appeal. The opinion of "one" man is still not something that can define a creative line. They're driving Shostakovich to the point of suicide; people say that they have put a ban on playing Shostakovich over the radio.

[...]

H[ead] of the GUGB Sec[ret] Polit[ical] Department
St[ate] Security Commissar 2nd Rank
Molchanov

In music, the campaign launched against the Shostakovich pieces effectively favored one side in the controversies of the 1920s between those who advocated that Soviet music build on the most advanced, modernist art, and their opponents who believed it should be based on folk traditions, on the songs written for the masses, or some other such readily comprehensible and melodic musical tradition (there had been analogous debates in art, literature, etc.). The various antimodernist lobbies welcomed the attacks on Shostakovich. Yet the rivalry was not completely resolved with this campaign and resurfaced exactly twelve years later in the famous TsK resolution, dated 10 February 1948, "On the opera *A Great Friendship* [*Velikaia druzhba*] by V. Muradeli" (see Chapter 23). In the following memorandum we see how, as the anti-Formalist campaign was pursued, not all intellectuals simply fell into line. Sollertinsky, one of those who resisted renouncing modernist music, was Shostakovich's close friend and mentor, a former member of the Bakhtin circle, and a music critic and theorist of a modernist orientation. It should be noted, also, that Shostakovich was never arrested or purged in the wake of the *Pravda* articles.

· 100 ·

Memorandum from TsK VKP(b) Department of Cultural-Educational Work Deputy Head A. I. Angarov to the TsK VKP(b) secretaries "On the discussion among musicians on the subject of the *Pravda* article on Formalism in music."
AP RF, f. 3, op. 35, d. 32, ll. 44–48. Original. Typewritten.
20 March 1936

The editorials in *Pravda* ("Muddle Instead of Music" and "Balletic Falsity") provoked the greatest animation among musicians of all tendencies and specialties. Meetings organized by the Moscow and Leningrad composers' unions devoted to discussion of these articles took place in overflowing halls. Discussion of the *Pravda* articles was especially lively among the composers and music scholars of Moscow and Leningrad but also in a number of musical-opera theaters (Moscow's Bolshoi Theater and Nemirovich-Danchenko Theater, Leningrad's Maly Opera Theater and Leningrad's Bolshoi Theater).

In the first few days of the discussion, most of the speeches suffered from abstractness and were declarative in nature, but at subsequent meetings the discussion acquired a more concrete nature. The overwhelming majority of speakers recognized without qualification the correctness and timeliness of *Pravda's* criticism. However, individual participants in the discussion in Moscow and Leningrad attempted to gloss over the significance of the articles in *Pravda* and to interpret them as an attempt at bad administering in the arts, and so forth.

Direct statements of disagreement with the *Pravda* articles were made by Sollertinsky and Rabinovich at meetings of Leningrad critics and music scholars. At a meeting on 5 February 1936, a music scholar (non-Party) stated that he disagreed with *Pravda* in its assessment of Shostakovich's opera *Lady Macbeth of Mtsensk District*, which he considers a brilliant work. At the same meeting, Sollertinsky stated that he intended to quit the music front. The statements by Sollertinsky and Rabinovich were condemned by the meeting. The same thoughts, but in more tempered form, were expressed by the Leningrad pianist and critic Druskin, who spoke out sharply against Dzerzhinsky's opera *Quiet Flows the Don*. All three—Sollertinsky, Rabinovich, and Druskin—are radical formalists wholly oriented toward Western European musical modernism. Their speeches evoked a sharp rebuff on the part of those gathered and were condemned in a resolution of the plenum of Leningrad critics and music scholars dated 7 February 1936.

A tight group of former ideologues and leaders of the Russian Association of Proletarian Musicians (RAMP [sic]),[6] including the f[ormer] general secretary of this association L. Lebedinsky, the critic and music scholar Shteinpress, and the historian Keldysh, spoke at the discussion of Moscow composers.

In his speech, L. Lebedinsky denied that Soviet music had any accomplishments to its credit and made an attempt to focus Soviet composers exclusively toward the art of the deceased composer Davidenko and his tendency (RAMP), which was condemned by a decision of 23 April 1932. Lebedinsky asserted that "some of Davidenko's magisterial works are the very Soviet classics that will live for ages."

[. . .]

Among the positive speeches, we should note the speech of Prof. Neigauz, a very prominent Soviet pianist.[7] Prof. Neigauz subjected the conceit and arrogance that is still widespread on the music front to harsh criticism and stated that Shostakovich should have been grateful to *Pravda* for rousing him to new life and pointing out the correct paths of creativity. Protesting Formalism in musical creativity, Neigauz considers the articles in *Pravda* a "call to great art." "The appearance of these articles," says Neigauz, "despite their harshness, despite the fact that they have struck painfully at our entire 'musical estate,' is a joyous, life-affirming phenomenon."

At the composers' discussion, the major theoreticians of Formalism in music kept their counsel. The desire to keep their counsel is characteristic for quite a number of composers and music scholars from both Moscow and Leningrad. The acknowledged head of the so-called "Moscow school" of Formalists, the major composer of symphonies N. Ia. Miaskovsky, former leader of the Association of Contemporary Music (ASM), which has joined an international association of bourgeois modernist-musicians, he did not even show up for the discussion, which lasted for three days. In the same fashion his students, the composer Shebalin and others, did not speak. In Leningrad, the most visible of the theoreticians of Formalism, the music scholar B. V. Asafiev (Igor Glebov), author of *On Stravinsky* [*Kniga o Stravinskom*], *Musical Form as Process* [*Muzikal'naia forma kak protsess*], and so forth, is getting off with silence. Characteristic is the unique artistic "double-dealing" of Asafiev, who propagates Formalism, extols the trans-sense music of the German Expressionists Schoenberg and Alban Berg, but himself, as a composer, composes music that is relatively accessible. It must, however, be borne in mind that Shostakovich was reared specifically on the theoretical compositions of Asafiev, who is the author of a number of complimentary articles about Shostakovich (including about *Lady Macbeth of Mtsensk District*).

There is undoubtedly a conspiracy of silence among the Formalists of various tendencies, even those who have been enemies in the past. By way of example I can point to the Leningrad professor Shcherbachev, who is Shostakovich's artistic opponent but who in the hallways spoke out in his defense. Also Shostakovich's opponent is Miaskovsky, who in private conversations even before the appearance of the *Pravda* articles harshly condemned the ballet *Limpid Stream*. The day *after Pravda's* statement, Miaskovsky occupied a position of "friendly neutrality" toward Shostakovich. The conduct of all these individuals is nothing but a covert form of sabotage of the Party's instructions. In essence it stems from the principle of noninterference by the Party in the internal affairs of art.

In the course of the entire discussion, musicians' corporate, workshop biases, which hinder the development of straightforward Bolshevik self-criticism, still had a powerful effect. This circumstance was commented on by a number of speakers, and on the last day of the discussion the criticism took on a more direct and specific nature.

In no event should the discussion of the *Pravda* articles be considered exhausted at this point. The most prominent formalists have yet to disarm. Many artistic issues of Socialist Realism in music have only been posed and await resolution. The TsK VKP(b) Department of Cultural-Educational Work has proposed that the organizations of musicians and composers hold further discussion of all these issues on the basis of an analysis of specific works of musical art.

  Dep[uty] Head of the TsK VKP(b) Cultural-Educational
  Department
  Angarov

The following report, which was drafted early in December 1935, i.e., on the eve of the mid-thirties revolution in Soviet culture, concerns the world of Soviet art but is indicative of the point already made—the extent to which those participating in the aesthetic debates of the 1930s were largely promoting positions held by them in the debates of the 1920s, though in many instances these positions now had to be presented obliquely or in watered-down versions. Among those figuring in this document, Shterenberg, Ehrenburg, and Deineka had all been closely linked with the leftist avant-garde of the 1920s while those mentioned as "leading artists in MOSKh" were all traditionalists who enjoyed the patronage of leading Party figures.

· 101 ·

Special Report from the GUGB NKVD SSSR Secret Political Department to the TsK VKP(b) on the conference of Moscow artists. AP RF, f. 3, op. 35, d. 43, ll. 2–4. Original. Typewritten.

2 December 1935

The attention of Moscow artists is focused on the creative conference taking place at the present time on the theme, "The Problem of the Soviet Portrait."

The conference sessions of 19 November and 29 November went beyond the framework of the originally assigned theme and the conference turned into a general creative discussion on the topic of the paths of Soviet painting.

A pivotal moment in the work of the conference was the speech by a distinguished figure in art, the paint[er] Shterenberg, on 19 November 1935, former director of the Soc[iety] of Easel Painters (OST), which existed before the TsK resolution of 23 April 1932 on restructuring literary and artistic organizations.

Shterenberg's speech was sharply indicative. Shterenberg, in very harsh formulations, advanced a demand for freedom of creative groupings and came down hard on the leadership of the Mosc[ow] Assoc[iation] of Soviet Artists (MOSKh), accusing it of stifling creative competition and of foisting on all artists the tastes and aims of the group in whose hands the MOSKh leadership was held at the present moment, a group of former members of the Association of Artists of Revolutionary Russia.

Shterenberg stated that the MOSKh leadership had led to real artists going hungry, that he personally had gone hungry for two years, and that the TsK VKP(b) resolution of 23 April 1932 was a failure, since, in his opinion, what had been achieved in the artistic sphere was "commercial" rather than Socialist Realism.

The continuation of Shterenberg's speech took place on 27 November. Declaring at the start that he recognized several points in his first speech as in error, for instance his statement that artists, in particular he himself, were going hungry, Shterenberg, continuing his speech, made counterrevolutionary assertions to the effect that there is no freedom of creativity in Soviet reality, that creativity is confined within a narrow framework and that creativity has turned into "venal labor."

Shterenberg's speech enjoyed a great success with the audience, his speech was interrupted several times by applause and approving shouts.

On 27 November, at a session of the conference, the writer I. Ehrenburg, who on a number of points supported Shterenberg's aims, spoke. Ehrenburg declared the leading group of MOSKh—Brodsky, Katsman, A. Gerasimov, and others—the "rear guard of Soviet art," which for some reason that no one can understand had elevated itself to the avant-garde, and stated that the art of this group cannot be great revolutionary art since the torments of questioning and the raptures of achievement are unknown to it.

Ehrenburg's speech enjoyed major success. The following incident is characteristic: the artist Bogorodsky shouted from his seat that Ehrenburg was speaking that way because his wife was studying with Picasso (a radically leftist French artist in terms of formal approach). This shout aroused tremendous indignation from the hall, and to cries of "Down with that," "Away with him," "Beat him," "Hooligan with a Party ticket," and so forth, Bogorodsky had to leave the meeting.

On 29 November, Mikhoels, an artist from the Jewish Chamber Theater, and Deineka the artist spoke in the discussion, having also successfully supported Shterenberg. In particular, to the complete surprise of the MOSKh leadership and the conference presidium, Deineka stated that "we have artists who hold the sources of material goods in their hands and sit on presidiums," while a seat on the presidium should be not for them but for Shterenberg, whom artists respect because they have learnt, and continue to learn, a great deal from him.

To a significant degree, the success of Shterenberg's speech can be explained by the circumstance that the C[entral] O[ffice] of MOSKh (the management organization of the Moscow Union of Artists) ended 1935 with a major financial loss, and owes artists under its contracts and for the work performed as much as 100,000 rubles. Debts to individual artists have not been paid for from three to six months or so.

[. . .]

In circles close to Shterenberg, they are repeating what he said about TsK VKP(b) instructor Com. Dinamov supposedly telling Shterenberg about the impending removal of the current MOSKh leadership. This rumor, like the restraint of the principal speaker at the conference, Beskin (head of the painting department at Narkompros) regarding the group of Katsman, Brodsky, and others, have been interpreted as a sign of an anticipated restoration of previously existing artistic groups and organizations.

The conference continues. The next session will be held on 9 December 1935.

>H[ead] of the GUGB Sec[ret] Polit[ical] Department
>G. Molchanov

Our next document comes from a mere year after the preceding one, and in comparing them one gets a good sense of the changes in the art world wrought by the anti-Formalist campaign.

· 102 ·

Memorandum from Chairman P. M. Kerzhentsev of the Committee on Arts Affairs under the SNK SSSR to I. V. Stalin and V. M. Molotov on the need to remove artistic compositions of the Russian avant-garde from museum exhibitions. RGASPI, f. 17, op. 163, d. 1108, ll. 125–126. Original. Typewritten.
19 May 1936

To Com. I. V. Stalin
To Com. V. M. Molotov

In the last twenty to twenty-five years, our country's two foremost museums, the St[ate] Tretiakov Gallery and the Russian Museum, have been filled with compositions of a Formalist and naturalist kind. Insignificant in their artistic importance and, in a number of instances, simply harmful compositions, they take up, however, to this day, a significant portion of the museums' exhibition space (for instance, compositions by the Jack of Diamonds [*Bubnovyi valet*] group[8] and other Formalist cliques). I am attaching photographs of a number of these kinds of pictures). At the same time, many pictures, sculptures, and drawings by the best Russian realist masters of the nineteenth and twentieth centuries are being kept in storerooms.

Thanks to the large number of Formalist compositions, the Soviet period is represented falsely in the Tretiakov Gallery.

The inadmissibly low level of many compositions supposedly characterizing the Soviet period is especially startling in comparison with the marvelous exhibit of I. Repin. This kind of "picture" naturally evokes sharp responses among worker visitors.

Hence arises the task of reviewing the appropriate sections of our museums in order to preserve in the exhibition halls the best realistic compositions of our era and in part those compositions by prominent masters that are close to realism.

The review must now touch on only the two museums (Tretiakov Gallery and Russian Museum) and only the pictures of the last twenty to twenty-five years.

As for works that are subject to removal from exhibition but are at the same time material for art-historical study, it makes sense to separate them in a special building closed to the mass viewer.

Along with this rehanging of pictures, and based on the experience of the Repin exhibit, the Committee on Arts Affairs, for the purposes of propaganda for realist art, proposes organizing several exhibitions of this nature—Surikov, Rembrandt, and so forth.

I request approval for the following resolution:

1. Approve the proposal of the Committee on Arts Affairs to remove from the general exhibition halls of the Tretiakov Gallery and Russian Museum (in Leningrad) compositions of a Formalist and crudely naturalistic nature from the last twenty-five years.

2. Approve the organization by the Committee on Arts Affairs of special exhibitions of the realist artists Repin, Surikov, and Rembrandt.[9]

Kerzhentsev

During the course of 1936 a number of programmatic articles establishing the new line appeared in *Pravda*, prepared either by the Committee for Arts Affairs under Kerzhetsev or by the Committee on Cinema headed by Boris Shumiatsky. The following year the anti-Formalist campaign focused on another branch of the arts, cinema, and the main target was another major name, Sergei Eisenstein.

Eisenstein, who had not been able to complete a single project for a feature film since *The General Line* (*General'naia linia,* also known as *The Old and the New* [*Staroe i novoe*]) of 1929, was assigned the task in 1935 of making a film about Pavlik Morozov, a legendary young Pioneer who had died a martyr's death at the hands of the kulaks after denouncing his own father to the authorities as involved in a kulak conspiracy (this official version of the circumstances of Pavlik's death, incidentally, was false in many of its claims). As the film's title suggests (it is taken from a short story by Ivan Turgenev), however, Eisenstein's conception of the film was not circumscribed by his instructions to eulogize an official hero who was as it were the patron saint of purging. On 5 March 1937, two days after the end of the Central Committee plenum which established the official rationale for the Great Purge, came a memorandum from State Administration of Cinematography Head B. Z. Shumiatsky to the members of the Politburo of the TsK VKP(b) on the situation surrounding the production of Eisenstein's film *Bezhin Meadow* [*Bezhin lug*].

Though the film was subsequently banned by a Politburo decree, as the following documents suggest, not all official decisions were merely top-down, and there was maneuvering and dissent even during these most "totalitarian"-seeming times. Eisenstein had many influential supporters and they enlisted Lion Feuchtwanger among others in their struggle to prevent the film from being banned. Feuchtwanger was a popular German novelist and leader of the international antifascist alliance of intellectuals. Though resident in France since the Nazi takeover of 1933, he was a co-editor of the Moscow-sponsored and published German language journal *Das Wort* [*The Word*] (1936–1939). At this time (1937) he was particularly powerful in the Soviet context in that he had been essentially commissioned to write a rejoinder (*Moscow, 1937*) to Andre Gide's *Back from the USSR*, which had caused a scandal in Soviet Russia with its negative account of Gide's visit there in 1936.

· 103 ·

Report by State Administration of Cinematography Head B. Z. Shumiatsky to members of the TsK VKP(b) Politburo on the situation concerning S. M. Eisenstein's production of *Bezhin Meadow*. TsA FSB RF, d. R-4377, t. 2, ll. 228–228v. Copy. Typewritten.
5 February 1937

To the TsK VKP(v)
To Com. I. V. Stalin
To Com. V. M. Molotov
To Com. A. A. Andreev

S. Eisenstein has been producing a film of kolkhoz life, *Bezhin Meadow*, for more than a year and a half.

We have already redone this film several times, for the director had given in it frankly mistaken and Formalist interpretations.

However, we have liberal patrons who literally gape at Eisenstein and know only one thing—how to praise every single work of his, even if it is frankly erroneous.

A few days ago, we, the Union's cinema leadership, had occasion to encounter at our All-Union production conference a line of organized "defense" for Eisenstein from our principled critics. Representing this line at the conference were the leaders of our Moscow film studio, Mosfilm, who spoke at this conference and outside of it in open defense of Eisenstein's mistakes. A number of other individuals tacitly defended him, too, including some who are not even cinematographers (Angarov, Tamarkin).

Even the specialized arts press did not publish our criticism of the politically evil-smelling works and mistakes of Eisenstein. I'm certain that this was done out of considerations of piety toward him.

But what was our amazement when today we read in the organ of the All-Union Committee on Arts [Affairs], in *Sovetskoe iskusstvo* [*Soviet art*] (no. 6/352, 5 February 1937), the apologetic review by Lion Feuchtwanger supposedly about Eisenstein's *Bezhin Meadow*, although this film is only 60–70 percent shot, has not been edited at all, and in addition according to our existing rules cannot be shown even in separate parts to anyone, especially a foreigner.

In this instance we have a disgraceful attempt to appeal to foreign public opinion regarding our assessments of Soviet films.

This could happen because we have in Moscow *a number of individuals who overtly and covertly are conducting a campaign of struggle supposedly in defense of Eisenstein,* in this way helping some scoundrel abroad wage this very campaign in defense of Eisenstein against a nonexistent enemy.

Among these individuals there are several writers, several cinematographers, and, as is attested to by the compliant placement of Feuchtwanger's discussion about an as yet nonexistent film on the pages of the organ of the All-Union Committee on Arts [Affairs], several workers from the Arts Committee.

If in this case we were talking only about Mosfilm workers who have taken in this matter an unprincipled line by appealing to Feuchtwanger regarding our assessments of Eisenstein's mistakes, I could resolve this matter by taking organizational measures against our workers.

In this instance, however, we are dealing with a small group of workers from a number of spheres of the arts and several workers from the press, a clique that is taking on a politically dangerous character.

I request that this matter be sorted out at the TsK.

I am attaching a copy of a conversation between an employee of *Sovetskoe iskusstvo* and Feuchtwanger and my critique of the defense of Eisenstein and clips from his *Bezhin Meadow* at the Eighth All-Union Cinema Conference.

B. Shumiatsky

Exactly one month later the Politburo resolved to ban the film and in so doing attacked it sharply on political grounds. Such attacks, coming in the spring of 1937 when the Great Purge was at its height, could have had the most dire consequences for those involved in making the film, though Eisenstein was never purged.

· 104 ·

Resolution of the TsK VKP(b) Politburo on the ban on the production of *Bezhin Meadow*. RGASPI, f. 17, op. 3, d. 984, l. 18. Original. Typewritten.
5 March 1937

No. 46, p. 82—*On the production by director S. Eisenstein of the film* Bezhin Meadow, *on the viewing of startups [sic][10] from this film, and on its screenplay.*
 1. Ban this production in view of the film's anti-artistic nature and blatant political bankruptcy.
 2. Instruct Com. Shumiatsky not to allow film studios to release films into production, as in the given instance, unless they have given preliminary approval of the exact screenplay and dialogue.
 3. Suggest to Com. Shumiatsky that in the future he permit the production of films only if they follow completely the screenplays, dialogue, and general projects he has approved.
 4. Require Com. Shumiatsky to clarify the present resolution to the cinema's creative personnel and to impose an administrative fine on the guilty parties in this prolonged delay in banning this mistaken production.

This resolution, which had been prompted by Eisenstein's old enemy Shumiatsky, was opposed by many intellectuals, as Shumiatsky reports to Molotov here:

· 105 ·

Memorandum from State Administration of Cinematography Head B. Z. Shumiatsky to V. M. Molotov, on the reaction of some of the cultural public to the Politburo TsK VKP(b) resolution banning the production of *Bezhin Meadow*.
TsA FSB RF, d. R-4377, t. 2, ll. 230–230v. Copy. Typewritten.
28 March 1937

To Com. Molotov.

The ban of production work on the film *Bezhin Meadow* was met by certain elements that do not share the Party's line in matters of art literally with bestial fury. Without risking coming out openly against the TsK decision, they are mobilizing all their forces to discredit this decision by slandering us—those carrying out this decision.

The matter is reaching the point where at the Writers Union, in concealment from its secretary Com. Stavsky, a meeting has already been held of some writers and playwrights in order to work out a line of defense for Eisenstein and to discredit me as the stifler of the "brilliant world artist S. Eisenstein." We have been told that through the German writer Lilo Damert, who left to go abroad a few days ago, a request has been sent to Feuchtwanger regarding defending Eisenstein, for which his supporters (Com. Sokolovskaia), during Feuchtwanger's visit with us (February 1937), without letting me know, showed him clips from this defective film and, as I have written to you, foreseeing the banning of this production, insisted that Feuchtwanger come out in our press with a promotional article about the defective *Bezhin Meadow* as a masterpiece.

Worst of all, though, is the fact that this entire company is actively supported by certain organs of our press, with the exception of *Pravda*. They, for example the newspaper *Izvestia*, are doing this by means of total silence about the decision of the Party's TsK banning *Bezhin Meadow*.

No less infuriating is the position of the TsK's Department of Cultural-Educational Work head, Com. Angarov, and the head of the film sector of the department, Com. Tamarkin. Instead of helping us convey the TsK decision on *Bezhin Meadow*, Comrades Angarov and Tamarkin are using their position as Party workers to give Eisenstein's entire clique a weapon to defame us politically, to defame Party members working in film who are implementing the Party line in the matter of Eisenstein's anti-Soviet production. And this at a time when so recently Com. Tamarkin demanded of me in writing that we "don't kill" Eisenstein but let him continue producing *Bezhin Meadow*.

This entire revolt by representatives of the petty bourgeois bohemia led a few days ago to the point where, at our Moscow studio [Mosfilm], the administration in the persons of Comrades Babitsky and Sokolovskaia collected for a viewing of Eisenstein's banned *Bezhin Meadow* not only cinematographers but also writers, especially apologists for the "genius" Eisenstein. At this viewing not only was material from a film banned by the TsK shown but Eisenstein was also given an opportunity to deliver an extended report about what he had not yet shot. Eisenstein gave his speech the character of an appeal against the production ban.

After this viewing, the studio's administration gathered in their office a group of Eisenstein supporters—Vs. Vishnevsky, B. Lapin, Z. Khatsrevin, and several others—for a closed meeting.

I request your instructions.

B. Shumiatsky

One year after the above alarming development in cinema, a Politburo resolution closed the Meyerhold Theater, one of the few experimentalist theaters remaining. The closure of the Meyerhold Theater marks a stage in the progressive demise of Meyerhold which began in earnest with the *Pravda* article "Muddle Instead of Music," an attack not only on Shostakovich but also on "Meyerholditis." But since then the mechanism for conducting the anti-Formalist campaign had been radicalized. The *Pravda* article had launched an ideological purge entailing discussions and mass meetings but virtually no repressions of the individuals named. By late 1936 the campaign had taken a more sinister turn and Meyerhold was ultimately to be its victim. After his theater was closed, in June 1939 he was arrested and in February 1940 shot.

· 106 ·

Resolution of the TsK VKP(b) Politburo on the closure of the Vs. Meyerhold State Theater (GOSTIM). RGASPI, f. 17, op. 3, d. 994, ll. 52–53. Original. Typewritten. Published in *Pravda*, 8 January 1938; *Teatr* [Theater], no. 1 (1938): 5.

7 January 1938

No. 56, p. 252—*On eliminating the Vs. Meyerhold Theater.*

Approve the following decree for the All-Union Committee on Arts Affairs under the SNK SSSR:

The Committee on Arts Affairs under the SNK SSSR determines that the Meyerhold theater has completely backslid to positions alien to Soviet art and has become alien for the Soviet viewer:

1. Throughout its entire existence, the Meyerhold Theater has been unable to free itself from thoroughly bourgeois Formalist positions alien to Soviet art. As a result of this, in the service of Left Art's love of stunts and Formalist capering, even classical works of Russian drama have been presented in the theater in a distorted, anti-artistic form, perverting their ideological essence (*Inspector General* [*Revizor*], *Woe to Wit* [*Gore umu*], *Death of Tarelkin* [*Smert' Tarelkina*],[11] etc.);

2. The Meyerhold Theater has proved itself totally bankrupt in producing the plays of Soviet dramaturgy. The production of these plays has offered a perverted, slanderous picture of Soviet reality permeated with [ambiguity and even outright][12] anti-Soviet ranting (*The Suicide* [*Samoubiitsa*], *A Window on the Village* [*Okno v derevniu*], *Commander of the Second Army* [*Komandarm II*],[13] etc.);

3. In the last few years, Soviet plays have completely disappeared from the theater's repertoire, [a number of the best actors have left the theater,] and Soviet playwrights have turned their backs on the theater, which has isolated itself from all the public and artistic life of the Union;

4. For the twentieth anniversary of the October Revolution, the Meyerhold Theater not only did not prepare a single production but made a politically hostile attempt to produce Gabrilovich's play *One Life* [*Odna zhizn'*], which perverts in an anti-Soviet way the [celebrated work] of art by N. Ostrovsky, *How the Steel Was Tempered* [*Kak zakalialas' stal'*].[14]

Apart from everything else, this production was an abuse of state funds on the part of the Meyerhold Theater, which has gotten used to living off state monetary subsidies.

In view of all this, the Committee on Arts Affairs under the SNK SSSR resolves:

a. to eliminate the Vs. Meyerhold Theater as alien to Soviet art;

b. to use the theater's troupe in other theaters;

c. to discuss separately the matter of the possibility of Vs. Meyerhold continuing to work in theater.

The anti-Formalist campaign was one of the central events in the cultural life of the 1930s, which left its mark on Soviet culture for the rest of the Stalin period. Thereafter, the element of fear that became ingrown among intellectuals became fundamental to Soviet cultural life, regardless of whether at a given moment there were purges or not.

CHAPTER THIRTEEN

The Campaign for a Patriotic Culture

1936 saw another significant shift in cultural policy, the turn to nationalism. The Communist Party had come to power with an ideology that rejected the old regime and all it stood for, and the prerevolutionary regime was variously labeled a "prison of the ethnic nations," a hateful empire, a police state, and a backward country; but in this year a campaign was launched to struggle against what was called an "irreverent attitude towards the past." The past of Russia now acquired positive coloration, and cultural workers were instructed to mine it for examples of "the heroism of the people," and of the "wisdom" of its leaders (tsars) who had fought to "strengthen the state," to unify it and protect its independence from external enemies. In consequence, the "beautiful music," "realistic art," and "cinema accessible to the masses" demanded in the rhetoric of the anti-Formalist campaign were directly identified with the national (by which was especially meant a largely Russian) tradition. The progressive evolution to be seen in Eisenstein's change of subject matter from the revolutionary themes of the 1920s to rulers of the Russian nation (Alexander Nevsky, Ivan the Terrible) is indicative of this shift.

A prominent casualty of the shift was Demian Bedny. Bedny, a popular poet from prerevolutionary times who had been close to Lenin and Stalin, did not understand the ideological shifts that were taking place in the 1930s. He had also made the mistake of being somewhat familiar in addressing Stalin, naively assuming that their collaboration before the Revolution gave him that right. In the late 1920s and early 1930s this had led to a break in relations in a heated exchange of letters (see docs. 28, 29, and 30). At this later time Bedny became the scapegoat of the campaign to "affirm the heroic past"; as is clear in the Politburo documents, there were political as well as ideological reasons why he in particular was singled out.

The ban on the opera *The Bogatyrs* [Bogatyri] for which Bedny had written the libretto was but one of many events that signaled a shift from a more communist internationalist and even Popular Frontist Soviet culture to one that claimed the Soviet Union as the true bearer of the Russian national tradition (clearly the growing threat of war played some role in the shift). The *bogatyr* was the fantastic knight of Russian fairy tale and folk epic, genres which at this time were being revived. Surviving bards of the folk tradition were commissioned to write new (pseudo-)epics which, using traditional folk forms and motifs, extolled the glories of the new regime, its economic achievements and leaders, while simultaneously recounting the dastardly deeds of their enemies. Bedny's parody of the *bogatyrs* in his libretto was seen as a defamation of a newly revered tradition and potentially also of the leadership itself (he had wrongly assumed that one could mock the Russian past in 1936 as he had in 1919 and even 1929). Consequently, although Bedny had been a literary mainstay of prerevolutionary *Pravda* he was made an example of, and in 1938 expelled from the Writers Union. A. Tairov who staged the operetta at his Kamernyi Theater was a leading modernist director and as such a rival of Meyerhold.

· 107 ·

Resolution of the TsK VKP(b) Politburo on banning D. Bedny's play *The Bogatyrs*. RGASPI, f. 17, op. 3, d. 982, l. 40. Original. Typewritten.
14 November 1936

No. 44, p. 202—*On the play* The Bogatyrs *by Demian Bedny.*
Approve the following draft resolution from the Committee on Arts Affairs:

In view of the fact that Demian Bedny's comic opera, produced under the supervision of A. Ya. Tairov at the Chamber Theater using music by Borodin,

a. is an attempt to extol the brigands of Kievan Rus' as a positive revolutionary element, which contradicts history and is thoroughly false in its political tendency;

b. indiscriminately blackens the *bogatyrs* of Russia's storied past, whereas in the national imagination the most important *bogatyrs* are the bearers of the heroic characteristics of the Russian people;

c. gives an antihistorical and mocking depiction of Old Russia's acceptance of Christianity, which was in reality a positive stage in the history of the Russian people, since it helped bring the Slavic peoples closer to peoples of a higher culture,

The Committee on Arts Affairs under the SNK SSSR resolves:

1. To remove *The Bogatyrs* from the repertoire as alien to Soviet art.
2. To propose to Com. Kerzhentsev that he write an article in *Pravda* in the spirit of the present decision.

Bedny was widely disliked in intellectual circles. He was close to all the leaders in the Kremlin and until his falling-out with Stalin had lived there. But he was also a somewhat primitive poet who wrote crude agitational verses (even Lenin, who was very much in favor of agitational poetry, admitted that his were crude). Essentially a mouthpiece of the Party line, he had written his most popular poetry during the Civil War. Consequently, in the reactions to his downfall recorded below one can find much malicious glee. Yet we also see in this document glee at the predicament of Tairov, who directed the production but who was himself far from a "crude" agitationalist or purveyor of the Party line. This glee was expressed not only by personnel from the MKhAT and the Bolshoi Theater, which were more traditional so that one could predict that they would be in favor of attacks on modernist "Formalism," but also by Meyerhold.

· 108 ·

Report from the GUGB NKVD SSSR Secret Political Department "On the responses of writers and arts workers to the removal of D. Bedny's 'The Bogatyrs' from the repertoire." [No later than 16 November 1936]. TsA FSB, f. 3, op. 3, d. 121, ll. 98–107. Copy. Typewritten.

A. *Tairov* (stunned by the committee's resolution removing *The Bogatyrs* announced that he was ill—a heart attack. Art workers went to see him at home and expressed their sympathy. According to A. Koonen, many people visited, as one does the recently deceased):

"I made a major mistake. I take all responsibility, despite the fact that the Committee on Arts Affairs, which passed the performance, approved it. My mistake consists in the fact that I as an artist should have foreseen all the consequences.

"It's insulting that my mistake is being taken as a sortie, which is how they are writing about it.

"The mistake occurred because I put great trust in Demian Bedny who is an old Communist. How could I have imagined that D. Bedny's text constituted a harmful tendency, how could I be a commissar for D. Bedny? This mistake was not made in *An Optimistic Tragedy* [*Optimisticheskaia tragedia*][1] or in *Homeland* [*Rodina*], where the authors are less authoritative and I subjected their plays to the criticism of authoritative officials.

"I will go to the TsK VKP(b), where, I hope, they will understand me. There I will raise the issue of how new shows need to be shown not only to the committee but to the TsK as well.

"This is essential for a guarantee.

"What really frightens me is whether they will let me keep working. What infuriates me is the desire to set me up as a renegade from the people. This is so dreadful I can't even think about it calmly."

[...]

Tsenin, Honored Artist of the Kamernyi Theater:

"Until the monarchy in our theater ends, all questions will be decided single-handedly by Tairov, who does not take into account the theater's leading personnel, and the theater will be plagued by political debacles."

Gersht, director at the Chamber Theater:

"The resolution is fundamentally correct. We are supposed to stage *Eugene Onegin* [*Evgenii Onegin*]. I predict that there will be the same story with that as there has been with *The Bogatyrs.*"

Demian Bedny. Demian Bedny is utterly shaken by the resolution of the Committee on Arts Affairs. For three days he did not go out at all, received no one, and only yesterday called in SSP Secretary Stavsky for a confidential talk. From all that follows it is clear that Demian Bedny, while reluctant to appeal personally to the TsK VKP(b) secretaries, wishes to use Stavsky to convey his explanations and justifications. Stavsky, finding Demian Bedny in a state of utter distraction, brought along a stenographer to give the report on this talk a documentary nature.

The general sense of Demian Bedny's explanations on the subject of *The Bogatyrs,* as set down in the transcript, is approximately the following. The farcical tone of the piece and the treatment of *The Bogatyrs* are explained by the character of the music. Thus, for instance, the "bogatyrs" sing arias from popular operettas. The farcical display of Old Russia's acceptance of Christianity and its incorrect interpretation is explained by the habit of antireligious propaganda that lingers on in Demian Bedny's practice. On the other hand, he was let down by works in his possession on historical issues that are far from Marxist in orientation.

Admitting that he made a huge mistake, Demian Bedny explains it by his failure to understand the material and by his own stupidity. However, in the conversation he frequently returned to the role of the oversight organs and indicated that at the very beginning of his work on *The Bogatyrs,* a year and a half ago, the original text did not satisfy him, it seemed frivolous and stupid, but Tairov and Litovsky encouraged him, convincing him that the text was turning out brilliantly for a stage piece.

Shortly before the performance, a fairly well-worked text was submitted to the Committee on Arts Affairs, where Kerzhentsev, Boiarsky, and Orlovsky looked at it, but from there the piece was returned only with a note from Kerzhentsev saying that it was boring and rather crude. Therefore further correction of the text followed along the line of cuts and excision of single sentences.

Demian Bedny also cites the fact that he set forth his concept of *The Bogatyrs* in an article he submitted to *Pravda,* where no comments of any kind were made about the essence of his concept, and consequently he considered the text of *The Bogatyrs* to be absolutely approved.

In making all these references, Demian Bedny stressed, "I have an artist's mind, not a leader's."

Demian indicated that he was having an attack of diabetes. He talked about how he didn't want to die branded as an enemy of the Party and would like, if he couldn't go back to literature as a creative person, then at least to be used as a book specialist, at the Chamber of Books [national bibliographic center], for instance.

Furthermore, asking to speak off the record, Demian said that his library was his enemy. He had been told this, but he hadn't understood it. He declared he was going to burn his library. Then he emphasized that what he feared most was that, notwithstanding all his past career, he would be condemned as an enemy of the Party acting to encourage the enemies of communism. He declared that he was afraid that if such an opinion took hold about him he would be deported from Moscow.

Demian Bedny remained in this extremely demoralized state even after his meeting with Stavsky, which evidently did not do any good to cheer him up.

Stanislavsky, People's Artist of the USSR:

"The Bolsheviks are brilliant. Everything the Kamernyi Theater does isn't art. It's Formalism. It's pragmatic theater, it's Koonen's theater."

Leonidov, People's Artist of the USSR:

"When I read the committee's resolution, I lay down in bed and threw my feet up in the air I was so delighted. They really gave Litovsky, Tairov, and Demian Bedny a good bashing. It's worse than MKhAT-2."

Yanshin, Hon[ored] Artist of MKhAT:

"The play is a very bad one. I'm very pleased with the resolution. You can't hold on that long by worthless means. Now all the worthlessness of Tairov's system has been fully exposed. The sooner they shut down the theater the better. If they've shut down MKhAT-2, then this one should have been closed a long time ago."

Khmelev, Hon[ored] Artist of MKhAT:

"A perfectly correct decision. The leadership sees where the real art is and where it's profanation. After this decision we should expect the elimination of the Kamernyi Theater. There's nothing more for that theater to do."

Kedrov, Hon[ored] Artist of MKhAT:

"If they shut down the Kamernyi Theater, there'll be one less bad theater."

Stanitsyn, Hon[ored] Artist of MKhAT:

"This is a theater where they act badly, sing badly, and dance badly. It needs to be closed."

Markov, head of the MKhAT lit[erary] section:

"This is vile speculation in the names of Borodin and Palekh. A repulsively awful performance. The resolution is wholly justified."

Izrailevsky, head of the MKhAT musical section, Hon[ored] Artist:

"All the shows at the Kamernyi Theater are strictly Formalism. Nowhere else could its workers apply their talents. All its life the theater has not given any satisfaction."

Samosud, art[istic] director of the Bolshoi Theater:

"The resolution is absolutely correct. The Kamernyi Theater isn't a theater. Tairov is a deceiver. The idea of *The Bogatyrs* production is fallacious. Demian Bedny offered me this play back at the Mikhailovsky Theater, but I rejected it."

Meyerhold, People's Artist of the Republic:

"At last they've given Tairov the bashing he deserved. I keep a list of Tairov's banned plays, and *The Bogatyrs* will be the pearl on this list. Demian did get what he deserved. But the most important thing is that the committee, and Boiarsky personally, is to blame for it all. He is persecuting me. As long as there is that kind of leadership on the committee, art will not develop."

Natalia Sats, Hon[ored] Art[ist] of the Rep[ublic], artistic director of the Central Children's Theater:

"Tairov made a mistake. He used Borodin's unfinished music. He should not have depended on Demian Bedny because he's a bad playwright. Inviting the Palekh artists to participate plays on the form without a chance of justifying it with content. The theater can't tell the viewer anything."

Sadovsky, People's Artist of the RSFSR, artist of the Maly Theater:

"A sensible resolution. They were right to slap Tairov and Demian Bedny on the wrists. You shouldn't distort the history of the great Russian people."

Trenev, playwright, author of *Liubov' Iarovaia:*

"I was very cheered by the resolution. I take pride in it, as a Russian.

You shouldn't spit in our face. I myself couldn't go to the performance, so I sent my wife and daughter. They couldn't sit through it, they left in disgust. That's how sickening an impression it makes."

[. . .]

P. Romanov, writer, prose writer:

"They did right slamming them. Demian takes advantage of his award, his connections, and his crude ways. This time it flopped. That's for one, and secondly, it's very good that they stood up for Russian folklore and the Russian *bogatyrs.* We need to find Russian heroes, too."

Gorodetsky, poet:

"I can't sympathize with repressions of any kind, but I like the fact that they are striking against the mockery of folklore and not at themes from it. One should not treat the people's history like that, and I like it even more that they struck at Tairov: he's a scoundrel."

Vsev[olod] Vishnevsky, playwright:

"It serves Demian right, he can quit the hack work. This is history's lesson: 'Don't lay a finger on our people.' History will still stand us in good stead, and very soon. An opera is being prepared, *Minin [and] Pozharsky*—salvation from the interventionists." (This opinion of the decision did not keep Vishnevsky from going to see Tairov to express his sympathy.)

[. . .]

I. Trauberg, director, author of the screenplay *Counterplan* [*Vstrechnyi*]:

"The Soviet state is becoming more and more national and even nationalistic. Because of this, utterly unexpected things find a defense among the Party leadership. It's getting harder and harder to work, especially when so many leading people—including members of Glavrepertkom and the Committee on Arts Affairs—can't decide correctly on the meaning of a play, which they have to withdraw after it's been approved."

S. Klychkov, writer:

"But actually, it could be, anything could be. After all the great Russian people number a hundred million, and of course they have a right to an art greater than what you find on boxes of powder and kiosks *à la russe.* Someday they may dare call me a Russian writer. Russian art cannot be thrown under the tail of a Mansi saga.

"To whom did they give the Russian epic to desecrate? Tairov the Kike and Bedny the Puny. What else beside satire could you expect from Bedny, who's mainly a pamphleteer? Some smart refined person is picking them up by the ass, though, and shaking all the extra stink out of them . . .

"I hope that it will be easier for writers to write the truth, but critics are going to have to admit their mistakes."

[. . .]

Iu. Olesha, writer:

"The play is not the main thing here. Demian got too fussy and Demian got a slap in the kisser. Today him, tomorrow someone else. There's nothing in particular to rejoice about. Demian is paying for his past sins."

[. . .]

Kozlovsky, artist of GABT:

"There's no doubt the play was read before in the government, so why didn't they ban it before the production? Tairov is a great talent, and this resolution isn't going to kill him."

Kaverin, director at TRAM:

"The resolution is correct, everyone realizes that, and if many are refraining from harsh criticism of Tairov, it's only because, really, every theater has its own 'little *bogatyrs.*'"

Eisenstein, Honored Figure of the Arts and film director:

"I didn't see the show, but I'm extremely pleased if only because they gave Demian a good drubbing. That's just what he needs, he's got a swelled head. It's also good that they laid into that toady Litovsky, who came a cropper with his laudatory article. In this whole affair what interests me is one question, Where were they before, when they allowed this counterrevolutionary play on the stage?"

Leonid Sobolev, author of *Major Overhaul* [*Kapital'nyi remont*]:

"I was just at Tairov's. People have been visiting him ever since morning. Right as I arrived at Tairov's, Vs. Vishnevsky was leaving. Alisa is terribly upset and dispirited, she says everyone's coming to see him now as if it were a funeral. I feel sorry for Tairov, even though I think the resolution is correct. After all, when a book is published that distorts history, reality, and so on, we don't release it to the reader, but the multitudinous viewer is being educated in the theater, too. It's strange—where was Kerzhentsev before? If the play was rehearsed and was already running as a completed performance for the viewer, that means the Committee on Arts Affairs approved the show and approved it highly. Even the press praised both the play and the production. They say that Molotov and Voroshilov saw *The Bogatyrs.* Clearly they uncovered distortions in the play."

[. . .]

Isidor Kleiner, theoretician and theat[er] critic:

"The story of the production of *The Bogatyrs* is instructive and useful for dramaturgy and for the theatrical art. True, Tairov had written approval of the production from Glavrepertkom. All was 'in order.' So that Litovsky is no less responsible than he is. Today there was an emergency meeting with Angarov in connection with this story. There was a new 'battle of Kerzhenets.'

"Well, but Demian probably isn't going to be rich anymore. They've calculated he managed to get 250 rubles per performance. And there were seven or eight paid performances."

[. . .]

Svobodin, artist in the Operetta Theater:
"The committee's decision is correct. Tairov's theater is hanging by a thread. It would have been shut down long ago if it weren't for Litvinov, who was protecting it."

[. . .]

Dzerzhinsky, composer, composer of *Quiet Flows The Don:*
"I've been planning to write an opera entitled 'Pugachev.' After this resolution of the committee, I don't know what I should do. I'd like to talk with one of the leading comrades. Now you have to approach any historical theme with maximum caution."

[. . .]

Orbeli, academician, director of the Hermitage (after a meeting of the Arts Committee):
"What conclusions? The resolution is marvelous. Although Demian Bedny should be getting more of a beating than Tairov. You can't finish off Tairov. Meyerhold infuriated me. It was the speech of a hooligan. It was tomfoolery."

[. . .]

Lenin, Honored Artist of the Maly Theater:
"The production has been canceled. Good for them. Under Tsar Nicholas there was one censor who could decide issues single-handedly, but our censors were intimidated by Demian Bedny and let the show through."

[. . .]

D. N. Morozov, playwright:
"Tairov wanted to earn himself political capital on D. Bedny's play and 'broke his fast.' Actually, could you really expect high-quality artistic output from D. Bedny? Signing a poster is a long way from genuine dramaturgy. But the fact that the play was canceled, Kerzhentsev is to blame for this at the least. The play was canceled, of course, at the 'boss's' instruction. And rightly so. It's time to speak out about culture."

[. . .]

Litovsky, chairman of Glavrepertkom:
"I'm not going to speak at a non-Party meeting. At a meeting of Party members I will say that not only Litovsky but the committee as well is to blame: Kerzhentsev, Boiarsky, as well as Gorodinsky, who approved the production."

M. Bulgakov, author of *Days of the Turbins:*
"This is a rare instance when Demian, despite his character, is not going

to be gloating. This time he himself has fallen victim—he's not going to be chortling over anyone else. Let him feel it for himself."

> Head of the GUGB Sec[ret] Political Department
> Commissar of St[ate] Security 2nd rank
> Molchanov

Bedny made several attempts to rehabilitate himself after this attack, but to no avail. When he tried to publish an antifascist fable in *Pravda* and it was submitted to Stalin for approval Stalin took great pleasure in responding to Bedny personally and mocking him:

· 109 ·

Note from I. V. Stalin to *Pravda* Editor-in-Chief L. Z. Mekhlis on D. Bedny's fable "Struggle or Die" ("Boris' ili umirai"). RGASPI, f. 71, op. 10, d. 130, l. 100. Copy. Typewritten.
20 July 1937

Com. Mekhlis!
To your inquiry about Demian's fable "Struggle or Die," I'm replying in a letter addressed to Demian, which you can read to him.
To our newly appeared Dante, i.e., Conrad, that is to say . . . Demian Bedny.
Your fable or long poem, "Struggle or Die," in my opinion, is an artistically mediocre critique. As a criticism of fascism, it is pale and unoriginal. As a criticism of the Soviet order (don't joke!), it is stupid, albeit transparent.
Since we (Soviet people) have no shortage of literary rubbish as it is, it is hardly worthwhile to multiply the deposits of this type of literature with yet another fable, so to speak. . . .
I realize, of course, that I must beg Demian-Dante's pardon for the necessary candor.

> Respectfully,
> I. Stalin

Stalin was doubtless aware of the blow he was delivering to the former close, and therefore powerful, friend of the Bolshevik leaders. He kept a close watch on Bedny, as the following document prepared for him reveals. Yet, and this was quite common, although the material gathered on Bedny was more than enough, by the standards of those times, to get him arrested, Stalin did not authorize it, and though Bedny was temporarily expelled from both the Party (he had been a member since 1912) and the Writers Union, he was never purged and died in 1945. One can only speculate about why some intellectuals were purged while others, who seemed equally vulnerable, were not, but this case seems indicative of the strong element of the arbitrary in the history of the purges.

· 110 ·

Report from the NKVD GUGB SSSR to I. V. Stalin on the poet D. Bedny. TsA FSB RF, f. 3, op. 5, d. 262, ll. 57–60. Original. Typewritten.
9 September 1938

Demian Bedny (Efim Alekseevich Pridvorov) is a poet and member of the Union of Soviet Writers. Expelled from the VKP(b) in July of this year for "drastically expressed moral depravity."

D. Bedny has had close ties with the leaders of right wing and Trotskyite organizations. D. Bedny has a drastically anti-Soviet inclination and is malicious with respect to the VKP(b) leadership. On this subject, A. I. Stetsky, an arrested participant in the anti-Soviet organization of right-wing forces, has testified:

"Before 1932, the main task I set before the groups of right-wing forces that I headed in Moscow and Leningrad consisted in recruiting new people into our organization. Among writers I established a close political connection then with Demian Bedny, who was and remains someone hostile to Soviet power. I had several conversations with Demian Bedny that were openly anti-Soviet in character. He was acutely annoyed by what he felt was insufficient attention to his person. In our further meetings, when our political like-mindedness began to make itself clear, Demian Bedny roundly cursed Stalin and Molotov and extolled Rykov and Bukharin. He stated that he would not accept Stalinist socialism. He conceived his play *The Bogatyrs* as a counterrevolutionary allegory on how "they are dragging our peasants into socialism by force."

D. Bedny's embitteredness is characterized by the following statements he made among persons close to him:

"I've become an outsider, I've gone out of print. The era of Demian Bedny is over. Do you really not see what's going on here? The entire old guard is being cut off. The old Bolsheviks are being exterminated. They're destroying all the best of the best. In whose interests is it to exterminate the entire generation of Lenin? Who needs that? They're persecuting me, you see, because I have the halo of the October Revolution on me."

D. Bedny systematically expresses his bitterness against Comrades Stalin and Molotov and other leaders of the VKP(b).

"The clampdown and terror in the USSR are such that literature and scholarship are impossible, free research is impossible. Not only do we have no history, we don't even have a history of the Party. The history of the Civil War has to be tossed into the stove as well—you can't write it. It turns out I've been going along with a party of which 99.9 [percent] are spies and provocateurs. Stalin is a horrible man and is often guided by his personal grudges. All great leaders have always created around themselves brilliant cohorts of associates. But what has Stalin created? He has wiped out everyone, there is no one, they have all been destroyed. There has not been the likes of this since Ivan the Terrible."

[. . .]

Since the KPK [Party Control Commission] decision to expel him from the Party, D. Bedny has been in an increasingly embittered state. He mocks the KPK resolution: "At first they cheapened me—announced I was morally depraved, and then they declare I'm a Turkish spy."

Several times D. Bedny has spoken of his intention to commit suicide.

> Assistant to the head of NKVD First Admin[istration],
> Fourth Section
> St[ate] Security Captain
> V. Ostroumov

The demand for "Soviet patriotism" which became one of the main consequences of the campaigns of 1936–1938 became a fundamental principle of the new aesthetic doctrine, Socialist Realism. It became an official requirement that a Socialist Realist work exemplify *narodnost'* in all its meanings, having to do with "popular," "folk," "of the common man," "people's," "national," and "state," and here, as with Socialist Realism in general, involved all four of them.[2] Thus the concept entailed not just simplicity and accessibility, and even not just love for the "socialist motherland," but also love for its history. This history was now represented as a line of continuity from the ancient past in Kievan Rus' through to Soviet times.

CHAPTER FOURTEEN

The Censorship

Censorship is generally seen as a defining feature of Soviet cultural life. Glavlit, the Main Administration for Matters Concerning Literature and Publishing Houses (Glavnoe upravlenie po delam literatury i izdatel'stv) was the main censorship body in Soviet Russia and all printed material had to bear its authorization number, hence it was a body of ongoing concern to the Party leadership (as can be seen in docs. 59, 60, and 61). Of particular interest is the following document from the Politburo archives, the report of the head of Glavlit, Boris Volin, an old Bolshevik who in the 1920s had been one of the most militant members of RAPP.

· 111 ·

Excerpt from Glavlit's memorandum to the TsK VKP(b) Politburo on the work and new tasks of the censorship organs. AP RF, f. 3, op. 34, d. 37, ll. 25–36.
Original. Typewritten.
9 April 1933

Exactly two years ago (5 April 1931), the TsK Politburo issued a detailed directive "on strengthening political oversight over the output of the periodical and nonperiodical press."[1]
[. . .]
Soon after this directive (three months later) Glavlit's leadership was changed. Not only was Glavlit's leadership changed but virtually all of Glavlit's work was reorganized.
In this period of time, the Party's TsK paid significant attention to the work of our publishing houses, holding hearings on them at Kultprop and

in the Orgburo and Politburo. Glavlit feels it must inform the Politburo how it has fought over the last two years for the quality of our book, journal, newspaper, and also fine art output and radio broadcasts, for the quality of our entire press. Glavlit is our Soviet censor. Glavlit, guided by the above-mentioned Politburo directive, is carrying out in its work the instructions contained in such Party documents as Com. Stalin's letter, the TsK resolution "On the work of Gosizdat," on *Young Guard* [*Molodaia gvardia*], on Narkompros, on textbooks, on poster literature, on the restructuring of literary organizations, and so on.

I
The Functions of Glavlit

Glavlit performs preliminary and subsequent censorship for all forms of publishing. Preliminary censorship examines publishing both in the interests of protecting state secrets and in the interests of preventing the commission of politically harmful, illiterate hack works—or individual sections in them—that distort Soviet reality. This function of preliminary censorship has vindicated itself in full. The editorial staffs in our publishing houses are still so imperfect and at times even simply weak that our censors represent a supplemental mobilization of Bolshevist vigilance on a front as important as is the front of our publishing in the broadest, most all-encompassing sense of the word. The responsibility of the organs of preliminary oversight is tremendous. For if there is the slightest breach in our publishing (a novel, poem, article, book, caricature, illustration, label, disclosure of state secret, etc.) a claim could be made against Glavlit: after all, Glavlit's authorization number is everywhere.

Whether or not a given doubtful item gets permission to be published depends ultimately on preliminary censorship. However, the quality even of our people is far from perfect. True, their vigilance is especially acute and mobilized. They are not guided by the need to mandatorily put out an issue of a magazine or fulfill some publishing plan (in quantity), they are not bound by an agreement with a printer and author, and so on. Therefore, they are freer in their opinions of a given piece, they are more objective and materially disinterested. Nonetheless, though, although the quantity and quality of undesirable and harmful omissions on the part of the preliminary censorship are decreasing, there have been omissions and mistakes, and not just a few.

[. . .]

Given the current condition of its apparatus, Glavlit can cover with subsequent oversight up to 70 percent of the printed output of the RSFSR.

Glavlit's work is exceptionally intense and operational. We receive the first copies of a print run and within twenty-four hours must have an opinion about the literature we have received today. Otherwise, the book, brochure, poster, or magazine, goes to Kogiz [Cooperative Organization of State Publishing Houses], stores, kiosks, and subscribers, and then it is very hard to snatch anything back.

Glavlit, along with its censorship repression, is conducting important educational and organizational work. Preliminary censorship summarizes the shortcomings of the work of editors, publishing houses, and the like and reports about this to their boards as well as the Party organizations, makes reports at production conferences, and so on.

In the event of the discovery of grave oversights, Glavlit exerts influence on the censor by administrative means, takes the printers to court, reports on the censor as well as on the editor and the author (if they are Party members) to the Party organization or organs of the C[ontrol] C[ommission]. All this very seriously mobilizes the responsibility of our publishing, raises their vigilance, and improves the quality of their work.

Glavlit brings the most instructive, important, and serious breaches in the publishing and editorial business immediately to the knowledge of the TsK secretaries and Kultprop by attaching the corresponding literature.

I must emphasize that the instructions of preliminary censorship, as well as of Glavlit, are finally being accepted (not without significant resistance) by publishers and editors. Instances of their protesting to the TsK are highly insignificant and usually end in approbation on the part of Kultprop and Agitmass [Department of Agitation and Propaganda] (art publishing) of Glavlit's action.

II
The Practical Work of Glavlit

[...]

Glavlit is finally censoring all the foreign press that reaches the Union. There is a sizable group of workers who know several languages apiece and who work both in the Post Office and in the Glavlit apparatus. Glavlit also gives permission for the export of manuscripts, and so on.

[...]

Among our best and most prominent writers, there are none who have been hurt by Glavlit and are sharply displeased with our censorship. Authors usually accept individual comments from Glavlit that improve the text politically. Publishers do not exactly welcome Glavlit, for a censor, of course, causes them quite a few unpleasantnesses of a political and material nature. Authors and editors affected by Glavlit's influence frequently think that it is not they who are to blame for their political mistakes but Glavlit for discovering them.

<...>²

Glavlit Head B. Volin

Glavlit was responsible not only for censoring prior to publication but also for censoring books already released. During the turbulent 1930s when the number of "enemies of the people" kept snowballing and more and more historical events or personalities were proscribed, there was a frenzy of purging in library collections that was directed by lists compiled by Glavlit. Sometimes, however, zealous "local workers" destroyed books or sections of books on their own initiative, actions that are here labeled "deviations" (*peregiby*). In such instances TsK bodies became involved, as we see in the following document. This document might seem to be intended to liberalize publishing, given that it seeks to abolish ludicrously excessive vigilance in censorship, a curious position in the worst year of the Great Purge, but it will be noted that the resolution is actually to give censorship over completely to the oversight of the Central Committee.

· 112 ·

Resolution of the TsK VKP(b) Orgburo "On eliminating Glavlit's sabotaging system of withdrawing literature." RGASPI, f. 17, op. 114, d. 635, ll. 16–17. Original. Typewritten.
9 December 1937

No. 77, p. 75g—*On eliminating Glavlit's sabotaging system of withdrawing literature (Com. Mekhlis).*

The TsK VKP(b) condemns Glavlit's practice of arbitrary, bordering on sabotage, mass withdrawal of literature. For example, in the Tatar Republic a collection of algebraic problems by Shaposhnikov and Valtsov and a collection of problems in geometry by Rybkin et al. were withdrawn. In Bashkiria they withdrew a Party charter, a resolution of the Seventeenth Congress of the VKP(b), and works by Lenin and Stalin. The situation is no better in Dagestan, where enemies deprived the republic's workers of the classics of Marxism-Leninism translated into local languages. In all these instances the literature was withdrawn on the grounds that at the end of the books the names were listed of translators who had turned out to be politically tainted.

The withdrawal of books as a kind of exhibitionist vigilance, in particular under the pretext of the translator's faultiness, has led in the national republics to overzealous bunglers and wreckers withdrawing a huge portion of the standard textbooks, Russian classics, and even official Party documents.

Apart from that, Glavlit has been publishing in huge print runs for wide use lists of authors, books, and brochures that are supposed to be removed. Summary lists include insignificant, trifling little books by local authors whom no one has ever read. The authors of these, it could be said, little books, never considered themselves writers. In its wrecking actions, Glavlit has enrolled them as "writers."

This criminal practice has only played into the hands of our enemies.

The VKP(b) Central Committee resolves:

1. To ban henceforth the withdrawal of any literature without a special decision of the TsK VKP(b). Only Glavlit and its local organs henceforth can withdraw literature, in each individual case with the sanction of the TsK.

The withdrawal of books and brochures written by local authors and published by local publishing houses shall be brought about, in each individual case, at the decision of the regional Party committee, district Party committee, and the TsK of the Communist Parties of the national republics.

2. To forbid the unauthorized publication by Glavlit in large print runs of various kinds of lists of withdrawn literature. Henceforth the lists of literature subject to withdrawal for various reasons, including outdated literature, shall be released as needed, and in each individual case with the permission of the TsK.

Soviet censorship was not only a matter of Glavlit. TsK functionaries of all levels also performed censorship functions. For example, Agitprop officials often found occasion to correct censorship work done by Glavlit. The following document concerns two famous Soviet satirists, Erdman and Mass. Nikolai Erdman was a popular writer particularly noted for his plays *The Mandate* (*Mandat*, 1925) and *The Suicide* (*Samoubiitsa*, 1928). The year following this document, in 1934, the two co-authored the script for G. Aleksandrov's popular musical comedy *The Happy-Go-Lucky Guys* (*Veselye rebiata*). One is struck in the following document by the efforts to take responsibility away from Gorky for publishing the offending Erdman and Mass piece in an almanac he edited and to assign blame to his co-editor Averbakh who had by now fallen from grace but had been very powerful only a year earlier as a leader of RAPP.

· 113 ·

Memorandum from TsK VKP(b) Department of Cultural-Educational Work Head A. I. Stetsky to the TsK VKP(b) secretaries on the publication of the anti-Soviet tales of V. Z. Mass and N. R. Erdman and on progress in the preparations for the Writers' Congress. RGASPI, f. 17, op. 163, d. 985, ll. 150–151. Original. Typewritten. On the first page of the memorandum there are two instructions: "To Molotov, Voroshilov, Kuibyshev, M. Gorky, I. St[alin]"; "Averbakh must be punished. Molotov," and the results of the voting on this matter: Kaganovich, Stalin, Voroshilov, and Ordzhonikidze—in favor.

22 May 1933

To Com. Stalin and Com. Kaganovich

The almanac *The Sixteenth Year* [*God shestnadtsatyi*] has come out under the editorship of Gorky, Averbakh, and others. Averbakh edited it here.

This miscellany should have been held back. I did not do this only because it came out on the very day of Gorky's arrival here and this would have been a very nasty surprise for him.

The miscellany includes "A Meeting on Laughter" [*Zasedanie o smekhe*] by Mass and Erdman, which is a malicious insult against us. I should add that the basis for Mass and Erdman's work is a certain counterrevolutionary joke.

The same insulting nature pertains to a fairytale by the same authors, "The Law of Gravity" [*Zakon tiagotenia*].

Averbakh is primarily responsible for this. It is one of the manifestations of time-serving from which he has yet to free himself. Even now Averbakh continues to engage in political intrigue all over the place. Almost all the Communist writers (with the exception of Afinogenov, Kirshon, and Makariev) have turned away from him. This doesn't bother him. He clutches at Gorky's authority and hides behind it, surrounding himself with non-Party people, which is facilitated by the inaction of the Organizing Committee and the placidity of Gronsky (Gronsky has gotten the idea into his head that he is going to the congress having eliminated cliquishness and therefore does not want to notice Averbakh's work). As a result, the non-Party writers are disoriented.

The faction meetings held at Kultprop put the Communist writers on their feet, and they have taken up preparing for the congress and working with the non-Party writers. The congress is supposed to be held on 20 June. In my opinion and the opinion of the faction, there are no grounds for postponing it. Some preparatory work has been done by the Organizing Committee (discussion of creative issues). As far as the structure of the union goes, the issue has been clarified and developed. The theses of the reports will be ready in the next few days.

Most important, though, the writers have made all their plans around the congress in June. If it is postponed, then it should be to autumn, because you can't get writers together in the summer. Therefore I believe we can stay permanently with this date.

Most important now is to hold several meetings with the non-Party writers in order to clarify what they want from the congress, what problems concern them.

I will take this up in the next few days.

In view of the fact that writers are very interested in rural issues, I have asked Com. Yakovlev to hold a discussion at the Organizing Committee with thirty to forty writers. This would be good and would clarify many things for them.

> TsK VKP(b) Kultpropotdel Head
> A. Stetsky

Kerzhentsev, who prepared the following stinging memorandum on Bulgakov, had in the 1920s been one of the leading theoreticians of Proletkult [Proletarian Culture, a cultural organization], especially in the area of the theater and mass spectacle, and as such an opponent of Bulgakov's approach. However, his denunciation of Bulgakov is couched in terms of "Party criticism" with casuistic (though perceptive) readings of his play's subtexts. One should note here how Stalin supports Kerzhentsev's proposal to not merely ban the play but make MKhAT renounce it "consciously."

· 114 ·

Memorandum from Chairman P. M. Kerzhentsev of the Committee on Arts Affairs under the SNK SSSR, to I. V. Stalin and V. M. Molotov on M. A. Bulgakov's play, *A Cabal of Hypocrites (Molière)* [*Kabala sviatosh (Mol'er)*]. RGASPI, f. 17, op. 163, d. 1099, ll. 96–98. Original. Typewritten. On the first page of the memorandum is Stalin's instruction: "To Molotov. I think Com. Kerzhentsev is right. I'm in favor of his proposal. I. Stalin" and the signatures of V. M. Molotov, L. M. Kaganovich, A. I. Mikoyan, V. Ya. Chubar, K. G. Voroshilov, M. I. Kalinin, and G. K. Ordzhonikidze.

29 February 1936

To Com. I. V. Stalin
To Com. V. M. Molotov
On M. Bulgakov's Molière (at the MKhAT annex)

1. *What was the author's political intent?* M. Bulgakov wrote this play in the years 1929–1931 (Glavrepertkom permission dated 3 November 1931), i.e., during that period when a number of his plays were removed from the repertoire or not allowed to be performed (*Zoika's Apartment* [*Zoikina kvartira*], *Crimson Island* [*Bagrovy ostrov*], *Flight* [*Beg*], and at one time, *The Brothers Turbin* [*Brat'ia Turbiny*—sic]).[3] In his new play he wanted to show the fate of a writer whose ideology runs counter to the political order and whose plays are banned.

It is on this level that Bulgakov interprets this "historical" play from the life of Molière. A secret "cabal" run by priests and ideologists of the monarchist regime is waging a battle against a talented writer. Fighting Molière are the leaders of the royal musketeers—the king's privileged guard and police. Slander is spread about Molière's family life, etc. At one point only the king stands up for Molière and defends him against the persecutions of the Catholic church.

Molière utters lines like this: "All my life I have licked his [the king's] spurs and thought only one thing: don't crush me. . . . And here he has crushed me anyway. . . ." "Did I perhaps fail to flatter you enough? Did I perhaps fail to lick enough? Your Excellency, where will you find another sponger the like of Molière?" "What must I do to prove I'm a worm?"

This scene concludes with a cry: "I hate arbitrary tyranny!" (Repertkom corrected it to "royal" tyranny).

Despite the whole veil of hints, the political meaning Bulgakov invests in his work is sufficiently clear, although most viewers may never even notice these hints.

He wants to evoke in the viewer an analogy between the writer's status under the dictatorship of the proletariat and under the "arbitrary tyranny" of Louis XIV.

2. *What does Molière make of itself as a dramatic work?* This is a cleverly crafted play in the spirit of Dumas or Scribe, with effective theatrical scenes, loose ends, duels, betrayals, offstage events, confessions in Catholic churches, meetings in the underground room of the "cabal's" members wearing black masks, etc.

It is a play about a brilliant writer, about one of the most avant-garde fighters for the new bourgeois culture in opposition to the sway of the priests and aristocracy, about one of the most vivid realists of the eighteenth century, who struggled steadfastly for materialism over religion, for simplicity over depravity and affectation. But where is Molière?

There is no trace of the writer Molière in Bulgakov's play. What is shown, to the philistine's satisfaction, is a mediocre actor tangled up in his family affairs and sponging off the crown—and only that.

On the other hand, Louis XIV is brought out as a true "enlightened monarch," an enchanting despot who stands several heads taller than everyone around him and who shines like the sun in the literal and figurative sense of the word.

Inasmuch as it is Molière's family life that is taken as the basis of the plot, the entire play is reduced to a mediocre bourgeois drama.

If we set aside the author's political hints and the apotheosis of Louis XIV, the play is a total ideological vacuum—the play poses no problems, does nothing to enrich the viewer, but then it skillfully offers up poison drops in an opulent but barren flower.

3. *What has the theater done* with this poisonous barren flower? It did not want to emphasize the political hints and has tried not to notice them. Having no ideological material in the play, the theater followed the line of least resistance. It strove to make out of the production a luxurious spectacle and to attract by the artistry of the players' acting.

All the theater's energy went into *externals*. The sets (Viliams), costumes, and mise-en-scène—all this has as its aim amazing the viewer with the costly genuine brocade, silk, and velvet. (It's no accident the production cost 360,000 rubles, whereas *The Storm* [*Groza*]⁴ cost 100,000 rubles.)

All the *outward* effects are especially emphasized and played out (the scene of dinner at the palace, the meeting of the "cabal" underground, the confession in the cathedral to organ and choral accompaniment, etc.).

The technically brilliant acting of Bolduman (Louis XIV) bears the same quality of outward show and extolling the image of the king while concealing the genuine features of "enlightened" despotism and coarseness. The comicality of Yanshin (Buton) is also conveyed through externals (the device of repeating the same little words and gestures over and over) without any deepening of the image. In Molière, Stanitsyn makes strident use of the same superficial technical devices (for example, he hiccups, which particularly contradicts the very type of Molière the brilliant *actor*). Livanov builds his role on his surface good looks.

As a result, we have a luxurious, at times technically brilliant production but one that completely distorts the period and images of the leading historical figures of that era. The viewer sees the wise monarch Louis and the pathetic writer Molière, who is ruined by his family drama and by the roots [*sic*][5] of some secretive "cabal."

The ideological content of the production is on the level of the novels of Dumas *fils*. A lamentable result after four years' work by the MKhAT annex, which has given us so many examples of profoundly ideological and strongly realistic productions.

4. *My suggestions:* Have the MKhAT annex remove this production not by formal prohibition but through the theater's conscious rejection of this production as mistaken and distracting them from the line of Socialist Realism. For this, place in *Pravda* a sharp editorial on *Molière* in the spirit of these comments of mine and analyze the production in other organs of the press.

Let the theaters see from the example of *Molière* that we are trying to achieve not outwardly brilliant productions where the acting is technically clever, but productions that are ideologically saturated, realistically full-blooded, and historically accurate—from the leading theaters *especially*.

Kerzhentsev

It was more customary for Politburo interventions in theater productions to take the form of establishing a "commission" to review a particular play. The commission would comprise "theater specialists" plus Voroshilov or Yenukidze. Generally, if they did not ban outright a play that seemed dubious politically they would suggest changes that would make it more acceptable. Suggested alterations might be relatively minor but in some instances they involved drastically altering the plot or the director's conception for the staging so that the commission effectively became co-authors. The following ruling on a play by Lev Slavin provides a good example of this.

· 115 ·

Memorandum of a Commission of the Politburo of TsK VKP (b) "On the issue of the performance by the Vakhtangov Theater of L. I. Slavin's play *The Foreign Collegium* [*Inostrannaia kollegiia*]." AP RF, f. 3, op. 34, d. 221, l. 17. Copy. Typewritten.
19 February 1933

Allow the Vakhtangov Theater to perform L. Slavin's play *A Foreign Collegium* provided they observe the following conditions:

a. Change the play's title: instead of "A Foreign Collegium," call it "Intervention" [*Interventsiia*], which fits the play's content.

b. Call the character of Marshal Franchet d'Espery simply a general, and not of the French army but a "general of the troops or army of the Entente."

c. Toss out of the scene at French counterintelligence:

1. the taking of bribes by the chief of counterintelligence (mandatory) and

2. the taking by Ksidias the mother of money for turning in Communists (this is up to the theater, since there is nothing political in this).

d. Bondarenko, the head of the partisan brigade, should straighten up, giving him a more military bearing and reserve (Bondarenko, a sailor commanding revolutionary troops attacking Odessa, is much too slack).

In Bondarenko's speech, substitute "Entente" in the places about the French army and French command. Clean up individual phrases elsewhere in the play as well, replacing everywhere sentences about France and the French army with the Entente.

e. Cut Selesten's speech on the ship's gangway to a third in its propaganda section and throw out mentions in it of France, replacing them with the Entente.

Yenukidze
Voroshilov
Bubnov

As the documents in this collection suggest, censorship had turned into virtually a routine activity for Stalin and the Politburo, one in which virtually every member was involved. This was particularly true of censoring films. As is well known, Stalin and his entourage attended regular screenings of new films in the Kremlin. Not a single film could be released without his approval. Generally the result was that a film was passed for release on condition that it be reworked in specific ways set out in instructions formulated during screenings for Politburo members. But sometimes Stalin took offense at a particular film, which could mean very serious consequences for those who made it. The following two documents from the Politburo archives illustrate the two most common outcomes of these Kremlin screenings.

The first document concerns filmic representation of the Cheliuskin Expedition of 1933–1934, an iconic event in Soviet political culture. The expedition's 104 members, stranded on an ice floe after its boat sank in the ice during a voyage through the Northeast Passage under Otto Shmidt, were rescued in a series of extremely hazardous and highly publicized airlifts.

· 116 ·

Resolution of the TsK VKP(b) Politburo "On the motion picture 'Cheliuskin.'"
RGASPI, f. 17, op. 3, d. 948, l. 13. Original. Typewritten.
29 June 1934

No. 10 p. 50/32—*On the motion picture* Cheliuskin.
Propose to the Cinema Administration:
1. Expand the motion picture *Cheliuskin,* including in it all the significant moments without exception in the voyage of the *Cheliuskin* (a) especially about the difficulties of the struggle of the *Cheliuskin* and its crew with the icy elements in the ocean; (b) do more to reflect the inner life of Shmidt's camp on the ice, in particular, the role of the Party group, as well as of the women; (c) give a fuller picture of the totality of the measures to organize assistance from Moscow for the Shmidt camp; (d) reflect more the broad, mass nature of the meeting of *Cheliuskin* men and workers of the USSR all along the way to Moscow.
2. After making the indicated corrections, present *Cheliuskin* for viewing by the TsK commission, and only after its approval release the film to the cinemas.

The following document records a meeting of 1941 between Andrei Zhdanov (who had delivered the Party's keynote address at the Writers Union congress in 1934 and was at this time the chief Party spokesman, other than Stalin, on ideological matters), and leading filmmakers. It shows how the Party assumed priority in arbitrating aesthetic issues.

· 117 ·

Uncorrected transcript of introductory remarks by TSK VKP(b) Secretary A. A. Zhdanov at a meeting of cinematographers at the TsK VKP(b). RGASPI. f. 77 op. 1, ll. 1a-7.
14 May 1941

Comrades, the Central Committee has decided to call a meeting of creative workers in Soviet cinematography in order to discuss with you the most imminent and painful issues in the creative work of cinematography workers.

[. . .]

If we take films not released to the screen or released with a great number of changes, it must be said that all these films suffer from a fairly low level from the standpoint of ideological content and sometimes from dragging in ideological and moral tendencies alien to us. This is especially unpleasant and incorrect considering that the modern era, the modern period, it imposes on our screen, on our cinema, as the most critical form of our art in terms of political propaganda and education of the masses, particular responsibilities in connection with the war, in connection with our tasks in the sphere of building a Communist society, in connection with the tasks set by the Eighteenth Party Conference. All the tasks of educating the masses, they are posed right now the most intensely and from this standpoint one would like to consult, clarify, and verify what the reasons are for these failures, what are the reasons are for the fact that the ideological content and artistic value of many of our films are not at the proper level.

I want to say just a few words about why the TsK VKP(b) has been forced to ban a few films due to ideological tendencies somewhat alien to us. I'm not going to go into *The Law of Life* [*Zakon zhizni*] because enough has been written about this; I will talk about a film like *At a Distant Outpost* [*Na dal'nei zastave*], why it did not hit the mark. This film did not hit the mark because it very wrongly and distortedly distributes the chiaroscuro between our people, the border guards, waging the fight against defectors and spies, especially English spies and this figure of the enemy, the English spy. Our border guards, Red Army soldiers, are shown as the worst louts, the worst simpletons, whom it's no sin to dupe. The spy is shown as a strong person with strong, tough virtues and qualities. In the final analysis, a summary of this film, the square root of this film, comes down to the fact that this spy was caught because there was supposed to be a happy ending. His capture is not properly motivated, it absolutely does not follow from the entire inner dynamic of events and circumstances that go with the film.

In connection with *The Law of Life*, Comrade Stalin at a meeting of writers indicated that Avdeenko's[6] sin consists not in the fact that he draws the enemy as a great man, rather his sin consists in the fact that Avdeenko was showing our people as sorry specimens and, consequently, from this standpoint, he had absolutely not understood and had distorted our Soviet reality to the advantage of our enemies. He depicted the Bolsheviks as sorry specimens and our enemies as men of action and very strong people. Also following this path in a more softened form were the authors of quite a few films I have already spoken about. For example, in *At a Distant Outpost*, the dragging in of all kinds of banality, the lowering of the ideological level of our Soviet citizens, the dragging in of theory and practice, the Don Juanist tendencies that are in *The Law of Life*, the dragging in of Artsybashevism.[7]

And then many of the films released to the screen suffer from an easy and poorly motivated explanation for our Soviet reality. When our people are depicted in film, they turn into heroes, into distinguished people, without the slightest effort. This kind of development of our Soviet people is effected without the slightest difficulty, without the slightest effort of will, energy, persistence, or other qualities of human character. They cannot help but disenchant people and engender among young people a casual attitude toward our Soviet reality, they present things as very easy in terms of rising up in the world and of creating a lifelike portrait.

Therefore we must discuss together the matter of how to improve the ideological content and artistic quality of our films, how to avoid failures on this front, how to get rid of defective products, how to raise our cinematography to a new level so that the defective products are reduced to a minimum, if not eliminated altogether.

This is the matter on which the Central Committee feels it essential to consult with the comrades.

A few words as a way of raising the issue—this is with regard to comedies. If in the sphere of artistic films we have quite a few failures, then with respect to comedies this situation is getting even worse. For a long time we have not had Soviet comedies, with the exception of a few films. Here it emerges that having achieved a certain level in the creation of our Soviet film comedies, the latest films, they seem to try to reach this level and then return to the initial step. I want to say about the recent new film *Hearts of Four* [*Serdtsa chetyrekh*].[8] We saw this film a few days ago. The plot takes just ten minutes, but when this matter gets spread out to an hour and a half, the comedic dynamic, the comedic method itself, turns into its exact opposite, into something boring. These attempts to amuse the public by all manner of falling into the water, splashing people in the face from goblets, and so forth, all these simplistic devices are very trivial, they cannot raise or arouse enthusiasm. Then the general backdrop of the comedy—

one is in love, and another, then they switch roles and one loves another woman, then the two fall in love with sisters, then they switch roles—it's a fairly familiar and well-known theme and quite worn out. Moreover, all these romances are presented against a backdrop of idleness, a backdrop of that sweet indolence, on the basis of military camp and vocations, the muses from which it all originates. Red commanders are depicted in the guise of attractive, fun-loving military who are busy courting and then perform all kinds of services—there is idleness all around.

Does this really correspond to Soviet life? What does this attest to? It attests to a certain dangerous detachment from reality.

But at the same time, take the decisions of the Eighteenth All-Union Party Conference and the shortcomings revealed there. Could one not collect a lot of material and themes there for a good Soviet comedy, if only on issues of purity, stocktaking, and so on? Couldn't you create here an effective, on-target comedy? No, they take these banal materials and create hour-and-a-half comedies and then expect success. Therefore we obviously have not been lucky with Soviet comedy.

CHAPTER FIFTEEN

Presenting the Image of the Leader

Censorship is generally looked at in terms of its negative aspect—banning. Yet as an institution for ideological harmony one should also see it as potentially having a constructive impact on society. One example of this would be the way the main Soviet censorship bodies (from Glavlit to the Politburo) played an active role in establishing the national image of the Party leader. In this chapter we present four documents, each concerning a different branch of the arts (painting, theater, literature, and film). In two of them we see how censorship bodies move to ban representations of the leader but in the other two, by contrast, they seek to foster the particular image presented.

The resolution contained in the first document might seem bizarre were it not for the sensitive nature of the portrait to be censored. Kirov, the head of the Party in Leningrad, had been assassinated in December 1934, an event which continues to occasion speculation about Stalin's possible involvement but which Stalin himself used as justification for the subsequent Great Purge.

· 118 ·

Memorandum from TsK VKP(b) Department of Culture and Propaganda of Leninism Head A. I. Stetsky to the TsK VKP(b) Politburo on the painting by the artist N. Mikhailov on the theme of the funeral of S. M. Kirov. AP RF, f. 3, op. 35, d. 45, ll. 26–27. Original. Typewritten. On the memorandum are the following instructions: "To Molotov, Voroshilov, Kaganovich. I. Stalin"; "Read. *In favor* of the proposal to *arrest* Mikhailov. Molotov" and "Need to arrest this Mikhailov. K. Voroshilov." Beneath the last instruction there is also the signature "Kaganovich."

23 January 1935

To the Politburo of TsK VKP(b)

Since this morning, the Party group of the board of the Moscow Union of Artists has been meeting on the subject of Mikhailov's counterrevolutionary picture (Volter, Bogorodsky, Riazhsky, Lvov, Lekht, Viazmensky, etc.). Called in after that were the prominent artists Yuon, Mashkov, S. Gerasimov, A. Gerasimov, P. Kuznetsov, Lentulov, Katsman, Moor, Favorsky, and Perelman. Com. Bubnov and I spoke with them.

Yuon, who is the leading expert on painting and had not seen Mikhailov's picture before, immediately drew our attention to the skeleton and, as a specialist, gave a detailed analysis, declaring that this could in no way be an "accident," that this was a definite intention.

Other prominent specialists have arrived at the same conclusion, drawing our attention to other details as well in the figure of death given in the picture: to the fact that the details of its feet, limbs, and so forth are given in different colors and patches, which in no way ties in with the bed curtain, that the very folds are unnatural, that on the head of this death the shine and color of the hard part of the skull is emphasized and this could not be a human head; and then the spine is distinctly outlined.

Yuon went on to say that this picture was made especially for photography, since the very choice of colors is built on the figure of death, which stands out most distinctly when photographed and published in the press.

A meeting was then held of the Union's board of forty artists. Mikhailov was called in. The artists themselves questioned him about all the picture's details as well as his biography. At first Mikhailov was defiant and arrogant, declaring that he saw nothing bad in the painting, that it was a sketch, and he threatened to shoot himself. Under cross-examination by specialists, especially Yuon, Lentulov, Gerasimov, Moor, and others, he finally declared that his skeleton had in fact come about as a result of his enthusiasm for mysticism and that this would be a lesson for him from now on.

The questioning of Mikhailov by the artists from the standpoint of his biography brought out the fact that his father was a quartermaster in Kazan, that he himself had gone from Kazan to the East with the Whites in 1918. He had gone with them as far as Vladivostok, there obtained a Polish passport allegedly from the artist Shabel-Tabulevich (who is now also in Moscow and who must be checked out—A. S.), set off with this passport to Harbin, where he worked as a theater artist, and later was in China. He returned to the USSR in 1923.

[...]

After the speeches, the attached resolution was approved unanimously to applause. It must be added that in the picture of the execution of the Paris Communards by this same Mikhailov a skull can be seen behind the group of Communards being executed.

I think that in view of the circumstances brought to light in Mikhailov's case, he must be arrested and a thorough search conducted at his place.

I request permission to give the corresponding instructions to the NKVNudel.

> Head of the TsK VKP(b) Department of Culture and
> Propaganda of Leninism
> A. Stetsky

The image of a national leader was of paramount importance to the Party leadership and any particular version would be always scrutinized with attention to the tiniest detail. The following memorandum from Kerzhentsev regarding guidelines for a competition for the best play to commemorate the twentieth anniversary of the Revolution marks the first time that it was openly permitted to represent Lenin on the stage. Stalin personally crossed his own name out of the draft resolution on the guidelines (text in brackets in the document). Nevertheless, starting from the mid-thirties it became impossible to put Lenin on stage without Stalin.

· 119 ·

Memorandum from P. M. Kerzhentsev, Chairman of the Committee on Arts Affairs under the SNK SSSR, to I. V. Stalin and V. M. Molotov with proposals for the organization of a competition for the best play and screenplay on the October Revolution. RGASPI, f. 17, op. 163, d. 1101, ll. 54, 66. Original. Typewritten.

19 February 1936

To Com. I. V. Stalin
To Com. V. M. Molotov
On the matter of the organization of a closed competition for a play and screenplay about the October Revolution *in connection with the twentieth anniversary of the October revolution,* advance the following considerations:

1. *The Task*
Show the role of Lenin [and Stalin] in the preparation and conduct of the October Revolution, and highlight the Party's organizing role.

The pivotal point of the play and screenplay should be the proletarian October Revolution as a decisive stage in the history of mankind.

Lenin may be shown in the play and the screenplay.

[. . .]

Kerzhentsev

Determining the image of the leader became a prerogative of the Politburo (and in effect of Stalin). No changes or additions to this image could be made without Stalin's permission. In the following document it will be noted that here the Politburo is even attacking Lenin's widow, Nadezhda Krupskaia, for playing a consultative role, *without Politburo supervision,* in the writing of a fictionalized account of the family of Lenin.

· 120 ·

Resolution of the TsK VKP(b) Politburo on M. S. Shaginyan's novel *A History Exam (Bilet po istorii)*. RGASPI, f. 17, op. 3, d. 1001, l. 14. Original. Typewritten.

5 August 1938

No. 63, p. 73—On Marietta Shaginyan's novel *A History Exam,* part 1, The Ulianov Family [*Sem'ia Ul'ianovykh*].

Having familiarized ourselves with the first part of Marietta Shaginyan's novel *A History Exam* (subtitled "The Ulianov Family"), as well as with the circumstances surrounding this novel's appearance, the TsK VKP(b) has established that Shaginyan's book, while pretending to give a biographical documentary novel about the life of the Ulianov family, as well as about the childhood and youth of Lenin, is a politically harmful and ideologically hostile work. It has been deemed a crude political error on the part of the editor of *Red Virgin Soil* [*Krasnaia nov'*], Com. Yermilov, and the former director of GIKhL [State Publishing House for Literature], Com. Bolshemennikov, to allow Shaginyan's novel to be published.

We condemn the conduct of Com. Krupskaia who, having received the manuscript of the novel from Shaginyan, not only did not stand in the way of the novel's appearance but on the contrary did everything to encourage Shaginyan, gave positive reviews of the manuscript, and consulted with Shaginyan on the factual aspect of the life of the Ulianov family and therefore bears full responsibility for this book.

We consider the conduct of Com. Krupskaia so much the more inadmissible and tactless because Com. Krupskaia did everything without the knowledge or consent of the TsK VKP(b), behind the back of the TsK VKP(b), thereby transforming a general Party matter—the compilation of works on Lenin—into a private family matter and acting in the role of monopolistic interpreter of the circumstances of the public and private life and work of Lenin and his family, for which the TsK has never given anyone the rights.

The TsK VKP(b) resolves:

1. to remove Com. Yermilov from his post as editor of *Red Virgin Soil*;
2. to reprimand former GIKhL Director Com. Bolshemennikov;
3. to point out to Com. Krupskaia the errors she has committed;
4. to prohibit the publication of works about Lenin without the knowledge and consent of the TsK VKP(b);
5. to remove Shaginyan's book from use;
6. to suggest that the Board of the Union of Soviet Writers reprimand Shaginyan.

The following document shows the material rewards to be gained by film directors and actors who represented key moments in Soviet history in a way acceptable to the Soviet leadership. The films *Lenin in 1918* [*Lenin v 1918 godu*] and *Man with a Rifle* [*Chelovek s ruzh'em*] feature Lenin, and in fact Shchukin is being rewarded for his depiction of Lenin. The film *Shchors* is about a legendary commander from the Civil War.

· 121 ·

Resolution of the TsK VKP(b) Politburo on material incentives for cinematography workers. RGASPI, f. 17, op. 3, d. 1008, l. 10. Original. Typewritten.
23 March 1939

No. 1. p. 49—*On issuing raised wages to movie directors and camera operators and prizes to the artist Com. Shchukin.*

Permit the chairman of the Committee on Cinematography Affairs to make a payment for the staging of the following moving pictures:

1. *Lenin in 1918*—to director M. I. Romm, 100,000 rubles; to cameraman B. I. Volchek, 30,000 rubles;

2. *Shchors*—to director A. P. Dovzhenko, 100,000 rubles; to cameraman Iu. I. Yekelchik, 30,000 rubles;

3. *Man with a Rifle*—to director S. I. Yutkevich, 75,000 rubles; to cameraman Zh. K. Martov, 25,000 rubles;

4. Award a prize to Com. Shchukin of 20,000 rubles by economizing on the funds of the Cinema Committee.

The material and symbolic awards (dachas, state honors, etc.) handed out to cultural workers were in function directives indicating the current interpretations of the correct ideological and aesthetic parameters for works of art, censorship being another. But Stalin's ideological and aesthetic tastes were absolute and in consequence Stalin was both chief censor and chief patron in the arts.

CHAPTER SIXTEEN

Stalin as Patron-Potentate

Within Stalin's correspondence, the letters from intellectuals could largely be categorized as essentially complaints or requests—petitions, a genre which in the circumstances usually necessitated an obsequious tone. The following letter from Mikhail Bulgakov which recounts his misadventures in applying for an external passport so that he could travel abroad provides a vivid example of the sort of demeaning protestations of loyalty and praise for the leader to which most supplicants were reduced.

· 122 ·

Letter from M. A. Bulgakov to I. V. Stalin. AP RF, f. 3, op. 34, d. 206, ll. 37–38v. Original. Typewritten. On the first page of the letter, across the first two paragraphs, Stalin has written sweepingly: "Confer."
Moscow, 11 June 1934

---

from the playwright and director of the Gorky MKhAT SSSR Mikhail Afanasievich Bulgakov
Deeply respected Iosif Vissarionovich!
Permit me to inform you of what has happened to me.
1.
In late April of this year I sent to the Chairman of the Government Commission that administers the Art Theater an application in which I asked for permission for a two-month trip abroad, accompanied by my wife Elena Sergeevna Bulgakova, as well as permission to exchange Soviet for foreign currency in the quantity that I find necessary for the trip.

In the application I indicated the purpose of my trip—to compose a book about my journey through Western Europe and brief treatment in the south of France.

Since I truly am suffering from exhaustion of the nervous system, in connection with my fear of being alone, I also asked for permission for my wife to accompany me, while at the same time leaving here, for the time of our trip, my seven-year-old stepson, whom I am supporting and bringing up.

After sending the application, I began waiting for one of two answers, that is, permission for the trip or denial, believing there could be no third.

However, something I hadn't anticipated happened, that is, a third.

On 17 May, I received a telephone call (I didn't ask who it was), inquiring whether I had submitted an application for foreign travel.[1]

Moreover, the following conversation took place:

"Did you submit an application concerning foreign travel?"

"Yes."

"Go to the Foreign Department [INO] of Mosgubispolkom [Moscow Region Executive Committee] and fill in a form for yourself and your wife."

"When do I need to do this?"

"As quickly as possible, since your case will be examined on the 21st or 22nd."

In a fit of joy, I didn't even ask who was speaking with me, I immediately showed up with my wife at the Ispolkom INO and there gave my name. When the employee heard I had been called in to the INO by telephone, he suggested that I wait and went into the next room, and returning, asked me to fill out forms.

Upon their completion, he took them, attaching to them two photos apiece, and took no money, saying:

"The passports will be free."

He did not take our Soviet [internal] passports, saying:

"That's later, when you do the exchange for external ones."

Then he added the following word for word:

"You will get your passports very soon, since there are instructions concerning you. You could have received them today, but it's too late now. Call me on the morning of the 18th."

I said:

"But the 18th is a weekend."

Then he answered:

"Well then, the 19th."

On the morning of the 19th, in response to our call, the following was said:

"Still no passports. Call toward the end of the day. If the passports are here, the passport officer will issue them to you."

After a call toward the end of the day it became clear there were no passports, and it was suggested we call on the 23rd.

On 23 May I personally appeared with my wife at the INO, moreover I learned that there were no passports. Here the employee began making inquiries by telephone about them, and then suggested we call on 25 or 27 May.

Then I was put somewhat on my guard and asked the employee whether there definitely was an instruction about me or had I misunderstood on 17 May.

The reply I received to that was this:

"You realize yourself I can't tell you whose instruction it is, *but there is an instruction concerning you and your wife,* just as there is concerning the writer Pilnyak."

At that any doubts I might have had fell away, and my joy was boundless.

Soon after came yet another confirmation of the existence of permission for me. I received a report from the Theater that the following was said in the TsIK secretariat:

"The Bulgakovs' case is being settled."

At that time they congratulated me that my writer's dream of so many years of a trip, so essential to every writer, had come true.

At the same time the Ispolkom's INO kept putting off an answer concerning passports from one day to the next, which I regarded with total equanimity, believing that no matter how much they put it off, there would be passports.

On 7 June, a courier from the Art Theater went to the INO with a list of artists who were supposed to get foreign passports. The Theater kindly put me and my wife on this list, although I had submitted our application separately from the Theater.

In the afternoon the courier returned, moreover even from his distraught and confused face I could see that something had happened.

The courier informed me that passports had been issued to the artists, that he had them in his pocket, but with regard to me and my wife he said that we had been DENIED passports.

The next day, without the slightest delay, INO was informed that Citizen M. A. Bulgakov had been denied permission for the right to travel abroad.

After this, so as not to have to listen to expressions of sympathy, amazement, and so forth, I went home, understanding just one thing, that I had landed in a grievous, ridiculous position unbefitting my age.

2.

The insult inflicted on me at INO Mosoblispolkom is all the more serious because my four years of service at MKhAT give it no grounds for this, which is why I am asking for you to intercede.

... I can hope to receive permission for foreign travel as easily as my comrades at work in MKhAT can do this.

The sole reason for this, I assume, can be just one: doesn't there exist in the organs that control foreign travel the assumption that if I leave for a short trip I will remain abroad permanently?

If that is so, then I, accepting responsibility for my words, am informing you that this assumption has absolutely no basis, not even an imaginary one.

I am not even talking about the fact that in order to depart for abroad after my deceptive petition I would have to part my wife from her child, thereby placing her in a horrific position, destroying the life of my family, making me personally scuttle my own repertoire at the Art Theater, and disgracing myself—and most importantly, all this for no good reason.

What is important here is something else: I cannot comprehend why I, in appealing to the Government with a petition so important for me, should inevitably put false information in it.

I don't understand why, if one thing was intended, another was solicited.

And I have proof of the fact that I don't understand this.

Exactly four years ago I went to the Government with a petition in which I begged for either permission to leave the Union indefinitely or permission to go to work at MKhAT.

Having contemplated at the time an open-ended departure, in view of my personal circumstances as a writer, I did not write about a two-month trip.

Now, though, in 1934, having decided on a short trip, I am asking for it.

I have neither guarantees, nor warrantors.

I am asking you to review my case—involving a trip with my wife to France and Italy to compose a book, from the second half of July through September of this year.

Mikhail Bulgakov

Permanent address: 3 Nashchokinsky Avenue, Apt. 44, Moscow 19, tel. 58-67.

Temporary (from 14 June to 15 July): Hotel Astoria, MKhAT *Days of the Turbins* Tour, Leningrad.

The following document, a letter to Stalin from Lily Brik, with whom the poet Vladimir Mayakovsky had been involved for much of the 1920s in a ménage à trois, has not been hitherto known. Mayakovsky had committed suicide in 1930 and some critics had assumed he should be attacked as unstable and an avant-gardist. But Stalin's response to the Brik letter became known to the entire country a few weeks after he received hers, presented in the form of his famous pronouncement about Mayakovsky, published in *Literary Gazette* on 12 December 1935: "Mayakovsky was and remains the best and most talented poet of our Soviet epoch. Indifference to his memory and his works is a crime." With this statement Stalin not only instantly canonized Mayakovsky, but also became virtually the only remaining defender of those who wanted to continue the tradition of the avantgarde from the 1920s (if in a watered-down version). It should be recalled, however, that the articles in *Pravda* that launched the anti-Formalist campaign, a campaign that was essentially directed against modernist tendencies (see Chapter 12), appeared only a month after this statement was published, one of many facts that should complicate any account of Stalin's role in Soviet cultural history.

· 123 ·

Letter from L. Yu. Brik to I. V. Stalin. AP RF, f. 45, op. 1, d. 729. Copy. Typewritten.
24 November 1935

Dear Comrade Stalin,

Since the death of the poet Mayakovsky, all matters connected with the publication of his poetry and the perpetuation of his memory have been consolidated with me.

I have his entire archive, his drafts, notebooks, and manuscripts, all his things. I am editing his works. People have been coming to me for materials, information, and photographs.

I am doing everything in my power to see that his poems are published, his things preserved, and the constantly mounting interest in Mayakovsky is satisfied at least in part.

And interest in Mayakovsky is mounting with each passing year.

His poems have not only not become dated, but today they are absolutely topical and are a very powerful revolutionary weapon.

Nearly six years have passed since the day of Mayakovsky's death and he has yet to be replaced by anyone. He remains, as he was, the most important poet of our Revolution.

Far from everyone understands this, however.

It will soon be six years since the day he died, and only half of his *Complete Collected Works* have come out, and that with a print run of only 10,000 copies.

Negotiations have been going on for more than a year over a one-volume edition. The material was submitted long ago, but the book has not even been typeset.

His children's books are not being reprinted at all.

There are no books by Mayakovsky in the stores. They are impossible to purchase.

After Mayakovsky's death, a Government resolution proposed organizing a Mayakovsky room at the Komakademia [Communist Academy], where all his materials and manuscripts would be gathered. So far there is still no such office.

The materials are scattered. Some are in the Moscow Literary Museum, which has absolutely no interest in them. This is obvious if only because the museum's bulletin makes almost no mention of Mayakovsky.

A few years ago the District Soviet of the Proletarsky District suggested to me that they restore Mayakovsky's last apartment and, attached to it, organize a district library in Mayakovsky's name.

A while later I was informed that the Moscow Soviet had refused the money, though the money required was very little.

It is a small wooden house with four apartments (15 Gendrikov Lane, Taganka). One of the apartments was Mayakovsky's. The library was supposed to be housed in the others. The District Soviet was undertaking to find new housing for the few residents.

The apartment is very characteristic for Mayakovsky's daily life—plain, modest, clean.

The little house could be razed any day. Rather than regret this for the next fifty years and try to gather objects bit by bit from the daily life and work environment of the Revolution's great poet, wouldn't it be better to restore all this while we are still alive?

We are grateful now for that inkpot, for that desk and chair, which they display for us in the Lermontov house in Piatigorsk.

Discussion has been raised many times about renaming Triumfalnaya Square in Moscow and Nadezhdinskaia Street in Leningrad Mayakovsky Square and Street. This, too, however, has not come about.

This is the main thing. I am not mentioning a number of minor facts. As an example: on the instruction of Narkompros, "*Lenin*" and "*Good*" [*Khorosho*] have been thrown out of the modern literature textbook for 1935. They are not even mentioned.

All this taken together points to the fact that our institutions do not realize the immense significance of Mayakovsky—his propaganda role, his revolutionary relevance. They underestimate the exceptional interest there is in him among Komsomol and Soviet youth.

Therefore they publish him very little and very slowly, instead of publishing his selected poems in a print run of hundreds of thousands.

Therefore they take no care to collect all the materials related to him before they are lost.

They don't think about preserving the memory of him for up and coming generations.

I cannot overcome this bureaucratic disinterest and resistance alone. After six years of work I turn to you, since I see no other means of realizing Mayakovsky's enormous revolutionary legacy.

    L. Brik

My address:
    11 Ryleev Street, Apt. 3, Leningrad
    telephones: Smolny switchboard, 25-99
    and Nekrasovskaia ATS 2-90-69

Written on the letter is Stalin's instruction from no earlier than 29 November 1935: "Com. Yezhov! I ask you to look at Brik's letter. Mayakovsky was and is the best and most talented poet of our Soviet era. Indifference to his memory and works is a crime. Brik's complaints, I think, are correct. Contact her (Brik) or summon her to Moscow, bring Tal and Mekhlis in on the case, and please, do everything we have neglected to do. If my help is needed, I'm ready. Greetings! I. Stalin."

The famous Ukrainian film director Aleksandr Dovzhenko had already established a relationship with Stalin before writing the following letter. When he was having trouble getting approval for the script *Aerograd* (1935), a film set in the Far East which he both wrote and directed, he appealed directly to the Kremlin. Stalin endorsed the script and, while pinning the Order of Lenin on Dovzhenko in 1935, suggested that he make a film about the Ukrainian Civil War commander Shchors as a "Ukrainian Chapaev" (a reference to the film *Chapaev* of 1934 about a legendary Russian Civil War commander which had become the canonical example of Socialist Realist cinema). However, this politically sensitive assignment proved problematical and negotiations with senior officials over the script dragged on for three years before the film was completed in 1939.

· 124 ·

Letter from A. P. Dovzhenko to I. V. Stalin. AP RF, f. 3, op. 35, d. 75, ll. 50–53.
Copy. Typewritten.
26 November 1936

Moscow, 47/24 Herzen Street
Deeply esteemed Iosif Vissarionovich,

It is very hard and even frightening for me to judge what reading my letter evokes in you—fury or a smile of irony. Nonetheless, I can no longer keep from writing you about what is literally oppressing me and preventing me from working on the completion of *Shchors*.

In submitting the scenario to the GUK [State Administration of Cinematography] leadership, I myself stated that the image of Shchors I have is not sufficiently polished. This happened not out of carelessness or frivolity but from incorrect advice given me by the Ukrainian leadership in resolving the image of Shchors as a fighter with the Trotskyite command. This mistake led to an impoverishment of Shchors, an impoverishment of the dramatic conflict. I felt this, but by then I needed help and consultation here in Moscow.

[. . .]

I had the misfortune to speak in a discussion at a House of Cinema and to make a number of critical comments on the reasons for our lag in film production, which the TsK knows about. I think this is what destroyed me. Com. Shumiatsky, who hates criticism, especially from his workers, did not come to the discussion, but at an open Party meeting at his office at GUK he routed me and discredited me politically, declaring to the meeting that my screenplay was taking so long to finish as a result of the presence in it of a number of major faults up to and including the insinuation of SR [Socialist Revolutionary] ideology, letting the meeting understand that this was not just his personal opinion but also the opinion of the top leadership.

At that time the GUK already knew that you had read the screenplay.

Right now I have two written conclusions from GUK, or rather three, if you also count the first one issued me "in error" and confiscated the next day, i.e., the day you requested the screenplay. The third, additional conclusion, says that "the impoverishment of Shchors's image and the abundance of colors and attention given to the figure of Bozhenko create a situation when it seems, and not without foundation, that the author evidently sympathizes more with Bozhenko than Shchors."

[. . .]

Iosif Vissarionovich, this is all wrong. It's wrong.

I did not hear one warm word about a single bit of the screenplay at

GUK. I'm feeling a chill from the staff of the directors, and working is no fun.

[. . .]

Forgive me, dear Iosif Vissarionovich, if I don't believe you saw an insinuation of SR ideology in my admittedly incomplete work.

I am a Soviet art worker. This is my life, and if I am doing it wrong, then it is due to a shortage of talent or development, not malice.

I bear your refusal to receive me as a great sorrow.

But *Nikolai Shchors* will be magnificent, profound, and exciting. I have almost accomplished this now in the screenplay, and I have many more fine thoughts ahead.

Deeply respecting you,
A. Dovzhenko

So called "collective letters" to the leader, a genre that was to become popular under Brezhnev and Gorbachev, were very rare in the 1930s. At that time intellectuals were generally apprehensive about "collective consequences" if a jointly signed letter was received unfavorably; they could be greater than for an individual's letter because of the probable suspicion that the signatories might represent a clandestine organization. Dissatisfaction with the situation in film was nevertheless so great by the end of the decade that several prominent directors, all of whom had produced Soviet classics, sent the following joint letter to Stalin (one could speculate as to whether this letter is symptomatic of the officially sponsored reaction within culture against the deleterious effects of the purge era, to be seen in literature in doc. 87):

· 125 ·

Letter from a group of cinematographers to I. V. Stalin. [No later than 13 July 1940]. AP RF, f. 3, op. 35, d. 64, ll. 81–83. Original. Typewritten.

Dear Iosif Vissarionovich!

After great hesitations, we have decided to write to you. More than once in the last two years we have asked ourselves the question of the possibility of this appeal. The fact that beneath it stand our signatures and no others is not a result of the fact that we are connected in any special way; we work in different studios, we have different creative paths, and the sole thing we have in common is our awareness of our responsibility for our cause.

We know how excessively busy you are. And nonetheless we are obliged to ask you to read this letter.[2] We purposely have not discussed it with any of our comrades and have not "gathered signatures." At the same time, though, we are convinced that every cinema worker would say the same thing we are saying.

The state of affairs in the film art seems to us very alarming. Three or four good pictures come out in a year. All the rest are exceptionally wretched, gray, boring, often illiterate and banal.

Technically, all the pictures without exception are at an extremely low level. The projection and mass reproduction are so poor that the people are seeing these pictures in an even worse, totally distorted form.

Cinematography has been transformed from the youngest, most militant, impassioned, joyous, and cheerful art into gray, doctrinaire rumination. Although it is the sharpest weapon after print in the hands of the Party, cinematography is not accomplishing its tasks for the country.

The moral condition of creative workers is very difficult.

What are the reasons for all this?

First. The unprecedented pressure of self-criticism and the inexplicable mistrust of the cinema's leadership for its own cadres.

Second. The main link of film art: the screenplay business is in a catastrophic condition. The huge, overwhelming majority of screenplays that go into production are of very low quality.

This is happening above all because of the persistent poisoning in cinematography of the creative atmosphere, which is steadily being replaced by bureaucratic relations. The planning and acceptance of screenplays is ruled by excessive caution, bad taste, and a vulgar understanding of the tasks of art. Screenplays pass through a huge number of offices, each of which has the right to make corrections to its own taste. The screenplays lose their individuality. The existing system of payment for the writer's labor—as a result of the abolition of copyright—has led to a complete leveling that benefits only hacks and bad workmen.

Third. The same reasons make the director's creative work in production very hard. The people creating pictures of major political significance intended to resolve major artistic and political questions in art have been placed in conditions of petty-minded oversight and arrogant mistrust, and thereby deprived of the opportunity to develop creatively in full.

Fourth. Cinema technology has lagged behind impermissibly, and as we know, the cinematic art and its progress depend wholly on technology. We have lost the opportunity to use the arsenal of technical means that make foreign films look so attractive. [. . .]

Fifth. The organized system of leadership for cinematography is founded on a complete confounding of the issues of art and the cinematography industry. The tremendous confusion regarding these issues allows for no possibility of discovering who's right and who's wrong. Centralization has been taken to the absurd. Studios operating with tens of millions of rubles and in fact creating works of cinema art have lost the opportunity to resolve their own financial, creative, or organizational problems essential for operative work. Even issues of rhyme in a lover's song are subject to coordination, consultation, sanctioning, and approval from all offices right up to the chairman of the committee.

Sixth. Relations between the leadership and artists of Soviet cinema have reached the limits of the impossible. Cinematography's leadership does not understand that in twenty-two years the Party reared cadres of genuine Party and non-Party Bolshevik workers in Soviet cinema. Instead of relying on these cadres in all their activities, they, the leadership, are pushing them away, looking on cinema artists as a gang of idlers, self-seekers, bohemians.

[. . .]

Dear Iosif Vissarionovich! We know that you follow the work and successes of Soviet cinema with love. We are afraid of losing this love of yours, which is always the love of the people. It is for this reason that we cannot shut ourselves up each in his own work, cannot fail to be alarmed at the general fate of Soviet cinematography.

We feel we do not have the right to remain silent. Each of us, like the entire mass of creative workers in the cinema, is prepared to give all our efforts to justify the people's faith.

We ask for your intercession. Moreover, if you, dear Iosif Vissarionovich, find it possible to receive a group of artists from Soviet cinematography and speak with them about these matters, that would be a tremendous happiness for each of them and would play a decisive role in the development of the Soviet cinema art.

Trauberg, Mikh. Romm, Al. Kapler, Sergei Vasiliev, F. Ermler, Gr. Aleksandrov

Stalin's responses to his correspondents are of particular interest. The following note by Stalin is addressed to Afinogenov, a former prominent member of RAPP and a leading Soviet playwright of the "psychological realist" school. His plays, and especially *Fear* (*Strakh*, 1930), an expose of the "bourgeois" intelligentsia at a time of militant proletarianization, were performed in scores of theaters throughout the country. *Deceit* (*Lozh'*), finished in 1933, was being rehearsed by MkhAT and a Kharkov theater. In the play Afinogenov exposed double dealing among members of the Party Opposition resulting in crimes, wrecking, and deceit, and warned that this climate of insincerity and intrigue could infect others around them. But, as in *Fear*,

Afinogenov resisted depicting his negative characters as cardboard villains (Stalin was frequently troubled when in works of art the "enemies" emerged as more colorful and interesting than the heroes, and this is one cause for his reservations here). Moreover, in the play the protagonist, Nina, is plagued by doubts and agonizes over whether to denounce an "enemy" to whom she is attached, to the point where she can stand it no longer and commits suicide.

· 126 ·

Note from I. V. Stalin to A. N. Afinogenov with comments on his play *Deceit*. [No earlier than 2 April 1933]. RGASPI, f. 558, op. 1, d. 5088, ll. 118–118v.

Com. Afinogenov!

The play's conception is a rich one, but its staging is not rich. For some reason, *all* the Party men you have came out as monsters, physical, moral, and polit[ical] monsters (Gorchakova, Viktor, Kulik, Seroshtanov). Even Riadovoy sometimes looks imperfect in some way, almost retarded. The only person who carries out a logical and thoroughly considered line (of double-dealing) is Nakatov. He's the most "integrated."

What was the purpose of Nina's shooting [herself]? It only confuses the matter and spoils all the music.

Kulik should have been contrasted to another *honest, unstained worker selflessly devoted to the cause* (open your eyes and you'll see that we have such workers in the Party).

You should have had in the play a meeting of workers where they expose Viktor, overthrow Gorchakova, and restore the truth. This is even more essential because you don't have any *actions* in the play at all, there are only *conversations* (if you don't count Nina's senseless and unnecessary shooting).

You succeeded, I think, with the types of the *father, mother, and Nina*. But they are not thoroughly worked out, not fully sculpted.

Nearly every hero has his own (conversational) style. But these styles are not worked out, they're stilted and sloppily conveyed. Evidently you were in a hurry to finish the play.

Why is Seroshtanov depicted as a physical monster? You don't think, do you, that only physical monsters can be devoted Party members?

The play cannot be released in this form.

Let's talk [about this] if you like.

    Greetings!
    I. Stalin

P.S. It is in vain that you go on about the "leader." This is not good and perhaps not decent. It's not a matter of the "leader" but of the collective leader—the Party's TsK.

I. St[alin]

The following letter in which Stalin comes out in defense of Leonid Sobolev, a mediocre writer, is curious because it appears that Stalin is undermining the standard demand of the literary bureaucracy that writers produce novels about Soviet production and construction, or even that he is advocating creative freedom! However, it can also be read as symptomatic of a waning of interest around 1935 in themes having to do with economic development and a shift to emphasizing as topics for literature the Civil War and other military or historical themes.

· 127 ·

Note from I. V. Stalin to SSP Secretary V. P. Stavsky on the writer L. S. Sobolev.
AP RF, f. 45, op. 1, d. 1118, l. 149. Copy. Typewritten.
10 December 1935

Com. Stavsky!
Pay attention to Com. Sobolev. He is indisputably a major talent (judging from his book, *Major Overhaul* [*Kapital'nyy remont*]). As is evident from his letter, he is capricious and uneven (he does not recognize "the turning back"). However these characteristics, in my opinion, are present in all major literary talents (with perhaps a few exceptions).
There is no need to require him to write a second *Major Overhaul*. Nothing necessitates it. There is no need to require him to write about kolkhozes or Magnitogorsk. One cannot write about such things out of duty.
Let him write *what* he wants and *when* he wants.
In short, let him run wild. . . . And protect him.

Greetings!
I. Stalin

The film *Shchors* (see also doc. 124) which Stalin critiques in the following note was one of many films and literary works from this period that contributed to mythologizing the Civil War. As we see here, he was little concerned with aesthetic aspects of a given work, but more that the historical account be "truthful," that it conform with the official version.

· 128 ·

Note from I. V. Stalin to State Administration of Cinematography Head B. Z. Shumiatsky concerning the screenplay for the film *Shchors*. AP RF, f. 3, op. 35, d. 75, l. 56. Copy. Typewritten.

9 December 1936

Com. Shumiatsky!

1. Shchors came out too crude and uncouth. Shchors's true face must be restored.

2. Bozhenko did not come out in full. The author evidently sympathizes more with Bozhenko than Shchors.

3. Shchors's staff is nowhere to be seen. Why?

4. It cannot be that Shchors had no tribunal, otherwise he would not have started executing fighters over trifles (a tobacco pouch, etc.).

5. It is not good that Shchors looks less cultured and cruder than Chapaev. It's unnatural.

I. Stalin

In the culture of the thirties the new (revised) history of the Party was needless to say no less important than the mythologized version of the Civil War. Stalin was personally involved in a series of decrees and publishing ventures which progressively reviewed the standard account of Party history, a process that culminated in 1938 with the publication of the *Istoria Vsesoiuznoi Kommunisticheskoi Partii (Bolshevikov): Kratky kurs* [*History of the Communist Party of the Soviet Union (Bolsheviks): Short Course*], a book about which there has been continued speculation as to precisely what role Stalin played in its composition. The *Short Course* was to remain authoritative for the rest of the Stalin period and became a primer at all schools and universities. Here Stalin discusses one of the many films of the 1930s which present the new take on recent Party history, Ermler's *The Great Citizen* (*Veliky grazhdanin*), a thinly disguised political biography of Sergei Kirov (called Shakhov in the film). Since Kirov's murder in 1934 was frequently used as a justification of the terror, Stalin's concern with this film was even more politically motivated than usual. The Piatakov-Radek trial mentioned in this document, the second of the three show trials, was held in Moscow between 23 and 30 January 1937. The seventeen defendants were charged with industrial wrecking and espionage allegedly done at the behest of Trotsky and the German government.

· 129 ·

Note from I. V. Stalin to the State Administration of Cinematography Head B. Z. Shumiatsky concerning the screenplay for *The Great Citizen*. RGASPI, f. 71, op. 10, d. 127, ll. 188–189. Printed text.
27 January 1937

To B. Shumiatsky

I've read Com. Ermler's screenplay *(The Great Citizen)*. It is indisputably well put together politically. Its literary merits are also indisputable.

There are errors, however.

1. The representatives of the "opposition" look older than the TsK representatives physically and in the sense of Party seniority. This is not typical and does not correspond to reality. Reality gives the opposite picture.

2. Zhelyabov's portrait needs to be eliminated. There is no analogy between the terrorist-pygmies from the camp of Zinovievites and Trotskyites and the revolutionary Zhelyabov.

3. Mentions of Stalin must be deleted. The Party's TsK should be substituted for Stalin.

4. Shakhov's murder should not serve as the center and high point of the screenplay: any terrorist act pales before the facts disclosed at the trial of Piatakov and Radek.

The struggle between the two programs, the two aims, should be the screenplay's center and high point: one program is for the victory of socialism in the USSR, the elimination of all remnants of capitalism, the independence and territorial integrity of the USSR, antifascism and rapprochement with nonfascist states against the fascist states and against war, for the policy of peace; the other program is for the restoration of capitalism in the USSR and the undoing of the socialist achievements, against the independence of the USSR and for the dismemberment of the USSR for the benefit of the fascist states, for rapprochement with the most powerful fascist states against the interests of the working class and to the detriment of the interests of the nonfascist states, for the exacerbation of the military threat and against the policy of peace.

The situation must be presented in such a way that the struggle between the Trotskyites and the Soviet government looks not like a struggle for power between two coteries, of which one "is lucky" in this struggle and the other is "unlucky," which would be a crude distortion of reality, but as a struggle between two programs, the first of which corresponds to the interests of the Revolution and is supported by the people and the second contradicts the interests of the revolution and is rejected by the people.

However, it follows from this that the screenplay will have to be redone, making it more contemporary in its content, reflecting all the main things that were revealed by the Piatakov-Radek trial.

With Com[munist] greeting
I. Stalin

At the same time as so much attention was being devoted to Party history, historians of the nation were increasingly required to incorporate their accounts of prerevolutionary Russia into a single heroic narrative that culminated in Stalin's socialist state while, in turn, Soviet culture was inflected with Russian national motifs. Particularly popular as subjects for cultural production were Russian tsars and military commanders, and the accounts of their achievements were often structured as allegories for current situations or Party leaders. The following document concerns a film about the last years of the famous Russian military commander Suvorov and his victories over Napoleon.

· 130 ·

Note from I. V. Stalin to SNK SSSR Committee on Cinematography Affairs Chairman I. G. Bolshakov concerning the screenplay for *Suvorov*. RGASPI, f. 71, op. 10, d. 127, ll. 389–390. Copy. Printer's copy.
9 June 1940

To Com. Bolshakov.

The screenplay for *Suvorov* suffers from inadequacies. It is thin and not rich in content. It is time to stop depicting Suvorov as a kindly old man who occasionally crows "Cock-a-doodle-do" and keeps repeating "Russian," "Russian." This is not where the secret of Suvorov's victories lies.

The screenplay does not reveal the specific features of Suvorov's military policy and tactics: (1) a correct estimate of his opponent's shortcomings and an ability to take full advantage of them, (2) a well thought-out and bold attack combined with a flanking maneuver to strike at the opponent's rear, (3) an ability to choose experienced and bold commanders and direct them at the object of the strike, (4) an ability to boldly advance those who distinguish themselves to higher posts, going against the requirements of the "rules on ranks," reckoning little with the official seniority and origins of those he promotes, (5) an ability to support strict, truly iron discipline in the army.

Reading the screenplay, you might think that Suvorov turned a blind eye to discipline in the army (that he did not value discipline highly) and that he took the upper hand not thanks to these characteristics of his military policy and tactics but primarily by his goodness toward the soldiers and bold cunning with regard to the opponent bordering on a certain adventurism. This is a misunderstanding, of course, to say the least.

These comments also refer to the well-known play *Suvorov* being presented at TsDKA [M. V. Frunze Central House of the Red Army].

I. Stalin

The new line on culture that was introduced in the mid-1930s involved not only a return to Russian national values but also encouragement of a new interest in national identity among members of the republics that made up the Soviet Union—one, however, in which their republican identity was seen as distinctive but at the same time involved with, or structurally subordinated to, the overall national narrative of the Soviet state. Stalin's response recorded below to the film *Georgy Saakadze* provides a good example of this. Part I of *Georgy Saakadze,* an epic of seventeenth-century Georgia with a screenplay by Anna Antonovskaya and Boris Cherny (an adaptation of her novel) was one of several historical films produced at this time for each of the major national republics. It was directed by the prominent Stalinist director Mikhail Chiaureli, came out in 1942, and was awarded a Stalin Prize, as was Part II, released in 1943. In the film Saakadze is represented as the wise unifier of Georgia, who is prepared to sacrifice anything for that cause, a role Stalin saw himself as playing for the entire Soviet Union. Chiaureli, a Georgian, was the director who did most for establishing the screen image of Stalin (particularly in his infamous later film, *The Fall of Berlin* [*Padenie Berlina*] of 1948).

· 131 ·

Note from I. V. Stalin to SNK SSSR Committee on Cinematography Affairs Chairman I. G. Bolshakov concerning screenplays for the motion picture *Georgy Saakadze*. RGASPI, f. 71, op. 10, d. 127, ll. 399–400. Printer's copy.

11 October 1940

To Com. Bolshakov
Copy: Leonidze
Copy: Antonovskaya and Cherny

A few days ago I received two screenplays on the theme of *Georgy Saakadze:* one by Antonovskaya and Cherny, the other by Leonidze.

In my opinion, Leonidze's screenplay is unsuccessful. It is poor in its artistic aspects. It is somewhat primitive in terms of the selection and use of historical material.

The screenplay by Antonovskaya and Cherny is free of similar shortcomings. However it has another shortcoming. It ends with the victory as the apotheosis of Saakadze's policy and Saakadze himself. Such a finale, though, as we know, does not correspond to historical reality and creates a false impression of Georgia's past. In fact, as history tells us, Saakadze's policy, although it was progressive from the standpoint of Georgia's future prospects, suffered a defeat (and Saakadze himself perished), since Georgia in the time of Saakadze had still not matured enough for that kind of policy, i.e., for its unification into a single state by means of affirming tsarist absolutism and eliminating the power of the princes. The reason is clear: the princes and feudalism proved more powerful, and the tsar and nobility weaker, than Saakadze had assumed. Saakadze felt this inner weakness of Georgia and conceived the idea of getting around that by attracting to the cause an outside (foreign) power. But the foreign power could not compensate for the country's internal weakness. And that is what occurred, as we know. Given these insoluble contradictions, Saakadze's policy had to—and in fact did—suffer defeat.

I think that this historical truth should be restored in the screenplay by Antonovskaya and Cherny.

And if it is restored, the screenplay of Antonovskaya and Cherny could be characterized as one of the best works of Soviet cinematography.

    I. Stalin

In the following document Stalin critiques a film on Komsomol life which was directed by Aleksandr Stolper and Boris Ivanov but banned in 1941, causing quite a stir. His remarks on the screenplay were typical of the directives he had given since at least 1931 about how to represent historical reality "truthfully," and how to depict negative characters.

· 132 ·

Uncorrected transcript of I. V. Stalin's speech at the session of the TsK VKP(b) on the motion picture *Law of Life* [*Zakon zhizni*] based on a screenplay by A. O. Avdeenko. RGASPI, f. 77, op. 1, d. 907, ll. 72–82. Copy. Typewritten.

9 September 1940

Here there are various issues, and these issues are of grave importance for the development of literature. I want to express myself on an issue that has nothing to do with Avdeenko's book—on the approach to literature. There is an approach to literature that is truthful and objective. This truthful and objective approach, does it mean that it may or must be impartial—simply draw or photograph? Can you place a living person, a writer who wants to be truthful and objective, on the same footing as a camera? By no means. That means truthfulness and objectivity have to be living, not impassive. This is a living person, he sympathizes with someone, is not particularly taken by one of his heroes. This means truthfulness and objectivity are truthfulness and objectivity that serve some class.

Plekhanov said that literature cannot exhibit a tendency [*sic*],[3] but when he decoded this, it emerged that literature has to serve certain conditions, a certain class, a certain society. Therefore, literature cannot be a camera. That's not how truthfulness should be understood. There cannot be literature without passion, it sympathizes with someone, despises someone. I think that we must approach an assessment of literature from this point of view—from the point of view of truthfulness and objectivity.

There is a demand for works to represent the enemy for us in all his most important aspects. Is this right or wrong? Wrong. There are different ways of writing—the way of Gogol, or of Shakespeare. They have outstanding heroes—negative and positive. When you read Shakespeare or Gogol, or Griboedov, you find one hero with negative features. All the negative features are concentrated in one individual. I would prefer a different manner of writing—the manner of Chekhov, who has no heroes but rather gray people who nevertheless reflect the main course of life. This is another manner of writing.

I would prefer we were given enemies not as monsters but as people hostile to our society but not lacking all human traits. The very worst scoundrel has human traits, he loves someone, respects someone, wants to sacrifice himself for someone. He has some human qualities. I would prefer it if enemies were shown to be strong. What would be the advantage if we declared loudly that there was a struggle of capitalism with socialism and suddenly smashed something puny. And the enemies made a lot of noise about not being so weak. Could it be that there were no strong people? Why not depict Bukharin,[4] no matter how monstrous he was, yet he has some human features. Trotsky is an enemy, but he is[5] a capable person, undoubtedly he should be depicted as an enemy with negative features, but as one who also has positive qualities because undoubtedly he had them.

Here my concern is not at all that Avdeenko depicts enemies decently, but that he leaves our brother in the shadow. We need truthfulness depicting the enemy in a full-fledged way, not only with negative traits but with positive traits as well, which were, for example, persistence, consistency, the daring to go against society. These traits are attractive, so why not depict them?

[. . .]

Peering into [other's] souls is not my business, but I don't want to be naive. I think that he [Avdeenko] is someone of the hostile rabble of Sarkisov and Kabakov, and he has verbal exchanges with our enemies: "I'm living among fools, still they let my works through, they don't notice, I get money, and whoever needs to will understand, as to the fools—to hell with them, let them remain fools."

We will note here that Stalin's primary object in his criticism of the film is the *screenplay,* the text, as was absolutely typical. The writer Konstantin Simonov in his memoirs recounts how, immediately after the TsK session at which this film was banned at Stalin's behest and Avdeenko, the author of the scenario, subjected to strong criticism, Stalin was asked what to do with the film's two directors who were waiting there. Stalin, making a casual circular motion of his hand in imitation of the way film winds around in the projector, remarked: "But who are they? They just set rolling what he had written for them."[6]

CHAPTER SEVENTEEN

Reports on Writers from the NKVD and Soviet Officials

One of the central questions in analyzing Soviet cultural politics has always been the degree to which the Party elite were informed of the real situation within culture and the mood of intellectuals. Were they, for example, so cut off that they were hostage to their apparatus for surveillance and purveying information? Documents in the Politburo archives reveal that the leadership were provided with fairly detailed information, though one must not assume that the NKVD reports were not edited or in some way slanted for the purposes of their compilers, or of the leadership.

· 133 ·

Memorandum from the NKVD Administration for Leningrad Oblast to A. A. Zhdanov, "On negative and counterrevolutionary manifestations among the writers of Leningrad." Published in *Zvezda*, 1994, no. 8, pp. 73–80. On the memorandum text here are numerous underlinings by A. A. Zhdanov. On the first page there is the stamp of the Special Sector of the Leningrad Oblast Party Committee and Municipal Party Committee of the VKP(b) dated 2 June 1935, "To be returned." Original. Typewritten.
28 May 1935

To VKP(B) Oblast Party Committee Secretary Com. Zhdanov
Smolny

Agent materials that have come into the SPO UNKVD [People's Commissariat of Internal Affairs Administration] for L[eningrad] O[blast] recently on the activities of the Leningrad Union of Soviet Writers, as well as materials from the investigation into the case against the c[ounter]r[evolutionary] nationalist group of young writers, point to just how detached the Union's Party leadership is from the mass of writers, the extreme weakness of the mass-political educational work, the ignoring of work with young writers, and the absence of real political direction for the work of the literary circles at factory and plant enterprises in Leningrad.

[...]

The Leningrad Union almost never arranges readings or selections of new unpublished works. Writers gather in private apartments. So, for instance: the apartments of the writers Tikhonov, Kazakov [sic],[1] Zabolotsky, Oleynikov, Venus whom we deported, and the critic Manuilov are the site of private gatherings of Leningrad writers where they read and discuss individual as yet unpublished works.

[...]

"Evenings at the club are boring, deserted, and cold, and no one listens to the reports" (statement by the writer Kuklin).

"Creative life in our club is being replaced by banquets, dinners, and general reports. The leadership is detached from us, it doesn't know what we find meaningful" (statement by the writer N. Nikitin).

The Union sections, with the exception of the critics' section, are not functioning.

The work methods of Gorelov, the senior secretary of the Union of Soviet Writers and a form[er] activist of the Literary Front, evoke negative attitudes among the majority of the unaffiliated writers.

Since the very first days of the Union's existence, Gorelov has replaced the board's work with his own personal administration, which is leading to a break with the mass of writers.

Writers Union Chairman Tikhonov has frequently complained in conversation with writers Fedin, Slonimsky, Kazakov, and oth[ers] that "in the time of the union's existence he hadn't been given a single document for signature." "The decisions of a great number of fundamental literary matters by the 'secretariat' were frivolous, and the explanation of these matters by Gorelov and Bespamiatny (sec[retary] of the Par[ty] group) has misled me."

According to Kazakov, he made several attempts to speak to Gorelov on this subject, but the latter always refused to have these conversations.

[...]

With respect to the Party group in the Union of Soviet Writers, there is also an absence of leadership for the mass literary movement in Leningrad, which is leading to socially hostile elements penetrating into the movement's leadership.

The writer Tveriak, whom we arrested in the case against the c[ounter]r[evolutionary] nationalistic group, indicated in the investigation that members of the group were trying to take over literary circles with their counterrevolutionary influence:

". . . The purpose of this group was supposed to be the fight for asserting our nationalistic ideas in literature. In doing so, Dmitrochenko indicated that our work should follow along the line of literary circles and take them over with our influence. As an example he cited RAPP, which, according to him, was strong because it rested on the mass of literary circles. . . ." (Tveriak's test[imony], 5 April 1935).

A check of the leaders of Leningrad literary circles showed that most of them—78 percent (43 of 55) are unaffiliated and only 6, or 11 percent, are members or candidates for the Party, and six, also 11 percent, are members of Komsomol.

In a number of large Leningrad plants and factories, the leaders of the literary circles are socially hostile and anti-Soviet individuals:

Rozhdestvensky is a poet, he guides a circle at the Lenin Club, in the past he was closely linked with Gumilyov, who was shot in connection with the Tagantsevsky case; with Khodasevich, an emigrant, with Kliuev, who has been imprisoned in a concentration camp for c[ounter]r[evolutionary] activities, and with O. Mandelshtam, who was exiled for c[ounter]r[evolutionary] activities.

Rozhdestvensky is the author of a number of counterrevolutionary poems which are being disseminated in manuscript form.

[. . .]

Based on their literary qualifications, most leaders of literary circles are individuals unsuited for this work.

Of the 55 leaders, only 9, or 16 percent, are members of the Union of Soviet Writers, moreover most of them are not leading Leningrad writers, and 13, or 24 percent, are candidates for membership in the Writers Union. Of the remaining number of circle leaders, most are literature teachers in the schools and workers in cultural institutions who do not have the necessary training to lead circles.

[. . .]

> Head of the NKVD Adm[inistration] for L[eningrad] O[blast]
> Zakovsky
> Head of the Secret Polit[ical] Dep[artment] of the L[eningrad] O[blast] UNKVD
> Lupekin

Often NKVD reports were essentially prepared for particular cases under scrutiny and were clearly structured as prosecutorial documents intended to vindicate repressive measures, as in the following document in which the NKVD purports to have uncovered an "underground organization" among writers:

· 134 ·

Special report from the GUGB NKVD SSSR Secret Political Department "On the anti-Soviet group of writers N. S. Postupalsky, P. S. Karaban (Shleiman), and V. I. Narbut." TsA FSB RF, f. 3, op. 3, d. 121, ll. 61–69. Original. Typewritten. The following instruction appears on the special report: "Send to Comrades Yagoda, Agranov, Prokofiev. Secr[et] Polit[ical] Department Head G. Molchanov."

25 June 1936

---

1. *Postupalsky,* Igor Stefanovich, twenty-nine years old, non-Party, poet and translator of Ukrainian literature (4 Sadovo-Samotechnaia Street, apt. 7).

2. *Karaban* (Shleiman), Pavel Solomonovich, forty-five years old, non-Party, writer and translator from Ukrainian. Before 1934, he lived in the Ukraine and was linked with a number of prominent Ukrainian writers who were subsequently repressed. Since his arrival in Moscow has been working as a translator at Gosizdat (15 Khavsky Lane, apt. 2).

3. *Narbut,* Vl[adimir] Iv[anovich], poet, for[mer] VKP(b) member, expelled from the Party in 1931 for treacherous conduct during the arrest of Denikin counterintelligence in 1919, for[mer] dir[ector] of the Zemlia i Fabrika [Land and Factory] publishing house, for[mer] ch[ief] of the TsK VKP(b) press department. Mem[ber], Union of Sov[iet] Writers (15 Kursova Lane).

The initiative for the group's creation lies with Postupalsky, who in early August 1935 proposed to Karaban and the poet Turganov, who works primarily as a translator, { . . . } organizing a literary group that was independent of the Union of Soviet Writers for writers close in spirit.

Somewhat later, V. Narbut joined the group, quickly taking the leading position in the group.

At a meeting on 23 October 1935, the group, at Karaban's suggestion, was named the "Association of Old Men."

At systematically organized gatherings of the group, general political and public-literary issues were discussed in an anti-Soviet spirit, moreover the initiative for the discussion of these issues, as a rule, lies with Postupalsky and Narbut.

[. . .]

On 23 January 1936, a meeting was held of group members Postupalsky, Karaban, and Turganov together with the Ukrainian writers Kopylenko, Panch, and Pervomaisky, during which they discussed the situation in literature and in the Union of Sov[iet] Writers. During it, Kopylenko and Panch shed a tendentious light on the situation with literature in the Ukraine, and in their assessments expressed views and moods that coincide with the views of the group's members.

At a meeting of the group held on 1 May in the apartment of Bagritsky's widow . . . Postupalsky once again posed the question of the need to create a special writers' organization to counterbalance the Union of Soviet Writers.

[. . .]

Most recently, this group's activeness has increased significantly.

Gatherings of the group have begun to occur more often (9 May, 24 May, 28 May, 17 June, 22 June), and questions of the further expansion and organizational planning of the group have become the subject of constant discussions at said gatherings.

At a meeting of the group on 24 May, the Ukrainian poet Bazhan spoke on the topic of nationalism and expressed the thought that nationalistic aspirations always lead to a political struggle for independence.

[. . .]

"Ukrainian affairs involving the removal of thousands of people here are still fast in our memory. What does all this mean? Each nation and ethnic group wishes to be independent, to have its own ruler. This is planted in the consciousness of people who love their fatherland. Try to propose to the Germans that they become our subjects and that in exchange each person will receive all manner of goods—and they won't agree, even the unemployed won't want it. This needs to be remembered. Here people have been executed for this, but that is, after all, the only solution."

At the same meeting, I. Postupalsky said that the new constitution may facilitate their group's further growth:

"Don't forget that there will be a new constitution, and then we can spread our influence in an organized fashion. I'm not going to speak now, but there are still active people here who can fight, we just need to find them and combine our efforts."

[. . .]

At a gathering of the group on 17 June, I. Postupalsky spoke out in a sharply anti-Soviet spirit on the matter of the new constitution and once again spoke about the need to immediately set about extending the group's ties:

"In the constitution there are many words that yield nothing in life. All these freedoms are forgeries, and all this will soon be clear to the entire nation. I even composed a verse:

>"Under the new constitution
>There'll be no prostitution,
>Since by itself the constitution
>Is pure and simple prostitution.

"Still, though, right now we could be trying to say something, and when we do speak, lots of people will come to us immediately. Our task must be the creation of a small union on the scale of Moscow, Leningrad, Kiev,

Kharkov, and Tiflis. That would be enough. If there were about forty people, then we would have enormous influence. And the deadline—no later than January–February 1937. The summer we're using entirely for this purpose."

>Head of the SPO GUGB NKVD 6th Department
>Captain of State Security
>Stromin

The following report on the writer Isaak Babel is important for the way it reveals the extent to which this leading Soviet writer moved among the Party and secret police elite (and this was not untypical). In this instance, many of his closest Party associates had, unfortunately for him, fallen out of favor and were being repressed. The list includes Ivan Smilga, a hero of the Civil War now accused of Trotskyism, Aleksandr Voronsky, a Party literary theoretician and the most important publisher and patron of fellow-traveler literature during the 1920s when he edited, inter alia, the leading literary journal *Red Virgin Soil* (*Krasnaia nov'*), and Genrikh Yagoda, the head of the secret police who was sentenced in the Bukharin show trial of 1938. Also mentioned in this document are Andrei Malraux and André Gide, French writers whom Babel invited to dinner during their visits to the USSR. Gide was invited to the Soviet Union in 1936 in the expectation that he would write favorably about his visit (a frequent motive in inviting prominent Western intellectuals for visits). Instead, he published an attack, *Back from the USSR* (*Au retour de l'URSS*), causing a scandal.

· 135 ·

Dispatch from the First Section of the GUGB NKVD SSSR Secret Political Department on the moods of I. E. Babel in connection with the arrests of the former oppositionists. TsA FSB RF, f. 3, op. 3, d. 65, ll. 225–228. Original.
Typewritten.
5 July 1936

On 27 June, Emmanuel telephoned the office of A. N. Pirozhkova (an engineer at Metroproekt, I. E. Babel's wife, non-Party). Over the telephone she told him: "I'm awfully glad to hear your voice. I was very worried about you. I wanted to call, but I just couldn't take the chance, since I was certain they would tell me you weren't there." Emmanuel made a date that same day to stop by for her after work. He stopped by and started to see her home. Emmanuel asked why she had been so worried. Pirozhkova said: "What, can it be you don't know anything? I'm truly amazed they haven't gotten to you. Masses of people have been arrested. I have the impression that everyone to a man who had any connection at all to the Trotskyites has been arrested." To his question of who it was who'd been arrested, Pirozhkova answered: "Of my friends they've taken Marusia Solntseva, Efim and Sonia Dreitser, Okhotnikov's last wife Shura Solomko, Lialia Gaevskaia, and also Iasha Okhotnikov was arrested again." Pirozhkova had got the impression that they were arresting everyone to a man, and she was even concerned for herself and Babel.

Pirozhkova relates that she asked Babel: "Can't they arrest you?" To which Babel replied: "As long as the old man (Gorky) was alive, that was impossible. And now it's still difficult." They were told by Sonia Dreitser about the arrest of Efim Dreitser, Pirozhkova was herself convinced of Sonia's arrest when she went to visit her and found the room sealed. About the arrest of Marusia Solntseva, Babel was informed by her current husband, Dzhango Goglidze (Gogoberidze). This latter is a member of the Party, he was very indignant at the arrest of Solntseva and asked Babel several times to intervene in this matter. He (Goglidze) said to Babel, "They are always viewing Solntseva as an adjunct—either to Okhotnikov or to Lominadze. But she is her own person."

Pirozhkova related that Babel consulted with her and decided to intervene in this case. Babel decided to choose specifically for intervention Maria Solntseva, of whose innocence he was more certain than with respect to the others. Babel decided to go to Gorky when Com. Yagoda was there and speak with him in the presence of Nadezhda Alekseevna Peshkova, whom Yagoda regards well.

Pirozhkova related that André Gide had dinner at their place (Babel's) on 26 June of this year. Besides him, Eisenstein and some French writer dined, too. Living with Babel in his apartment is André Malraux's brother, Rolland Malraux, who has stayed to work in the USSR as a film director.

Em[manuel] asked: "You mean Gide and Babel's other French friends know about these arrests?" Pirozhkova replied that she thought they didn't. According to Pirozhkova, André Gide throughout the entire dinner spoke about his delight at what he had seen in the USSR, he spoke about everything with delight. After he left, Babel asked Pirozhkova whether she understood what Gide had been talking about (she is studying French). Pirozhkova replied that she had understood he was delighted with everything going on here. Then Babel told her: "Don't you believe this delight. He's as crafty as a devil. We still don't know what he's going to write when he gets home. It's not so easy to guide him. In comparison with him, Gorky is a country sexton. When he gets back to France, he (Gide) could come out with something diabolical."

Emmanuel and Pirozhkova, conducting this conversation on Nogin Sq[uare], suddenly ran into Babel, who was waiting for a tram. Pirozhkova told Babel: "This is Roman, who it turns out wasn't arrested." Babel asked Em[manuel] jokingly: "Aren't you ashamed you weren't arrested?" He asked Em[manuel] whether he was working. Em[manuel] replied he wasn't. He asked: "They won't give you a job or you aren't looking for one?" Em[manuel] replied that he just couldn't seem to get a job. Then Babel said: "That may be what's saved you, since you're not on anyone's books anywhere." The threesome walked as far as Babel's apartment and he invited Em[manuel] to have dinner with them. Babel started questioning Em[manuel] about the arrests. Em[manuel] replied that he hadn't seen anyone for a long time and had learned of the arrests only today, from Pirozhkova. Babel asked whether Em[manuel] knew any of the former Trotskyites who had not been arrested so far. Em[manuel] replied that because they were neighbors and old friends, he occasionally stopped by to see N. V. Poluyan and knew that she had not been arrested.

Babel questioned Emmanuel about Smilga—where he was and how long his sentence was. Babel said he simply could not find out or understand the reasons for the latest mass arrests, but even if there were weighty reasons for this, what could people like Iashka Okhotnikov and Noy Bliskavitsky [sic][2] have to do with these matters? "After all, they've spent these three years in solitary confinement. For Okhotnikov and for Noy Bliskavitsky, another arrest and another sentence mean expulsion from life," said Babel. "In essence, this is a slow execution."

"If we need to settle Kolyma," said Babel, "they could simply suggest people go there to work in such a way that they could not refuse."

When Babel went into his room, Pirozhkova repeated a number of vile rumors she'd heard from Babel about the VKP(b) leadership in connection with Gorky's death.

Immediately after dinner, Babel went to his room to sleep and in parting invited Em[manuel] to stop by.

To Babel's [sic][3] question as to whether he knew about the fate of A. K. Voronsky, Babel replied: "Certainly, of course I know. Voronsky was expelled from the Party, but he also wasn't arrested and they even let him keep his apartment."

>Assist[ant] to the head of the SPO GUGB 1st Sec[tion]
>Sen[ior] Lieutenant of St[ate] Security
>Bogen

A report on Babel submitted several months later was even more dangerous, revealing as it did his positive evaluations of Trotsky and Trotsky's associates Sokolnikov and Mrachkovsky, not to mention Kamenev.

· 136 ·

Summary by the GUGB NKVD SSSR Secret Political Department on the moods of I. E. Babel in connection with the conclusion of the trial of the so-called "Anti-Soviet United Trotskyite-Zinovievite Center." RGASPI, f. 57, op. 1, d. 64, ll. 93–94. Original. Typewritten. On the first page of the summary there are the following instructions: "To Com. Yezhov. Ya. Agranov, 22 September 1936."

22 September 1936

After the publication of the sentence of the Military Board of the Sup[reme] Court against the participants in the Trotskyite-Zinovievite bloc, a source, while in Odessa, met with the writer Babel in the presence of film director Eisenstein. The conversation took place in the hotel room where Babel and Eisenstein were staying.

Concerning primarily the results of the trial, Babel said:

"You cannot imagine or appreciate the scale on which people perished and what significance this has for history.

"This is a terrible business. You and I, of course, know nothing, whether or not there has been a struggle with the 'boss' due to the personal attitudes of a number of people toward him.

"Who made the Revolution? Who was in the first Politburo?"

At this, Babel picked up a sheet of paper and began writing out the names of the TsK VKP(b) and Politburo members from the first years of the Revolution. Then he began gradually crossing out the names of those who had died, left, and finally, those who had been through the last trial. After this, Babel tore up the sheet with his jottings and said:

"You realize who is now being shot or is on the verge of it: Lenin was very fond of Sokolnikov because he's a very smart man. True, Sokolnikov is a 'great skeptic' and an office man who literally detests mass work. For Sokolnikov, the only authority that could exist was Lenin's, and his whole struggle is the struggle against Stalin's influence. That's why this relationship came about between Sokolnikov and Stalin.

"But take Trotsky. You cannot imagine his charm and the strength of his influence on the people he met. Trotsky will indisputably continue the struggle and many will support him.

"Of those shot one of the most remarkable figures is Mrachkovsky. He himself is a worker, he was the organizer of the partisan movement in Siberia; he's a man of exceptional strength of will. People have told me that shortly before his arrest he had an eleven-hour discussion with Stalin.

"I'm very sorry for the people executed because these were real people. Kamenev, for example, after Belinsky[4] he's our most brilliant connoisseur of the Russian language and literature.

"I don't think this is the counterrevolutionaries' struggle, I think it's a struggle with Stalin based on personal relationships.

"Can you imagine what's going on in Europe and how they're going to feel about us now? I know that after the execution of Kamenev, Zinoviev, and the others, Hitler said: 'Now I'm executing Thälmann.'

"What alarming times! I feel horrible!"

During Babel's statements, Eisenstein made no objections.

>Dep[uty] Head of the GUGB Sec[ret]-Polit[ical] Department
>Senior Major of State Security
>V. Berman

The following document provides a further example of the closeness of many writers to the Soviet secret police, but this time the writers had in the 1920s been leaders of RAPP which represented a very different literary orientation than that of Babel. In addition to Kirshon's alleged closeness to Genrikh Yagoda, the head of the NKVD, Averbakh was linked to Yagoda by family ties. Yagoda was dismissed on orders from Stalin and Zhdanov that were sent in a telegram from Sochi of 25 September 1936. Subsequently, Yagoda, together with Kriuchkov, Gorky's former secretary (also mentioned in this document), Bukharin, Radek, and other members of an alleged "Right-Trotskyite Bloc" were tried at the third and culminating show trial of March 1938 and condemned to death.

· 137 ·

Statement by P. F. Yudin to TsK VKP(b) Secretaries I. V. Stalin and L. M. Kaganovich on the playwright V. M. Kirshon. AP RF, f. 3, op. 34, d. 256, ll. 15–16. Original. Typewritten. On the statement there are many penciled underscores, probably made by Stalin or his assistant, A. N. Poskrebyshev.

23 April 1937

To TsK VKP(b) Secretaries Com. Stalin
Com. Kaganovich

I submitted the attached statement to the Party group of the Writers Union.

On 20 April, this statement was considered at a closed session of the Party group of the Writers Union's presidium.

At this session, a repugnant picture of Kirshon's political and personal disintegration emerged.

For several years, Kirshon has virtually been living at Yagoda's. He has taken part, along with Kriuchkov and others, in all kinds of drinking parties. Kirshon has become so attached to and has been so dragged down by Yagoda that he himself had trouble explaining what made him get so close to Yagoda. All he could say was that he thought Yagoda's way of life fully corresponded to the ethics of senior Soviet leaders.

Yagoda's generosity to and concern for Kirshon have reached the point that when Kirshon went to the plenum in Minsk with several writers, Kirshon was met at the train station in Minsk by a group of senior NKVD workers, who drove him to the NKVD hotel (or apartment building) in their vehicles.

Even more outrageous things have come to light about the political ties between Kirshon and Averbakh.

Comrades Panfyorov and Fadeev have stated that Averbakh, Kirshon, and others in their circle have held discussions of a Trotskyite nature. At one of their gatherings in Averbakh's apartment, they discussed the matter of the contrast between M. Gorky and Com. Kaganovich.

Discussions have been held that were aimed against Com. Kaganovich.

The anti-Party activities have also come to light of Averbakh, Kirshon, and others who stood close to Kriuchkov in his attempts to do everything possible to bring Gorky into conflict with the Union's Party group; in particular, their powerful efforts to poison Gorky against Communist writers were unleashed before the writers' congress.

In my opinion, Kirshon has disintegrated in all respects, he is someone alien to the Party and linked with the criminal activities of Yagoda, Averbakh, Kriuchkov, and others.

In addition to Bruno Yasensky and Afinogenov, Mints has been very close to this company; he is a two-faced Janus, the toady of Yagoda and Kriuchkov.

P. Yudin

A second aspect of the campaign against Averbakh and Kirshon is the partial dismantling of the Gorky legacy. Gorky, as mentioned, had been a patron of Averbakh. In the aftermath of the 1932 resolution abolishing all independent writers' organizations and founding the single Writers Union, Averbakh had been resistant to the demise of RAPP and fallen out with the Party faction, making his situation precarious. Gorky took him under his wing and had him play an active role in one of his pet projects, the *History of the Factories* (*Istoria fabrik i zavodov*), a project launched in 1931. The history sought to have all the major factories and many industrial enterprises (such as railways) produce a collectively written history of each individual enterprise, frequently with much of the history written by workers themselves or based on their recollections, though to varying degrees guided, edited or ghost written by designated writers or Party historians. Two blue-ribbon volumes published in this series were *The Stalin White Sea–Baltic Canal* (*Belomor-Baltiisky kanal imeni Stalina*) and *The People of Bolshevo* (*Bol'shevtsy*). The first described how convicts (many of them political prisoners) laboring on the canal in one of the earliest Gulags transformed themselves through labor into politically conscious and productive Soviet citizens (several famous Soviet writers and photographers contributed to this glossy volume); the second was an account of how wayward youths were reformed in a special labor colony. Both books had previously been assiduously promoted but were banned in the aftermath of Yagoda's arrest.

· 138 ·

Memorandum from SSP Secretary V. P. Stavsky to I. V. Stalin on the writers' discussion of the decisions of the February–March (1937) Plenum of the TsK VKP(b) and the activities of L. L. Averbakh and V. M. Kirshon. AP RF, f. 3, op. 34, d. 256, ll. 58–61. Original. Typewritten. On the statement are underscores in pencil, probably made by Stalin or his assistant, A. N. Poskrebyshev.

3 May 1937

To the TsK VKP(b)
To Comrade I. V. Stalin

Discussion of the decisions and instructions of the VKP(b) Central Committee plenum began at a citywide gathering of writers, on 2–5 April of this year. This discussion raised the level of political activism for writers and led to the development of genuine criticism and self-criticism, something we have never had to a sufficient extent in the Union of Soviet Writers.

The writers harshly and rightly criticized their own union and its leadership for a lack of political concern, an absence in many cases of class vigilance, and for organizational muddle-headedness, which in the final analysis has helped class enemies penetrate literature and be active among writers.

The writers spoke with special harshness about the subversive activity in the literature of Averbakh and his accomplice Kirshon and others.

In connection with this, as well as with the statement by Comrade Yudin, the Party group of the SSP board subjected the activities of Kirshon, as Averbakh's closest comrade-in-arms, to a thorough examination.

At a gathering of Moscow playwrights lasting several days that began immediately after the Party group's session, the exposure of the Averbakh group unfolded even more. Only now has the subversive wrecking activity of this Averbakh group become fully evident to the Union of Soviet Writers.

After the TsK VKP(b) decision to restructure the literary organizations, Averbakh and people of like mind applied all their efforts to sabotaging this decision's implementation. With this goal in mind, as is now evident from the confessions of Kirshon, Bruno Yasensky, and Korabelnikov, as well as the confirmations of Fadeev, Bela Illes, and others, the Averbakh group has for a long time been holding its illegal, factional, anti-Party meetings in the apartments of Averbakh, Kirshon, and, subsequently, Yagoda.

At these illegal, anti-Soviet gatherings, means and methods of fighting the Party line in literature were worked out. Thus, Averbakh essentially forced a group of writers (including Fadeev, B. Illes, Sholokhov, and others) to write a letter to the TsK VKP(b) on their disagreement with the decision to eliminate RAPP.

There it was agreed, at Averbakh's initiative, to call A. M. Gorky to the defense of RAPP, i.e., against the TsK VKP(b) decision. Subsequently the group reached an agreement and unleashed wrecking work to bring A. M. Gorky into conflict with the Party group of the Union of Soviet Writers and the non-Party writers into conflict with the Communists. Relying on the support of Yagoda, who became their own man in A. M. Gorky's home, and having surrounded A. M. Gorky with "their own men," also with the help of P. Kriuchkov, the Averbakh group managed to get some unaffiliated workers to break away from the Communists and to make Gorky, who was receiving one-sided information daily, very unfavorably inclined toward the Party group and the Communist writers. This found its expression in A. M. Gorky's articles entitled "Literary Amusements" [*Literaturnye zabavy*], whose point was aimed mainly at the Communist writers (Fadeev, Panfyorov, Gladkov, Vishnevsky, and others). As we know, his "Literary Amusements" ceased publication after the *Pravda* editors published an open letter from F. Panfyorov to A. M. Gorky.

The Averbakh group's audacity reached the point where at the group's gatherings there was vile compromising of Comrade L. M. Kaganovich, as was brought out at a session of the Party group.

The Averbakh group exploited the NKVD—its funds and connections—to create its own center parallel to the Union of Soviet Writers. It concentrated its activities in the editorial offices on the publication of its book about the White Sea—Baltic Canal, and later on the Bolshevo Commune. In the process, there was also pressure on non-Party workers from several former NKVD workers (Yagoda and his retinue).

After Averbakh was sent to the Urals to work, Kirshon took charge of the group's efforts aimed at returning Averbakh to literature. They tried to bring Averbakh to the writers' congress as a delegate. Rumors were sown among the writers about how Averbakh would be back any day. Gorky kept getting asked to make efforts on behalf of Averbakh's return. Averbakh was proposed for a job in the editorial offices of *People of the Second Five-Year Plan* [*Liudi vtoroi piatiletki*].

Until the day of Averbakh's arrest, Kirshon defended him as an "honest Bolshevik and Party man." He was echoed by Bruno Yasensky and others.

The composition of the Averbakh group attracts the most serious attention:

—Ivan Makariev, for[mer] secretary of RAPP, a Trotskyite terrorist, now arrested by the NKVD;

—D. Maznin, a critic close to Averbakh, a Trotskyite, now arrested by the NKVD;

—Pikel, shot in 1936;

—Bruno Yasensky, recommended to the VKP(b) by the spy Dombal, traveled with him through Tajikistan, himself gave a recommendation to the Shimkeviches, two spies, to enter the USSR, offered his apartment in Moscow for a long time to the executed provocateur and spy Vandursky, and so on;

—Kirshon, being connected with Yagoda and Averbakh in the closest possible way, broke from the Party organization and the workers, disrupted the work of the drama section of the Writers Union, committed a number of criminal acts in conducting the playwrights' monetary affairs, and so on.

All these facts characterize the true face of the Averbakh group and its activities—the most subversive wrecking.

Only now, Comrade Stalin, in connection with the full exposure of this hostile gang that has been so active in literature, will the TsK VKP(b) decision of 23 April 1932 be implemented in full.

During discussion of the decisions of the TsK VKP(b) Plenum, the activities of the literary-artistic journals and publishers, which are functioning extremely unsatisfactorily, were subjected to harsh and justified criticism.

Comrade Stalin, I beg of you to receive a group of Communist writers (Vishnevsky, Fadeev, Panfyorov, Lakhuti, and others) in the very near future.

With Communist greeting
Vl. Stavsky

To some extent Party influence on members of the Writers Union was affected by organs of the TsK such as Agitprop and the Department of Cultural-Agitational Work, and by functionaries of the Union itself, as can be seen here:

· 139 ·

Memorandum from the TsK VKP(b) Department of Cultural-Educational Work to the TsK VKP(b) secretaries on the discussion by writers of the sentence in the case of the so-called "Trotskyite-Zinovievite Center." RGASPI, f. 17, op. 120, d. 257, ll. 14–19. Original. Typewritten.
29 August 1936

To the secretaries of the TsK VKP(b)
To Com. L. M. Kaganovich
To Com. A. A. Andreev
To Com. N. I. Yezhov

On 25 and 26 August, a meeting was held of the Party group of the Union of Soviet Writers Board which was devoted to a discussion of the sentence against the Trotskyite-Zinovievite terrorists and the article in the press signaling the lack of self-criticism in the Union of Soviet Writers.

These gatherings have great significance for the life of the Writers Union. The circumstance that the bandit Pikel was a member of the Union and that a number of double-dealers and traitors have been discovered in the Union (Serebriakov, Selivanovsky, Grudskaia, Troshchenko, Tarasov-Rodionov, et al.) has forced the Party group to take a close look at both its own work and its own ranks. The self-criticism in the Union was headed up by the board's secretary, Com. Stavsky. In the course of the discussion, a number of important facts were uncovered. In 1928, the writer Ivan Kataev (Party member since 1919) traveled to Lipetsk to see the exiled Trotskyite Voronsky and to pick up directives on the work of the literary group Crossing [*Pereval*].[5] Kataev maintained active ties with condemned Trotskyites, rendering them financial assistance. He rendered financial aid to condemned Trotskyites Mirov and Maleev as well. The latter wrote a short book praising the executed Smirnov, who was then the director of a combine factory. The book never saw the light of day as a result of Glavlit's intervention. Kataev has consistently patronized the writer Zarudin, a Trotskyite expelled from the Party. In 1932 Iv. Kataev announced the liquidation of the literary group Crossing. In fact, the group continued to exist with Voronsky's active participation. The group has tried to obtain a publishing organ under the name "The Thirties," right up until recently, when Ivan Kataev and Pilnyak tried persistently to obtain permission to publish a miscellany under this title. By a decision of the Party group, it was resolved *to expel Ivan Kataev from the Party*. At a session of the Party group, the work of magazines and the *Literary Gazette* were subjected to harsh criticism. . . .

Communists' work with the unaffiliated was subjected to harsh criticism. Facts were cited: Inber is now living at the dacha of Party member Bespalov. Inber is a relative of Trotsky, his cousin's daughter. Inber gave a bad speech at a meeting of writers, and in the hallways she said she had been forced to speak. While living in the same house with her, Bespalov did nothing to prepare her speech.

The Party organization work of the Writers Union's board was subjected to harsh criticism. [. . .]

[. . .]

Presidium

On 25 August, a meeting was held of the SSP Presidium at which the Supreme Court's sentence against the Trotskyite-Zinovievite Center was discussed. [. . .]

V. Inber admitted that her speech at the meeting had been bad and said that she was Trotsky's relative and so ought to have come out especially decisively demanding the execution of the counterrevolutionary assassins.

The other writers expressed their unanimous approval of the Supreme Court's sentence.

It should be noted, however, how bad Olesha's speech was; he defended Pasternak, who in fact did not sign the demand for the execution of the counterrevolutionary terrorists, saying that Pasternak was a perfectly Soviet man but he could not sign a death sentence with his own hand. Olesha was one of those writers who had been welded together by the Trotskyite terrorist Shmidt and who had prepared the assassination attempt against Com. Voroshilov (Babel, Malyshkin, Valentin Kataev, Nikulin, and Olesha have drunk with Shmidt). Olesha drew no conclusions for himself from this fact. He tried to vindicate himself by saying that he had known nothing, that he viewed Shmidt only as a man with a heroic military past, although he himself indicated that he was sometimes amazed by the great ambition in Shmidt. [. . .]

[. . .]

The writer Fedin, who was on the Union presidium, did not speak. Most of the speakers indicated that lately an improvement had been noted in the work of the Union of Soviet Writers.

Dep[uty] Head of the TsK VP(b) Department of Cultural-
Educational Work
A. Angarov
Head of the Literature Sector
V. Kirpotin

The following document containing evidence of dissident views among intellectuals was read by Party leaders. Yet hardly even one of those writers identified as having made politically dangerous remarks was arrested. This is but one of many instances which suggest that the expressed attitudes on the part of intellectuals towards the Soviet regime were generally not the reason for their arrest. Otherwise put, and as we have already noted, there was a strong element of the arbitrary in who was repressed and who not. Of the writers cited here, Tarasov-Rodionov who made perfectly loyal comments was repressed, while Pasternak who demonstrated his independence was not touched.

The archive of the FSB (the present-day acronym for the secret police) contains reports prepared especially for Stalin on what particular writers were saying, reports that one might have expected to result inevitably in their being shot, or at least arrested, but they were not. Here we will cite excerpts from the files of Mikhail Svetlov and Iosif Utkin.[6]

> Mikhail Svetlov: "What's going on? They are nabbing everyone, literally everyone. It's terrifying. The arrests are assuming hyperbolic dimensions. The Peoples Commissars and their dep[uties] have moved to Lubianka [headquarters of the secret police]. But what is both ludicrous and tragic is that we are walking around as this is going on and don't understand a thing. Why, what is it for? [. . .] All I understand is that there has been an epochal shift, that we already live in a new epoch, that we are just the pitiful remnants of the epoch that has died, that there is nothing left of the old Party, there's a new Party with new people. They have replaced us [. . .] These are not court trials but organized killings, so what then could we expect from them? There's no Communist Party any more, it has been transformed and has nothing in common with the proletariat."[7]

> Iosif Utkin: "Here the revolution is entering a Bonapartist phase [. . .] The enemy could not cause us as much evil as Stalin has done with his open trials [. . .] When I read a newspaper I say: 'God, what cynicism, what black Asiatic cynicism in our politics!' They declared democracy and parliamentarism but at sessions of the Supreme Soviet not a single question has been raised about the mass disappearance of deputies and ministers. The deputy prime minister disappears, Kossior, a member of the all-powerful Politburo, yet there are no questions, no announcements, no inquiries."[8]

Even though all these statements were known to Stalin, not one of these poets was touched and they remained in Soviet literature, occupying respected positions. One can only speculate as to the reasons why these figures, and so many more in comparable positions, were not arrested, but clearly one is that people were arrested for more pragmatic reasons having to do with, for example, the political purposes of the highest leadership at any given moment. The leadership had at their disposal dossiers with incriminating material on most figures of any significance in Soviet public life, and failing that they could always fabricate such material to suit their purposes. This was an important factor in their enjoying so much power.

· 140 ·

Special report from the GUGB NKVD SSSR Secret Political Department on the moods among writers. AP RF, f. 45, op. 1, d. 174, ll. 53–58. Original. Typewritten. On the report are the following notes: "From Com. Yezhov," "To Com. Stalin," and signatures: "St[alin]," "Read, M[olotov]," "Kaganovich."

9 January 1937

In the last few days, the attention of literary circles has been attracted by three facts: Fadeev's article concerning Savin's book *Nafta* (*Pravda,* 8 December 1936), I. Lezhnev's article, "A Bacchanalia of Republications" ["*Vakkhanaliia pereizdanii*"] (*Pravda,* 15 December 1936), and the harsh criticism of Pasternak's conduct in Stavsky's report at a citywide meeting of writers devoted to the extraordinary session of the Soviets.

Fadeev's article was perceived as a Stavsky-inspired attack against a specific portion of the most prominent fellow-traveler writers.

Vs. Ivanov: "I'm stunned by Stavsky's uncomradely attitude. Two points are especially insulting: first, they ascribe to me personal motivations; second, this is, after all, a letter to Stavsky, he did not answer me, and it lay there for a long time, and then suddenly he released it. Most piquant here is the fact that Fedin and Tolstoy acted exactly the same way, but there's not a murmur about them. It's clear the 'job' was aimed at me."

I. Selvinsky: "I used to believe Stavsky, but now I see that he is nothing but a provocateur. He sold out Pilnyak when he confessed his sins, and now he's betraying Ivanov.

"Now I understand a few things. When I had troubles with the censor, I went to see Stavsky. I happened to meet Aseev at the door, and he asked me why I'd come. I said, 'To gnaw something off of the censor.' 'Ah,' he said, 'this question interests me, let's go together.' We walked in and there sat Surkov, and a few minutes later Kirsanov came in, also completely by accident. Stavsky said, 'This is good, all the poets at once.'

"I said that soon we'd have the Constitution—freedom of speech, an act of the greatest trust in us, but the censor is untrusting.

"What would you think. Soon a rumor was going around that the poets of a delegation had gone as a delegation to ask for the repeal of censorship on the basis of the Constitution. Clearly Stavsky went to see someone and presented everything in that guise.

"On top of this they need to create the impression that all is not well and that their post therefore is a battle post so they are essential. They are deceiving the true leadership, and they have been looking to create an incident for a long time.

"Lezhnev's article 'Bacchanalia of Republications was greeted hostilely. In the main the objections are not against the article's ideas but against a number of imprecisions in the article which are being characterized as intentional reconsiderations.

[. . .]

P. Antokolsky (poet): . . .

In his criticism of Pasternak's conduct, Stavsky pointed out that in hallway conversations Pasternak had tried to vindicate A. Gide.

B. Pasternak (talking about this hallway conversation with the critic Tarasenkov): ". . . It's simply funny. Tarasenkov walks up to me and asks, 'Isn't it true what they say, that Gide is a scoundrel?'

"And I say, 'What are you and I going to say about Gide? We have *Pravda*'s official opinion. And then what were all these people doing latching on to him? He wrote what he thought and had every right to do so. We didn't buy him.'

"But Tarasenkov went after me: 'Ah, so that's it, you mean they've bought us. You and I are bought.'

"I said: 'We're a different matter, we're living in the country, we have obligations to it.'"

Vsevolod Ivanov: "In reporting about the congress, Stavsky in general gave such a depressing report that everyone went away with a heavy heart. His report was politically incorrect. He cursed all Muscovites, but the Muscovites are Soviet literature, too. And he praised some unknown provincials. Stavsky has been abandoned. The writers have turned away from him. The fact that all the major writers were demonstratively absent from the meeting proves what they think of Stavsky and the Union. It was the same with the reply to *Pravda*. Pasternak's outburst was no accident. It's the expression of how most major writers feel."

Pav. Antokolsky: "Pasternak is three times right. He doesn't want to be a petty liar. Gide saw what was basic—that we are petty, cowardly creatures. We should be proud to have such a powerful comrade."

Al. Gatov (poet): "Pasternak has now been elevated to the level of leader, he dared, he is uncowed and unafraid to take risks. What is also important is that this isn't Vasiliev, you can't put him in prison. But in essence this is how genuine poets should act. Let them dare lay a finger on him, and all Europe will rise up. Everyone admires him."

S. Budantsev: "What has been proclaimed is attention to the individual, and in a writer this has to be expressed in concealing everything human in the individual. Ten years ago it was incomparably freer. Right now, many of us face the question of leaving this life. Only now is Mayakovsky's tragedy becoming particularly clear; evidently he saw further than we did. Pasternak has become the expresser of the opinion of all honest writers. Naturally, he'll be a martyr—such is the lot of honest men."

In the light of the writers' moods characterized above, a number of reports take on special interest that pointed to the fact that Peredelkino (the writers' colony outside Moscow), where Vs. Ivanov, B. Pilnyak, B. Pasternak, K. Fedin, L. Seifullina, and other prominent writers live, is becoming the center of a special writers' community that is attempting to be independent of the Union of Sov[iet] Writers.

A few days ago, the following people gathered at Selvinsky's dacha: Vsevolod Ivanov, Vera Inber, Boris Pilnyak, and Boris Pasternak—and he read them four thousand lines from his long poem, *Cheliuskiniana*.

"The reading," Selvinsky relates, "evoked great excitement, serious creative enthusiasm, and even helped establish amicable relations. For instance, Vs. Ivanov and B. Pilnyak had been feuding for a long time and weren't talking to each other, but after this evening they started talking again. There is creative communication; readings are becoming part of the daily life of the colony," says Selvinsky. His very real composition excited everyone, creative interests were sparked that had been on ice since the quasi-literary discussions about criticism, union tactics, and so on. A vital stream appeared.

An analogous reading of Seifullina's new play for Vakhtangov's theater was organized at Vs. Ivanov's dacha. Present were Ivanov, Pilnyak, Seifullina, Vera Inber, Zazubrin, Afinogenov, Perets Markish, Aduev, Selvinsky, and Pasternak and his wife.[9]

After the play reading, which was extremely unsuccessful, Ivanov took the floor and gave comradely but harsh criticism. Everyone but Zazubrin expressed themselves in the same tone; Zazubrin attempted to smooth over the situation and advised Seifullina to read her play to the Vakhtangov group anyway. This evoked a general protest in the spirit of protecting Seifullina as a comrade from a mistake and from unnecessary diminishment of her authority in the theater.

In the discussion after the reading nearly everyone talked about how tired they were of the "pseudo-social turmoil" that followed along the official line. Many are offended, irritated, and absolutely do not believe in the sincerity of the leadership of the Union of Soviet Writers, and they have latched onto their Peredelkino friendship as the genuine life of writers pursuing their own interests.

Head of the GUGB 4th Department
Commissar of St[ate] Security 3rd Rank
Kursky

CHAPTER EIGHTEEN

Petitions to Stalin

An important aspect of the bizarre dialogue between Soviet power and the intellectuals was the petition to Stalin on behalf of those arrested, an act of civic courage. In this chapter we present a selection written by figures of different orientations and employing different strategies in the hope of achieving their ends.

The first of these is from the famous poet Anna Akhmatova. In the fall of 1935 her son, Lev Gumilyov, and her common-law husband, Nikolai Punin, were arrested. She immediately went to Moscow from Leningrad to try to obtain their release, and wrote a very short letter to Stalin swearing that neither of them was a conspirator or state criminal. She then had Pasternak, who was in favor with Stalin at the time, write a letter to Stalin on their behalf. In the following letter Pasternak thanks Stalin for their speedy release, taking the opportunity to express his position on some other issues.

· 141 ·

Letter from B. L. Pasternak to I. V. Stalin. [No earlier than 5 December 1935]. AP RF, f. 5, op. 1, d. 788, ll. 107–110v. Original. Typewritten. On the letter is an instruction: "My archive. I. Stalin."

Dear Iosif Vissarionovich!

I am tormented by the fact that I did not follow through at the time on my first wish and did not thank you for the marvelous, lightning-quick release of Akhmatova's relatives, but I was hesitant to disturb you a second time and decided to keep to myself this feeling of fervent gratitude, and I am certain that you will hear of this in any case, in some unknown way.

One more heavy feeling. At first I wrote you in my usual way, with digressions and verbosity, yielding to something hidden that apart from what everyone knows and everyone shares ties me to you. But I was advised to shorten and simplify the letter, and I was left with the horrible feeling that I had sent you something that wasn't my own, something alien.

I have long dreamed of offering up to you some modest fruit of my labors, but all this is so untalented that my dream obviously will never come true. Or should I be bolder here and, without giving it long thought, follow my first impulse?

Georgian Lyrics [*Gruzinskie liriki*][1] is a weak and derivative work, the honor and merit for which belongs wholly to the authors themselves, especially the marvelous poets. In conveying Vazha Pshavela, I consciously deviated from faithfulness to the form of the original, on the basis of considerations I dare not weary you with, in order to convey more freely the spirit of the original which is bottomless and thunderous in its beauty and thought.

In conclusion, I fervently thank you for your recent words about Mayakovsky. They correspond to my own feelings, I love him and have written an entire book about him. But even indirectly your lines about him had a saving effect on me. Of late, under the influence of the West, [people] have been inflating [my significance] terribly and according [me] exaggerated significance (it even made me ill): they began suspecting serious artistic power in me. Now, since you have put Mayakovsky in first place, this suspicion has been lifted from me, and with a light heart I can live and work as before, in modest silence, with the surprises and mysteries without which I would not love life.

> In the name of this mysteriousness,
> fervently loving and devoted to you

B. Pasternak

Petitions were also sent by foreign writers. The following document is a desperate attempt by the French writer Romain Rolland to save Bukharin. Any letter from Rolland might have been assumed to have some weight in that at the time he was a key player in the antifascist movement and a valued supporter of the Soviet Union, where he was consequently very much in favor so that his books were published in large editions. But the gesture probably has to be seen as quixotic. Rolland also wrote a letter to Stalin on 4 August 1937 protesting the arrest of Aleksandr Arosev, the head of the All-Union Society for Cultural Relations with Foreign Countries (VOKS), which organized trips by foreigners to the Soviet Union, and the arrest of Arosev's wife.[2]

· 142 ·

Letter from R. Rolland to I. V. Stalin, translated from French into Russian by the writer's wife, M. P. Rolland-Kudasheva. AP RF, f. 45, op. 1, d. 795, ll. 143–144.
The autograph signature is on ll. 142–142v. Handwritten.
Villeneuve (Vaud) Villa Olga, 18 March 1937

Dear Comrade Stalin,

I turn to you once again, using the permission you granted me when, two years ago, I had the opportunity to talk with you.

On the eve of the trial of Bukharin, and in no way disputing the evidence gathered against him, I appeal to your lofty humanitarian spirit and understanding of the higher interests of the USSR.

A mind on the order of Bukharin's is a kind of wealth for his country, he can and should be preserved for Soviet scholarship and thought. If he could, on the basis of the most harmful ideologies, overstep himself in a criminal manner, it is these ideologies that should be punished, but a man of scholarly value who has been misled by them should be spared. He, having admitted his mistake and regretted it, could help tear the mask off these ideologies and wage an energetic battle against them.

In the century and a half since the Revolutionary Tribunal of Paris sentenced the brilliant chemist Lavoisier to death, we, the most fiery revolutionaries, the most loyal to the memory of Robespierre and the Great Committee of Public Safety, have always bitterly regretted and felt remorse for this punishment.

Allow me also to remind you of a name dear to us both: our mutual friend Maxim Gorky. I often saw Bukharin at his house, I saw the close friendship that bound them. May the memory of it save Bukharin! In the name of Gorky, I beg you to spare him. No matter how guilty he is, he is a man of another breed than the defendants in the previous trial. He could still bring honor to Soviet thought and attest in history to your spirit of magnanimity.

I beg you to believe, dear Comrade Stalin, in my sincere devotion.

Romain Rolland

Bruno Yasensky, who wrote the following petition to Stalin on his own behalf, was a Polish Communist who emigrated to the Soviet Union in 1929 and became secretary of the International Association of Revolutionary Writers (MORP). In 1932–1933 he published *A Man Changes His Skin* [*Chelovek meniaet kozhu*], which depicts the bitter class struggles in Tadzhikistan as the republic moves towards a socialist society. The petition to Stalin proved of no avail: Yasensky was arrested in 1937 and executed as a Trotskyite in 1941.

· 143 ·

Letter from B. Yasensky to I. V. Stalin. TsA FSB RF, D. R-3482, ll. 38–41. Copy. Typewritten.
Moscow, 25 April 1937

Dear Iosif Vissarionovich!

I feel guilty for taking up your time with my personal matters. But the Party legitimately demands of us Soviet writers the creation (in particular for the twentieth anniversary of October) of politically topical, artistically conscientious works of literature. Since the publication of my last big novel, *A Man Changes His Skin,* I have been working for more than two years on a new novel aimed against the enemies of the people—the Trotskyites—and their master—German fascism. In this work I contrast two worlds, the worlds of communism and fascism, and I attempt against this backdrop to reveal the methods of underground work of the Gestapo and its agents here in our country—Trotskyite traitors. It's a complex and difficult theme. During the time I've been working, I have had occasion several times to rework and restructure the novel, in particular after the latest trial against enemies of the people Piatakov, Radek, and others, which exposed an entire set of new facts. This also explains why my work on the novel has dragged on somewhat. Nonetheless, I have already prepared for publication the first volume of the novel, which I will begin to publish with the April issue of *Novy mir.* I would very much like to finish in the next few months the second (final) volume as well, so that the novel as a whole could see the light of day before the Twentieth Anniversary of October.

Neither the Writers Union nor anyone else has helped me in this work. I think that I have a legitimate wish at the very least that they not hinder me in this. Unfortunately, one of the directors in our section of comrades who was instructed to get involved in literature, Com. P. Yudin, understands his assignment otherwise. In the 23 April issue of *Pravda* this year, in his article "Why RAPP Had to Be Eliminated" [*Pochemu RAPP nado bylo likvidirovat'*], Com. Yudin aligns me with that enemy of the people the Trotskyite Averbakh, advancing a monstrous and defamatory accusation against me as a Communist:

"Averbakh, Kirshon, Afinogenov, and Bruno Yasensky have in essence started down the path of resisting the decision of the Party's TsK. This group of dethroned 'literary leaders' continued its group activities even after the TsK resolution...."

Everyone, including Com. Yudin, knows perfectly well that I arrived in the USSR only two and a bit years before RAPP was eliminated, that I was never part of the RAPP leadership, I never published a single line in a RAPP periodical, and for the entire time RAPP existed not a single line ever appeared in the RAPP press about my literary works. Knowing how zealously the leading On Guard [*Na postu*] group engaged in self-publicity for their works, it is rather hard to explain such persistent silencing of my creative work if I had actually belonged to this leading group. On the contrary, my harsh speeches against Libedinsky, who at the time was defending [his] *Birth of a Hero* [*Rozhdenie geroia*], and in particular my statement in the press against RAPP's silencing of Mayakovsky, by no means gained for me the favor of the leading On Guard group, whose creative orientation was most vividly embodied by Com. Fadeev.

Thus, without every having been a "literary leader," which Com. Yudin is attempting to make me into in retrospect, I lost nothing from the elimination of RAPP, if I can put it so jokingly, "but my chains."

If anyone ever elevated and "crowned" me, it was Com. Yudin himself, who published an article in *Pravda* shortly before the writers' congress where he raised me to the rank of leading Communist writers who had achieved the greatest artistic perfection. At that time, Com. Yudin was secretary of the Organizing Committee and evidently would not have raised me like that knowing I was waging a battle against a decision of the Party's TsK.

What has changed since that time? What do my "crimes" consist of that are now giving Com. Yudin the right to put me together with enemies of the people and to do that on the pages of *Pravda?*

My "crime" consisted in the fact that after RAPP was eliminated I continued to feel that Com. Fadeev had not wholly freed himself from cliquish On Guardist methods of leadership. And when Com. Yudin, in his capacity as secretary of the Organizing Committee, fell wholly captive to Com. Fadeev, I had the rashness to speak out at one of the plenums against him, Com. Yudin, criticizing his incorrect theory about two streams in the Union of Soviet Writers, and later, on the eve of the writers' congress, to sign along with Gladkov, Sholokhov, Bakhmetiev, Afinogenov, and Kirshon a letter to the secretaries of the Party's TsK criticizing the activities of the Organizing Committee headed by Com. Yudin.

Com. Yudin, who has tried to seal shut the mouth of self-criticism with the odious label of "groupism," cannot forgive me these two "crimes."

After the writers' congress, I threw myself into my creative work, taking no part in any literary tussles. The novel I am starting to publish right now will demonstrate clearly how conscientiously I have carried out the Party's instructions.

L. Averbakh's arrest presented Com. Yudin with a long-awaited occasion to stain my literary and political name.

A few months ago, responding to the vile attacks by Mr. Valevsky in the Polish Sejm, *Pravda* listed my name alongside the name of Levanevsky and other Poles who have gained a true homeland in the USSR and who have earned the love of the broad masses of the Soviet people. I do not feel that I have as yet earned this love, but I know that all my life and in all my work I shall try to earn it. The day before yesterday the same readers of *Pravda* suddenly learned that this same Bruno Yasensky has turned out to be a comrade-in-arms of the traitor-Trotskyite Averbakh in his struggle against the Party's TsK. And all this on the grounds of a completely unreasoned, completely unfounded, personal statement by Com. Yudin. One wonders, who needs this? Who does it serve to increase the cadres of Trotskyite traitors at the expense of completely untainted Communist writers who have never had any political ties whatsoever with the Trotskyite bandits and who have never manifested the slightest deviations from the Party's general line?

Com. Yudin's bald-faced accusation can have only one result: undermining my creative work. Now I will have to set aside the novel and get busy searching for printed proof that I have never belonged to the Averbakh group, to dig around in old journals, to dredge up five-year-old conversations with individual comrades, to account for and explain myself at a dozen meetings. You yourself realize that it makes almost no sense to try to continue work on a novel under such conditions. Thus, for the Twentieth Anniversary I will not be able, no matter how much I would like, to submit a finished work mobilizing the reader to fight enemies of the people and their accomplices. Com. Yudin who, while working in the press department of the TsK and being to a certain extent in charge of literature, never even took the least interest in what I've been writing does not care one way or the other about this. But are these kinds of methods of "literary leadership" in the interests of our Party?

This is what I would like to ask you, and this is why I decided to take up your time with my letter.

With Communist greeting
B. Yasensky

In the following letter from Zinaida Raikh, the wife of Meyerhold, to Stalin one will note how, in seeking to enlist Stalin's aid for the embattled Meyerhold, she tries to discredit those opposed to Meyerhold by emphasizing that they are from RAPP and have been exposed in a campaign of that year as "Trotskyites."

· 144 ·

Letter from the actress Z. N. Raikh to I. V. Stalin. AP RF, f. 3, op. 34, d. 188, ll. 22–25. Copy. Typewritten.
29 April 1937

Dear Iosif Vissarionovich!

I have been writing you a letter in my mind for more than year, since Furer's speech against Meyerhold—in the spring of 1936.

I didn't hear it, my son heard it. He came home with clenched fists in his pocket and said: now Furer is my enemy forever. But I know this speech (the content)—he purposely juggled the facts.

I have been arguing with you in my mind constantly, constantly trying to prove that sometimes you are not right in art.

I have been living in it for more than twenty years; Tolstoy (forgive me for saying "and I," almost like Khlestakov) spent fifteen years writing his essay on "Art"; you were preoccupied with other matters (art [is part of] the superstructure) and are right according to the law you have set for yourself, and you are right in your own way—herein lies your power—and I recognize it.

But Tolstoy rejected art, and you have to understand its *full force* and not limit it to your own tastes. Forgive my impertinence—I take the responsibility—no one would ever say an impertinence to you—I was raised on "Neighboring Mills" [*Blizhnie mel'nitsy*] (described in V. Kataev's novel, *A Lonely Sail Gleams* [*Beleet parus odinokii*]). I am the daughter of a worker—right now this is the most important thing for me—and I have faith in my "class instinct"; it guided me when I helped Meyerhold in his struggle with RAPP.

It is guiding me now to this letter to you, and I am obliged by my conscience to tell you everything I know. "What I know" isn't all that much, but *I will tell you everything when we meet. I have many "projects" in mind, but probably not everything is correct. You will sort it out and think it over yourself.*[3]

Right now I have two matters for you. The first is to bring the entire truth about the death of Yesenin and Mayakovsky out in the open. This will take a great deal of time (studying all the materials), but I will tell you absolutely everything and point out all the roads. They are—this only became clear to me a few days ago—"Trotskyite." I always felt about Volodia Mayakovsky that they were RAPPish; his family (mother and sister) felt this as well. Yesenin's death—also a matter of Trotskyite hands, which I did not sense—I was blind (many had sand thrown in their eyes and emotions). Now it is clear to me, too, but this takes such great tact and caution: I don't have that. I want you to "unravel" this, for I am powerless alone. I don't want Yesenin's grave to be a "sacred grave for pilgrimage," that there should be a cross there put by his mother, but rather that there should be a good Soviet monument, and for Bukharin's idiotic mistake with the "Angry Comments" [*zyle zametki*] to be corrected, and for Trotsky's "regret" about the "unprotected children" to be unmasked as not genuine "humanity" but "politicized humanity."

Dear Iosif Vissarionovich, I have a very happy "façade of a biography," but it is only a façade and so I always find in myself many true words and feelings that many people lack.

They have so endlessly, endlessly deceived you, they have hidden things and lied that you are dealing correctly with the masses now. For you I too right now am the voice of the masses, and you have to listen to the bad and the good from me. You can sort out what's right and what's wrong for yourself. I have faith in your sharpness. What proofs? I know when they were selecting for the Pushkin Committee you nominated Meyerhold and they responded by agreeing to meet with him when he wrote to you; you didn't meet with him because we weren't summoned to the congress when the Constitution was being approved. It was a kind of slap that only Kerzhentsev's hand could do, but were we insulted?! Kerzhentsev cursed Meyerhold as practically an "enemy of the people"—that's no joke, who did that? The offense has to be untangled completely.

But you understood Mayakovsky. You understood Chaplin, and you will understand Meyerhold, too. A hostile hand has led you away from him, as it has us from you.

Now the second matter and the main one for me right now, for in it is the pledge of my recuperation, for right now I am very ill—my brain and nerves are ill from all that is going on.

At a literary gathering at Gorky's you advised Seifullina to write a play. This is a writer of tremendous conscience but pride as well (both of them are proud people—both Meyerhold and Seifullina). I don't have that kind of pride, I have purpose—if I'm doing something I don't stop and I continue without letup, for, as it seems to me, I am living not for fame but for *life*. They are both a hundred times more talented than I—that's not the point right now. *The point is for "Natasha" to be passed, for it to exist. You ordered it and you will accept it. Without your help, nothing will come of it.* This play, as I understand and feel it, is (1) about Soviet humanism, (2) about the new Soviet woman-builder, (3) about the new man in our era.

What needs to be done to give birth to this wonderful child?

There is still a lot of work, but they are both in a hurry—I am complaining to you about them. I have borne an unbearable burden of work for my woman's shoulders, and I am tired. How should I help—we can't rush *Natasha*'s birth, it's not ready yet, not only I but everyone interested in it being good needs to think through a great deal, decide a great deal, understand a great deal.

I am hiding this letter to you from both Seifullina and Meyerhold.

I am sending you the play, the discussions after its first showing in the minutes, my speech was in an almost half-mad state, but much in it seems right to me, other than the crude form, which you will understand and forgive, but they still didn't understand and cursed in "RAPPish" fashion. That's not important. I've put up with too much to be delicate now. Help me to be delicate, too. "Where was I to learn to express the right feeling right away?" That's what it says in the play and that's what I'll say. But I'm not trying to vindicate myself, I'm going to educate myself in this, too—not to be harsh. *I've also thought of having a meeting with you on 5 May, if you can. A meeting together with (1) Mayakovsky's mother and his sisters, (2) Meyerhold and Seifullina.* I'm going to write to Nikolai Ivanovich Yezhov right now about organizing this meeting, and I will send it to him along with this letter. Please, send me a short telegram, to the Leningrad Soviet Building, 13 Karpovka, apartment 20, Leningrad. I hope I'm well. I have to be.

Sincere greetings.
Zinaida Raikh

The following petition to Stalin from Mikhail Bulgakov, requesting the release of N. Erdman, is noteworthy for its calm and dignified tone, which contrasts with that of some other petitions printed here.

· 145 ·

Letter from M. A. Bulgakov to I. V. Stalin. TsA FSB RF, d. N-8620, t. 1, l. 41. Original. Typewritten. On the letter is a stamp for its receipt at the TsK VKP(b) Special Section on 7 February 1938, the note "NKVD," evidently written in A. N. Poskrebyshev's hand, and a stamp for the letter's receipt at the Eighth Section of the Eighth Department of the GUGB NKVD on 11 March 1938.
Moscow, 4 February 1938

To Iosif Vissarionovich Stalin
from playwright Mikhail Afanasievich Bulgakov
Deeply esteemed Iosif Vissarionovich!

Allow me to make of you a request concerning the playwright Nikolai Robertovich Erdman, who has served out his three-year term of exile in Yeniseisk and Tomsk and is at the present time residing in Kalinin.

Confident that literary gifts are extraordinarily valuable in our society, and knowing at the same time that the writer N. Erdman is now deprived of any opportunity to apply his abilities as a result of the negative attitudes that have been created toward him and that have received such expression in the press, I am allowing myself to ask that you turn your attention to his fate.

I live in hope that the lot of the writer N. Erdman will be alleviated if you were to find it necessary to consider this request, and I fervently ask that N. Erdman be given the opportunity to return to Moscow and to labor unimpeded in literature, thereby leaving behind his condition of isolation and spiritual oppression.

M. Bulgakov

Here we see a letter from the head of the Writers Union, Stavsky, to the head of the secret police, Yezhov, requesting that the situation of Mandelshtam be regularized. Mandelshtam was subsequently arrested and perished in the camps.

· 146 ·

Petition from SSP Secretary V. P. Stavsky to USSR People's Commissar of Internal Affairs N. I. Yezhov on the poet O. E. Mandelshtam. V. Shentalinskiy, *Raby svobody v literaturnykh arkhivakh KGB* (Moscow, 1995), p. 242. Original. Typewritten.
16 March 1938

Esteemed Nikolai Ivanovich!

Among some writers, the issue of Osip Mandelshtam is being discussed very nervously.

As we know, for obscene and slanderous verse and anti-Soviet agitation, Osip Mandelshtam was exiled to Voronezh three or four years ago. His term of exile is over. Right now he and his wife are living outside Moscow (outside the "zone").

In fact, however, he is often in Moscow with friends, mostly writers. He is supported, money is collected for him, he has been made into a "martyr"—the brilliant unrecognized poet. Valentin Kataev, I. Prut, and other writers have spoken out openly in his defense, spoken out sharply.

For purposes of improving this situation, O. Mandelshtam has been given support through Litfond. However, this does not resolve the entire Mandelshtam matter.

The matter does not only or mostly concern an author of obscene, slanderous verse about the Party leadership and the entire Soviet people. The matter concerns the attitude toward Mandelshtam of a group of prominent Soviet writers. So I have turned to you, Nikolai Ivanovich, with a request for help.

Of late, O. Mandelshtam has written several poems. However, they are not of any special value—even according to the general opinion of comrades whom I asked to read them (in particular, Com. Pavlenko, whose review I attach).

I ask you once again to help solve this matter of Osip Mandelshtam.

With Communist greeting
V. Stavsky

In the following document we see an example of a positive outcome of a petition, in this case by the MKhAT theater director Nemirovich-Danchenko. On the letter are the following instructions by Stalin: "(1) If we can, we should free her and return her to Moscow. (2) Don't arrest Professor Britske and the others yet" and A. N. Poskrebyshev's notation "Instruction given Com. B[eria]. 8 January 1939."

· 147 ·

Letter from V. I. Nemirovich-Danchenko to I. V. Stalin. AP RF, f. 3, op. 35, d. 18, l. 73. Original. Typewritten.

6 January 1939

Dear, fervently loved Iosif Vissarionovich!

The musical theater named after me is losing a magnificent artist, the singer *Galemba*.[4] She has been exiled while remaining at liberty merely for her husband's misdemeanors, it seems. I don't know exactly, but judging by the lightness of the punishment and the nature of her personality, her guilt is not such that there would be any shame in requesting *a complete pardon*.

I have decided to do this. It is very frustrating if *such an artist* were lost due to the drastic change in climate and separation from her beloved theater.

Forgive me for this letter. Believe me that it is dictated exclusively by my devotion to the theater and my deep faith in your fairness.

    Entirely yours
    Vl. Nemirovich-Danchenko

Sofia Mikhailovna Golemba. Place of exile—Atbasar.

The following petition comes from Viktor Vinogradov, one of the most distinguished Russian linguists of the twentieth century. His career demonstrates how in some instances talent and determination enabled those repressed not merely to survive but actually to make major contributions to Soviet culture. Vinogradov went on to produce *The Russian Language* (*Russky iazyk: Grammaticheskoe uchenie o slove*) in 1947, which was awarded a State Prize in 1951. In 1952 he became the editor of *Russian Linguistics* (*Russkoe yazykoznanie*) and in 1959 director of the Institute for the Russian Language of the Academy of Sciences. Some have also speculated that he was involved in preparing Stalin's essay of 1950, "Marksizm and Problems of Linguistics" [*Marksizm i voprosy iazykoznania*] which put an end to the sway in that discipline of the school of Niklai Marr.

· 148 ·

Letter from V. V. Vinogradov to I. V. Stalin. [No earlier than 5 February 1939]. AP RF, f. 3, op. 58, d. 159, ll. 66–67. Copy. Typewritten. On the copy of the letter there are an instruction in red pencil from Stalin: "Grant request of Prof. Vinogradov. I. St[alin]" and the signatures of V. M. Molotov, L. M. Kaganovich, A. A. Zhdanov, N. S. Khrushchev, and K. E. Voroshilov.

Deeply esteemed Iosif Vissarionovich!

I am turning to you as the organizer of Soviet science and its guide *with a request to improve the conditions of my scientific work if my work is necessary and useful to the Soviet people,*[5] the Soviet state. In the conditions of my present-day life it is almost impossible for me to continue and definitely impossible for me to finish major research on the Russian language (some of my work has seen the light—and is attached herewith).

In 1934, *by a resolution of the OGPU Board I was exiled for three years to Kirov (formerly Viatka).* In 1936 *after a review of the case I was freed from exile and have been living ever since in Mozhaisk* (outside the hundred-kilometer zone around Moscow). All these years I have been working honestly and with all my powers for the benefit of Soviet scholarship and Soviet culture. Any Soviet specialist in Russian philology can give an assessment of the quality of my works. In the last five years, I have published and prepared for publication six books (of them, three are textbooks for institutions of higher learning) and nine major scientific research articles (a total of nearly 200 galley sheets). Moreover, I am one of six authors of the *Explanatory Dictionary of the Russian Languages* [*Tolkovy slovar russkogo yazyka*] (vols. 1 and 2 have come out). In 1936–1937, at the invitation of Narkompros, I organized a section on Pushkin's language for the All-Union Pushkin Exhibition, which has now been transformed, at government behest, into the Pushkin Museum.

Separated from the capital's libraries and archives, forced to spend eight hours on the train trip, having no legal opportunities for working in Moscow, I am suffering from the duality of my position. I am writing Russian language courses for institutions of higher learning, but meanwhile I am deprived of the opportunity to teach in those institutions. I am engaged in scholarly research, but I can barely take advantage of Moscow's scholarly treasure houses. I am considered a major linguist, but I do not have the professional rights of any Soviet scholar.

I beg of you to grant me a residency permit for Moscow in my wife's room. Your trust will give me new strength for even more intensive work to the glory of Soviet scholarship and the Soviet people.

Prof. Vikt. Vinogradov

My address: Viktor Vladimirovich Vinogradov, 28 2nd Zheleznodorozhnaia Street, Mozhaisk, Moscow Oblast.

CHAPTER NINETEEN

The Stalin-Sholokhov Exchange

Mikhail Sholokhov, the Nobel laureate, was virtually a unique phenomenon among Soviet writers, partly because of his enormous prestige. The following document (together with doc. 150, a letter from Sholokhov to Stalin) provides some insight into the murkiness and arbitrariness of the purges in the Soviet countryside. Sholokhov's native village of Veshensk was in the Don Cossack area. However, as the document also indicates, Sholokhov as the author of what had been deemed the great Soviet novel, *Quiet Flows the Don* (*Tikhy Don*), published between 1928 and 1940, was virtually immune from purging and hence almost uniquely in a position to protest local miscarriages of justice. Sholokhov's correspondence with Stalin is voluminous and has been published elsewhere.[1] Here we publish just three letters from Stalin's personal archive.

· 149 ·

Letter from V. P. Stavsky to I. V. Stalin. AP RF, f. 45, op. 1, d. 827, ll. 32–36.
Notarized copy.
16 September 1937

To the TsK VKP(b)
To Comrade I. V. Stalin
In connection with the alarming reports about the conduct of Mikhail Sholokhov I went to see him at the village of Veshensk.

Sholokhov did not go to Spain to the International Writers' Congress.[2] He explains this by "the complexity of my political position in Veshensk District."

So far M. Sholokhov has not published either the fourth volume of *Quiet Flows the Don* or the second volume of *Virgin Soil Upturned* [*Podniataia tselina*]. He says that the circumstance and conditions of his life in Veshensk District have deprived him of the opportunity to write.

I had to read three hundred pages of the typed manuscript of the fourth volume of *Quiet Flows the Don*. One gets a depressing impression from his picture of the devastation of the Tatar village, the death of Daria and Natalia Melekhova, the overall tone of devastation, and a hopelessness to be found on all three hundred pages; in this gloomy tone even the flash of patriotism (against the English) and the anger against the generals that Grigory Melekhov harbors are lost.

M. Sholokhov told me that ultimately Grigory Melekhov abandons his weapon and the struggle:

"I just can't make him be a Bolshevik."

What are Sholokhov's Veshensk circumstances? Three months ago the form[er] secretary of the Veshensk District Party Committee VKP(b), Lugovoi—Sholokhov's closest political and personal friend—was arrested. Before and after a group of workers in the district was arrested (for[mer] h[ead] of the dis[trict] pre[paratory] dep[artment] Krasiukov, for[mer] chair[man] of the dis[trict] Party ex[ecutive] com[mittee] Lygachev [*sic*],[3] and others)—all of them are accused of belonging to a counterrevolutionary Trotskyite organization.

M. Sholokhov told me flat out:

"I don't believe in Lugovoi's guilt, and if they condemn him, that means I'm guilty, too, and they'll condemn me. After all, we've been doing everything together in the district."

Recalling Lugovoi, he found in him only positive traits; he especially praised the passion with which Lugovoi fought enemies of the people Sheboldaev, Larin, and their stooges.

With great irritation bordering on hostility, M. Sholokhov spoke:

"I still don't know how the region's officials will turn out for me.

"The second secretary just arrived, Ivan Ulianych Ivanov, spent two days here, we drank vodka together and talked; how well he spoke. I was already thinking he was stronger than Yevdokimov, and now he's turned out to be an enemy of the people and now he's being arrested!

"Look what's going on! They put pressure on us about the sowing and harvest, but they're letting the grain rot in Bazki. Tens of thousands of poods are rotting in the open air!"

The next day I verified these words of Sholokhov. Indeed, at Bazki on the banks of the Don lie (some of it trampled) about ten thousand tons of wheat. Tarpaulin has been sent in only in the last few days (after the rains). The wreckers from the Grain Union have been arrested.

M. Sholokhov spoke bitterly about how an NKVD district worker was following him and gathering all kinds of gossip about him and his relatives.

In an outburst of candor M. Sholokhov said:

"Thoughts are occurring to me such that later I myself am frightened by them."

I took this as an admission of thoughts about suicide.

I asked him point-blank, "Haven't you thought that your enemies in the district are arming around you and that it's advantageous to your enemies for you not to write? If you don't write, that means your enemy has to some extent got what he was after!"

Sholokhov paled and softened. From our further conversation it is quite obvious that lately he has made some crude political mistakes.

1. Receiving a letter (on cigarette paper) in early August from for[mer] head of the dis[trict] pro[curement] department Krasiukov in exile, he didn't show it to anyone and took it out for the first time only in the conversation with me. And that was by way of an argument in support of Lugovoi. In his letter, Krasiukov wrote that he was innocent, that the investigation was wrong and criminal, etc.

To my question of whether he had made a copy of this letter Sholokhov said he had, but he hadn't given it either to Com. Yevdokimov or to the district Party committee.

2. As one of the seven members of the district Party committee, Sholokhov is doing no Party work, he's never at the kolkhozes, he stays home or goes hunting, and also listens to reports from "his" men.

Kolkhoz farmers from the Sholokhov Kolkhoz have expressed extreme dissatisfaction with the fact that he has forgotten them and hasn't been there for many months:

"What else does he want in life? His house is a two-story palace, a man and woman to farm it, an automobile, two horses, cows, a pack of dogs, and he's constantly grumbling, sitting at home."

3. At the oblast' conference, Sholokhov was selected for the Secretariat [of the area Party committee], but he hasn't stopped by there once.

In the oblast' (Rostov on Don), the attitude toward Sholokhov is extremely leery.

Com. Yevdokimov said:

"We don't want to surrender Sholokhov to our enemies, we want to tear him away from them and make him ours!"

At the same time Com. Yevdokimov also added:

"If it weren't Sholokhov with his name, he would have been arrested long ago." Com. Yevdokimov, whom I told all about my conversation with Sholokhov, said that Lugovoi still hasn't confessed, despite the clear facts of wrecking and the numerous testimonies against him. The attention of the NKVD's area administration has been brought to the quality of the investigation.

The enemies operating in the district have evidently hidden behind Sholokhov's back, played on his vanity (the district Party committee bureau has met several times at Sholokhov's home) and are attempting even now to use him as their intercessor and defender.

The best thing would be for Sholokhov (who even now is under the influence of his wife's family, who are direct bearers of counterrevolution) to leave the village for an industrial center, but he is decisively opposed to this, and I was powerless to convince him of this.

Sholokhov stated decisively and categorically that he has no disagreements of any kind with the policy of the Party and the government, but the Lugovoi case raises major doubts for him as to the actions of the local authorities.

Complaining that he can't write, M. Sholokhov for some reason found it necessary to mention that he had just sent abroad parts of the fourth volume, but they had been held in Moscow (by Glavlit) and inquiries have come to him from abroad: Where's the manuscript? Has something happened?

Sholokhov admitted and promised to correct his mistakes both with respect to Krasiukov's letter and with respect to his public-Party work. He said that he felt better after our conversation.

We agreed that he would write more often and he would come to Moscow in the near future.

But the main thing is that his casting about, his isolation (due to his own fault), and his doubts raise serious concerns, and it is about this that I am reporting.

With Com[munist] greeting
Vl. Stavsky

On the copy of the letter the following instruction from Stalin is reproduced from the unpreserved original: "*Com. Stavsky!* Try to summon Com. Sholokhov to Moscow for a couple of days. You can use my name. I'm not against speaking with him. I. Stalin."

Stalin made special efforts with Sholokhov and often invited him to visit. These visits became almost yearly and took place either in Stalin's study at the Kremlin or at his dacha. In Stalin's study they often discussed Sholokhov's complaints and sometimes his attempts at "redressing an injustice" were successful. After one such meeting (of 4 November 1937), Sholokhov wrote the following letter to Stalin:

· 150 ·

Letter from M. A. Sholokhov to I. V. Stalin. AP RF, f. 45, op. 1, d. 827, ll. 41–61. Original. Typewritten.
Veshenskaia Station, 16 February 1938

Dear Com. Stalin!

After the release from arrest of Veshensk RK VKP(b) Secretary Lugovoi, RIK Chairman Logachev, and Representative Krasiukov of the Com[mittee for] Procure[ment under the] SNK, the Rostov Obkom Partburo approved a decision to return Lugovoi and the others to their former work. In this decision, the following was written: ". . . Materials from the inquiry have established that Comrades Lugovoi, Logachev, and Krasiukov were maliciously accused by participants in c[ounter]r[evolutionary] right-wing Trotskyite and SR—White Guard organizations for their own base and hostile purposes."

This formulation is incorrect in its essence and was conceived in order to erase the traces of the enemy's work. What could be simpler: enemies slandered Veshensk Communists, which is why they are enemies, because they slander; the slandered are rehabilitated; the error of the Rostov Obkom and the oblast UNKVD [People's Commissariat of Internal Affairs Administration] has been erased by a decision of the TsK. Whereas in fact it was all otherwise. The Obkom (the former enemies in it are still there) created a case against Lugovoi and the others knowing full well that Lugovoi and the others have no part in enemy work, the enemies expelled them from the Party, and the enemies sitting in the organs of the Rostov Oblast NKVD forced others who had been arrested to give false testimony against Lugovoi, Logachev, and Krasiukov. And not only were a few who had been arrested forced to commit slander; they tried by every means and method to obtain the same false testimonies from Lugovoi, Logachev, and Krasiukov themselves. To a certain extent they succeeded here, too: broken under torture, Logachev gave false testimonies against many honest Communists, including me, and even accused himself. Logachev, who like all those others arrested, was literally being tortured in the Novocherkassk prison (I will return to the methods of investigation and interrogation practiced at Azovo-Chernomorie at the end of the letter), gave exactly the testimonies being tortured out of him.

At the oblast Party committee and oblast UNKVD, there was and is a lingering, powerful, closed-rank, and diabolically conspiratorial group of enemies of all ranks who have set as their goal the rout of Bolshevik cadres throughout the region. It—this group—has achieved much, especially in the northern districts of the region, where the enemy of the people Lukin and his helpers have done some very thorough work. The Veshensk case is direct proof of this. However, Lugovoi and the other Veshenskites have been freed, thanks to your intervention, but hundreds of other Communists imprisoned as enemies of the Party and the people languish in prisons and exile to this day.

It is time to untangle this web for good, Com. Stalin! We cannot have a state of affairs when, for example, Lugovoi is freed and restored to the Party but those who were arrested and condemned "for ties to enemy of the people Lugovoi" are still suffering and bearing unmerited punishment. Those who consciously imprisoned honest Communists must not go unpunished. For now, though, the situation remains as before: the innocent are jailed, the guilty are flourishing, and no one thinks of calling them to account.

In my two meetings with you, I could not consistently and cogently tell you about everything that went on previously in the region and what is happening at the present time. Allow me now to tell you about all this.

[. . .]

We need to put an end to the shameful system of torture applied to those arrested. We cannot allow uninterrupted interrogations that last for five to ten full days. This method of inquiry disgraces the glorious name of the NKVD and allows no opportunity to establish the truth.

Investigators' unmonitored work provides a wide opportunity for enemies who have made their way into the investigative apparatus to create their own terrible cases. . . .

[. . .]

We must painstakingly review the cases of those condemned in Rostov Oblast last year and this, since many of them have been imprisoned for no reason. Imprisoned and at the mercy of our enemies.

The cases of those removed during the purge of the rear must also be reviewed. They not only removed White Guards, émigrés, and executioners, in short, those who had to be removed, but under this rubric brought in genuinely Soviet people: young brigade leaders, tractor drivers, livestock breeders. This is also the method of enemy work, the desire to instill in the Cossack population hostile feelings for Soviet power, to engender a consciousness of uncertainty and alarm. The enemies have achieved their goals. Among the people in the northern dis[tricts] of the Don, people say without a shadow of irony: "Mine [my relatives] were taken away when the second levy was passing through."

From the mouths of kolkhoz farmers I know I myself have heard more than once that they are living in a unique state of "mobilization readiness"; they always have a supply of dry biscuits and a change of clean linen in the event of arrest. What earthly good could this do, Com. Stalin? Hasn't this circumstance contributed to the fact that last year's magnificent crop was scarcely harvested, a huge quantity of grain rotted in the field, the seed wasn't preserved, and the plowing wasn't finished for the spring sowing?

Dear Com. Stalin! I ask you personally—you have always been attentive toward us—I ask the TsK, make a full investigation of our affairs!

Bring to the attention of N. I. Yezhov the content of my letter, after all he took the first initiative in untangling the Veshensk web, and send a commission made up of big men from our Party, real Communists who can untangle this web completely. The oblast Party committee has never done anything and never will! I already told Yevdokimov, "Why doesn't the oblast Party committee take any measures to free from the prisons those who are jailed in connection with Lugovoi, who was imprisoned by our enemies?" He answers, "Did you tell Yezhov about this? Well, that's enough. What can I do?" He can imprison people, but he can't talk about releasing those who were wrongly imprisoned. Then why could he ask about Shatsky, Semiakin, and Shestovaia, "But weren't they imprisoned for nothing? Weren't they slandered?"

Send M. F. Shkiryatov on the cases of the arrested Communists. He knows a great many people here from 1933, and it will be easier for him to orient himself, and also one of Com. Yezhov's deputies. Let them familiarize themselves with the Rostov cases and take a good close look at Yevdokimov! He's crafty—that lame old fox! He's an old hand at Cheka work so why couldn't he see the enemy work on the part of Pivovarov, Kravtsov, Shchatsky, Larin, Semiakin, Shestovaia, Lukin, Kasilov, and all the others who have latched onto him on all sides? I can't believe it, Com. Stalin! But if Yevdokimov is not an enemy but simply a sorry old geezer, then is this really the kind of leader we need in our oblast, where the political situation is so extremely complicated and where so many enemies have been such bastards.

In the last five years I've barely managed to write half a book. In the kind of situation there was in Veshensk, not only was it impossible to work productively but even living was immeasurably hard. It's pretty hard even now. My enemies are still spinning a black web around me. Since Timchenko and Kravchenko's departure, their assistants have continued to conduct active work. Familiarize yourself with the statement I am enclosing and you will see it's the same old story. The RK [Raion Committee] brought to the attention of the d[istrict] d[ivision] of the NKVD the actions of this "politically mature" scoundrel Sidorov, who terrorized the collective farmers, passing himself off as a "secret agent" of the NKVD.

The results of the inquiry conducted by NKVD worker Kostenko are indicated in this statement. Yevdokimov knows about this, too. However, Sidorov has yet to be called to account. You could never recount it all, Com. Stalin, this will have to do.

I will deliver the letter myself. If you find you need me, Poskrebyshev will find me. If I don't see you, I implore you to inform me through Poskrebyshev of your decision. I firmly shake your hand.

M. Sholokhov

The next meeting took place on 31 October 1938. Stalin made such efforts with Sholokhov in part because he thought he was a truly great and loyal writer, and Stalin, in this respect typical of the times, had great faith in the power of literature. He recurrently expected a great book from Sholokhov that would support his regime, first a book on the kolkhoz system and then, after World War II, Stalin hoped that Sholokhov would write a twentieth-century *War and Peace* that might give him prominence. Sholokhov never met this latter expectation but he responded to Stalin's attentions with expressions of devotion to him personally, as can be seen in our last Sholokhov document from the 1930s.

· 151 ·

Letter from M. A. Sholokhov to I. V. Stalin. AP RF, f. 45, op. 1, d. 827, ll. 87–88. Handwritten. On the typewritten copy of M. A. Sholokhov's letter that was made for the leader's ease of reading and attached to the handwritten letter, there is a note from Stalin: "My archive. I. Stalin."

Veshenskaia, 11 December 1939

Dear Com. Stalin!

On 24 May 1936 I was at your dacha. If you remember, at the time you gave me a bottle of brandy. My wife took it away from me and firmly stated: "This is a memento, and you can't drink it!" I wasted loads of time and eloquence trying to convince her. I said the bottle might break by accident, that its contents might turn sour in time, I said anything I could think of! With the repulsive stubbornness that is inherent in all women, probably, she insisted: "No! No and no!" In the end, I did get her, my wife, to give in: we agreed to drink the bottle when I finish *Quiet Flows the Don*.

Over the last three years, at the hard moments of my life (and I, like every person, have had plenty), I have often tried to infringe on the integrity of your gift. My wife has fought off all my attempts fiercely and methodically. In a few days, after thirteen years' work, I will finish *Quiet Flows the Don*. And since this coincides with your birthday, I will wait until the 21st and then, before taking a drink, I will wish what the old man in the little article attached to this letter wishes.

I am sending it to you because I don't know whether *Pravda* will print it.

Yours M. Sholokhov

Sholokhov was feigning modesty in doubting that his "little article" would be published: on 23 December 1939 *Pravda* printed it as "On the Simple Word." The article, dedicated to Stalin's jubilee, anticipates that on December 21 "an old man" will sit down at table with his family, pour a glass of vodka for each adult, and propose a toast with the words: "Now Stalin is sixty. He's a good man. God grant him the best of health and that he should live on this earth as many years more as he has lived [so far]." Such sentiments were of course conventional for these occasions, and though the irony of wishing an unnaturally prolonged life for one responsible for shortening the lives of so many may not be lost on readers of these documents, one has to appreciate that Sholokhov was operating within a very different, and unique cultural ecosystem. Like so many of the other intellectuals whom we have seen in Part Two maneuvering in the interests of themselves or their own coteries, he knew the discourse, the rules, and the magic "simple word."

III
The Forties

Introduction: The Culture of Late Stalinism, 1941–1953

The period of Soviet political and cultural history conventionally referred to here as the forties includes the Great Patriotic War (i. e., the period of Soviet engagement in the Second World War, 1941–1945) and the postwar period (1945–1953). It can be said without exaggeration that the late Stalinist period is the least studied of Soviet history. By comparison with the dynamic revolutionary era of the 1920s, the horrific paroxysms of state terror that marked the 1930s, or the dramatic revelations and de-Stalinization during Khrushchev's "thaws," this period appears static, like stiff lava that had been hardened during the years of war (though in Soviet history textbooks it used to be called the "era of accomplishments"). The last years under Stalin cannot be compared (as some have) with the era of Brezhnevian "stagnation," in which there were attempts, albeit half-hearted, at economic reforms, and yet in these years literature and culture developed in quite interesting ways (despite the censorship), there was ongoing political struggle, and the intellectual and cultural elites were permeated with dissident thought.

The perception that creative artistic endeavor was stifled after the war explains the lack of interest in late Stalinism. It explains it, though really this neglect is not justified inasmuch as the forties occupy a special place in Soviet history. In the last analysis, it was in the name of the "superstability" and full governability that came about after the war that the terror of the 1930s had been undertaken. On the other hand, without this kind of "stability" there would not have been the "thaws" of the second half of the 1950s and the early 1960s. At the same time, one must see the specific characteristics of the era under examination:

it worked out its own special forms for governing society, the specific features of the Soviet mentality, and its own forms of functioning for social institutions and mechanisms, which may not have been as dynamic as earlier versions but undoubtedly possessed their own internal logic.

The main thing that distinguished this era from previous and subsequent eras was the formation of an entirely new sociopolitical context, which gave rise to corresponding forms of ideological and cultural representation. One of these was the "routinization of terror," which ceased to be looked upon as terror and was not perceived in the mass consciousness as such. This "routinization" was conditioned by a completely new situation: *for the first time, power did not have to prove its legitimacy*. It was this need for legitimization (though not exclusively, of course) that helps explain both the collisions of the 1920s and the dramas and tragedies of the 1930s. This aim was not achieved as a result of the terror of the 1930s but was achieved as a result of war, which rendered the Stalinist regime wholly legitimate. During the war the system not only withstood the test of its stability but became stronger, and the issue of succession, both in the context of Party history per se and in the context of Russia's overall history, had now been resolved, to use Stalinist terminology, "finally and irrevocably." This enabled a displacement of former emphases in Soviet rhetoric and practices and led in turn to the formation of a Soviet imperial consciousness that asserts itself even today (this phenomenon was born not in the 1930s but precisely during late Stalinism). The Soviet victory and national consolidation in the war also mitigated somewhat the trauma of the 1920s and 1930s in the mass consciousness, and led to the development of new ways of demonstrating power and the functioning of institutions of power, including in the sphere of culture. This interpretation of late Stalinism necessitates rejecting two commonplaces in the historiography: first, the persistent view of the war as an era of some kind of "thaw" coming after the "freezes" of the latter half of the 1930s; and second, the standard account of so-called Zhdanovism.

Regarding the first—as materials from the Politburo show, the war did not bring with it any "ideological indulgence" whatsoever. The "cultural front" remained strictly administered *throughout* the war, including in its initial stage. It is another matter that during the early war years (definitely until the middle of 1943) the actual *content* of "ideological work" changed drastically. At that time Soviet official rhetoric emphasized the role of the Russian people in the war effort and the "popular," "patriotic" nature of the military struggle against the Nazi invaders, not the role of the Party in conducting the war, or even the role of Stalin himself. The rhetoric of "class struggle" that had been dominant in the 1920s and 1930s was almost wholly supplanted by a traditional nationalistic rhetoric. These developments are not, however, grounds for alleging that there was any "ideological confusion" during the first years of the war, any "latitude permitted in the official press," to say nothing of a "thaw" or any "ideological retreat." The materials of the Central Committee give no grounds for conclusions of this kind. On the contrary, the speed and effectiveness with which the "ideological restructuring" came about during the first days of the war allow us to conclude that the process was well controlled and well monitored. The prerequisites for this ideological shift had been created long before the war (so that there was no "confusion" here as well). The rejection of traditional ideological rhetoric was a sign not of any slackening but in fact of a strengthening of the regime, and it played an enormous role in the legitimation of power that took place as a result of the victory in the war. The new cult of "holy war" and victory, largely derived from prerevolutionary Russian tradition, persisted in the media and the official platform for half a century and essentially replaced the cult of the Revolution. This cult was conditioned primarily by the status of the war and victory themselves in Soviet history: they made the regime wholly legitimate and in this sense wholly "popular." The postwar decade is the best proof of this.

In discussing this decade we should, secondly, distinguish between the "Zhdanov era" and "Zhdanovism." The former refers to a specific historical period (conventionally, up until Zhdanov's death in 1948), when several Central Committee resolutions were passed on issues in literature, cinema, theater, and music. These documents, in whose development and passage Andrei Zhdanov, the TsK secretary for ideology and culture, took a very active part, represent a bloc of "ideological resolutions" by which, according to the standard account in Western historiography, the state hoped to curb the intelligentsia, rescind the freedoms allegedly granted during the war years, and show the new generation of young men returned from the war that their experience of independent thinking and action, their fearlessness, their familiarity with the West, and so forth, were not only no longer needed but were marks of what was effectively political disloyalty. This standard account represents the goal of the "ferocious ideological actions" taken during 1946–1948 as one of reversing history, curbing liberalization, and returning to society the climate of fear it had experienced during the 1930s. In this sense, "Zhdanovism" meant the demise of widespread "expectations and hopes" for an "easing of the regime."

In reality, however, in the wake of the terror of the 1930s the intelligentsia (like any other strata of Soviet society) was in no need of "curbing." Any indications of dissident thought remained, as before, in the private sphere, with no public outlet whatsoever. As for "expectations and hopes" for improvement in society—such improvements as occurred were to be found almost wholly in the material sphere, in daily life, and not in politics and ideology. The new generation that came of age during the war was wholly Soviet.

It should be noted that the very term "Zhdanovism" (if we are talking not about the purely chronological designation of the period under examination) is misleading. The system of governance during the Stalinist era (including control over ideology and culture) presumed a peculiar decision-making process in which no single functionary at any level (including Zhdanov) had the final word. As the Politburo materials show, all "final words," indeed in some sense all "words," were Stalin's personally. Stalin would "pronounce" his decisions in the course of various types of meetings, and only then were they formulated (or not formulated, depending on what status Stalin gave them) in the form of Central Committee resolutions. The fact that after the war the state's goals were achieved almost exclusively through the use of resolutions (ten years before, in 1936, the same functions had been filled by lead articles in *Pravda* in combination with outright terror) attests to the fact that the system had achieved maximum efficiency, confirming yet again that the impetus for such actions was not only the desire to "intimidate society."

There was, however, some element of intimidation in the passage of the "Zhdanov resolutions" in 1946. It could even be argued that they were not in fact aimed at "correcting the situation" in a given area of culture (be it literature, theater, cinema, or music). Three points need to be made here.

First, these resolutions "resolved" virtually nothing. Suffice it to recall the less-verbose resolutions of previous years, which contained serious political directives or concrete measures. There is none of this in the resolutions of the latter half of the 1940s. They contain either decisions that effectively mean just transfers of nomenklatura cadres, or else inadequate measures that do not adequately address the alleged problem (such as the closing down of the journal *Leningrad*).

Secondly, these resolutions arguably contain nothing new. All the aesthetic prejudices of the Stalinist leadership that inform them (the rejection of avant-garde music, the attitude toward Acmeism or the Serapion brothers) had been widely proclaimed back in the 1930s, and these resolutions of the mid-1940s sometimes just literally repeated ten-year-old invectives.

Thirdly, a distinct feature of these "Zhdanovist" resolutions is their inordinately swollen "establishing" sections, which (as is obvious from transcripts of meetings at the Central Committee) most often simply contain a word-for-word repetition of Stalin's invectives, even retaining the leader's intonations (e.g., the famous diatribes about Zoshchenko and Akhmatova, Eisenstein and Shostakovich). These "establishing sections" were significantly more important than the sections containing the actual resolutions.

The only thing new in these resolutions is the actual disclosure of the censorship mechanism, which had been painstakingly concealed earlier, in resolutions of the 1920s and 1930s. In essence, these later ones are ordinary "censorship" resolutions and as such similar to the hundreds of such resolutions on various issues which had been approved by the Politburo, Orgburo, and Central Committee Secretariat on various issues, with one major difference: previously, such resolutions had been *restricted,* secret documents; by contrast, the resolutions of 1946–1948 are *public* documents. And the most important thing the later, "Zhdanovist" resolutions have in common is the new function of such documents: they both affirm a new procedure rendering discussions of culture public and create a kind of discursive matrix for them. They "resolve" nothing precisely because their goal is not subject to verbal expression but is inherent in them. These are symbolic documents that signify the state's new status: virtually the sole public function of the state becomes *the demonstration of itself* (all other functions, from disciplinary to economic, have become completely concealed).

The resolutions of the "Zhdanov era" could also be seen as preliminary (reconnaissance) steps, as a kind of "ideological limbering up" for the later campaign against "cosmopolitanism" (up to and including the "Doctors Plot"). At the same time, this highly consequential campaign must be considered both in its international context (the peak of the Cold War) and in its domestic political context, the context of preparation for a new wave of terror from which the country was rescued only by Stalin's death.

CHAPTER TWENTY

The Literary Front: The War

The archives of Stalin's Politburo offer a unique opportunity not only to view the decision-making mechanism and approval process in action but also to understand why the leadership came to make certain decisions. We have organized this section so that the documents are framed by two secret police reports on the attitudes of writers. The first of these is from mid-1943, when there was a turning point (at the time not yet fully recognized) in the course of the war. Writers' reactions to the recent disbanding of the Comintern and the intensification of nationalist propaganda provide a broad spectrum of the opinions reigning among writers, from the Trotskyite and internationalist to the extreme nationalist and anti-Semitic.

· 152 ·

Special Report from the NKGB SSSR Counterintelligence Administration, "On anti-Soviet manifestations and negative political moods among writers and journalists." [No later than 24 July 1943]. TsA FSB RF, f. 4, op. 1, d. 159, ll. 168–179. Copy. Typewritten. 1. On the first page there is an instruction from the administration's head, P. V. Fedotov, on sending the document to People's Commissar V. N. Merkulov and his first deputy, B. Z. Kobulov.

Lately { . . . } on the part of individual writers and journalists there have been noted various negative manifestations and political tendencies connected with their assessment of the international, domestic, and military situation of the USSR.

Hostile elements have been expressing defeatist moods and attempting to influence those around them in an anti-Soviet spirit.

For example,

I. P. Utkin, poet, former Trotskyite. "If this were 1927, I'd be very pleased at the situation that's come about on the front now (Utkin means the impossibility of achieving victory by the forces of the Red Army alone). Now, though, the current situation is going to do a lot to help everything fall into place. . . .

"I prefer Switzerland to our state. There at least there's no death penalty, there they don't cut people's heads off. There they don't remove prisoners in groups of forty echelons to remote places, to certain death. . . .

"We have as terrible a regime as in Germany. . . . All and everything has been crushed. . . . We're supposed to vanquish German fascism and then vanquish ourselves. . . .

". . . What a situation Russia is in! It's terrible to think. No art, no culture.

"Any independence the bureaucracy running the government kills in the womb. Their ideal is for the Russian people to become a single flock of sheep. This ideal has nearly been achieved. . . .

"The logical path begun with the policy proclaimed [by Stalin] 'to build socialism in one country' is complete. . . . Out of his socialism has come the country's monstrous impoverishment. And private agriculture will probably have to be revived, or else the country will never make its way out of poverty. And men will be coming back from the front who will want, at long last, to live better, more freely. . . .

". . . We need to be saving Russia, not conquering the world. . . . Now we have a hope of living in a free democratic Russia, for without allies we are not going to be able to save Russia, and this means we must agree to concessions. And all this cannot help but lead to internal changes, herein lies the logic and inertia of events. Much has to change. Just take the Party's name, which reflects its ideology: the Communist Party. There would be nothing surprising if after the war it were called the 'Russian Socialist Party.' . . .

"We have yet to see how the state form of our life will change, the paradoxical situation of having the 'best constitution' along with the worst regime cannot continue indefinitely. A regime that totally tramples human freedom. . . ."

N. P. Nikandrov, writer, former Socialist Revolutionary: "Last summer we were waiting for the war's end and liberation from twenty-five years of servitude, this year, this summer, the liberation will take place, only somewhat differently than we had thought. Bolshevism will be disbanded, like the Comintern, under pressure from our ally states. . . .

"Right now, first and foremost, we must expect reforms in agriculture—there, private initiative must be introduced and credit partnerships created in place of the kolkhozes. Then there must be reforms in the sphere of trade. In the sphere of morality, the Jews must be destroyed or somehow restricted first of all. The Jewish question is a military issue for every Russian...."

M. A. *Svetlov,* poet, once part of a Trotskyite group: "Before I thought we were fools—we were shouting that the Revolution was dying, that we would end up under the thumb of world capitalism, that the theory of socialism in one country would be the death of Soviet power. Then I decided, We're fools, what are we shouting for? Nothing terrible has happened. But now I think, My God, we really were smart, in fact, we predicted and foresaw all this, we were shouting, crying, warning, people were looking at us like we were Don Quixotes, we were made fun of. And then we ourselves believed that we were Don Quixotes . . . but now it's turned out that we were right. . . .

"There's not much of anything good or intelligent in this finale. The revolution has ended at the point where it began. Now there is a quota for Jews, a table of ranks, epaulettes, and other 'delights.' Even we never foresaw this kind of a turnabout...."

B. S. *Valve,* literary scholar: "Ultimately it is an irony of fate that we are shedding blood and destroying our country for the sake of strengthening Anglo-American capitalism. . . . Hitlerism has won its historical role, for it saved capitalism from ruin, created a circumstance in which even our country, capitalism's enemy, not sparing its own belly, came to defend it, capitalism, from ruin, to strengthen it, submitting to it. . . .

"The future is very gloomy. All the most important processes in people's consciousness and in politics have to be viewed as concessions to Hitler (the raising of national self-awareness) or capitalism (the disbanding of the Comintern), a rejection of the goals of world revolution. . . .

"German fascism is a logical reaction to our socialism. Ultimately, there are two types of socialism: Nazism and Bolshevism are dueling for world supremacy. History engendered German fascism so that it could put an end to Bolshevism, but Hitler . . . conceived of a foolish idea—to go against history's prescription and raise his hand against the master—capitalism. The master, however—Anglo-American capitalism—proved just as intelligent and was able to parry the blow and send Nazism against its legitimate opponent—us. Now matters stand such that the master is winning, for he is helping us against Germany, but he is in no hurry to rout Germany, because he wants to exhaust more certainly both types of the socialism he detests...."

A. E. *Kolbanovsky,* journalist, editorial associate of *The Latest News* [*Poslednie izvestia*] radio committee: ". . . The war is going to continue for a very long time and will not bring us victory. We are much weaker than the Germans. There is no second front, nor will there be one, our allies are ready to betray us at any moment by reaching an agreement with Hitler at our expense. We can expect tremendous privations, people will be dying at the fronts in vain, and we here, in the rear, will starve, swell up from hunger and cold, perish from fascist bombs. . . .

"The statement from Sovinformburo [Soviet Information Bureau] on the second anniversary of the war about the impossibility of defeating the enemy without a second front is an official admission of our weakness and the utter inevitability of our defeat. Therefore there is no point in working, making every effort, starving, enduring privations. . . .

"Our propaganda is obtuse and undistinguished. I cannot read without malice what is being written in the newspapers and Informburo reports, what we broadcast over the radio. It's the same stock, stupid, repulsive lie. I curse my profession of journalist. We aren't writing what's happening, we're writing what we've been told to from above, what they're forcing us to write about. . . . I'm tired of the perpetual lying, this pressure from above, these undistinguished, obtuse idiot censors and political editors who are killing vital thought and forcing us to lie stupidly and obtusely in line with the norm."

[. . .]

K. A. *Trenev*, writer, former Kadet [Constitutional Democrat]: ". . . Stalin's answers (concerning the disbanding of the Comintern) were written terribly muddle-headedly, illogically, inconsistently. . . . On the one hand, he talks about wiping out the slander against the activities of the Comintern; on the other, that the Comintern has been eliminated so as not to inhibit the struggle against Hitlerism (in saying this Trenev spoke out very harshly about [Stalin] personally). . . . Under pressure from England and the United States, at last, the parasites have been dispersed. . . .

[. . .]

". . . As for our country, it is in no condition to withstand any more war, especially since not very many are likely to agree to fight to preserve the existing regime. . . . We have to be logical. The Comintern has been disbanded, and the 'Internationale' has to be reexamined; the Allies cannot possibly like it. . . ."

Among some of the writers there has been an intensification of so-called democratic tendencies, the expression of hopes for fundamental changes in the Soviet order as a result of the war, and in individual instances outright insistence on the restoration of capitalism in the USSR.

Among them are:

[. . .]

M. A. *Nikitin*, writer: "Does our state really not see the general disenchantment with the Revolution? Are reforms really not going to be undertaken after the war? We can't go on like this. If we can't right now, then we have to tomorrow. So much blood has been shed, and blood yields its own fruits. . . . The misfortunes that the war has brought must be redeemed by an improvement in living conditions and politics. The bureaucrats are living off the people. . . . The Revolution has not justified the forces and sacrifices expended on it. We need reforms, transformations. Otherwise we won't be able to rise out of this abyss, out of the devastation the war has cast us into. Our industry is growing, but agriculture is melting away before our eyes. This disproportion demands correction. . . ."

K. I. Chukovsky, writer: "Soon we must expect even more decisions to the benefit of our masters (the Allies), our fate is in their hands. I'm glad a sensible new era is beginning. They will teach us culture. . . ."

L. V. Soloviev, writer, war correspondent, author of the play *Field Marshal Kutuzov* [Fel'dmarshal Kutuzov]: "We have a catastrophic situation with respect to food, there is nothing to feed the population or even the army. Without the Americans' help we would have given up the ghost long ago. Everything here is in disarray. The peasant men and women in the countryside don't want to work.

"We have to disband the kolkhozes, then the situation will change. The Allies will probably press [Stalin] on this matter and might get what they want, the way they got the Comintern disbanded. . . .

"The Russian people are bearing the brunt of the war, they have borne unprecedented sacrifices. And what will they get in the event of victory? Another series of Five Year Plans, famines, and lines. Our prospects are sad, and I'd rather not think about what's going to happen tomorrow. . . ."

G. I. Maksimov, journalist, VKP(b) member: "The Russian muzhik in the occupied regions is in a quandary now. He doesn't want the Germans to stay in Russia, and he doesn't want the return of Soviet power with its kolkhozes and intolerable state supply system. Our government ought to have eliminated the kolkhozes back at the beginning of the war, and if the muzhik believed that this was sincere and permanent he would have gone to fight the Germans for real. Now he's fighting reluctantly, his arm's twisted, but he is the main force in our army, everything is resting on him."

S. M. Bondi, professor and Pushkin scholar: "I regret over and over again the antidemocratic shifts that are taking place here and that can be observed from one day to the next. Take the mounting national chauvinism. What has provoked it? Above all, the moods in the army, which are anti-Semitic, anti-German, anti with respect to all the national minorities, about whom legends are being composed saying that they are insufficiently valorous, and our government is wholly agreeing to these moods of the army, making no attempt to reeducate it or change its nature.

"Most important is to preserve the army's battle-readiness, its readiness to fight, as for the war's goals, it's best not to think about them. This is how you create a simulacrum of a military caste, which naturally does not fit into the framework of a democracy.

"For the Bolsheviks, a serious crisis has ensued, a terrible impasse. They're not going to be able to come out of it with their head held high, they'll have to crawl on all fours, and then for only a very brief while. After the Comintern there will be a liquidation of a more serious order. . . . This is not a concession, it's not even a reform, it's an entire revolution. It's the rejection of Communist propaganda in the West as an obstacle to the ruling classes, it is the rejection of the forcible overthrow of the public order of other countries. Not bad for a start. . . .

"Here you have the first creative thing the Germans and their war have yielded. . . ."

S. T. Morozov, journalist, grandson of manufacturer Savva Morozov: "We are all broken, crushed men. It could never occur to any of us that he might legitimately take part in the public, political life of the country. Meanwhile, it is clear that after the war life in the country has to change drastically, under the Allies' influence the government will be forced to decisively alter its domestic course. It is highly likely that opposition parties will arise in the country. . . . I would like for the government right now, during the war, to make a promise to organize life in the country after the war on other principles. Such a statement would help us, it would make each person feel that he was fighting for an improvement in his position, in his own interests."

Ya. E. Golosovker, poet-translator and literary historian, arrested and convicted of Trotskyite activity: "The Soviet order is a despotism, economically the costliest and most unproductive system possible, a predatory economy. Hitler will be beaten and the Allies may be able to put pressure on us and attain a minimum of freedoms. . . ."

Banding together on the grounds of a commonality of anti-Soviet moods, some elements among writers hostile to the Soviet order are making attempts to create, under the guise of literary circles, political factions, opposing them to Soviet public life, counting on winning specific positions in the state, and expressing hopes for the elimination or alteration of the Soviet order.

Such attempts are illustrated by the following examples:

P. A. Kuzko, writer, formerly belonged to the Socialist Revolutionaries: [. . .]

"Apart from [Stalin] the people have nominated their own leaders—Zhukov, Rokossovsky, and others. These leaders are beating the Germans and after the victory they will demand a place for themselves in the sun. . . . One of these popular generals will become dictator, or else demand changes in the country's administration. . . . The mass of soldiers, after they've returned from the war and seen that agriculture cannot be restored under collectivization, will overthrow Soviet power . . . as a result of the war the Communist Party's hegemony will fall and give way to the hegemony of a peasant party, which will create a new state and free the people from the kolkhozes. . . .

"I understand full well that right now we cannot begin with excessively drastic statements, but we need to be clear that today's literature, which distorts and embellishes reality for the good of the powers that be, has to be destroyed because it is false and perverts men's minds. . . .

"Forces discontented with the war are accumulating in the country. . . . The Allies are doing a poor job of exerting their influence; if they applied real pressure we might have hope of some easing, emancipation. . . .

"We must not waste time . . . if we are to latch onto some spot in the leadership. This might stand us in very good stead. We must use the Soviet public just as it is using us. . . .

"We have to be the new thing that replaces today's bureaucratic Soviet junk. We are those who realize, for instance, that today's literature is bureaucratized and soulless, who clearly see that today's apparatus of officials, today's Party hierarchy, has to be destroyed. All these 'we,' who understand more than all the well-intentioned and right-thinking officials, must surge upward on the wave of wartime and postwar events. . . .

"There is no Soviet power. There is a kind of conglomerate of diverse aspirations and a chief of everything. There is a tsar over the tsardom, in which there is no unity. . . . An infinite number of officials, who must be fought, an infinite herd of the Party fellowship, is not a political whole. All these people long ago forgot and spat upon socialist, communist ideas. . . .

[. . .]

V. B. Shklovsky, writer, former Socialist Revolutionary: "Right now I'd like to gather a solid, energetic core of writers, as there once was around Mayakovsky, and truly, genuinely illuminate and show the war. . . .

"When you come right down to it, I'm sick and tired of everything, I feel as if no one trusts me personally, I have no desire to work, I'm tired, and everything can go the way it's going for all I care. It doesn't matter, none of us has the strength to change anything without a directive from above. . . .

"As before I'm tormented most of all by the same thought: victory will not yield anything good, it will not bring any changes whatsoever to the order, it will not yield an opportunity to write as one pleases and print what's been written. But without victory it's all over, we're done for. That means there is no solution. Our regime has always been more cynical than any that has ever existed, but the anti-Semitism of the Communist Party—that's just too charming. . . .

". . . I have no hope for favorable influence from the Allies. They will be declared imperialists from the moment peace talks begin. The present-day moral poverty will flourish after the war."

P. B. Krasnov, journalist: ". . . Our situation from this point on is going to become unbearable. A country bled dry cannot withstand a new onslaught of Hitlerites. I have all my hopes on England and America, which will deal the Germans the decisive blow. But it is obvious that neither England nor America wants to give the Stalinist government their full backing. They are trying to bring about a 'peaceful revolution' in the USSR. One of its links is the Comintern's elimination. If Stalin does not agree to all of England and America's demands, they could throw Russia into Germany's hands, which would be a catastrophe. . . .

"My sympathies have always been on the side of the democratic powers. . . . In the event of victory for Soviet power, there is only one thing left for me, an old democrat and pupil of V. G. Korolenko—suicide! [. . .]

". . . I'm prepared to endure the war another three years if necessary, let millions more men perish if only as a result the despotic, penal order in our country is broken. Believe me, dozens of my comrades think just as I do, who, like me, have only the Allies to count on, their victory over both Germany and the USSR, . . ."

Individual prominent writers and poets have adopted a vague, wait-and-see political position, have not published any significant works during the war, and have not specified their attitude toward the war with Germany.

In their close circle, these writers and poets ascribe their creative passivity during the war to the strict measures of the censor and their reluctance to "adapt." Most of them maintain anti-Soviet positions.

Thus, for example:

K. A. Fedin, writer, before 1918 imprisoned in Germany, admirer of "German culture," has made several trips to Germany and was closely linked with associates of the German embassy in the USSR: ". . . Everything Russian perished for me long ago with the coming of the Bolsheviks; now a new era must ensue when the people will go hungry no more and will not strip themselves of everything so that a handful of people (Bolsheviks) can prosper.

"For the blood shed in the war, the people will demand payment, and something will happen here. . . . Perhaps blood will be shed again. . . .

". . . I am now going to write about Gorky only for money; this topic no longer excites or interests me. I was quite insulted by how things turned out with my play. For the same kind of drivel (*The Invasion* [*Nashestvie*]), Leonov received a prize, but that's understandable—it was necessary to bow down at their feet, and he did, he tacked on a final scene that's nothing but a hymn [to Stalin], and this is how they repaid him for bowing.

"I, naturally, will never diverge from my line, no matter what it costs me. I will bow down to no one, nor will I make any attempt to fit in. . . .

[. . .]

"We won't be able to do anything without America. Only once we have sold ourselves and our entire people to the Americans, lock, stock, and barrel, will we be able to extricate ourselves from the horror of the devastation.... By surrendering our honor, transforming ourselves into beggars, and begging with outstretched hand—that's the guise in which we now stand before America. We must bow down to it; we will be walking around on a leash like trained dogs....

"... I'm very much afraid that after the war all our literature so far will be simply crossed out. They've broken us of thinking. If you look at what has been written these last two years, it's nothing but exclamation points.... And Leonov's article in *Izvestia*—'Holy Hatred' [*Sviataia nenavist*]—evokes a feeling of disgust and revulsion.... You can't go on shouting endlessly, 'Homeland, my Homeland!' with a sob, manneredly, the way Leonov does it.... I reread Maupassant's story 'Whiskers' ["La moustache"]. That's how one ought to write about war—not head-on but subtly, intelligently, and this produces a tremendous impression. But they won't let us write like that.

"One must wait to keep from putting one's foot in it" (stated Fedin regarding his refusal to edit a German antifascist journal).

B. L. Pasternak, poet: "I've now completed a new translation of Shakespeare's *Antony and Cleopatra* and I would like to meet with Riskey (the British press attaché) for practice in English.

"... You can't meet with anyone you please. For me he is a person, a foreigner, not some diplomat.... You can't write what you please, everything is dictated in advance.... I don't like so-called war literature, and I'm not opposed to the war.... I want to write, but they won't let me write what I please about how I perceive the war. But I don't want to write directed by a traffic policeman: this is all right but that isn't. But here they say—write this way, not that.... I'm doing translations, do you think it's because I like it so much? No, it's because I can't do anything else....

"I have a long tongue, I'm not Marshak, he knows how to do what's required, but I don't know how to adapt and I don't want to. I'm going to speak publicly, even though I know it could end badly. I have a name and I want to write, I'm not afraid of the war, I'm prepared to die, prepared to go to the front, just let me write what I see, not along conventional lines...."

A group of writers returning to Moscow from Chistopol was furnished with a special steamer. Wishing to thank the ship's crew, the group of writers decided to leave them a book of comments. This idea met with a fervent response.... When they brought this to Pasternak, he offered this comment: "I want to swim and I also thirst for freedom of the press."

Pasternak evidently seriously considers himself a silenced poet-prophet, therefore he has moved off to the sidelines, declining to give a direct answer to the questions posed by the war, and is engaged in translations of Shakespeare, retaining his "poetic individuality" far removed from the fates of the country and the people. As if to say the people and their fate can keep to themselves, and I'll keep to myself...."

N. N. *Aseev,* poet: [...]

"... I cannot write genuinely optimistic verse since they don't provide for me as they should, and I'm not a poet but a beggar in the church porchway. I have to go around from morning until night begging for a ration. I encounter heartlessness everywhere. Everything here has been overly bureaucratized.... One has no choice but to darken the doorsteps of all kinds of officials.... We don't have a Writers Union. There are clever individuals who have fallen in step, but there is no opening for real writers and poets.... Here they consciously skirt and conceal what Mayakovsky said and against which he fought all his life—against poetry being timeserving."

[...]

A. G. *Glebov,* writer, expelled from the VKP(b): "... The hopelessly difficult position of Soviet writers.... There's nowhere to publish, they pay crumbs, the writer encounters the censor's horns at every step.... If I knew that the general situation was not going to change in the next five to ten years, I would retrain from writer to at least bookkeeper, and my son, who has an interest in literature, I would try to do everything I could to divert him from it.... I've been writing a novel for a long time 'for my soul,' in which I freely say everything I want to say...."

Not only this, but among prominent writers other political moods have been remarked as well that reflect their assessment of the contemporary situation.

Let us cite the most characteristic statements.

A. N. *Tolstoy,* writer: "We're already concerned about having human military reserves—in the event that when the war comes to an end we still have to fight the Allies over dividing up and rearranging Europe....

"In the near future we will have to permit private initiative, a new NEP, without which we won't be able to restore and revive the economy and circulation of goods...."

L. M. *Leonov,* writer: "I'm very worried by the last part of the document (the Sovinformburo report of 22 June 1943). I think we're standing on the brink of refusing the Allies' help for us.... [Stalin's] reply to Roosevelt was clearly unsatisfactory for 'Democracies.' Roosevelt, as many have told me, demanded the disbanding of the kolkhozes, and [Stalin] replied that this was one of the cornerstones of the Soviet order.... We could have agreed to some reorganization in agriculture, for the personal incentives kolkhoz farmers had even before the war, and especially now, have become very weak....

"We are evidently irritating our allies with our curtness in posing the issues of Poland, the Baltic states, Ukraine, and so forth. We could have refrained from all this to a certain degree. Otherwise it's odd: we ourselves say we can't defeat Germany without a second front, but we're playing a risky game with this second front...."

N. F. Pogodin, writer: ". . . The most terrible life lessons the country has been given, which nearly ended, literally, in the chance surrender of Moscow, which the Germans did not attempt on 15–16 October 1941, simply because they did not believe our total lack of any kind of organization, should speak to one thing above all: things cannot go on like this, we cannot live like this anymore, we won't survive like this. . . .

"Something is wrong with the mechanism itself; it's on the verge of jamming and creaking. Something is wrong here in the system itself. What's good is good, and for many of us it's excellent, but we've had to take the bad in such doses that you just can't understand how and when this could have happened. . . ."

S. N. Sergeev-Tsensky, writer.

Running like a red thread through all his statements is the idea that here he is, Tsensky, the oldest Russian writer, an artist of the word, who all his life has had to break through the debris of misunderstanding of the significance of the writer, his role. He ascribes this especially to the Soviet period, "when many non-Russian people came to literature and journalism, kikeifying Ehrenburgs who don't understand the significance of the artist. They're political hacks and demand the same from all the other writers." Setting himself up in contrast to the "Ehrenburgs," the newspapermen, Tsensky has stated: 'It was impossible to work in Moscow, editorial offices were besieged with requests to write an article. And I so wanted to tell them I'm a writer, not a journalist, that I have more important and necessary things to do. . . ."

In his public practice Tsensky does not deviate from these views of his. Thus, according to the poet Mark Tarlovsky, when the TsK of the Party in Kazakhstan invited him to edit the text of a letter from the Kazakh people to the Kazakh fighters, Tsensky declined this work, stating that this was not the business of a writer. . . .

Speaking about the war, Tsensky . . . has stated that as a result of the war there will be a period of lawlessness for many long years. . . ."

S. N. Golubov, writer, author of the novel *General Bagration:* ". . . After the war everyone is going to be harnessed without letup to the reconstruction of the country's economy, to stopping the gaps. . . . Any changes whatsoever in the direction of improving life and liberating thought and creativity are ruled out for us, for the state has its own inertia that has established itself once and for all. Even if it wanted to, the state could not make even small concessions in public life and kolkhoz existence, the economy, for this could form a crack through which all the pent-up dissatisfaction would surge. There is no light at the end of the tunnel. . . .

After the appeal to Com. [Shcherbakov], Golubov declared: "Where else but here could a writer be asked such a wild question: Is he going hungry? Our demands on life have dropped so low that a writer can be done a great favor by a pood of potatoes and a pair of trousers. . . . Here in the interests of propaganda I became useful to them—and they were kind to me, but if it hadn't been for this, no one would ever have taken an interest in me. . . ."

A. P. Dovzhenko, Ukrainian writer and film director: ". . . We need to publish and in general legitimize all those writers, the nationalist-émigrés, who did not show themselves to be on the side of the fascists, in order to win them over and pull them over to our side. We're poor, every creative individual is priceless to us—why should we rob ourselves? . . .

"The Ukrainian girls who fell in love with Germans and married them are not guilty of a lack of patriotism, the guilty ones are those who did not inculcate this patriotism in them, i.e., we ourselves, the whole Soviet system of education, which was unable to arouse in someone a love for his homeland, a sense of duty, patriotism.

"There can be no question of any punishment, everyone must be forgiven as long as they did not engage in spying. . . .

"The theme of exposing the defectiveness of Soviet education, the uselessness of the Soviet pedagogue, the mistakenness of the propaganda, and the tragic results of all this must be a basic theme of Soviet art, literature, and film for the near future. . . .

". . . What disturbs me the most are the losses we are accepting in order to succeed in the attack. Our forces are not so great, we must economize on them both for the war with Germany and for the defense of our prestige against the 'Allies' after war's end, and therefore it hardly makes sense to spend these forces in a difficult attack. Wouldn't it be better to continue merely to maintain the front lines until a more propitious time—until winter or the Allies' attack on the continent of Europe? . . .

". . . I'm outraged that they have created a Polish division and not formed Ukrainian national units. . . ."

F. V. Gladkov, writer: "Just think, twenty-five years of Soviet power, and even before the war people were going around in rags, starving. . . . In cities like Penza and Yaroslavl, in 1940 people were swelling up from malnutrition, you couldn't have dinner or even get bread. This leads to very grave thoughts: Why did they make a revolution if twenty-five years later people were starving just as much before the war as they are now. . . ."

P. A. Pavlenko, writer, correspondent for *Red Star* [*Krasnaia zvezda*], VKP(b) member: ". . . It is now clear that we are not going to be able to drive the German out of Russia without the Allies. Our might has been powerfully undermined. . . . Ultimately, our fate now depends on the conduct and good will of the Allies. . . ."

I. L. Selvinsky, poet, correspondent for military newspaper in the Kuban: ". . . The mood in our units is not great. People are tired of the war, the German is still strong and fighting persistently.... If things go on like this any longer, there will be no end to the war...."

[...]

Writers manifesting harshly anti-Soviet moods are being actively scrutinized.

On the basis of agent materials attesting to attempts at organized anti-Soviet work, measures have been taken to activate a working over and preparations for operational elimination.

NKGB SSSR 2nd Department 3rd Section Dep[uty] Head
St[ate] Security Major
Shubnyakov

Interestingly enough, although these statements by writers differ virtually not at all from the statements of the 1930s, repressions were almost never applied to their authors (of course, the accuracy of such special reports was far from 100 percent). The increased complaints against the censorship can be explained by its inevitable tightening under wartime conditions, which, in turn, confirms yet again the idea that the war did not bring with it any "ideological relaxation." It is also obvious that the subsequent interpretation of "Zhdanovism" as a reaction against the "expectation of political freedoms after the war," against the fact that "after the war life in the country must change drastically," was born specifically out of the statements just reproduced, which attest to the "negative political moods among writers and journalists." Meanwhile, the state read something else in these moods: overt nationalism and anti-Semitism, a readiness for loyal service, a longing for the "old days." It is characteristic that only a few of the writers had a proper grasp of the situation and gave accurate prognoses: "We must vanquish German fascism and then vanquish ourselves" (Iosif Utkin), "The revolution has ended at the point where it began" (Mikhail Svetlov), "I have no hope of any favorable influence from the Allies. They'll be declared imperialists the moment peace talks begin. The current moral poverty will flourish after the war" (Viktor Shklovsky).

The state responded to these moods by tightening censorship. It should be recalled, however, that the censorship was aimed ultimately not so much at the writer (a point constantly emphasized) as at "protecting" the reader (this is, so to speak, the "positive" aspect of censorship). Soviet censorship dealt quite successfully with that function. In this sense, the "Zhdanov era" began long before 1946.

The Literary Front: The War 365

On 25 September 1940, TsK administrator D. Krupin sent Zhdanov a memorandum "On Anna Akhmatova's poetry collection." It pointed out that "there are no poems with a revolutionary and Soviet theme or about the people of socialism in the collection. All this passed Akhmatova right by and 'did not merit' her attention"; that everything in her book was "old 'tunes,'" "poetic litter"; that her "'artistic images . . . are borrowed from ecclesiastical literature." Later on the memorandum gave about thirty excerpts from the book, and the document concluded with a demand: "Akhmatova's poems must be taken out of distribution." On the document is an instruction from Zhdanov addressed to the directors of TsK Agitprop: "Comrades Aleksandrov and Polikarpov. On the heels of Churilin's 'verse,' *Soviet Writer [Sovetsky Pisatel']* is publishing the 'verse' of Akhmatova. They say that the editor of Sovetsky Pisatel' is simultaneously running the Molodaia Gvardia publishing house. It is simply a disgrace when these collections, if one can call them that, are brought out. How could this 'lechery of Akhmatova's with a prayer to the glory of God' be published? Who promoted it? What is Glavlit's position? Clarify this and submit proposals. Zhdanov."[1]

The TsK Secretariat's resolution on A. Akhmatova's poetry collection, *From Six Books* [*Iz shesti knig*], followed just a month later. It characterized the publication of the collection as a "crude mistake" by the publishing house; the book itself was called a "collection of ideologically harmful, religious-mystical verse"; the editors were reprimanded "for carelessness and a frivolous attitude toward their duties"; and it was suggested that Glavlit "strengthen its political oversight over the literature put out in the country." The final point of the instruction (which was written on the text of the document by A. A. Andreev himself, then a TsK secretary and chairman of the Party Control Committee) proclaimed: "Seize Akhmatova's book of verse."[2] The "Akhmatova question" had been decided, but six years later, when a resolution was passed on the journals *Star* [*Zvezda*] and *Leningrad*, Zhdanov repeated—publicly, this time—his characterization of Akhmatova's poetry as "lechery with a prayer to the glory of God."

Beginning in mid-1943, the nature of the censor's work began to change. It did not become harsher but it did become more public (as we know, previously it had been completely hidden). Now the campaigns of destruction began at publication and were followed by the book's public rout. This is what happened with Konstantin Fedin's *Gorky Among Us* [*Gor'ky sredi nas*]. This is also how it was with

Mikhail Zoshchenko's *Before Sunrise* [*Pered voskhodom solntsa*]. The publication of that novella, which had been supposed to begin with issues 6–9 of *October* [*Oktiabr'*], was unexpectedly halted. Zoshchenko immediately sent Stalin the following letter.

· 153 ·

Letter from M. M. Zoshchenko to I. V. Stalin. RGASPI, f. 17, op. 125, d. 460, ll. 1a-1. Handwritten.
26 November 1943

Dear Iosif Vissarionovich!
   Only extreme circumstances have allowed me to turn to you.
   I have written a book, *Before Sunrise*.
   This is an antifascist book. It was written in defense of reason and its rights.
   In addition to an artistic description of life, the book has a scientific theme about Pavlovian conditioned reflexes.
   This theory has been thoroughly tested on animals. I have evidently succeeded in proving its beneficial applicability to human life as well.
   In doing so, I have patently exposed Freud's crudest ideological errors.
   And this to an even greater degree has proved the tremendous truth and significance of Pavlov's theory, which is simple, precise, and true.
   The editors of *October* gave my book for review to Academician A. D. Speransky several times, both during the period when I was writing the book and upon completion of work. The scientist acknowledged that the book was written in accordance with the facts of modern science and was worthy of publication and attention.
   They began printing the book. However, without waiting for the end, critics took a negative view of it. And printing was halted.
   It seems unfair to me to judge a book on the basis of its first half, for in the first half there is no resolution of the issue. There only the materials are cited, the problems posed, and the method revealed in part. Only in the second half of the book does the artistic and scientific part of the research get developed and the corresponding conclusions get drawn as well.
   Dear Iosif Vissarionovich, I would not have dared to disturb you if I did not hold the deep conviction that my book, which proves the might of reason and its triumph over the basest forces, is needed in our day. It may even be needed by Soviet science.
   For the sake of the scientific theme I have allowed myself to write more frankly perhaps than is usually accepted. However, this was essential for

my arguments. It occurs to me that this frankness of mine only intensified the satirical aspect—the book ridicules falsity, vulgarity, and immorality.

I am making bold to ask you to read my work, or else to give instructions that it should be checked more thoroughly and, in any event, checked in its entirety.

I will take into account all comments that may be made in the process, with gratitude.

I sincerely wish you health.

Mikh. Zoshchenko

Moscow, Hotel Moskva
No. 1038. Mikhail Mikhailovich Zoshchenko

No answer followed, but devastating reviews of the book did, immediately, as did criticism of the novella at a session of the presidium of the Union of Soviet Writers where the work of *October* was discussed. Zoshchenko sent a penitential letter to the TsK:

· 154 ·

Statement by M. M. Zoshchenko to the TsK VKP(b). 8 January 1944. RGASPI, f. 17, op. 125, d. 460, ll. 7–8. Original. Typewritten.

8 January 1944

To the Party TsK
To A. S. Shcherbakov

I considered my book *Before Sunrise* beneficial and necessary in our day. But I did not aim to get it published, thinking that the book was not for the masses, in view of its extreme complexity. The lofty, unanimous praise from many knowledgeable people changed my intention.

Subsequent harsh criticism confused me; it was unexpected.

After painstakingly going over my work, I discovered that the book has significant defects. They arose by force of the new genre in which my book was written. There was not the proper combination of science and literature. Obscurities, omissions, and gaps appeared. They distorted my intention over and over again and disoriented the reader. The new genre proved faulty. Such diverse elements need to be combined more circumspectly and more precisely.

Two examples:
1. The gloomy perception of life referred to the hero's illness. Liberation

from this gloominess was the main theme. In the book this was not made clear enough.

2. Labor and a connection with the collective in many instances bring more benefit than research on the psyche. However, severe forms of psychoneurosis are not cured by this method. This is why the method of clinical treatment is shown. In the book, this is not stipulated.

The book's complexity did not allow me (and others) to uncover mistakes immediately. And I must now confess that the book should not have been printed in the form it is now in.

I am deeply dispirited by the failure and by the fact that my experiment was conducted inopportunely. There is some consolation for me in the fact that this work was not my main work. During the war years I have done a great deal of work in other genres. I sincerely ask that you forgive me my blunder—it was caused by the extreme difficulty of the task, which evidently was beyond my powers.

I have been working in literature for twenty-three years. All my thoughts have been directed at making my literature fully comprehensible to the mass reader. I will try henceforth to make my work necessary and useful to the people. I will make amends for my unintentional guilt.

In late November I had the imprudence to write a letter to Com. Stalin.

If my letter was transmitted, then I must ask that this confession of mine be made known to Com. Stalin. That is, of course, if you find it necessary. I feel guilty and awkward for having the temerity to disturb Com. Stalin and the TsK a second time.

Mikh. Zoshchenko

If a more detailed explanation of the mistakes made in the book is required, I will make it. Right now I am afraid to trouble you with an extensive statement.

M. Z.

Moscow, Hotel Moskva
No. 1038. Mikh. Zoshchenko

No one, however, had any intention of forgiving Zoshchenko his "blunder." On the contrary, we are looking merely at the prelude to the beginning of a campaign. The main Party journal, *Bolshevik*, published an article, "On one harmful novella," which was signed by a group of "rank-and-file Leningrad readers." This essentially directive article was published on Zhdanov's own order, after he proposed in his instruction on the text of the article "to strengthen the *attack* on

Zoshchenko, who needs to be pecked at until there's not even a wet spot left from him." The conflict began to involve details (discussions with literary officials from the TsK and Writers Union), which have come to light thanks to the following document:

· 155 ·

Transcript of a conversation between M. M. Zoshchenko and an associate of the NKGB SSSR Leningrad Administration. RGASPI, f. 17, op. 125, d. 460, ll. 10–16. Copy. Typewritten.
20 July 1944

During a conversation with M. M. Zoshchenko on 20 July of this year, he was asked a number of questions, the answers to which give an idea of his moods and views.

1. What were the reasons for the first speech against your novella *Before Sunrise*?

Answer: "... I was made to understand clearly that it was not just a matter of the novella. An attempt was being made to bring me down in general, as a writer."

2. Who had an interest in this? Your literary enemies?

Answer: "... No, here we could only be talking about corresponding moods at the top. The problem is that many of my works have been reprinted abroad. Often these reprints have been done in bad faith. New dates have been put under stories written long ago. This was bad faith on the part of the 'reprinters,' but I couldn't fight it. And since the Russian man is being described now otherwise than he is described in my stories, this has made people want to 'bring me down,' since my entire writing output, not only the novella *Before Sunrise*, has been condemned at the top. Then there was a turnabout in attitudes toward me."

3. What do you think of Yegolin's article in *Bolshevik*?

Answer: "... I consider it dishonest, since before the critical attacks by the press Yegolin held a different opinion of my novella. Yunovich (ed[itor] of *October*) can confirm this. Yegolin approved the novella. But when they started berating it, Yegolin turned yellow. He was afraid I would 'betray' him by telling about his opinion at the session of the Writers Union presidium where I was berated. Seeing that I did not betray him in my speech, Yegolin came up to me after the session and said quietly, 'It's a good novella.'"

4. Have you ever told anyone subsequently about Yegolin's behavior?
Answer: "I told Polikarpov."

5. How did Polikarpov look on what you had to say?

Answer: "He took an unusual interest in what I had to say and said that he had other materials as well confirming what I'd said and attesting to the fact that some leading Party workers were following an incorrect line. Polikarpov demanded that I write about this and submit a statement about Yegolin's behavior."

6. Why did he demand a written statement from you?
Answer: "He said he would send it on to Shcherbakov."

7. Did you submit this statement?
Answer: "No, I felt sorry for Yegolin."

8. Did Polikarpov insist ultimately that you submit the statement?
Answer: "He shouted at me, demanding that I submit a statement, but I didn't do it."

9. How do you intend to behave toward Yegolin?
Answer: "I'll write a novella in which I'll tell the whole story of my novella *Before Sunrise*. In the novella I'll quote Yegolin—I'll quote all the ugliness of his behavior."

10. Will he recognize himself in that novella?
"Indisputably, since I'll write candidly about everything."

11. Have there been other examples of this kind of double-dealing assessment of your work?
"Yes. In particular I can name Shklovsky as our literature's Bulgarin. Before the 'rout' he praised the novella, but later at the session of the Union's Presidium he berated it. I caught him out in his lie, right there at the session."

12. What does Tikhonov think of your novella?
"He praised it. Later at a session of the presidium he explained to me that he had been 'ordered' to berate the story, which he did, but not very meanly. Later, when the transcript was printed in *Bolshevik*, I was amazed when I saw Tikhonov severely criticizing me. I started asking him what provoked this 'change of front'? Tikhonov started 'apologizing,' inconsistently explained that he had been 'required' to strengthen his criticism, 'ordered' to criticize it harshly—so he was forced to criticize, fulfilling an order, even though he didn't agree with it."

13. How do you regard the removal of your stories from *Leningrad*?
"It can all be explained by the fact that in Leningrad everyone is always looking over their shoulder at Moscow, in this case at Yegolin's article, because they don't know Moscow's true attitude toward me."

14. And what is the attitude toward you now in Moscow?
"It's good. I judge this on the basis of what Tikhonov said. When I saw him in Moscow, Tikhonov said that I had already 'come out of the spin.' Later, on his last trip, he told me again that Yegolin's article was nonsense and the attitude toward me, regardless of that article, couldn't be better."

15. Were you talking about the attitude of writers or the official attitude?

"Tikhonov was suggesting it was the attitude 'at the top.'"

16. Are there facts confirming what Tikhonov said?

"Yes, there are. Not long ago, *Izvestia* came to see me and asked me if I could put out regularly my sharp satirical feuilleton in my old format. Obviously this was cleared beforehand with the TsK, there's no other way to explain the daily calls asking me to get them the feuilletons as quickly as possible."

17. What kind of material are you planning to give them?

"Very pointed material, in my old satirical manner, castigating our shortcomings. One of these feuilletons is a pointed story about a beginning writer and a bad editor who spoils the work, obviously, it's about art and its goals.

"The story of this beginning writer tells about how a steamer sank, but the editor, afraid to have anything said about the wreck of a steamer, corrects the manuscript and renders the story meaningless by replacing the narration about the wreck of the steamer with a story about the wreck of a rowboat."

18. Will they let a feuilleton like that through?

"Not in Leningrad, since they don't know the new order coming out of Moscow: relentlessly expose our shortcomings."

19. What do you think of the general state of our literature?

"I think that Soviet literature right now is a sorry spectacle. The cliché rules in literature, everything is written on the basis of cliché. Therefore even our capable writers are writing badly and tediously."

20. What do you think of the Party's leadership of literature?

"It's easier to guide industry and railroads than it is art. Our leaders frequently do not have a deep understanding of the goals of the arts."

21. What do you think of the fate of writers during the revolutionary years?

"The poets turned out to be less stable than the prose writers, and there were many tragic deaths among the poets: Mayakovsky, Yesenin, and Tsvetaeva committed suicide; Kliuev and Mandelshtam died in exile; and Khlebnikov and Blok died tragically (the latter poured out his medicine during his fatal illness because he did not want to live);

"of the young people—Kornilov, Vasiliev, and others also ended tragically—never got used to the times."

22. Do you consider the reason for Mayakovsky's death clear now?

"It is going to remain puzzling. It's curious that the revolver Mayakovsky used to shoot himself had been given to him by the well-known Chekist Agranov."

23. Can we assume from this that Mayakovsky's suicide was provoked?

"It's possible. In any event, it had nothing to do with women. Veronika Polonskaia, about whom there are so many different surmises, told me that she had not been intimate with Mayakovsky."

24. Whose fate seems tragic to you, if you happen to be talking about writers now alive?

"I am particularly concerned about the fate of Yury Olesha, who was living in Ashkhabad. He used to say that catastrophe was waiting for him—he was right."

25. What do you think about the rest of your life?

"I need to bide my time. Right after the war the literary situation will change, and all the obstacles that have been put before me will fall. Then I'll start publishing again. In the meantime I'm not going to change in any way, I'm going to stick to my positions. Especially since the reader knows and likes me. Recently I spoke at a military evening with Prokofiev and Miroshnichenko. I was greeted by an ovation, a deafening ovation.

"Bear in mind, moreover, that they were berating not only me. I was soothed, for instance, by Leonov and D. Bedny. Leonov said: 'It will all pass. They didn't publish me for two years, and then all the locks were broken through at once.'

"Bedny said: 'They didn't publish me for four years, then everything changed. My only regret is that I was forced to sell my library.'

"The only hard part, really, will be the money. Actually, I've always had a hard time with that, my print runs have always been limited. The only thing that makes it easier is the limit."

26. Besides *Izvestia*, do you propose to appear in print anywhere else?

"My stories have been accepted by Golubeva at *Star*. She sent them to Moscow, but there hasn't been an answer from Moscow yet. Actually, I don't think they'll approve them, since Golubeva mutilated them with her editing, she wanted to put them in a condition to make sure they would pass."

27. Do you believe you've done everything you could to defend *Before Sunrise?*

"I've done everything I could, but I haven't been lucky. Academician Speransky and I wrote a letter to Comrade Stalin, but the letter was sent just when Comrade Stalin had gone to Teheran, and it fell into the hands of Shcherbakov, who was standing in for Comrade Stalin. But Shcherbakov, understandably, dealt with it differently than Comrade Stalin would have."

28. What's your opinion of the current leadership in the Writers Union?

"It's an odd thing: many people attacked Fadeev before, but now everything in Moscow has changed: Moscow likes Fadeev, you see, but not

Tikhonov, since Fadeev is someone who loves Soviet literature, whereas Tikhonov is a cold, indifferent man.

"Polikarpov is an abrupt, direct man, as can be seen from the instance when he demanded that I write a statement about Yegolin's double-dealing."

29. What is your opinion of the general political situation today?

"The news from the front gladdens me. The statement by the German General Hoffmeister shows that Germany's demise is imminent. Stalin saw it all brilliantly. His confidence at the most difficult time was stunning, at a time when nearly all Soviet people thought that ruin was inevitable, that the state's demise was imminent."

30. Do you think that after the war the political situation in literature will change?

"Yes. Literature will be told to write more cruelly and mercilessly about our shortcomings."

31. Do you think you will travel to Moscow in the near future?

"No."

These are the main issues touched upon during the conversation.

As can be seen, Zoshchenko considered the disgrace that had befallen him in the context of his colleagues' misfortunes. Around him people were quite uneasy. Simultaneously with Zoshchenko's story, a new book of verse by Nikolai Aseev, *Years of Thunder* [*Gody groma*], was also banned. In a memorandum addressed to TsK Secretary A. Shcherbakov, G. Aleksandrov, head of the Propaganda and Agitation Department of the TsK, wrote that the collection included "politically erroneous poems" in which Aseev "slanderously depicts our Soviet rear," where "a fetal existence, Asiatic savagery, and a lack of culture" reign, then asserts that "hatred for the enemy is transient, that once we are rid of him we will be people again."[3] Shcherbakov forwarded the letter to TsK Secretary Georgii Malenkov, who also took an active part in literary affairs. Two months later, Malenkov chaired a session of the TsK Secretariat where they considered the latest poems by Ilya Selvinsky. Selvinsky subsequently recalled how Stalin suddenly appeared in the hall and sinisterly said: "This man must be treated with care, he was much loved by Trotsky and Bukharin."[4] The "scrutiny of art" in the TsK Secretariat concluded with the following resolution:

· 156 ·

Resolution of the TsK VKP(b) Secretariat "On I. Selvinsky's poem, 'To Whom Did Russia Sing Lullabies' ["Kogo baiukala Rossia"]." 10 February 1944. RGASPI, f. 17, op. 116, d. 144, ll. 20–21. Original. Typewritten.

10 February 1944

No. 144, p. 104g—On I. Selvinsky's poem, "To Whom Did Russia Sing Lullabies."

Note that I. Selvinsky's poem, "To Whom Did Russia Sing Lullabies," published in *Banner* [*Znamia*] (no. 7–8 [1943]), contains crude political errors. In this poem Selvinsky slanders the Russian people. The appearance of this poem, as well as his political harmful works "Russia" [*Rossia*] and "Episode" [*Epizod*], attest to serious ideological errors in Selvinsky's poetry that are inadmissible for a Soviet writer, especially a writer who is a VKP(b) member.

Dismiss Com. Selvinsky from his job as war correspondent until Com. Selvinsky proves through his art his ability to understand correctly the life and struggle of the Soviet people.

It is hard to name a single leading Soviet writer of prose or poetry who did not attract the ire of the TsK during the war years. Virtually all Soviet writers, one way or another, were "guilty" during the war, including the most eminent among them. It is entirely possible that this is why it was decided to pay attention to organizing an actual institute for the operation of literature. This was primarily a matter of the literary journals. Two documents (presented here) were approved one after the other. The first is on TsK oversight of journals:

· 157 ·

Resolution of the TsK VKP(b) Secretariat "On oversight of literary-artistic journals." RGASPI, f. 17, op. 116, d. 140, ll. 15–16. Original. Typewritten.

2 December 1943

No. 140, p. 98g—*On oversight of literary-artistic journals.*

Note that the TsK VKP(b) Propaganda and Agitation Administration and its press department are providing poor oversight over the content of journals, especially literary-artistic ones. Only weak oversight could lead to such politically damaging and anti-artistic works as Zoshchenko's *Before Sunrise* and Selvinsky's poem "To Whom Did Russia Sing Lullabies" getting into journals.

Require Comrades Aleksandrov and Puzin to organize oversight over the content of journals so as to exclude the appearance in the press of politically dubious and anti-artistic works.

Assign oversight within the TsK VKP(b) Propaganda and Agitation Administration of *New World* [*Novy mir*] to Com. Aleksandrov, *Banner* to Com. Puzin, and *October* to Com. Fedoseev. Establish that those watching over these journals bear full responsibility before the TsK VKP(b) for the journals' content.

The second resolution dealt with making the journals' editorial offices more accountable:

· 158 ·

Resolution of the TsK VKP(b) Secretariat "On increasing the responsibility of the secretaries for the literary-artistic journals." RGASPI, f. 17, op. 116, d. 140, ll. 20–21. Original. Typewritten.

3 December 1943

No. 140, p. 128g—*On increasing the responsibility of the secretaries for the literary-artistic journals.*

The TsK VKP(b) notes that the senior secretaries of the literary-artistic journals *October* (Com. Iunovich), *Banner* (Com. Mikhailova), and *New World* (Com. Shcherbina), who were appointed by the Central Committee to improve the work of the literary-artistic journals and improve the supervision of the journals' editorial staff and their work with the author collective, have been performing the duties assigned to them poorly. The editorial boards of journals are not doing their job, the manuscripts coming into the editorial offices are not being discussed, and the work with the author collective has been set up in an unsatisfactory way. The journals' senior secretaries treat manuscripts coming into the editorial offices uncritically, and they're not making high demands on the quality of published works or their ideological and political content. As a result of the irresponsible attitude of the journals' secretaries toward the publication of artistic works, gray, unpolished, and sometimes even harmful works are getting into print. *October* published the anti-artistic, vulgar novella by Zoshchenko, *Before Sunrise; Banner,* Selvinsky's politically harmful poem "To Whom Did Russia Sing Lullabies."

The TsK VKP(b) resolves:

1. To require the senior secretaries of all the literary-artistic journals to raise their demands on the quality of the works published in the journals and to establish working procedures for manuscripts that come into the

editorial offices that fully exclude the appearance in the journals of antiartistic and politically harmful works.

2. To warn the senior secretaries of the literary-artistic journals that they are personally responsible to the TsK VKP(b) for the supervision of the journals and for their ideological and political orientation and content.

Did this tightening up of responsibility lead to the changes demanded? We can judge this using as an example one of the leading literary journals *Banner*. Half a year after the passage of the resolution on tightening control over the journals, a memorandum arrived addressed to Malenkov.

· 159 ·

Memorandum from the TsK VKP(b) Propaganda and Agitation Administration to TsK VKP(b) Secretary G. M. Malenkov "On *Banner*." RGASPI, f. 17, op. 117, d. 438, ll. 12–17. Original. Typewritten.

7 August 1944

To TsK VKP(b) Secretary Com. G. M. Malenkov

There are serious shortcomings in the work of the literary-artistic journal *Banner*. The TsK VKP(b)'s instructions to improve the work of the literary-artistic journals have been poorly implemented by the editors of *Banner*.

The editorial board of *Banner* created in 1940 is not functioning. The editorial board's members—Al. Isbakh, V. Lebedev-Kumach, V. Lugovskoi, and M. Sokolovsky—do not take any part in the work of the journal. During the war they have not published a single work in the pages of *Banner*.

The journal's senior secretary, Com. Mikhailova, as experience has shown, is incapable of ensuring the journal's being conducted at the proper ideological and literary-artistic level.

The Propaganda Administration has been forced in the process of preparing and putting out the next issues of the journal to correct crude errors committed by the journal's editors. Thus politically incorrect articles by Yuzovsky and Usievich, which were signed to be printed by the editors, have been held back. In his "Critic's Diary" [*Kriticheskii dnevnik*], Yuzovsky essentially comes out against ideology in art and makes fun of the positive illumination of Soviet reality in literature:

"The smug, mystical 'preordainedness' of mandatory success once the hero, about whom we know that he is for rather than against Soviet power, has taken up a cause, has given rise to varnishing and complacency in our literature."

In his article, Yuzovsky states that our prewar art did not arm the people's consciousness for the impending war. He writes:

"Pardon me, the viewer is in rapture, the viewer is being mobilized for the future struggle against fascist Germany. That's not true. We are witnesses. The viewer was demobilized, not mobilized. Tens of thousands of people emerged from the theater in a hat-tossing mood, and this is called educating for the coming war."

In his arguments about Mdivani's play *The Battalion Heads West* [*Batal'ion idet na Zapad*], Yuzovsky makes these malicious attacks:

"Spectacle was badly needed—the war had begun. The play had the instructive, result-oriented title *The Battalion Heads West*. We have to say, because it's instructive, albeit offensive, that while *The Battalion Heads West* was heading for stage, its authors and actors were evacuated east."

In her article about Gorbatov's *The Unbowed* [*Nepokorennye*] Usievich lays responsibility on Soviet power for the sufferings of our people who wound up under the Germans' dominion:

"Those left behind had to go through this first terrifying moment, this moment of tragic bewilderment, in isolation: how could our army, our hope and love, have been unable to resist, to defend our lives, our labor, our entire life, which we put so many years and so much labor and effort into building.... Those retreating were not strangers, they were not the people standing over him and answering for him. No, these were his own, his sons, his children, for whom he was answerable. He (Taras) was lonely in this moment, terrifyingly lonely, but he knew that he would have to account for this period of his life as well. To his men, to his children, to the power that he, Taras, had once won and that rested on him, to all those to whom he had answered all his life *and from whom he had demanded and would demand an answer*. Taras felt he was the master of everything that existed on his home turf, he felt that he, master Taras, was answerable for everything, but also that *they must answer to him*. This was a basic feature of Taras's patriotism."

For issue no. 5–6 (May) of the journal, the editors prepared a long poem by Yevg. Dolmatovsky, *The Leader* [*Vozhd'*], in which he inaccurately depicts the retreat of the Red Army during the first months of the war. To judge from this poem, the Red Army was constantly retreating and offering no resistance to the Germans, starting from our borders nearly to Moscow.

There continue to appear in the journal, weak, artistically gray sketches, short stories, and novels. Thus published in issue no. 11–12 for 1943 were empty, mannered stories by V. Shklovsky, "On Separations and Losses" [*O razlukakh i poteriakh*], and in issue no. 11–12 for 1943, vulgar, antiartistic stories by Ya. Kiselev ("Equal among Equals" [*Ravnyi sredi ravnykh"], "His Duty" [*Ego dolg*], "In the Hospital at Night" [*V gospitale noch'iu*]).

Banner's department of literary criticism is in a state of devastation. Many literary-critical articles offer nothing of journalistic or scholarly value, and in addition some of them are patently erroneous. Published in issue no. 9–10 of *Banner* for 1943 was an article by L. Polyak, "On the Lyrical Epos of the Great Patriotic War" [*O liricheskom epose Velikoi Otechestvennoi voiny*], in which the author makes incorrect insinuations about the characteristics and conditions of the development of Soviet poetry in the prewar era. Polyak writes: "During the difficult years of newly begun construction there existed an unwritten poetic charter which no one had drawn up but everyone tacitly recognized and which placed its veto on intimate-lyrical themes." And further: "Soviet poets of our day have freed themselves from the ascetic hobbles and iron fetters with which they inhibited themselves in the recent past." Later L. Polyak asserts: "The Great Patriotic War has intensified, honed, and filled with new content the patriotic feelings of Soviet man and has thereby finally removed the contradictions between 'one's own' personal interests and the interests of the nation, the homeland." This is saying that before the war there were serious contradictions between the personal interests of Soviet people and the interests of society and that these contradictions were finally removed only by the war. It was evidently clear to the journal's workers that these statements by L. Polyak were unacceptable. Therefore the editors have hidden behind their qualification about their disagreement with certain points in the article, not saying, however, which points they did not agree with. Three volumes of the journal have come out since the publication of L. Polyak's article, but the editors have yet to express their opinion of the article's mistaken points. In the same article Polyak extols I. Selvinsky as a poet who "seeks new but simple, genuine words of value." This was written after the TsK VKP(b) condemned I. Selvinsky's mistakes and those of the journal's editors, who had published I. Selvinsky's politically harmful poem, "To Whom Did Russia Sing Lullabies." Our attention is drawn to the ecstatic article by P. Antokolsky about Boris Pasternak (*Banner*, no. 9–10 [1943]). P. Antokolsky, while inflating and exaggerating in every possible way Pasternak's place and importance in Soviet poetry, writes: "Pasternak, who all his life has dealt with 'naturalness,' trying to achieve its extreme intensity, a stunningly sincere poet, has astonished us with the lightning bolts of his surmises. . . . Thus he lives among us, a superb lyric for whom each spring is a world event, as in early youth." And later: ". . . Everything in him intrigues, enchants, refuses to give a final answer, and over and over again promises to enchant."

The editors of *Banner* gladly publish the "critical" articles of V. Shklovsky, which present irresponsible chatter on the subject of literature.

The editors of *Banner* have no work plan, have not united writers around themselves, and are not facilitating the appearance of the needed artistic works on modern themes that would respond to the successes our people have achieved in the struggle against the German-fascist aggressors. The manuscripts of works being published are not discussed among the editors.

As a result of the editors' irresponsible and slipshod work, a significant part of the material is submitted to the typesetter in unpolished form, which entails additional correction on the galleys of the issue, disrupts the typesetter's work, and undermines the deadlines for putting out the journal. In the last few months absolutely impermissible delays have been observed for the journal: the advance copies of no. 1–2 (January–February) came out on 9 May and the full run on 12 June; the advance copies of no. 4 (April) came out on 8 July and the full run on 20 July.

In order to improve the work of *Banner*, the Propaganda Administration deems it proper to create a new editorial board consisting of the following: Tikhonov, Vishnevsky, Simonov, Ehrenburg, Timofeev, Tvardovsky, Tolchenov, and Orlova.

The writers Tikhonov, Simonov, Ehrenburg, and Tvardovsky have published a number of their own works in this journal: Tikhonov has published his poems here; Simonov has published poems, sketches, and a novella, *Days and Nights* [*Dni i nochi*]; Ehrenburg has also been connected with *Banner* for a long time, before the war he published here his *Fall of Paris* [*Padenie Parizha*] and during the war a number of sketches; Tvardovsky, short and long poems; Tolchenov could be a consultant for the journal on military matters. Approve V. V. Vishnevsky as editor-in-chief of *Banner*.

In view of the fact that Com. Mikhailova did not acquit herself well of the tasks assigned to her, remove her from her work at the journal. Appoint Com. Orlova, who now works as an instructor in the artistic literature department of the TsK VKP(b) Propaganda Administration, senior secretary of the journal's editorial office.

Since literary-artistic journals are organs of the Union of Soviet Writers Board, transfer the publication of *Banner* from Goslitizdat to Sovetsky Pisatel' publishing house.

The main task of *Banner* should be to rally writers writing about the Red Army and Navy. *Banner* should facilitate the appearance of artistic works on the Patriotic War and the military history of our people and publish political journalism on military education issues.

The draft of the TsK VKP(b) decision is attached.

G. Aleksandrov
P. Fedoseev
D. Polikarpov

Two weeks later, on 23 August 1944, the TsK Orgburo passed a resolution replacing the *Banner* leadership, having approved the changes proposed in the memorandum.[5]

The Politburo archives, however, give us a unique opportunity to look at the situation not only from the standpoint of the TsK but from the opposite side of the "barricades":

· 160 ·

Report from USSR State Security People's Commissar V. N. Merkulov to TsK VKP(b) Secretary A. A. Zhdanov on writers' political moods and statements. Published in *Rodina*, 1992, pp. 92–96. Original. Typewritten.
31 October 1944

To the TsK VKP(b)
To Com. A. A. Zhdanov

According to agent reports received at the NKGB SSSR, public discussion and criticism of politically harmful works by the writers Selvinsky, Aseev, Zoshchenko, Dovzhenko, Chukovsky, and Fedin have evoked a harsh and primarily hostile reaction among those individuals and widespread outcries in the literary world.

Poet N. N. Aseev, with regard to his summons to the TsK VKP(b), where his poems were subjected to criticism, stated:

[. . .]

"I know that I wrote poems the people need today. . . . We need to be patient and wait out the reaction that has spilled out all across the country.

"I'm still writing poems, but I'm not showing them. I don't have the right to betray myself, and these poems are objectionable."

Evaluating, in connection with this, the state of Soviet literature, Aseev says:

"In Russia, all writers and poets have been put into the service of the state, and they write what they're told to. Therefore literature here is official literature. What comes of that? The USSR as a state decisively influences the course of world life, but in front of foreigners I'm ashamed of this country's literature.

"Thank God Mayakovsky is gone. He couldn't have taken it. And a new Mayakovsky cannot be born. The soil is wrong. It's not fertile, it's not a yielding soil. . . .

". . . Never mind with the demobilization, men who have seen everything will return to life. These men will bring with them a new measure of things. It's important for a poet who has not traded in his talent for conventionalism to wait for that time to come. I don't know what kind of time it will be. I just believe that it will be a time of free poetry."

The writer M. M. Zoshchenko believes that the criticism and condemnation of his *Before Sunrise* was aimed not at the book but at him.

[. . .]

Zoshchenko gives the following evaluation of the state of Soviet literature:

"I believe that Soviet literature right now is a pitiful spectacle. Cliché reigns in literature. Therefore even capable writers write badly and tediously.

"Often leaders do not have a deep understanding of art's aims."

"Creativity must be free; but here it's by edict, by assignment, under pressure." On the question of his own plans for the future, Zoshchenko declares:

"I need to bide my time. Right after the war the literary situation will change, and all the obstacles that have been put before me will fall. Then I'll start publishing again. In the meantime I'm not going to change in any way, I'm going to stick to my positions. Especially since the reader knows and likes me."

According to reports received from Leningrad, Zoshchenko, while outwardly emphasizing his desire to restructure his art on relevant themes, continues to write and appear before listeners with works that reflect his pacifist world view (his stories "Strategic Assignment" [*Strategicheskaia zadacha*], "Cabbage Soup" [*Shchi*], and others).

The writer K. I. Chukovsky, concerning his tale "Let's Overcome Barmalei" [*Odoleem Barmaleia*], stated that a year ago the Presidium of the Union of Soviet Writers gave the book a good assessment because it is a real work of children's literature and he doesn't understand the drastic change in attitude toward it.

Chukovsky defines the situation in Soviet literature from hostile positions:

". . . They want to bring order to literature. The TsK frankly admits that the situation is clear to them in all spheres of life except literature. They want to force us writers to serve, like everyone else. For this an obtuse and limited man, Sergeant-Major Polikarpov, has been appointed. He will bring order, fine us, curse us, etc. Tikhonov will be a purely decorative figure. . . .

"Vapidity and gloom reign in the journals and publishing houses. Not one manuscript can be accepted independently. Everything has to be approved by the TsK, so the editorial offices have been transformed into dead offices, strictly for registration. Literature is undergoing the most awful centralization, it is being adapted to the goals of the Soviet empire.

"In democratic countries, which rest on the free will of the people, art flourishes naturally and freely. I am not surprised at what has happened to me now. What is despotism? It is the will of one man transferred to his intimates. One of his intimates took a dislike to me. I am living in an antidemocratic land, in a land of despotism, and therefore I must be prepared for all that despotism brings.

"For reasons I have already spoken of, i.e., in conditions of despotic rule, Russian literature has gone to seed and nearly perished. The recent celebration of Chekhov in which I, to my own surprise, took the most active part, eloquently showed what an abyss lies between pre-Soviet literature and the literature of our day. Then, an artist worked to the full extent of his talent, now he works by violating and demeaning his talent.

"The dependence of the current press has led to a silencing of talents and the squealing of time-servers—to our literature's shame before the entire civilized world.

". . . With all my heart I wish the death of Hitler and the defeat of his delusional ideas. With the fall of Nazi despotism, the world of democracy will come face to face with Soviet despotism. We will be waiting." When he learned that his "Reminiscences of Repin" [*Vospominaniia o Repine*] would not be printed in *New World,* Chukovsky stated indignantly:

"I am experiencing a sadistic pleasure listening to the editors turn themselves inside out in front of me as they inform me why my articles are not going to be published. Of late I have had returned to me from various places 11 accepted, typeset, or already proofed articles. This is a collection I'm going to save. When the weather is good, this collection will come in handy, as a living monument to refined persecution. . . . The writer Kornei Chukovsky is under a boycott. . . . There is lying, ridicule, and vileness everywhere."

The writer K. A. Fedin, in connection with the publication and criticism of his latest book, *Gorky Among Us,* [*Gor'ky sredi nas*] said:

"A rumor has reached me that my book was published specifically so that it could be criticized at every crossroad. That is why the editor's name does not appear on it—an unprecedented instance in our literary activity.

"If this is the case, then there is nowhere lower to fall in the moral sense. It means I have been cold-bloodedly and calculatedly, and evidently quite officially, provoked.

"It's one of two things. If the book is harmful, it should be banned. If it is not harmful, it should be published. But to publish so you can beat the harmful author with a rod—that is something the history of Russian literature has never before known."

Concerning an article in *Pravda* criticizing his book, Fedin states:

"Yury Lukin, who wrote the article with a prompter, is formally correct. By the formal point of view I mean the point of view of our government, which is probably progressive when it comes to the war, compelling writers to serve as soldiers without considering the fact that writers placed in the situation of soldiers are not shooting rifles. This is the eternal law of art, after all: it cannot withstand outside provocation, to say nothing of coercion.

"Ridiculous and blatantly fallacious are all the discussions of realism in our literature. Can there be a discussion of realism when the writer is forced to depict what is wished for but does not exist?

"All the discussions of realism in this situation are hypocrisy or demagoguery. The sad fate of literary realism under all types of dictatorship is identical.

"Realistic portraits of Remizov and Sologub are interpreted as a distortion of reality. One cannot write realistically even about the distant past, and what Lukin requires has obviously been incited; it is a demand for the falsification of history.

"Gorky—a man of great vacillations, a truly Russian, truly Slavic writer with all the abysses inherent in Russian talent—has already been licked clean, smoothed over, falsified, stretched into a straight Marxist thread by the various Kirpotins and Yermilovs.

"They want Fedin to occupy himself in the same way!"

Fedin expresses his attitude toward the modern aims of Soviet literature in the following manner:

"I sit in Peredelkino and entertain myself writing a novel that will never see the light of day if the current literary policy continues. This writing without hope has a luscious masochism to it. I may become an odious figure in literature, but I am a Russian writer and will remain such to my grave—loyal to the traditions of the writer's conscience. . . .

". . . There is no need to err, modern writers have been turned into gramophones. Records manufactured to meet the demand of the day are spinning on these gramophones, and they all wheeze absolutely identically.

"Leonov thinks he's some kind of special gramophone. He's wrong. *The Taking of Velikoshumsk* [*Vziatie Velikoshumska*] sounds exactly the same as *The Unbowed* (by B. L. Gorbatov) or *Rainbow* [*Raduga*] (by V. L. Vasilevskaia). To the musical ear this is unbearable.

"Let them close the doors to literature in my face, but I do not want to and will not be a gramophone. It is very hard for me to live. Hard, lonely, and desperate."

Film director A. P. Dovzhenko, while outwardly agreeing with the criticism of his novella for the screen *Ukraine in Flames* [*Ukraina v ogne*], continues to express veiled nationalistic moods. Dovzhenko has responded in hostile tones to individuals who have come out with criticism of his story, especially Com. Khrushchev and the leaders of Ukraine's

Union of Soviet Writers, who, according to him, before the discussion of the screenplay in the TsK VKP(b) gave it a positive evaluation.

"I'm not a politician. I'm prepared to admit that I can make mistakes. But why does it happen with us that at first everyone says, 'Fine, wonderful,' and then suddenly it turns out to be practically slander against Soviet power?

"I don't hold anything against Stalin and the TsK VKP(b), where they have always treated me well. I hold something against the Ukrainians—people who had the courage to defy Stalin and throw malicious slogans at me after all their admiration of the screenplay—these people cannot guide the war and the people. This is trash."

After a summons to the TsK VKP(b), Dovzhenko worked harder on new screenplays about Michurin and about Ukraine, secluded himself, and steadfastly declined to meet with Ukrainian workers in literature and art. According to agents' reports, in his new screenplay about Ukraine, he attempts to free himself of his characteristic nationalistic conceptions, however he has trouble doing this.

The poet I. L. Selvinsky, in connection with the discussion in the TsK VKP(b) Secretariat of his poem, "To Whom Did Russia Sing Lullabies," stated:

"I did not anticipate being called to Moscow for scrutiny. "To Whom Did Russia Sing Lullabies" is just a phase for me. I expected them to praise me at last because I still fight pretty well. I received two honors in two years and have been proposed for a third.

"I was called in to the TsK, they didn't yell at me very badly, they said I was a young Communist, it was all right, I'd straighten out. Now I think they'll stop scrutinizing me, not right away, of course, but in a little while. . . .

"I've been very unlucky for the last 15 years, ever since 'Pushtorg.' They keep pounding away at me. I have no hope of any particular success. Evidently such is my writing biography."

Summing up his thoughts about the situation in Soviet literature, Selvinsky says:

"I am afraid that we, our present-day literature, like medieval literature, are merely manure, fertilizer, for the literature that will come to be under communism.

". . . Right now one can create only according to strict orders and cannot do anything else. . . .

"I have no hope of any particular improvement (in the sense of creative freedom) after the war for myself, since I have seen the people who run art, and it's clear to me that they can and will want to direct only an art of perfect simplicity."

[. . .]

Discussion and criticism in the press of the works of the above-indicated authors has evoked widespread outcries among writers and has served as grounds for generalizations about the contemporary condition and aims of Soviet literature.

Several writers have reacted positively to the criticism of politically harmful works and condemn the creative positions of their authors.

The writer L. M. Leonov:
"Fedin's book about Gorky is bad. There's no excuse for publishing Gorky's letters and statements without taking into consideration that this ultimately distorts Aleksei Maximovich's image. Gorky did not immediately become the writer and teacher of life that the Soviet land esteems so highly. And it's tactless now, in the interests of a personal writer's biography, to publish what Gorky said at a completely different time, at a different stage in our public and literary life.

"I, too, have letters from Gorky, reminiscences of conversations with him, but I'm not handing this material over to the world because I want to preserve in the people an intact image of a great writer who arrived at a complete oneness with his people, with the Party, and with the Soviet state."

[. . .]

Playwright I. D. Volkov:
"Fedin was criticized too mildly, you could write more harshly about his book. He has two great sins. First of all, every page exudes the author's arrogant attitude toward Soviet power; secondly, the author separates life and literature and tries to prove that literature can develop along its own paths, independent of the life of the country. This view is absolutely mistaken and harmful.

"What is infuriating is that Fedin seems to be contrasting himself and the Serapion Brothers to all the rest of literature in the USSR, and not only the literature but also the social and political life of the state."

The writer P. F. Nilin:
"Fedin is not a real writer, his writing is an imitation, repeating the ideas and thoughts of foreign writers alien to us. Fedin somehow, without foundation, suddenly, occupied among us the place of 'great Russian writer'; he suffers from an exaggerated opinion of himself and has given us nothing consonant to our era. He is a pseudorevolutionary, not a people's writer. . . ."

Individual writers, considering the condemnation of works by Aseev, Zoshchenko, Fedin, and others correct, have expressed bitter dissatisfaction with the system of leadership in literature, which has been brought about, in their opinion, by incompetent individuals, a lack of authoritative instructions in the sphere of directing creativity, strictness of censorship, and unsatisfactory educational work among writers.

Literary critic I. G. Lezhnev: "Our literature is limited by specific historical conditions—international and domestic-political. These conditions have not allowed us to develop an art similar to the art of the past, with its criticism and advocacy. This must be admitted as inevitable. Under the above-noted conditions, can our literature develop? Yes, it can. However, it has been led into a narrow, more limited circle than the larger historical and social circle.

"The small circle is defined by the activities of the Agitation and Propaganda Administration. When Aleksandrov spoke at the Plenum, he called on writers to look farther and see more than the usual intellectual things. However, this is virtually not being done. Every attempt to look ahead is restricted and cut short by this same Aleksandrov.

"I'm not talking about the hostile books that were condemned, I'm talking about something else. Right now many writers are disoriented. Vsevolod Ivanov told me that it's impossible to write because 'there isn't any tuning fork.' He's prepared to go along with the Party, but he's accustomed to receiving instructions, not the cudgel.

"Instead of explaining to the writer the meaning of events and what problems need to be raised, they are jerking him around and in fact helping double-dealing anti-Party people.

"It works out that a hostile book like Fedin's can see the light of day but Party criticism of this book cannot (Lezhnev has in mind his article about Fedin's book which was not accepted at *Literature and Art* [*Literatura i iskusstvo*]).

"They won't let us develop criticism. They need to trust the writer if they want to get anything out of him. But there is no such trust. Our central newspapers and journals publish critical analyses of hostile books, but these are articles from the outside, not by critics. They don't derive from the writer milieu.

"Pathetic speeches are given at meetings, writers are exhorted to write, but they laugh at these speeches because they know that the TsK holds back any fresh word. As a result, people are tired of doing battle, are ceasing to write, and are degenerating.

"In this I see the main reason why our literature is not developing. It cannot develop either in this narrow circle, which is strangling it. People are afraid to write because they could be 'scrutinized.'

"There is a kind of craze for Party disaffiliation going on. Any mention of class struggle has to be slipped through as contraband."

Writer A. I. Erlikh:

"Our latest failures on the literary front are a direct result of the fact that people of a low level are sitting in the editorial offices. A good work cannot make its way because the editors are incapable of appreciating it, they think in stock phrases and are captive to the cliché. Not knowing how to think independently and not relying on themselves, they are under the thumb of the high-profile names and so often print hack work, politically low-quality rubbish, as long as it's signed by a more or less approved name—Zoshchenko, for instance.

"I am expressing my firm confidence that with the end of the war all these people whom the TsK's Propaganda Administration has entrusted with the leadership of literature and the press will be swept away—no trace of them will remain. They will be replaced by new people, talented, bold, understanding, politically stalwart."

Writer N. I. Virta:

"The writer now faces substantial obstacles in regard to censorship, and the writer's art depends too much on the chance opinion of various individuals.

"I do not agree when a murderous sentence against a given writer suddenly appears on the pages of the central newspapers. I feel that this kind of criticism is unnecessary and frequently even harmful. Individuals who write such reviews are incompetent judges and in any case bad critics."

Writer V. G. Lidin:

"Grandiose things are being accomplished. Our leaders do not have time for literature or our personal fates or for the fact that in our mighty land a writer cannot survive on his salary and serves literature as a zealot.

"But I dream that someday Stalin will invite writers in for a heart-to-heart conversation. Only will this conversation work out? Shaginyan, as the Party neophyte, will read a tract with citations from Marx, and Pavlenko will say that all of us Soviet writers aren't worth the paper we write on. It's bad that under the knout of RAPP, through the bureaucratic methods of the Writers Union's work, we have lost the writer's great gift, the gift of candor.

"The population in our country is 180 million, but there are probably no more than 150 writers actually writing. Given this disgraceful ratio, which speaks to a low level of humanist culture, the Party ought to guard its tiny gold reserve like the apple of its eye. But how many writers have been put out of commission during the war years, how many moral murders have been committed! I'm not talking about Chukovsky, who may have political sins to pay for. But here is Zoshchenko, who wrote one bad story. . . . Is this sufficient reason to break a man's back, to bury him morally, to defame him to the whole world? . . . No, we don't love literature. Writers are treated like enemies in principle, or day laborers, their punishment is fierce punishment for every error, intentional or not.

"Literature must be lifted up, once it has been offered relative independence within the framework of Soviet ideology and writers have been returned a sense of their own dignity. Returning it means rescuing writers from the kind of situation when any article in *Pravda* categorically determines a certain fate for a writer. A writer should not be defenseless in the face of criticism. . . ."

A somewhat unique position is held by the writer *Ilya Ehrenburg,* who condemns Aseev's antiwar poems while simultaneously expressing his dissatisfaction with the existing system of censorship and criticism:

"We have been ascribed great importance and they watch us vigilantly. Truthful literature is scarcely possible right now, it's all structured in the style of salutes, whereas truth is blood and tears.

"Very telling is the Zoshchenko, Selvinsky, Chukovsky, and Fedin story. In it you can see the administrative tyranny. Aseev is another matter, he wrote antiwar pieces during the war, and that got him into hot water.

"However, the cases of Zoshchenko-Selvinsky-Chukovsky-Fedin are something different. They're very crude in form. About ten years ago they could write the most negative articles about me, call me a bourgeois writer, and publish me all at the same time. Now it's different—once Zoshchenko or Chukovsky has been destroyed in *Pravda* or *Bolshevik,* no one is going to publish them, and this puts writers in a terrible position of social ostracism without evident guilt.

"We writers betrayed art for the newspaper for the duration of the war. This was a public necessity, a sacrifice, but no one appreciates this. Writers are treated the devil knows how.

"I am Ehrenburg, so a great deal is permitted me. I am respected in the country and at the front. But I cannot publish my best poems because they are pessimistic and insufficiently like the style of salutes. But after all, war engenders a great deal of sorrow in man. It has to be expressed."

Recently reports have been coming in concerning the writer *F. V. Gladkov* that testify to his possession of anti-Party views of Soviet literature's situation and the prospects for its development.

Thus, Gladkov says:

"In my *Oath* [*Kliatva*], everything that came out of writerly contemplation, political thought, the artistic image—everything was thrown out. And not by the censor but there, 'at the top,' by Aleksandrov's bureaucrats. I cannot and do not want to be a participant in applied literature, but only that kind of literature is legal now. . . .

"We old Bolsheviks have always fought for freedom of the creative life of the proletariat. But now old Bolsheviks are out of fashion, their revolutionary principles are of no use. . . .

"It's hard to write. Unbearably hard. But mainly—there's no one to talk to. People have been made scoundrels. . . .

"At one time the writer's profession was understood as a 'vocation,' now it is looked upon as bureaucratic service. The writer's labor is being used for blatant agitation; there is no assessment of a literary work on the basis of its artistic merits; literary fame is being artificially manufactured for people like Simonov and Gorbatov, while the genuine writers are in the shadow.

"The absence of creative interests and the indifference toward one another among writers is explained by the view of literature held by the leading comrades as subsidiary to politics. Literature has been deprived of all independence and so has lost its life's work. Artists are dragging out a pathetic existence in the creative sense; lackeys like Kataev and Virta, all kinds of clever and unprincipled people, are flourishing. . . .

"The form of oversight over literature by the Party's TsK is absolutely ruinous, this captious and nitpicking purge of every journal galley by instructors and Yegolin. . . .

"To say nothing of the fact that this delays journals coming out, levels and emasculates literature, and in addition does not spare us from mistakes (the example of Zoshchenko's story). . . . This kind of practice must be stopped if the comrades want our Great Union to have 'if not a great' than at least a major literature.

"I am not trying to console myself with illusions regarding changes in the literature business. We are all fertilizer for future literary harvests. Literature won't get back on its feet for twenty or thirty years. This will come about when the people in their mass, with open doors at the frontier, become cultured. Only then will the bureaucrats be driven out of the command posts. . . .

"Miserable is the position of the writer, who is witness to and participant in grandiose events but has his lips sealed and cannot express his writerly truth about these events. . . .

"In its day, literature has seen Benkendorfs of all stripes and nonetheless has been left alive. Our evil hour will pass as well. . . .

"They should know all this at the top, but they don't. There was a time when writers—including myself—had discussions with Stalin about literature, but now they don't let people in to see him, and even writers' letters don't reach him."

Anti-Soviet-inclined elements among writers assess the criticism and censorship of harmful works, as well as the situation in Soviet literature, from hostile positions, declaring that literature cannot exist and develop given the Soviet reality.

Poet I. P. Utkin:

"Leadership in the ideological sphere of life has been entrusted to people who not only do not love thought but are indifferent to it.

"All the poets resemble one another because they write in political formulas. The image has been banished because it seems dangerous; after all, the poetic image is not a multiplication table.

"I am useless because I am following my own poetic road and not surrendering my dignity. They would like to make Soviet poetry into Arakcheev colonies where each man steps on command as one. I as a poet am incapable of keeping in step and therefore am dangerous: after all, behind me stands the broad reader whose heart I can easily reach. This reader is a thinking, and therefore also dangerous, person, of course, from the standpoint of the Party bureaucrat.

"Administration of literature, administration of poetry! You can't administer poetry, you can create favorable conditions for it, and then it will flourish, but you can put a straitjacket on it and then it will be what is being printed in our journals. It has been transformed into a bureaucratic pennywhistle.

"Working Fedin over seems to have broken the 'meat grinder.' Somehow they couldn't make a cutlet out of Fedin. Vishnevsky and Tikhonov even praised him. And when it was all over arranged a banquet and drank with Fedin to his health. I look on such conduct as scoring off *Pravda*.

"But maybe they decided, in view of the lack of results from the massive bloodletting against Chukovsky, Aseev, and Zoshchenko, to reject this henceforth and try to discuss things differently. You still aren't going to correct us. They can't [do things] the way we do, and we don't want to [do things] the way they [want]. So what are they going to do with us? Publish us or not? They don't pay us anyway! They won't feed us? They will, it's not in their interest for us to kick the bucket."

Writer V. B. Shklovsky:

"In literature, especially war reporting, they select staff who are officially oriented people prepared to write under dictate. Fresh thought is an illness. Even Ehrenburg complained to me that the regulations are becoming increasingly bureaucratic.

"The working over, the scare tactics, and the prohibitions have eaten away at us so badly that they've ceased to frighten us, and people by tacit agreement have decided to pay no attention, not to react or participate in this spectacle. The blows have numbed everything so much that we no longer feel the blows.

"And ultimately, what is there to fear? There can't be anything worse than the situation literature now finds itself in. So why try, why beat each other up—that is how non-Party members have reasoned, so they didn't take on Fedin. Instead, Union [of Soviet Writers] employees gathered and scrutinized Fedin in front of him and scrutinized him gently, even praised him, and then they went and had a drink and took Fedin along with them.

"The Union is dead, everything is so dead that after Aseev, after Zoshchenko, after Selvinsky, after Chukovsky, Fedin no longer produced any action. That's it! Enough! We're sick of it! We really don't have to go—that's what people felt, and so they didn't.

"This working over isn't going to work anymore. They'll have to come up with something else."

Playwright N. F. Pogodin:
"There are many valuable thoughts and statements in Fedin's book. It should be on the desk of every writer. What is most valuable in it is the author's idea: 'A man should listen but not obey.'

"This book affirms the artist's right to think and write what he wants, without reckoning with 'decrees.'"

Writer S. N. Golubov:
"We have no criticism, nor could we, since no one is going to let us create any concepts, even philosophical ones.

"Right now it's become unbearably stuffy. We sit as in a dark cellar. They've smothered us so, we have nowhere else to go.

"When we had military defeats, the authorities lost their head a little, people wandered in different directions ideologically, and no one took any particular interest in us. Now that we're winning, though, these people are starting to close ranks again, and the old ideology has reappeared—class struggle and all that...."

Writer N. N. Shpanov:

[...]

"We live amid lies, pretence, and the vilest time-serving. Literature is run by cretins, and you have to fight for every line of yours, foaming at the mouth."

Writer L. A. Kassil:
"All works of contemporary literature are rot and trash. Literature's degeneracy has reached its limit. The Writers Union should be shut down immediately and writers given an opportunity to gather in groups in their apartments and discuss what they've written according to their own creative sympathies and views. This is the only way...."

Based on agent reports received, works alien to Soviet ideology by the writers Selvinsky, Aseev, Zoshchenko, Chukovsky, Fedin, and Dovzhenko have found approval among anti-Soviet-inclined students at the Literary Institute of the Writers Union, who are turning condemned works into "masterpieces" of contemporary literature, rejecting the principles of Socialist Realism, and attempting to work out "new theories" of the development of literature and art.

> People's Commissar for State Security of the USSR
> Merkulov

This compilation of writers' statements not only makes clear the conditions on the "literary front" as a result of the successive attacks against various "harmful" books and their authors but also gives us a picture, on the very eve of the onset of "Zhdanovism," of the full spectrum of unfulfilled hopes and unrealized myths.

Above all, we would point out the belief that "right after the war the literary situation will change" (M. Zoshchenko), that "with the demobilization, men who have seen everything will return to life. These men will bring with them a new measure of things" (N. Aseev). In essence, it was on this that the entire subsequent criticism of "Zhdanovism" as a reaction to these hopes was constructed: "They want to bring order to literature" (K. Chukovsky). It is here, long before the resolutions of the years 1946–1948, that we find the explanation for the coming "frosts" after the slight "thaw" of the first war years. "When we had military defeats, the authorities lost their head a little, people wandered ideologically in different directions, and no one took any particular interest in us. Now that we're winning, though, these people are starting to join together as one again, and the old ideology has reappeared—class struggle and all that. . . ." (S. Golubov). Meanwhile, a significant number remarked that something had gone wrong with "ideology" as such: "There is a kind of craze for Party disaffiliation going on. Any mention of class struggle has to be slipped through as contraband" (I. Lezhnev).

As the materials from the TsK archives show, "Zhdanovism" was not preceded by any kind of "thaw." In essence, the resolutions of the years 1946–1948 merely made public what had been known to a narrow circle of writers and had been concealed from the broad public under a mask of "the opinion of criticism and the Party press": the TsK guided literature brutally and consistently into whatever channel the state needed and stood behind each such "opinion." In mid-1944, two years before the resolution about *Star* and *Leningrad,* only a few understood that "There can't be anything worse than the situation literature now finds itself in" (V. Shklovsky).

CHAPTER TWENTY-ONE

The Literary Front: "Zhdanovism" and Beyond

In August 1945, A. Yegolin, the deputy head of TsK Agitprop (as well as an academician and literary scholar), sent TsK Secretary G. Malenkov the following document:

· 161 ·

Memorandum from TsK VKP(b) Propaganda and Agitation Administration Deputy Head A. M. Yegolin to TsK VKP(b) Secretary G. M. Malenkov on the situation in literature. RGASPI, f. 17, op. 125, d. 366, ll. 210–221. Original. Typewritten.
3 August 1945

To TsK VKP(b) Secretary Com. G. M. Malenkov

At your behest I am presenting material on literature, in connection with the report by the Sovetsky Pisatel' publishing house to the TsK VKP(b) Orgburo.

The overwhelming majority of Soviet writers, together with the entire people, took part in the war. During the Patriotic War significant works came out that responded to the people's thoughts and hopes. During the war Soviet people grew up spiritually and were tempered morally, and the life experience of Soviet writers was enriched. Several writers are now working on major works. Sholokhov is writing a novel, *They Fought for the Homeland* [*Oni srazhalis' za rodinu*], Fadeev is finishing a story, *Young Guard* [*Molodaia gvardia*]. V. Grossman is writing a novel, *Stalingrad*, L. Sobolev is publishing a novel, *Green Ray of Light* [*Zelenyi luch*]. Right now new, previously unknown people are entering literature:

Kalinin (a novel, *In the South* [*Na yuge*]), Ovechkin (a story, *Greetings from the Front* [*S frontovym privetom*]), the poets Zakharchenko, Gudzenko, Nikolaeva, and others.

There is every reason to expect a new surge, a flourishing of Soviet literature. At the Plenum after the war's end, Soviet writers declared that they were full of impressions and hoped to embody their experience in artistic creation. It would be a mistake to think, however, that a great national literature can be created only as a result of direct experience and empirical observations. Without a deep historical understanding of the events of the Patriotic War in all their interrelatedness, multifacetedness, and development, only superficial, immature works can be written. Only an artist armed with the method of Socialist Realism is capable of penetrating to the essence of vital phenomena, of seeing the sources and prospects for their movement and development.

Meanwhile the ideological backwardness and philosophical illiteracy of some writers leads them to create far-fetched, harmful, unscientific "theories." Thus, recently (6 April 1945), writer-Communist I. Selvinsky, speaking at an all-Russian conference on arts issues, stated that there is a contradiction between the method of Socialist Realism and those tasks which now face art, that modern art is cramped inside the confines of Socialist Realism, therefore Socialist Realism needs to be replaced with Socialist Symbolism. To back up his point of view, this writer declared all the Russian classic writers Symbolists, moreover Pushkin, according to the assertion of the newly fledged "theoretician," is the "acme of Symbolism." The author of this "theory" of Socialist Symbolism went on to establish that there was a "crisis in modern Soviet dramaturgy." The alleged reason for the crisis is that playwrights have been hampered by the narrow confines of Socialist Realism, which restricts their creative abilities. This attempt to reexamine the very foundations of our aesthetics is without a doubt profoundly mistaken and reactionary. Soviet writers must use truthful and therefore realistic images to show our people and the entire world the sources of our victory.

Unfortunately, some of our writers have not risen to the occasion of these goals. Instead of morally strengthening the people and calling them to victory by presenting the vanguard of Soviet society, in the most difficult periods of the war they themselves succumbed to panic and faintheartedness. Some, frightened by the difficulties, gave up in 1941–1942 and wrote nothing. Thus during those years K. Fedin, Vs. Ivanov, and V. Lugovskoi did not publish a single work of art, but "sat it out." Others created works that made the already difficult ordeals of the Soviet people even worse. N. Aseev, M. Zoshchenko, I. Selvinsky, and K. Chukovsky created harmful works lacking in ideals. Aseev's poems slanderously depicted our Soviet rear, and the life of workers was shown to be a "womb-like existence," "Asiatic barbarity," and a "lack of culture." During the toughest periods of the war, these writers forgot their writers' duty, forgot their responsibility to the people.

Some Soviet writers deviated from our ideology and began reexamining Soviet views of reality and social relations. During the years when the entire Ukraine was occupied by the Germans, Dovzhenko, in his novella for the screen for *Ukraine in Flames* and in his story, *Victory* [*Pobeda*], blamed Soviet power for the policy of struggling with class enemies, which allegedly divided the people and led to them forgetting their national feeling and national idea. Writer N. Shpanov, in his play *Medallion* [*Medal'ion*], attempted to idealize the commanders of the tsarist army and called upon Soviet commanders to learn duty and honor from old officers.

The unpublished version of V. Vishnevsky's play, *At the Walls of Leningrad* [*U sten Leningrada*], depicts a former White Guard and prince, now a reserve commander. He comes to see a Soviet officer-Communist when the Germans are already at the walls of Leningrad. He calls himself "a Russian who like many others, including people much more important, was wrong." Vishnevsky makes the former White Guard look like an honest, noble patriot. He teaches the Bolsheviks hatred for the Germans, which is evidently more organic in him than in the Bolsheviks since all his ancestors had fought the Germans. "My dear departed father, Prince Sergei Vasilievich, said, 'Keep an eye on Germany, keep an eye on it.'" And in reply to the big talk and exhortation of the former prince, who spent twenty-five years living under an assumed name, the officer-Communist says, "Why didn't you come to us in 1920? You're a crank."

In 1945, Sovetsky Pisatel' publishing house put out an ideologically tainted book by Y. Ryss, *At the City Gates* [*U gorodskikh vorot*].

Pointed out in a timely fashion to Sovetsky Pisatel' was the need for a substantial reworking of Yevgeny Ryss's *At the City Gates*, but it was limited merely to minor corrections. Yevg. Ryss's book reflects the author's panic in the initial period of the war. The book's hero, a fifteen-year-old worker youth, is given the psychology of a mortally terrified intellectual: "To this day I remember that feeling of agonizing, endless melancholy that would not let go of me for a minute" (p. 28); ". . . longing brought me nearly to the point of nausea, to a physical feeling of weakness and dizziness" (p. 30), etc. In moments of danger, Yevg. Ryss's hero behaves like a pathetic coward: he abandons his comrade in a desolate field while men are shooting; more than anything in the world he fears that when weapons are being passed out he will be given a rifle as well; at the moment of the German attack he "doesn't care what happens later," etc. The image of this fifteen-year-old sniveler, who in the tensest days of the war is idle and succumbs to gloomy presentiments, has nothing in common with the actual psychology of our young people. Yevg. Ryss takes pleasure in rummaging through his heroes' souls in moments of cowardice, terror, and panic, and loses all interest in them as soon as they overcome these feelings. In the chapter "German Carousel" ["*Nemetskaia karusel'*"] (pp. 129–141), the author painstakingly draws out the smallest nuances of the animal fear that grips the soldiers of the workers' battalion during an attack by German aviation. According to Yevg. Ryss's description, at the moment of the bombing, the men turn into a flock of sheep. Smelters abandon the trenches "without thinking, without reasoning, powerless to resist the urge to flee" (p. 136). "We didn't understand that the Germans had gone on the attack. But even if we had understood this, we still would have been so infinitely weak that we would only have been able to wait senselessly and obtusely" (p. 139). "I saw faces, pale and indifferent, hands dropped limply, and cloudy, unseeing eyes. I stood up. I didn't care what happened afterward.... Indifferently I thought how now the Germans would cross the river, jump the trench, capture the city.... My imagination went no further, my thoughts meandered limply, and I didn't care" (p. 140). Extremely wordily and eloquently, the author paints a picture of how a man under the influence of fear presses himself into the earth and loses his human face. But he does absolutely nothing to reveal which forces help these same men rise up from the earth and repulse the enemy's attack. If we are to believe Yevg. Ryss, soldiers are guided at that moment merely by a pure automatism of movement and their commander's shout: "'Step lively, step lively,' said Kalmykov, 'no sense lying about'" (p. 139). "And Kalmykov went off again, cursing for some reason. And the men gathered at their nests and set their bayonets on the parapets" (p. 141). In the first period of the Patriotic War, Yevg. Ryss sees nothing but confusion, distress, and anarchy.

The Leningrad literary-artistic journal *Star* has published several poems by local poets—Vladimir Livshits, Mikhail Dudin, Vsevolod Rozhdestvensky, Olga Berggolts—that are filled with motifs of suffering, death, and the sense of doom....

[...]

Recently N. Aseev submitted his long poem *Flame of Victory* [*Plamia pobedy*], written in the years 1942–1944, to *Banner's* editors for publication. In this poem, the author tells stories about many things—the prewar life of Soviet society, the first months of the war, the battle for Moscow, the Stalingrad epos—and discusses America and the postwar world. N. Aseev looks on all events with the eyes of the philistine. He judges prewar peacetime life by its concerts, soccer matches, fashion houses, and so forth. Aseev perceives the rout of the Germans outside Moscow as a miracle accomplished with the help of a harsh winter. He bows down before America, with pathos describes its democratic ways, and dreams of some foolish future biblical life, where "a single production plan will be created for the cooperation of all countries."

[. . .]

... there have been quite a few discussions among writers about their oppression by the censors and editors who give permission for artistic works to be released. Before it can be printed or performed on stage, a play has to go through these offices: Repertkom, the Committee on Arts Affairs, the republic administration, Iskusstvo publishing house, Glavlit, and the army or navy censor. Each of these organizations makes its own corrections or demands that the author make changes in the text.

Sometimes instead of a judgment based on principle about the ideological essence of a work of art, workers in the censorship organs or publishing houses make corrections that are nothing but petty oversight of the author. Some censors attempt to correct the play or novel with an instruction, forgetting that this is a work of art and that changes can destroy its integrity and diminish its emotional effect. Undoubtedly, the writers are correct in some part in their comments against the censor and editors. We do, unfortunately, have editors who take a crude and ignorant approach to matters of literary creation. But can this really serve as a basis for such incoherent speeches as Com. Vishnevsky, Party member and editor of *Banner*, allowed himself at the Writers Union Plenum? Com. Vishnevsky spoke quite tactlessly at the Plenum, demanding in essence bourgeois freedom of speech. Com. Vishnevsky declared:

"I spoke several times in Moscow this winter and summer at various Moscow gatherings and in my speeches I touched upon freedom of speech, which is so essential to us all. Thousands and thousands of people have understood correctly what I said, what I defend, what I think, and what I live by. I was speaking of the provision in the Stalin Constitution." Further, V. Vishnevsky began explaining in a highly confused manner what he had in mind in speaking about "freedom of speech." Freedom of speech "is the highest demand on yourself. Speak out, struggle with yourself if it's hard for you. Argue with yourself, but lay out everything you have in your soul and your heart—that is our demand. And respect, deeply respect, the speech of your comrade, the thoughts and feelings of your comrade writer, creator, artist. Think what it cost him to create his composition, his work. Try to understand him always for what is good, what is noble. Understand this and you will be fine."

V. Vishnevsky's speech at the plenum was preceded by a session of the Writers Union Presidium where V. Vishnevsky behaved provocatively and asserted: "We fought, we struggled, so give us freedom of speech." Although this speech was given a friendly rebuff at the Writers Union Plenum, nonetheless Vishnevsky's demagoguery left a definite mark on the literary world.

Such are some facts characterizing the moods of Soviet writers in recent years.

A. Yegolin

As can be seen, Yegolin's memorandum about the state of literature a year (!) before the resolution on *Star* and *Leningrad* not only named figures to be targeted in the subsequent campaign of summer—autumn 1946, but virtually formulated the principal charges that would be brought against them. It should be noted, however, that Yegolin is not saying anything new (for those familiar with TsK documents on matters of literature and art of the war period). The main emphasis in the memorandum is put on the "ideological failures" of the Leningrad poets. Here in detail, over many pages, he cites various "politically harmful" poems (we have shortened these extensive poetry citations in the document reproduced). It turned out that they had depicted the Leningrad blockade, the front, the rear, and the daily life of Soviet people "incorrectly and tendentiously," they had "slandered Soviet youth," and so forth. Meanwhile, as can be seen, there was still not the critical mass needed for the coming resolution. Criticized in the main were those who had been criticized before, during the war, or else young poets who were not yet known to the general reader. The TsK materials allow us to see how the clouds were gathering for the future resolution. Above all, an institution had been found to bear responsibility for the situation in literature—the thick journals (it should be recalled that the famous 1946 resolution was devoted above all to the literary journals, which were guilty of printing such writers as Akhmatova and Zoshchenko). It was Stalin who had pinpointed the guilty party in literature's misfortunes.

On 13 April 1946, the Politburo examined the issue of the future structure of the TsK apparatus. Zhdanov (TsK secretary responsible for ideology) and G. Aleksandrov (head of TsK Agitprop) were instructed "to submit proposals for undertakings to significantly improve the guidance of agitation work and to improve the apparatus of the Propaganda Administration of the TsK VKP(b)." Evidently, at this session of the Politburo, Stalin had expressed his own claims against the activities of the literary journals and criticism, which five days later, on 18 April 1946, Zhdanov diligently enumerated in his speech at a meeting of workers from the TsK apparatus on propaganda issues. He spoke after G. I. Vladykin, the recently appointed head of the literature department of the TsK Propaganda and Agitation Administration, had opened the session. Here we have fragments from the transcript of Zhdanov's speech:

· 162 ·

From the transcript of A. A. Zhdanov's speech at a meeting of TsK VKP(b) apparatus workers on propaganda issues. RGASPI, f. 17, op. 125, d. 377, ll. 35–37. Original. Typewritten.
18 April 1946

< . . . >

This matter was discussed after Comrade Stalin issued instructions regarding questions of improving work. Comrade Stalin criticized our thick journals quite harshly, moreover he questioned whether our thick journals ought to be cut back. This had to do with the fact that we cannot ensure that they are all run at the proper level. Comrade Stalin cited *New World* as the very worst of the thick journals, and after that *Star.* As for the best of the very best, Comrade Stalin names *Banner,* then *October, Star,* and *New World.* Comrade Stalin indicated that there are not enough talented works, significant works, for all four journals, and that this in itself shows that the number of journals is too great here. In particular he pointed to a number of weak works, he pointed to the fact that [Yagdfeld's] "Road of Time" ["*Doroga vremeni*"] and then Ivanov's "Outside Berlin's Walls" ["*Pod stenami Berlina*"] had appeared in *Star.* Comrade Stalin expressed a good opinion of "For Those in the Sea" ["*Za tekh, kto v more*"].

As for criticism, Comrade Stalin's assessment was to the effect that we have no criticism, and those critics who do exist are critics in the charge of the writers they serve, critic mercenaries out of friendship. Their task is to praise someone and curse all the rest, so if we want to talk about the reanimation of criticism, then we should not begin it with the reanimation of bureaucratic criticism. We have raised the issue of the thick journals concentrating on criticism, but nothing ever came of this, and criticism has not come back to life here.

Comrade Stalin raised the question of fine literature, of the state of film, the theaters, art, and fine literature. Comrade Stalin raised the question of us having to organize this criticism from here, i.e., from the Propaganda Administration. The Propaganda Administration should be the leading organ posing the issue of literary criticism. Therefore Com. Stalin raised the issue of creating this type of newspaper and creating cadres of critics around the Propaganda Administration and on the staff of the Propaganda Administration, for Com. Stalin spoke about how we needed an objective criticism independent of the writer, i.e., a criticism that could be organized only by the Propaganda Administration, an objective criticism regardless of individuals, unbiased, inasmuch as Com. Stalin said quite plainly that our present-day criticism is biased.

It seems to me that from this standpoint (I don't know whether Com. Vladykin has been brought up to date), Com. Vladykin's proposals begin somewhere else. Com. Vladykin proposes starting with what we have already done, i.e., spreading [the correct] literary criticism among writers, the Writers Union, etc. All this is necessary, of course, but this is not what is fundamental; here the fundamental flywheel that should drive this entire matter is the TsK Propaganda and Agitation Administration. Such is Com. Stalin's directive, and it must be reflected in the plan.

I don't know how prepared we are to submit proposals concerning the journals, or whether this should be included in the plan in such a way as to consider the journals from the standpoint of continuing with their position and other qualities.

A second issue concerning the organization of criticism through the efforts of the Propaganda Administration should be, . . . the best people on matters of ideology. He developed this basic idea of his in connection with the plan, too. Evidently we are still not carrying out this directive of Com. Stalin's. We have to implement it because only from us, of course, can genuine criticism come.

Departmental criticism (I have in mind *Literaturnaia gazeta* [*Literary Gazette*]) and the organ of the [Writers] Union must have a model of unbiased criticism—and we should provide them with such a model. Active intervention in creativity is connected first of all with the matter of criticism, which brings together different literary works, for I do not think that we should repeat the practice of such preventive editing. I think that we tie our hands greatly if we are going to edit preventively, i.e., bring the literary work here. Then we deprive ourselves of the opportunity to analyze and assess it critically.

But you, of course, can imagine that the matter of giving unbiased criticism and a genuine analysis of a given literary work requires the presence in the Propaganda and Agitation Administration of individuals who can be released into this arena without embarrassment, because it is perfectly obvious that people are going to pay heed to their voice, and they will be the masters of our writers' minds, they will have very great weight in our literary arena. Therefore we must equip ourselves with the best people to provide critical surveys. All the rest is auxiliary methods or in any case the kinds of methods that arise only out of strengthened Party leadership in this regard. [. . .]

The materials from the Politburo archives allow us to reject previous assumptions and substitute a more correct picture of the course of events. We can say for certain that it was in mid-1946 that the idea began to mature of a "major ideological resolution" that would concentrate on the work of the literary journals. The matter had a specific impetus. Here, as often happens, circumstances coincided with the interests of the participants in the events. The latter were, undoubtedly, decisive.

During this period, the struggle in the higher Party leadership for power and influence over Stalin intensified drastically. At one pole stood Malenkov and Beria; at the other, Zhdanov. In the period under consideration, Zhdanov's position was stronger than the position of his opponents. Behind Zhdanov, who for many years headed the Leningrad Party organization, stood the so-called Leningrad group of energetic young functionaries and technocrats who had distinguished themselves in Leningrad during the war. These people, as representatives of the "new generation" and protégés of Zhdanov, represented a real threat to the power of the "old guard." Stalin began to transfer many of them into the central state and Party organs, and continued doing so right up until Zhdanov's death in 1948. Malenkov and Beria then took revenge, provoking the so-called Leningrad Affair, as a result of which the entire "Leningrad group" in Moscow and the entire leadership of the Leningrad Party organization were wiped out. It is entirely possible that it was for political motives that Zhdanov decided to lead the struggle against the Leningrad intelligentsia (above all), in order to "cover" the Leningrad Party leaders responsible for the "failure of ideological work." By doing so, by taking the matter into his own hands, he removed his political opponents from ideological implementation and simultaneously absolved himself of any suspicion of any "Leningrad patriotism." This can also explain the special energy, aggression, and cruelty that Zhdanov brought to the ideological campaigns of the years 1946–1948; by attacking the intelligentsia he "covered" himself and those he had promoted for political reasons. As for the "impetus" for the resolution on *Star* and *Leningrad*, it presented itself at the same time: Zoshchenko's story for children, "Adventures of an Ape" ["*Prikliuchenia obez'iany*"] was republished in issue no. 5–6 of *Star* for 1946, having been published a year before in the children's magazine *Murzilka* (no. 5–6, 1945). The story provoked the ire of Stalin and was republished without the consent of the author, therefore the very fact of its publication can be viewed as a deliberate provocation.

Be that as it may, on 7 August 1946, Zhdanov received a memorandum from the leaders of Agitprop, G. Aleksandrov and A. Yegolin (Aleksandrov was Malenkov's protégé).

· 163 ·

Memorandum from the TsK VKP(b) Propaganda and Agitation Administration to TsK VKP(b) Secretary A. A. Zhdanov "On the unsatisfactory state of *Star* and *Leningrad*." RGASPI, f. 17, op. 117, d. 628, ll. 10–17. Original. Typewritten.

7 August 1946

The literary-artistic journals *Star* and *Leningrad* are being run in an entirely unsatisfactory fashion. Over the last two years, these journals have published a number of ideologically harmful and artistically very weak works.

In 1945, *Star* was publishing historical novels, for the most part. Very few works were published in the journal about the life of the Soviet people. Moods of decadence and decline were cultivated in *Star*'s pages. This was expressed especially vividly in the poetry of A. Akhmatova, I. Sadofiev, and M. Komissarova (no. 1, 1946).

A. Akhmatova's poem, "A Kind of Monologue" ["*Vrode monologa*"] is full of pessimism and disenchantment with life. Reality appears gloomy and sinister to Akhmatova, reminding her of a "black garden" and an "autumn landscape." The poetess perceives the city's sounds as if heard "from the other world" . . . and "permanently estranged." Akhmatova's sympathies and attachment are on the side of the past.

[. . .]

I. Sadofiev's poems are saturated with the same feeling of desperate longing as are the poems of Akhmatova. In M. Komissarova's poem "In the Heart's Voice" ["*Golosom serdtsa*"], the main motifs are grief about the past and the presentiment of death. . . .

[. . .]

In several works the theme of the Patriotic War and the heroic defense of Leningrad is put forward irresponsibly, at a low artistic level. The circle of people shown in these works is extremely narrow, limited primarily to the depiction of the aesthetic intelligentsia, which is not typical for Soviet reality. The authors assign to our intelligentsia features uncharacteristic of it and show it detached from the life of the country.

Thus, in G. Gor's novella *House on Mokhovaya* [*Dom na Mokhovoi*], the main hero is an artist who during the days of the war is concerned only about the fate of his pictures. Another hero of this story is a botanist concerned only with preserving his cacti. In A. Shtein's story "Swan Lake" ["*Lebedinoe ozero*"], a pilot is presented who is more interested in ballet, which he is constantly recalling, than aviation.

The genuine heroes of Leningrad's defense are not shown in the journal's pages.

In V. Knekht's novella *At the Nevsky Position* [*Na Nevskoi pozitsii*] (no. 2, 1945), the Leningraders' battle against the fascists during the blockade is only a backdrop for an adventure tale. The central place in the story is occupied not by the soldiers and officers of the Red Army but by the images of a photographer-artist and icon collector. In this story, St. George is proclaimed the symbol of the Russian army. . . .

Among works devoted to the war theme is also L. Maliugin's play *Old Friends* [*Starye druz'ia*] (no. 5–6, 1946). The cast of characters in it are young Soviet men and women who survived the blockade in Leningrad. The images created by L. Maliugin are not typical or characteristic for our young people. In this play, young people are shown as ideologically impoverished. Some of the girls work in hospitals, the boys were at the front, but they are little concerned about the fate of the homeland; the war has left almost no trace in their consciousness. They are continuing to live frivolously and to treat life frivolously. . . .

[. . .]

D. Ostrov's stories "Peace" ["*Mir*"] and "Escape" ["*Pobeg*"] (no. 1, 1946) emphasize the tenacity of the German officers and soldiers. "Escape" describes the steady resistance of German units surrounded by the troops of the Red Army. The Germans' tenacity is explained by the fact that they had a large supply of wine and were regularly furnished by plane with . . . prostitutes.

[. . .]

The author reduces the aim of the Soviet command guiding the rout of the surrounded hostile grouping to the destruction of German wine cellars and to the prostitutes servicing the German soldiers.

In no. 5–6 of *Star*, under the heading "Novelties of Children's Literature," is printed M. Zoshchenko's story, "Adventures of an Ape." The events Zoshchenko describes take place in a city in the rear during the war. While the city is being bombed, an ape runs away from the zoo, and finding itself on city streets, has a number of adventures. The author needed the description of the ape's escapades only in order to mockingly underscore the hardships of the life of our people during the war (food shortages, lines, etc.). The ape is starving and begins looking for food. Zoshchenko describes it like this:

"In town, where can she eat? There's nothing edible on the streets. She can't go into a cafeteria with her tail. Or a cooperative. Especially since she doesn't have any money. There aren't any discounts. She doesn't have ration cards. It's a nightmare. . . . She stopped in at a . . . store. She saw a big line. No, she didn't get in line. And she didn't start pushing people aside to get to the counter. She ran right over the customers' heads and up to the sales clerk. Jumped up on the counter. Didn't ask the price of a kilo of carrots, just grabbed a whole bunch of carrots and, as the saying goes, that's the last anyone ever saw of her. She ran out of the store quite pleased with her purchase. Well—she's an ape. She doesn't understand what's what. Doesn't see the sense of going without food."

At the end of the story the author cynically states that the ape, which had been taught and quickly grown used to wiping its nose with a handkerchief, not to take others' things, and to eat its kasha with a spoon, could serve as an example for people.

Zoshchenko's story is a faulty, far-fetched work. In Zoshchenko's depiction, Soviet people are very primitive and limited. The author makes our people look dumb.

Idealistic views of art are being propagandized on *Star*'s pages. L. Borisov's novella, *The Magician from Gel-Giu* [*Volshebnik iz Gel'-Giu*] (nos. 4, 5–6, 1946), is filled to the brim with appeals to abandon reality for the sphere of "sweet legends," "the world of fantasy and pure invention." The writer Grin, who is the hero of this novella, is idealized as the image of the dreamer, the man "not of this world," plunged into his own endless fantasies. The same propaganda of idealist aesthetics is objectively served by many of the critical articles in *Star*. S. Spassky, in his "Letter on Poetry" ["*Pis'mo o poezii*"], in speaking about several Soviet poets is completely silent as to the ideological content of their art and examines works of art exclusively from the formal aspect. The article's formalist tendencies are obvious.

* * *

The literary-artistic journal *Leningrad* is filled with material that just happened to come its way. In the last few years, the journal has not published a single full-fledged work of art. Frequently they print excerpts from novels that, because they're broken up, are of no interest whatsoever to readers.

Leningrad publishes barely artistic, ideologically faulty works. The journal has run quite a few works about the Patriotic War, but the courageous struggle of the Soviet people against the fascists has not found a worthy artistic expression on its pages. The few stories on this theme printed in *Leningrad* in the last two years were contrived, distorting and trivializing images of the soldiers of the Red Army.

S. Varshavsky and B. Rest's story "Incident over Berlin" ["*Sluchai nad Berlinom*"] (*Leningrad*, no. 3–4, 1946) shows Sergeant Korotkov, who, while flying off to carry out his military assignment, takes along a bottle of beer. Then it describes how this bottle of beer, which Korotkov has hidden in his jumpsuit, breaks during the flight and the shards of glass get stuck in his leg. The frightened sergeant, thinking he's wounded, informs his commander of this. When the plane returns to the airstrip, the "wounded man" is taken away to the hospital and only there is the whole misunderstanding cleared up.

M. Slonimsky's story "At the Outpost" ["*Na zastave*"] (no. 3–4, 1946) gives an extremely ordinary image of a Soviet officer. It describes the following incident. When abandoning his border outpost in 1941, together with the retreating troops, an officer hid a bottle of wine in the cellar of the building, hoping to drink it upon his return. As the author informs us, these hopes were not realized—the officer returned to the outpost at war's end, but the bottle was broken. Why all this is recounted is unknown.

The journal prints many poems, but the artistic level of most of them is very low. In "Sevastopol" [*Sebastpol*] (no. 1–2, 1946), I. Selvinsky describes his impressions from visiting a hero-city after its liberation by the Red Army. But the poet says nothing about the city's courageous defenders; he recalls merely how once in the years before the revolution he met a girl on the street. He describes this girl's appearance in a vulgar tone:

> Do you like girls with tans
> Darker than their orange hair?
> With eyes just like two ocean bays
> Around a colossal promontory?
> With shoulders
> Wider than their hips? ah?
> And a very pointy nose?

In issue no. 1–2 for 1946, there is a parody, A. Flit's "My Nekrasov" ["*Moi Nekrasov*"], in which the author attempts to make fun of E. Katerli's story about Nekrasov published in *Star*. However, the parody itself is nothing but a desecration of the great poet. "Nekrasov," writes A. Flit, "woke up with a belch and late. He was tormented by heartburn and the tsar's censor. All night he had dreamed of soaked apples and Nikitenko the censor. The pit of his stomach ached. He felt sour deep down inside. He'd been hiccupping since the night before. 'What am I going to tell the muzhik!?' thought Nikolai Alexeevich gloomily, drawing on his expensive, fragrant cigarette. His conscience and the serf-owning landowners tormented him. Nekrasov listlessly stuck his skinny yellow heels into his worn shoes and wended his way toward the window. He felt sick at the thought of his impotence in the face of the tsar and his toadies, and from the French cognac he'd been drinking the night before. Out the window Nekrasov saw the main entrance and a crowd of muzhiks. He sighed, with his yellow hand he dipped the nib of his pen in the ink, and yawning unconsciously and scratching, he wrote: 'Thoughts at the Main Entrance' ["*Razmyshlenia u paradnogo* pod"ezda"]. He felt like seeing Turgenev, but he was abroad. Nekrasov lay down on the sofa and turned his creased face toward the shabby wall. He couldn't sleep. Serfdom weighed upon him."

In issue no. 10 of the journal for 1940, in the parody section, there are poems composed by A. Khazin entitled "The Return of Onegin: Chapter Eleven. Fragments" ["*Vozvrashchenie Onegina: Glava odinnadtsataia. Fragmenty*"]. These poems describe with malicious mocking and scoffing the daily life of modern Leningrad. . . .

[. . .]

The criticism department is run quite unsatisfactorily in the journal. Reviews of the works of Leningrad writers are nearly exclusively laudatory in nature.

In the issues of the journal for 1946, the works of V. Rozhdestvensky, I. Avramenko, and Rakhmanov, were praised wildly and hoisted on a shield, and at the same time a work like V. Inber's *Leningrad Diary* [*Leningradsky dnevnik*] was the subject of coarse ridicule (no. 13–14, 1945, parody by A. Flit).

Several critical articles (*Banner*, no. 11, 1945, no. 2–3, 1946; *Literaturnaia gazeta*, 8 September 1945) have been published about the shortcomings of *Star* and *Leningrad*. However, even after these signals the quality of the journals did not improve, which points to the inability of the editors of *Star* and *Leningrad* to cope with the demands placed on them.

The Board of the USSR Union of Soviet Writers and its Leningrad division have turned the journals over to a group of writers, have not guided their work, and have not given them any assistance.

The Leningrad VKP(b) committee is not paying sufficient attention to the literary-artistic journals, is missing the major ideological errors in the content of the works published in *Star* and *Leningrad,* and is not supervising the editorial work.

A new editorial board must be approved for *Star* that is capable of improving the journal's work in a fundamental way.

As for *Leningrad,* its further existence should be deemed inexpedient.

A draft of the TsK VKP(b) resolution on *Star* and *Leningrad* is attached.

G. Aleksandrov
A. Yegolin

A day later, on 9 August 1946, there was a discussion of the journals at the Orgburo, participating in which were, besides Orgburo members, the leaders of TsK Agitprop, the Leningrad Party organization, the Leningrad journals, and the Writers Union. After Aleksandrov's report, the floor was turned over to the former editor of *Star,* Vissarion Sayanov. The uncorrected transcript picks up at the moment when Stalin demands explanations from Sayanov for the publication of Zoshchenko's story:

· 164 ·

Uncorrected transcript of the TsK VKP(b) Orgburo session "On *Star* and *Leningrad.*" RGASPI, f. 17, op. 117, d. 1032, ll. 45–67. Copy. Typewritten.
9 August 1946

SAYANOV. (The beginning was not transcribed.) My guilt is great because I obviously did not realize the extent to which the Party's and country's attention was riveted on our journal.
STALIN. Is this journal of yours published for children?
SAYANOV. No.
STALIN. Then why didn't you put it in a children's journal?
SAYANOV. It was published because of children.
STALIN. You don't have elementary standards. This is a silly story.
SAYANOV. Now that's obvious.
STALIN. That's how it is for everyone. Only later does it turn out they didn't see anything and it turns out they're writing trivia. Did you read the story?
SAYANOV. Yes.
STALIN. This is the silliest piece, it has nothing for the mind or the heart. It's a puppet-show anecdote. I can't understand why an unquestionably fine journal offered its pages to this trivial puppet-show piece. You have no standards for your writers, but the readers will.
SAYANOV. It seems to me that the problem here is that we haven't done enough ideological and educational work among the writers and that there is a certain mistaken notion among the bulk of writers that sometimes writers don't understand well enough the meaning of criticism based on principle, that some writers were looking over their shoulders too much at Western and American literature, that sometimes they underappreciated the creative riches in the heritage of our Russian and Soviet literature, that sometimes in some writers' circles there is a certain enthusiasm for modern Western writers. This can be explained by the fact that some writers believed that the role of the ideological, topical theme has been diminished.
A few pieces we returned, pieces that distorted our correct conception

ideologically. We pointed out their mistakes to the authors, but some writers felt that here the war had ended and now they would relax, now they needed to entertain the Soviet reader, they needed to give him the kind of works that he would read with pleasure. It is our fault that we were unable to distance our leading writers from these moods, that we were unable to work with them in the right way. This, it seems to me, is the main thing that needs to be said right now.

LIKHAREV. [. . .]

Our journal is a slim journal, it should be built primarily on the basic genre of the short story. This is very complicated. All is not entirely well with this literary genre. Our journal came out all during the blockade, it came out all during the war, but now we're suddenly finding things rather more complicated. Then we had a small collective. Then you could count the writers on two hands, but they were great creative writers with great possibilities. Now the undertaking has expanded somewhat, comrades have returned from other fronts, this is our great asset, but they cannot imagine what happened in Leningrad, they were on other fronts and have not perceived the Leningrad theme properly, so they can't come up with the works about Leningrad that we would like to see.

[. . .]

Concerning the failures which Com. Aleksandrov has quite justifiably pointed out to us, I am really not able in more detail . . .

STALIN. But did you read what was written? How could you have let it through?

LIKHAREV. I'm just about to tell you why this happened. The artist Raikin brought this work to Leningrad. He gave readings in the theater for two months and broadcast it over the radio. Glavrepertkom approved it.

STALIN. Who approved it?

LIKHAREV. Glavrepertkom, here in Moscow.

STALIN. Glavrepertkom gives approval for publication or for readings?

ZHDANOV. Is it a stage piece?

LIKHAREV. Yes. We made a mistake. We forgot that the printed word is more powerful than the spoken word. With respect to Nekrasov. This is a parody of a work on Nekrasov.

ALEKSANDROV. If you were to read this parody out loud you would be dragged off the stage. You end up with a parody of Nekrasov.

STALIN. Do you affirm that this is a parody of a parody?

LIKHAREV. There is such a book, it's a bad book.

STALIN. It's a trick, the author is using it as a cover.

LIKHAREV. We have many such pieces, I could go on.

ZHDANOV. You've also published several works by Zoshchenko, for example, "Journey to Olympus" [*Puteshestvie na Olimp*] [sic],[1] is this the same thing as "Journey of an Ape"?

STALIN. You walk on tiptoe in front of foreign writers. Is it worthy of a Soviet man to walk on tiptoe in front of foreign countries? This is how you cultivate servile feelings, this is a great sin.

LIKHAREV. Many translated works have been published.

STALIN. By doing this you are instilling a taste for excessive respect for foreigners. You're instilling the feeling that we are second-rate people and there the people are first rate, which is wrong. You are the pupils, they are the teacher. In its very essence, this is wrong.

LIKHAREV. I want to point out just one thing. . . .

STALIN. Speak with a little sharper tongue. Are you confused or are you in general agreement with the criticism?

LIKHAREV. I'll try now.

STALIN. Whatever you try, you have to speak more firmly.

LIKHAREV. Selvinsky's "In Sebastopol" [*V Sevastopole*] has a conclusion, he's recalling his youth in Sevastopol, recalling a young girl he saw there who called him sweet. He remembered that all his life. This is his poem.

STALIN. It's a trick.

LIKHAREV. I like our journal and I hope this journal is preserved.

STALIN. Should the journal guide the writers or should it trail behind them?

LIKHAREV. It should guide.

STALIN. Can it guide or not?

LIKHAREV. It should and it will.

STALIN. It hasn't managed so far.

LIKHAREV. I wanted to assure the comrades that we can do this if we have their trust. Beginning with the next issue the journal will be different. I have pieces that were conceived of in a new way, but you see it's not so easy for us to work.

STALIN. You want everything to be all right. I can see that. But you have to know how to make it so everything is all right.

LIKHAREV. We have to.

STALIN. Yes, you do.

LIKHAREV. It's very painful to deprive the city of its journal. We have to preserve it. Having no journal—we can't let that happen.

STALIN. Everyone is demanding that we improve the quality of our output: consumer goods, metal, and so forth. It follows, then, that the quality of literary output should be improved, and we want better works published, we want to emphasize quality.

PROKOFIEV. You have to bear in mind, comrades, that the Leningrad brigade of Soviet writers was in an exceptional situation: of the large number (right now this Leningrad brigade of Soviet writers numbers 274), the real writers among them, i.e., those directly creating Soviet literature, number approximately one-half.

STALIN. What, do you only publish Leningrad writers? Can you publish writers from other cities?

PROKOFIEV. Absolutely. I believe that our journals, just like the city of Leningrad, are all-Union journals and therefore I don't believe we can restrict ourselves to the confines of Leningrad.

STALIN. Will you be publishing Urals writers?

PROKOFIEV. We have been, we're publishing the poems of Siberian and Urals comrades. We're also thinking of bringing in Moscow writers, because we need to raise the prestige of our Leningrad journals.

STALIN. All you lack are enough of your own writers, evidently there are too few works?

PROKOFIEV. If we take the best works by Moscow and Urals writers, then we can forgo our Leningrad patriotism and push the Leningrad writers into the background.

STALIN. Who is this Yagdfeld of yours, a Leningrader?

PROKOFIEV. I don't know, he hasn't been in the Writers Union very long.

STALIN. What, do you like his works, can they be staged?

PROKOFIEV. When I read them, I felt these were romantic works.

STALIN. These are childish works, this is an unformed writer, a schoolboy. You should make it so that they keep an eye on your journal and learn from it.

PROKOFIEV. Evidently we lacked the taste.

STALIN. And the works to put in did too, evidently, for here you've dumped them all into one heap.

PROKOFIEV. Our journal is not a trash heap, we want our journal to be worthy of our city, but evidently this has not worked out.

STALIN. There's not enough material, evidently, and therefore, evidently, *Star* sometimes publishes remarkable pieces, absolute diamonds, and alongside the diamonds—manure.

PROKOFIEV. To your comment I can answer that half or three-quarters of our fault is lifted (laughter) because our work hasn't been entirely for naught. We've also published good things.

STALIN. Without question.

PROKOFIEV. I'm very glad of that. I feel that the shortcomings of the Leningrad brigade of writers, they are not inherent only to Leningrad.

STALIN. Unfortunately not, there are even more.

ZHDANOV. This cannot be reassuring.

STALIN. Still he's glad inside.

PROKOFIEV. If we had known we were going to be called to account, we wouldn't have made those kinds of mistakes in issues 5 and 6. We didn't know we would be at this kind of meeting. I believe that the purpose of the present meeting, the purpose is to give our *Star* and *Leningrad* help. We need help, Iosif Vissarionovich. I think that this help should be very real and effective. I feel that the Leningrad journals should be put under the same conditions as the Moscow journals. What good writer would agree to be in the journal when *Star*'s print run is 10,000 copies, if *Star* and *Leningrad* brought the state a loss of about 1 million rubles?

STALIN. That must mean the goods are bad. (Laughter.)

PROKOFIEV. There aren't any of our journals on the stands.

STALIN. Weren't you given paper?

PROKOFIEV. Yes. Take *October*. It has the following staff: besides the five department heads, besides the literary consultant, the head of the mass department, and so on, there are seven members of the editorial board. We have one editor and he is, as they say, a jack of all trades. There's more: a literary consultant, typesetter, managing editor. I feel that we should be given equal conditions.

STALIN. Aren't you going to tell us anything about *Leningrad*?

PROKOFIEV. *Leningrad* has grand traditions. It arose out of the journal *Chisel* [*Rezets*], which was the Rabkor organ, and after that it subsequently became *Leningrad*. We have conceived of it as a journal for the masses, a journal that ought to focus on the short story, in particular, but the journal's editors have allowed for excerpts to be taken out of larger works.

STALIN. Do you approve of this?

PROKOFIEV. No. The Union of Soviet Writers needs to focus on the short story. The short story genre here is not in very great esteem among writers. We have discussed both of our journals in the Writers Union more than a few times, but our criticism was not as severe as now. Evidently we have again lacked the courage in several instances to tell the truth, bearing in mind that the people with whom we work, they are right next to us and would be insulted, and this insult would not be forgiven till the end of time. We have several who take insults very hard.

STALIN. Mistrustful, thin-skinned people?

PROKOFIEV. Yes, and sometimes even minor criticism leaves a deep scratch.

STALIN. You shouldn't be afraid of that. How else can you educate people except with criticism?

PROKOFIEV. There has been criticism, but it hasn't been very effective.

STALIN. You were afraid they'd be insulted. You can't be afraid of insults.

MALENKOV. And you sheltered the people who were insulted. Zoshchenko was criticized, but you sheltered him.

PROKOFIEV. Then we need to pay attention to something else. Right now Zoshchenko has a third comedy running.

STALIN. A whole war went by, all the peoples were soaked in blood, and he didn't give us a single line. He writes some nonsense, it's an absolute mockery. The war is in full swing and he doesn't have a single word for or against, but he writes all kinds of cock-and-bull stories, nonsense that offers nothing for the mind or the heart. He wanders from place to place, pokes his nose in somewhere, then somewhere else, and you're perfectly complaisant. You wanted to make the journal interesting, so you gave him space, and because of that you can't print the works you do get from our people. That's not why we built the Soviet order, to teach people drivel.

PROKOFIEV. I wanted to raise another question about the drain of people from Leningrad. About twenty people have left.

STALIN. You present the account to Moscow, and maybe the people will return. They're leaving—what can you do? They're not serfs. In Moscow, evidently, things are in better shape.

PROKOFIEV. There are more opportunities for a writer than in Leningrad, if we're talking in human terms. And right now, if the Central Committee approves the TsK Agitprop's proposal regarding cutting Leningrad's journals, then I don't know what state the Leningrad literary brigade is going to find itself in. You can't throw the baby out with the bath water. I think that for a city like Leningrad, you can't leave [just] a journal like *Star*. You have to do everything possible so that both journals start functioning properly. We'll find the strength and the people so that both journals can exist.

I believe our Leningrad journals can raise themes with tremendous world resonance in a genuine way, profoundly, and with a knowledge of the Leningrad theme. We were all in Leningrad and saw all the misfortunes with the Leningraders, and our task, the task of the Leningrad division of the Union of Soviet Writers and of both journals, is to make this theme resonate in a genuine way. We don't have works that are grand and broad enough where this theme might resonate. We have Tikhonov's "Traits of the Soviet Man" [*Cherty sovetskogo cheloveka*] and Chukovsky's "This Happened in Leningrad" [*Eto bylo v Leningrade*], but I haven't found works that raise this theme in a genuine way. This kind of an attempt is being made among us in Leningrad, though. You see, Iosif Vissarionovich, Sayanov has written the first part of a trilogy about the Leningrad front. I think that this will be a work with a grand embrace of events.

MALENKOV. Why are you praising it in advance if you haven't read it?

PROKOFIEV. I'm talking about the theme. Leningrad's writers are taking up this theme. Vera Ketlinskaia has written a novel about Leningrad.

When I met her I said that she needed to work a lot, but the fact is that writers are beginning to do this.

STALIN. This is greatly to your advantage. There's a lot of material, but you're making poor use of these advantages. "Adventure of an Ape"—what is this, about Leningrad, does it raise Leningrad's authority?

PROKOFIEV. No. A few objections to the criticism. We approached with caution Borisov's novella, *The Magician from G[el-Giu]*. We printed the first part with cuts. When *Literaturnaia gazeta* published L. Rakhmanov's article recommending this novella, we felt that this was wrong. Now Borisov is writing the third part. At a meeting at the city Party Committee we said that he shouldn't write a third part, that one was enough.

STALIN. As a writer, Borisov is good, writes elegantly, has mastered literary language. This is not Yagdfeld.

PROKOFIEV. The theme he has chosen would be enough for Grin. That is my conviction.

With regard to poems. I believe it's no great sin that Anna Akhmatova's poems were published. This is a poetess with a small voice and conversations about sadness; they are inherent in the Soviet person as well.

STALIN. Anna Akhmatova, aside from the fact that she has an old name, what else do you find in her?

PROKOFIEV. You find several good poems in her compositions of the postwar period. There is "The First Long-Range" [*Pervaia dal'noboinaia*], about Leningrad.

STALIN. One-two-three and that's it.

PROKOFIEV. There are too few poems on topical themes, but she is a poetess with old foundations, with set opinions, and she can no longer give us anything new, Iosif Vissarionovich.

STALIN. Then let her publish somewhere else, why in *Star*?

PROKOFIEV. I must say that what we rejected at *Star* was published in *Banner*.

STALIN. We'll get to *Banner* as well, we'll get to them all.

PROKOFIEV. That would be very good. I want to ask you and the TsK secretaries to let us have our *Leningrad*, you don't need to shut down *Leningrad*. We will put these journals on the proper footing, so that there are more diamonds in *Star* and the trash is destroyed.

VS. VISHNEVSKY. [...]

... The writer brigade must be given specific goals. We're only just out of the war, and there is a lot we haven't yet managed to sort out. New people are coming to us. Many manuscripts are coming to us at the journals, many people are coming to us, and we need to speak with each one. And interesting people are coming. A few days ago a young poet came to see me. He has fine, clear eyes. I'm looking at him and I'm thinking, what does he need? It turns out, he's thinking about the fate of the younger generation and asking me to clarify the meaning of a few words, he says he was wounded and never got to the West and therefore couldn't feel the victory. People are asking thousands of questions. We have to work with them, we have to explain. I think that our comrade Leningraders, all of us, Prokofiev, Sayanov, Levonevsky, and Likharev, they have to make this work even more relevant, go outside the framework of Leningrad. Leningrad did not hesitate when it came time to help along other lines, it helped. We need to set writers the task of gathering and talking with small and large groups of people, putting conferences together, looking at what's being done at the lower levels. We don't have a good idea of readers' responses. This is a great crime on the part of our criticism. The sooner our press takes up this matter and makes authors read the responses of the people who know life and who have something genuine to say about the writers' work—without that we can't work.

About the short story. If we have to resolve this matter, then I have to say that so much of our powers, labor, and energy needs to be put into the story that it's simply hard to talk about. We need to publish a story that's no more than ten pages long, the story has to be placed in the central press, broadcast over the radio. . . .

STALIN. A good story, like a Chekhov story, will be broadcast over the radio, and people will listen to it with pleasure.

VISHNEVSKY. Comrade Stalin, so many prizes are given in your name, at least one story could be recognized.

STALIN. People are reluctant to write stories.

VISHNEVSKY. Because there's an economic aspect, too. Ten pages, that's a little more than a thousand rubles for the writer, who is an engineer of the human soul.

STALIN. Is the payment badly differentiated?

VISHNEVSKY. Yes. Let me cite the following facts. We have 8,600 authors working for the theater, cinema, stage, clubs, and so on. Of these, 93 percent receive 1000 rubles and less. This is not an engineer's rate, it's not a professor's rate, and this requires some thought. Further, if one analyzes all the points, analyzes everything more deeply, then I have to say that I have materials lying there from the first day of the blockade of Leningrad. Can I release them immediately? No, I can't, because I need to think through several things. When Vera Inber came out with her *Diary,* what did you do? You put out a parody of Vera Inber, a person who stood with you throughout the blockade, but you struck her so hard she could barely keep her feet. Now she has a prize, now no one is going to criticize her, but this, too, is wrong.

STALIN. Right.

VISHNEVSKY. The press should be the first to set an example and start a genuine, broad popular discussion of things. This would have great educative significance. In 1943, Zoshchenko was given a signal about what he had written, about his confession *Before Sunrise*. This is a man who stripped himself and everyone close to him to their dirty linen. When I read this story, I wrote an analysis of this work. This man began writing in 1923–1924. He has characters everywhere who are drunkards, cripples, invalids, he has fights and noise everywhere. And here you take his last story, "Adventures of an Ape," take it and make an analysis of it. You'll see that we're back to invalids, back to beer stands, back to brawls....

STALIN. And the bathhouse.

VISHNEVSKY. The bathhouse, absolutely correct. That's how it comes out with him. Here you've criticized me, and now you're in for it, esteemed ones. There should have been a very deep and serious conversations, someone should have said to him, What are you thinking of doing now?

STALIN. He's a preacher of an unideological approach.

VISHNEVSKY. He put out his last things without thought or plot.

STALIN. Nasty little pieces.

VISHNEVSKY. In 1942, people could barely stand because of dystrophy, the first issue was literally being carried by our comrades when I arrived in Leningrad and saw what was going on there, saw the conditions in which this journal was being put out. I must say that these journals are infinitely precious to us Leningraders, and I would personally ask that you consider both this point and our attachment to this journal, as well as our genuine problems and traditions. You don't have to shut down these journals.

STALIN. That's up to Zoshchenko.

VISHNEVSKY. Zoshchenko and others need to be watched, but the journal itself needs to be preserved. I think that if they make every effort and have our Moscow support, Leningraders will be able to correct the situation.

I wanted to ask a question, who should appoint the new leadership, especially for *Star*? I believe we're the owners, the Union of Soviet Writers. This is our journal, and Leningraders have to reckon with us. I think this journal should include Prokofiev, Ketlinskaia, and Berggolts, and there should be young people. We need to create a militant board. Muscovites can be included as well, that would be useful for communication.

I think you will take the lessons of today's meeting to heart and move forward.

Here we have been dancing around *Banner*. Our *Banner* brings the people about 1 million rubles profit, whereas you have about a million in losses. Take this information and write it down.

[...]

I ask you to leave us *Leningrad*, which is infinitely dear to us, but make a new staffing selection for the editorial board, help it. This is one of our first joys.

STALIN. If the journal goes, Leningrad will remain.

POPKOV. A few comments. First. I believe that the criticism given here in the speeches of Aleksandrov and several other comrades regarding the Leningrad journals is correct. What are the reasons for the shortcomings in the journals' work? I would consider it essential to note the following. The main reason is that there was no supervision [of] these journals either by the Party's City Committee or by the Union of Soviet Writers. In this half-year, we, the Party City Committee, did not find the time once to schedule an account or report from the editorial board and review the work plan. I'm thinking about the bureau of the Party City Committee, the editorial work plan of *Star* and *Leningrad*, it was never submitted once. This speaks for itself. On the part of the Union of Soviet Writers. I, Comrade Stalin, must provide some information. The last journal came out with a stamp that didn't say this was the organ of the Union of Soviet Writers, it came out with a stamp saying that it was an organ of the Union of Leningrad Writers. All the 1946 issues came out with the stamp of the Union of Leningrad Writers, not the Union of Soviet Writers. How is it that it was an organ of the Union of Soviet Writers and then suddenly became an organ of the Leningrad Writers? Who is to blame for this and what is the meaning of it? I believe we're to blame for overlooking this. Secondly, who was the instigator here? The instigators were Comrades Tikhonov and Sayanov, but they said nothing about it, and this has very substantial significance. As a result, the Union of Soviet Writers has practically stepped aside from this journal and ceased guiding it, stopped helping it. This is from the leadership standpoint.

Why they changed—there were reports on this from the Party's TsK. In particular, I issued an assignment to establish how it came about and at whose initiative. I asked Com. Kuznetsov to report on this subject, why and since when the literary journal *Star* had become the journal of the Union of Leningrad Writers. It turned out that there has not been any decision on this subject, but after a conversation between Sayanov and Tikhonov it was named the organ of the Union of Leningrad Writers. This is the first reason why the journal lost so much prestige.

The second reason. I believe that the editorial board is [to blame], in particular Com. Sayanov and the editorial board as it was then composed. Among them all Zoshchenko enjoys very great authority. Meanwhile, no one has mentioned this and, unfortunately, it has been like this to the present day. When they discussed the latest editorial staff, I wasn't there, but they all recommended Zoshchenko. After all, why did Zoshchenko's latest compositions appear in *Star?* Because none of them, none of the members of the editorial board, had the nerve to do this, seeing as how you feel that this is tsar and God and that even if he writes nonsense you don't consider it your honor and duty as a writer to call him to order. No one did this, no one has ever talked about this to anyone. Com. Vishnevsky is speaking fine right now, but before a good review of him appeared in *Pravda,* no one said anything or even criticized.

With respect to Akhmatova. Here too it came about that this was such greatness, such a poetess, how could we not publish her in our *Star*! This is the point, you see, Comrade Stalin. They bow down before them and are afraid to speak out. They have no genuine self-criticism or criticism, and when you come right down to it, they have transformed this journal into their own narrow circle of people who apparently cannot be criticized. And it is because of this that it came to pass that neither in this journal nor in *Leningrad* did we have genuine criticism revealing the shortcomings of a given work.

VOICE. *Leningrad Pravda* [*Leningradskaia Pravda*] publishing German's article [praised Zoshchenko].

POPKOV. Correct, that happened, they did praise him, and they didn't criticize him, which is why we have what we do.

MALENKOV. Why was Zoshchenko approved?

POPKOV. I must take the blame myself. I missed this decision of the Party City Committee, it happened when I wasn't there....

[...]

Speech by Com. TIKHONOV at the TsK VKP(b) Orgburo session of 9 August 1946, on the subject of Star and Leningrad

Leningrad's journals, of course, are not the journals of a provincial town, a small town. These journals, indeed, should be journals of world stature.

[...]

Anna Akhmatova is a separate matter, this is not just Leningrad. The younger generation thought she had died and suddenly saw a writer who had long followed her own political line. If she, despite her age, wrote poems which Prokofiev spoke about, that doesn't mean that after this she can then start resurrecting the old situation. Akhmatova has nothing new for us. Therefore we don't think there is any need to find space for anything that is not an apotheosis of a kind which she cannot be depended on for.

This provided a beginning which led to another mistaken situation, when people began getting mixed up in Leningrad's traditions, when people began moving from the [revolutionary] armored car to the Bronze Horseman [of Pushkin's eponymous poem].

Therefore, all these mistakes stem from a debilitated condition. Even in the ethical respect, these are very weak pieces. Moreover, foreign influence has been on the increase. It is. Thank God, now this is starting to die down, people are starting to understand that they shouldn't blindly follow Priestley, who lately has taken up all our journals and stages. But now writers understand this, that Priestley is not a great literary name but the product of a hasty, frivolous literary mercantilism that has arisen. This has now been made clear.

The journals also made a mistake when they promoted Balzac and other foreign writers. Of course, stories by our beginning authors don't stand up to criticism, but still that shouldn't have been done.

It seems to me we need to help Leningrad's journals. The fact that there is discussion and criticism of them going on here, this is a high honor, and this places much more responsibility on other journals as well as the Leningrad journals. Journals must become a brigade of real literature, of the greater political life.

STALIN. They must educate our young people.

TIKHONOV. Therefore we need to drastically strengthen the work of the editorial boards. We need to reinforce them with political workers, maybe even workers on a philosophical plane, it could be a senior editor, or a deputy, or a secretary. Without a doubt, though, this issue must be raised. But *Leningrad* should not be shut down because that would be a loss on our literary balance sheet. This means we won't surrender this "patch," as we used to say—this special parcel of the Leningrad defense, albeit small, but of great significance. Losing *Leningrad* would mean losing a piece of Soviet culture.

Speech by Com. SHIROKOV at the TsK VKP(b) Orgburo session of 9 August 1946, on the matter of Star and Leningrad

[. . .] Why have *Star* and *Leningrad* ended up in this unsightly shape? This can be explained in two ways: by the general principles of poor work by the journals' editors, and by insufficient guidance for the journals on the part of the propaganda department of the Party's City Committee. The journals' editorial boards did not organize an authors' collective. The work of the editorial boards lacks planning. Material comes into the editorial offices to a significant extent of its own accord. Editorial boards receive material that is what people bring to their offices, not what they should be asking for. Journals' editorial offices treat authors liberally. In selecting material they are guided not by notions of principle but by considerations of how not to offend someone, how not to wreck friendly relations with comrades. . . .

[. . .]

What did the propaganda department of the Party's Leningrad City Committee fail to do and what does the department bear responsibility for? We were unable to organize criticism of our journals' shortcomings in Leningrad newspapers. Our Leningrad press paid little attention to the journals. We were unable to solve the problem of editorial staffing in a timely fashion. The editorial boards work poorly. For instance, there are two people working on the *Star* editorial board—Sayanov and Prokofiev.

STALIN. They don't know how to set up the work. It can't be that there isn't anyone in Leningrad.

[. . .]

SHIROKOV [. . .] What should the propaganda department of the Party's Leningrad City Committee do to help the journal? Organize better writers' ideological and political training on a larger scale. In this regard we have done very little so far. True, we did organize a department for workers in the arts, including writers, at the University of Marxism-Leninism, but I must tell you frankly that writers don't always go to the department willingly to study. Right now we're conducting recruitment for the first year of university, and we have to accept 300 people. We have to offer more opportunities for writers to get into the university of Marxism.

STALIN. And drag them to school? That's going to be hard, they're grownups. Give them the textbooks, they'll read them, they'll figure it out themselves. Why drag them to school?

SHIROKOV. That won't work for them.

STALIN. They'll get interested and they'll read.

SHIROKOV. And we need to resolve the matter of the editorial staffs for *Star* and *Leningrad*.

MALENKOV. Who's the editor now?

SHIROKOV. Sayanov.

MALENKOV. Was there a decision about the editorial staff?

SHIROKOV. There was a decision about the new editorial board.

STALIN. Who was nominated editor?

SHIROKOV. They nominated the young writer Kapitsa. Based on certain ideas, we may have been mistaken, though. We worked from the following ideas. Com. Sayanov is a well-known man among writers, but he has little in the way of organizational abilities and makes few demands on writers.

STALIN. I don't think I've ever heard of such a writer.

SHIROKOV. Kapitsa is a young writer, he just had a work come out, *On the Open Sea* [*V otkrytom more*].

MALENKOV. Do writers recognize him?

STALIN. Will he have any authority among writers?

SHIROKOV. In Leningrad, when we discussed the issue of the editor, there were no objections among Leningrad writers.

STALIN. Maybe they took the approach that there was nothing to fear from a weak man. In the old days the tsar would put in an interloper, a weak man, to make it easier to put the squeeze on him. Could that be how matters stand?

SHIROKOV. I don't think so.

MALENKOV. But tell me, is this editorial staff operating or the old one?

SHIROKOV. Right now the old one.

MALENKOV. A new editorial staff was appointed two months ago, but the old one is still operating.

SHIROKOV. The next issue, number 6, was prepared by the old editorial staff, and they decided to see what they had started through to its conclusion.

ZHDANOV. At one time the Leningraders didn't leave so much as a wet spot from Zoshchenko.

STALIN. But people like Zoshchenko, they have power over the journal. What is this, a Leningrad journal or a journal of the Union of Soviet Writers?

SHIROKOV. No, it's not a Leningrad one.

STALIN. Do you want your decision confirmed?

ZHDANOV. Have you registered the new editorial staff or do both exist?

SHIROKOV. We made the decision ourselves.

MALENKOV. Made the decision to approve the editorial staff and brought in Zoshchenko.

STALIN. Is the Leningrad committee informed of your decision about the new editorial staff?

MALENKOV. This is what the Leningrad committee decided.

STALIN. What are you asking, that we approve this?

SHIROKOV. Judging from how the matter has been put in the TsK, evidently, we need to approve a more serious person as editor of *Star*, someone who is known not only in Leningrad but in the country, too. Kapitsa is known in Leningrad, but the country doesn't know him.

STALIN. Agitprop did not know of the intention to shut it down?

SHIROKOV. No.

The discussion concluded with passage of a decision to organize a commission to draw up a TsK resolution (which was approved five days later). The commission, under Zhdanov's leadership, included all the participants in the discussion except Stalin.[2] However, we can state that the issue of the document's status—the public (not classified, as before) TsK resolution (not Orgburo decision)—was decided by Stalin personally. And although in the course of the discussion virtually everything was stated that subsequently went into the resolution, the text of the document itself was restrained in its tone, even though in import it was harsher than what took place during the discussion at the Orgburo. We cite here the main, "constituting" portion of the resolution:

· 165 ·

Resolution of the TsK VKP(b) Orgburo "On the journals *Star* and *Leningrad*." RGASPI, f. 17, op. 116, d. 272, ll. 7–11. Original. Typewritten. Published with minor omissions in *Pravda*, 21 August 1946.

14 August 1946

No. 274, p. 1g—*On the journals* Star *and* Leningrad.

The TsK VKP(b) notes that the literary-artistic journals *Star* and *Leningrad* published in Leningrad are being run in a completely unsatisfactory fashion.

Recently, along with important and successful works by Soviet writers, many unprincipled, ideologically harmful works have appeared in *Star*. *Star's* crude mistake is providing a literary platform for the writer Zoshchenko, whose works are alien to Soviet literature. The editors of *Star* know that Zoshchenko has long specialized in writing vapid, contentless, vulgar pieces, in the advocacy of rotten unprincipledness, vulgarity, and apoliticalness calculated to disorient our young people and poison their minds. The latest of Zoshchenko's published stories, "Adventures of an Ape" (*Star*, no. 5–6, 1946) is a vulgar squib on Soviet daily life and Soviet people. Zoshchenko depicts Soviet ways and Soviet people in distorted caricature, slanderously presenting Soviet people as primitive, uncultured, and stupid, with philistine tastes and mores. Zoshchenko's maliciously hooliganish depiction of our reality is accompanied by anti-Soviet jabs.

Presenting the pages of *Star* to vulgarians and literary scum like Zoshchenko is even more impermissible because *Star's* editors are perfectly familiar with Zoshchenko's physiognomy and unworthy conduct during the war, when Zoshchenko, who did nothing to help the Soviet people in their struggle against the German aggressors, wrote a piece as loathsome as *Before Sunrise*, whose assessment, like the assessment of all of Zoshchenko's literary "creation," was given on the pages of *Bolshevik*.

Star is doing everything it can to popularize as well the works of the writer Akhmatova, whose literary and public-political physiognomy have been known to the Soviet public for a very long time. Akhmatova is a typical representative of the empty, unprincipled poetry alien to our people. Her poems, permeated with a spirit of pessimism and decadence, expressing the tastes of the old salon poetry which stagnated in the strongholds of bourgeois-aristocratic aestheticism and decadence, "art for art's sake," reluctant to walk in step with their people, are inflicting harm on the cause of educating our young people and cannot be countenanced in Soviet literature.

Giving Zoshchenko and Akhmatova an active role in the journal has undoubtedly introduced elements of ideological disarray and disorganization among Leningrad writers. Works have begun appearing in the journal that cultivate the spirit, uncharacteristic of Soviet people, of groveling before the modern bourgeois culture of the West. Works have begun being published that are permeated with longing, pessimism, and disenchantment with life (the poems of Sadofiev and Komissarova in no. 1, 1946, etc.). By running these works, the editors have aggravated their mistakes and lowered the journal's ideological level even more.

Having let works alien in the ideological respect penetrate the journal, the editors have also reduced their demands on the artistic qualities of the literary material they print. The journal has started being filled with plays and stories of little artistic merit (Yagdfeld's "Road of Time" [*Doroga vremeni*], Shtein's "Swan Lake" [*Lebedinoe ozero*], etc.). This lack of discrimination in the choice of materials for publication has led to a lowering of the journal's artistic level.

The TsK notes that *Leningrad*, which is constantly offering its pages to the vulgar and slanderous forays of Zoshchenko and the vapid, apolitical poems of Akhmatova, is being run especially badly. Like the editors of *Star*, the editors of *Leningrad* have committed major errors, having published several works permeated with the spirit of groveling toward everything foreign. The journal has printed several mistaken works ("Incident over Berlin" [*Sluchai nad Berlinom*] by Varshavsky and Rest, "At the Outpost" [*Na zastave*] by Slonimsky). In Khazin's poem, "Onegin's Return" [*Vozvrashchenie Onegina*], slander against contemporary Leningrad comes out in the guise of literary parody. *Leningrad* publishes mostly low-quality literary materials without content.

How could *Star* and *Leningrad*, which are published in Leningrad, a hero-city famous for its advanced revolutionary traditions, a city that has always been a hotbed of advanced ideas and advanced culture, let an unprincipledness and apoliticalness alien to Soviet literature get dragged into the journals?

What is the meaning of the mistakes made by the editors of *Star* and *Leningrad*?

The journals' supervising personnel and, above all, their editors, Comrades Sayanov and Likharev, have forgotten Leninism's thesis that our journals, whether scholarly or artistic, cannot be apolitical. They have forgotten that our journals are a powerful means of the Soviet state in the matter of educating Soviet people and especially the young, and therefore must be guided by what comprises the vital basis of the Soviet order—its policy. The Soviet order cannot allow youth to be educated in a spirit of indifference to Soviet policy, in a devil-may-care, unprincipled spirit.

The strength of Soviet literature, the most advanced literature in the world, consists in the fact that it is a literature that does not and cannot have other interests besides the interests of the people, the interests of the state. The aim of Soviet literature is to help the state correctly educate young people, respond to their demands, and educate a new generation to be bold, to believe in its cause, not to fear obstacles, and to be prepared to overcome all obstacles.

Therefore any advocacy of unprincipledness, apoliticalness, or "art for art's sake" is alien to Soviet literature and harmful to the interests of the Soviet people and state and has no place in our journals.

The lack of principles among the supervising workers at *Star* and *Leningrad* has also led to these workers placing at the basis of their relations with writers not the interests of the correct education of Soviet people and the political guidance of writers' activities but personal interests, interests of friendship. Out of reluctance to spoil friendly relations, criticism has grown dull. Out of fear of offending friends, clearly useless works have been allowed to go to press. This kind of liberalism, under which the interests of the people and the state, the interests of correctly educating our young people, are sacrificed to friendship and under which criticism is muffled, leads to writers ceasing to improve, losing the awareness of their own responsibility to the people, the state, and the Party, and ceasing to move forward.

All the above attests to the fact that the editors of *Star* and *Leningrad* have not dealt well with the task assigned to them and have made serious political mistakes in the supervision of the journals.

The TsK has established that the Board of the Union of Soviet Writers and, in particular, its chairman, Com. Tikhonov, have not taken any measures whatsoever to improve *Star* and *Leningrad* and not only have not fought the harmful influences of Zoshchenko, Akhmatova, and similar non-Soviet writers on Soviet literature but have even facilitated the penetration into the journals of tendencies and mores alien to Soviet literature.

The Leningrad City Committee of the VKP(b) has overlooked major mistakes by the journals, absented itself from supervision of the journals, and offered an opportunity for people alien to Soviet literature, like Zoshchenko and Akhmatova, to occupy a leading position in the journals. Moreover, while aware of the Party's attitude toward Zoshchenko and his "art," the Leningrad Party City Committee (Comrades Kapustin and Shirokov), while not having the right to do so, by a decision of the City Committee dated 28 January of this year, approved *Star's* new editorial board, onto which even Zoshchenko had been brought. In doing this the Leningrad city committee made a crude political mistake. *Leningrad Pravda* made a mistake when it ran a dubious laudatory review by Yury German about Zoshchenko's art in the issue dated 6 July of this year.

The TsK VKP(b) Propaganda Administration has not ensured proper oversight over the work of the Leningrad journals. [. . .]

Without a doubt, the initiative for the public insults against Akhmatova and Zoshchenko came from Zhdanov himself, who was trying his hardest to demonstrate his "objectivity" and "impartiality." The texts of the "explanatory" Zhdanov reports (the final point of the resolution on *Star* and *Leningrad* required "sending Com. Zhdanov to Leningrad to clarify the present TsK VKP(b) resolution") allow us to make this judgment. The day after the resolution was passed, Zhdanov was in Leningrad, where he spoke before Party activists and Leningrad writers on 15 and 16 August 1946. *Pravda* printed a detailed account of these activities, and a month later (21 September 1946) it published the actual text (an abbreviated transcript) of the reports Zhdanov had delivered in Leningrad. Comparing the text of the resolution and that of the reports "clarifying" it show that the invectives addressed against Zoshchenko and Akhmatova were Zhdanov's. The only other possible author could be Stalin himself, but a brief document preserved in the archive attests to the fact that Stalin, while approving the Zhdanov texts, was not their author:

· 166 ·

Note from I. V. Stalin to A. A. Zhdanov on the text of his report "On the journals *Star* and *Leningrad.*" AP RF, f. 45, op. 1, d. 732, l. 2. Handwritten.
19 September 1946

Com. Zhdanov! I've read your report. I think the report came out superbly. It needs to be published quickly and then come out in the form of a pamphlet. Look at my corrections in the text. Greetings!

I. Stalin

Stalin's corrections of the text of Zhdanov's reports were primarily stylistic in nature. The text the leader approved was not only published in *Pravda* two days later and immediately published as a brochure, but also became a mandatory attachment to the famous resolution. Two other documents that followed immediately after the resolution, in contrast, were never published. The first was the TsK Secretariat's resolution on the editorial board of *Star*, dated 30 August 1946. It not only defined how many and which departments the journals' editorial office was supposed to have but also appointed the heads of these departments and the members of the editorial board.[3] The second document was the TsK Orgburo's resolution, dated 13 September 1946, on the removal of the leadership of the USSR Writers Union. This resolution removed Nikolai Tikhonov from his post as chairman of the Writers Union Board and introduced a new system of leadership for the Union. A secretariat was formed led by a general secretary (as whom Aleksandr Fadeev was appointed), four of his deputies (Konstantin Simonov, Nikolai Tikhonov, Vsevolod Vishnevsky, Aleksandr Korneichuk), and eight secretariat members (Boris Gorbatov, Andrei Upit, Antanas Venclova, J. Semper, Simon Chikovani, Aibek, and Leonid Leonov).[4] These "organizational" and "staffing" shifts brought the postwar restructuring of literary institutions to an end.

Yet another document is to be found in the TsK archive:

· 167 ·

Letter from M. M. Zoshchenko to I. V. Stalin. RGASPI, f. 17, op. 125, d. 460, ll. 76–77. Copy. Typewritten.
27 August 1946

Dear Iosif Vissarionovich!

I have never been an anti-Soviet person. In 1918 I volunteered for the ranks of the Red Army and spent half a year at the front fighting the White Guard forces.

I descend from a noble family, but I have never been of two opinions—as to whom I should go with—the people or the landowners. I have always gone with the people. And no one can ever take that away from me.

I began my literary work in 1921. I began writing with the fervent wish to bring benefit to the people by making fun of everything appropriate to make fun of in the human character as formed by our past life.

No doubt I have made mistakes, falling too often into caricature, such as was required in the 1920s for satirical pamphlets. And if we're talking about my youthful stories, then a correction should be made for time. In a quarter-century even the attitude toward the word has changed. I used to work at the Soviet journal *Rowdy* [*Buzoter*], whose name at the time seemed neither base nor vulgar.

I have never been satisfied with my work in the sphere of satire. I have always tried to depict the positive sides of life. This wasn't easy to do, though, just as it's hard for a comic actor to play heroic roles.

However, step by step, I began avoiding satire and, beginning in 1930, I had fewer and fewer satirical stories.

I did this also because I saw what a dangerous weapon satire was. White

Guard publications frequently published my stories, distorting them over and over again, and often ascribing to me things I didn't write. In addition, they didn't date the stories, whereas our daily life has changed enormously over the course of twenty-five years.

All this has forced me to be cautious and, beginning in 1935, I stopped writing satirical stories, with the exception of newspaper feuilletons done on specific material.

During the Great Patriotic War, from the very first days, I worked actively in the journals and newspapers. My antifascist broadsheets were often read over the radio. My satirical antifascist review, *Under Berlin's Lime Trees* [*Pod lipami Berlina*], was performed on the stage of Leningrad's Komedia Theater in September 1941.

After that I was evacuated to Central Asia, where there were no journals or publishers, and willy-nilly I started writing screenplays for the studio located there.

As for my book, *Before Sunrise* (started during the evacuation), it seemed to me that this book was needed and beneficial during the war, for it revealed the sources of the fascist "philosophy" and exposed one of the components in the complicated sum that yet again was prompting people to reject civilization, to reject a higher consciousness and reason.

I was not alone in thinking this way. Tens of people discussed the book I had begun. In June 1943 I was called into the TsK and told to continue this work of mine, which had received high marks from scholars and authoritative people.

These people later retracted their opinion, and therefore I did not feel I could increase their cowardice or doubts with my complaints. And if I am reporting this now, then it is by no means by way of complaint but with the sole desire to show what kind of situation it was that led me to make the mistake, which was caused, probably, by a certain disjunction of mine from real life.

After the harsh criticism that appeared in *Bolshevik*, I decided to write for children and for the theaters, for which I had always had an inclination.

This small humorous story, "Adventures of an Ape," was written in early 1945 for the children's magazine *Murzilka*. And that was where it was published.

But I never submitted this story to *Star*. And it was reprinted there without my knowledge.

Naturally, I would never have placed this story in a thick journal. In isolation from children's and humorous stories, this story in a thick journal would undoubtedly create an awkward impression, as would any joke or caricature for children placed amid serious text.

However, this story of mine does not have any Aesopian language or any subtext. This is merely a funny picture for children, without the slightest malicious intention on my part. I give you my word of honor on this.

If I had wanted to depict satirically what I'm accused of, I could have done this much more wittily. In any event I would not have used this faulty method of veiled satire, a method which was completely exhausted back in the nineteenth century.

In identical measure in my other stories in which this method has been espied, I have not applied a satirical bent. And if people have tried yet again to see in my text certain supposedly shady sketchings, then this could only be a chance coincidence involving no evil plan or intention of mine.

I am not looking or asking for any improvements in my fate. And if I am writing you, then it is with the sole purpose of easing my pain somewhat. It was extremely hard on me to have you see me as a literary scoundrel, a base man, or a man who had surrendered his labor for the good of the landowners and bankers. This is an error. I assure you.

Mikh. Zoshchenko

Zoshchenko's motives in deciding to respond to the resolution with this letter, in which he in fact failed to recognize the sentence pronounced on him, more than likely lay in his emotional state. If we compare this letter with his letter to the TsK of 8 January 1944, which is cited above, we can see that the remorseful tone of the previous letter has been replaced by almost a challenge: an awareness that the "public civil punishment" which had already taken place freed the writer from any concern over the consequences of this step. Stalin was not the only one to read this letter; judging from notations on the first page of the document, so did A. Zhdanov, A. Kuznetsov, N. Patolichev, G. Popov, and G. Aleksandrov. No answer to the letter was forthcoming. Not that Zoshchenko was expecting one. This was a desperate gesture on his part.

Meanwhile, the problems with the journals did not end here. Two years later, from October to December 1948, the TsK Orgburo returned to the work of the journals ("on verifying implementation of the resolution on *Star* and *Leningrad*"). As we recall, during the discussion of these two journals in 1946, Stalin maliciously pronounced: "We'll get to *Banner*, as well, we'll get to them all." This time the object of the attacks was *Banner*, which was, without a doubt, the best postwar journal. The resolution deems the journal's work "unsatisfactory" and replaces the editorial board completely. When in January

1949, the campaign "to fight cosmopolitan critics" began, *Banner* was one of the most active participants in this persecution. Only the preamble to the resolution on *Banner* was published at that time.

· 168 ·

Resolution of the TsK VKP(b) Orgburo "On the journal *Banner*." RGASPI, f. 17, op. 116, d. 406, ll. 22–25. Original. Typewritten. Preamble to the resolution, published in *Kul'tura i zhizn'* [*Culture and Life*], 11 January 1949.
27 December 1948

No. 406, p. 9—*On the journal* Banner.

The TsK VKP(b) notes that the editors of *Banner* have not been coping well with the tasks set for it and in their work have committed several grave errors.

The editors did not draw the appropriate lessons from the TsK VKP(b) resolutions on *Star* and *Leningrad*. During 1948, *Banner* lowered the ideological and artistic quality of the materials it published. The journal published several ideologically defective works that were also inferior in the artistic respect.

The journal's major error is the publication of a novella by N. Melnikov (Mel'man), *The Editorial Office* [*Redaktsia*], in which the workers of our front-line press are depicted either as dullards and conceited petty tyrants, or else as gray, unremarkable men utterly indifferent to their cause. At the same time, the story involves the image of a soldier convicted of a breach of military duty. By depicting the just punishment he suffers as unmerited retribution, the author surrounds him with the halo of heroism.

E. Kazakevich's novella "Two in the Steppe" [*Dvoe v stepi*] testifies in detail to the ordeals of a faint-hearted man sentenced to the firing squad by a military tribunal for violating his military duty. The author morally justifies the coward's very serious crime, which led a military unit to perish. Yu. Yanovsky's stories "Heart of a Doctor" [*Serdtse vracha*] and "Blind Happiness" [*Slepoe schast'e*] lack verisimilitude and are built on tortuous psychological conjectures borrowed from examples of decadent bourgeois literature.

The editors did not direct poets' attention to the militant themes of the modern day. By offering a platform to verse permeated with the emotions of melancholy and grief, the editors helped some poets wander off into the narrow little world of their individual sufferings.

Publication of the indicated works testifies to the incorrect line that has been followed of late by the editorial board of *Banner*. The editors have retreated from the principle of literature's Bolshevik Party spirit, forgotten that literature is a powerful means of ideological education for the Soviet people, disdained vital truth, and offered the journal's pages to works whose authors, by depicting backward, inferior people, have elevated and transformed them into heroes.

The TsK VKP(b) especially points out the unsatisfactory state of the literary criticism department at the journal. The critical articles being published in the journal are distinguished by their low level; often, through their erroneous assessments of literary works, they disorient writers and push them onto an incorrect path. B. Kostelyanets's article about V. Panova's novel *Kruzhilikha* makes fun of Soviet readers' proper and natural desire to see full-fledged, spiritually healthy people as heroes of our literature, literary heroes lacking in any trait of ideological inferiority whatsoever the author contemptuously calls "ironed smooth." B. Runin's article about G. Konovalov's novel *University* [*Universitet*] regards the ideological restraint of the novel's heroes, representatives of advanced Soviet science, as a sign of their intellectual limitation.

The editors are relying on a narrow group of critics and are not raising on the journal's pages topical issues in the country's public and literary life. The journal has done little to help expose bourgeois cosmopolitanism and has not waged an active struggle against Formalism and naturalism in literature.

Lately the journal's work with authors has deteriorated. Submitted manuscripts are being edited carelessly and published in raw, imperfect form. In this way the editors are inculcating in young writers moods of self-assurance and failing to promote their ideological and artistic growth.

The TsK VKP(b) feels the practice that has come about at *Banner*, whereby the editorial board does not meet for long periods of time, does not discuss the works accepted for publication, and in essence absolves itself of responsibility for the journal's direction, having handed over leadership of the journal to the editorial staff, is wrong. [. . .]

As we can see, the TsK's censorship actions were aimed above all at neutralizing real (and more often, imaginary) criticism, which they detected everywhere—in a children's story by a famous writer or in a review of a novel by a little-known writer. Therefore there is nothing surprising in the fact that over the course of a few years resolutions were passed twice concerning the main (and, in essence, sole) satirical journal in the country, *Crocodile* (*Krokodil*). The first time it was the TsK Orgburo's resolution "On the journal *Crocodile*," dated 6 September 1948. It said that "the journal is being run in a totally unsatisfactory manner and is not a militant organ of Soviet satire and humor," that "the editors are detached from life" and publishing "untalented, antiartistic materials." Besides replacing the entire editorial board, as was usual in such instances, the resolution established a few "aesthetic standards" for "Soviet satire and humor": "We believe that the journal's main purpose is to fight the remnants of capitalism in people's consciousness. The journal should use the weapon of satire to expose the plunderers of public property, the self-seekers, the bureaucrats, the manifestations of conceit, servility, and baseness, to speak out in a timely way concerning critical international events, to subject the bourgeois culture of the West to criticism by demonstrating its ideological insignificance and degeneration."[5] This eloquent list exhausted the entire selection of "permitted" objects of "satire."

It is not surprising that three years later (as established by a resolution of what was now the TsK Secretariat, dated 26 September 1951, "On the shortcomings of the journal *Crocodile* and measures for its improvement"), it turned out the journal "is of very little interest," that on its pages "what is published is a great deal of contrived, contentless stories and verse, weak drawings and caricatures that have no serious public significance." This, of course, was stated not in order to develop genuine satire; on the contrary, the journal was accused of a terrible sin, "the blackening of Soviet reality": "Frequently in *Crocodile* individual negative facts are given out as general shortcomings of the work of state, trade union, and other organizations, which gives readers the wrong picture of the work of these organizations."[6]

The system of oversight of the literary process naturally affected literature itself. Scholars of Soviet literature have often noted the astonishing "slipperiness" of Socialist Realist texts: when a given work was analyzed, its date of publication played a large role. Books during the Soviet era were endlessly rewritten, over and over, by their authors "bearing in mind Party criticism," therefore even the classic texts of Soviet literature are known in several versions, which often differ significantly from one another. This practice reached its logical conclusion in the directives of the TsK: inasmuch as the thick journals have always played a central role in the literary process in Russia, the first publications took place as a rule in them, and only afterward was a work published as a separate edition, as a book. Now a new practice replaced this one:

· 169 ·

Resolution of the TsK VKP(b) Politburo "On the procedure for publishing works of artistic literature that have been published in journals." RGASPI, f. 17, op. 3, d. 1081, l. 37. Original. Typewritten.

12 May 1950

No. 74, p. 157—*On the procedure for publishing works of artistic literature that have been published in journals (Art. of 21 April 1950, pr. No. 500, p. 520-s).*

1. Deem it incorrect that publishing houses mechanically reprint artistic works from journals regardless of their ideological and artistic value and without doing any additional editorial work on them.

2. Propose to the directors of the publishing houses Sovetskii Pisatel', Goslitizdat, Molodaia Gvardia, Detgiz, and Iskusstvo that they abolish this incorrect practice and establish a procedure such that works published in literary-artistic journals and sent for publication as separate books be examined preliminarily for their substance at meetings of the editorial boards of the above-indicated publishing houses and subjected to expert review.

3. Deem it essential that artistic works published in journals as separate books shall henceforth be published only with the permission of one of the TsK VKP(b) secretaries.

Require that the TsK VKP(b) Propaganda and Agitation Section ensure strict implementation of the procedure established for publishing works that have been published in journals.

Such high status for a book (permission at the level of TsK secretaries!) should not mislead us. No matter how high the status of literature on the Stalinist Parnassus, "the most important of all the arts" remained Stalin's beloved cinema.

CHAPTER TWENTY-TWO

"The Most Important Art"

Without a doubt, the central event in Soviet cinema life of the 1940s was the edict that followed the success of the first part and the ban on the second part of Sergei Eisenstein's *Ivan the Terrible* (*Ivan Groznyi*). The ensuing chain of events peaked in the famous TsK resolution "On the film *A Grand Life* [*Bol'shaia zhizn'*]" approved in September 1946. TsK materials that have been preserved allow us not only to trace the chain of events whose initiator was Stalin personally but also to take a look at their context.

The problem of restoring the "authentic historical face of Tsar Ivan the Terrible" (as of other tsars and military leaders) had begun to preoccupy Stalin for some time. Long before the war (and specifically since the mid-1930s), a broad ideological campaign had been initiated—in historical scholarship, literature, art, and film—to reassess "Russia's historical past," which was deemed to have been presented too negatively in Marxist historiography. The greatest interest (due to its historic allusiveness, one assumes) was aroused by the "progressive tsar-reformers, the unifiers of the Russian lands," such as Ivan the Terrible and Peter the Great. Their historical contributions could be associated directly with Stalinist industrialization, the strengthening of centralization and statehood, and "military victories." Many writers and directors worked on those themes. Among writers, it is worth singling out above all Aleksei Tolstoy, who worked in the early 1940s on a play (subsequently his plans grew into a two-part drama) about Ivan the Terrible. The work, which Stalin had initiated personally, displeased the TsK apparatus, as a result of which the following document emerged:

· 170 ·

Note from TsK VKP(b) Secretary A. S. Shcherbakov to I. V. Stalin about A. N. Tolstoy's play *Ivan the Terrible*. Published in *Glasnost'*, 28 November–4 December 1991, no. 48.

28 April 1942

The Committee on Stalin Prizes for literature and art has nominated A. N. Tolstoy's play *Ivan the Terrible* [*Ivan groznyi*] for the 1941 Stalin Prize.

During the evaluation of the play, it was denied presentation of the Stalin Prize both because of formal concerns (the play has not been published or performed in a single theater, the Soviet public doesn't know it, the critics have not responded to it, etc.) and because of its essence, for the play distorts the historical face of one of the most prominent Russian state figures, Ivan IV (1530–1584).

However, in the instance of A. N. Tolstoy's *Ivan the Terrible*, we can scarcely limit ourselves to rejecting it for presentation for the Stalin Prize.

The problem is that *Ivan the Terrible* was written at the special request of the Committee on Arts Affairs, following TsK VKP(b) instructions on the need to restore to Russian history the authentic historical face of Ivan IV, which has been distorted by aristocratic and bourgeois historiography.

Ivan IV is the outstanding statesman of sixteenth-century Russia. He completed the progressive work begun by Ivan III, the creation of a centralized Russian state. Ivan IV, having successfully broken the resistance of the feudal lords, essentially eliminated the country's feudal fragmentation. Soviet literature and historical scholarship had literally never once been asked to restore the true face of this major Russian statesman. Therefore the staging of this play or its publication would increase the confusion in the minds of historians and writers on the issue of Russia's history in the sixteenth century and of Ivan IV.

In connection with what has been set forth here, we must ban the staging of A. N. Tolstoy's *Ivan the Terrible* in Soviet theaters, as well as ban this play's publication in print.

A. Shcherbakov

We will not go into the fate of A. Tolstoy's plays on stage. All we know is that he reworked his texts many times so that they would conform to the required "line," and in 1946 he received the Stalin Prize. Be that as it may, there was no reply forthcoming from Stalin to Shcherbakov's memorandum. More than a year later, A. Tolstoy personally addressed the leader in a letter:

· 171 ·

Letter from A. N. Tolstoy to I. V. Stalin. Published in *Glasnost'*, 28 November–4 December 1991, no. 48.

2 June 1943

Deeply esteemed Iosif Vissarionovich,

I have sent you my play, *Difficult Years* [*Trudnye gody*], the second part of the dramatic tale of *Ivan the Terrible*. The play covers the years 1567–1572, which have been the most obscure for Russian historiography, since the archival documents of the period have perished, or were consciously destroyed; only now have Soviet historians (Vipper, Bakhrushin, et al.) shed light on this era.

Difficult Years is an independent and complete play, which can go onto the stage apart from its connection with the first part.

The dramatic tale of *Ivan the Terrible* was begun during a very difficult time, October 1941 (with the play *The Eagle and Its Mate* [*Orel i orlitsa*]), when we needed with all our might and with all necessity to turn the history of Russian culture upside down, understand it in a new way, and enlist it as a weapon of struggle. The story of twenty-five years of Soviet history and our inexhaustible forces in this war have shown that the Russian nation—nearly alone among the European peoples to have remained for two millennia sovereign in its own land—harbors a powerful, national, unique culture, even if for a time it matured beneath an unsightly outward appearance. The ideas of the greatness of the Russian state, the reach of its aims, its desire for good, for moral perfection, its boldness in social revolutions, upheavals, and restructurings, its gentleness and at the same time its courage and persistence, the strength of its personalities—all this is special and Russian, and all this is expressed unusually vividly in the men of the sixteenth century. And the most vivid of the period's personalities is Ivan the Terrible. In him are concentrated all the unique qualities of the Russian nature, and from him, as from a spring, flow the streams and broad rivers of Russian literature. What did the Germans have to show for themselves in the sixteenth century? The classic philistine Martin Luther?

The first play, *The Eagle and Its Mate*, was for me an experiential understanding of Ivan the Terrible and the shaping of his character, and in it, as through a narrow crack, I crawled back to the sixteenth century in order to hear the voices and see the real faces of the people of that era.

The second play, *Difficult Years*, is a story about Ivan the Terrible's deeds. Naturally I did not even consider squeezing all his dealings and events into the play's 75 pages. Dramaturgy is limited by theatrical time, and in a historical play by the truth of the historical facts. In *Difficult*

Years I did not force the facts but went along with them, as from milestone to milestone, trying to understand their meaning, trying to uncover their causality, which was lost or distorted by nineteenth-century historians.

Dear Iosif Vissarionovich, my play, *Difficult Years,* is still lying without movement. I have addressed Com. Shcherbakov, but he gave me neither a positive nor a negative answer. The Committee on Arts Affairs has not taken any decision. The Maly Theater wants with all fervor to stage a performance of *Difficult Years,* which it could do in late November or December.

I beg of you, if you find the time, to read the play, which for me—in all my literary life—is the hardest and most precious work.

With deep respect
Aleksei Tolstoy

As can be seen, Tolstoy's letter reflects the "correctness" of the writer's take on the tsar's historical role. Couched in the Russian chauvinist rhetoric Stalin always liked, the "dramatic project" by A. Tolstoy, who had already been elevated to the rank of classic author of Soviet literature, eventually did pique the leader's interest. Finding time at the most critical moment of the war, Stalin finally read the plays and not only approved them but also made comments on them (evidently in oral form) and expressed a desire for their speediest possible completion, which was conveyed to the writer. A month later, on 16 October 1943, both plays lay on Stalin's desk, redone. The scenes in them of Kurbsky's flight to Lithuania had been added to. The second play concluded with a scene of Ivan the Terrible outside Moscow. Work on the plays continued and after another month, on 24 November of the same year, A. Tolstoy sent Stalin the final version with the added scenes of the princes' conspiracy in Moscow involving Kurbsky. The road to the audience was open for A. Tolstoy's plays. It was against this backdrop that Stalin approved Eisenstein's screenplay:

· 172 ·

Note from I. V. Stalin to SNK SSSR Committee on Cinematography Affairs Chairman I. G. Bolshakov concerning the screenplay of *Ivan the Terrible*. Published in *Glasnost'*, 28 November–4 December 1991, no. 48.
13 September 1943

To Com. Bolshakov.

The screenplay did not work out badly. Com. Eisenstein has coped with his assignment. Ivan the Terrible, as a progressive force for his era, and the *Oprichnina*, as his logical instrument, did not come out badly.

The screenplay should be put into production as quickly as possible.

    I. Stalin

It is interesting to note that in his screenplay Eisenstein did not take the same road as A. Tolstoy. Stalin read both texts virtually simultaneously, giving the go-ahead to both, and it is entirely possible that with the very same "desires" the leader might have created a previously prepared "master plot" for a narrative about his favorite tsar. What came next is well known: the first part of the film was highly esteemed and received the Stalin Prize First Class. The second part roused the leader's fury: "This isn't a film but some kind of nightmare!"[1] A letter to Stalin from a student and friend of Eisenstein, the film director Grigory Aleksandrov, of whom Stalin thought highly, sheds further light on events:

· 173 ·

Letter from G. V. Aleksandrov to I. V. Stalin. Published in *Glasnost'*, 28 November–4 December 1991, no. 48.
6 March 1946. Moscow.

Dear Iosif Vissarionovich!

Comrade I. G. Bolshakov has informed me of your negative opinion concerning the second part of S. M. Eisenstein's *Ivan the Terrible,* as well as of the TsK VKP(b) decision banning the film's release to the screen due to its unartistic and antihistorical nature.

The purpose of my letter is not to defend the film!

Exceptional and extraordinary circumstances force me to disturb you. Among the creative workers on *Ivan the Terrible,* both the first and the second part evoked harsh criticism. The second part was reproached especially harshly for the fact that the episode of Efrosinia Staritskaia overshadowed all of Tsar Ivan's statesmanlike activities; for the absence of popular scenes in the picture; and for the absence of Russian nature, architecture, and surroundings. They also reproached it for admiring the dreadful aspects of life, for its excessive display of religious moments instead of a display of the organization of the Russian state and preparation for the Livonian campaigns, instead of a display of the struggle for a route to the Baltic Sea.

Four months ago, the leadership of the Mosfilm Studio decided that the removed material cannot comprise an independent picture and correctly depict the career of Tsar Ivan. It was proposed to S. M. Eisenstein that he do more work on the film; film for it scenes of state activities and preparation for the Livonian war and combine the proposed third and second parts to make a single film that would conclude with "Victory by the Sea."

However, the director S. M. Eisenstein took this in a painfully negative way and asked the studio leadership to give him a chance to complete the second part according to the previously approved screenplay and not distort its basic plan.

The conferring of the Stalin Prize First Class on S. M. Eisenstein, the director and author of the first part of *Ivan the Terrible*, strengthened his conviction that he was right even more. We decided not to force him and to comply with S. M.'s request—to finish the film according to his plan and only after that take a final decision.

On 2 February, Eisenstein completed work on the film and submitted the material to the film laboratory, but a few hours after this (at a celebration on the occasion of Stalin Prizes being conferred on film workers), Eisenstein suddenly suffered a very serious attack of angina pectoris, which lasted thirty-six hours. Only timely intervention with medicine and the application of vigorous measures saved him from death.

Having been taken ill so suddenly, Eisenstein did not get to see the picture in finished form.

When he recovered from his attack, Eisenstein asked me to show the film to the Arts Council of the Film Committee.

Most of the members of the Arts Council had a negative opinion of the film and subjected it to harsh criticism—having noted, however, that the work was done very conscientiously, that it was original in its creative methods, new in its means of expression, and highly professional. Also noted were the great achievements in the area of creative and technical mastery of color filming according to the new method. The Arts Council decided to instruct the commission to come up with proposals for correcting and adding to the film, but Eisenstein's condition was so bad that there could be no question of any corrections or additions anytime soon.

Eisenstein insisted on being let out of the hospital so that the film could be shown to you, Iosif Vissarionovich. Your viewing of the film became his life's goal. This viewing worried him more than anything else.

He has invested more than five years of his life and labor in this film. He shot it under difficult conditions in Alma-Ata, and he had nothing else in life besides this film.

Postponing a viewing by you would have meant dragging out and intensifying S. M.'s worry, which was counterindicated for him.

After his daily and persistent demands, I asked Comrade I. G. Bolshakov to show you the picture.

The result of the viewing for him would be extremely surprising. Judging from what he has said, he anticipated favorable results and was certain of them.

News of such a negative assessment would unquestionably serve as cause for powerful worry, which for him at the given moment is akin to death.

Knowing you, Iosif Vissarionovich, as a man who is attentive to people and their misfortunes, a responsive and emotional man, and, on the other hand, having known the director Eisenstein for twenty-six years as an active figure in our cinematography, as a teacher of many now renowned masters, as a founder of Soviet cinematography, and, keeping in mind the extraordinary circumstances set forth above, I would be so bold as *to ask you, Iosif Vissarionovich, not to take a final decision on* Ivan the Terrible *until its author's recuperation.*

Once he has recuperated and has viewed his own work, Eisenstein may propose a version of the editing and corrections which will recover all the means and effort spent on this major work.

I am turning to you as the artistic director of the Mosfilm Studio and a former student of Eisenstein.

With deep respect and love for you,

Gr. Aleksandrov

Two months later, Eisenstein himself appealed to the leader.

· 174 ·

Letter from S. M. Eisenstein to I. V. Stalin. Published in *Glasnost'*,
28 November–4 December 1991, no. 48.
Moscow, 14 May 1946

Kremlin Hospital
Dear Iosif Vissarionovich!

I have not written you before, sensing and knowing how very busy you are and overburdened with the gravest affairs of state.

However, inasmuch as a lesser burden for you is hardly to be anticipated in the near future, I am nonetheless writing to you.

This concerns the second part of *Ivan the Terrible*.

We rushed its completion for the beginning of this year so much that at the moment of the film's completion (February of this year), the heart spasms that have happened to me due to overexhaustion in turn concluded in a heart attack (infarction)—and so I have been lying in the hospital for over three months.

The danger has passed now, and in the near future I will transfer to sanatorium treatment. Physically I will get better soon, but morally I am very much oppressed by the fact that you have still not seen the picture, which has been ready for several months—especially because you looked so benevolently on the first part.

Added to this as well are all kinds of vague and disturbing reports that have reached me that the "historical theme" seems to have been pushed back altogether from the field of attention to the second or third level.

I beg of you, therefore, dear Iosif Vissarionovich, if you could find a little free time, to see this work of mine and resolve my concern and alarm.

The picture is the *second* part of a contemplated *trilogy about Tsar Ivan*—between the first part, which you know, and a third, which has yet to be shot and will be devoted to the Livonian War.

In order to set off both these broad battle canvases, the present part was taken in a narrow cross-section: it is inside Moscow and its plot is constructed around the boyars' conspiracy against the unity of the Muscovite state and around Tsar Ivan overcoming sedition.

Forgive me for disturbing you with my request.

With sincere respect for you,

    Film director
    S. M. Eisenstein

Meanwhile, everything Stalin and Beria had stated immediately after viewing the second part of the film—Beria said that the scene of the *oprichniki* dancing in the film reminded him of a coven of witches, that Ivan was depicted as a "pathetic neurasthenic," and Stalin called Eisenstein's Ivan "weak-willed," comparing him with Hamlet, and the dance scene reminded him of the Ku Klux Klan—was repeated almost word for word publicly in the resolution on *A Grand Life*. Eisenstein and Nikolai Cherkasov (who played the part of Ivan) asked Stalin for a face-to-face meeting, which took place on the night of 25–26 February 1947, in the Kremlin.

· 175 ·

Authorized transcript of the conversation between I. V. Stalin, A. A. Zhdanov, and V. M. Molotov, and S. M. Eisenstein and N. K. Cherkasov, concerning *Ivan the Terrible*. 26 February 1947.[2] Published in D. Mar'iamov, *Kremlevskii tsenzor: Stalin smotrit kino* [The Kremlin censor: Stalin watches the movies] (Moscow: Kinotsentr, 1992), pp. 84–92.

We were summoned to the Kremlin for 11 o'clock.

At 10:50 we arrived in the waiting room. At exactly 11 o'clock Poskrebyshev emerged to take us into the office.

At the far end of the office were Stalin, Molotov, and Zhdanov.

We come in, greet everyone, sit down at the table.

Stalin. You wrote a letter. The answer was a little delayed. We're meeting with some delay. I thought of answering you in writing but decided it was better to have a talk. Since I'm very busy, there's no time, I decided, with great delay, to meet here. . . . I received your letter in November.

Zhdanov. You received it in Sochi.

Stalin. Yes, yes. In Sochi. What are you thinking of doing with the picture?

We talk about how we have cut the second part into two parts, which is why the Livonian campaign did not appear in this picture and there was a disproportion between its separate parts, and the picture needs fixing in the sense of cutting some of the material filmed and filming some more, mainly the Livonian campaign.

Stalin. Have you studied the history?

Eisenstein. More or less. . . .

Stalin. More or less? I know a thing or two about history, too. You've shown the *Oprichnina* improperly. The *Oprichnina* was the royal army. Unlike a feudal army, which could turn its banners around at any moment and leave the war, a regular army was formed, a progressive army. You have the *oprichniki* looking like the Ku Klux Klan. Eisenstein said that they wore white hoods, whereas ours wore black ones.

Molotov. That doesn't constitute a difference in principle.

Stalin. The tsar comes out in your film as indecisive, like Hamlet. Everyone suggests to him what should be done, but he can't make a decision himself. . . . Tsar Ivan was a great and wise ruler, and if he is compared with Louis XI (have you read about Louis XI, who prepared absolutism for Louis XIV?), then Ivan the Terrible and Louis are worlds apart. Ivan the Terrible's wisdom consisted in the fact that he insisted on a national point of view and wouldn't allow foreigners into his country, fencing the country off from the penetration of foreign influence. By showing Ivan the Terrible along that line, deviations and errors were committed. Peter I is also a great sovereign, but he treated foreigners too liberally, opened the gates too wide, and let foreign influence into the country, allowing the Germanizing of Russia. Catherine allowed this even more. And furthermore. Was the court of Alexander I really a Russian court? Was the court of Nicholas I really a Russian court? No. Those were German courts.

Ivan the Terrible's remarkable enterprise was the fact that he was the first to introduce a state monopoly on foreign trade. Ivan the Terrible was the first to introduce it; Lenin was the second.

Zhdanov. Eisenstein's Ivan the Terrible came out looking like a neurasthenic.

Molotov. In general, the stress was put on psychologism, on the excessive emphasis of inner psychological contradictions and personal sufferings.

Stalin. You need to show historical figures correctly in their style. So, for instance, in the first part, it's wrong that Ivan the Terrible spent so long kissing his wife. In those days that wasn't allowed.

Zhdanov. The picture was made with a Byzantine bias, and this wasn't the practice there, either.

Molotov. The second part is squeezed in by arches and cellars, there's no fresh air, there's none of Moscow's spaciousness, no display of the people. You can show conversations, you can show repressions, but not only that.

Stalin. Ivan the Terrible was very cruel. You can show that he was cruel, but you have to show why it was essential to be cruel.

One of Ivan the Terrible's mistakes was that he didn't finish off the five major feudal families. If he had wiped out these five boyar families, then there never would have been a Time of Troubles. But Ivan the Terrible would execute someone and then spend a long time repenting and praying. God hindered him in this matter. . . . He should have been even more decisive.

Molotov. Historical events need to be shown in the correct light. Here, for instance, there was the instance with Demian Bedny's play *The Bogatyrs*. In it Demian Bedny made fun of Russia's acceptance of Christianity, but the point is that for its historical stage, the acceptance of Christianity was a progressive phenomenon.

Stalin. Of course, we aren't very good Christians, but we can't deny the progressive role of Christianity at a certain stage. This event had very major significance because it meant the Russian state turning around to close ranks with the West, instead of orienting itself toward the East.

On relations with the East, Stalin says that having just freed himself from the Tatar yoke, Ivan the Terrible rushed to unite Russia in order to be a bulwark against possible Tatar incursions. Astrakhan was subdued, but it could attack Moscow at any moment. The Crimean Tatars could do this, too.

Stalin. Demian Bedny imagined the historical prospects incorrectly. When we moved the monument to Minin and Pozharsky closer to the Cathedral of Vasily the Blessed, Demian Bedny protested and wrote how the monument should be thrown out altogether and in general we should forget about Minin and Pozharsky. In reply to this letter I called him an "Ivan who does not remember his kin." We can't just toss out history. . . .

Stalin goes on to make several comments concerning the interpretation of Ivan the Terrible's image and talks about how Maliuta Skuratov was a major military leader and perished heroically in the war with Livonia.

Cherkasov, in reply to the idea that criticism helps and that Pudovkin after criticism made a good film, *Admiral Nakhimov,* said: "We are confident that we will do no worse, for I am working on the image of Ivan the Terrible not only in film but in the theater, I have come to love this image and feel that our refashioning of the screenplay can prove correct and truthful."

To which Stalin replied (addressing Molotov and Zhdanov): "Well, what do you say, let's try it."

Cherkasov. I'm sure the remake will succeed.

Stalin. May God grant you a new year every day. (He laughs.)

Eisenstein. We're saying that in the first part several moments succeeded, and that gives us confidence that we can do the second part, too.

Stalin. We're not talking about what succeeded and was good, right now we're only talking about the shortcomings.

Eisenstein asks whether there are going to be any other special instructions regarding the picture.

Stalin. I'm not giving you instructions, I'm expressing a viewer's remarks. Historical images have to be depicted truthfully.

[. . .]

Cherkasov says that he has played most of the tsars and even played Peter I and Aleksei.

Zhdanov. Down the line of succession. You followed the succession . . .

Stalin. Historical figures have to be shown truthfully and powerfully. (To Eisenstein.) Look at Alexander Nevsky—did you invent him? That came out wonderfully. The most important thing is observing the style of the historical era. A director can retreat from history; it's wrong if he's simply going to copy down details from historical material, he has to work with his imagination, but keeping within the limits of the style. A director can vary within the limits of the style of the historical era.

Zhdanov says that Eisenstein got carried away with shadows (which distract the viewer from the action) and with Ivan the Terrible's beard, that Ivan raises his head too often to let us see the beard.

Eisenstein promises in the future to cut back on Ivan's beard.

Stalin. (recalling individual performers in the first part of *Ivan the Terrible*). Kurbsky is magnificent. Staritsky (the actor Kadochnikov) is very fine. He's very good at catching flies. What a man! A future tsar, and he catches flies with his hands!

You have to give details like that. They reveal the essence of a man.

[. . .]

Stalin. . . . Well, then, that means the matter's decided. What do you think, comrades (he turns to Molotov and Zhdanov), should we give Cherkasov and Eisenstein a chance to finish the film?—and he adds: Tell Comrade Bolshakov this.

Cherkasov asks about certain particulars of the picture and about the appearance of Ivan the Terrible.

Stalin. The appearance is right, no need to change it. It's a good appearance for Ivan the Terrible.

Cherkasov. Can the scene of Staritsky's killing be left in the screenplay?
Stalin. You can leave it. There were killings.
Cherkasov. In the screenplay we have a scene where Maliuta Skuratov chokes Metropolitan Filipp.
Zhdanov. That was in the Tver Otroch Monastery?
Cherkasov. Yes. Should we keep that scene?

Stalin said they should keep the scene, that that would be historically correct.

Molotov says that repressions in general can and should be shown, but it has to be shown why they were committed, in the name of what. To do this you have to show the state's activities more broadly and not limit it just to scenes in cellars and enclosed spaces, but show broader state activities.

Cherkasov expresses his thoughts concerning the remade future screenplay, the future second part.

Stalin. How will the picture end? What's the best way to make the next two pictures, that is, the second and third parts? How are we thinking about doing this in general?

Eisenstein says that it's better to combine the cut material from the second part with what was left in the screenplay—and one big picture.

Everyone agrees with this.

Stalin. How will we have the film end?

Cherkasov says that the film will end with the rout of Livonia, the tragic death of Maliuta Skuratov, and the march to the sea, where Ivan the Terrible stands by the sea surrounded by his troops and says, "We stand at the seas now and forever!"

Stalin. And that's what happened, and even a little more.

Cherkasov asks whether the draft of the new screenplay for the film should be shown to the Politburo for approval.

Stalin. You don't have to present the screenplay, sort it out yourselves. It's hard to judge from a screenplay usually, easier to talk about the finished work. (To Molotov.) You probably really want to read the screenplay.

Molotov. No, I'm working in a slightly different area. Let Bolshakov read it.

Eisenstein says it would be good if they didn't rush with this picture.
This remark gets a lively response from everyone.

Stalin. In no event should you rush, and in general we're going to shut down rushed pictures and not release them. Repin worked on his *Zaporozhtsy* [*Zaporozhye Cossacks*] for eleven years.

Molotov. Thirteen years.

Stalin (insistently). Eleven years.

Everyone comes to the conclusion that only through prolonged work can good pictures in fact be made.

Concerning *Ivan the Terrible,* Stalin said that if it takes a year and a half or two years, or even three years, to make the film, then do it in that length of time, just make sure the picture is made well, that it's made "sculpturally." Generally speaking, right now we should be improving quality. Let there be fewer pictures, but of higher quality. Our viewer has matured, and we have to show him good output.

They say that Tselikovskaia was fine in other roles. She acts well, but she's a ballerina.

We reply that in Alma-Ata we couldn't call in another actress.

Stalin says that a director should be adamant and demand what he needs, whereas our directors give in too easily on their demands. It sometimes happens that a great actor is needed, but someone acts who doesn't suit a given role because he demands to and they let him act that role, and the director agrees.

Eisenstein. They couldn't let the actress Gosheva go from the Art Theater to Alma-Ata for filming. We searched for our Anastasia for two years.

Stalin. The artist Zharov approached his role in *Ivan the Terrible* incorrectly, frivolously. He's a frivolous military commander.

Zhdanov. He's not Maliuta Skuratov, he's some kind of "top hat!"

Stalin. Ivan the Terrible was more of a national tsar, more prudent, he never allowed foreign influence into Russia, whereas that Peter—he opened the gates to Europe and let in too many foreigners.

Cherkasov talks about how, unfortunately, and to his shame, he didn't see the second part of *Ivan the Terrible*. When the picture was edited and shown, he was in Leningrad at the time.

Eisenstein adds that he too did not see the picture in its final form, since immediately after its completion he fell ill.

This arouses great surprise and animation.

The conversation ends with Stalin wishing them success and saying: "May God help you!"

We shake hands and leave. At 0:10 the conversation ends.

Addition to the B. N. Agapov transcript, made by S. M. Eisenstein and N. K. Cherkasov:

Zhdanov also said that "the film has too much misuse of religious rituals."

Molotov said that this "lends a patina to mysticism, which should not be emphasized so strongly."

Zhdanov says that "the scene in the cathedral, where the 'cave rite' takes place, is shown too broadly and is distracting."

Stalin says that the *oprichniki* during the dancing look like cannibals and remind him of some kind of Phoenicians or Babylonians.

When Cherkasov said that he'd been working on the image of Ivan the Terrible for a long time, both in film and the theater, Zhdanov said: "I've been reigning peacefully for over five years."

In parting, Stalin inquired about Eisenstein's health.

This meeting took place half a year after the resolution on the film *A Grand Life,* which absorbed the irritation that had accumulated in the Stalinist leadership over the state of Soviet film. Undoubtedly, Stalin remained the central figure. His retinue were merely giving voice to the leader's directives, couching them in the form of resolutions. One such resolution (secret) was passed shortly before the resolution on *A Grand Life.* It concerned Vsevolod Pudovkin's film *Admiral Nakhimov.*

· 176 ·

Resolution of the TsK VKP(b) Secretariat on the film *Admiral Nakhimov*.
RGASPI, f. 17, op. 116, d. 262, ll. 73–74. Original. Typewritten.
11 May 1946

No. 262, p. 366g—*On the film* Admiral Nakhimov.

1. The TsK VKP(b) notes that the film *Admiral Nakhimov*, produced by director Pudovkin based on a screenplay by Lukovsky, has serious shortcomings that diminish the film's artistic value. The film exhibits a disregard for historical truth. The scene of the Sinope naval battle, which is basic to the film, is not developed and remains incomplete; the historical fact of Nakhimov's capture of the commander of the Turkish navy and his staff is not reproduced; the town of Sinope after the battle is shown poorly. The defense of Sebastopol is depicted schematically and not convincingly enough. The reasons for the Russians sinking their own fleet during the Sebastopol raid are not explained at all. Nakhimov's action in the defense of Sebastopol are shown less vividly than in other scenes of the picture.

2. The TsK VKP(b) instructs the Ministry of Cinematography (Com. Bolshakov) to remake *Admiral Nakhimov* along the following lines:

a. add a scene about Nakhimov's capture during the Battle of Sinope of the Turkish admiral Osman Pasha, his staff, and the English officers assigned to him, in doing so quote what Nakhimov said to the Turkish admiral about how Turkey should always be in peace and friendship with Russia and how Turkey itself was to blame for its defeat, having started a risky war with Russia.

Show Nakhimov's humane treatment of the Turkish captives and the civilian population of Sinope;

b. show Sinope and the harbor before the battle, as well as the remnants of the Turkish squadron and Sinope burning as a result of the fighting;

c. give a more vivid and grand picture of Nakhimov's victorious squadron returning to Sebastopol after the Sinope victory;

d. remake the scene of the conversation between Nakhimov and Menshikov so as to restore the historical truth, i.e., so that Nakhimov's proposal to seize the Bosporus and the Dardanelles quickly is motivated by the need to shut off access to the Black Sea to the English and French fleet, which consisted then of screw steamers and in its technical features surpassed the Russian fleet, which consisted of sailing vessels;

e. add to the picture a scene showing the meeting of the admirals and top officers before the beginning of the siege of Sebastopol, at which Kornilov and Nakhimov convincingly cite arguments about the need to implement Menshikov's order to sink the Russian fleet in view of the obvious superiority of the English-French squadron's screw steamers over the sailing vessels of the Russian fleet;

f. show more vividly the defense of Sebastopol and Nakhimov's role in organizing the battle for Sebastopol;

g. include an additional episode on the capture by the popular Sebastopol hero, the sailor Koshka, of an English officer, who had been captured earlier and released by Nakhimov at Sinope among the English instructors of the Turkish fleet.

3. Finish the remake of *Admiral Nakhimov* in four months' time.

As can be seen, the TsK had been transformed into an institution of "creative censorship"; it did not simply ban something but actually prescribed how it should be filmed.

An important question is the matter of Stalin's role in the decision-making process in the sphere of culture. This refers in particular to the era that has been given the name "Zhdanovism." Actually, Zhdanov's role here was not decisive. Unquestionably, it was Stalin who not only initiated the various decisions but also directly dictated and pronounced them. We have seen this from several coincidences in the documents and transcripts of discussions referring to literature. The situation in cinema is even more instructive: in the archive there is a transcript of a speech by Stalin at a session of the TsK Orgburo (dated 9 August 1946) at which a decision was approved instructing the TsK Secretariat to prepare a resolution on the film *A Grand Life* (this occurred immediately in the wake of consideration of the *Star* and *Leningrad* case). We will cite this transcript in full in parallel with fragments from the text of the resolution published several days afterward:

· 177 ·

Corrected transcript of I. V. Stalin's speech at the session of the TsK VKP(b) Orgburo on the film *A Grand Life*. 9 August 1946. RGASPI, f. 558, op. 1, d. 5325, ll. 23–27. Copy. Typewritten.

Excerpt from a resolution of the TsK VKP(b) Orgburo "On the film *A Grand Life*." 4 September 1946. Published in *Kul'tura i zhizn'*, 10 September 1946; *Literaturnaia gazeta*, 14 September 1946.

We have viewed this film, we have viewed its first part, too. The first part is better, though it too has provoked criticism. Right now by

How are we to explain such frequent instances of the production of false and erroneous films? Why have the famous Soviet directors

association I link this film with Eisenstein's *Ivan the Terrible* (the second part) and Pudovkin's *Admiral Nakhimov*. You get the general impression that the producers and directors are doing very little work on the subjects they are trying to demonstrate and are treating their obligations very lightly, sometimes lightly to the point of criminality, I would say. People are not studying their subject, don't have a good picture of the matter, but they're writing screenplays. This is an unconscientious attitude.

Take the good producers and directors, and also the American Charlie Chaplin. For a few years the man is silent, works hard, conscientiously studies the technique and details of the matter, because nothing can be studied without details, and you can't make a good film without details. Details have to be studied. And here good producers and directors work for years on a film, two, three, four years, because they have a very scrupulous and conscientious attitude toward what they're doing. We have poets, for example, who can write two long poems in a month, but take Goethe, he worked on *Faust* for thirty years, that's how honestly and conscientiously he regarded what he was doing. A light attitude toward what they're doing on the part of authors of some works is the basic sin that leads directors and producers to releasing these kinds of films. Just take *Admiral Nakhimov*. Pudovkin is a capable producer and director, he knows Comrades Lukov, Eisenstein, Pudovkin, Kozintsev, and Trauberg, who in the past created pictures of high quality, suffered failure?

The problem is that many masters of cinematography, producers, directors, and screenplay authors treat their obligations lightly and irresponsibly and do not work in good conscience on the creation of their films. The main shortcoming in their work consists in the fact that they do not study the matter they take up.

< ... >

Ignorance of their subject and a frivolous attitude on the part of screenwriters and directors toward what they are doing comprise one of the main reasons for the release of unfit films.

what he's doing, but this time he didn't take the time to study the matter as he should have. He decided this: I am Pudovkin, they know me, I'll write it and the public will "swallow" it, they're going to watch any film. People are starving, there's lots of curiosity and inquisitiveness, so naturally they're going to watch it. Meanwhile, people's tastes have become more expert, and they aren't going to "swallow" just anything. People are starting to distinguish the bad from the good and are making new demands. And if this matter is to go any farther, and we Bolsheviks are going to try to develop tastes in our viewers, I'm afraid they're going to take some of our screenwriters, producers, and directors out of circulation.

In the film *Nakhimov* there are also elements of an unconscientious approach by the producers to the study of the subject they wanted to show. They try to get by with all kinds of trifles, they showed a few paper ships, and the rest was dancing, various trysts, all kinds of episodes to engage the viewer. This really is not a film about Nakhimov but a film about something or other with a few episodes about Nakhimov. We sent the film back and told Pudovkin that he hadn't studied this matter, didn't even know the history, didn't know that the Russians were at Sinope. The matter is depicted as if the Russians weren't there. Russians took lots of Turkish generals prisoner, but the film doesn't con-

Thus film director V. Pudovkin decided to make a film about Nakhimov, but he did not study the details of the matter and distorted the historical truth. He ended up with a film not about Nakhimov but about balls and dances with episodes from Nakhimov's life. As a result, such important historical facts as that the Russians were at Sinope and that an entire group of Turkish admirals led by their commander were taken captive in the Battle of Sinope were left out of the film.

vey this. Why? We don't know. Maybe because this takes a lot of work and it's much easier to show dancing. In short, it's an unconscientious attitude toward what the man has taken up, something that was going to be shown throughout the world. If a man respected himself, he wouldn't do this, he would have produced the film differently. But Pudovkin evidently doesn't care how viewers and public opinion might respond to him.

Or the other film, Eisenstein's *Ivan the Terrible*, the second part. I don't know whether anyone has seen it, but I have—a vile thing! The man got completely distracted from the history. He depicted the *oprichiniki* as rotten scoundrels, degenerates, something like the American Ku Klux Klan. Eisenstein didn't realize that the troops of the *Oprichnina* were progressive troops. Ivan the Terrible relied on them to gather Russia into a single centralized state, against the feudal princes, who wanted to fragment and weaken it. Eisenstein has an old attitude toward the *Oprichnina*. The attitude of old historians toward the *Oprichnina* was crudely negative because they equated the repressions of Ivan the Terrible with the repressions of Nicholas II, and got completely away from the historical circumstances in which this occurred. In our era, there is a different view of the *Oprichnina*. Russia fragmented into feudal principalities, i.e., into several states, had to unite if it didn't want to fall under the Tatar

Director S. Eisenstein, in the second part of *Ivan the Terrible*, exposed his ignorance in his depiction of historical facts, presenting the progressive force of Ivan the Terrible's *oprichniki* in the guise of gangs of degenerates, similar to the American Ku Klux Klan, and Ivan the Terrible, a man with a powerful will and character, as weak of character and will, something like Hamlet.

yoke a second time. This is clear to everyone else and it ought to have been clear to Eisenstein, too. Eisenstein can't help but know this because there is a literature to this effect, whereas he depicted degenerates of some kind. Ivan the Terrible was a man with a will and character, but in Eisenstein he's a weak-willed Hamlet. This is Formalism now. What do we care about Formalism—give us the historical truth. Studying takes patience, and some of our producers don't have enough patience and therefore they mix everything up into a single whole and present it as a film: here you are, "swallow it," especially since it has Eisenstein's stamp on it. How are we supposed to teach people to treat their obligations and the interests of the viewers and the state conscientiously? After all, we want to educate our youth on the truth, not distort the truth.

Finally, the third film, *A Grand Life*. What's depicted there, of course, is not a grand life at all. Everything is taken in order to interest the undemanding viewer. One likes the harmonica and the gypsy songs. There is that. Another likes cabaret songs. There's that, too. A third likes a few discussions on diverse topics. And there's that. A fourth likes drinking—and in the film there's a worker you can't get to wake up unless he smells vodka and hears the clinking of glasses and then he quickly jumps up. There's that. There are amorous escapades, too. After all, viewers

What do the sins and deficiencies of *A Grand Life* consist of?

The film depicts only one minor episode in the first assault on the reconstruction of the Donbass, which does not give a correct picture of the actual range and significance of the reconstruction work carried out by the Soviet state in the Don basin. In addition, the restoration of the Donbass occupies a small part in the film, while the main attention is paid to the primitive depiction of all kinds of personal sufferings and scenes from daily life. In view of this, the film's content does not correspond to its title.

have all kinds of tastes. There's also a little about reconstruction, however, even though it's a film about the reconstruction of the Donbass the process of the Donbass's restoration takes up only one eighth, and it's all given in a toylike, humorous form. It's simply painful when you look, can it really be that our producers, who live among golden men, among heroes, can't depict them as they should but must necessarily dirty them? We have good workers, damn it! They showed themselves in the war, they came back from the war and should especially show themselves in the reconstruction. This film smells of the old ways, when instead of an engineer they put in an unskilled worker, as if to say, you're ours, worker, you're going to guide us, we don't need an engineer. They kick out the engineer, put in a simple worker, and he's supposedly doing the guiding. It's the same in this film, they make an old worker into a professor. The workers had moods like these in the first years of Soviet power, when the working class took power for the first time. That happened, but it was wrong. How much time has passed since then! The country has risen to unprecedented heights with the help of mechanization. We've started producing seven to eight times more coal than in the old days. Why? Because all labor has been mechanized, because coal-cutters are doing all the work. All the devices, taken together, comprise a system of mechanization. If it

Moreover, the film's title, *A Grand Life,* sounds like a mockery of Soviet reality.

The film obviously mixes up two different eras in the development of our industry. According to the level of technology and culture of production shown in *A Grand Life,* the picture reflects more the period of the Donbass's restoration after the end of the Civil War, not the modern Donbass with its advanced technology and culture created during the years of Stalin's Five Year Plans. The film's authors create a false impression for the viewer, as if the restoration of the Donbass mines after their liberation from the German aggressors and coal mining were being carried out in the Donbass not on the basis of modern advanced technology and the mechanization of labor processes but by the application of crude physical force, long since outdated technology, and conservative work methods. In this way the film distorts the prospects for the postwar reconstruction of our industry based on advanced technology and a high culture of production.

[. . .]

A Grand Life preaches backwardness, a lack of culture, and ignorance. The film's producers show in a completely unmotivated and wrong way the mass advancement to supervisory posts of technically illiterate workers with backward views and attitudes. The film's director and screenwriter didn't understand that in our coun-

weren't for mechanization, we would simply perish. All this has been achieved with the help of machines.

What kind of reconstruction is shown in the film where not a single machine figures? It's all as of old. People simply have not studied the matter and don't know what reconstruction means under our conditions. They've confused what took place after the Civil War, in 1918–1919, with what is taking place, say, in 1945–1946. They've confused one with the other.

People now say that the film needs fixing. I don't know how to do this. If it's technically possible, it should be done, but what will be left there? The gypsy stuff has to be tossed out. The fact that eight young girls happen to show up and turn everything around in the Donbass, that's a fairytale, that's something unthinkable. That has to be fixed, too. The fact that people are living in terrible conditions, almost out in the open, that the engineer in charge of the mine doesn't know where to sleep, all that will have to be thrown out. This may happen here and there, but it isn't typical. We've built entire towns in the Donbass, not all of that was blown up. If this film gets called the first assault on reconstruction, then interest will drop off, but in any case, this is not a grand life after the Second World War. If the film is called *A Grand Life,* then it's going to have to undergo cardinal changes. You're going to have to bring in other new actors (although the actry it is cultured, modern people who know what they're doing who are highly valued and boldly promoted, not backward, uncultured people, now that Soviet power has created its own intelligentsia, it's clumsy and absurd to depict the promotion of backward and uncultured people to supervisory posts as a positive phenomenon.

A Grand Life gives a false, distorted depiction of Soviet people. The workers and engineers who are restoring the Donbass are shown as backward, uncultured people with very low moral qualities. Most of their time the film's heroes spend doing nothing, engaged in idle talk and heavy drinking. According to the film's conception, the best people are the inveterate drunkards.

tors act pretty well). The whole spirit of haphazard work, as if we didn't need educated people, didn't need engineers—those stupidities have to be thrown out. What's left then? The film can't be released like this, and 4,700,000 rubles have gone to waste. If it can be fixed, fix it, please. But it's going to be very hard, everything has to be turned completely around. It will be a new film in essence. You watch, we suggested to Pudovkin that he fix his *Admiral Nakhimov,* he asked for six months, but he's evidently not going to be able, since he has to turn everything completely around. He approached this major problem lightly, and now his film still isn't ready, and he's essentially remaking it. Here too, everything is going to have to be turned completely around. Let them try, maybe they'll succeed.

As can be seen, the text of the official resolution was a kind of "corrected transcript" of Stalin's speech, which once again puts in question the definition of the era under consideration as "Zhdanovist."

Stalin took a lively interest in film. Not only because he ascribed to it a major ideological role, but also because the screen became for him (especially in the postwar years) nearly the sole projection of reality. Characteristic in this sense are the references to the "ignorance" of the directors, who are supposedly unfamiliar with "reality"—the reality Stalin "knew," having created it in his own imagination (be it the reconstruction of the Donbass or the times of Ivan the Terrible or of Admiral Nakhimov). On the other hand, Stalin demands "verisimilitude on the screen." Significant in this sense is the special resolution of the TsK Politburo, dated 30 January 1950, about a ban on the release of the film *Fishermen of the Caspian (Rybaki Kaspia).* This short documentary from the Nizhnevolzhskaia Film Studio was banned on orders from the Ministry of Cinematography. However, the matter was not simply brought up for consideration by the Politburo, rather a special text of the report was approved for publication in the central newspapers. As appears from this, the director Ia. Bliokh,

> on the basis of an approved screenplay for the short documentary *Fishermen of the Caspian,* in this film was supposed to truthfully show the wealth of the Caspian Sea as the Soviet Union's largest fishing base, to show the development of the state and kolkhoz fishing economy in the Caspian Sea, new advanced methods of fishing, and the application of mechanization in the fishing business.
>
> The director Bliokh was irresponsible and unconscientious toward the work assigned to him, he allowed crude dramatizations in the film, violating the frequent instructions he had on this score from the USSR Ministry of Cinematography on the impermissibility of dramatizations in documentary cinematography, thereby distorting real life by showing faked episodes. Thus, for instance, in showing sturgeon and beluga fishing, the director Bliokh used previously caught fish and artificially attempted to create the impression of real fishing, misleading with his dramatization the Soviet viewer, who in documentary cinematography is supposed to see life in its documentary precision. This hack approach to showing the labor of the fishermen of the Caspian Sea manifested by the director Bliokh led to other serious mistakes as well.
>
> Instead of a truthful display of the organization of labor among Caspian Sea fishermen, as well as advanced methods of fishing and fish processing, the film reproduces the old backward fishing technology based on manual labor. The short film does not show modern mechanized fishing, nor does it show the largest state fish processing plants equipped with modern, first-class technological equipment, or the high mechanization of fish processing technology.
>
> As a result of this unconscientious and hack approach to carrying out his important assignments, the director Bliokh created a short film that does not meet the high political and cultural demands of the Soviet viewer.[3]

One should not doubt that the pseudonym "Soviet viewer" conceals Stalin himself. This is given away not only by the text's style (with Stalin's favorite definition "hack"), but also by the familiar optics: the "false" episodes are those that are dramatized, whereas the "truthful" would be the pictures of "first-class technological equipment" not found in the film. In other words, the demand for verisimilitude instead of truth.

Stalin did not view cinema merely as a politician would. Let us recall his reply to Eisenstein, which was characteristic in this sense: "I'm not giving you instructions, I'm expressing the remarks of a viewer." Stalin did not consider himself a censor, but he did not consider himself a simple "Soviet viewer" either. He considered himself a legitimate co-author of the films, and, most importantly, their producer. This is why Stalin's influence is so distinct not only on the content of films but also on the politics of Soviet film production as a whole.

The postwar years went down in the history of Soviet cinema for their low yield. The small number of films produced in the country was explained not only economically, not only politically (censorship considerations: a smaller number of films is easier to monitor), but also "aesthetically." As is evident from the statements of his cited above, Stalin was utterly convinced of the principle, the fewer, the better. He thought that if there were a larger production of films, directors would do "hack work," and if they produced fewer pictures more rarely, then this small number would be "high quality." This idea was repeated by Stalin, as we recall, not only in connection with film but also in connection with literature (he justified the closing down of *Leningrad* specifically by the fact that the journal was printing "all kinds of nonsense" because there was simply not enough "high-quality material"). In the cinema, this approach ended in an abrupt cutback in film production.

On 16 December 1946, the Politburo passed a resolution "On major shortcomings in the organization of film production and mass facts of the squandering and theft of state funds in film studios," which was drawn up in the form of a resolution of the USSR Council of Ministers. The document gave an "economic basis" for the cutback in film production and established a system whereby the Ministry of Cinematography was supposed to "present for Government approval every full-length feature film." The system of "thematic plans" that had been approved by Stalin previously now was not only intensified but also interconnected with plans for the production and release of films which also could be changed only at the Government level.[4]

Every year, the "thematic production plans" approved by the Politburo became harsher and stricter, and a Politburo resolution dated 4 June 1948, "On the production plan for artistic, documentary, and genre films for 1948," contained the following preamble:

> The TsK VKP(b) believes that the film production plan for 1948 proposed for scrutiny by the TsK testifies to the fact that there is in the USSR Ministry of Cinematography an incorrect emphasis on releasing a large number of films to the detriment of their quality, as a result of which the ideological and artistic level of many motion pictures does

not meet the growing demands of Soviet viewers. The pursuit of quantity in films gives rise to the necessity of bringing into film production directors with little experience who put out weak pictures, on the production of which extremely large sums are spent that are not recouped by the proper income to the state from the running of the films due to the poor attendance of movie houses by viewers. The TsK VKP(b) feels it is necessary to decisively raise the quality of the films released by reducing their quantity and by bringing the best directorial and acting forces into the production of films.[5]

Later the deputy head of TsK Agitprop, Dmitry Shepilov, in his *Memoirs* (*Vospominania*), described the discussion of this draft Politburo resolution in Stalin's office (Shepilov considered all such discussions official sessions of the Politburo) as follows:

> At the Politburo session of 11 June 1948, during the consideration of the production plan for films, Stalin said approximately the following (I'm quoting from the notes I kept from that session): "The film ministry is carrying out an incorrect policy in film production. They keep trying to produce more and more pictures. Their expenditures are high. The waste great. They don't worry about their budget. While we could be getting 2 billion in net profit from the cinema. They want to make sixty films a year. That's not necessary. It's incorrect policy. We need four or five artistic films a year, but good ones, remarkable ones. Plus a few newsreels and popular science pictures. But we're going about cinema extensively, as if it were agriculture. We need to make fewer films, but good ones. And expand the cinema's network, print more copies. We can't compare with the United States in the cinema. They have completely different goals for cinema. There they make a lot of pictures and take in tremendous income. We have different goals. Here I'm looking at the production plan for films. What a lot of nonsense they've got planned! < . . . > Here they have *Night of the Commander* [*Noch' polkovodtsa*]. Why? It's pointless. They'll end up with nonsense. Or *Fellow Travelers* [*Sputniki*]. Pointless. Or *Tale of Tsar Saltan* [*Skazka o tsare Saltane*]. What do we need this for? The film about Matrosov came out badly. We shouldn't be letting the republics have their way, they're spending a lot of money on cinema. And what are they putting out? Here they want to make *Raid on the Carpathians* [*Reid na Karpaty*]. What for? Vershigora is going to lie. Or *Zaslonov*. What is that? A hymn to arbitrariness. Or a film about the Nakhimovites. What on earth can you say about the Nakhimovites? There are so many military themes. We need *A Great Force* [*Velikaia sila*]. I just don't like the director. It would be good if Pyriev took over. < . . . > In general, all the important pictures have to be en-

trusted to experienced directors. There's Romm, who's good, Pyriev, Aleksandrov, Ermler, Chiaureli. Entrust those to them. Men like that won't let us down. Give them the color films, too. That's an expensive trick. Kozintsev is good. Lukov needs to be driven out. Pudovkin is good. Here we have Bolshakov . . . going on and on about how we need workers promoted for the job, how we should be entrusting young people. Well, you can make experiments like this at your own expense, not the state's. As regards documentaries: we need a picture about Lenin. Only it should be given to Romm. But here we have Belyaev. I don't know Belyaev. Or give Pyriev the one about Lenin. . . ."[6]

Stalin's commentaries on the production plans for films (and each such review of plans for the coming year ended in drastic cutbacks) say what a real "Soviet manager," like a factory director or kolkhoz chairman, is made of. Compensation, actually, followed immediately: several times in the years 1948–1949 the Politburo passed special resolutions "On the release to the screen of foreign films from the trophy fund." These resolutions for screen release let out dozens of "trophy films" that fell into two categories: "for broad distribution" and "for restricted screenings." Moreover, each time it required "instructing the USSR Ministry of Cinematography (Com. Bolshakov), in conjunction with the TsK VKP(b) Propaganda and Agitation Department, to make the necessary editorial corrections in the films, after providing each film with an introductory text and painstakingly editing the subtitles."[7]

Stalin's demands on the cinema probably revealed more fully than anything else his attitude toward art as a whole. Here we see combined his political demands on the cinema as a means of propaganda (use of the screen for the purpose of advancing various political and ideological goals); his aesthetic preferences (the demand for "verisimilitude" and the simultaneous strict subordination of depicted reality to the "proper" reality—according to the formula of Socialist Realism: "the truth of life" and simultaneously "life in its revolutionary development"); and, finally, his economic pragmatism (the desire for the most economical production of a few "film masterpieces" a year and the necessity of turning a profit—flooding the screen with "trophy films"). On the basis of this kind of political-aesthetic and economic plan, Soviet cinema was doomed to extinction. And that is exactly what happened in the postwar decade.

CHAPTER TWENTY-THREE

"Moments Musicaux"

AS in other spheres of art, in music the era of late Stalinism continued the line marked out back in the 1930s. The pivotal point here was the famous TsK resolution, dated 10 February 1948, "On the opera *A Great Friendship* [*Velikaia druzhba*] by V. Muradeli." We know that on 5 January 1948, Stalin and a group of Politburo members attended the Bolshoi Theater and saw *Friendship of Nations* [*Druzhba narodov*], which evoked great distaste in the leader. The TsK apparatus immediately began work to "correct errors on the musical front" and seek out the guilty parties. The very next day, on 6 January, Zhdanov held a meeting on opera at the Bolshoi Theater. Two days later, a document came out in his name, which he sent to Stalin, Molotov, Beria, Mikoyan, Malenkov, and Voznesensky:

· 178 ·

Explanatory memorandum from TsK VKP(b) Propaganda and Agitation Administration Deputy Head D. T. Shepilov to TsK VKP(b) Secretary A. A. Zhdanov concerning the circumstances surrounding permission for production of V. I. Muradeli's opera *A Great Friendship*." AP RF, f. 3, op. 35, d. 32, ll. 92–93. Copy. Typewritten.
9 January 1948

To TsK VKP(b) Secretary Com. A. A. Zhdanov
The attached draft notes addressed to you were prepared by the Arts Section of the Propaganda Administration (Com. Lebedev) and presented to Com. Aleksandrov.

As can be seen from the text, the draft notes prepared by Com. Lebedev did not fully disclose the politically mistaken content of the opera *Commissar Extraordinary* [*Chrezvychainyi komissar*] (*A Great Friendship*) and the fundamental shortcomings of its musical-vocal forms. However, the draft notes did characterize the opera as faulty and from this assessment the appropriate conclusions were drawn.

As has now become clear, this note from Com. Aleksandrov was not sent to you and on the questions it poses no measures were taken to ban work on the opera or seize the opera's published score.

D. Shepilov

This self-vindicating letter accompanied the document itself, which matured in the TsK apparatus and was not put in motion until Stalin himself got involved in the matter.

· 179 ·

Draft memorandum from the TsK VKP(b) Propaganda and Agitation Administration to TsK VKP(b) Secretary A. A. Zhdanov on a ban on the production of V. I. Muradeli's *A Great Friendship*. [No earlier than 1 August 1947, and no later than 9 January 1948]. AP RF, f. 3, op. 35, d. 32, ll. 86–88. Original. Typewritten.

To TsK VKP(b) Secretary Com. A. A. Zhdanov

On instruction from the Committee on Arts Affairs under the USSR Council of Ministers, the USSR Muzfond publishing house has released 400 copies of the score (libretto and music) of V. Muradeli's opera *Commissar Extraordinary* (libretto by G. Mdivani). This opera is being prepared for performance at the present time by about twenty of the country's opera theaters, including the Bolshoi Theater of the USSR. This opera will be the principal work staged in opera theaters for the thirtieth anniversary of the October Socialist Revolution.

The Propaganda Administration has familiarized itself with the content of this opera and feels that it is faulty and gives a distorted notion of the Bolsheviks' struggle in the northern Caucasus in the years 1919–1920 and of the revolutionary activities of Com. Ordzhonikidze during those years.

The content of this opera in brief is the following: a young Lezgin, Murtaz, and a Cossack girl, Galina, fall in love at first sight. As he is trying to get into the encampment for a tryst with Galina, Murtaz kills a sentry and hides in Galina's house. Cossacks appear at the dwelling led by the White

Guard officer Pomazov. They are looking for Murtaz and express their hatred for the mountain dwellers who have risen up at Ordzhonikidze's call to the defense of Soviet power. Pomazov is calling for a struggle against the mountain dwellers and for the murder of Ordzhonikidze (the commissar extraordinary). Galina's mother discovers Murtaz in the house by accident. Galina's furious father, Fedor, and the other Cossacks fall upon Murtaz. However, Pomazov, learning of Murtaz's love for Galina, suggests to Murtaz that he kill Ordzhonikidze, for which he promises to arrange his marriage to Galina. The entire specified scene (chorus, orchestra) creates a distorted notion, as if all the Cossacks rose up as a monolithic reactionary mass against Soviet power.

Murtaz sets out for the mountains, where in his father's hut he meets Ordzhonikidze, who is calling upon the mountain dwellers to rise up. In contrast to the previous scene, the mountain peoples are shown in this scene as a unified revolutionary mass. The opera's authors show no class differentiation among the mountain dwellers. And if in the previous scene all the Russians, in the grip of the somber emotion of vengeance, are depicted only in black, then all the mountain dwellers are shown in idyllic tones, as bearers of a bright, progressive principle.

That night, Murtaz's father has him guide Ordzhonikidze out of the village. En route, Murtaz fires at Ordzhonikidze, but misses. In a cave where mountain shepherds are sheltering from a storm, Murtaz shows up, followed by Ordzhonikidze. To Murtaz's surprise, Ordzhonikidze extends his hand to him and says: "You have a strong arm, comrade, but a bad aim." After talking with the mountain dwellers, Ordzhonikidze goes to bed, demonstratively turning his back to Murtaz. In the next scene, Murtaz repents his action and true to his love for Galina once again comes to the Cossack encampment. For incomprehensible reasons, Galina's father greets Murtaz joyously, from his short aria we learn about his unexpected defection to Ordzhonikidze's side. However, Fedor's and Murtaz's joy is premature: Pomazov shows up and demands that Murtaz keep his promise to kill the commissar, threatening otherwise to take his revenge on Galina. The final scene depicts "The Gathering of the Peoples," of which the bulk shown are dzhigit [skilled horse riders] mountain dwellers and the rest are a group of Cossacks and Red Army soldiers who have turned up seemingly from nowhere. Everyone joyously greets Ordzhonikidze. Pomazov is present, and seeing that Murtaz has not kept his promise, fires at Ordzhonikidze himself. Murtaz shields the commissar with his body and dies from Pomazov's bullet.

In this concluding scene, the authors show that the leading revolutionary force is not the Russian people but the mountain dwellers (Lezgins and Ossetians). With the exception of the young girl Galina, who participates only in the development of the love intrigue, we do not meet a single positive Russian character in the opera. Ordzhonikidze is developed not as the leader of the Bolshevik-oriented mountain-dwelling and Cossack poor, not as the organizer of partisan struggle in Denikin's rear, as actually happened, but merely as the leader of the mountain dwellers. In addition, in several arias Ordzhonikidze mentions that he is the envoy of Lenin and Stalin.

It should be noted as well that if the music characterizing the commissar and the mountain dwellers makes broad use of national melodies and is, on the whole, successful, the musical characterization of the Russians lacks any national coloring, is pale, and one often hears alien oriental intonations.

For my part, I would consider it essential to confiscate the published scores of *Commissar Extraordinary* and instruct the Committee on Arts Affairs (Com. Khrapchenko) to ban work on the opera based on the published score.

G. Aleksandrov

Thus, storm clouds began gathering over Muradeli's opera even before the leader attended the Bolshoi Theater. However, the day after Shepilov's explanatory note to the TsK, a four-day (10–13 January) "conference of figures in Soviet music" opened, in which the leading Soviet composers and musicians took part.[1] At this conference (minutes of the meeting were published at the time) an argument broke out between the song writers, who defended the "national traditions" of the officially supported "melodic" "Russian national music" (Vladimir Zakharov, Tikhon Khrennikov, et al.), and composers whom Zhdanov accused of formalism and of being "antipopular" (Dmitry Shostakovich, Sergei Prokofiev, Aram Khachaturian, Nikolai Miaskovsky, Vissarion Shebalin). The latter held leading positions in the Organizing Committee of the USSR Union of Composers. The result of the conference was a TsK Politburo resolution, dated 26 January 1948, "On a change in leadership of the Committee on Arts Affairs under the USSR Council of Ministers and of the Organizing Committee of the USSR Union of Soviet Composers." This resolution routed the Composers' Union's Organizing Committee and organized a new one, which did not include any "Formalist composers" (Tikhon Khrennikov and Vladimir Zakharov were placed at the head of the new Organizing Committee); the same changes were made in the Music Section of the Committee on Stalin Prizes.

This Politburo resolution stated:

The Organizing Committee of the Union of Soviet Composers was pursuing a fundamentally incorrect line in the sphere of Soviet music. Instead of developing Soviet music in the spirit of Socialist Realism, lofty ideas, and the people, and improving the artistic mastery of Soviet composers, the Organizing Committee was transformed into a hotbed of the Formalistic, antipopular trend in Soviet music, which has been condemned by the Party and which has inflicted serious damage on Soviet music's development. The Organizing Committee not only failed to help creative discussions, criticism, and self-criticism develop among Soviet composers but, on the contrary, cultivated ways alien to the Soviet public of restricting criticism and self-criticism and facilitated unrestrained praise of a small group of composers in the interest of friendly relations. In view of all the above, the Organizing Committee of the Union of Soviet Composers and its presidium shall be disbanded.[2]

What came next is well known. Two weeks later, *Pravda* published the TsK resolution on the opera *A Great Friendship,* which concluded the cycle of attacks against avant-garde music that began in 1936 with "Muddle Instead of Music" [*Sumbur vmesto muzyki*], again in *Pravda*.[3] In this purely aesthetic sense, according to Mikhail Svetlov, "The revolution has ended at the point where it began."

CHAPTER TWENTY-FOUR

"The Revolution Has Ended at the Point Where It Began"

Late Stalinism caps the process that got under way in the 1930s and that has become known as "The Great Retreat," a name given it by Nicholas Timasheff in his classic work so titled (1946). We have observed this process over the course of the entire Stalinist era. In the postwar years, however, it received a mighty boost thanks above all to the war and the victory. This meant not only a pragmatic return to the ideological doctrine of "Great Russia" but also the total rejection after the war of many elements of Marxist class rhetoric that were still characteristic for the 1930s. The campaign "against toadying to the West" and "in affirmation of Russian priorities" in culture and science that was unleashed in the years 1947–1948 was brought to its conclusion in 1949 with the "struggle against cosmopolitanism," which was blatantly anti-Semitic in nature. The final campaign lasted all the way up until the well-known "Doctors' Plot" and Stalin's death, which, as many sources confirm, saved the Jews from mass deportation from the European part of the country. Although these tendencies made themselves felt in open form after the war, they were already palpable during the war. Highly characteristic in this sense is a letter from film director Mikhail Romm, which he sent to Stalin in early 1943:

· 180 ·

Letter from M. I. Romm to I. V. Stalin.
8 January 1943, Tashkent

Dear Iosif Vissarionovich!

I have long wanted to write you this letter. However, conscious of what majestic world-scale labors rested on your shoulders, I simply could not bring myself to address you. The matter has gone so far, however, that I cannot avoid this letter.

Dear Iosif Vissarionovich! Have you ever asked yourself why during the war you never saw a single picture by Eisenstein, Dovzhenko, Ermler, Kozintsev and Trauberg, myself, Aleksandrov, Raizman (*Mashen'ka* was begun long before the war), Kheifits, and Zarkhi (*Sukhe-Bator*, too, is essentially a prewar movie), and several other major artists? After all, it cannot be that these men, so closely bound to the Party, cultivated by the Party, after creating before the war such pictures as *The Battleship Potemkin* [*Bronenosets "Potemkin"*], *Alexander Nevsky*, *The Great Citizen* [*Velikii grazhdanin*], *Shchors*, *Trilogy About Maxim* [*Trilogia o Maksime*], *Lenin in October* [*Lenin v oktiabre*], *Lenin in 1918* [*Lenin v 1918*], *Deputy from the Baltic* [*Deputat Baltiki*], and so on, that these men would not or could not work for the homeland at the most serious time. No, what has happened is that your beloved offspring—Soviet cinematography—is right now in an unprecedented state of disarray, distress, and decline.

I'll begin with myself, although the matter, in essence, is not about me. A little more than two years ago I was appointed artistic director of cinematography. [Romm has in mind the fact that he was appointed Deputy Chair of the Council on Artistic Questions of the Committe on Cinematic Affairs] Simultaneously, other major directors were appointed artistic directors of studios. This endeavor, undoubtedly dictated by the Party's TsK and you personally, we, the creative workers of cinematography, greeted with enthusiasm, we saw it as a new era in cinema. We took up this hard and thankless work so unfamiliar to us, and I'll be blunt, by the sweat of our brow we made up for the innumerable mistakes made before us by Bolshakov and thus spanned the gap that for years had separated the leadership of cinematography from the main body of creative workers. And lately now I've found myself in an incomprehensible situation. I am working in an atmosphere of blatant ill will on the part of Bolshakov and his deputy Lukashev. Moreover, I have got the impression that I am in tacit disfavor. All the most important questions directly affecting artistic leadership are being decided not only apart from me but without even informing me of the decisions. Without my participation, screenplays are being approved, pictures put into production, directors appointed, without my participation pictures are being approved, rejected, or remade, without my participation workers in the artistic organs of cinematography are being appointed and replaced, including the artistic directors of studios and even workers in my apparatus. To all the questions of principle and practice I have posed, Com. Bolshakov has not felt it necessary even to reply, and among other things I did not receive an answer to my question of when I will get the chance to make a picture and exactly which one.

It has reached the point that the workers around me look at me with disbelief, unable to comprehend what is going on. Directors, cameramen, and actors come to me with many essential creative questions. I can't give them any answers, since my instructions often lead to total disorientation due to discrepancies with the instructions from Bolshakov, which are unknown to me and are made apart from me.

If it were only a matter of me—only of my own difficult condition—then perhaps I would not have had the nerve to write you in these times. But we are not talking about me personally. Thus, the artistic director of our major Alma-Ata film studio, Ermler, is in the same lamentable situation. Everything I have written about myself applies in full measure to him, too. The most important issues of artistic practice for the studio he runs are being decided without his participation. It has reached the point that by order of Bolshakov Ermler's deputies for artistic direction, Trauberg and Raizman, were removed, and Pyriev was appointed in their place, moreover no one consulted Ermler on this matter, no one explained to him the reasons for this exceptional undertaking or even found it necessary to inform him of this. Being in Tashkent, Ermler had a talk with me. His morale is extremely low.

The same thing is being experienced not only by artistic directors but also by a number of other major directors. Today I received a tragic letter from the creator of the *Trilogy About Maxim*—Kozintsev. He complains of unbearable treatment, total disorientation, speaks about how he feels like a "former" man and is simply going to perish. His story is truly outrageous, and not his alone.

Dear Iosif Vissarionovich! We ask ourselves, what's going on? What offense was committed against the Party and Soviet power by Ermler, Romm, Kozintsev, Trauberg, and the many others whose names I am not mentioning only because they have not spoken with me personally or written to me, but whose situation and mood I know all too well. Among us there is not a single person who has not asked many times to go to Moscow and the front. But we continue to sit in the rear, cut off from the central organs of the Party, receiving from the Committee not guidance but orders, bureaucratic shouts, and streams of incomprehensible and ill-willed instructions. A gloomy atmosphere of slander, apparatus secrecy, and bureaucratism, which had disappeared over the last four or five years, is beginning to be reborn in new forms with all its typical "charms": favorites, groveling, mysterious shifting around, conceit, petty tyranny, and vindictiveness. We look with envy upon workers in other areas who are living a full, joyous life, despite all the deprivations of wartime, giving their full-fledged labor to the homeland.

[...]

I will not allow myself to take up your attention with an enumeration of the many facts illustrating the bureaucratism, organizational confusion, formal resolution of questions, and so on. People are going to perish. The most prominent directors, whose names are known not only to any Pioneer in our country but also in America and England and throughout the world—these directors find themselves in such a state that, if nothing changes literally in the near future, the country may lose these artists for good. It may already be too late to get them back on their feet. As for our young people, it's already too late to help here, I think. We have lost half of our scarce replacements.

I beg of you, Iosif Vissarionovich, to summon to Moscow, to the Party's TsK, the artistic directors of the major studios: Ermler, Yutkevich, Chiaureli, Aleksandrov, as well as me and the directors Eisenstein, Kozintsev, and Trauberg. Ukrainian cinematography can be represented at this meeting by Dovzhenko, who is in Moscow.

I would close my letter at this, for I am convinced that such a meeting would bring clarity to all questions and give us political and creative guidance for a long time to come. But there is one more question which I have no one to ask except you. In the last few months, there have been fifteen to twenty shifts and removals of important workers in cinematography (artistic directors, members of the editorial board of the Screenplay Studio, deputy directors of film studios, heads of screenplay departments, etc.). All these shifts and removals cannot be explained by any political or practical considerations. But since all the workers removed were Jews and the people who replaced them were not Jews, then after the first period of disbelief some people began ascribing these shifts to anti-Jewish trends in the leadership of the Committee on Cinematography Affairs. Monstrous though this sounds, more and more new instructions from the Committee daily add fodder to these conversations, which have simply become hard to dispute.

Checking myself, I became convinced that in the last few months I have very often had occasion to be reminded of my Jewish heritage, although in twenty-five years of Soviet power I have never given it a thought, for I was born in Irkutsk, grew up in Moscow, speak only Russian, and have always felt myself a Russian, a full-fledged Soviet man. If even I am having these kinds of thoughts, that means things are very bad in cinematography, especially if we recall that we are waging a war against fascism, which has drawn anti-Semitism on its banner.

Dear Iosif Vissarionovich! Twice in my life I have turned to you in a difficult moment. If I am in any way wrong now, if there is something I don't understand, I beg of you to explain to me, a member of the Party and a director, the error I have made.

Forgive me for taking up your time, which is so valuable for all progressive mankind, with my letter.

    Stalin Prize laureate
    Mikhail Romm

The "Russian question" in Soviet cinema that arose during the war is only one episode[1] of what had gone on in other spheres of art as well. It should be pointed out that at this time anti-Semitism was still quasi-official. A definite shift, which virtually legalized state anti-Semitism, occurred in connection with the so-called Jewish Anti-Fascist Committee case. Beginning in late 1948, one secret Politburo resolution after another was passed aimed at shutting down all organs of Jewish culture in the country. Thus, on 25 November 1948, the Politburo passed a resolution shutting down the Der Emes publishing house, "in connection with the fact that the circle of readers of literature in the Yiddish language is extremely insignificant and most of the books put out by the Der Emes publishing house are not in distribution."[2] On 8 February 1949, a Politburo resolution was passed "On the disbanding of associations of Jewish writers and on stopping publication of miscellanies in the Yiddish language."[3] The day after this resolution, on 9 and 10 February 1949, a closed Party meeting was held at the USSR Writers Union at which Writers Union Secretary Anatoly Sofronov gave a pogrom-like, frankly anti-Semitic report, "On a certain antipatriotic group of theater critics." There it was decided to examine issues of membership in the Party "for participants in the antipatriotic group of critics," who were accused of a "conciliatory attitude toward the criminal activities" of the writers and poets Itzik Fefer, Perets Markish, and Lev Kvitko, the literary critic Isaak Nusinov, and others who had been arrested in the case of the Jewish Anti-Fascist Committee. On 9 March 1949, at a Party meeting, all the "antipatriot-critics" were expelled from the Party.[4] Politburo archives preserved not only the documents testifying to the participation of the top Party leadership in unleashing the anti-Semitic campaign but also of writers who took an active part in slandering their colleagues. Characteristic in this sense is a letter from USSR Writers Union General Secretary

Aleksandr Fadeev, in which he talks about two of his colleagues from the Writers Union:

· 181 ·

Statement from SSP General Secretary A. A. Fadeev to the TsK VKP(b) secretaries on the "antipatriotic group of critics" participants B. L. Dairedzhiev and I. L. Altman. 21 September 1949. AP RF, f. 3, op. 34, d. 189, ll. 12–15. Original. Typewritten.

21 September 1949

To the VKP(b) TsK
To Comrade I. V. Stalin
To Comrade G. M. Malenkov
To Comrade M. A. Suslov
To Comrade G. M. Popov
To Comrade M. F. Shkiryatov

In connection with the exposure of groups of antipatriotic critics in the Union of Soviet Writers and the All-Russian Theatrical Society, I draw the attention of the TsK VKP(b) to two representatives of this criticism in need of additional political verification, inasmuch as many facts about them lead one to assume that these are two-faced men.

B. L. Dairedzhiev, VKP(b) member since 1919. Dairedzhiev made his appearance in literary criticism during the existence of RAPP, as an active "figure" in the anti-Party group Litfront, whose leaders were enemies of the people Kostrov, Bespalov, and Zonin. In the early 1930s, he published a Trotskyite book, *On the Sandbar* [*Na otmeli*], with a foreword by the now-arrested A. Zonin, a book containing slanderous assertions about the degeneration of the Party. It's hard to imagine how Dairedzhiev held onto his Party card during those years, being the author of this hostile book.

Now that he has been expelled from the Party, Dairedzhiev has attempted to vindicate himself by saying that the book needs to be approached historically and that in its day it was not judged in the same way, as proof of which he cited excerpts from an article of the period printed in the RAPP journal. After checking, it came out that Dairedzhiev had quoted excerpts from an article by enemy of the people A. Selivanovsky.

After publication of *On the Sandbar*, Dairedzhiev disappeared for a few years from the pages of the press and surfaced shortly before the war, when he presented to the Writers Union a disparaging, ultraleft book about Sholokhov that never saw the light of day.

During the Great Patriotic War, Dairedzhiev again showed no signs of life, but after the war he began to appear rather actively in the press and at meetings with articles that aimed to discredit the themes of Soviet patriotism in literature and overthrow many of the best works of Soviet literature.

In 1948, I removed from a collection of critical works Dairedzhiev's essay about Belinsky, in which, claiming to explain Belinsky to the modern day, Dairedzhiev concentrated all his false pathos on Belinsky's struggle with "kvass [Russian populist] patriotism," casting aspersions in passing on contemporary criticism for not struggling against "kvass patriotism." With its methods of dragging out hostile little ideas, this essay by Dairedzhiev bears a thoroughly double-dealing nature.

Like several other representatives of antipatriotic criticism, Dairedzhiev preferred to pursue his occupation somewhere far from Moscow in the literature of one of the fraternal republics, counting on it having weaker oversight over his activities. Thus for several months Dairedzhiev "worked" in Tadzhikistan, where he subjected to ridicule and disarray performances of the Russian theater in Stalinabad based on the plays of Soviet playwrights and supported inside the theater people who held to the same line. The newspaper *Communist of Tadzhikistan* [*Kommunist Tadzhikistana*] of 10 April 1949, revealed this hostile activity of Dairedzhiev's in a major article, "Decisively Expose Rootless Cosmopolitans and Their Accomplices" ["Reshitel'no razoblachit' bezrodnykh kosmopolitov i ikh posobnikov"].

Having been exposed in all these actions, Dairedzhiev refuses to admit anything and slithers out of any criticism.

I. L. Altman was born in Orgeev (Bessarabia). His career began with the Left SRs in the years 1917–1918. He joined the VKP(b) as of 1920. He belonged to the anti-Party group in literature, Litfront. He began his literary activity with a major work on Lessing in which he set forth his view of the West's primacy over Russia in all spheres of ideology. Having been before the war an editor of *Theater* [*Teatr*], he pursued a line leading to the discrediting of Soviet dramaturgy on modern themes, together with the critics Gurvich, Yuzovsky, and so on, and in particular printed Borshchagovsky's disparaging article against Korneichuk's play *In Ukraine's Steppes* [*V stepiakh Ukrainy*]. For distorting the Party line in matters of theater and dramaturgy, he was removed from his position as editor of *Theater* by a resolution of the TsK VKP(b).

In 1937, while I. L. Altman was head of the literature and art department at *Izvestia*, he received a severe reprimand for a dubious "typo" in *Izvestia* (in 1944 the reprimand was lifted).

The Secretariat of the Union of Soviet Writers was unable to clarify the nature of the conflict in which during the Great Patriotic War I. Altman was removed from his job in the political organs and army press and discharged from the army before war's end.

In his literary criticism and public activities of the postwar years, Altman occupied a double-dealing position, while depicting himself in oral conversations as an enemy of antipatriotic criticism, nowhere in the press or at meetings did he speak out against them, slithering like a snake between the antipatriotic line he in fact supported and the Party statement of the issue. Thanks to this double-dealing line, Altman managed to create in the literary world a notion of his supposedly greater closeness to the Party line than that held by his cosmopolitan friends, although in fact he was following a much more cleverly masked hostile line.

We need to verify additionally the facts of Altman's close contact with bourgeois Jewish nationalists in the Jewish theater and in the Moscow section of Jewish writers, inasmuch as Altman's close connection with these circles is widely known in the literary world. Com. A. E. Korneichuk has informed me that Altman by private means, taking advantage of his familiarity with and connections among prominent figures in literature and art, distributed subscriptions to the Jewish theater, i.e., actively supported this artificial method of assistance for the theater by means of "private philanthropy" rather than by improving its repertoire and the quality of its performances.

Like Dairedzhiev, Altman, having been exposed for his hostile literary-critical activities, is not admitting to his actions and is trying to slither out of criticism.

At the present time, by decision of the Party organization of the Union of Soviet Writers, Dairedzhiev and Altman have been expelled from the Party and are "struggling" at higher levels for a repeal of the decision of the SSP Party organization.

For my part I feel that there is no place for Dairedzhiev and Altman in the Party and I ask the TsK VKP(b) to allow the Secretariat of the Union of Soviet Writers to raise before the Presidium the issue of expelling Dairedzhiev and Altman from the Writers Union.

A. Fadeev

The Jewish Theater mentioned in the letter was also shut down in late 1949. The reasons for the shutdown are by now familiar: "The theater has not justified itself in the financial respect and cannot operate on a self-financing basis in the future. < ... > The financial troubles of the Moscow Jewish Theater can be explained by the completely unsatisfactory attendance at its performances. The theater has a limited contingent at viewers < ... > the theater can put on only evening performances for adult viewers, since children do not attend the Jewish theater and morning performances do not have good box office returns. Nor does the Jewish Theater have opportunities to tour in other cities."[5]

Meanwhile, in 1949, Stalin was still not prepared to take the decisive step with respect to Soviet Jews. For the next three years the balancing act continued—all the way up to the beginning of the Doctors' Plot in January 1953, when a situation was created in the country such that the Jewish pogroms could begin. The anti-Semitic campaign was unleashed rather half-heartedly, but simultaneously prominent representatives of Jewish culture continued to take active part in official life. Above all we are referring to Ilya Ehrenburg. His fate in connection with the so-called the Jewish Anti-Fascist Committee Affair, whose members were accused of spying for English, American, and Israeli intelligence, was decided by Stalin. In a list presented to the leader by USSR State Security Minister V. Abakumov in early 1949 of people selected for arrest in this case, Ehrenburg's name was one of the first. "According to agent reports"—it mentioned in the list in particular—"while in Spain in 1937, Ehrenburg in conversation with the French writer and Trotskyite André Malraux made hostile attacks on Comrade Stalin. . . . During the period 1940–1947, as a result of measures carried out by the Cheka, Ehrenburg's anti-Soviet statements against the policy of the VKP(b) and the Soviet state were recorded." However, after checking off many other names on the list and writing the first letters of the word "Ar[rest]," opposite Ehrenburg's name Stalin left only an odd half-question mark. Next to it was a note from Stalin's personal secretary A. Poskrebyshev: "Com. Abakumov informed."[6] Ehrenburg's name continued to figure in Politburo materials—by special resolutions he was added to all kinds of delegations going abroad, to the Presidium of the Committee for the Defense of Peace, and so on. By doing this Stalin took advantage of Ehrenburg's authority with evidently one sole purpose—to support the appearance of an absence of state anti-Semitism in the country. It is worth noting that it was Ehrenburg who several years later coined the one word that will forever remain the sign of the era that followed immediately after Stalin's death: "The Thaw."

Notes

PART ONE: INTRODUCTION

1. A. Lunacharsky, "Iskusstvo, molodezh' i zadachi khudozhestvennoi raboty sredi molodezhi" [Art, youth, and the tasks of artistic work among youth], in *Komsomol, na front iskusstva! Materialy pervogo vsesoiuznogo soveshchania po khudozhestvennoi rabote sredi molodezhi* [Komsomol, to the art front! Materials from the first all-union conference on artistic work among youth] (Moscow, 1929), p. 29.

CHAPTER 1. "PROHIBIT TRAVEL . . ."

1. RGASPI, f. 17, op. 3, d. 21, l. 3.
2. RGASPI, f. 17, op. 3, d. 26, l. 2.
3. V. I. Lenin, *Polnoe sobranie sochineny v 55 tomakh* [Complete works], vol. 51 (Moscow, 1975), p. 694.
4. RGASPI, f. 17, op. 3, d. 160, l. 4.
5. RGASPI, f. 17, op. 3, d. 161, l. 2.
6. RGASPI, f. 17, op. 3, d. 161, l. 2.
7. RGASPI, f. 17, op. 3, d. 49, l. 3.
8. RGASPI, f. 17, op. 3, d. 161, l. 2.
9. RGASPI, f. 17, op. 3, d. 187, l. 1.
10. RGASPI, f. 17, op. 3, d. 187, l. 2.

CHAPTER 2. "THE UTTERLY INDECENT PROPOSAL TO PRESERVE THE BOLSHOI THEATER"

1. [Document footnote:] For example, pay for themselves by having opera singers and ballerinas participate in all different kinds of concerts and such.
2. RGASPI, f. 17, op. 3, d. 251, l. 4.
3. AP RF, f. 3, op. 35, d. 4, ll. 8–10.
4. RGASPI, f. 17, op. 3, d. 253, l. 4.

5. RGASPI, f. 17, op. 3, d. 261, l. 4.

6. The honorary title "academic" was awarded to theaters deemed exemplary. Usually there were institutes or (if they were opera theaters) conservatories attached to them.

7. RGASPI, f. 17, op. 3, d. 319, l. 3.

8. The workers' strip was a section in a theater set aside for workers, where tickets were either free or heavily subsidized.

9. RGASPI, f. 17, op. 3, d. 518, l. 2.

10. RGASPI, f. 17, op. 3, d. 785, l. 7.

11. The concept of the "Great Retreat" was advanced and argued in Nicholas Timasheff, *The Great Retreat: The Growth and Decline of Communism in Russia* (New York, 1946).

CHAPTER 3. ORGANIZING THE "ARTISTIC MILIEU"

1. RGASPI, f. 17, op. 3, d. 302, l. 2.
2. RGASPI, f. 17, op. 3, d. 304, ll. 4, 12.
3. RGASPI, f. 17, op. 3, d. 308, l. 5.
4. RGASPI, f. 17, op. 3, d. 312, l. 4.
5. RGASPI, f. 17, op. 112, d. 608, l. 4.
6. RGASPI, f. 17, op. 3, d. 487, l. 3.
7. RGASPI, f. 79, op. 1, d. 293, l. 1.
8. RGASPI, f. 79, op. 1, d. 293, l. 1.
9. RGASPI, f. 17, op. 60, d. 805, ll. 46–46v.

CHAPTER 4. THE ORGANIZATION OF PROLETARIAN ART

1. Entry of 9 December 1926 in Walter Benjamin, *Moscow Diary*, ed. Gary Smith, translated by Richard Sieburth (Cambridge, Mass.: Harvard University Press, 1986), p. 15.

2. RGASPI, f. 17, op. 3, d. 655, l. 6.

3. RGASPI, f. 17, op. 113, d. 341, l. 3.

4. RGASPI, f. 17, op. 3, d. 697, l. 10.

5. There is a file in the M. I. Kalinin collection: "Materials on the accusation of anti-Semitism against GABT [State Academic Bolshoi Theater] director Golovanov" (RGASPI, f. 78, op. 1, d. 294), which tells the story of this issue. The file includes numerous issues of *Komsomolskaia pravda* (Komsomol truth) from between 5 April and 12 May 1928, aimed against N. S. Golovanov, and other materials. The conflict at GABT became so acute that the Golovanov matter was considered three times in the Politburo. The first time, on 10 January 1929, in connection with the 25 December 1928 issue of *Komsomolskaia pravda*, it was decided: "a) to deem that the revived campaign of persecution and boycott against Golovanov, who has already borne his punishment for past mistakes, is not justified by the circumstances of the case and is incorrect, b) to propose to *Komsomolskaia pravda* and all other organs of the Soviet press (*Pravda, Izvestia, Rabochaia Moskva* [Workers' Moscow], *Rabochaia gazeta* [Workers' newspaper], etc.) that they not allow this kind of campaign to go ahead" (RGASPI, f. 17, op. 3, d. 721, l.

4). On 15 December 1929, Stalin once again raised the issue "On Golovanov" in the Politburo. The order said: "Instruct a commission made up of Comrades Kaganovich, Bubnov, and Shkiryatov to examine the issue at the base of the exchange of opinions in the Politburo. Com. Kaganovich shall convene the commission" (f. 17, op. 3, d. 768, l. 1). The last instruction is dated 30 December. It says: "Instruct the TsK Secretariat to examine the proposal of Com. Kaganovich's commission" (f. 17, op. 3, d. 771, l. 6). On 5 January 1930, the TsK Secretariat resolved: "a) to state that the government's resolution halting the campaign of persecution and boycott against Golovanov has not been implemented; b) to indicate to Comrades Raskolnikov and Pshebyshevsky that they have not taken any measures to implement the government's resolution, and c) to require Narkompros to take all necessary measures to ensure elementary working conditions in the conservatory, Sofil, etc." (f. 17, op. 113, d. 812, l. 17).

CHAPTER 5. "GORKY, WHOM NO ONE TAKES SERIOUSLY IN POLITICS"

1. RGASPI, f. 17, op. 3, d. 304, l. 4.
2. RGASPI, f. 17, op. 33, d. 243, l. 1.
3. RGASPI, f. 17, op. 3, d. 272, l. 2.
4. RGASPI, f. 17, op. 3, d. 301, ll. 6–12.
5. RGASPI, f. 17, op. 3, d. 660, l. 4.
6. RGASPI, f. 17, op. 3, d. 687, l. 1.
7. Ivan Gronsky, *Iz proshlogo . . . Vospominania* [From the past . . . Reminiscences] (Moscow, 1991), pp. 151–152.

CHAPTER 6. WORK WITH THE "ANTI-SOVIET INTELLIGENTSIA"

1. RGASPI, f. 17, op. 112, d. 474, l. 4.
2. RGASPI, f. 17, op. 3, d. 514, l. 3.
3. RGASPI, f. 17, op. 113, d. 728, ll. 229–229v.
4. RGASPI, f. 17, op. 113, d. 727, l. 12.
5. On 27 May 1926, Glavlit sent the following circular around to the publishing houses: "Secret. Henceforth you are not to allow works by B. Pilnyak in the thick Party-Soviet magazines and collections and you are to cross the name of said writer off the list of collaborators for these magazines. Head of Glavlit (Lebedev-Poliansky)." See A. Blium, "'Zvezda' v gody Bol'shogo terrora: Khronika repressivnoi tsensuroi (po materialam sekretnykh doneseny Lengorlita i Glavlita)" [*Star* in the years of the great terror: A chronicle of repressive censorship (from materials in secret reports of Lengorlit and Glavlit)], *Star*, no. 11 (1993): 171.
6. On the history of the story's publication, see T. F. Pavlova, "'Pil'niak zhul'ichaet i obmanyvaet nas . . .' (K istorii publikatsii 'Povesti nepogashennoi luny' B. Pil'niaka)" ['Pilnyak is behaving like a scoundrel and deceiving us . . .' (Toward a History of the Publication of 'Tale of the Unextinguished Moon' by B. Pilnyak)], in: *"Iskliuchit' vsiakie upominania . . .": Ocherki sovetskoi tsenzury* ["Exclude any mention . . .": Sketches of Soviet censorship] (Minsk, 1995), pp. 65–75.
7. RGASPI, f. 17, op. 3, d. 590, l. 4.
8. RGASPI, f. 17, op. 3, d. 655, l. 6.

9. On 24 November 1927, TsKK VKP(b) Secretary N. M. Yanson had informed Stalin that "the investigation . . . led to Com. Lunacharsky. However, since Com. Lunacharsky is not in Moscow at the present time and we are not going to be able to question him, we will have to postpone until his return from abroad." After the explanation that took place on 30 December 1927, the TsKK VKP(b) Partkollegia resolved "to indicate to Com. Lunacharsky that the TsK VKP(b) Politburo's resolution was divulged because he had informed theater workers of the upcoming viewing of the play by members of the Politburo commission." This finding against the people's commissar of education was approved by the Politburo on 16 February 1928 (prot. no. 19, p. 18) (AP RF, f. 3, op. 34, d. 221, ll. 11–12).

10. A letter from Glavrepertkom Chairman V. Yu. Mordvinkin to S. N. Krylov, dated 26 November 1927, explained the motives and circumstances of allowing the play. See *Schast'e literatury. Gosudarstvo i pisateli. 1925–1938: Dokumenty* [Happiness for Literature: The State and the Writer, 1925–1938] (Moscow, 1997), pp. 44–48.

11. AP RF, f. 3, op. 34, d. 241, l. 83. Published in Russian in *Istochnik*, no. 5 (1996): 114.

12. RGASPI, f. 17, op. 3, d. 724, l. 5. Published in Russian in *Istochnik*, no. 5 (1996): 115.

13. For more details on this campaign, see *Novoe o Zamiatine* [New Facts about Zamyatin], edited by L. Geller (Moscow, 1997).

14. L. Gumilevsky, "Sud'ba i zhizn'" [Destiny and life], in Andrei Platonov, *Vospominania sovremennikov: Materialy k biografii* [Reminiscences of contemporaries: materials for a biography] (Moscow, 1994), p. 74.

15. RGASPI, f. 17, op. 3, d. 858, l. 6.

16. Quoted from G. Belaia, *Don-kikhoty 20-x godov* [Don Quixotes of the 1920s] (Moscow, 1989), pp. 274–276.

17. AP RF, f. 45, op. 1, d. 201, l. 28.

18. *Osobaia papka* ("special file"), indicating that this part of the resolution is highly secret. It is omitted here since it was not declassified.

18. On the "Anthroposophists' case," see John Malmstad, "Andrei Belyi i antroposofia" [Andrei Bely and anthroposophy], *Minuvshee: Istorichesky al'manakh* [The past: A historical almanac] 6 (1988): 7–53; Malmstad, "K biografii Andreia Belogo" [For a biography of Andrei Bely], ibid., 12 (1993): 342–36.

19. The statements cited in the report of the members arrested on 10 December 1931 from the circle of followers of V. Khlebnikov—the Oberiu (Association for Real Art) poet A. I. Vvedensky and the poet and linguist A. V. Tufanov—are taken from the minutes of their interrogations. On the "Oberiu case," see "Razgrom OBERIU: Materialy sledstvennogo dela" [The rout of Oberiu: materials from the investigation], *Oktiabr'*, no. 11 (1992): 189–203.

CHAPTER 7. THE DEMISE OF RAPP

1. "Za proletarskuiu literaturu" [For proletarian literature] (Editorial), *Pravda*, 18 April 1931.

2. RGASPI, f. 17, op. 3, d. 875, l. 11.

3. The words in italics were added by Stalin; the words in brackets were crossed out by him.

4. *Recte* RAPM, RAPP's counterpart in music.

5. *Recte* RAPM.

CHAPTER 8. THE WRITERS' CONGRESS

1. "Ivan Gronsky: Iz pisem 1972 goda" [Ivan Gronsky: From the letters of 1972] in Evgeny Dobrenko (ed.), *Izbavlenie ot mirazhei: Sotsrealizm segodnia* [Rescue from the mirages: Socialist Realism today] (Moscow, 1990), pp. 119–122.

2. The report to the Congress of the Party leader K. Radek on international literature.

3. The draft text ends here.

4. On the special report, there is the following instruction: "Send out to Comrades Yagoda, Agranov, Prokofiev. SPO GUGB Dep. Head Liushkov."

5. The Bolshevo Commune was a reformatory for wayward youth.

6. Bogdanovism refers to the beliefs of A. A. Bogdanov, an early Bolshevik who ran the Capri school together with Lunacharsky and was attacked for "Godbuilding" heresy.

7. Lev Gumilevsky's "Dog's Lane" (1927), a novella about sexual mores, occasioned a press campaign at the time against sexual license in the young.

8. [Document footnote:] She's referring to Pilnyak's new story, in which he depicts a congress of agronomists in Cen[tral] Asia. The congress is limp, uninteresting, but as soon as one of the delegates makes a statement rejecting the aim of the main speaker, the congress comes to life. Seifullina { . . . } feels this is an analogy to Bukharin's report.

CHAPTER 9. THE GORKY FACTOR

1. In the pre-congress days starting in spring 1934, the SPO OGPU (from July 1934, the SPO GUGB NKVD SSSR) organized a regular (once every two to three days) practice of informing the Narkomat leadership and, accordingly, the TsK VKP(b), on the moods of the writers, the progress of the elections that were held among writers in enterprises and conferences, the composition of delegates, and so on. On this special report there is the following instruction: "Send to Comrades Yagoda, Agranov, Prokofiev. SPO GUGB Head G. Molchanov."

2. Usievich was an editor of *Literary Critic*, essentially the only major journal of literary theory in the thirties and one where G. Lukács and his associates were prominent contributors.

3. The italic date and signature were added to the letter by A. M. Gorky's secretary.

CHAPTER 10. THE UNION OF SOVIET WRITERS

1. The bracketed text in the draft of the letter, prepared by A. M. Gorky in the Crimea on 7 November 1935, was crossed out by the author. For the published draft of the letter, see *Izvestia TsK KPSS*, no. 11 (1990): 217–219.

2. The reference to Feuchtwanger's book is presumably to his *Moscow 1937*, which was essentially commissioned as a response to Gide's hostile *Back from the USSR* (1936).

3. *Recte* "Comments on the Synopsis of the Textbook on the History of the USSR" and "Comments on the Synopsis of the Textbook on Modern History," first published on 27 January 1936 in *Pravda* and *Izvestia*.

4. In the above attack on Lukács the Russian text recurrently critiques his understanding of what is *narodnyi* in literature, what is *narodnost'*. These two terms have been translated as "national" or "national character," but the reader should be aware that this is an imprecise translation. *Narodny* is a word formed from *narod*, meaning "the people," but in Stalinist discourse it had a range of meanings, including "popular," "folk," "of the common man," "peoples'," "national," and "state." As Kirpotin and Fadeev use these words above, and is typical of Stalinist discourse from the second half of the thirties, all these meanings are conflated. *Narodnost* (or *narodny*) functioned as a key value of Soviet culture that signified at the same time both loyalty to the regime and the essential quality of its people, with ever stronger tinges of Great Russian chauvinism.

5. RGASPI, f. 17, op. 116, d. 61, l. 6.

CHAPTER 11. STALIN AND THE MOSCOW ART THEATER

1. See: RGASPI, f. 17, op. 3, d. 888, l. 10; RGASPI, f. 17, op. 162, d. 14, l. 146.

2. In the left margin of the special report, opposite the remarks of M. P. Maksakova and D. D. Golovin, there is a note in pencil written by V. M. Molotov: "To Com. Mogilny. Report this by telephone to Com. Kerzhentsev and get his suggest[tions] today. M[olotov]. Contact Kerzhentsev regarding Gol[ovin] and Mes[serer]. Com. Kerzhentsev must submit the corresponding draft. Mol[otov]." On 3 June 1937, the Politburo approved a resolution conferring awards on D. D. Golovin, G. V. Zhukovsky, and S. M. Messerer.

CHAPTER 12. THE ANTI-FORMALIST CAMPAIGN

1. RGASPI, f. 17, op. 3, d. 973, l. 3.

2. The writer Olesha is concerned for the fate of the film *A Strict Youth* (*Strogy iunosha*) for which he wrote the scenario; it was indeed to be banned, as he feared. The remarks about Mayakovsky refer to the fact that this leading exponent of Left Art was suddenly praised by Stalin in a remark published in *Literaturnaia gazeta* on 12 December 1935 in which Stalin declared: "Mayakovsky was and remains the best, most talented poet of our Soviet epoch; indifference to his memory and works is a crime." This remark encouraged other poets from the former Left Art group, such as N. Aseev, to believe that they, too, would be more positively evaluated, but such proved not to be the case.

3. Babel's reference to Budenny is to the fact that this hero and veteran commander of the Red Cavalry in the Civil War attacked Babel savagely for his representation of the war in his cycle of short stories *Red Cavalry* [*Konarmiia*].

4. *Quiet Flows the Don*, an opera by Ivan Dzerzhinsky based on M. Sholokhov's Soviet classic novel of that name, was promoted by the leadership as a positive countermodel to *Lady Macbeth*.

5. In the text, Lezhnev's name is circled, and opposite the writer's statement are two checkmarks, probably made by someone in the GUGB NKVD SSSR leadership.

6. *Recte* RAPM throughout the document.

7. Neigauz was close to Pasternak.

8. Jack of Diamonds was a prerevolutionary group of Futurist artists.

9. Repin, Surikov, and Rembrandt were all artists championed at this time as "realists."

10. "*puskov*": probably *recte* "clips" ("*kuskov*").

11. *Woe to Wit*, staged in 1928, was Meyerhold's free adaptation of A. Griboedov's classic drama *Woe from Wit*. *Death of Tarelkin,* staged in 1922, was an adaptation of A. Sukhovo-Kobylin's play of 1869.

12. Bracketed words in the rest of the document (other than English titles of works) were added by V. M. Molotov to the draft resolution submitted by P. M. Kerzhentsev.

13. N. Erdman's *The Suicide* (1928) was prepared by Meyerhold for production but banned in 1932. R. Akulshin's *A Window on the Village*, a political review, was staged on 8 November 1927 as part anniversary celebrations of the Revolution. Selvinsky's tragedy *Commander of the Second Army* (1928) was staged by Meyerhold in 1929.

14. *How the Steel Was Tempered* (1932–1934), Nikolai Ostrovsky's semiautobiographical novel, was one of the most celebrated exempla of Socialist Realism. In the mid-thirties Ostrovsky was promoted as a national hero and Meyerhold was preparing a stage version of the novel for the twentieth anniversary of the Revolution in 1937.

CHAPTER 13. THE CAMPAIGN FOR A PATRIOTIC CULTURE

1. *An Optimistic Tragedy* (1933) by Vs. Vishnevsky presents a heroic account of the Civil War and was one of the most canonical Soviet dramas.

2. See above, Chapter 10, note 4.

CHAPTER 14. THE CENSORSHIP

1. See above, doc. 60.

2. The rest of the text deals with the work of the Glavlit apparatus and its local organs and the proposal to create an all-union censorship organ.

3. *Recte Days of the Turbins* [*Dni Turbinykh*].

4. *The Storm* (1859) is the most famous play by Aleksandr Ostrovsky, who was particularly promoted in Stalinist Russia as a "realist" dramatist.

5. "*orniami*": obviously *recte* "machinations" ("*kozniami*").

6. A. O. Avdeenko's script for *Law of Life,* a film from Mosfilm on Komsomol behavior, had been severely criticized by Stalin the previous year (see doc. 132).

7. Artsybashev was a "decadent" writer of the prerevolutionary period.

8. *Hearts of Four* was a comedy with a plot not unlike Lubitsch's *Ninotchka*—a highly rational and hard-working young woman (in this case a mathematician) is dismissive of boy-craziness and attention to one's appearance (seen in her younger sister) until she falls in love (with a Red Army commander). Then follows

a situation comedy with misunderstandings, etc., involving herself, her sister, and their respective love interests before the happy ending when love triumphs.

CHAPTER 16. STALIN AS PATRON-POTENTATE

1. In the original, the two pages following this are lost. Their text, in double square brackets, is cited from a handwritten draft of the letter that was also not preserved in full, without the concluding part of the letter, in the writer's personal archive (See OR GPB, f. 562, k. 19, ed. khr. 33).
2. Throughout the document, the italicized text was underscored by A. N. Poskrebyshev.
3. In the course of revision, the text was corrected to read: "cannot fail to exhibit a tendency."
4. In preparation of a fair copy, "Miliukov" was substituted.
5. In preparation of a fair copy, the word "was" was substituted.
6. Konstantin Simonov, "Glazami cheloveka moego pokoleniia" (in the eyes of someone of my generation) *Znamia*, no. 4 (1988): 71–72.

CHAPTER 17. REPORTS ON WRITERS FROM THE NKVD AND SOVIET OFFICIALS

1. *Recte* M. E. Kozakov throughout.
2. *Recte* "Bliskavetsky" throughout.
3. *Recte* "Emmanuel's."
4. Vissarion Belinsky (1811–1848) was a leading Russian critic whose advocacy of a social message in literature was seen by Soviet theorists as a model of the "realist" approach.
5. Crossing was a literary group that formed in 1924 under the sponsorship of the literary journal *Krasnaia nov'*, whose editor, A. Voronsky, was dismissed in 1927 as a Trotskyite. Crossing's literary position was relatively centrist; it called for greater literary "mastery" such as one found in the classics of Russian and Western literature, and decried what they saw as a lowering of standards in proletarian literature.
6. TsA FSB RF, f, 3, op. 5, d. 262, ll. 87–89, 93–96, 100–102.
7. TsA FSB RF, f. 3, op. 5, d. 262, ll. 95–96.
8. TsA FSB RF, f. 3, op. 5, d. 262, ll. 101–102.
9. The play by Lidia Seifullina discussed at the Peredelkino reading was probably her *Natasha* (1937).

CHAPTER 18. PETITIONS TO STALIN

1. Pasternak's collection of translations, *Georgian Lyrics*, was published in 1935.
2. Translation from the French: AP RF, f. 45, op. 1, d. 795, ll. 147–148.
3. Italicized text in the body of the letter was evidently underlined in pencil by Stalin or his assistant A. N. Poskrebyshev.
4. Italicized text in the body of the letter was underlined by A. N. Poskrebyshev.

5. Italicized text in the body of the letter was underlined by A. N. Poskrebyshev. A comment in the upper part of the latter is also his: "From Prof. of the Russian Language Vinogradov."

CHAPTER 19. THE STALIN-SHOLOKHOV EXCHANGE

1. Iury Murin, ed., *Pisatel' i vozhd': Perepiska M. A. Sholokhova s I. V. Stalinym: 1931–1950 gody. Sbornik dokumentov iz lichnogo arkhiva I. V. Stalina* [The writer and the leader: Correspondence of M. A. Sholokhov with I. V. Stalin. Selected documents from the personal archive of I. V. Stalin] (Moscow, 1997).
2. The International Writers' Conference in Spain was the second of the Soviet-sponsored antifascist Congresses for the Defense of Culture (the first had been in Paris in June 1935). This one was held in Valencia and Madrid during a critical phase of the Spanish Civil War.
3. *Recte* Logachev.

CHAPTER 20. THE LITERARY FRONT: THE WAR

1. RGASPI, f. 17, op. 117, d. 192, ll. 149–152.
2. RGASPI, f. 17, op. 116, d. 60, l. 53.
3. RGASPI, f. 17, op. 125, d. 212, ll. 96–99.
4. See L. Ozerov, *Il'ia Sel'vinsky: Ego trudy i dni* [Ilia Selvinsky: His works and times] (Moscow, 1973), pp. 8–9.
5. RGASPI, f. 17, op. 116, d. 168, l. 2.

CHAPTER 21. THE LITERARY FRONT: "ZHDANOVISM" AND BEYOND

1. Should be "Incident on Olympus" ["Proisshestvie na Olimpe"] (*Leningrad*, no. 3–4, 1946).
2. RGASPI, f. 17, d. 272.
3. RGASPI, f. 17, d. 275, ll. 90–91.
4. RGASPI, f. 17, d. 277, l. 34.
5. RGASPI, f. 17, d. 375, ll. 13–14.
6. RGASPI, f. 17, d. 618, ll. 53–54.

CHAPTER 22. "THE MOST IMPORTANT ART"

1. For more detail on the circumstances of the work on the film, see Leonid Kozlov, "The Artist and the Shadow of Ivan," in *Stalinism and Soviet Cinema*, ed. Richard Taylor and Derek Spring (London, 1993), pp. 109–130.
2. The transcript was made by B. N. Agapov from the words of S. M. Eisenstein and N. K. Cherkasov and authorized by them.
3. RGASPI, f. 17, op. 3, d. 1079, ll. 81, 204–205.
4. RGASPI, f. 17, d. 1062, ll. 87–90.
5. RGASPI, f. 17, d. 1071, ll. 14–15.
6. *Voprosy istorii*, no. 5 (1998): 24–25.
7. RGASPI, f. 17, op. 3, d. 1072, ll. 31–32.

CHAPTER 23. "MOMENTS MUSICAUX"

1. For more detail, see Leonid Maksimenkov, "'Partia—nash rulevoi.' Postanovlenie TsK VKP(b) ot 10 fevralia 1948 g. ob opere Vano Muradeli 'Velikaia druzhba' v svete novykh arkhivnykh dokumentov" ["The Party is our guide": The resolution of the TsK VKP(b) of 10 February 1948 on Vano Muradeli's opera *A Great Friendship* in light of new archival documents], *Muzykal'naia zhizn'*, nos. 13–14, 15–16 (1993): 34–39.

2. RGASPI, f. 17, op. 3, d. 1069, ll. 3–4.

3. For more detail, see Leonid Maksimenkov, *Sumbur vmesto muzyki: Stalinskaia kul'turnaia revoliutsia, 1936–1938* [Muddle instead of music: The Stalinist cultural revolution] (Moscow, 1997).

CHAPTER 24. "THE REVOLUTION HAS ENDED AT THE POINT WHERE IT BEGAN"

1. For more detail, see E. Levin, "Kratky kurs istorii 'Rusfil'ma'" [Short course in the history of Rusfilm], *Iskusstvo kino* [Art of the cinema], no. 9 (1994): 129–133.

2. RGASPI, f. 17, op. 3, d. 1073, l. 22.

3. RGASPI, f. 17, d. 1074, l. 24.

4. TsAOD Moscow, f. 8131, op. 1, d. 19, 21, 22, 23.

5. AP RF, f. 3, op. 35, d. 18, ll. 138–139.

6. Andrei Artizov and Oleg Naumov, *Vlast' i khudozhestvennaia intelligentsia: Dokumenty TsK RKP(b)-VKP(b), VChK–OGPU–NKVD o kul'turnoi politike, 1917–1953 gg.* (Power and the creative intelligentsia: Documents [of the Communist Party and the secret Police] on cultural policy, 1917–1953), (Moscow, 1999), p. 709 n. 47.

Glossary of Names

Note: All names cited in the book are listed here. In cases where it has not been possible to ascertain with certainty the identity of the person cited, that person is listed with no biographical information.

Abakumov, Viktor Semyonovich (1908–1954). USSR State Security Minister. Arrested and shot.

Aduev (pseudonym of Rabinovich), Nikolai Alfredovich (1904–1950). Soviet satiric poet, playwright.

Afinogenov, Aleksandr Nikolaevich (1904–1941). Soviet playwright.

Agranov, Yakov Saulovich (pseudonym of Yankel Shmaevich Sorenson) (1893–1938). Deputy to the Commissar for Internal Affairs. Highly trusted by Stalin and Yagoda. Used his connections with artistic circles to gain useful intelligence. Repressed.

Aibek (pseudonym of Musa Tashmukhamedov) (1904/05–1968). Leading Soviet Uzbek writer.

Akhmatova, Anna Andreevna (pseudonym of Anna Andreevna Gorenko) (1889–1966). Major lyric poet. In 1946 she and Mikhail Zoshchenko were targeted in a cultural purge and expelled from the Writers Union.

Akulov, Ivan Alekseevich (1888–1937). OGPU deputy head. Appointed State Prosecutor in 1933. Repressed.

Aleksandrov, Georgy Fyodorovich (1908–1961). Philosopher, Party functionary.

Aleksandrov (pseudonym of Keller), Vladimir Borisovich (1898–1954). Literary critic.

Aleksandrov (pseudonym of Mormonenko), Grigory Vasilievich (1903–1984). Film director and associate of Eisenstein in the 1920s.

Alekseev, Pyotr Alekseevich (1849–1891). Russian worker and revolutionary.

Alexander I (1777–1825). Tsar 1801–1825.

Alexander Nevsky (1220–1263). Medieval Russian prince and military commander.

Altman, Iogan Lvovich (1900–1955). Literary and theater critic. In the 1930s an editor of the journal *Teatr*. In the late 1940s accused of cosmopolitanism.

Andreev, Andrei Andreevich (1895–1971). Secretary of the Central Committee, member of the Politburo. In the mid 1930s the main supervisor of literary and artistic affairs for the Politburo.

Angarov (pseudonym of Zykov), Aleksei Ivanovich (1898–1937). Deputy head of the Central Committee Department of Cultural-Educational Work. Repressed.

Antokolsky, Pavel Grigorievich (1896–1978). Poet, translator.

Antonovskaya, Anna Arnoldovna (1885–1967). Soviet writer.

Apletin, Mikhail Yakovlevich (1885–1981). VOKS deputy chairman, secretary of the International Association of Revolutionary Writers (MORP), in the 1930s Chairman of the International Committee of the Union of Soviet writers.

Arkadiev, Mikhail Pavlovich (1896–1937). Party functionary, diplomat, director of the Moscow Art Theater. Repressed.

Arosev, Aleksandr Yakovlevich (1890–1938). Writer, publisher. VOKS chairman. Repressed.

Arsky, Pavel Aleksandrovich (1886–1967). Poet, novelist, playwright.

Artsybashev, Mikhail Petrovich (1878–1927). Russian novelist.

Asafiev, Boris Vladimirovich (literary pseudonym Igor Glebov) (1884–1949). Composer, musicologist, academician.

Aseev, Nikolai Nikolaevich (1889–1963). Poet. Close associate of Mayakovsky, member of LEF.

Avdeenko, Aleksandr Ostapovich (born 1908). Soviet writer.

Averbakh, Leopold Leopoldovich (1903–1937). Literary critic. Leader of RAPP. Repressed.

Avramenko, Ilya Kornilevich (1907–1973). Soviet poet.

Babel, Isaac Emmanuilovich (1894–1940). Major Soviet author of short stories, plays, and film scripts. Repressed.

Babeuf, François Noël (1760–1797). French revolutionary, organizer of an uprising against the Directory.

Badaev, Aleksei Egorovich (1883–1951). Party functionary.

Bagritsky (pseudonym of Dziubin), Eduard Georgievich (1895–1934). Soviet poet.

Bakaev, Ivan Petrovich (1887–1936). In 1925–1927 a leader of Trotskyite opposition. Party functionary. Repressed.

Bakhmetiev, Vladimir Matveevich (1885–1963). Writer.

Bakhtin, Mikhail Mikhailovich (1895–1975). Major literary theorist.

Balmont, Konstantin Dmitrievich (1867–1942). Major early Symbolist poet.

Barbusse, Henri (1873–1935). French novelist and journalist. He brought the pacifist and leftist groups in which he played a leading role into the Communist orbit.

Bazhan, Mykola Platonovich (1904–1983). Leading Soviet Ukrainian poet and public figure.

Bedny, Demian (Pridvorov, Yefim Alekseevich) (1883–1945). Poet and fabulist.

Beilis, Mendel (1873–1934). Jewish defendant in the infamous 1913 ritual murder trial.

Bekker, Mikhail. Literary critic. Repressed.

Belinsky, Vissarion Grigorievich (1811–1848). Leading Russian literary critic of the nineteenth century.

Bely, Andrei (pseudonym of Boris Nikolaevich Bugaev) (1880–1934). Leading Symbolist poet, novelist, literary critic, and memoirist.

Benjamin, Walter (1892–1940). Prominent German literary and cultural critic.

Benkendorf, Aleksandr Khristoforovich (1785–1844). Head of the secret police under Nicholas I.

Berezovsky, Feoktist Nikolaevich (1877–1952). Soviet prose writer.

Berg, Alban (1885–1935). Austrian composer.

Berggolts, Olga Fedorovna (1910–1975). Soviet poet.

Beria, Lavrenty Pavlovich (1899–1953). USSR People's Commissar for Internal Affairs. In 1953 arrested and shot.

Beskin, Emmanuil Martynovich (1877–1940). Theater critic.

Bespalov, Ivan Mikhailovich (1900–1937). Literary critic and functionary. Editor-in-chief of Goslitizdat. Repressed.

Bezymensky, Aleksandr Ilyich (1898–1973). Soviet poet.

Bill-Belotserkovsky (pseudonym of Belotserkovsky), Vladimir Naumovich (1884–1970). Soviet playwright.

Bliokh, Yakov Moiseevich (1895–1957). Documentary film director.

Bloch, Jean Richard (1884–1947). French essayist, novelist, and playwright.

Blok, Aleksandr Aleksandrovich (1880–1921). Leading Symbolist poet.

Bobrov, Sergei Pavlovich (1889–1971). Soviet writer and translator.

Bogdanov (pseudonym of Malinovsky), Aleksandr Aleksandrovich (1873–1928). Prominent Communist revolutionary, philosopher, founder of the Proletkult.

Bogorodsky, Fedor Semyonovich (1895–1959). Soviet artist.

Boiarsky (pseudonym of Shumshelevich), Yakov Iosifovich. (1890–1940). Chairman of the Central Committee of Rabis, manager of the Moscow Art Theater.

Bolduman, Mikhail Panteleimonovich (1898–1983). One of the leading actors of Moscow Art Theater.

Bolshakov, Ivan Grigorievich (1902–1980). In 1939 appointed Chairman of the Sovnarkom USSR Committee on Cinematographic Affairs, and in 1946 Minister of Cinematography, USSR.

Bondi, Sergei Mikhailovich (1891–1983). Pushkin scholar.

Borisov, Leonid Ilich (1897–1972). Soviet writer.

Borodin, Aleksandr Porfirievich (1833–1887). Major Russian composer.

Borshchagovsky, Aleksandr Mikhailovich (born 1913). Theater critic and writer. In the late 1940s accused of cosmopolitanism.

Bozhenko, Vasily Nazarovich (1871–1919). Military commander during the Civil War in Ukraine.

Brezhnev, Leonid Ilyich (1906–1982). Party leader. General Secretary 1964–1982.

Brik (Kogan), Lilya Yurievna (1893–1978). Wife of Osip Brik, muse of Vladimir Mayakovsky, and a sister of Elsa Triolet (French author and wife of Louis Aragon).

Brodsky, Isaac Izrailevich (1884–1939). Soviet painter.

Bruni, Lev Aleksandrovich (1894–1948). Soviet painter.

Bryusov, Valery Yakovlevich (1873–1924). Major Symbolist poet, novelist, and literary critic.

Buachidze, M. (1905–1937). Literary critic. Repressed.

Bubnov, Andrei Sergeevich (1883–1938). People's Commissar for Education from 1929. Repressed.

Budantsev, Sergei Fedorovich (1896–1940). Writer.

Budberg, Maria Ignatievna (née Zakrevskaya, first marriage to Benkendorf) (1892–1974). Translator, secretary of Maxim Gorky.

Budenny, Semyon Mikhailovich (1883–1973). Soviet military commander famous for Civil War victories.

Bukharin, Nikolai Ivanovich (1888–1939). Party leader and theoretician. Repressed.

Bulgakov, Mikhail Afanasievich (1891–1940). Leading Soviet novelist and playwright.

Bulgakova, Elena Sergeevna (1893–1970). Third wife of Mikhail Bulgakov.

Bulgakova (Belozerskaya), Liubov Yevgenievna (1895–1987). Second wife of Mikhail Bulgakov.

Bunin, Ivan Alekseevich (1870–1953). Major Russian writer. Emigrated 1920.

Bystriansky (pseudonym of Vatin), Vadim Aleksandrovich (1880–1940). Journalist. Party functionary.

Chaliapin, Fyodor Ivanovich (1873–1938). One of the greatest Russian opera singers.

Chapaev, Vasily Ivanovich (1887–1919). Military commander and legendary hero of the Civil War.

Chaplin, Charles (1889–1977). Great American actor, film director and producer.

Chekhov, Anton Pavlovich (1860–1904). Great Russian writer.

Chekhov, Mikhail Aleksandrovich (1891–1955). Russian actor. Emigrated 1928.

Cherkasov, Nikolai Konstantinovich (1903–1966). Theater and film actor. Starred in the title roles in Sergei Eisenstein's *Alexander Nevsky* and *Ivan the Terrible*.

Cherniavsky, L. Soviet writer. VOKS deputy chairman.

Chernyshevsky, Nikolai Gavrilovich (1828–1889). Major Russian writer and socialist activist.

Chiaureli, Mikhail Edisherovich (1894–1974). Soviet film director.

Chicherin, Georgy Vasilievich (1872–1936). Commissar of Foreign Affairs from 1918 to 1930.

Chikovani, Simon Ivanovich (1902–1966). Soviet Georgian poet.

Chubar, Vlas Yakovlevich (1891–1939). State and Party functionary. Repressed.

Chukovsky, Kornei Ivanovich (pseudonym of Nikolai Vasilievich Korneichukov) (1882–1969). Prominent writer and literary critic.

Chukovsky, Nikolai Korneevich (1904–1965). Soviet writer. Kornei Chukovsky's son.

Chumandrin, Mikhail Fedorovich (1905–1940). Soviet writer.

Conrad, Joseph (pseudonym of Jósef Teodor Konrad Korzeniowski) (1857–1924). Polish-born English novelist and short story writer.

Dairedzhiev, Boris Leonidovich (1902–1955). Literary critic. In the late 1940s accused of cosmopolitanism.

Damert, Lilo. German writer.

Davidenko, Aleksandr Aleksandrovich (1899–1934). Soviet composer.

Davydov, L. Head of the Foreign Department of the Cheka.

Deborin (pseudonym of Yoffe), Abram Moiseevich (1881–1963). Russian Marxist philosopher and protégé of Plekhanov. Elected to the Academy of Sciences in 1929 but in the early 1930s attacked for "Menshevizing idealism."

Deineka, Aleksandr Aleksandrovich (1899–1969). Prominent Soviet painter. Founding member of the Society of Easel Painters (1925–28), in October group (1928–30), and the Russian Association of Proletarian Artists (1931–32).

Derzhanovsky, Vladimir Vladimirovich (1881–1942). Composer and critic. In 1920s editor-in-chief of the journal *Sovremennaia muzyka* and one of the leaders of the modernist Association of Contemporary Musicians (ASM). Close to Prokofiev.

Dinamov, Sergei Sergeevich (1901–1939). Literary scholar and critic. Repressed.

Dobronitsky, K. Soviet writer.

Dolmatovsky, Evgeny Aronovich (1915–1994). Soviet poet.

Dostoevsky, Fyodor Mikhailovich (1821–1881). Great Russian writer.

Dovzhenko, Aleksandr Petrovich (1894–1956). Leading Soviet Ukrainian film director and writer.

Drozdov, Aleksandr Mikhailovich (1895–1963). Soviet writer.

Druskin, Mikhail Semyonovich (1905–1991). Soviet musicologist, critic, and music pedagogue.

Dudin, Mikhail Aleksandrovich (1916–1993). Soviet poet.

Dumas, Alexandre Sr., known as Dumas père (1802–1870). French writer.

Dzerzhinsky, Felix Edmundovich (1877–1926). Bolshevik leader, founder and head of the first Soviet secret police organization (VChK–GPU–OGPU).

Dzerzhinsky, Ivan Ivanovich (1909–1978). Soviet composer.

Ehrenburg, Ilya Grigorevich (1891–1967). Major Soviet writer, journalist, and public figure.

Eideman (pseudonym of Eidemanis), Robert Petrovich (1885–1937). Soviet Latvian poet. Repressed.

Eikhenbaum, Boris Mikhailovich (1886–1959). Literary historian and theorist. A key figure in the Formalist school of literary scholarship, he became a target of official attacks during the postwar anticosmopolitan campaign.

Eisenstein, Sergei Mikhailovich (1898–1948). Leading Soviet film director and theorist.

Engels, Friedrich (1820–1895). With Marx the founding theoretician of Marxism.

Erdman, Nikolai Robertovich (1900–1970). Soviet playwright.

Erlikh, Aron Isaevich (1896–1963). Soviet writer.

Ermler, Fridrikh Markovich (1898–1967). Soviet film director.

Es-Khabib Vafa. Playwright.

Fadeev (pseudonym of Bulyga), Aleksandr Aleksandrovich (1901–1956). Soviet writer and functionary, member of the Central Committee of the Communist Party. In 1946–1953 General Secretary of the Union of Soviet Writers.

Favorsky, Vladimir Andreevich (1886–1964). Soviet artist.

Fedin, Konstantin Aleksandrovich (1892–1977). Soviet writer.

Fedoseev, Pyotr Nikolaevich (1908–1990). Philosopher, Party functionary. In 1943–1946 first deputy head of the Central Committee's Agitprop. In 1945–1949 editor-in-chief of the Party theoretical journal *Bolshevik*.

Fefer, Itzik (Isaac Solomonovich) (1900–1952). Soviet Jewish poet. Repressed.

Feuchtwanger, Lion (1884–1958). Prominent German writer and antifascist activist. In mid-1930s close to the Soviet Union.

Fischer, Ernst (1899–1972). Austrian art and literary theoretician, aesthetician, and public figure. In 1938–1945 lived in the USSR.

Flakserman, A. Lunacharsky's secretary.

Flit, Aleksandr Mikhailovich. Soviet humorist.

Forsh, Olga Dmitrievna (1873–1961). Soviet historical novelist.

France, Anatole (pseudonym of Jacques Anatole François Thibault) (1844–1924). Writer, critic, a major figure of French literature in the late nineteenth and early twentieth centuries.

Frunze, Mikhail Vasilievich. (1885–1925). Professional revolutionary and military commander. In 1921 elected to the Central Committee and in January 1925 became the Chairman of the Revolutionary Military Council.

Glossary of Names

Gabovich, Mikhail Markovich (1905–1965). Ballet soloist of the Bolshoi Theater.

Ganetsky (pseudonym of Fiurstenberg), Yakov Stanislavovich (1879–1937). Prominent Party figure and diplomat. Repressed.

Gatov, Aleksandr Borisovich (1899–1972). Soviet poet and translator.

Gavronsky, Aleksandr Osipovich (1894–1956). Film director. Repressed.

Gerasimov, Aleksandr Mikhailovich (1881–1963). Leading Soviet painter and functionary. In 1940s and 1950s President of the Academy of Fine Arts of the USSR.

Gerasimov, Sergei Vasilievich (1885–1964). Leading Soviet painter.

Gerasimova, Valeria Anatolievna (1903–1978). Soviet writer.

German, Yury Pavlovich (1910–1967). Soviet writer.

Gersht, Meer Abramovich (born 1908). Stage director. In 1930s director at the Kamernyi Theater.

Gide, André (1869–1951). French writer and a leader of French liberal thought. Controversial for his espousal of communism and his subsequent disavowal of it in 1936 after a visit to the Soviet Union.

Gladkov, Fyodor Vasilievich (1883–1958). Major Soviet novelist and public figure.

Glebov, Anatoly Glebovich (1899–1964). Soviet playwright.

Goffenshefer, Veniamin Tsezarevich (1905–1966). Soviet literary critic.

Gogol, Nikolai Vasilievich (1809–1852). Famous Russian author of prose and drama.

Golemba, Sofia Mikhailovna (1904–1970). Opera soloist of the Nemirovich-Danchenko Music Theater.

Golodny (pseudonym of Epshtein), Mikhail Semyonovich (1903–1949). Soviet poet.

Golosovker, Yakov Emmanuilovich (1890–1967). Philologist, philosopher, literary historian, translator. In the Gulag, 1936–42.

Golovanov, Lev Viktorovich (born 1926). Ballet soloist of the Bolshoi Theater.

Golovanov, Nikolai Semyonovich (1891–1953). Bolshoi Theater conductor (from 1915) and artistic director (1948–1953).

Golovin, D. D. Opera soloist of the Bolshoi Theater. Repressed.

Golubov, Sergei Nikolaevich (1894–1962). Soviet historical novelist.

Gor, Gennady Samoilovich (1907–1981). Soviet writer.

Gorbachev, Mikhail Sergeevich (born 1931). Party and State leader. General Secretary 1985–1991.

Gorbatov, Boris Leontievich (1908–1954). Soviet prose writer.

Gorbunov, Kuzma Yakovlevich (1903–1986). Soviet writer.

Gorchakov, Nikolai Mikhailovich (1898–1958). Moscow Art Theater director.

Gorelov, Anatoly Efimovich (1904–1995). Literary critic and functionary. In

1930s a prominent official of the Leningrad Branch of the Union of Soviet Writers. In the Gulag, 1937–1954.

Gorky, Maxim (pseudonym of Aleksei Maksimovich Peshkov) (1868–1936). Major writer, playwright, public figure. Played a leading role from 1931 in Soviet literature and culture. Proclaimed "founder of Socialist Realism."

Gorodetsky, Sergei Mitrofanovich (1884–1967). Poet.

Gorodinsky, Viktor Markovich. Music critic.

Gosheva, Irina Prokofievna (1911–1988). Soviet actress.

Grib, Vladimir Romanovich (1908–1940). Literary scholar.

Griboedov, Aleksandr Sergeevich (1795–1829). Russian dramatist and diplomat.

Gronsky, Ivan Mikhailovich (1894–1985). Party and literary functionary. In 1930s the key figure in the Organizational Committee of the Soviet Writers Union, editor-in-chief of *Izvestia* and *Novyi mir* until May 1937. Repressed.

Grossman, Vasily Semyonovich (1905–1964). Soviet writer.

Grzhebin, Zinovy Isaevich (1877–1929). Publisher.

Gudzenko, Semyon Petrovich (1922–1953). Soviet poet.

Gumilevsky, Lev Ivanovich (1890–1976). Soviet writer.

Gumilyov, Lev Nikolaevich (1912–1992). Akhmatova's son.

Gumilyov, Nikolai Stepanovich (1886–1921). Major poet and literary critic. Akhmatova's first husband and one of the founders of the Acmeist movement. Repressed.

Gurvich, Abram Solomonovich (1897–1962). Soviet literary critic. In late 1940s accused of cosmopolitanism.

Gusev, Sergei Ivanovich (pseudonym of Yakov Davidovich Drabkin) (1874–1933). In 1925–1926 head of the Press Department of the Communist Party's Central Committee.

Guzovskaia, Olga Vladimirovna (1883–1962). Actress and stage director. From 1920 to 1932 in emigration.

Hidas, Antal (1899–1980). Hungarian writer. Lived in Soviet Union from 1926–1959. In the Gulag 1938–1944.

Hitler, Adolf (1889–1945).

Illés, Bela (1895–1974). Hungarian writer. From 1923 to 1945 lived in Soviet Union.

Ilyenkov, Vasily Pavlovich (1897–1967). Soviet writer.

Imas. Deputy head of the Administration of Theatrical Institutions of the Commissariat of Enlightenment of the RSFSR.

Inber, Vera Maikhailovna (1890–1972). Soviet poet.

Ionov (pseudonym of Bernshtein), Ilya Ionovich (1887–1942). Proletarian poet. Head of the Petrograd branch of Gosizdat.

Glossary of Names

Isbakh, Aleksandr Abramovich (pseudonym of Isaac Abramovich Bakhrakh) (1904–1977). Novelist, journalist. Repressed.

Istomin, Konstantin Nikolaevich (1887–1942). Soviet painter.

Ivanov, Boris (born 1918). Soviet film director.

Ivanov, Vsevolod Viacheslavovich (1895–1963). Soviet writer.

Ivan the Terrible (1530–1584). Tsar 1533–1584.

Ivanov-Razumnik (pseudonym of Ivanov), **Razumnik Vasilyevich** (1878–1946). Literary critic.

Izrailevsky, B. L. Head of the musical section of the Moscow Art Theater.

Kachalov (pseudonym of Shverubovich), **Vasily Ivanovich** (1875–1948). Leading actor of the Moscow Art Theater where he worked from 1909.

Kadochnikov, Pavel Petrovich (1915–1988). Soviet actor.

Kaganovich, Lazar Moiseevich (1893–1991). Party leader and member of the Politburo.

Kalinin, Anatoly Veniaminovich (born 1916). Soviet writer.

Kalinin, Mikhail Ivanovich (1873–1946). Public figure and titular head of the Soviet state.

Kallinikov, Iosif Fyodorovich (1890–1934). Russian writer. Emigrated to Prague after the Revolution.

Kamenev (pseudonym of Rozenfeld), **Lev Borisovich** (1883–1936). Communist Party leader. Together with Stalin and Zinoviev formed the ruling Party triumvirate after Lenin's death. Also headed the Akademia Publishing House. Repressed.

Kantorovich, Vladimir Yakovlevich (1901–1977). Writer, essayist, journalist, critic.

Kapitsa, Pyotr Iosifovich (born 1909). Soviet writer.

Kapler, Aleksei Yakovlevich (1904–1979). Soviet film scriptwriter.

Kapustin, Yakov Fedorovich (1904–1950). Party functionary. Secretary of Leningrad City Committee of the Communist Party. Repressed.

Karaban (pseudonym of Shleiman), **Pavel Solomonovich**. Soviet writer and translator.

Karakhan (pseudonym of Karakhanian), **Lev Mikhailovich** (1889–1937). Soviet diplomat. Deputy People's Commissar of Foreign Affairs.

Karamzin, Nikolai Mikhailovich (1766–1826). Writer, historian. Main exponent of Russian Sentimentalism and author of a monumental *History of the Russian State*.

Karavaeva, Anna Aleksandrovna (1893–1979). Soviet writer.

Kassil, Lev Abramovich (1905–1970). Children's writer.

Kataev, Ivan Ivanovich (1902–1939). Writer. Member of the Pereval group. Repressed.

Kataev, Valentin Petrovich (1897–1986). Novelist and playwright.

Katsman, Yevgeny Aleksandrovich (1890–1976). Soviet painter.

Kaverin, Fyodor Nikolaevich (1897–1967). Stage director.

Kazakevich, Emmanuil Genrikhovich (1913–1962). Soviet writer.

Kedrov, Mikhail Nikolaevich (1893/94–1972). Actor (from 1924) and director (1946–1955) of the Moscow Art Theater.

Keldysh, Yury Vsevolodovich (1907–1995). Musicologist.

Kemenov, Vladimir Semyonovich (1908–?). Art historian. Director of VOKS and Vice President of the Academy of Fine Arts of the USSR.

Kerzhentsev (pseudonym of Lebedev), Platon Mikhailovich (1881–1940). Party and state functionary. Chairman of the Committee on Arts Affairs under Sovnarkom of USSR.

Khachaturian, Aram Ilyich (1903–1978). Prominent Soviet composer and public figure.

Khalatov, Artemy Bagratovich (pseudonym of Artashes Bagirovich) (1894–1938). Chairman of the board of Gosizdat. Repressed.

Khalturin, Stepan Nikolaevich (1856–1882). Russian revolutionary. Member of the People's Will group.

Khatsrevin, Zakhar Lvovich (1903–1941). Soviet writer.

Khazin, Aleksandr Abramovich (1912–1976). Poet, humorist.

Kheifits, Iosif Efimovich (1905–1995). Soviet film director.

Khlebnikov, Velimir (pseudonym of Viktor Vladimirovich Khlebnikov) (1895–1922). Leading Futurist poet and theoretician of trans-sense literature.

Khmelev, Nikolai Pavlovich (1901–1945). Leading actor of the Moscow Art Theater where he worked from 1924.

Khrapchenko, Mikhail Borisovich (1904–1986). Literary scholar and Communist Party functionary. In 1938–1948 Chairman of the Committee on Arts Affairs under Sovnarkom USSR. Academician.

Khrennikov, Tikhon Nikolaevich (born 1913). Soviet composer. From 1948 to 1991 head of the Union of Soviet Composers.

Khrushchev, Nikita Sergeevich (1894–1971). Soviet leader. First Secretary of Moscow City and Regional Party Committee 1935–38; First Secretary Ukrainian Party Committee 1938–1946, 1948–49; First Secretary of the Moscow Party Organization and Secretary of the Central Committee 1949–53; First Secretary of the Communist Party 1953–64.

Khvylevy, Mykola (1893–1933). Prominent Ukrainian writer and publicist of the Ukrainian cultural renaissance of the 1920s.

Kirov, Sergei Mironovich (1886–1934). Party leader. Assassinated while head of the Leningrad Party Committee.

Kirpotin, Valery Yakovlevich (1898–1997). Critic, literary historian. In 1930s a secretary of the Organizational Committee of the Union of Soviet Writers and the head of the Literature Department of the Central Committee's Agitprop.

Kirsanov, Semyon Isaakovich (1906–1972). Soviet poet.

Glossary of Names 493

Kirshon, Vladimir Mikhailovich (1902–1938). A leader of RAPP. Playwright. Repressed.

Kleiner, Isidor Mikhailovich (1893–1971). Theater critic and theoretician.

Kliuev, Nikolai Alekseevich (1884–1937). Poet. Repressed.

Klychkov, Sergei Antonovich (1889–1937). Writer. Repressed.

Knekht, V. A. Writer.

Knipper-Chekhova, Olga Leonardovna (1868–1959). Anton Chekhov's wife and leading actress of the Moscow Art Theater which she joined in 1898.

Knorin (pseudonym of Knorinsh), Vilhelm Georgievich (1890–1938). Party functionary. From 1935 head of the Central Committee's Agitprop. Repressed.

Kobulov, Bogdan Zakharovich (1904–1953). A top official in state security organs. Arrested and shot.

Kogan, Pyotr Semyonovich (1872–1932). Literary critic.

Kolbanovsky, A. E. Journalist.

Kolegaev, Andrei Lukich (?1937). Party functionary. Repressed.

Koltsov (pseudonym of Fridliand), Mikhail Efimovich (1898–1940). Leading journalist in *Pravda* and other central press organs. Head of the publishing conglomerate Zhurgaz. Editor of *Ogonek* (*The Little Fire*), *Krokodil* (*Crocodile*), *Za rubezhom* (*Abroad*), and other journals. Head of the Foreign Commission of the Writers Union 1935–1938 and active in the international antifascist campaign and the Spanish Civil War. Repressed.

Komissarova, Maria Ivanovna (1904–1994). Soviet poet.

Kon, Feliks Yakovlevich (1864–1941). Prominent Party figure.

Kondratiev, Nikolai Dmitrievich (1892–1938). Prominent Russian economist. In 1930 proclaimed a "kulak-professor" and the leader of an alleged anti-Soviet "peasant party." Repressed.

Konovalov, Grigory Ivanovich (1908–1987). Soviet writer.

Koonen, Alisa Georgievna (1889–1974). Actress. Aleksandr Tairov's wife.

Kopylenko, Aleksandr Ivanovich (1900–1958). Soviet Ukrainian writer.

Korabelnikov, Grigory Markovich (1904–1990). Literary critic.

Koreneva, Lidia Mikhailovna (1885–1982). Actress. From 1904 in Moscow Art Theater.

Korneichuk, Aleksandr Evdokimovich (1905–1972). Soviet Ukrainian playwright, literary functionary, and public figure.

Kornilov, Boris Petrovich (1907–1938). Poet. Repressed.

Korobov, Yakov Evdokimovich (1874–1928). Soviet writer.

Korolenko, Vladimir Galaktionovich (1853–1921). Russian writer and prominent public figure.

Kosarev, Aleksandr Vasilievich (1903–1939). In 1930s General Secretary of the Komsomol Central Committee. Repressed.

Kostelyanets, Boris Osipovich (1912–1980). Soviet literary critic.

Kostrov, Taras (pseudonym of Aleksandr Sergeevich Martynovsky) (1901–1930).

Journalist, one of the founders of *Komsomolskaia Pravda* and editor-in-chief of the journal *Molodaia gvardia*.

Kozakov, Mikhail Emmanuilovicvh (1897–1954). Soviet writer.

Kozintsev, Grigory Mikhailovich (1905–1973). Soviet film director.

Kozlovsky, Ivan Semyonovich (1900–1993). Opera soloist of the Bolshoi Theater.

Krasin, Leonid Borisovich (1870–1926). State and Party functionary. Diplomat.

Krestinsky, Nikolai Nikolaevich (1883–1938). Party and State functionary. Repressed.

Krinitsky, Aleksandr Ivanovich (1894–1937). Party functionary. In 1926–1929 head of the Central Committee Agitprop.

Kriuchkov, Pyotr Petrovich (1889–1938). Gorky's secretary. Repressed.

Krupin, Dmitry Vasilievich (1895–1982). Party functionary.

Krupskaia, Nadezhda Konstantinovna (1869–1939). Lenin's wife.

Krylov, S. N. Deputy chief of the Central Committee Agitprop.

Krzhizhanovsky, Gleb Maksimilianovich (1872–1959). Revolutionary dignitary. Scholar. Party and state functionary.

Kuibyshev, Valerian Vladimirovich (1888–1935). State and Party functionary, a leading figure of Stalinist industrialization.

Kuklin, Georgy Osipovich (1903–1939). Writer. Member of Pereval group. Repressed.

Kuprin, Aleksandr Ivanovich (1870–1938). Russian writer. In emigration 1919–1937.

Kurbsky, Andrei Mikhailovich (1528–1583). Russian prince. Military commander.

Kusevitsky, Sergei Aleksandrovich (1874–1951). Musician, conductor. Emigrated 1920.

Kusikov (pseudonym of Kusikian), Aleksandr Borisovich (1896–1977). Russian poet-imagist. Emigrated to Paris 1924.

Kuzko, Pyotr Avdeevich (1884–1969). Soviet writer.

Kuznetsov, Aleksei Aleksandrovich (1905–1950). Party functionary. In 1938–1945 Secretary of the Leningrad City and Regional Party committees. In 1945–1949 Secretary of the Party's Central Committee. Repressed.

Kuznetsov, Pavel Varfolomeevich (1878–1968). Soviet painter.

Kvitko, Lev Moiseevich (1890–1952). Soviet Jewish poet. Repressed.

Lakhuti, Abolgasem Akhmedzade (1897–1957). Leading Tajik Soviet poet who wrote in Persian. A Party member.

Lapin, Boris Matveevich (1905–1941). Soviet writer.

Larin, Yury (pseudonym of Lurie Mikhail Zalmanovich) (1882–1932). Economist. Party and state functionary. A founder of Gosplan.

Latsis, Asja (Anna Ernestovna) (1891–1979). Latvian actress. Theater director and love of Walter Benjamin in 1920s.

Lavoisier, Antoine Laurent (1743–1794). French chemist.

Lavrenev, Boris Andreevich (1891–1959). Soviet playwright.

Lebedev-Kumach, Vasily Ivanovich (1898–1949). Poet. Lyricist for the most popular songs of the Stalin era.

Lebedev-Polyansky, Pavel Ivanovich (1881–1948). Critic, academician. Head of Glavlit in the 1920s.

Lebedinsky, Lev Nikolaevich (1904–1991). Musicologist, critic. General Secretary of the Russian Association of Proletarian Musicians (RAPM).

Lekht, Fridrikh (Ferdinand) Karlovich (1887–1961). Soviet painter.

Lelevich, G. (pseudonym of Labori Gilelevich Kalmanson) (1901–1937). Soviet poet, critic, and activist for proletarian literature. One of the founders of the RAPP journal *Na postu*. Repressed.

Lenin (pseudonym of Ulyanov), **Vladimir Ilyich** (1870–1924).

Lentulov, Aristarkh Vasilievich (1882–1943). Soviet painter.

Leonidov, Leonid Mironovich (1873–1941). Actor. Joined the Moscow Art Theater in 1903.

Leonidze, Georgy Nikolaevich (1899–1966). Soviet Georgian poet.

Leonov, Leonid Maksimovich (1899–1994). Soviet novelist, playwright.

Lepeshinskaia, Olga Vasilievna (born 1916). Ballet soloist of the Bolshoi Theater.

Lermontov, Mikhail Yurievich (1814–1841). Famous Russian Romantic poet and prose writer.

Lessing, Gotthold Ephraim (1729–1781). Dramatist, aesthetician, and critic of the German Enlightenment.

Levidov, Mikhail Yulievich (1891–1942). Playwright and journalist.

Levin, Fedor Markovich (1901–1972). Literary critic. In the 1930s an editor of the journal *Literaturnoe obozrenie* (*Literary Review*). In the late 1940s accused of cosmopolitanism.

Lezhnev, A. (pseudonym of Abram Zelikovich (Zakharovich) Gorelik) (1893–1938). Literary critic, member of the group Pereval. Repressed.

Lezhnev, I. (pseudonym of Isai Grigorievich Altshuler) (1891–1955). Literary critic and journalist.

Liashko (pseudonym of Liashchenko), **Nikolai Nikolaevich** (1884–1953). Soviet writer.

Libedinsky, Yury Nikolaevich (1898–1959). Soviet writer and critic. A leader of RAPP.

Lifshits, Mikhail Aleksandrovich (1905–1983). Literary scholar, aesthetician, associate of Lukács, and a leading theorist of Marxist aesthetics who wrote for *Literaturnyi kritik* (*Literary Critic*).

Likharev, Boris Mikhailovich (1906–1962). Soviet poet. Editor-in-chief of the journal *Leningrad*.

Litovsky, Osaf Semyonovich (1892–1971). Journalist and theater critic. In 1930–1937 Head of Glavrepertkom.

Litvinov, Maksim Maksimovich (pseudonym of Meer-Genokh Movshevich Vallakh) (1876–1951). Prominent Bolshevik and diplomat.

Liubimov-Lanskoy (pseudonym of Gelibter), Evsei Osipovich (1883–1943). Soviet stage director.

Liushkov, Genrikh Samoilovich (1900–1945). Deputy head of the NKVD SSSR Secret Political Department.

Livanov, Boris Nikolaevich (1904–1972). Leading Soviet actor. Joined the Moscow Art Theater in 1924.

Livshits, Vladimir Aleksandrovich (born 1913). Soviet children's poet.

Lominadze, Vissarion (Beso) Vissarionovich (1897–1935). Party functionary. Committed suicide.

Louis XIV (1638–1715). King of France 1643–1715.

Lubitsch, Ernst (1892–1947). German film director. Worked in United States from 1921.

Lugovskoi, Vladimir Aleksandrovich (1901–1957). Soviet poet.

Lukács, Georg (György) (1885–1971). Prominent Hungarian literary historian, essayist, critic, and literary theoretician, an influential figure in Western Marxism. In 1933 Lukács emigrated to the Soviet Union where he wrote for *Literaturnyi kritik*. After World War II he returned to Hungary.

Lukin, Yury Borisovich (1907–1995). Literary critic.

Lukov, Leonid Davidovich (1909–1963). Soviet film director.

Lunacharsky, Anatoly Vasilievich (1875–1933). Prominent Bolshevik leader and public figure. In 1917–1929 People's Commissar of Enlightenment.

Luppol, Ivan Kapitonovich (1896–1943). Literary scholar. Academician. Director of the Gorky Institute of World Literature (IMLI). Repressed.

Luther, Martin (1483–1546).

Luzgin, Mikhail Vasilievich (1899–1942). Soviet writer.

Makariev, Ivan Sergeevich (1902–1958). In 1925–1932 Secretary of RAPP. Repressed in 1937–1955.

Maksakova, Maria Petrovna (1902–1974). Opera soloist of the Bolshoi Theater.

Maksimov, G. I. Journalist.

Malakhov, Sergei Arsenievich (1902–1973). Soviet critic and poet.

Malenkov, Georgy Maksimilianovich (1902–1988). Party functionary. Member of the Central Committee from 1939.

Malinovskaia, Elena Konstantinovna (1875–1942). After the Revolution Commissar of Moscow Theaters. In 1920s and 1930s manager of the Bolshoi Theater.

Maliugin, Leonid Antonovich (1909–1968). Soviet playwright. In late 1940s accused of cosmopolitanism.

Malraux, André (Georges) (1901–1976). French novelist, adventurer, art historian, and statesman. Although aware of Stalin's crimes, in the 1930s he praised the Soviet system and backed many antifascist and leftist causes. With Louis Aragon, he founded the International Association of Writers for the Defense of Culture.

Malyshkin, Aleksandr Georgievich (1892–1938). Soviet writer.

Mandelshtam, Osip Emilievich (1891–1938). Major poet and essayist. Repressed.

Mann, Klaus (1906–1949). German writer. Son of Thomas Mann. Was a guest at the First Congress of Soviet Writers.

Manuilov, Viktor Andronikovich (1903–1987). Literary scholar.

Margueritte, Victor (1866–1942). French writer.

Mariengof, Anatoly Borisovich (1897–1962). Poet and playwright.

Markish, Perets Davidovich (1895–1952). Soviet Jewish poet. Repressed.

Markov, Pavel Aleksandrovich (1897–1980). Theater critic. In 1925–1962 head of the Moscow Art Theater literary department.

Marr, Nikolai Yakovlevich (1864/65–1934). Prominent linguist.

Marshak, Samuil Yakovlevich (1887–1964). Leading Soviet children's poet and translator.

Martov, Zhozef Klimentievich (1900–1972). Soviet cameraman.

Marx, Karl (1818–1883).

Mashkov, Ilya Ivanovich (1881–1944). Soviet painter.

Mass, Vladimir Zakharovich (1896–1979). Soviet poet and playwright.

Matrosov, Aleksandr Matveevich (1924–1943). Famous Soviet infantry soldier during World War II whose legendary bravery in a battle near Pskov won him the distinction Hero of the Soviet Union.

Maupassant, Guy de (1850–1893). Major French writer.

Mayakovsky, Vladimir Vladimirovich (1893–1930). Leading Futurist poet. Committed suicide in 1930 but five years later Stalin pronounced him "the best and most talented poet of the Soviet era."

Maznin, Dmitry Mikhailovich (1902–1938). Soviet poet and critic. Repressed.

Mdivani, Georgy Davidovich (1905–1981). Soviet Georgian playwright.

Medvedev, Pavel Nikolaevich (1891/92–1938). Literary scholar and critic of the Bakhtin circle. Repressed.

Mekhlis, Lev Zakharovich (1989–1953). Party and State functionary. Editor-in-chief of *Pravda* 1930–1937. Deputy People's Commissar of Defense and chief of the Main Political Administration of the Red Army (1937–1940) and Minister of State Control (1945–1949).

Melik-Pashaev, Aleksandr Shamilievich (1905–1964). From 1931 conductor of the Bolshoi Theater.

Melnikov, Naum Dmitrievich (pseudonym of Melman) (born 1918). Soviet writer.

Menshikov, Aleksandr Sergeevich (1787–1869). Prince. Admiral. During the Crimean War commander of the Crimean Army and Black Sea Fleet.

Menzhinsky, Viacheslav Rudolfovich (1874–1934). Deputy head (under Dzerzhinsky) and head (after his death) of OGPU.

Merkulov, Vsevolod Nikolaevich (1895–1953). USSR People's Commissar for State Security of the NKVD and KGB. Arrested and shot along with L. Beria.

Meshcheriakov, Nikolai Leonidovich (1865–1942). Revolutionary, journalist. From 1918 head of Gosizdat.

Messerer, Sulamith (1908–2004). Ballet soloist of the Bolshoi Theater. Emigrated 1980.

Meyerhold, Vsevolod Emilievich (1874–1940). Prominent and influential avant-garde stage director and leading figure in revolutionary theater. Repressed.

Miaskovsky, Nikolai Yakovlevich (1881–1950). Soviet composer and pedagogue.

Mikhoels (pseudonym of Vovsi), Solomon Mikhailovich (1890–1948). Leading Soviet Jewish actor, director, pedagogue, and public figure. Artistic director of the Moscow Jewish Theater, head of Jewish Anti-Fascist Committee.

Mikitenko, Ivan Kondratevich (1897–1937). Ukrainian writer. One of the leaders of VUSPP (All-Ukrainian Association of Proletarian Writers). Repressed.

Mikoyan, Anastas Ivanovich (1895–1978). Prominent Party leader. Member of Politburo in 1935–1966.

Minin, Kuzma (?—1616). Russian leader who rallied an army to defend the country against a Polish invasion.

Mints, Isaak Izrailevich (1896–1991). Soviet historian. Academician.

Miroshnichenko, Grigory Ilyich (1904–1985). Soviet writer.

Mirsky, Dmitry Petrovich (Sviatopolk-Mirsky, Prince D. P.) (1890–1939). Literary critic and scholar. Fought for the White Army in the Civil War, in emigration in London 1922–1931. Repressed.

Mitrofanov, Aleksandr Georgievich (1899–1951). Soviet writer.

Molchanov, Georgy Andreevich (1897–1937). Chief of the Secret Political Department of OGPU.

Molchanov, Ivan Nikandrovich (1903–1958). Soviet poet.

Molotov (pseudonym of Skriabin), Viacheslav Mikhailovich (1890–1986). Prominent Bolshevik leader. Party and state functionary.

Moor (pseudonym of Orlov), Dmitry Stakhievich (1883–1946). Soviet graphic artist.

Mordvinkin, Vladimir Yurievich. In 1920s head of Glavlit, later chairman of Glavrepertkom.

Morozov, Pavlik (Pavel Trofimovich) (1918–1932). A legendary young Pioneer who (according to the somewhat questionable official account) died a martyr's death at the hands of kulaks after denouncing his own father to the authorities for his involvement in a kulak conspiracy.

Morozov, S. T. Journalist, grandson of the industrialist Savva Morozov.

Morozov, Savva Timofeevich (1862–1905). A prominent Russian industrialist and patron of the arts who gave money to the revolutionary cause.

Moskvin, Ivan Mikhailovich (1874–1946). A leading actor in the Moscow Art Theater which he joined in 1898.

Mrachkovsky, Sergei Vitalievich (1888–1936). Military commander and Party functionary. Repressed.

Glossary of Names

Munblit, Georgy Nikolaevich (1904–1995). Literary critic and scriptwriter.

Muradeli, Vano Ilyich (1908–1970). Soviet composer.

Nakhimov, Pavel Stepanovich (1802–1855). Admiral in the Imperial Russian Navy.

Napoleon I (1769–1821). Emperor of the French 1803–1815.

Narbut, Vladimir Ivanovich (1888–1944). Soviet poet. Repressed.

Neigauz, Genrikh Gustavovich (1888–1964). Prominent pianist close to Pasternak.

Nemirovich-Danchenko, Vladimir Ivanovich (1859–1943). Russian stage director, co-founder (with K. Stanislavsky) and director of the Moscow Art Theater.

Nicholas I (1796–1955). Tsar 1825–1855.

Nikandrov (pseudonym of Shevtsov), Nikolai Nikandrovich (1878–1964). Soviet writer.

Nikitin, Mikhail Aleksandrovich (1902–?). Soviet writer.

Nikitin, Nikolai Nikolaevich (1895–1963). Soviet writer.

Nikolaeva (pseudonym of Volyanskaya), Galina Yevgenievna (1911–1963). Soviet writer.

Nikulin, Lev Veniaminovich (1891–1967). Soviet writer.

Nilin, Pavel Filippovich (1908–1981). Soviet writer.

Novikov-Priboy (pseudonym of Novikov), Aleksei Silych (1877–1944). Soviet writer.

Nusinov, Isaak Markovich (1889–1950). Literary scholar and critic. Repressed.

Olesha, Yury Karlovich (1899–1960). Major Soviet prose writer and dramatist.

Oleynikov, Nikolai Mikhailovich (1898–1942). Soviet poet. Was close to the Absurdist literary group Oberiu.

Orbeli, Iosif Abgarovich (1887–1961). Academician. In 1934–1951 Director of the Hermitage.

Ordzhonikidze, Grigory Konstantinovich (Sergo) (1886–1937). State and Party functionary, one of the leading figures of Stalinist industrialization.

Oreshin, Pyotr Vasilievich (1887–1938). Russian poet. Repressed.

Orlov, Nikolai Andreevich (1892–1964). Pianist. Emigrated in 1922.

Osmerkin, Aleksandr (1892–1953). Soviet artist.

Ostrov, Dmitry Konstantinovich (1906–?). Soviet writer.

Ostrovsky, Nikolai Alekseevich (1904–1936). Major Soviet writer. Author of canonical Socialist Realist novel *How the Steel Was Tempered* (*Kak zakalialas' stal'*).

Ovechkin, Valentin Vladimirovich (1904–1968). Soviet writer and essayist.

Ozerov, Nikolai Nikolaevich (1887–1953). Opera soloist of the Bolshoi Theater.

Panch, Petro (pseudonym of Panchenko, Petro Iosifovich) (1891–1978). Soviet Ukrainian writer.

Panfyorov, Fedor Ivanovich (1896–1960). Soviet writer. From 1931 editor-in-chief of the journal *Oktiabr'*.

Panova, Vera Fyodorovna (1905–1973). Soviet writer.

Pasternak, Boris Leonidovich (1890–1960). Major poet and prose writer.

Patolichev, Nikolai Semyonovich (1908–1989). Party functionary. Secretary of the Central Committee of the Communist Party.

Pavlenko, Pyotr Andreevich (1899–1951). Soviet writer.

Perelman, V. N. Soviet painter.

Pereverzev, Valerian Fedorovich (1882–1968). Literary scholar. Repressed.

Pervomaisky, Leonid Solomonovich (pseudonym of Ilya Shlemovich Gurevich) (1908–1973). Soviet Ukrainian writer.

Peshkova (Vvedenskaya), Nadezhda Alekseevna (1901–1971). Maxim Gorky's daughter-in-law.

Petrov-Vodkin, Kuzma Sergeevich (1878–1938). Prominent Russian and Soviet painter.

Piatakov, Georgy (Yury) Leonidovich (1890–1937). Soviet and Party functionary. Repressed.

Picasso, Pablo (1881–1973). Famous avant-garde painter.

Pikel, Richard V. (?–1936). Literary critic. Head of Zinoviev's Secretariat. Repressed.

Pilnyak (pseudonym of Vogau), **Boris Andreevich** (1894–1937). Major early Soviet writer. Repressed.

Pirozhkova, Antonina Nikolaevna (born 1912). Isaac Babel's wife.

Platonov (pseudonym of Klimentov), **Andrei Platonovich** (1899–1951). Major Soviet writer.

Plekhanov, Georgy Valentinovich (1856–1918). Revolutionary figure considered the "father of Russian Marxism."

Pletnev, Valerian Fedorovich (1886–1942). Soviet critic. In 1921–1932 head of Proletcult.

Pogodin (pseudonym of Stukalov), **Nikolai Fyodorovich** (1900–1962). Soviet playwright.

Poincaré, Raymond (1860–1934). French prime minister (1913–1914) and president (1913–1920).

Pokrovsky, Mikhail Nikolaevich (1868–1932). Leading Soviet historian. Deputy Commissar of Enlightenment (Narkompros).

Polikarpov, Dmitry Alekseevich (1905–1965). Party functionary and historian. In 1944–1946 Senior Secretary of the Union of Soviet Writers.

Politkovsky, V. M.

Polonskaia, Elizaveta Grigorievna (1890–1969). Soviet poet and translator.

Polonskaia, Veronika Vitoldovna (1908–1994). Actress. One of Mayakovsky's loves.

Polonsky (pseudonym of Gusev), Viacheslav Pavlovich (1886–1932). Influential critic and journalist. In 1920s editor-in-chief of the journals *Novyi mir* (*New World*) and *Pechat i revoliutsia* (*Press and Revolution*).

Polyak, Lidia Moiseevna (1899–1995). Literary critic.

Popkov, Pyotr Sergeevich (1903–1950). Party functionary. After World War II First Secretary of the Leningrad City and Regional Party Committees. Repressed.

Popov, Georgy Mikhailovich (1906–1968). Party functionary. After World War II First Secretary of Moscow City and Regional Party Committees and Secretary of the Central Committee of the Communist Party.

Poskrebyshev, Aleksandr Nikolaevich (1891–1965). Stalin's personal secretary.

Postupalsky, Igor Stefanovich (1907–1989). Soviet poet and translator.

Postyshev, Pavel Petrovich (1887–1939). Party functionary. Repressed.

Pozharsky, Dmitry Mikhailovich (1578–1642). Russian military commander who with Minin helped drive out the invading Poles.

Pravdukhin, Valerian Pavlovich (1892–1939). Soviet writer and literary critic. Repressed.

Prishvin, Mikhail Mikhailovich (1873–1954). Russian and Soviet writer.

Prokofiev, Aleksandr Andreevich (1900–1974). Soviet poet. A leading figure in the Leningrad Writers Union.

Prokofiev, Sergei Sergeevich (1891–1953). Major Soviet composer.

Prut, Iosif Leonidovich (1900–1996). Soviet playwright.

Pshebyshevsky (Pshibyshevsky), B. S.

Pudovkin, Vsevolod Illarionovich (1893–1953). Major Soviet film director.

Punin, Nikolai Nikolaevich (1888–1953). Avant-garde art critic. In 1920s influential member of Fine Art Section of the Commissariat of Enlightenment (Narkompros). Akhmatova's husband.

Pushkin, Aleksandr Sergeevich (1799–1837). Russia's national poet.

Puzin, Aleksei Aleksandrovich (1904–1987). In 1940–1944 deputy head of the Central Committee's Agitprop.

Pyriev, Ivan Aleksandrovich (1901–1968). Soviet film director.

Rabichev, N. N. Party functionary. In 1920s and early 1930s deputy head of the Central Committee's Department of Culture and Propaganda.

Rabinovich, Dmitry. Music critic.

Radek (pseudonym of Sobelson), Karl Berngardovich (1885–1939). Party activist, journalist. Repressed.

Radishchev, Aleksandr Nikolaevich (1749–1802). Author of *A Journey from Petersburg to Moscow* (*Puteshestvie iz Peterburga v Moskvu*) (1790).

Radlov, Nikolai Ernestovich (1889–1942). Soviet graphic artist and art critic.

Raikh, Zinaida Nikolaevna (1894–1939). Actress. The first wife of Yesenin and later wife and leading actress of Meyerhold. Brutally murdered after his arrest.

Raizman, Yuly Yakovlevich (1903–1994). Soviet film director.

Rakhmanov, Leonid Nikolaevich (1908–1988). Soviet writer.

Ramzin, Leonid Konstantinovich (1887–1948). Heating engineer. Key figure in the Industrial Party show trial of 1930.

Raskolnikov (pseudonym of Ilyin), Fyodor Fyodorovich (1892–1939). Party and military functionary.

Reich, Bernhard (1894–1972). Theater critic and husband of Asja Latsis.

Rembrandt van Rijn (1606–1669). Renowned Dutch artist.

Remizov, Aleksei Mikhailovich (1877–1957). Russian writer. Emigrated 1921.

Repin, Ilya Yefimovich (1844–1930). Leading realist artist especially known for his historical and genre paintings.

Rest, B. (1907–?). Soviet writer and scriptwriter.

Riabushinsky, Pavel Pavlovich (1871–1924). Russian entrepreneur. Emigrated after the Revolution.

Riazhsky, Georgy Geogievich (1895–1952). Soviet painter.

Rimsky-Korsakov, Nikolai Andreevich (1844–1908). Major Russian composer.

Robespierre, Maximilien (1758–1794). One of the leading figures of the French Revolution.

Rodov, Semyon Abramovich (1893–1968). Soviet poet and literary critic. Active member of RAPP.

Rolland, Romain (1866–1944). French novelist with Communist sympathies. Active in the antifascist movement.

Rolland-Kudasheva, M. P. Romain Rolland's wife.

Romanov, Panteleimon Sergeevich (1884–1938). Soviet writer.

Romm, Mikhail Ilyich (1901–1971). Soviet film director.

Rozental, Mark Moissevich (1906–1975). Soviet philosopher.

Rozhdestvensky, Vsevolod Aleksandrovich (1895–1977). Soviet poet.

Rudzutak, Yan Ernestovich (1887–1938). State and Party functionary. Repressed.

Runin, Boris Mikhailovich (1912–1994). Literary critic.

Rykov, Aleksei Ivanovich (1881–1938). One of the Party leaders, member of the Politburo and the head of the Soviet government. Repressed.

Ryss, Yevgeny Samuilovich (1908–1973). Soviet writer and theater critic.

Saakadze, Georgy (1580–1629). Georgian military commander and political leader.

Sadofiev, Ilya Ivanovich (1889–1965). Soviet poet.

Sadovsky, Prov Mikhailovich (1874–1947). Artist of the Maly Theater.

Sakhnovsky, Vasily Grigorievich (1886–1945). Director of the Moscow Art Theater. Theater critic and pedagogue.

Saltykov-Shchedrin, Mikhail Yevgrafovich (1826–1889). Major Russian satirical writer.

Samosud, Samuil Abramovich (1884–1964). Conductor and artistic director of the Bolshoi Theater.

Sannikov, Grigory Aleksandrovich (1899–1969). Soviet poet.

Sats, Igor Aleksandrovich (1903–1979). Literary scholar. Worked in *Literaturnyi kritik* and *Novyi mir.*

Sats, Natalia Ilyinichna (1903–1993). Founder and artistic director of the Central Children's Theater.

Savin, Lev (pseudonym of Lev Savelievich Moiseevich) (1891–?). Soviet writer.

Sayanov (pseudonym of Makhlin), Vissarion Mikhailovich (1903–1959). Soviet writer.

Schoenberg, Arnold (1874–1951). Austrian composer.

Seifullina, Lidia Nikolaevna (1889–1954). Soviet writer.

Selivanovsky, Aleksei Pavlovich (1900–1938). Literary critic. One of the leaders of RAPP. Repressed.

Selvinsky, Ilya (Karl) Lvovich (1899–1968). Soviet poet.

Semenko, Mikhail Vasilievich (1892–1937). Leading Ukrainian Futurist poet. Repressed.

Semper, Johannes (1892–1970). Soviet Estonian writer.

Semyonov, Sergei Aleksandrovich (1893–1942). Soviet writer.

Senchenko, Ivan Yefimovich (1902–1975). Soviet Ukrainian writer.

Serafimovich, Aleksandr (pseudonym of Aleksandr Serafimovich Popov) (1863–1949). Soviet writer.

Serebriansky, Mark Isaakovich (1900/01–1941). Soviet literary critic.

Sergeev-Tsensky (pseudonym of Sergeev), Sergei Nikolaevich (1875–1958). Soviet writer.

Shaginyan, Marietta Sergeevna (1888–1982). Soviet novelist and essayist.

Shakespeare, William (1564–1616).

Shaporin, Yury Aleksandrovich (1887–1966). Soviet composer.

Shaumian, Stepan Georgievich (1878–1918). Revolutionary leader.

Shaw, George Bernard (1856–1950). Irish dramatist, literary critic, a socialist spokesman, and a leading figure in the twentieth-century theater.

Shcherbakov, Aleksandr Sergeevich (1901–1945). Party functionary.

Shcherbina, Vladimir Rodionovich (1908–1989). Literary scholar and critic.

Shchors, Nikolai Aleksandrovich (1895–1919). Military commander during the Civil War in Ukraine.

Shchukin, Boris Vasilievich (1894–1939). Soviet actor. The first major interpreter of the role of Lenin in theater and cinema.

Shebalin, Vissarion Yakovlevich (1902–1963). Soviet composer.

Shepilov, Dmitry Trofimovich (1905–1995). Party functionary. In 1940s head of the Party's Central Committee Department of Propaganda and Agitation (Agitprop).

Shershenevich, Vadim Gabrielovich (1893–1942). Poet and translator.

Shirokov, Ivan Mikhailovich (1899–1984). In 1945–1946 Secretary of the Leningrad City Committee of the Party.

Shishkov, Viacheslav Yakolevich. (1873–1945). Writer.

Shkiryatov, Matvei Fedorovich (1883–1954). Party and state functionary.

Shklovsky, Viktor Borisovich (1893–1984). Literary critic, writer. One of the leading figures of the Formalist school. In the 1930s he turned to film criticism and script writing.

Shmidt, Otto Yulievich (1891–1956). Geologist. Academician and polar explorer.

Shmidt, Vasily Vasilievich (1886–1938). Party functionary. Repressed.

Sholokhov, Mikhail Aleksandrovich (1905–1984). Leading Soviet writer.

Shostakovich, Dmitry Dmitrievich (1906–1975). Great Soviet composer.

Shpanov, Nikolai Nikolaevich (1896–1961). Soviet writer.

Shtein, Aleksandr Petrovich (1906–1973). Soviet playwright.

Shteinpress, Boris Solomonovich (1908–1986). Musicologist.

Shterenberg, David Petrovich (1881–1948). Soviet painter.

Shukhov, Ivan Petrovich (1906–1977). Soviet writer.

Shumiatsky, Boris Zakharovich (1886–1938). In 1930s head of the State Administration of Cinematography.

Simonov, Konstantin Mikhailovich (1915–1979). Soviet poet, novelist, playwright, and literary functionary.

Skuratov-Belsky, Grigory Lukyanovich (Maliuta Skuratov) (?–1573). A nobleman and the leader of the *Oprichnina* terror under Ivan the Terrible.

Skvortsov-Stepanov, Ivan Ivanovich (1870–1928). Party journalist and functionary.

Slavin, Lev Isaevich (1896–1984). Soviet writer.

Slonimsky, Mikhail Leonidovich (1897–1972). Soviet writer.

Smelyakov, Yaroslav Vasilievich (1912/13–1972). Soviet poet.

Smidovich, Pyotr Germogenovich (1874–1935). Party functionary.

Smilga, Ivan Tenisovich (1892–1938). Military commander and Party functionary. Repressed.

Smirnov, Aleksandr Petrovich (1878–1938). State and Party functionary. Repressed.

Sobolev, Leonid Sergeevich (1898–1971). Soviet writer and literary functionary.

Sofronov, Anatoly Vladimirovich (1911–1990). Soviet poet, playwright, and literary functionary. In the 1940s one of the leading figures in the "struggle against cosmopolitanism."

Sokolnikov, Grigory Yakovlevich (pseudonym of Girsh Yankelevich Brilliant) (1888–1939). Prominent Bolshevik. Repressed.

Sollertinsky, Ivan Ivanovich (1902–1944). Musicologist, was close to Shostakovich and Bakhtin.

Sologub (pseudonym of Teternikov), Fyodor Kuzmich (1863–1927). Symbolist poet and novelist.

Soloviev, Leonid Vasilievich (1906–1962). Soviet writer.

Sosnovsky, Lev Semyonovich (1886–1937). Prominent journalist in 1920s. Repressed.

Glossary of Names

Spassky, Sergei Dmitrievich (1898–1956). Soviet writer and translator.

Speransky, Aleksei Dmitrievich (1887/88–1961). Soviet physiologist. Academician.

Stalin (pseudonym of Dzhugashvili), **Iosif Vissarionovich** (1879–1953).

Stanislavsky (pseudonym of Alekseev), **Konstantin Sergeevich** (1861–1938). Prominent stage director and the founder, with Nemirovich-Danchenko, of the Moscow Art Theater.

Stanitsyn, Viktor Yakovlevich (1897–1976). Moscow Art Theater actor and director.

Stavsky (pseudonym of Kirpichnikov), **Vladimir Petrovich** (1900–1943). Soviet writer and functionary. In 1930s General Secretary of the Union of Soviet Writers.

Stetsky, Aleksei Ivanovich (1896–1938). Party functionary. In 1930s head of the Central Committee Department for Culture and Propaganda (Kultprop).

Stolper, Aleksander Borisovich (1907–1979). Soviet film director.

Stravinsky, Igor Fedorovich (1882–1971). Famous modernist composer.

Subotsky, Lev Matveevich (1900–1959). Soviet literary critic. In 1930s editor-in-chief of *Literaturnaia gazeta*.

Sudakov, Ilyia Yakovlevich (1890–1969). Russian stage director. Worked in Moscow Art Theater, TRAM, and the Maly Theater.

Sukhovo-Kobylin, Aleksandr Vasilievich (1817–1903). Russian playwright.

Surikov, Vasily Ivanovich (1848–1916). Russian painter of historical subjects.

Surkov, Aleksei Aleksandrovich (1899–1983). Soviet poet and literary functionary.

Suslov, Mikhail Andreevich (1902–1982). Party functionary, secretary of the Central Committee.

Sutyrin, Vladimir Andreevich (1902–1976). Soviet critic and writer. One of the leading figures of RAPP.

Suvorov, Aleksandr Vasilievich (1730–1800). Russian military commander.

Svetlov (pseudonym of Sheinsman), **Mikhail Arkadievich** (1903–1964). Soviet poet.

Svidersky, Aleksei Ivanovich (1878–1933). State and Party functionary and diplomat. In late 1920s–early 1930s the head of Glaviskusstvo for the Russian Federation.

Svobodin, Nikolai Kapitonovich (1898–1973). Soviet actor.

Syrtsov, Sergei Ivanovich (1893–1937). Party and state functionary. Repressed.

Tairov, Aleksandr Yakovlevich (1885–1950). Prominent stage director, founder, and artistic director of the Kamernyi Theater.

Tal, Boris Markovich (1898–1938). Head of the Central Committee Department of the Press and Publishing, member of the editorial board of *Pravda*. Repressed.

Tamarkin, E. M. Head of the film section of the Central Committee's Department of Cultural and Educational Work.

Tarasenkov, Anatoly Kuzmich (1909–1956). Literary critic.

Tarasova, Alla Konstantinovna (1898–1973). Soviet actress. From 1916 worked in the Moscow Art Theater.

Tarasov-Rodionov, Aleksander Ignatievich (1885–1937). Soviet writer. Repressed.

Tarkhanov (pseudonym of Moskvin), Mikhail Mikhailovich (1877–1948). One of the leading actors of the Moscow Art Theater.

Tarlovsky, Mark Arievich (1902–1952). Soviet poet and translator.

Thälmann, Ernst (1886–1944). German communist leader.

Tikhonov, Nikolai Semyonovich (1896–1979). Soviet poet and public figure.

Tikhonov (pseudonym of Serebrov), Aleksandr Nikolaevich (1880–1956). After the Revolution head of the publishing house Vsemirnaia Literatura (World Literature). In 1920s editor-in-chief of the journal *Russkii sovremennik* (*Russian Contemporary*). In the 1930s head of the Akademia Publishing House.

Timasheff, Nicholas S. (Nicholas Sergeevich) (1886–1970). Son of the Minister of Trade under the last tsarist government. Emigrated in 1922. American sociologist. Known for *The Great Retreat* (1947) in which he argued that Soviet society had abandoned its revolutionary course and was returning to the cultural and social practices of tsarist Russia.

Timofeev, Leonid Ivanovich (1904–1984). Literary scholar.

Tolstoy, Aleksei Nikolaevich (1882–1945). Leading Soviet novelist.

Tolstoy, Lev Nikolaevich (1828–1910). Great Russian writer.

Tomsky (pseudonym of Efremov), Mikhail Pavlovich (1880–1936). Leader of the Soviet trade unions. Committed suicide.

Trauberg, Ilya Zakharovich (1905–1948). Soviet film director, playwright, and critic.

Trauberg, Leonid Zakharovich (1902–1990). Soviet film director and pedagogue.

Tregub, Semyon Adolfovich (1907–1975). Literary critic.

Trenev, Konstantin Andreevich (1876–1945). Soviet playwright.

Troshchenko, E. D. Prose writer.

Trotsky (pseudonym of Bronshtein), Lev Davidovich (1879–1940). Bolshevik leader. His faction called the United Opposition lost a power struggle with Stalin in 1927. Exiled to Alma-Ata, then deported 1928. Assassinated by a Stalinist agent in Mexico.

Tseitlin, M. Senior editor of *Literaturnaia gazeta*.

Tselikovskaia, Liudmila Vasilievna (1919–1992). Soviet actress.

Tsenin, Sergei Sergeevich (1884–1964). Artist of the Kamernyi Theater.

Tsvetaeva, Marina Ivanovna (1892–1941). Major Russian poet. In 1922–1939 lived in emigration. Personal tragedy and ostracism drove her to suicide in 1941.

Tufanov, Aleksandr Vasilievich (1878–1941). Avant-garde poet and linguist.

Turganov, Boris Alexandrovich (1901–?). Soviet poet and translator.

Turgenev, Ivan Sergeevich (1818–1883). Major Russian writer.

Glossary of Names

Tvardovsky, Aleksandr Trifonovich (1910–1971). Major Soviet poet and public figure.

Tveriak (pseudonym of Solovyov), Aleksei Artamonovich (1900–1937). Soviet writer. Repressed.

Tychina, Pavlo Grigorovych (1891–1967). Major Soviet Ukrainian poet and public figure.

Tynyanov, Yury Nikolaevich (1894–1943). Major literary scholar and writer.

Unshlikht, Iosif Stanislavovich (1879–1938). Military commander and one of the founders of the Cheka. Repressed.

Upit, Andrei Martynovich (1877–1970). Soviet Latvian writer and public figure.

Uritsky, Moisei Solomonovich (1873–1918). Russian revolutionary. Head of Petrograd Cheka.

Ushakov, Nikolai Nikolaevich (1899–1973). Soviet poet and translator.

Usievich, Elena Feliksovna (1893–1968). Daughter of Felix Kon. In 1930s influential literary critic and senior editor of the journal *Literaturnyi kritik*.

Utkin, Iosif Pavlovich (1903–1944). Soviet poet.

Vakhtangov, Yevgeny Bagrationovich (1883–1922). Prominent Soviet stage director.

Vaks, B. Playwright and critic.

Valve (Valbe), Boris Solomonovich (1889/90–?). Literary scholar.

Vardin, Illarion (pseudonym of I. V. Mgeladze) (1890–1943). Literary critic and journalist. One of the founders of RAPP and the journal *Na postu*. Repressed.

Vareikis, Iosif Mikhailovich (1892–1939). Party functionary. Repressed.

Varshavsky, S. P. (1906–1980). Soviet writer and playwright.

Vasilevskaia, Vanda Lvovna (1905–1964). Polish and Soviet writer.

Vasiliev, Pavel Nikolaevich (1910–1937). Soviet poet. Repressed.

Vasiliev, Sergei Dmitrievich (1900–1959). Soviet film director.

Vazha Pshavela (pseudonym of Luka Pavlovich Razikashvili) (1861–1915). Major Georgian poet.

Venclova, Antanas (1906–1971). Soviet Lithuanian writer and public figure.

Vengerova, Zinaida Afanasievna (1867–1941). Historian of West European literature.

Veresaev (pseudonym of Smidovich), Viktor Viktorovoch (1867–1945). Russian and Soviet writer.

Vershigora, Pyotr Petrovich (1905–1963). Soviet military commander and writer.

Vesely, Artem (pseudonym of Nikolai Ivanovich Kochkurov) (1899–1939). Soviet writer. Repressed.

Vinogradov, Anatoly Kornelievich (1888–1946). Soviet writer.

Vinogradov, Viktor Vladimirovich (1894/95–1969). Prominent linguist and literary scholar. Academician.

Virta, Nikolai Yevgenievich (1906–1976). Novelist, playwright, journalist.

Vishnevsky, Vsevolod Vitalievich (1900–1951). Soviet playwright and script writer.

Vladykin, Grigory Ivanovich. In 1940s head of the Literature Department of the Central Committee Propaganda and Agitation Administration (Agitprop).

Voitinskaia, Olga Sergeevna (1905–1968). Philosopher.

Volchek, Boris Izrailevich (1905–1974). Soviet cameraman.

Volin, Boris (pseudonym of Boris Mikhailovich Fradkin) (1886–1957). Journalist. Head of Glavlit from 1931 to 1935.

Volkov, I. D. Playwright.

Volodarsky, V. (pseudonym of Moisei Markovich Goldshtein) (1891–1918). Russian revolutionary.

Voloshin, Maximilian Aleksandrovich (1877–1932). Russian poet.

Voronsky, Aleksandr Konstantinovich (1884–1937). In 1920s influential literary critic, founder and the editor-in-chief of the leading literary journal *Krasnaia Nov'*. Repressed.

Voroshilov, Kliment Yefremovich (1881–1961). Party and military leader, member of the Politburo.

Voznesensky, Nikolai Alekseevich (1903–1950). Economist, academician, Party and state functionary. In the 1940s member of Politburo, in 1938–1949 chairman of Gosplan. Repressed.

Vurgun, Samed (pseudonym of Samed Yusif ogly Vekilov) (1906–1956). Leading Soviet Azerbaijani poet.

Vvedensky, Aleksandr Ivanovich (1901–1941). Avant-garde poet and leading member of the Russian Absurdist literary group Oberiu.

Wrangel, Pyotr Nikolaevich (1878–1928). Baron. Russian general, one of the leaders of the White Army during the Civil War.

Yagdfeld, Grigory Borisovich (1908–1969). Soviet playwright.

Yagoda, Genrikh Grigorievich (1891–1938). Head of the Soviet secret police between 1934 and 1936.

Yakovlev (pseudonym of Epstein), **Yakov Arkadievich** (1896–1938). Party functionary. Repressed.

Yakubovsky, Pyotr Filippovich (1860–1911). Russian poet.

Yanovsky, Yury Ivanovich (1902–1954). Soviet Ukrainian writer.

Yanshin, Mikhail Mikhailovich (1902–1976). One of the leading actors of the Moscow Art Theater.

Yanson, Nikolai Mikhailovich (1882–1938). Party functionary. Repressed.

Yaroslavsky, Emelian Mikhailovich (pseudonym of Minei Izrailevich Gubelman) (1878–1943). Party functionary, historian, and journalist.

Yasensky, Bruno (Bruno Jasien'ski) (1901–1941). Poet and writer. Polish Communist who emigrated to the Soviet Union in 1929 and became Secretary of the International Association of Revolutionary Writers (MORP). Repressed.

Glossary of Names 509

Yashvili, Paolo (Pavel) Dzhibrazlovich (1895–1937). Prominent Georgian poet. Friend of Pasternak. Repressed.

Yavich, Avgust Yefimovich (1900–1979). Soviet writer.

Yegolin, Aleksandr Mikhailovich (1896–1959). Literary scholar. In 1944–1947 deputy head of the Central Committee Propaganda and Agitation Administration (Agitprop).

Yekelchik, Yury Izrailevich (1907–1956). Soviet cameraman.

Yenukidze, Avel Sofronovich (1877–1937). Party and state functionary. Repressed.

Yermilov, Vladimir Vladimirovich (1904–1965). Literary critic and functionary. Leading figure in RAPP. In the 1940s editor-in-chief of *Literaturnaia gazeta*.

Yesenin, Sergei Alexandrovich (1895–1925). Major early Soviet poet.

Yezhov, Nikolai Ivanovich (1895–1939). Party functionary and head of the secret police in 1936–39. A central figure of the Great Terror. Repressed.

Yudin, Pavel Fedorovich (1891–1968). Philosopher, academician, party functionary. In 1930s one of the leading figures of the Soviet literary scene.

Yunovich, M. M. Editor of the journal *Oktiabr'*.

Yuon, Konstantin Fyodorovich (1975–1958). Prominent Soviet painter.

Yutkevich, Sergei Iosifovich (1904–1985). Soviet film director.

Yuzovsky, Iosif Ilyich (1902–1964). Theater and literary critic.

Zabolotsky, Nikolai Alekseevich (1903–1958). Major poet.

Zakharchenko, Vasily Dmitrievich (born 1915). Soviet poet.

Zakharov, Vladimir Grigorievich (1901–1956). Soviet composer and the author of folk-based patriotic songs.

Zamoisky (pseudonym of Zevalkin), Pyotr Ivanovich (1896–1958). Soviet writer. In 1920s one of the leaders of VOKP (The All-Russian Union of Peasant Writers).

Zamyatin, Yevgeny Ivanovich (1884–1937). Major writer and essayist, the author of dystopian novel *My* (*We*). Emigrated 1931.

Zarkhi, Natan Abramovich (1900–1935). Soviet script writer.

Zarudin, Nikolai Nikolaevich (1899–1937). Soviet writer, member of Pereval. Repressed.

Zaslavsky, David Iosifovich (1880–1965). Soviet journalist.

Zazubrin (pseudonym of Zubtsov), Vladimir Yakovlevich (1895–1938). Soviet writer. Repressed.

Zharov, Aleksandr Alekseevich (1904–1984). Soviet poet.

Zhdanov, Andrei Aleksandrovich (1896–1948). Party functionary. Secretary of the Central Committee. Leading Party spokesman on ideological and cultural issues whose pronouncements in the 1940s and attacks on modernist cultural figures gave the decade the name "the Zhdanov era."

Zhelyabov, Andrei (1850–1881). Member of the "People's Will," who took part in three attempts on the life of Alexander II. Along with his lover, Sofia Perovskaya, he organized the assassination of the tsar on 1 March 1881.

Zhiga (pseudonym of Smirnov), Ivan Fedorovich (1895–1949). Soviet essayist.

Zinoviev (pseudonym of Radomyslsky), Grigory Yevseevich (1883–1936). Party leader. Chairman of the Petrograd Soviet after the October Revolution and head of the Communist International from 1919 to 1926. Member of the Trotskyite United Opposition 1925–1927. Repressed.

Zlatogorova, Bronislava Yakovlevna (1905–1995). Opera soloist of the Bolshoi Theater.

Zonin, A. I. (1901–1962). Soviet writer and critic.

Zoshchenko, Mikhail Mikhailovich (1895–1958). Leading Soviet humorist. In 1946 he and Anna Akhmatova were targeted in a cultural purge and expelled from the Writers Union.

Zweig, Stefan (1881–1942). Austrian biographer, poet, and novelist.

Documents

Document 1. Memorandum from VChK Chairman F. E. Dzerzhinsky to the TsK RKP(b) with objections to the intercessions of RSFSR people's commissar of education on behalf of art figures going abroad, 19 April 1921.
Document 2. Memorandum from RSFSR People's Commissar of Education A. V. Lunacharsky to the Politburo of the TsK RKP(b) on the procedure for allowing art world figures to travel abroad [Not before 12 May 1921].
Document 3. Letter from Deputy VChK Chairman I. S. Unshlikht and VChK Foreign Department (INO) Head L. Davydov to the TsK RKP(b), 18 May 1921.
Document 4. Letter from A. V. Lunacharsky to the TsK RKP(b), 7 June 1921.
Document 5. Letter from INO [Foreign Department] VChK Head L. Davydov to the TsK RKP(b), 28 June 1921.
Document 6. Letter from A. V. Lunacharsky to RSFSR Narkomindel, 8 July 1921.
Document 7. Letter from A. V. Lunacharsky to the TsK RKP(b), 11 July 1921.
Document 8. Note from V. R. Menzhinsky to V. I. Lenin, 11 July 1921.
Document 9. Letter from A. M. Gorky to V. I. Lenin [Not before 12 July 1921].
Document 10. Letter from A. V. Lunacharsky to TsK RKP(b), 16 July 1921.
Document 11. Note from L. B. Kamenev to V. M. Molotov [No later than 23 July 1921].
Document 12. Resolution of the Politburo of the TsK RKP(b) on L. B. Kamenev's proposal to reconsider the previous resolution banning A. A. Blok from foreign travel, 23 July 1921.
Document 13. Memo from V. I. Lenin to V. M. Molotov, 12 January 1922.
Document 14. Letter from A. V. Lunacharsky to V. I. Lenin, 13 January 1922.
Document 15. Letter from A. V. Lunacharsky to V. M. Molotov, 14 January 1922.
Document 16. Resolution of the Politburo of the TsK RKP(b) on the closure of the Bolshoi and Mariinsky theaters, 2 November 1922.
Document 17. Resolution of the Politburo of the TsK RKP(b) on the academic theaters, 2 July 1925.
Document 18. Memo from L. D. Trotsky to the Politburo of the TsK RKP(b) on young writers and artists, 30 June 1922.

Document 19. Report from TsK RKP(b) Agitation and Propaganda Department Deputy Head Ya. A. Yakovlev to I. V. Stalin on the situation among writers [No later than 3 July 1922].

Document 20. Memorandum from I. V. Stalin to the Politburo of the TsK RKP(b) on the subject of L. D. Trotsky's proposals on young writers and artists, 3 July 1922.

Document 21. Resolution of the Politburo of the TsK RKP(b) "On Party policy in the sphere of literature," 18 June 1925.

Document 22. From a letter from a group of artists to I. V. Stalin [No later than 3 February 1926].

Document 23. Resolution of the Politburo of the TsK VKP(b) "On writers' organizations," 5 May 1927.

Document 24. Letter from the Proletarian Theater Association to I. V. Stalin [December 1928].

Document 25. Letter from I. V. Stalin to playwright V. N. Bill-Belotserkovsky, 1 February 1929.

Document 26. Letter from I. V. Stalin to the Communist writers of RAPP, 28 February 1929.

Document 27. Excerpt from an uncorrected shorthand report of I. V. Stalin's speech at a meeting with Ukrainian writers, 12 February 1929.

Document 28. Resolution of the TsK VKP(b) Secretariat "On the feuilletons of Com. Demian Bedny, 'Climb down off the Stove' ["*Slezai s pechki*"] and 'Without Mercy' ["*Bez poshchady*"]," 6 December 1930.

Document 29. Letter from D. Bedny to I. V. Stalin, 8 December 1930.

Document 30. Letter from I. V. Stalin to D. Bedny, 12 December 1930.

Document 31. Resolution of the TsK RKP(b) Politburo on the essays of A. M. Gorky, 31 July 1920.

Document 32. Letter from A. M. Gorky to A. I. Rykov, 1 July 1922.

Document 33. Letter from I. V. Stalin to A. M. Gorky, 11 June 1929.

Document 34. Letter from I. V. Stalin to A. M. Gorky, 24 October 1930.

Document 35. Letter from A. M. Gorky to I. V. Stalin, 2 November 1930.

Document 36. Letter from I. V. Stalin to A. M. Gorky [No later than 15 December 1930].

Document 37. Letter from I. V. Stalin to A. M. Gorky, 10 January 1931.

Document 38. Resolution of the TsK VKP(b) Politburo "On the speeches against Maxim Gorky by certain Siberian writers and literary organizations," 15 December 1929.

Document 39. Letter from A. M. Gorky to I. V. Stalin, 8 January 1930.

Document 40. Resolution of the Politburo TsK VKP(b) on B. A. Pilnyak's "Tale of the Unextinguished Moon," 13 May 1926.

Document 41. Postal telegram from A. V. Lunacharsky to A. I. Rykov on the GPU prohibition of M. A. Bulgakov's *Days of the Turbins*, 27 September 1926.

Document 42. Memorandum from TsK VKP(b) Orgburo member and RSFSR People's Commissar for Agriculture A. P. Smirnov to the TsK VKP(b) Politburo concerning lifting the ban on *Days of the Turbins*, 8 October 1927.

Document 43. Letter from A. V. Lunacharsky to I. V. Stalin, 12 February 1929.

Document 44. Letter from Deputy Chief of Agitpropotdel TsK VKP(b) S. N. Krylov to V. M. Molotov, 16 November 1927.

Document 45. Letter from A. Ya. Tairov to M. P. Tomsky, 19 November 1927.
Document 46. Memorandum from M. P. Tomsky to V. M. Molotov, 21 November 1927.
Document 47. Resolution of the Politburo TsK VKP(b) on banning M. Yu. Levidov's play *Conspiracy of Equals,* 24 November 1927.
Document 48. Report from P. M. Kerzhentsev, Deputy Head of Agitprop TsK VKP(b), to the Politburo of the TsK VKP(b) on M. A. Bulgakov's *Flight* [No later than 6 January 1929].
Document 49. Note from RSFSR Glaviskusstvo Head A. I. Svidersky to TsK VKP(b) Secretary A. P. Smirnov on his meeting with M. A. Bulgakov, 30 July 1929.
Document 50. Note from TsK VKP(b) Secretary A. P. Smirnov to the TsK VKP(b) Politburo concerning M. A. Bulgakov's petition, 3 August 1929.
Document 51. Letter from M. A. Bulgakov to I. V. Stalin, 30 May 1931.
Document 52. Letter from E. I. Zamyatin to I. V. Stalin, June 1931.
Document 53. Letter from B. A. Pilnyak to I. V. Stalin, 4 January 1931.
Document 54. Letter from I. V. Stalin to B. A. Pilnyak, 7 January 1931.
Document 55. Note from I. V. Stalin to M. S. Shaginyan concerning her novel *Hydrocentral,* 20 May 1931.
Document 56. Letter from K. S. Stanislavsky to I. V. Stalin, 29 October 1931.
Document 57. Letter from I. V. Stalin to K. S. Stanislavsky, 9 November 1931.
Document 58. Note from I. V. Stalin to the editors of *Red Virgin Soil* concerning A. P. Platonov's "To Advantage" [*Vprok*] [May 1931].
Document 59. From a report by Glavlit Chief P. I. Lebedev-Poliansky to the Orgburo TsK VKP(b) "On the activities of Glavlit" [No later than 7 March 1927].
Document 60. Resolution of the Politburo TsK VKP(b) on the reorganization of Glavlit, 3 September 1930.
Document 61. Resolution of the Politburo of the TsK VKP(b) "On strengthening political oversight over the output of the periodical and nonperiodical press," 5 April 1931.
Document 62. From a report by the OGPU Secret Political Department "On anti-Soviet activity among the intelligentsia in 1931" [No earlier than 10 December 1931].
Document 63. OGPU special memorandum "On writers' responses to the assistance rendered by the government to the son of writer M. E. Saltykov-Shchedrin," March 1932.
Document 64. Resolution of the TsK VKP(b) Politburo "On restructuring literary and arts organizations," 23 April 1932.
Document 65. Resolution of the TsK VKP(b) Orgburo on measures to implement the resolution of the TsK VKP(b) Politburo "On restructuring literary and arts organizations," 7 May 1932.
Document 66. Letter from A. A. Fadeev to TsK VKP(b) Secretary L. M. Kaganovich, 10 May 1932.
Document 67. Letter from V. M. Kirshon to I. V. Stalin and L. M. Kaganovich [No earlier than 26 May 1932].
Document 68. Memorandum from TsK VKP(b) Kultpropotdel Deputy Head N. N. Rabichev to the TsK VKP(b) secretaries "On the progress of the plenum of the writers' organizing committee," 1 November 1932.

Document 69. Memorandum from I. M. Gronsky to the TsK VKP(b) secretaries on preparations for the All-Union Writers' Congress, 16 March 1933.

Document 70. Letter from A. A. Zhdanov to I. V. Stalin [28 August 1934].

Document 71. Note from GUGB NKVD SSSR Secret Political Department Deputy Head G. Liushkov to USSR People's Commissar of Internal Affairs G. G. Yagoda on the discovery of an underground leaflet at the All-Union Writers' Congress, 20 August 1934.

Document 72. Special report from the GUGB NKVD SSSR Secret Political Department "On the progress of the All-Union Congress of Soviet Writers" [No later than 31 August 1934].

Document 73. Special report from the GUGB NKVD SSSR Secret Political Department "On the progress of the All-Union Congress of Soviet Writers," 31 August 1934.

Document 74. Letter from A. M. Gorky to the TsK VKP(b) [30 August–1 September 1934].

Document 75. Report from the GUGB NKVD SSSR Secret Political Department "On writers' attitude toward the recent writers' congress and toward the new leadership of the Union of Soviet Writers" [No earlier than 9 September 1934].

Document 76. Letter from A. M. Gorky to I. V. Stalin, 25 January 1932.

Document 77. Letter from A. M. Gorky to I. V. Stalin, 24 March 1932.

Document 78. Letter from A. M. Gorky to I. V. Stalin, 28 February 1933.

Document 79. Letter from I. V. Stalin to A. M. Gorky [No earlier than 1 March 1933].

Document 80. Special Report from GUGB NKVD SSSR Secret Political Department "On progress in the preparations for the First Congress of the Union of Soviet Writers" [No earlier than 10 July 1934].

Document 81. Letter from A. M. Gorky to I. V. Stalin, 2 August 1934.

Document 82. Letter from A. M. Gorky to I. V. Stalin [No earlier than 7–10 March 1936].

Document 83. Letter from A. M. Gorky to TsK VKP(b) Secretary A. A. Andreev, 8 December 1935.

Document 84. Memorandum from SSP SSSR Secretary A. S. Shcherbakov to I. V. Stalin on the situation in literature, 2 January 1936.

Document 85. Report from the SSP SSSR Organizing Committee Secretary P. F. Yudin to I. V. Stalin on the request of writer E. I. Zamyatin to be accepted as a member of the Union of Soviet Writers, 14 June 1934.

Document 86. Memorandum from TsK VKP(b) Secretary A. A. Andreev to I. V. Stalin on Soviet writers' awards [July 1938].

Document 87. Memorandum from TsK VKP(b) Press and Publishing Department Head A. E. Nikitin to the TsK VKP(b) secretaries "On the situation in the Union of Soviet Writers," 28 February 1938.

Document 88. Statement from *Literary Gazette* editor O. S. Voitinskaia to A. A. Zhdanov on the situation in the SSP SSSR [Before 15 March 1938].

Document 89. Memorandum from TsK VKP(b) Secretary A. A. Andreev to I. V. Stalin on the conference with writers [No earlier than 27 March 1938].

Document 90. Excerpt from a memorandum from SSP SSSR Secretaries A. A. Fadeev and V. Ya. Kirpotin to the TsK VKP(b) secretaries "On the Anti-Party Faction in Soviet Criticism," 10 February 1940.

List of Documents

Document 91. Memorandum from TsK VKP(b) Department of Cultural Educational Work Head A. S. Shcherbakov to the TsK VKP(b) secretaries on the situation at MKhAT, 3 August 1935.

Document 92. Memorandum from TsK VKP(b) Department of Cultural-Educational Work Head A. S. Shcherbakov to the TsK VKP(b) secretaries on the situation at MKhAT, 17 September 1935.

Document 93. Letter from K. S. Stanislavsky to I. V. Stalin, 1 January 1936.

Document 94. Memorandum from TsK VKP(b) Department of Cultural-Educational Work [Kultprosvetotdel] Head A. S. Shcherbakov to I. V. Stalin on the situation at MKhAT, 8 January 1936.

Document 95. Excerpt from a letter from MKhAT director M. P. Arkadiev to I. V. Stalin, 26 April 1937.

Document 96. Resolution of the TsK VKP(b) Politburo "On undertakings to mark the seventy-fifth anniversary of K. S. Stanislavsky's birth," 19 January 1938.

Document 97. Special Report from the GUGB NKVD SSSR Secret Political Department on the reaction of the artists of the Bolshoi Theater to the awarding of orders and the bestowing of honorary titles, 3 June 1937.

Document 98. Memorandum from P. M. Kerzhentsev, chairman of the Committee on Arts Affairs under the SNK SSSR, to I. V. Stalin and V. M. Molotov on his conversation with D. D. Shostakovich, 7 February 1936.

Document 99. Report from the GUGB NKVD SSSR Secret Political Department on responses from writers and arts workers to articles in Pravda about the composer D. D. Shostakovich [No later than 11 February 1936].

Document 100. Memorandum from TsK VKP(b) Department of Cultural-Educational Work Deputy Head A. I. Angarov to the TsK VKP(b) secretaries "On the discussion among musicians on the subject of the *Pravda* article on Formalism in music," 20 March 1936.

Document 101. Special Report from the GUGB NKVD SSSR Secret Political Department to the TsK VKP(b) on the conference of Moscow artists, 2 December 1935.

Document 102. Memorandum from Chairman P. M. Kerzhentsev of the Committee on Arts Affairs under the SNK SSSR to I. V. Stalin and V. M. Molotov on the need to remove artistic compositions of the Russian avant-garde from museum exhibitions, 19 May 1936.

Document 103. Report by State Administration of Cinematography Head B. Z. Shumiatsky to members of the TsK VKP(b) Politburo on the situation concerning S. M. Eisenstein's production of *Bezhin Meadow*, 5 February 1937.

Document 104. Resolution of the TsK VKP(b) Politburo on the ban on the production of *Bezhin Meadow*, 5 March 1937.

Document 105. Memorandum from State Administration of Cinematography Head B. Z. Shumiatsky to V. M. Molotov, on the reaction of some of the cultural public to the Politburo TsK VKP(b) resolution banning the production of *Bezhin Meadow*, 28 March 1937.

Document 106. Resolution of the TsK VKP(b) Politburo on the closure of the Vs. Meyerhold State Theater (GOSTIM), 7 January 1938.

Document 107. Resolution of the TsK VKP(b) Politburo on banning of D. Bedny's play *The Bogatyrs*, 14 November 1936.

Document 108. Report from the GUGB NKVD SSSR Secret Political Department

"On the responses of writers and arts workers to the removal of D. Bedny's 'The Bogatyrs' from the repertoire" [No later than 16 November 1936].

Document 109. Note from I. V. Stalin to *Pravda* Editor-in-Chief L. Z. Mekhlis on D. Bedny's fable "Struggle or Die" [*Boris' ili umirai*], 20 July 1937.

Document 110. Report from the NKVD GUGB SSSR to I. V. Stalin on the poet D. Bedny, 9 September 1938.

Document 111. Excerpt from Glavlit's memorandum to the TsK VKP(b) Politburo on the work and new tasks of the censorship organs, 9 April 1933.

Document 112. Resolution of the TsK VKP(b) Orgburo "On eliminating Glavlit's dangerous system of withdrawing literature," 9 December 1937.

Document 113. Memorandum from TsK VKP(b) Department of Cultural-Educational Work Head A. I. Stetsky to the TsK VKP(b) secretaries on the publication of the anti-Soviet tales of V. Z. Mass and N. R. Erdman and on progress in the preparations for the Writers' Congress, 22 May 1933.

Document 114. Memorandum from Chairman P. M. Kerzhentsev of the Committee on Arts Affairs under the SNK SSSR, to I. V. Stalin and V. M. Molotov on M. A. Bulgakov's play, *A Cabal of Hypocrites (Molière)* [*Kabala sviatosh (Mol'er)*], 29 February 1936.

Document 115. Memorandum of a Commission of the Politburo of TsK VKP (b) "On the issue of the performance by the Vakhtangov Theater of L. I. Slavin's play *The Foreign Collegium* [*Inostrannaia kollegia*]," 19 February 1933.

Document 116. Resolution of the TsK VKP(b) Politburo "On the motion picture 'Cheliuskin,'" 29 June 1934.

Document 117. Uncorrected transcript of introductory remarks by TSK VKP(b) Secretary A. A. Zhdanov at a meeting of cinematographers at the TsK VKP(b), 14 May 1941.

Document 118. Memorandum from TsK VKP(b) Department of Culture and Propaganda of Leninism Head A. I. Stetsky to the TsK VKP(b) Politburo on the painting by the artist N. Mikhailov on the theme of the funeral of S. M. Kirov, 23 January 1935.

Document 119. Memorandum from P. M. Kerzhentsev, Chairman of the Committee on Arts Affairs under the SNK SSSR, to I. V. Stalin and V. M. Molotov with proposals for the organization of a competition for the best play and screenplay on the October Revolution, 19 February 1936.

Document 120. Resolution of the TsK VKP(b) Politburo on M. S. Shaginyan's novel *A History Exam (Bilet po istorii)*, 5 August 1938.

Document 121. Resolution of the TsK VKP(b) Politburo on material incentives for cinematography workers, 23 March 1939.

Document 122. Letter from M. A. Bulgakov to I. V. Stalin, 11 June 1934.

Document 123. Letter from L. Yu. Brik to I. V. Stalin, 24 November 1935.

Document 124. Letter from A. P. Dovzhenko to I. V. Stalin, 26 November 1936.

Document 125. Letter from a group of cinematographers to I. V. Stalin [No later than 13 July 1940].

Document 126. Note from I. V. Stalin to A. N. Afinogenov with comments on his play *Deceit* [lozh'] [No earlier than 2 April 1933].

Document 127. Note from I. V. Stalin to SSP Secretary V. P. Stavsky on the writer L. S. Sobolev, 10 December 1935.

List of Documents 517

Document 128. Note from I. V. Stalin to the State Administration of Cinematography Head B. Z. Shumiatsky concerning the screenplay for the film *Shchors*, 9 December 1936.

Document 129. Note from I. V. Stalin to the State Administration of Cinematography Head B. Z. Shumiatsky concerning the screenplay for *The Great Citizen*, [*Veliky grazhdanin*] 27 January 1937.

Document 130. Note from I. V. Stalin to Committee on Cinematography Affairs Chairman I. G. Bolshakov concerning the screenplay for *Suvorov*, 9 June 1940.

Document 131. Note from I. V. Stalin to SNK SSSR Committee on Cinematography Affairs Chairman I. G. Bolshakov concerning screenplays for the motion picture *Georgy Saakadze*, 11 October 1940.

Document 132. Uncorrected transcript of I. V. Stalin's speech at the session of the TsK VKP(b) on the motion picture *Law of Life* [*Zakon Zhizni*] based on a screenplay by A. O. Avdeenko, 9 September 1940.

Document 133. Memorandum from the NKVD Administration for Leningrad Oblast to A. A. Zhdanov, "On negative and counterrevolutionary manifestations among the writers of Leningrad," 28 May 1935.

Document 134. Special report from the GUGB NKVD SSSR Secret Political Department "On the anti-Soviet group of writers, N. S. Postupalsky, P. S. Karaban (Shleiman), and V. I. Narbut," 25 June 1936.

Document 135. Dispatch from the First Section of the GUGB NKVD SSSR Secret Political Department on the moods of I. E. Babel in connection with the arrests of the former oppositionists, 5 July 1936.

Document 136. Summary by the GUGB NKVD SSSR Secret Political Department on the moods of I. E. Babel in connection with the conclusion of the trial of the so-called "Anti-Soviet United Trotskyite-Zinovievite Center," 22 September 1936.

Document 137. Statement by P. F. Yudin to TsK VKP(b) Secretaries I. V. Stalin and L. M. Kaganovich on the playwright V. M. Kirshon, 23 April 1937.

Document 138. Memorandum from SSP Secretary V. P. Stavsky to I. V. Stalin on the writers' discussion of the decisions of the February–March (1937) plenum of the TsK VKP(b) and the activities of L. L. Averbakh and V. M. Kirshon, 3 May 1937.

Document 139. Memorandum from the TsK VKP(b) Department of Cultural-Educational Work to the TsK VKP(b) secretaries on the discussion by writers of the sentence in the case of the so-called "Trotskyite-Zinovievite Center," 29 August 1936.

Document 140. Special report from the GUGB NKVD SSSR Secret Political Department on the moods among writers, 9 January 1937.

Document 141. Letter from B. L. Pasternak to I. V. Stalin [No earlier than 5 December 1935].

Document 142. Letter from R. Rolland to I. V. Stalin, 18 March 1937.

Document 143. Letter from B. Yasensky to I. V. Stalin, 25 April 1937.

Document 144. Letter from the actress Z. N. Raikh to I. V. Stalin, 29 April 1937.

Document 145. Letter from M. A. Bulgakov to I. V. Stalin, 4 February 1938.

Document 146. Petition from SSP Secretary V. P. Stavsky to USSR People's Commissar of Internal Affairs N. I. Yezhov on the poet O. E. Mandelshtam, 16 March 1938.

Document 147. Letter from V. I. Nemirovich-Danchenko to I. V. Stalin, 6 January 1939.

Document 148. Letter from V. V. Vinogradov to I. V. Stalin [No earlier than 5 February 1939].

Document 149. Letter from V. P. Stavsky to I. V. Stalin, 16 September 1937.

Document 150. Letter from M. A. Sholokhov to I. V. Stalin, 16 February 1938.

Document 151. Letter from M. A. Sholokhov to I. V. Stalin, 11 December 1939.

Document 152. Special Report from the NKGB SSSR Counterintelligence Administration, "On anti-Soviet manifestations and negative political moods among writers and journalists" [No later than 24 July 1943].

Document 153. Letter from M. M. Zoshchenko to I. V. Stalin, 26 November 1943.

Document 154. Statement by M. M. Zoshchenko to the TsK VKP(b), 8 January 1944.

Document 155. Transcript of a conversation between M. M. Zoshchenko and an associate of the NKGB SSSR Leningrad Administration, 20 July 1944.

Document 156. Resolution of the TsK VKP(b) Secretariat "On I. Selvinsky's poem, 'To Whom Did Russia Sing Lullabies'" ["Kogo baiukala Rossiia"], 10 February 1944.

Document 157. Resolution of the TsK VKP(b) Secretariat "On oversight of literary-artistic journals," 2 December 1943.

Document 158. Resolution of the TsK VKP(b) Secretariat "On increasing the responsibility of the secretaries for the literary-artistic journals," 3 December 1943.

Document 159. Memorandum from the TsK VKP(b) Propaganda and Agitation Administration to TsK VKP(b) Secretary G. M. Malenkov "On *Banner*," 7 August 1944.

Document 160. Report from USSR State Security People's Commissar V. N. Merkulov to TsK VKP(b) Secretary A. A. Zhdanov on writers' political moods and statements, 31 October 1944.

Document 161. Memorandum from TsK VKP(b) Propaganda and Agitation Administration Deputy Head A. M. Yegolin to TsK VKP(b) Secretary G. M. Malenkov on the situation in literature, 3 August 1945.

Document 162. From the transcript of A. A. Zhdanov's speech at a meeting of TsK VKP(b) apparatus workers on propaganda issues, 18 April 1946.

Document 163. Memorandum from the TsK VKP(b) Propaganda and Agitation Administration to TsK VKP(b) Secretary A. A. Zhdanov "On the unsatisfactory state of *Star* and *Leningrad*," 7 August 1946.

Document 164. Uncorrected transcript of the TsK VKP(b) Orgburo session "On *Star* and *Leningrad*," 9 August 1946.

Document 165. Resolution of the TsK VKP(b) Orgburo "On the journals *Star* and *Leningrad*," 14 August 1946.

Document 166. Note from I. V. Stalin to A. A. Zhdanov on the text of his report "On the journals *Star* and *Leningrad*," 19 September 1946.

Document 167. Letter from M. M. Zoshchenko to I. V. Stalin, 27 August 1946.

List of Documents

Document 168. Resolution of the TsK VKP(b) Orgburo "On the journal *Banner*," 27 December 1948.

Document 169. Resolution of the TsK VKP(b) Politburo "on the procedure for publishing works of artistic literature that have been published in journals," 12 May 1950.

Document 170. Note from TsK VKP(b) Secretary A. S. Shcherbakov to I. V. Stalin about A. N. Tolstoy's play *Ivan the Terrible* [*Ivan grozny*], 28 April 1942.

Document 171. Letter from A. N. Tolstoy to I. V. Stalin, 2 June 1943.

Document 172. Note from I. V. Stalin to SNK SSSR Committee on Cinematography Affairs Chairman I. G. Bolshakov concerning the screenplay of *Ivan the Terrible*, 13 September 1943.

Document 173. Letter from G. V. Aleksandrov to I. V. Stalin, 6 March 1946.

Document 174. Letter from S. M. Eisenstein to I. V. Stalin, 14 May 1946.

Document 175. Authorized transcript of the conversation between I. V. Stalin, A. A. Zhdanov, and V. M. Molotov, and S. M. Eisenstein and N. K. Cherkasov, concerning *Ivan the Terrible*, 26 February 1947.

Document 176. Resolution of the TsK VKP(b) Secretariat on the film *Admiral Nakhimov*, 11 May 1946.

Document 177. Corrected transcript of I. V. Stalin's speech at the session of the TsK VKP(b) Orgburo on the film *A Grand Life* [*Bol'shaia zhizn'*], 9 August 1946; excerpt from a resolution of the TsK VKP(b) Orgburo "On the film *A Grand Life*," 4 September 1946.

Document 178. Explanatory memorandum from TsK VKP(b) Propaganda and Agitation Administration Deputy Head D. T. Shepilov to TsK VKP(b) Secretary A. A. Zhdanov concerning the circumstances surrounding permission for production of V. I. Muradeli's opera *A Great Friendship* [*Bol'shaia druzhba*]," 9 January 1948.

Document 179. Draft memorandum from the TsK VKP(b) Propaganda and Agitation Administration to TsK VKP(b) Secretary A. A. Zhdanov on a ban on the production of V. I. Muradeli's *A Great Friendship* [No earlier than 1 August 1947, and no later than 9 January 1948].

Document 180. Letter from M. I. Romm to I. V. Stalin, 8 January 1943.

Document 181. Statement from SSP General Secretary A. A. Fadeev to the TsK VKP(b) secretaries on the "antipatriotic group of critics" participants V. L. Dairedzhiev and I. L. Altman, 21 September 1949.

Index

Abakumov, Viktor Semyonovich, 472, 483
Acmeism, 21, 351
Admiral Nakhimov, 442, 445–50, 454
Aduev, Nikolai Alfredovich, 321, 483
"Adventures of an Ape" (Zoshchenko), 401–4, 413, 415, 421, 426–27
Aerograd, 288
Afinogenov, Aleksandr Nikolaevich, 156–57, 266, 292–94, 312, 321, 326, 483
Agapov, B. N., 445, 481*n*2
Agitation and Propaganda Administration. *See* Agitprop
Agitmass (Department of Agitation and Propaganda), 263
Agitprop: and Akhmatova, 365; and artistic literature previously published in journals, 431; and Bulgakov's *Days of the Turbins*, 93–94; and Bulgakov's *Flight*, 98–103; and censorship and criticism generally, 123, 265, 398–401; and films, 458, 460–62; and Glavlit, 123; and journals, 374–75, 402–7, 412, 431; and Levidov's *Conspiracy of Equals*, 94–96; Lezhnev on, 386; reorganization of, 148; Shepilov as head of, 457–58; and writers during post–World War II period, 393–98; and Writers Union, 315
Agranov, Yakov Saulovich, 305–7, 310–11, 371, 477*n*1, 483
Agriculture, 337–38, 353, 354, 356, 357–58, 361
Aibek, 425, 483
Akademia Publishers, 110, 180–81, 204
Akhmatova, Anna Andreevna: biographical information on, 483; and Fadeev, 209; journals publishing writings by, 398, 417, 421–24; petitions to Stalin after arrest of family members of, 322–23; Popkov on, 417; Stalin's diatribe against, 351; Veresaev on silence of, 125
—works: "The First Long-Range," 413; *From Six Books*, 365; "A Kind of Monologue," 402
AKhRR (Association of Artists of Revolutionary Russia), 45–48
Akulov, Ivan Alekseevich, 222, 483
Akulshin, R., 479*n*13
Aleksandrov, Georgy Fyodorovich: and Akhmatova, 365; and Aseev, 373; biographical information on, 483; on Eisenstein's *Ivan the Terrible*, 436–38; and journals, 375–79, 398, 402–8, 416; Lezhnev on, 386; and opera, 459, 460–62; and Zoshchenko, 427
Aleksandrov, Grigory Vasilievich, 265, 290–92, 458, 465, 467, 483
Aleksandrov, Vladimir Borisovich, 211, 214, 483
Alekseev, Pyotr Alekseevich, 73, 483
Alexander I, Tsar, 441, 442, 483
Alexander Nevsky, 148, 249, 442, 483
Alexander Nevsky (film), 465
All-Russian Theatrical Society, 469
All-Russian Union of Peasant Writers (VOKP), 150, 153
All-Russian Union of Soviet Writers (VSSP), 155
All-Russian Union of Writers (VSP), 36, 37, 109, 150, 200

All-Union Association of Proletarian Writers (VAPP), 40, 52, 150
All-Union Association of Proletarian Writers Associations (VOAPP), 152
All-Union Central Board of Trade Unions, 25
All-Union Congress of Proletarian Writers, 52
All-Union Council of the National Economy, 26
All-Union Society for Cultural Relations with Abroad (VOKS), 113, 115, 324
Altman, Iogan Lvovich, 470–71, 484
Andreev, Andrei Andreevich, 40, 195–97, 201–15, 217–18, 243–44, 316–17, 365, 484
Angarov, Aleksei Ivanovich, 236–38, 246, 316–17, 484
Anna Karenina, 224
Anthroposophists, 132
Anti-Formalist campaign, 146, 191, 229–49, 251, 286, 429
Anti-Semitism, 209, 354, 356, 358, 364, 464, 467–72, 471–72, 474*n*5
Antifascism, 191, 426. *See also* Fascism
Antokolsky, Pavel Grigorievich, 320, 378, 484
Antonovskaya, Anna Arnoldovna, 298–99, 484
Antony and Cleopatra (Shakespeare), 360
Apletin, Mikhail Yakovlevich, 220, 484
Architects Union, 154
Arkadiev, Mikhail Pavlovich, 222, 223–26, 484
Armored Train 14-69 (Ivanov), 64, 65, 103
Arosev, Alexandr Yakovlevich, 324, 484
Arsky, Pavel Alexandrovich, 55, 484
"Art" (Tolstoy), 328
Art for art's sake, 421, 423
Artists and art associations, 45–48, 239–42
Artists Union, 154
Artsybashev, Mikhail Petrovich, 274, 479*n*7, 484
Asafiev, Boris Vladimirovich, 238, 484
Aseev, Nikolai Nikolaevich: biographical information on, 484; censorship and criticism of, 232, 319, 373, 380–81, 385, 388, 390, 394–95; as Futurist, 36; and Kliuev, 171; and Left Art group, 478*n*2; and Organizing Committee of Writers Union, 154; on post–World War II period, 380–81, 392; and publishing house initiative group, 38; students' approval of, 391; during World War II, 361, 394–97
—works: *Flame of Victory*, 396–97; *Years of Thunder*, 373
ASM (Association of Contemporary Music), 238
Association of Artists of Revolutionary Russia (AKhRR), 45–48
Association of Contemporary Music (ASM), 238
Association of Old Men, 305–6
At a Distant Outpost, 273, 274
At the City Gates (Ryss), 395–96
At the Nevsky Position (Knekht), 403
"At the Outpost" (Slonimsky), 405, 422
At the Walls of Leningrad (Vishnevsky), 395
Attila (Zamyatin), 110–11
Avdeenko, Aleksandr Ostapovich, 274, 300–301, 479*n*6, 484
Averbakh, Leopold Leopoldovich: arrest of, 315, 327; and Bedny, 70; and Bill-Belotserkovsky, 58; biographical information on, 484; death of, 142, 147; and Erdman and Mass satires, 265–67; and Fadeev, 176; and founding of Writers Union, 160; and Gorky, 144, 176, 179, 181, 315; and Gronsky, 159; and Kirshon, 312; literary career of, 142; political campaign against, 311–15; and RAPP, 160, 265, 312, 326; and restructuring of literary and arts organizations (1932), 151, 154, 156–57, 312; and Yagoda, 311; and Yasensky, 327
Avramenko, Ilya Kornilevich, 406, 484
Awards: for films, 218, 298, 436, 437; for Soviet writers, 201–2, 359, 433

Babel, Isaac Emmanuilovich: biographical information on, 484; and Eisenstein, 147, 308, 310, 311; and Gorky, 169, 191, 308; and Kamenev, 309, 310; and Malraux, 191; *Red Cavalry* by, 478*n*3; and Shmidt, 317; and secret policy, xv, 307–11; on Shostakovich, 232; and Trotsky, 309, 310; and Writers' Congress, 169; Zenkevich on possible censorship of, 233
Babeuf, François Noël, 95, 484
Babitsky, 246–47
Back from the USSR (Gide), 147, 478*n*2
Badaev, Aleksei Egorovich, 18, 484
Bagritsky, Eduard Georgievich, 305–6, 484
Bakaev, Ivan Petrovich, 18, 484

Bakhmetiev, Vladimir Matveevich, 153, 154, 188, 326, 484
Bakhtin, Mikhail Mikhailovich, 236, 484
Bakrushin, 434
Ballet, 31, 227, 228, 229–30, 235, 238. *See also* Bolshoi Theater; Leningrad ballet
Balmont, Konstantin Dmitrievich, 9, 14, 16, 484
Baltic states, 361
Balzac, Honoré de, 211
Banker (Korneichuk), 224
The Banner/Znamia, 374–80, 396, 399, 406, 413, 415, 427–29
Banning. *See* Censorship
Barbusse, Henri, 87, 484
"The Barefoot Truth" (Vesely), 89
The Battalion Heads West (Mdivani), 377
The Battleship Potemkin, 465
Bazhan, Mykola Platonovich, 306, 485
The Bedbug, 235
Bedny, Demian, 68–75, 147, 169, 175, 249–60, 372, 441–42, 485
Before Sunrise (Zoshchenko), 366–75, 381, 414–15, 421, 426
Beilis, Mendel, 18, 485
Bekker, Mikhail, 153, 485
Belgoskino film studio, 132
Belinsky, Vissarion Grigorievich, 212, 310, 470, 480n4, 485
Bely, Andrei, 15, 132–33, 159, 485
Belyaev, 458
Benefit (Platonov), 211, 214
Benjamin, Walter, 50, 53, 485
Benkendorf, Aleksandr Khristoforovich, 389, 485
Berezovsky, Feoktist Nikolaevich, 154, 485
Berg, Alban, 238, 485
Berggolts, Olga Fedorovna, 396, 415, 485
Beria, Lavrenty Pavlovich, 201, 332, 401, 439–40, 459, 485
Berman, V., 310–11
Beskin, Emmanuil Martynovich, 55, 241, 485
Bespalov, Ivan Mikhailovich, 120, 317, 469, 485
Bespamiatny, 303
Bezhin Meadow, 142–43, 242–47
Bezymensky, Aleksandr Ilyich, 154, 167, 174, 175, 178, 485
Bill-Belotserkovsky, Vladimir Naumovich, 55–60, 79, 104, 154, 485
Birth of a Hero (Libedinsky), 326
"Blind Happiness" (Yanovsky), 428
Bliokh, Yakov Moiseevich, 455, 485

Bliskavetsky, Noy, 309
Bloch, Jean Richard, 170, 485
Blockade, 103
Blok, Aleksandr Alexandrovich, 12–17, 19–22, 371, 485
Bobrov, Sergei Pavlovich, 36, 485
Bogatyrs (Bedny), 147, 250–59, 441–42
Bogdanov, Aleksandr Alexandrovich, 37, 477n6, 485
Bogen, 307–9
Bogorodsky, Fedor Semyonovich, 240, 277, 485
Boiarsky, Yakov Iosifovich, 220, 253, 254, 257, 485
Bolduman, Mikhail Panteleimonovich, 269, 485
Bolotnikov, A. A., 186
Bolshakov, Ivan Grigorievich, 297–99, 436, 438, 443, 444, 458, 465–66, 486
Bolshemennikov, A. P., 280
Bolshevik, journal, 368–70, 388, 426
Bolshevism, ix, xii–xiii, 354, 388
Bolshoi Theater, 23–31, 53, 216, 227, 228, 236, 251, 254, 256, 459, 460, 462
Bolt (ballet), 230
Bondi, Sergei Mikhailovich, 356–57, 486
Boris Godunov (Pushkin), 224
Borisov, Leonid Ilich, 171, 404, 413, 486
Borodin, Aleksandr Porfirievich, 250, 254, 486
Borshchagovsky, Aleksandr Mikhailovich, 470, 486
Bozhenko, Vasily Nazarovich, 289, 295, 486
Break (Lavrenev), 64
Brezhnev, Leonid Ilyich, 290, 347, 486
Brik (Kogan), Lilya Yurievna, 285–88, 486
Britske, Professor, 332
Brodsky, Isaac Izrailevich, 171, 240, 241, 486
Broido, G. I., 51, 90
Bruni, Lev Alexandrovich, 48, 486
Bryusov, Valery Yakovlevich, 20, 36, 38, 486
Buachidze, M., 157, 486
Bubnov, Andrei Sergeevich, 153, 154, 222, 271, 475n5, 486
Budantsev, Sergei Fedorovich, 176, 320–21, 486
Budberg, Maria Ignatievna (née Zakrevskaya), 191, 486
Budenny, Semyon Mikhailovich, 478n3, 486
Budnov, 277

Bukharin, Nikolai Ivanovich: and Bedny, 68, 259; biographical information on, 486; and Gorky, 79, 145; image of, in art, 301; and intelligentsia in 1919–1921, 8, 16; on proletarian writers, 40–41, 45; Raikh on, 329; Rolland's petition for, 323–24; and Selvinsky, 373; as Stalin's rival, ix, 108; trial of, 146–47, 311; and Writers' Congress (1934), 166, 167, 169, 171, 174, 175–76, 177, 178, 477n8

Bulgakov, Mikhail Afanasievich: on Bedny's *Bogatyrs*, 257–58; biographical information on, 486; censorship attempts against, 88, 91–94, 98–104; confiscation of diaries of, 105; foreign travel requests by, 104–8, 282–85; illness of, 106–8, 283; persecution of, 105, 106–7, 150; petition to Stalin by, on behalf of Erdman, 330–31; and Stalin, 55, 56–57, 61, 64–66, 91, 93–94, 105–9, 135, 282–85
—works: *Crimson Island,* 57, 103, 268; *Days of the Turbins,* 54, 57, 64–66, 91–94, 98, 101, 103, 257, 268; *Fatal Eggs,* 125–26; *Flight,* 53–57, 65, 66, 98–104, 268; *Heart of a Dog,* 126; *Molière,* 217–18, 220, 268–70; *Notes on Cuffs,* 126; "To the Government of the USSR," 105; *Zoika's Apartment,* 268

Bulgakova, Elena Sergeevna, 282–85, 486
Bulgakova (Belozerskaya), Liubov Yevgenievna, 108, 486
Bunin, Ivan Alekseevich, 14, 486
Bystriansky, Vadim Alexandrovich, 34, 486

"Cabbage Soup" (Zoshchenko), 381
Capitalism, 354, 355
Catherine the Great, 441
Censorship: and Agitprop, 123, 265; of anti-Soviet intelligentsia in 1920s, 54, 88–136; of Bulgakov's *Molière*, 268–70; of Erdman and Mass, 265–67; of films, 142–43, 242–47, 271–75, 383–84, 435–58; in Germany, 233; and Glavlit, 110, 122–29, 153, 261–65, 397; of journals, 398–425, 427–31; under Nicholas I, 257; and Politburo in 1920s, 88–91, 97–98, 104–5, 122, 124, 127–30, 351; and Politburo in 1930s, 245–47, 261–65, 270–75, 351; and presentation of image of leader, 276–81; Stalin's role in, xiii–xiv, 89, 117, 122, 141, 271–72; Trotsky on, 34, 35; during World War II, 360, 364–92, 397–98; and Zhdanovism, 351, 364, 398–425. *See also specific authors, artists, film directors, and music composers*

Central Committee of Soviet Communist Party: and Bolshoi Theater, 25, 27; and censorship during World War II, 351, 374–80, 381; and culture in 1930s, 140, 141; during NEP era, 5; and films, 273–75, 445–46; and Glavlit, 265; and Great Purge, 242; and intelligentsia during Civil War era, 8, 9–16, 19–21; and journals, 374–80, 428–29; and RAPP, 150–51; resolution (1932) of, on literary and artistic organizations, 5–6, 151–53, 163; resolutions of generally, 350; role of generally, in culture system, x–xii; and writers during World War II, 380–92; and Writers Union, 161; and Zhdanov resolutions, 349–51; and Zoshchenko's *Before Sunrise,* 367–68, 374, 375

Chaliapin, Fyodor Ivanovich, 10, 486
Chamber of Books, 253
Chamber Theater, 9, 94–96, 240, 250, 252
Chapaev, 288
Chapaev, Vasily Ivanovich, 288, 295, 487
Chaplin, Charles, 329, 448, 487
Cheka (VChK), 8–14, 17–19, 472
Chekhov, Anton Pavlovich, 87, 216, 300, 382, 414, 487
Chekhov, Mikhail Aleksandrovich, 57, 58, 487
Cheliuskin, 272
Cheliuskiniana (Selvinsky), 321
Cherkasov, Nikolai Konstantinovich, 440–45, 481n2, 487
Cherniavsky, L., 95, 220, 487
Cherny, Boris, 298–99
Chernyshevsky, Nikolai Gavrilovich, 73, 74, 212, 487
Chiaureli, Mikhail Edisherovich, 298, 458, 467, 487
Chicherin, Georgy Vasilievich, 14–15, 487
Chikovani, Simon Ivanovich, 425, 487
Children's literature, 123, 133, 135, 381, 401–4, 426–27
Children's theater, 192, 254
Chisel, 411
Chronicle/Letopis, 110
Chubar, Vlas Yakovlevich, 268, 487
Chukovsky, Kornei Ivanovich, 135, 356, 380–82, 387–92, 394, 487
Chukovsky, Nikolai Korneevich, 412, 487
Chumandrin, Mikhail Fedorovich, 154, 160, 189, 487

Church and Revolution, 18
Churilin, 365
Cinema. *See* Films
Circle (Krug) publishing house, 39, 51, 125
Civil War era in Russia, 3–4, 7–22
Class struggle, 41–42, 211–12, 349
"Climb Down off the Stove" (Bedny), 68–73
Club for Masters of Culture, 183–85
Cold War, 351
Comintern, disbanding of, 352, 353, 354, 355, 356, 357, 359
Commander of the Second Army (Selvinsky), 238, 479n13
Commissar Extraordinary (Muradeli), 459–63
Commissariat (later Ministry) of Culture, xii, xvi
Commission to Improve Scholars' Living Conditions (KUBU), 18
Committee on Arts Affairs: and Bedny's *Bogatyrs*, 251–53, 255, 256; and Bulgakov's *Molière*, 267–70; and censorship, 397; and closing of Meyerhold State Theater, 247–48; and Eisenstein's *Bezhin Meadow*, 244; founding and power of, 145–46, 148, 228, 229; and opera, 460, 462; and plays commemorating twentieth anniversary of Revolution, 278; and removal of avant-garde artwork from museums, 241–42; and A. N. Tolstoy's plays on Ivan the Terrible, 433, 435
Committee on Cinema, 242, 243–47
Communist International, 77
Communist of Tadzhikistan, 470
Composers Union, 152, 462–63
Congresses for the Defense of Culture, 191, 481n2
Conrad, Joseph, 112, 487
Conspiracy of Equals (Levidov), 57, 94–95
Constructivists, 50, 146, 150
Counterplan (Trauberg), 255
Crimea, 190
Crimson Island (Bulgakov), 57, 103, 268
Criticism of literature. *See* Literary criticism
Crocodile, 429–30
Crossing literary group, 40, 150, 153, 155, 316, 480n5
Cultural revolution, 3, 5–6, 33, 49, 50–75
Czechoslovakia, 148

Dairedzhiev, Boris Leonidovich, 469–71, 487
Damert, Lilo (German writer), 246, 487
Davidenko, Aleksandr Aleksandrovich, 237, 487

Davydov, L., 11–12, 14, 487
Days and Nights (Simonov), 379
Days of the Turbins (Bulgakov), 54, 57, 64–66, 91–94, 98, 101, 103, 257, 268
Dead Souls (Gogol), 107, 214
Death of Tarelkin (Sukhovo-Kobylin), 248, 479n11
Deborin, Abram Moiseevich, 156, 487
Deceit (Afinogenov), 292–94
Deineka, Aleksandr Aleksandrovich, 239, 240, 487
Depths, 126
Deputy from the Baltic (Zarkhi), 465
Der Emes publishing house, 468
Derzhanovsky, Vladimir Vladimirovich, 235, 487
Detgiz publishing house, 431
Diary (Inber). *See Leningrad Diary*
Difficult Years (Tolstoy), 434–35
Dinamov, Sergei Sergeevich, 153, 169, 176, 240, 487
Dmitrochenko, 304
Dobronitsky, K., 234, 487
Doctors' Plot, 351, 464, 472
"Dog's Lane" (Gumilevsky), 477n7
Dolmatovsky, Evgeny Aronovich, 377, 488
Dombal, 315
Dostoevsky, Fyodor Mikhailovich, 125, 488
Dovzhenko, Aleksandr Petrovich: biographical information on, 488; censorship and criticisms of generally, 380; Romm on, 465, 467; and *Shchors*, 280, 281, 288–90, 294–95, 465; students' approval of, 391; and *Ukraine in the Flames*, 383–84, 395; and *Victory*, 395; wages for, 281; on World War II period, 363
Dreitser, Efim and Sonia, 308
Drozdov, Aleksandr Mikhailovich, 36, 488
Druskin, Mikhail Semyonovich, 237, 488
Dudin, Mikhail Aleksandrovich, 396, 488
Dumas, Alexandre, Jr. (Dumas fils), 270
Dumas, Alexandre, Sr. (Dumas père), 269, 488
Dzerzhinsky, Felix Edmundovich, 8, 9–10, 488
Dzerzhinsky, Ivan Ivanovich, 237, 257, 478n4, 488

The Eagle and Its Mate (Tolstoy), 434
Earth (Virta), 225
The Editorial Office (Melnikov), 428
Ehrenburg, Ilya Grigorevich, 36, 177, 239, 240, 362, 379, 388, 472, 488

Eideman, Robert Petrovich, 196, 488
Eikhenbaum, Boris Mikhailovich, 135, 488
Eisenstein, Sergei Mikhailovich: award for, 436, 437; and Babel, 147, 308, 310, 311; on Bedny's *Bogatyrs*, 256; *Bezhin Meadow* by, 142–43, 242–47; biographical information on, 488; films by generally, 249, 465; as Formalist, 230; and Gide, 147; illness of, 437–39; *Ivan the Terrible* by, 432, 435–45, 448, 450–51, 481n2; and Shumiatsky's death, 148; and Stalin, 435–45, 455, 467; and Zhdanovism, 351
Engels, Friedrich, 210, 488
England, 354, 359
Erdman, Nikolai Robertovich, 117–19, 265–67, 330–31, 479n13, 488
Erlikh, Aron Isaevich, 386–87, 488
Ermler, Fridrikh Markovich, 290–92, 295–97, 458, 465–67, 488
"Escape" (Ostrov), 403
Es-Khabib Vafa, 55, 488
Eugene Onegin, 252
Excelsior, 82
Explanatory Dictionary of the Russian Languages, 334
Expressionism, 231

Fadeev, Aleksandr Aleksandrovich: and Averbakh, 176, 312, 314; and awards for Soviet writers, 201; biographical information on, 488; and demise of RAPP, 155–56; and Gorky, 180, 181, 187, 188; literary career of, 177, 187, 188; and *Literary Critic*, 209–15; and *narodnost*, 478n4; and On Guard group, 326; and Organizing Committee of Writers Union, 154, 159, 160; and Platonov's "To Advantage" in *Red Virgin Soil*, 120–21; on proposed explusion of Dairedzhiev and Altman from Writers Union, 469–71; and RAPP, 180; on Savin's *Nafta*, 319; and Stalin, 315; suicide of, 209; and Writers' Congress (1934), 172, 174–75; and Writers Union, 142, 148, 155, 209, 372–73, 425; *Young Guard* by, 393
The Fall of Berlin (Chiaureli), 298
Fall of Paris (Ehrenburg), 379
Fascism, 195, 206, 214, 325, 353, 354, 364, 382, 467. *See also* Antifascism; Germany
Fatal Eggs (Bulgakov), 125–26
Faust (Goethe), 448
Favorsky, Vladimir Andreevich, 277, 488

Fear (Afinogenov), 292
Federation of Unions of Soviet Writers (FOSP), 49, 50–52, 150
Federatsia publishers, 111
Fedin, Konstantin Aleksandrovich: biographical information on, 488; censorship and criticism of, 380, 385, 388, 390; and Germany, 359; *Gorky Among Us* by, 359, 365, 382–83, 385, 386; Ivanov on, 319; and Organizing Committee of Writers Union, 153, 154; and Peredelkino (writers' colony), 321; Pogodin on, 391; students' approval of, 391; and World War II, 359–60, 394; and Writers Union, 204, 206, 303, 317; and Zamyatin, 201
Fedoseev, Pyotr Nikolaevich, 376–79, 488
Fefer, Itzik, 468, 488
Fellow Travelers, 457
Fellow travelers. *See* Intelligentsia
Feuchtwanger, Lion, 147, 206, 244, 246, 478n2, 488
Field Marshal Kutuzov (Soloviev), 356
Films: *Admiral Nakhimov* by Pudovkin, 442, 445–50, 454; awards for, 281, 298, 436, 437; *Bezhin Meadow* by Eisenstein, 142–43, 242–47; censorship and criticisms of, 142–43, 242–47, 271–75, 383–84, 435–58; collective letter to Stalin from cinematographers, 290–92; and Committee on Arts Affairs, 229; directors of generally, 131–32, 457–58, 465; documentaries, 458; *Fishermen of the Caspian*, 454–55; *A Grand Life*, 432, 440, 445, 451–54; *The Great Citizen*, 295–97, 465; image of leader in, 280–81; *Ivan the Terrible* by Eisenstein, 432, 435–45, 448, 450–51; and Orgburo, 447–56; and Politburo, 454–58; Romm on, 465–68; *Shchors* by Dovzhenko, 280, 281, 288–90, 294–95, 465; Shumiatsky as head of cinema, 148, 242, 243–47, 289, 295–97; and Stalin, 243–44, 271–72, 274, 288–92, 294–301, 435–45, 447–58, 465–68, 479n6; in United States, 457; wages for directors and camera operators, 281. *See also* specific films and film directors
"The First Long-Range" (Akhmatova), 413
First Studio of the Art Theater, 9, 10, 11–12
Fisher, Ernst, 210, 489
Fishermen of the Caspian, 454–55
Flakserman, A., 11, 13, 15, 20, 489
Flame of Victory (Aseev), 396–97
The Flea (Zamyatin), 111, 112

Flight (Bulgakov), 53–57, 65, 66, 98–104, 268
Flit, Aleksandr Mikhailovich, 405–6, 489
"For Those in the Sea," 399
The Foreign Collegium (Slavin), 271
Formalism, 68, 146, 149, 230, 236–38, 241–43, 248, 253–54, 429, 462, 463. *See also* Anti-Formalist campaign
Forsh, Olga Dmitrievna, 209, 489
FOSP (Federation of Unions of Soviet Writers), 49, 50–52, 150
France, 191
France, Anatole, 78, 489
Freud, Sigmund, 366
Friendship of Nations, 459
From Six Books (Akhmatova), 365
Frunze, Mikhail Vasilievich, 40, 45, 89, 90–91, 196, 489
FSB, 318. *See also* Secret police
Futurists, 4, 36, 50, 479n8

Gabovich, Mikhail Markovich, 227, 489
Gabrilovich, 248
Gaevskaia, Lialia, 308
Ganetsky, Yakov Stanislavovich, 79, 489
Gatov, Aleksandr Borisovich, 233–34, 320, 489
Gavronsky, Aleksandr Osipovich, 131, 489
Geiki, A., 18–19
General Bagration (Golubov), 362
The General Line (Eisenstein), 242
Georgian Lyrics (Pasternak), 323, 480n1
Georgy Saakadze (Chiaureli), 298–99
Gerasimov, Aleksandr Mikhailovich, 240, 277, 489
Gerasimov, Sergei Vasilievich, 277, 489
Gerasimova, Valeria Anatolievna, 209, 489
German, Yury Pavlovich, 417, 423, 489
Germany: censorship in, 233; Communist Party in, 174; and espionage in Soviet Union, 296; fascism in, 195, 206, 214, 325, 353, 354, 364, 382; Fedin in, 359; and Hitler, 192, 311, 354, 357, 382; invasion of Czechoslovakia by, 148; and Nazism, 148, 224, 349, 354, 382; publishers in, 18, 78; in World War II, 349, 353, 354–55, 357, 359, 361–64, 373, 395. *See also* World War II
Gero, D., 48
Gersht, Meer Abramovich, 252, 489
Gide, André, 147, 308, 320, 478n2, 489
GIKhL (State Publishing House for Literature), 280
Gladkov, Fyodor Vasilievich, 188, 314, 326, 363, 388–89, 489

Glaviskusstvo, 53
Glavlit, 110, 122–29, 153, 261–65, 316, 339, 365, 397, 475n5
Glavrepertkom (Central Repertoire Commission): and Bedny's *Bogatyrs*, 255, 256, 257; and Bulgakov's *Day of the Turbins*, 91, 92; and Bulgakov's *Molière*, 217, 268; and Erdman's *The Suicide*, 117; and Bulgakov's *Flight*, 103; and Levidov's *Conspiracy of Equals*, 95; and Litovsky, 223; Orgburo's review of, 97–98; and Proletarian Theater Association, 54–55; and Raikin, 408; Veinshtok on, 132; and Zamyatin's *Attila*, 111
Glebov, Anatoly Glebovich, 55, 361, 489
Goethe, Johann Wolfgang von, 448
Goffenshefer, Veniamin Tsezarevich, 235, 489
Goglidze, Dzhango, 308
Gogol, Nikolai Vasilievich, 107, 118, 214, 300, 489
Golemba, Sofia Mikhailovna, 333, 489
Golodny, Mikhail Semyonovich, 489
Golos Truda (Voice of Labor) publishing house, 125
Golosovker, Yakov Emmanuilovich, 357, 489
Golovanov, Lev Viktorovich, 227, 490
Golovanov, Nikolai Semyonovich, 474–75n5, 490
Golovanovism, 53, 56
Golovin, D. D., 227, 228, 478n2, 490
Golubov, Sergei Nikolaevich, 362–63, 391, 392, 490
Good (Mayakovsky), 287
Gor, Gennady Samoilovich, 403, 490
Gorbachev, Mikhail Sergeevich, ix, x, 200, 290, 490
Gorbatov, Boris Leontievich, 377, 383, 425, 490
Gorbunov, Kuzma Yakovlevich, 14, 157, 180, 181, 490
Gorchakov, Nikolai Mikhailovich, 217–18, 490
Gorelov, Anatoly Efimovich, 303, 490
Gorky, Maxim: and Averbakh, 312, 315; and Babel, 308; biographical information on, 490; and Bukharin, 79, 145, 324; and cliquism, 176; on Club for Masters of Culture, 183–85; critics of, 176–77; death of, 142, 145, 182, 187–88, 309; encyclopedic works by, 180, 181, 312–13; and Erdman and Mass satires, 265–67; and Erdman's *The Suicide*, 118; Fedin's *Gorky Among Us*, 359, 365,

382–83, 385, 386; and intelligentsia during Civil War era, 7, 8, 16–20; and Leonov, 385; "Literary Amusements" by, 185–87, 314; in 1930s, 143–45, 179–97; on patronage, 189–90, 196; patronage by, 179–81, 187, 312; and Peredelkino (writers' village), 143, 183–84; Platonov on, 214; and Politburo, 76–79, 84–85; political mistakes by, 174; and RAPP, 144, 153, 182–83, 314; role of, in culture system of 1920s, 5, 13–14, 36, 45, 76–87; Siberian writers' criticisms of, 84–86; and Socialist Realism, 139, 164, 182, 187, 194; and Socialist Revolutionaries, 77–78, 83–84; and Stalin, 78–87, 143–44, 178–94, 324; on training for writers and critics, 196; and Vasiliev, 185–87; and Writers' Congress (1934), 139, 165–70, 172, 174, 177, 182, 187; and Writers Union, 143–44, 154, 172–73, 195–97; on Zamyatin's *Attila*, 111
Gorky Among Us (Fedin), 359, 365, 382–83, 386
Gorodetsky, Sergei Mitrofanovich, 36, 233, 255, 490
Gorodinsky, Viktor Markovich, 257, 490
Gosheva, Irina Prokofievna, 444, 490
Gosizdat (State Publishing House), 18–19, 38–39, 52, 90, 126, 262, 305
Goslitizdat, 379, 431
GPU (State Political Administration), 81, 91–92, 170, 190
Graft/Privoi, 126
A Grand Life (Lukov), 432, 440, 445, 451–54
The Great Citizen (Ermler), 295–97, 465
A Great Force, 457
A Great Friendship (Muradeli), 236, 459–63
Great Purge (1937–1938), 139, 142–43, 145–49, 202, 226, 242, 245, 264, 276, 340–42
Great Retreat, 464–72
Grechishnikov, Vladimir, 188–89
Green Ray of Light (Sobolev), 393
Greetings from the Front (Ovechkin), 394
Grib, Vladimir Romanovich, 211, 490
Griboedov, Aleksandr Sergeevich, 300, 479n11, 490
"Grigory Pugachev" (Yavich), 88, 125
Gronsky, Ivan Mikhailovich: and Averbakh, 159, 266; biographical information on, 490; condemnation of, to Gulag, 162; and Gorky, 87, 184; as *Izvestia* editor-in-chief, 87, 162; and Organizing Committee of Writers Union, 87, 141–42, 153, 154, 157–58, 160, 162; and RAPP, 162–63; on Socialist Realism, 162–65; and Writers' Congress (1934), 165–66
Grossman, Vasily Semyonovich, 234, 393, 490
Grudskaia, A. Ya., 316
Grzhebin, Zinovy Isaevich, 18–19, 490
Gudzenko, Semyon Petrovich, 394, 490
GUGB (Central Directorate of State Security): on Bedny, 251–60; on conference of Moscow artists (1935), 239–41; and Gorky's "Literary Amusements," 186–87; on honors for theater performers, 227–28; on Shostakovich, 231–35; and Writers' Congress (1934), 168–78. See also NKVD (People's Commissariat for Internal Affairs)
GUK (State Administration of Cinematography), 289–90, 295–98
Gumilevsky, Lev Ivanovich, 175, 477n7, 490
Gumilyov, Lev Nikolaevich, 322, 490
Gumilyov, Nikolai Stepanovich, 21, 304, 490
Gurvich, Abram Solomonovich, 470, 490
Gusev, Sergei Ivanovich, 51, 177, 490
Guzovskaia, Olga Vladimirovna, 490
Gzovskaia, 9, 13

The Happy-Go-Lucky Guys (Aleksandrov, Erdman, and Mass), 265
Hatred (Shukhov), 187, 189
"Heart of a Doctor" (Yanovsky), 428
Heart of a Dog (Bulgakov), 126
Hearts of Four (Yudin), 274–75, 479–80n8
Hidas, Antal, 157, 491
A History Exam (Shaginyan), 279–80
History of the Civil War (Gorky), 180, 181
History of the Communist Party of the Soviet Union (Bolsheviks): Short Course (Stalin), 141, 260, 295
History of the Factories (Gorky), 180, 312–13
Hitler, Adolf, 192, 311, 354, 357, 382, 491. See also Nazism
Hoffmeister, General, 373
Homeland, 252
Homemaking, 73
House of Arts, 110
House of Mokhovaya (Gor), 403
How the Steel Was Tempered (Ostrovsky), 248, 479n14
Hydrocentral (Shaginyan), 116–17

Illés, Bela, 157, 314, 491
Ilyenkov, Vasily Pavlovich, 154, 491
Imaginists, 36
Imas, 220, 491
"In the Heart's Voice" (Komissarova), 402
In the South (Kalinin), 394
In Ukraine's Steppes (Korneichuk), 470
Inber, Vera Maikhailovna, 317, 321, 406, 414, 491
"Incident over Berlin" (Varshavsky and Rest), 404–5, 422
Ingots (Panfyorov), 66, 182, 187, 188–89
Inspector General (Gogol), 248
Intelligentsia: arrests of, during Civil War era, 8; censorship and persecution of anti-Soviet intelligentsia in 1920s, 88–136; deportation of, 7, 112; "fellow travelers" and NEP, 4–5, 32–49; foreign travel requests by and emigration of, 4, 7–22, 104–8, 112–16, 282–85; hierarchical system of patronage and arbitration for, xv, 142–43; and Kadet Party (Constitutional Democratic Party), 8; OGPU report on, 130–33; Politburo on fellow travelers, 42–43; role of, xiv–xv; struggle between proletarian writers and fellow travelers, 4–5, 39–40, 42–43, 109, 136
International Society of Revolutionary Writers (MORP), 191, 220, 325
International Writers' Conference (Spain), 337, 481n2
The Invasion (Leonov), 359
Ionov, Ilya Ionovich, 34, 180–81, 491
Irinin, 181
The Iron Flood (Serafimovich), 182
Isbakh, Aleksandr Abramovich, 376, 491
Iskusstvo publishing house, 397, 431
Istomin, Konstantin Nikolaevich, 491
Ivan the Terrible, 249, 432–45, 450–51, 454, 491
Ivan the Terrible (film) (Eisenstein), 432, 435–45, 450–51, 481n2
Ivan the Terrible (A. Tolstoy), 432–34, 436
Ivanov, Boris, 299–301, 491
Ivanov, Vsevolod Viacheslavovich: *Armored Train 14-69* by, 64, 65, 103, 399; biographical information on, 491; Gorky on, 82; and Organizing Committee of Writers Union, 154, 159–60; and Peredelkino (writers' colony), 321; and Pilnyak, 321; and proletarian writers, 36; and Society for the Development of Russian Culture, 38; and Stavsky, 319, 320;

during World War II, 386, 394; and Writers Union, 203, 207
Ivanov-Razumnik, Razumnik Vasilyevich, 135, 494
Izrailevsky, B. L., 254, 494
Izvestia: and Altman, 470; and Bedny, 68–70; and *Bezhin Meadow*, 143, 246; Gronsky as editor-in-chief of, 87, 162; and Kerzhentsev, 146; Leonov's "Holy Hatred" in, 360; and literary criticism, 215; and Pilnyak, 114, 115; and Zoshchenko, 371, 372

Jack of Diamonds group, 241, 479n8
Japan, 192
Jewish Anti-Fascist Committee affair, 468, 472
Jewish pogroms, 472. *See also* Anti-Semitism
Jewish Theater, 471–72
Jews. *See* Anti-Semitism
Journals, 204–6, 374–80, 381, 389, 398–425, 427–31. *See also specific journals*
"Journey to Olympus" (Zoshchenko), 408–9

Kabakov, 301
Kachalov, Vasily Ivanovich, 218, 491
Kadet (Constitutional Democratic) Party, 8, 355
Kadochnikov, Pavel Petrovich, 443, 491
Kaganovich, Lazar Moiseevich: and Averbakh group, 314; and Bedny, 72; biographical information on, 491; and Bolovanov, 475n5; and Bulgakov, 104, 268; and Gorky, 84, 180, 184; and Kirshon, 311–12; and Mikhailov's painting of Kirov's funeral, 277–78; and Moscow Art Theater, 219–20; on national culture, 64; and Pilnyak, 116; and RAPP, 151, 162; and Trotskyite-Zinovievite Center, 316–17; and Vinogradov, 334; and Writers' Congress (1934), 165–66; and Writers Union, 155–57, 159–60, 202–8; and *Young Guard*, 89
Kalinin, Anatoly Veniaminovich, 394, 491
Kalinin, Mikhail Ivanovich, 28–29, 31, 116, 120, 268, 491
Kallinikov, Iosif Fyodorovich, 125, 491
Kamenev, Lev Borisovich: and arrests of Kadet Party members, 8; and Babel, 309, 310; biographical information on, 491; and Blok's request for foreign travel, 21; defeat of, 5; execution of, 311; and

Gorky, 181; and proletarian writers, 40; and publishing houses, 38, 39; and theaters, 29, 30; trial of, 146; and Vesely, 89
Kamernyi Theater, 250, 252–54
Kantorovich, Vladimir Yakovlevich, 233, 491
Kapitsa, Pyotr Iosifovich, 419, 492
Kapler, Aleksei Yakovlevich, 290–92, 492
Kapustin, Yakov Fedorovich, 423, 492
Karaban, Pavel Solomonovich, 305–7, 492
Karakhan, Lev Mikhailovich, 11, 492
Karamzin, Nikolai, 73, 492
Karavaeva, Anna Aleksandrovna, 157, 209, 492
Kasilov, 342
Kassil, Lev Abramovich, 176–77, 291, 492
Kataev, Ivan Ivanovich, 316, 492
Kataev, Valentin Petrovich, 209, 317, 328, 332, 389, 492
Katerli, E., 405
Katsman, Yevgeny Aleksandrovich, 240, 241, 277, 492
Katya Dolga (Korobov), 66–67
Kaverin, Fyodor Nikolaevich, 256, 492
Kazakevich, Emmanuil Genrikhovich, 428, 492
Kedrov, Mikhail Nikolaevich, 254, 492
Keldysh, Yury Vsevolodovich, 237, 492
Kemenov, Vladimir Semyonovich, 211, 212, 492
Kerzhentsev, Platon Mikhailovich: and Bedny's *Bogatyrs*, 251, 253, 256, 257; and Bill-Belotserkovsky, 60; biographical information on, 492; on Bulgakov's *Flight*, 98–103; on Bulgakov's *Molière*, 267–70; career of, 145–46; and Committee on Arts Affairs, 145, 148, 241–42; and Levidov's *Conspiracy of Equals*, 95; and Meyerhold, 329; and Moscow Art Theater, 222, 225–26, 478n2; and nationalities policy, 93, 94; and play commemorating twentieth anniversary of Revolution, 278; on removal of avant-garde artworks from museums, 241–42; and Shostakovich, 230–31
Ketlinskaia, Vera, 412–13, 415
Khachaturian, Aram Ilyich, 462, 492
Khalatov, Artemy Bagratovich, 79, 492
Khalturin, Stepan Nikolaevich, 73, 492
Khanaev, 228
Khatsrevin, Zakhar Lvovich, 247, 492
Khazin, Aleksandr Abramovich, 406, 422, 492
Kheifits, Iosif Efimovich, 465, 492

Khlebnikov, Velimir, 371, 476n19, 492
Khlestakov, 328
Khmelev, Nikolai Pavlovich, 254, 492
Khodasevich, 304
Khrapchenko, Mikhail Borisovich, 462, 492
Khrennikov, Tikhon Nikolaevich, 462, 493
Khrushchev, Nikita Sergeevich, 162, 334, 347, 493
Khvylevy, Mykola, 206, 493
"A Kind of Monologue" (Akhmatova), 402
Kirov, Sergei Mironovich, 116, 211, 276, 277–78, 295–96, 493
Kirpotin, Valery Yakovlevich, 142, 153–58, 210–15, 317, 383, 478n4, 493
Kirsanov, Semyon Isaakovich, 319, 493
Kirshon, Vladimir Mikhailovich, 154, 156–58, 266, 311–16, 326, 493
Kiselev, Ya., 377–78
Kleiner, Isidor Mikhailovich, 256–57, 493
Kliuev, Nikolai Alekseevich, 171, 304, 371, 493
Klychkov, Sergei Antonovich, 255, 493
Knekht, V. A., 403, 493
Kniga (Book) publishing house, 125
Knipper-Chekhova, Olga Leonardovna, 216, 218, 493
Knorin, Vilhelm Georgievich, 51, 493
Kobulov, Bogdan Zakharovich, 352, 493
Kogan, Pyotr Semyonovich, 181, 493
Kogiz (Cooperative Organization of State Publishing Houses), 263
Kolbanovsky, A. E., 354–55, 493
Kolegaev, Andrei Lukich, 30, 493
Kolkhozes, 354, 361, 362
Kolos (Ear of Grain) publishing house, 124–25
Koltsov, Mikhail Efimovich, 191, 192, 493
Komedia Theater, 426
Komissarova, Maria Ivanovna, 402, 422, 493
Komsomol (Communist Union of Youth), 38, 89, 299–301
Komsomolskaia Pravda, 215
Kon, Feliks Yakovlevich, 209, 493
Kondratiev, Nikolai Dmitrievich, 82–83, 493
Konovalov, Grigory Ivanovich, 429, 494
Konstromoltsy group, 131
Koonen, Alisa Georgievna, 193, 251, 253, 494
Kopylenko, Aleksandr Ivanovich, 305, 494
Korabelnikov, Grigory Markovich, 314, 494
Koreneva, Lidia Mikhailovna, 217–18, 494

Korneichuk, Aleksandr Evdokimovich, 207, 224, 425, 470, 471, 494
Kornilov, Admiral, 446–47
Kornilov, Boris Petrovich, 371, 494
Korobov, Yakov Evdokimovich, 66–67, 494
Korolenko, Vladimir Galaktionovich, 359, 494
Kosarev, Aleksandr Vasilievich, 154, 494
Kostelyanets, Boris Osipovich, 429, 494
Kostenko, 343
Kostrov, Taras, 469, 494
Kozakov, Mikhail Emmanuilovicvh, 134, 303, 494
Kozelkov, 153
Kozintsev, Grigory Mikhailovich, 448, 458, 465–67, 494
Kozlovsky, Ivan Semyonovich, 256, 494
KPK (Party Control Commission), 260
Krasikov, 18
Krasin, Leonid Borisovich, 11, 13, 494
Krasiukov, 337–40
Krasnaia nov', 480n5
Krasnov, P. B., 358–59
Krestinsky, Nikolai Nikolaevich, 78, 494
Krinitsky, Aleksandr Ivanovich, 95, 96, 494
Kriuchkov, Pyotr Petrovich, 81, 311, 312, 314, 494
Krupin, Dmitry Vasilievich, 365, 494
Krupskaia, Nadezhda Konstantinovna, 30, 135, 280, 494
Kruzhilikha (Panova), 429
Krylov, S. N., 94–96, 494
Krzhizhanovsky, Gleb Maksimilianovich, 51, 494
Ku Klux Klan, 440, 450
Kuibyshev, Valerian Vladimirovich, 40, 116, 266, 494
Kuklin, Georgy Osipovich, 303, 494
Kultprop (Department of Culture and Propaganda), 119, 129, 141, 142, 153, 261, 263, 266
Kuprin, Aleksandr Ivanovich, 14, 495
Kurbsky, Andrei Mikhailovich, 435, 443, 495
Kurs, A. L., 85
Kusevitsky, Sergei Aleksandrovich, 9, 495
Kusikov, Aleksandr Borisovich, 36, 495
Kuzko, Pyotr Avdeevich, 357–58, 495
Kuznetsov, Aleksei Aleksandrovich, 416, 427, 495
Kuznetsov, Pavel Varfolomeevich, 48, 277, 495
Kvitko, Lev Moiseevich, 468, 495

Lady Macbeth of Mtsensk District (Shostakovich), 145, 146, 229, 233, 234, 237, 238, 478n4
Lakhuti, Abolgasem Akhmedzade, 196, 234, 315, 495
Lapin, Boris Matveevich, 176, 247, 495
Larin, V. F., 25, 26, 495
Larin, Yury, 342, 495
The Last of the Udegs (Fadeev), 187, 188
The Latest News, 354
Latsis, Asja (Anna Ernestovna), 53, 55, 495
Lavoisier, Antoine Laurent, 324, 495
Lavrenev, Boris Andreevich, 64, 65, 495
"The Law of Gravity" (Mass and Erdman), 266
The Law of Life (Avdeenko), 273, 274, 299–301, 479n6
The Leader (Dolmatovsky), 377
Lebedev, 459–60
Lebedev-Kumach, Vasily Ivanovich, 376, 495
Lebedev-Polyansky, Pavel Ivanovich, 34, 61, 90, 95, 122–26, 495
Lebedinsky, Lev Nikolaevich, 237, 495
LEF (Left Front in Art), 40, 50, 150
Left Art group, 478n2
Lekht, Fridrikh (Ferdinand) Karlovich, 277, 495
Lelevich, G., 40–41, 75
Lenin, Vladimir Ilyich: and Bedny, 68, 249, 257; biographical information on, 495; and Blok, 15–17, 20–21; and Bolshoi Theater, 23–27, 30; dates of rule of, ix; death of, ix; documentary on, 458; and Gorky, 76, 77, 78; on Great Russians' national pride, 75; illness of, 23; image of, as leader, 278–81; and intelligentsia during Civil War era, 7, 8, 17–19; on Lukács, 211; on proletariat, 62, 75; role of generally, in culture system, 4; scholarly publications on, 210; and Sokolnikov, 310; on Tolstoy, 211–12
Lenin (Mayakovsky), 287
Lenin in 1918, 280, 281, 465
Lenin in October, 465
Leningrad (journal), 350, 365, 370, 392, 398, 402, 404–25, 427, 428, 456
Leningrad Affair, 401
Leningrad ballet, 31
Leningrad Diary (Inber), 406, 414
Lentulov, Aristarkh Vasilievich, 277, 495
Leonidov, Leonid Mironovich, 218, 253, 495

Leonidze, Georgy Nikolaevich, 299, 495
Leonov, Leonid Maksimovich: award for, 359; biographical information on, 496; censorship of, 372; on communism and fascism, 206; and Gorky, 385; and Organizing Committee of Writers Union, 154; Voitinskaia on, 207; on World War II, 361; and Writers' Congress, 173–74; and Writers Union, 425; and Zoshchenko, 372I
—works: "Holy Hatred" in *Izvestia*, 360; *The Invasion*, 359; *Polovchan Gardens*, 225; *The Taking of Velikoshumsk*, 383
Lepeshinskaia, Olga Vasilievna, 227, 496
Lermontov, Mikhail Yurievich, 213, 496
Lessing, Gotthold Ephraim, 470, 496
"Let's Overcome Barmalei" (Chukovsky), 381
Levanevsky, 327
Levidov, Mikhail Yulievich, 94–98, 496
Levin, Fedor Markovich, 83, 211, 496
Lezhnev, A., 232–33, 496
Lezhnev, I., 198, 319, 320, 386, 392, 496
Liashko, Nikolai Nikolaevich, 38, 496
Libedinsky, Yury Nikolaevich, 142, 157, 159, 160, 189, 326, 496
Lidin, V. G., 387–88
Lifshits, Mikhail Aleksandrovich, 210–12, 496
Likharev, Boris Mikhailovich, 408–9, 422, 496
Limpid Stream (Shastkovich), 229–30, 235, 238
Linguistics, 333–35
"Literary Amusements" (Gorky), 185–87, 314
Literary Association of the Red Army and Navy (LOKAF), 155
Literary circles, 304, 319
Literary Critic, 209–15, 477n2
Literary criticism, 197–99, 209–15, 378, 386, 391, 399–401, 429
Literary Gazette/Literaturnaia gazeta, 52, 111, 150, 157, 185–87, 191–93, 205–8, 212, 317, 400, 406, 413, 478n2
Literary Heritage, 157
Literary Review/Literaturnoe obzrenie, 210, 211, 215
Literary Studies/Literaturnaia ucheba, 86
Literature and Art, 386
Literature and Revolution (Trotsky), xvi, 32–33
Litfront, 469, 470

Litovsky, Osaf Semyonovich, 220, 223, 253, 256, 257, 496
Litovtseva, 219
Litvin, 228
Litvinov, Maksim Maksimovich, 257, 496
Liubimov-Lanskoy, Evsei Osipovich, 55, 496
Liubov Yarovaia (Trenev), 224
Liushkov, Genrikh Samoilovich, 168, 496
Livanov, Boris Nikolaevich, 270, 496
Livshits, Vladimir Aleksandrovich, 396, 496
Logachev, 337, 340, 481n3
LOKAF (Literary Association of the Red Army and Navy), 155
Lominadze, Vissarion (Beso) Vissarionovich, 308, 496
A Lonely Sail Gleams (Kataev), 328
Long, R., 182
Louis XI, King of France, 441
Louis XIV, King of France, 268, 269, 270, 441, 496
The Lower Depths (Gorky), 78
Lubitsch, Ernst, 479n8, 496
Lugovoi, 337, 339–42
Lugovskoi, Vladimir Aleksandrovich., 376, 394, 496
Lukács, Georg (György), 209–13, 477n2, 478n4, 496–97
Lukin, Yury Borisovich, 382–83, 497
Lukov, Leonid Davidovich, 448, 458, 497
Lukovsky, 446
Lunacharsky, Anatoly Vasilievich: and artists, 48; biographical information on, 497; and Bolshoi Theater, 24–29, 31; and Bulgakov, 92–94; and Capri school, 477n6; and Gorky, 79; and intelligentsia during Civil War era, 3, 8–16, 18–20, 22; and Levidov, 95; and Pilnyak, 90; and Politburo, 27, 476n9; and proletarian writers, 40–41; and writers organizations, 51
Lupekin, 302–4
Luppol, Ivan Kapitonovich, 196, 497
Luther, Martin, 434, 497
Luzgin, Mikhail Vasilievich, 157, 497

Magazines. See Journals; *and specific periodicals*
The Magician from Gel-Giu (Borisov), 404, 413
Magnitostroi, 159, 160
Mahogany (Pilnyak), 111, 113, 114, 196

Major Overhaul (Sobolev), 256, 294
Makariev, Ivan Sergeevich, 157, 190, 266, 315, 497
Maksakova, Maria Petrovna, 228, 478*n*2, 497
Maksimov, G. I., 356, 497
Malakhov, Sergei Arsenievich, 211, 497
Maleev, 316
Malenkov, Georgy Maksimilianovich: and Aleksandrov, 402; and anti-Party faction in Soviet criticism, 210–15; and *Banner*, 376–79; biographical information on, 497; and Leningrad affair, 401; and opera, 459; and proposed expulsions from Writers Union, 469–71; and Sayanov, 412; and Selvinsky, 373; and *Star*, 420; and writers during post–World War II period, 393–98; and Zoshchenko, 417
Malinovskaia, Elena Konstantinovna, 26, 497
Maliugin, Leonid Antonovich, 403, 497
Malraux, André (Georges), 170, 191–92, 308, 472, 497
Maly Theater, 218, 236, 254, 435
Malyshkin, Aleksandr Georgievich, 154, 317, 497
A Man Changes His Skin (Yasensky), 325
Man with a Rifle (Yutkevich), 280, 281
The Mandate (Erdman), 265
Mandelshtam, Osip Emilievich, 304, 331–32, 371, 497
Mann, Klaus, 171, 497
Manuilov, Viktor Andronikovich, 303, 497
Margueritte, Victor, 126, 497
Mariengof, Anatoly Borisovich, 36, 497
Mariinsky theater, 29–30
Markish, Perets Davidovich, 321, 468, 497
Markov, Pavel Aleksandrovich, 218, 254, 497
Marr, Nikolai Yakovlevich, 333, 497
Marshak, Samuil Yakovlevich, 360, 498
Martov, Zhozef Klimentievich, 281, 498
Marx, Karl, 210, 387, 498
Mashbits-Verov, 110
Mashen'ka, 465
Mashkov, Ilya Ivanovich, 277, 498
Mass, Vladimir Zakharovich, 265–67, 498
Matrosov, Aleksandr Matveevich, 457, 498
Maupassant, Guy de, 360, 498
Mayakovsky, Vladimir Vladimirovich: biographical information on, 498; and Brik, 285–88; as Futurist, 36; and Gorky, 176–77; home of, 287; and LEF (Left Front in Art), 40; on poetry, 361; publication of works by, after his death, 286–88; and RAPP, 150, 326; Shostakovich compared with, 231, 235; Stalin on, 232, 286, 288, 323, 329, 478*n*2; suicide by, 21, 150, 285, 286, 321, 328–29, 371–72, 380
Maznin, Dmitry Mikhailovich, 315, 498
Mdivani, Georgy Davidovich, 377, 460, 498
Medallion (Shpanov), 395
Medvedev, Pavel Nikolaevich, 135, 498
"A Meeting on Laughter" (Mass and Erdman), 266
Mekhlis, Lev Zakharovich, 70, 187, 188, 258, 264, 288, 498
Melik-Pashaev, Aleksandr Shamilievich, 227, 498
Melnikov, Naum Dmitrievich, 428, 498
Mensheviks, 83–84
Menshikov, Aleksandr Sergeevich, 446–47, 498
Menzhinsky, Viacheslav Rudolfovich, 14, 16, 498
Merkulov, Vsevolod Nikolaevich, 380–92, 498
Meshcheriakov, Nikolai Leonidovich, 34, 498
Messerer, Sulamith, 228, 478*n*2, 498
Meyerhold, Vsevolod Emilievich: anti-Formalism campaign against, 230, 232, 233, 247, 251; arrest and execution of, 247; and *The Bedbug*, 235; on Bedny's *Bogatyrs*, 254, 257; Bill-Belotserkovsky on, 57, 58; biographical information on, 498; and Erdman's *The Suicide*, 479*n*13; Gorky on, 193; and Ostrovsky's *How the Steel Was Tempered*, 479*n*14; and Pushkin Committee, 329; and RAPP, 328; on Shostakovich, 235; on Tairov, 147; wife's petition to Stalin for, 328–30; *Woe to Wit* by, 248, 479*n*11
Meyerhold Theater, 247–48
Miaskovsky, Nikolai Yakovlevich, 238, 462, 498
Michurin, 384
Mikhailov, N., 277–78
Mikhailova, E. N., 375, 376, 379
Mikhailovsky Theater, 254
Mikhoels, Solomon Mikhailovich, 240, 498
Mikitenko, Ivan Kondratevich, 157, 499
Mikoyan, Anastas Ivanovich, 268, 459, 499
Minin, Kuzma, 442, 499

Minin and Pozharsky, 255
Ministry of Culture. *See* Commissariat (later Ministry) of Culture
Mints, Isaak Izrailevich, 312, 499
Miroshnichenko, Grigory Ilyich, 372, 499
Mirov, 316
Mirsky, Dmitry Petrovich, 187–88, 207, 499
Mitrofanov, Aleksandr Georgievich, 173, 499
Mogilny, 478n2
Molchanov, Georgy Andreevich, 173–78, 231–35, 239–41, 251–58, 305, 477n1, 499
Molchanov, Ivan Nikandrovich, 189, 499
Molière (Bulgakov), 217–18, 220, 268–70
Molodaia Gvardia publishing house, 365, 431
Molotov, Viacheslav Mikhailovich: and anti-Soviet intelligentsia in 1920s, 94–96, 105, 116, 120; and Bedny, 72, 73, 256, 259, 260, 441; biographical information on, 499; and Bolshoi Theater, 23–24, 28; and Bulgakov's *Molière,* 268–70; censorship by, 89, 90; and confidentiality of Politburo's work, 97; and Eisenstein, 243–46, 440–45; and Erdman and Mass satires, 266–67; and intelligentsia during Civil War era, 11–14, 21; and *Literary Critic,* 210–15; and Mikhailov's painting of Kirov's funeral, 277–78; and Moscow Art Theater, 119, 222, 225, 226, 478n2; and museums, 241–42; and opera, 459; and plays commemorating twentieth anniversary of Revolution, 278; publication of speeches of, in *Literary Gazette,* 206; and Shostakovich, 230–31; Stalin on, 83; and Vinogradov, 334; and Writers' Congress (1934), 170; and Writers Union, 205–8
Moor, Dmitry Stakhievich, 277, 499
Mordvinkin, Vladimir Yurievich, 95, 499
Mordvinov, 219
Morning Frosts, 36
Morozov, D. N., 257
Morozov, Pavlik, 242, 499
Morozov, Savva Timofeevich, 357, 499
MORP (International Society of Revolutionary Writers), 191, 220, 325
Moscow 1937 (Feuchtwanger), 147, 478n2
Moscow Art Theater: Arkadiev as director of, 223–26; and Bedny, 251; and Bulgakov's *Days of the Turbins,* 91, 92, 94; and Bulgakov's *Flight,* 100, 102–3; and Bulgakov's *Molière,* 217–18, 267, 269–70; Bulgakov's work at, 105, 107, 284–85; candidates for director of, 220, 223; compared with Kamerny Theater, 253; and Erdman's *The Suicide,* 117–19; foreign tour by, 9, 57; founding of, 216; and Gosheva, 444; honors for performers at, 226–28; problems of, 53, 219–20, 224–25; productions of, 91, 92, 102–3, 111, 117–19, 216, 217–18, 224–25; renaming of, after Gorky, 87; salaries at, 225; Stanislavsky and Nemirovich-Danchenko as founders and directors of, 8, 117–19, 147, 216–24, 226
Moscow Association of Soviet Artists (MOSKh), 239–41
Moscow Diary (Benjamin), 50, 53
Moscow Press House, 36, 37
Moscow Trade Union of Writers, 7
Moscow Union of Artists, 240, 277–78
Mosfilm (Moscow Film Studio), 143, 244, 246–47, 438, 479n6
MOSKh (Moscow Association of Soviet Artists), 239–40
Moskvin, Ivan Mikhailovich, 8, 499
Mountains (Zazubrin), 181
Movies. *See* Films
Mrachkovsky, Sergei Vitalievich, 309, 310, 499
Munblit, Georgy Nikolaevich, 234, 499
Muradeli, Vano Ilyich, 236, 459–63, 499
Murzilka, 402
Museums, 241–42
Music and music organizations, 152, 153–54, 235–38, 351, 459–63. *See also* Opera; *and specific composers*
Muzfond publishing house, 460
"My Nekrasov" (Flit), 405–6

Nafta (Savin), 319
Nakhimov, Pavel Stepanovich, 446–50, 454, 499
Napoleon I, Emperor of the French, 297, 499
Narbut, Vladimir Ivanovich, 178, 305–7, 499
Narkomfin, 39
Narkompros (People's Commissariat of Education): and artists' associations, 47; and Bolshoi Theater, 25–27, 31; and Bulgakov, 91–94; and Glavlit, 262; and Golovanov, 475n5; and Gorky, 78; and intelligentsia during Civil War era, 9–14, 16, 19–20; and Osinksy, 27; painting department of, 241; and Pushkin Exhibition, 334; and writers' organizations, 51; and Zamyatin, 112

Narodnost, 147, 260, 478n4
Natasha (Seifullina), 329–30, 480n9
Nationalism, 249–60, 306, 348–49, 352, 364, 379
Naturalism, 146, 149, 234, 429
Nazism, 148, 224, 349, 354, 382. *See also* Germany; Hitler, Adolf
Nebolsin, 227
Neigauz, Genrikh Gustavovich, 237, 499
Nekrasov, 405–6, 408
Nemirovich-Danchenko, Vladimir Ivanovich, 8, 216–20, 222, 223, 332–33, 500
NEP (New Economic Policy), 3, 4–5, 32–49, 88, 110, 151–52, 190
New Russia, 90
New World, 90–91, 125, 204 375, 382, 399
Newspapers. *See specific newspapers*
Nicholas I, Tsar, 257, 441, 500
Night of the Commander (Selvinsky), 457
Nikandrov, Nikolai Nikandrovich, 353–54, 500
Nikitin, A. E., 202–5
Nikitin, Mikhail Aleksandrovich, 355–56, 500
Nikitin, Nikolai Nikolaevich, 36, 303, 500
Nikolaeva, Galina Yevgenievna, 394, 500
Nikulin, Lev Veniaminovich, 159, 160, 317, 500
Nikulin, Yury, 177
Nilin, Pavel Filippovich, 385, 500
Ninotchka, 479n8
NKGB: on writers during World War II, 352–64, 380–92; and Zoshchenko, 369–73
NKID (People's Commissariat of Foreign Affairs), 115
NKP (People's Commissariat of Enlightenment), 93–94, 128, 129, 222
NKVD (People's Commissariat for Internal Affairs): and anti-Formalism campaign, 231; and denunciation of rivals by cultural figures, 147; and Gorky, 185–87; and Mikhailov, 278; and Selvinsky, 206; and Sholokhov, 338, 339, 340–43; on writers, 140, 173–78, 201, 302–21; and Writer's Congress, 140, 173–78. *See also* GUGB (Central Directorate of State Security)
NKVT (People's Commissariat of Foreign Trade), 78
Notes on Cuffs (Bulgakov), 126
Novaia Moskva, 126

Novikov-Priboy, Aleksei Silych, 169, 174, 500
Novy mir. See *New World*
Nusinov, Isaak Markovich, 468, 500

Oath (Gladkov), 388
October/Oktiabr', 173, 366, 367, 369, 375, 399, 411
October group, 39
Ogiz (Amalgamated State Publishing House), 129, 130
OGPU (Unified State Political Directorate), 89, 105, 129–35, 171, 334
Okhotnikov, Yakov (Yasha), 308, 309
The Old and the New (Eisenstein), 242
Old Friends (Maliugin), 403
Olesha, Yury Karlovich, 175, 177, 231–32, 256, 317, 372, 478n2, 500
Oleynikov, Nikolai Mikhailovich, 303, 500
On Guard group, 326
On Guard, 39, 49, 160
On Literary Guard/Na literaturnom postu, 58–60, 69, 158
On the Open Sea (Kapitsa), 419
On the Sandbar (Dairedzhiev), 469
One Life (Gabrilovich), 248
"Onegin's Return" (Khazin), 422
Opera, 145, 146, 147, 192, 229–36, 250–58, 459–63
An Optimistic Tragedy (Vishnevsky), 252, 479n1
Orbeli, Iosif Abgarovich, 257, 500
Ordzhonikidze, Grigory Konstantinovich (Sergo), 268, 460–62, 500
Oreshin, Pyotr Vasilievich, 160, 171, 500
Organizing Committee of Writers Union, 87, 141–42, 153–55, 157–58, 160, 162, 165, 266, 267, 326
Orgburo: and *Banner*, 380; and censorship, 124, 351; and films, 447–56; and Glavlit, 122, 262, 264–65; and Glavrepertkom, 97–98; and journals, 418–24, 427–30; and *Literary Critic*, 215; and literature in 1930s, 140; and Lunacharsky, 13; and *New World*, 204; and publishing houses, 262; and restructuring literary and arts organizations in 1932, 152, 153–55; and VAPP (All-Union Association of Proletarian Writers), 52
Orgkom, 176, 189
Orlov, Nikolai Andreevich, 10, 500
Osadchy, P. S., 82
Osinksy, 27
Osmerkin, Aleksandr, 48, 500

OST (Society of Easel Painters), 239
Ostroumov, V., 259–60
Ostrov, Dmitry Konstantinovich, 403, 500
Ostrovsky, Aleksandr, 479n4
Ostrovsky, Nikolai Alekseevich, 248, 479n14, 500
"Outside Berlin's Walls" (Ivanov), 399
Ovechkin, Valentin Vladimirovich, 394, 500
Ozerov, Nikolai Nikolaevich, 227, 500

Painting and painters, 239–41, 277–78
Pakhiev, P., 18
Palekh, 254
Panch, Petro, 305, 500
Panfyorov, Fedor Ivanovich: on Averbakh and Kirshon, 312; biographical information on, 501; and Gorky, 144, 182–83, 187, 188–89, 314; *Ingots* by, 66, 182, 187, 188–89; and Organizing Committee of Writers Union, 157–58; and restructuring of literary and arts organizations in 1932, 151, 154; and Stalin, 315; and Writers' Congress, 170, 172–75
Panfyorovism, 234
Panova, Vera Fyodorovna, 429, 501
Party Control Commission (KPK), 260
The Party Leads (Tychina), 206
Pasternak, Boris Leonidovich: Antokolsky on, 378; biographical information on, 501; and censorship, 360; at Congress for the Defense of Culture (1935) in Paris, 191; *Georgian Lyrics*, 323, 480n1; and Gide, 320; on Gorky's "Literary Amusements," 186–87; leadership of, 320–21; and Mayakovsky, 323; Olesha's defense of, 317; and Peredelkino (writers' colony), 321; and Platonov, 214; political independence of, 318; and Stalin, 322–23; Stavsky's criticism of, 319, 320; on World War II, 360; and Writers' Congress, 175–77; and Writers Union, 207, 235; and Zamyatin, 200, 201; Zenkevich on, 233
Patolichev, Nikolai Semyonovich, 427, 501
Patriotic culture campaign, 249–60
Patronage: by Gorky, 179–81, 187, 312; Gorky on, 189–90, 196; hierarchical system of, xv, 142–43; in 1930s generally, 216; Stalin as patron-potentate, 282–301
Pavlenko, Pyotr Andreevich, 153, 154, 201, 209, 332, 363, 387, 501
Pavlov, Ivan, 366
"Peace" (Ostrov), 403
Peasant (Molchanov), 189

The People of Bolshevo, 313
People of the Second Five-Year Plan, 315
Peredelkino (writers' village), 143, 183–84, 204, 321
Perelman, V. N., 277, 501
"Pererva" (Bedny), 73
Pereverzev, Valerian Fedorovich, 156, 501
Periodicals. *See* Journals; *and specific periodicals*
Pervomaisky, Leonid Solomonovich, 305, 501
Peshkova, Nadezhda Alekseevna, 83, 308, 501
Peter the Great, Tsar, 432, 442
Petersburg House of Writers, 36
Petrograd Association of Proletarian Writers, 36
Petrov-Vodkin, Kuzma Sergeevich, 135, 501
Petrovsky, V., 168–71, 173–78
Photography, 229, 277
Piatakov, Georgy (Yury) Leonidovich, 78, 296, 325, 501
Picasso, Pablo, 240, 501
Pikel, Richard V., 95, 315, 316, 501
Pilnyak, Boris Andreevich: arrest of, 116; biographical information on, 501; censorship of, 89–91, 113–16, 475n5; foreign travel requests by, 112, 113–16; on Frunze's death, 196; and Gorky, 85; and Ivanov, 321; and miscellany titled "The Thirties," 316; and Peredelkino (writers' village), 321; and Politburo, 38; and RAPP, 109; and Stalin, 36, 59, 113–16, 135, 174–75; and Stavsky, 319; Trotsky on, 34; and Writers' Congress (1934), 174–75, 477n8
—works: *Mahogany*, 111, 113, 114, 196; "The Tale of the Unextinguished Moon," 89–91, 475n6; *The Volga Runs into the Caspian Sea*, 114
Pirozhkova, Antonina Nikolaevna, 307–9, 501
Pivovarov, 342
Platonov, Andrei Platonovich, 119–22, 210, 211, 214, 234, 501
Plays and playwrights. *See specific plays, playwrights, and theaters*
Plekhanov, Georgy Valentinovich, 300, 501
Pletnev, Valerian Fedorovich, 40, 501
Poetry and poets, 213–14, 234, 361, 371, 389–90, 478n2. *See also specific poets*
Pogodin, Nikolai Fyodorovich, 206, 362, 391, 501

Poincaré, Raymond, 82, 501
Pokrovsky, Mikhail Nikolaevich, 79, 82, 501
Poland, 325, 361
Police. *See* Secret police
Polikarpov, Dmitry Alekseevich, 365, 369–70, 373, 376–79, 381, 501
Politburo: and anti-Semitism, 468–69; and Bedny, 250–51; and Bolshoi Theater and academic theaters, 24, 25, 28–31; and Bulgakov, 91–94, 98–104; and censorship in 1920s, 88–91, 97–98, 104–5, 122, 124, 127–30, 351; and censorship in 1930s, 245–47, 261–65, 270–75, 351; during Civil War era, 7, 8–9, 12–13, 16, 21–22; and Committee on Arts Affairs, 229; and Composers Union, 462–63; confidentiality of work of, 97; and cultural policy of 1930s, 140, 141; and decision-making procedure, 24; and Ehrenburg, 472; and Eisenstein, 243–47; and film censorship and criticism, 454, 456–58; and Gorky, 76–79, 84–85; and journals, 398–99, 431; and Levidov, 97–98; and Meyerhold Theater, 247–48; and Mikhailov's painting of Kirov's funeral, 277–78; and Moscow Art Theater, 119; during NEP era, 33–35, 37–45; and presentation of image of leader, 279–81; and proletarian writers, 39–45, 48–49, 52–53; on publication of literature previously published in journals, 431; and RAPP, 151–53, 162–63; reprimand of Lunacharsky by, 27; on restructuring literary and arts organization (1932), 151–53; role of generally, in culture system, x–xii; and Stanislavsky, 226; on Voronsky's removal from editorial board of *Red Virgin Soil*, 52; on writers organizations, 50–52; and Writers Union, 139
Politkovsky, V. M., 227–28
Polonskaia, Elizaveta Grigorievna, 36, 501
Polonskaia, Veronika Vitoldovna, 372, 501
Polonsky, Viacheslav Pavlovich, 90, 95, 501–2
Polovchan Gardens (Leonov), 225
Poluyan, N. V., 309
Polyak, Lidia Moiseevna, 378, 502
Popkov, Pyotr Sergeevich, 416–17, 502
Popov, Georgy Mikhailovich, 427, 469–71, 502
Popov-Dubovsky, V. S., 95
Popular Front, 191

Poskrebyshev, Aleksandr Nikolaevich: biographical information on, 502; and Bulgakov's letter to Stalin, 331; and Ehrenburg, 472; and Gorky's letter to Stalin, 180; and petition to Stalin on Mandelshtam, 332; and Sholokhov, 343; and Stavsky's memo on Averbakh and Kirshon, 313; and Sutyrin, 120; and Yudin's statement on Kirshon, 311; and writers' conference (1938), 209
Postupalsky, Igor Stefanovich, 305–7, 502
Postyshev, Pavel Petrovich, 159–60, 162, 164, 180, 502
Pozharsky, Dmitry Mikhailovich, 442, 502
Pravda: anti-Formalist campaign by, 146, 229–38, 242, 247, 286; and Bedny, 68–70, 147, 250, 251, 258; and Bulgakov's *Molière*, 270; editors of, 153, 187; and Eisenstein, 246; on Fedin's *Gorky Among Us*, 382–83; on formalism in music, 236–38; function of, in 1930s, 350; and Gide, 320; and Gorky, 19, 77–78, 314; on journals, 424; Lezhnev's article in, 319; Lidin on, 387–88; literary section of, and literary criticism, 198, 210, 215; on opera, 463; and Pilnyak, 135; Popkov on, 417; on proletarian literature, 150; on RAPP, 325–26; Sholokhov's "On the Simple Word" in, 344; on Shostakovich, 146, 191, 229–35, 238; Stalin's articles in, 192; and Stavsky, 199; on Ukrainian writers, 93–94; Utkin on, 390; and Yasensky, 188, 326, 327; on Zoshchenko, 423
Pravdukhin, Valerian Pavlovich, 169, 175, 502
The Present, 85
Prishvin, Mikhail Mikhailovich, 159–60, 168–69, 502
Prokofiev, Aleksandr Andreevich, 177, 186, 305–7, 372, 409–13, 415, 418, 477n1, 502
Prokofiev, Sergei Sergeevich, 462, 502
Proletarian Theater, 53–55, 58
Proletarian writers: and cultural revolution, 49, 50–75; during NEP era, 4–5, 39–45; Politburo resolution (1925) on, 39–45, 48–49; and Stalin, xv–xvi, 53–75; struggle between fellow travelers and, 4–5, 39–40, 42–43, 109, 136; Trotsky on, xv–xvi. *See also* RAPP (Russian Association of Proletarian Writers)
Proletarianization, xvi, 33

Proletariat, 32–33, 41–42, 62, 73–74, 75
Proletkult (Proletarian Culture), 4, 32, 33, 36, 40, 50, 85, 267
Propaganda and Agitation Administration. *See* Agitprop
Prut, Iosif Leonidovich, 332, 502
Pshavela, Vazha, 323
Pshebyshevsky (Pshibyshevsky), B. S., 153, 475*n*5
Publishing: and Glavlit, 122, 124–25, 261–65; Gorky on, 18–19, 180–81; of literature previously published in journals, 431; and Politburo, 38–39, 51, 52, 90, 128–29; Pravdukhin on, 169; during World War II, 381; Yakovlev on, 36–38. *See also* Censorship; Journals; *and specific publishers*
Pudovkin, Vsevolod Illarionovich, 442, 445–50, 454, 458, 502
Punin, Nikolai Nikolaevich, 322, 502
Pushkin, Aleksandr Sergeevich, 177, 213, 214, 224, 329, 334, 356, 394, 417, 502
Pushkin Museum, 334
Puzin, Aleksei Aleksandrovich, 375, 502
Pyriev, Ivan Aleksandrovich, 457, 458, 466, 502

Quiet Flows the Don (Dzerzhinsky), 232, 237, 257, 478*n*4
Quiet Flows the Don (Sholokhov), 336, 337, 339, 343–44, 478*n*4

Rabichev, N. N., 153, 154, 159–60, 502
Rabinovich, Dmitry, 237, 502
Radek, Karl Berngardovich, 166, 169, 175, 296, 311, 325, 502
Radishchev, Aleksandr Nikolaevich, 73, 74, 502
Radlov, Nikolai Ernestovich, 135, 502
Raid on the Carpathians, 457
Raikh, Zinaida Nikolaevna, 193, 328–30, 502
Raikin, 408
Rainbow (Vasilevskaia), 383
Raizman, Yuly Yakovlevich, 466, 503
Rakhmanov, Leonid Nikolaevich, 406, 413, 503
Raltsevich, V. F., 157
RAMP. *See* Russian Association of Proletarian Musicians
Ramzin, Leonid Konstantinovich, 83, 503
RAPP (Russian Association of Proletarian Writers): and "anti-Soviet writers," 109, 111, 150; and Bolshevization of literature, 5, 39; demise of, 141, 150–61, 312, 314, 325–26; and Gorky, 144, 153, 182–83, 314; influence and success of, 150–51; leadership of, 142, 180, 311; and LEF (Left Front in the Arts), 50, 150; Lidin on, 387; and literary circles, 304; and Mayakovsky, 150, 326; and Meyerhold, 328; and Politburo, 151–53, 162–63; purge of leaders of, in 1930s, 147; and Socialist Realism, 163–65; and Stalin, 55–61, 79, 119–21, 162–64; and VAPP, 40, 52, 150; and Writers' Congress (1934), 167; and Writers Union, 142, 143, 144, 153, 172
Raskolnikov, Fyodor Fyodorovich, 95, 475*n*5, 503
Reader and Writer, 52
Realism. *See* Socialist Realism
Red Cavalry (Babel), 478*n*3
Red Field, 88
Red Poppy, 235
Red Star, 363
Red Virgin Soil, 35, 40, 52, 88, 90, 120–21, 125, 280
Reich, Bernhard, 55, 503
Relics (Kallinikov), 125
Rembrandt van Rijn, 242, 479*n*9, 503
"Reminiscences of Repin" (Chukovsky), 382
Remizov, Aleksei Mikhailovich, 15, 383, 503
Repertkom, 119, 268, 397
Repin, Ilya Yefimovich, 241, 242, 444, 479*n*9, 503
Rest, B., 404–5, 422, 503
Resurrection (Tolstoy), 100, 102
"The Return of Onegin" (Khazin), 406
Riabushinsky, Pavel Pavlovich, 87, 503
Riazhsky, Georgy Geogievich, 277, 503
Rimsky-Korsakov, Nikolai Andreevich, 231, 503
RKI (Worker-Peasant Inspection), 29
"Road of Time" (Yagdfeld), 399, 422
Robespierre, Maximilien, 95, 503
Rodchenko, M., 48
Rode, A. S., 18
Rodov, Semyon Abramovich, 40, 503
Rokossovsky, 357
Rolland, Romain, 114, 308, 323–24, 503
Rolland-Kudasheva, M. P., 324, 503
Romanov, Panteleimon Sergeevich, 13, 255, 503

Romm, Mikhail Ilyich, 281, 290–92, 458, 464–68, 503
Roosevelt, Franklin D., 361
ROPKP (Russian Union of Proletarian-Kolkhoz Writers), 150, 154, 155
Rosko, G. E., 18–19
Rost, 158
Rowdy, 425
Rozental, Mark Moissevich, 186, 211, 503
Rozhdestvensky, Vsevolod Aleksandrovich, 304, 396, 406, 503
Rudder/Rul', 85
Rudnikov, 14
Rudzutak, Yan Ernestovich, 116, 503
Runin, Boris Mikhailovich, 429, 503
Russian Association of Proletarian Musicians (RAMP), 152, 153, 235, 237
Russian Association of Proletarian Writers. See RAPP (Russian Association of Proletarian Writers)
The Russian Language (Vinogradov), 333
Russian Contemporary, 180
Russian Linguistics, 333
Russian Museum, 241–42
Russian Union of Proletarian-Kolkhoz Writers (ROPKP), 150, 154, 155
Rykov, Aleksei Ivanovich, 31, 77–78, 83, 91–92, 259, 503
Ryss, Yevgeny Samuilovich, 395–96, 503

Saakadze, Georgy, 299, 503
Sadofiev, Ilya Ivanovich, 402, 422, 503
Sadovsky, Prov Mikhailovich, 254, 503
Sakhnovsky, Vasily Grigorievich, 218, 219, 504
Saltykov-Shchedrin, Mikhail Yevgrafovich, 134–35, 504
Samosud, Samuil Abramovich, 254, 504
Sannikov, Grigory Aleksandrovich, 232, 504
Sanprosvet (Sanitary Enlightenment) theater, 107
Sapozhnikov, P. F., 95
Sarkisov, 301
Sats, Igor Aleksandrovich, 211, 504
Sats, Natalia Ilyinichna, 254, 504
Savelyev, M. A., 70
Savichev, M., 131
Savin, Lev, 319, 504
Sayanov, Vissarion Mikhailovich, 232, 407–8, 412, 416, 418, 419, 422, 504
Scapegoat literary group, 131
Schoenberg, Arnold, 238, 504
School of Scandal (Sheridan), 110

Secret police: and anti-Formalism campaign, 231; on Babel, xv, 307–11; on Bedny, 251–60; and Bulgakov's *Days of the Turbins,* 91–92; on conference of Moscow artists (1935), 239–41; denunciation of rivals by cultural figures to, 147; and Gorky, 81, 185–87; on honors for theater performers, 227–28; and Mikhailov, 278; and Selvinsky, 206; and Shostakovich, 231–35; torture by, 170, 340–41; and Writers' Congress (1934), 140, 143, 168–78, 477n1; on writers during World War II, 352–64, 380–92; on writers in 1930s, 140, 143, 148, 173–78, 201, 302–21; and Writers Union, 148, 168–78; and Yavich's "Grigory Pugachev," 88; and Zoshchenko, 369–73
Seifullina, Lidia Nikolaevna, 154, 175, 321, 329–30, 477n8, 480n9, 504
Selivanovsky, Aleksei Pavlovich, 156, 157, 316, 469, 504
Selvinsky, Ilya (Karl) Lvovich: biographical information on, 504; censorship and criticism of, 373–74, 375, 378, 380, 384, 388, 390, 394; and NKVD, 206; on Socialist Realism, 394; on Stavsky, 319–20; students' approval of, 391; on World War II, 363–64; and Writers' Congress, 175–76
—works: "To Whom Did Russia Sing Lullabies," 374, 375, 378, 384; *Cheliuskiniana,* 321; *Commander of the Second Army,* 238, 479n13; "Sevastopol," 405, 409
Semenko, Mikhail Vasilievich, 169–70, 504
Semiakin, 342
Semper, Johannes, 425, 504
Semyonov, Sergei Aleksandrovich, 38, 504
Semyonova, N., 55
Senchenko, Ivan Yefimovich, 206, 504
Serafimovich, Aleksandr, 144, 154, 182–83, 188, 504
Serapion Brothers, 36, 38, 351
Serebriansky, Mark Isaakovich, 157, 504
Sergeev-Tsensky, Sergei Nikolaevich, 362, 504
"Sevastopol" (Selvinsky), 405, 409
Shaginyan, Marietta Sergeevna, 36, 38, 116–17, 174, 186, 192, 279–80, 387, 504
Shakespeare, William, 111, 211, 300, 360, 504
Shakespeare-Bandzho literary group, 131

Shaporin, Yury Aleksandrovich, 235, 504
Shaposhnikov, 264
Shaumian, Stepan Georgievich, 80, 504
Shaw, George Bernard, 114, 504
Shchatsky, 342
Shchedrin, 118
Shcherbakov, Aleksandr Sergeevich: and Aseev's *Years of Thunder*, 373; biographical information on, 504; and Department of Cultural-Educational Work of Central Committee, 142; and Golubov, 362; on Moscow Art Theater, 217–20; and Shostakovich, 238; and Stanislavsky, 222–23; on A. N. Tolstoy's plays on Ivan the Terrible, 433, 435; and Writers' Congress, 174, 176; and Writers Union, 142, 197–200; and Zoshchenko, 367–68, 370, 372
Shcherbina, Vladimir Rodionovich, 375, 505
Shchors (Dovzhenko), 280, 281, 288–90, 294–95, 465
Shchors, Nikolai Aleksandrovich, 288, 289, 505
Shchukin, Boris Vasilievich, 280, 281, 505
Shebalin, Vissarion Yakovlevich, 462, 505
Shepilov, Dmitry Trofimovich, 457–60, 462, 505
Sheridan, Richard, 110
Shershenevich, Vadim Gabrielovich, 36, 505
Shestovaia, 342
Shimkeviches, 315
Shirokov, Ivan Mikhailovich, 418–20, 423, 505
Shishkov, Viacheslav Yakolevich, 135, 505
Shkiryatov, Matvei Fedorovich, 342, 469–71, 475n5, 505
Shkliar, N., 177
Shklovsky, Viktor Borisovich, 232, 358, 364, 370, 377, 378, 390, 392, 505
Shmidt, Otto Yulievich, 272, 505
Shmidt, Vasily Vasilievich, 39, 317, 505
Sholokhov, Mikhail Aleksandrovich: Arkadiev's interest in, 225; biographical information on, 505; Dairedzhiev's book on, 469; foreign travel request by, 82; and Gorky, 82, 180, 181; and Organizing Committee of Writers Union, 326; political mistakes by, 338–39; prestige of, 336, 343; and RAPP, 314; Stalin-Sholokhov exchange, 336–44; Stavsky on, 336–37
—works: "On the Simple Word," 344; *Quiet Flows the Don* by, 336, 337, 339, 343–44, 478n4; *They Fought for the Homeland*, 393; *Virgin Soil Upturned* by, 187, 189, 337
Short Course (Stalin), 141, 260, 295
Short stories, 411, 414. *See also specific authors*
Shostakovich, Dmitry Dmitrievich, 145, 146, 191, 192, 229–38, 351, 462, 505
Shpanov, Nikolai Nikolaevich, 391, 395, 505
Shpitsberg, 17–18
Shtein, Aleksandr Petrovich, 403, 422, 505
Shteinberg, A., 233
Shteinpress, Boris Solomonovich, 237, 505
Shterenberg, David Petrovich, 48, 239–40, 505
Shubnyakov, 352–64
Shukhov, Ivan Petrovich, 187, 189, 505
Shumiatsky, Boris Zakharovich, 148, 242–47, 289, 295–97, 505
Shushkanov, N., 157
Shvartsbakh, O., 170–71
Siberian writers, 84–86, 410
Sidorov, 342
Simonov, Konstantin Mikhailovich, 301, 379, 425, 505
Skuratov-Belsky, Grigory Lukianovich (Maliuta Skuratov), 442, 443, 444, 505
Skvortsov-Stepanov, Ivan Ivanovich, 79, 90, 97, 505
Slavin, Lev Isaevich, 232, 270–71, 505
Sletov, P., 175
Slonimsky, Mikhail Leonidovich, 153, 154, 179, 181, 201, 303, 405, 422, 505
Smelyakov, Yaroslav Vasilievich, 171, 186, 505
Smidovich, Pyotr Germogenovich, 79, 506
Smilga, Ivan Tenisovich, 309, 506
Smirnov, Aleksandr Petrovich, 92, 104–5, 506
Smithy literary organization, 39, 40, 150, 153
Sobolev, Leonid Sergeevich, 206, 209, 256, 294, 393, 506
Socialist Realism: beginning of policy of, 142, 149; description of, 139–40, 260; evolution from "realism" to, 210; and films, 458; and Gorky, 139, 164, 182, 187, 194; Gronsky on, 162–65; in music, 238, 463; and *narodnost, narodnyi*, 260; and Ostrovsky's *How the Steel Was Tempered*, 479n14; and painting, 240, 242; and patriotic culture campaign, 260; in

Socialist Realism (*continued*)
post–World War II period, 394; and RAPP, 163–65; Selvinsky on, 394; and Stalin, 162–64, 187; writers' responses to generally, 155; and Writers Union, xiii, 6, 139
Socialist Revolutionaries, 77–78, 83–84
Society for the Development of Russian Culture, xv, 37–38
Society of Easel Painters (OST), 239
Society of Honorary Bell Ringers (Zamyatin), 112
Sofronov, Anatoly Vladimirovich, 468, 506
Sokolnikov, Grigory Yakovlevich, 31, 309, 310, 506
Sokolovskaia, E. K., 246–47
Sokolovsky, M., 376
Solitude (Virta), 225
Sollertinsky, Ivan Ivanovich, 230–31, 236, 237, 506
Solntseva, Marusia, 308
Sologub, Fyodor Kuzmich, 12, 14–16, 19–20, 125, 383, 506
Solomko, Shura, 308
Soloviev, Leonid Vasilievich, 356, 506
Sosnovsky, Lev Semyonovich, 27, 506
Sovetsky Pisatel' publishing house, 169, 365, 379, 393, 395, 431
Soviet Art, 143, 210, 244
Soviet Siberia, 85
Sovnarkom, 17, 23
Spanish Civil War, 481*n*2
Spassky, Sergei Dmitrievich, 404, 506
Speransky, Aleksei Dmitrievich, 366, 372, 506
Spiridonov (Sayanin), 80
Stalin, Iosif Vissarionovich: and Afinogenov, 292–94; and "anti-Soviet intelligentsia," 93–94, 105–22, 134–35; and artists and writers during NEP era, 36–38, 45–49; and Averbakh and Kirshon, 313–15; and awards for Soviet writers, 201–2; and Bedny, 68–75, 249–50, 251, 258–60; biographical information on, 506; and Bolshoi Theater, 29, 30, 31; and Bulgakov, 55, 56–57, 61, 64–66, 91, 93–94, 105–9, 135, 282–85; and Bulgakov's *Molière*, 268–70; and censorship, xiii–xiv, 89, 117, 122, 141, 271–72, 366–67; changing role of, in culture system, xv–xvi, 33, 140–41; Comintern disbanded by, 355; and cultural revolution, 5–6, 33, 53–68; culture of High Stalinism (1932–1941), 139–49; dates of rule of, ix; death of, ix, 140, 351, 464, 472; decision-making power of, 350; and Eisenstein, 243–44, 435–45, 455; and Erdman and Mass satires, 266–67; and films, 243–44, 271–72, 274, 288–92, 294–301, 435–45, 447–58, 465–68, 479*n*6; and Gorky, 78–87, 143–44, 178–94, 324; introduction to, 139–49, 347–51; and Jewish pogroms, 472; and journals, 398–99, 407–25, 427; and Kirov's assassination, 276; and Kirshon, 311–12; and *Literary Critic*, 210–15; on Mayakovsky, 286, 288, 323, 329, 478*n*2; and Mikhailov's painting of Kirov's funeral, 277–78; and Moscow Art Theater, 216–28; and museums, 241–42; and NKVD reports on writers during 1930s, 302–21; and opera, 459–60; and Pasternak, 322–23; as patron-potentate, 282–301; petitions to, on behalf on those arrested, 322–35; and play commemorating twentieth anniversary of Revolution, 278; and presentation of image of leader, 276–81; and proletarian literature, 53–75, 119–21; and proletarianization, xvi; and proposed expulsions from Writers Union, 469–71; and RAPP, 55–61, 79, 119–21, 162–64; and Sholokhov, 336–44; *Short Course* by, 141, 260, 295; and Shostakovich, 230–31; and Socialist Realism, 162–64, 187; and A. N. Tolstoy, 434–36; and World War II, 373; and Writers' Congress (1934), 165–68; and Writers Union, 197–205, 208–9; and Zhdanov, 424; and Zhdanovism, 447–56; and Zoshchenko, 411–12, 420, 425–27. *See also* Great Purge (1937–1938)
The Stalin White Sea–Baltic Canal, 313, 314
Stalingrad (Grossman), 393
Stanislavsky, Konstantin Sergeevich, 8, 117–19, 147, 216–24, 226, 253, 506
Stanitsyn, Viktor Yakovlevich, 217–18, 220, 254, 269–70, 506
Star, 90, 365, 372, 392, 396, 398, 399, 401–4, 406–28
Staritsky, 443
State Academy of Artistic Societies, 47–48
Stavsky, Vladimir Petrovich: on Averbakh and Kirshon, 313–15; biographical information on, 506; and Gorky, 180, 181, 183; and Great Purge, 202; and Ivanov, 319, 320; literary career of, 177; and Or-

ganizing Committee of Writers Union, 154; on Pasternak, 319, 320; petition to secret police by, on behalf of Mandelshtam, 331–32; and Pilnyak, 319; and *Pravda*, 199; and RAPP, 180; Selvinsky on, 319–20; on Sholokhov, 336–39; and Sobolev, 294; and Writers' Congress, 169, 170, 172, 174, 175, 176; and Writers Union, 142, 148, 155, 182, 197, 199–200, 202–5, 208–9, 246, 316

Stetsky, Aleksei Ivanovich: and Bedny, 259; biographical information on, 506; and Erdman and Mass satires, 266–67; and Gorky, 84, 184; on Mikhailov's painting of Kirov's funeral, 277–78; and Organizing Committee of Writers Union, 153, 154; and RAPP, 158, 162; and Stanislavsky, 119; and Writers' Congress, 165, 175, 176

Stolper, Aleksandr Borisovich, 299–301, 306

Storm (Bill-Belotserkovsky), 58

The Storm (Ostrovsky), 269, 479n4

Stradivarius Quartet, 10

"Strategic Assignment" (Zoshchenko), 381

Stravinsky, Igor Fedorovich, 238, 506

A Strict Youth (Olesha), 478n2

Stromin, 305–7

"Struggle or Die" (Bedny), 258

Subotsky, Lev Matveevich, 166, 506

Sudakov, Ilyia Yakovlevich, 218, 506

The Suicide (Erdman), 117–19, 248, 265, 479n13

Sukhe-Bator, 465

Sukhovo-Kobylin, Aleksandr Vasilievich, 479n11, 507

Surikov, Vasily Ivanovich, 242, 479n9, 507

Surkov, Aleksei Aleksandrovich, 319, 507

Suslov, Mikhail Andreevich, 469–71, 507

Sutyrin, Vladimir Andreevich, 119–21, 157, 181, 507

Suvorov, 297–98

Suvorov, Aleksandr Vasilievich, 148, 297–98, 507

Svetlov, Mikhail Arkadievich, 318, 354, 364, 463, 507

Sviatopolk-Mirsky, Prince. *See* Mirsky, Dmitry Petrovich

Sviderskiy, Aleksei Ivanovich, 53, 57, 104–5, 507

Svobodin, Nikolai Kapitonovich, 257, 507

"Swan Lake" (Shtein), 403, 422

Symbolism, 21, 394

Syrtsov, Sergei Ivanovich, 84, 507

Tagantsevsky, 304

Tairov, Aleksandr Yakovlevich, 96–97, 147, 193, 250–57, 507

The Taking of Velikoshumsk (Leonov), 383

Tal, Boris Markovich, 288, 507

"The Tale of the Unextinguished Moon" (Pilnyak), 89–91, 475n6

Tale of Tsar Saltan, 457

Tamarkin, E. M., 246, 507

Tarasenkov, Anatoly Kuzmich, 320, 507

Tarasov-Rodionov, Aleksander Ignatievich, 316, 318, 507

Tarasova, Alla Konstantinovna, 218, 507

Tarkhanov, Mikhail Mikhailovich, 218, 507

Tarlovsky, Mark Arievich, 362, 507

Teleshova, 219

Thälmann, Ernst, 311, 507

Theater journal, 470

Theater of Worker Youth (TRAM), 107, 256

Theaters. *See* Bolshoi Theater; Moscow Art Theater; and *specific theaters, plays and playwrights*

They Fought for the Homeland (Sholokhov), 393

"This Happened in Leningrad" (Chukovsky), 412

Tikhonov, Aleksandr Nikolaevich, 180, 181, 370–71, 373, 507

Tikhonov, Nikolai Semyonovich: and *Banner*, 379; biographical information on, 507; and Fedin, 390; and journals, 417–18, 423; and Organizing Committee of Writers Union, 154; and Serapion Brothers, 36; "Traits of the Soviet Man" by, 412; and writers' circles, 303; and Writers Union, 423, 425; and Zamyatin, 201

Timasheff, Nicholas S. (Nicholas Sergeevich), 464, 507

Timchenko, 342

Timofeev, Leonid Ivanovich, 379, 508

"To Advantage" (Platonov), 119–21

"To the Government of the USSR" (Bulgakov), 105

"To Whom Did Russia Sing Lullabies" (Selvinsky), 374, 375, 378, 384

Tolchenov, M. P., 379

Tolstoy, Aleksei Nikolaevich: award for, 433; biographical information on, 508; Ivanov on, 319; Nikulin on, 177; on Saltykov, 134–35; and Stalin, 434–36; on Stalin, 134; on World War II, 361; Yakovlev on, 36; and Zamyatin, 201

—works: *Difficult Years,* 434–35; *The Eagle and Its Mate,* 434; *Ivan the Terrible,* 432–34, 436
Tolstoy, Lev Nikolaevich, 100, 102, 211–12, 328, 508
Tomsky, Mikhail Pavlovich, 40, 78, 79, 96–97, 104, 508
Torture, 170, 340–41
Toward a History of Realism (Lifshits), 212
"Traits of the Soviet Man" (Tikhonov), 412
TRAM (Theater of Worker Youth), 107, 256
Translations and translators, 178, 264, 305, 360
Trauberg, Ilya Zakharovich, 255, 290–92, 508
Trauberg, Leonid Zakharovich, 448, 465–67, 508
Tregub, Semyon Adolfovich, 210, 508
Trenev, Konstantin Andreevich, 254–55, 355, 508
Tretiakov Gallery, 241–42
Trilogy About Maxim (Kozintsev and Trauberg), 465, 466
Troshchenko, E. D., 157, 316, 508
Trotsky, Lev Davidovich: and Babel, 309, 310; and Bedny, 68; biographical information on, 508; and Blok, 21; defeat of, ix, 5, 50; and Golovin, 228; and Gorky, 77–78; image of, in art, 301; and Inber, 317; *Literature and Revolution* by, xvi, 32–33; and Piatakov-Radek trial, 296; on proletariat, xv–xvi, 32–33; Raikh on, 329; and Selvinsky, 373; supporter of, 52; and writers and artists during NEP era, 33–35, 37–39, 41
Trotskyite-Zinovievite Center, 316–17
Tseitlin, M., 186, 508
Tselikovskaia, Liudmila Vasilievna, 444, 508
Tsenin, Sergei Sergeevich, 252, 508
Tsvetaeva, Marina Ivanovna, 371, 508
Tufanov, Aleksandr Vasilievich, 133, 476n19, 508
Turganov, Boris Alexandrovich, 305, 508
Turgenev, Ivan Sergeevich, 242, 406, 508
Tvardovsky, Aleksandr Trifonovich, 379, 508
Tveriak, Aleksei Artamonovich, 303–4, 508
26 Communards (Spiridonov), 80
"Two in the Steppe" (Kazakevich), 428
Tychina, Pavlo Grigorovych, 206, 207, 508
Tynyanov, Yury Nikolaevich, 135, 508

Ukraine, 61–68, 93–94, 104, 206, 207, 305, 361, 363, 383–84, 395, 467
Ukraine in the Flames (Dovzhenko), 383–84, 395
Ulianov, 73
The Unbowed (Gorbatov), 377, 383
Under Berlin's Lime Trees (Zoshchenko), 426
Union of Soviet Writers. *See* Writers Union
United States, 114, 354, 359–60, 457
University (Konovalov), 429
Unshlikht, Iosif Stanislavovich, 11–12, 508
Untimely Thoughts (Gorky), 76
Upit, Andrei Martynovich, 425, 508
Uritsky, Moisei Solomonovich, 18, 508
Ushakov, Nikolai Nikolaevich, 178, 508
Usievich, Elena Feliksovna, 186, 209, 211, 213–14, 376, 377, 477n2, 508
Utkin, Iosif Pavlovich, 318, 353, 364, 389–90, 508

Vagramov, Fyodor, 55
Vainer, L., 48
Vakhtangov, Evgeny Bagrationovich, 321, 509
Vakhtangov Theater, 271, 321
Vaks, B., 55, 509
Valevsky, 327
Valtsov, 264
Valve (Valbe), Boris Solomonovich, 354, 509
Vandurdursky, 315
VAPP (All-Union Association of Proletarian Writers), 40, 52, 150
Vardin, Illarion, 40, 509
Vareikis, Iosif Mikhailovich, 40, 45, 173, 187, 188, 509
Varshavsky, S. P., 404–5, 422, 509
Vasilevskaia, Vanda Lvovna, 383, 509
Vasiliev, Pavel Nikolaevich, 175, 185–87, 371, 509
Vasiliev, Sergei Dmitrievich, 290–92, 509
Vasilkovsky, G., 189
Vazha Pshavela, 323, 509
VChK (Cheka). *See* Cheka (VChK)
Veis, D. L., 19
Venclova, Antanas, 425, 509
Vengerova, Zinaida Afanasievna, 14, 509
Veresaev, Viktor Viktorovoch, 125, 509
Vershigora, Pyotr Petrovich, 457, 509
Vesely, Artem, 40, 82, 89, 509
Victory (Dovzhenko), 395

Vinogradov, Anatoly Kornelievich, 181, 509
Vinogradov, Viktor Vladimirovich, 333–35, 509
Vipper, 434
Virgin Soil Upturned (Sholokhov), 187, 189, 337
Virta, Nikolai Yevgenievich, 213, 225, 387, 389, 509
Vishnevsky, Vsevolod Vitalievich: and *Banner*, 379, 397; on Bedny's *Bogatyrs*, 255, 256; biographical information on, 509; creative leave for, 203, 205; and Eisenstein, 247; on Fedin, 390; on freedom of speech, 397–98; and Gorky, 176, 189, 314; Popkov on, 417; during post–World War II period, 413–15; and Stalin, 315; and Writers Union, 425
—works: *At the Walls of Leningrad*, 395; *An Optimistic Tragedy*, 252, 479n1
Vladykin, Grigory Ivanovich, 399, 400, 509
VOAPP (All-Union Association of Proletarian Writers Associations), 152
Voices of the Depths (Bill-Belotserkovsky), 58
Voitinskaia, Olga Sergeevna, 205–8, 509
VOKP (All-Russian Union of Peasant Writers), 150, 153
VOKS (All-Union Society for Cultural Relations with Abroad), 113, 115, 324
Volchek, Boris Izrailevich, 281, 509
The Volga Runs into the Caspian Sea (Pilnyak), 114
Volin, Boris, 95, 153, 154, 261, 509
Volkov, I. D., 385, 510
Volodarsky, V., 110, 510
Voloshin, Maximilian Aleksandrovich, 125, 510
Volter, A. A., 277
Voronsky, Aleksandr Konstantinovich, 34, 38–40, 52, 90–91, 156, 309, 480n5, 510
Voroshilov, Kliment Yefremovich: assassination attempt against, 317; and Bedny's *Bogatyrs*, 256; biographical information on, 510; and Bolshoi Theater, 29, 31; and Bulgakov's plays, 92, 104, 268–70; and censorship of theater productions, 268, 270, 271; and Erdman and Mass satires, 266–67; and Levidov's *Conspiracy of Equals*, 97; and Mikhailov's painting of Kirov's funeral, 277–78; and Pilnyak, 116; and Platonov's "To Advantage," 120; and Slavin's *Foreign Collegium*, 271; and Vinogradov, 334
Vorovsky, 14
Voznesensky, Nikolai Alekseevich, 196, 459, 510
VSP (All-Russian Union of Writers), 36, 37, 109, 150, 200
VSSP (All-Russian Union of Soviet Writers), 155
Vurgun, Samed, 234, 510
Vvedensky, Aleksandr Ivanovich, 133, 476n19, 510

Wages: of authors, 414; for film directors and camera operators, 281
War Communism (1917–1921), 3–4
We (Zamyatin), 111, 200
Western-bourgeois, 147
"Whiskers" (Maupassant), 360
A Window on the Village (Akulshin), 248, 479n13
"Without Mercy" (Bedny), 68–70, 72, 73
Woe from Wit (Griboedov), 479n11
Woe to Wit (Meyerhold), 248, 479n11
Workers Newspaper, 53
Working class. See Proletariat
World War II: Allies in, 354, 356, 358, 359–60, 361, 363, 364; censorship during, 360, 364–92, 397–98; Germany in, 349, 353, 354–55, 357, 359, 361–64, 373, 395; in literature, 394–97, 402–5, 412–13; nationalist propaganda during, 348–49, 352, 355; Nazi invasion of Czechoslovakia, 148; and routinization of terror, 348; Russia in, 354–59, 361–64, 373, 377, 378, 395; and Stalin, 373; writers' attitudes during, 352–64, 380–93; Zhdanovism after, 349–51, 364
Wrangel, Pyotr Nikolaevich, 98, 510
Writers. *See specific writers and playwrights*
Writers' Congress (1934), 139, 140, 143, 162–78, 182, 187, 272
Writers' Publishing House, 111
Writers Union: and anti-Semitism, 209, 468; and Bedny, 250, 259; budget of, 195, 196; and Eisenstein, 246; exclusions from, 185; and Fadeev, 142, 148, 155, 209, 372–73, 425; and Fedin, 390; Foreign Commission of, 191; founding of, xiii, 6, 52, 87, 139, 141, 143, 145, 152; and Gorky, 143–44, 154, 172–73, 195–

Writers Union (*continued*)
97; and journals, 406, 407, 411, 415, 416, 423; Kassil on, 391; leadership of, 20, 141–42, 148, 153–55, 172–73, 182, 188, 190, 199–200, 202, 208–9, 303, 372–73, 425; Lidin on, 387; and literary criticism, 400; Literary Institute of, 391; Nikitin's criticisms of, 202–5; NKVD report on, 302–4; Organizing Committee of, 87, 141–42, 153–55, 157–58, 160, 162, 165; Party members in, 207, 208; and Peredelkino writers' community, 321; proposed expulsion of Dairedzhiev and Altman from, 469–71; and RAPP, 142, 143, 144, 153, 172; removal of Stavsky from leadership of, 208–9; and secret police, 148; and Shaginyan, 280; Shcherbakov on, 197–200; and Socialist Realism, 139; and Stalin, 197–205, 208–9; status and privilege of members of, 161; and Stavsky, 142, 148, 155, 182, 197, 199–200, 202–5, 208–9, 246, 316; and training for writers, 196; and Trotskyite-Zinovievite Center, 316–17; and Vishnevsky on freedom of speech, 397–98; Voitinskaia's criticisms of, 205–8; during World War II, 361. *See also* Writers' Congress

Yagdfeld, Grigory Borisovich, 399, 410, 413, 422, 510
Yagoda, Genrikh Grigorievich, 88, 168, 305–7, 311–15, 477*n*1, 510
Yakovlev, Yakov Arkadievich, 30, 35–38, 267, 510
Yakubovsky, Pyotr Filippovich, 40, 510
Yanovsky, Yury Ivanovich, 428, 510
Yanshin, Mikhail Mikhailovich, 253, 269, 510
Yanson, Nikolai Mikhailovich, 476*n*9, 510
Yaroslavsky, Emelian Mikhailovich, 70, 72, 510
Yasensky, Bruno, 157, 188, 207, 312, 314, 315, 325–27, 510
Yashvili, Paolo (Pavel) Dzhibrazlovich, 207, 510
Yavich, Avgust Yefimovich, 125, 510
Years of Thunder (Aseev), 373
Yegolin, Aleksandr Mikhailovich, 369–70, 373, 389, 393–98, 402–6, 510
Yekelchik, Yury Izrailevich, 281, 510
Yenukidze, Avel Sofronovich, 25, 27, 28, 29, 154, 270–71, 511

Yermilov, Vladimir Vladimirovich, 157, 172, 198, 280, 383, 511
Yesenin, Sergei Alexandrovich, 36, 185, 328–29, 371, 511
Yevdokimov, 337, 338–39, 342, 343
Yezhov, Nikolai Ivanovich: and Babel, 310–11; biographical information on, 511; and Brik's petition on Mayakovsky, 288; and Mandelshtam, 331–32; and Moscow Art Theater, 217–20; and Raikh, 330; and Trotskyite-Zinovievite Center, 316–17; and Veshensk web, 342; and writers in 1930s, 319–21; and Writers Union, 202–5
Young Guard (Fadeev), 393
Young Guard/molodaia guardia journal, 89, 126, 262
Yudin, Pavel Fedorovich, 170, 176, 186–88, 201, 311–13, 325–27, 511
Yunovich, M. M., 369, 375, 511
Yuon, Konstantin Fyodorovich, 277, 511
Yutkevich, Sergei Iosifovich, 281, 467, 511
Yuzovsky, Iosif Ilyich, 376–77, 470, 511

Zabolotsky, Nikolai Alekseevich, 209, 303, 511
Zakharchenko, Vasily Dmitrievich, 394, 511
Zakharov, Vladimir Grigorievich, 462, 511
Zakovsky, 302–4
Zamoisky, Pyotr Ivanovich, 153, 154, 511
Zamyatin, Yevgeny Ivanovich, 109–13, 135, 150, 200, 201, 511
Zaporozhye Cossacks, 444
Zarkhi, Natan Abramovich, 465, 511
Zarudin, Nikolai Nikolaevich, 316, 511
Zaslavsky, David Iosifovich, 153, 511
Zaslonov, 457
Zazubrin, Vladimir Yakovlevich, 179, 181, 321, 511
Zemlia i Fabrika (Land and Factory) publishing house, 111, 305
Zenkevich, P., 178, 233
Zharov, Aleksandr Alekseevich, 171, 175, 178, 444, 511
Zhdanov, Andrei Aleksandrovich: and Akhmatova, 365, 424; biographical information on, 511; and Central Committee, 148, 349; death of, 349, 401; and Eisenstein's *Ivan the Terrible*, 440–45; and films, 272–75; on journals, 399–406, 408, 410, 420, 424; and literary criticism, 398–402; and *Literary Critic*

journal, 210–15; NKVD report on writers to, 302–4; and opera, 459–62; and press and publishing houses, 141; and Stalin, 424; status of, in post–World War II period, 401; and Vinogradov, 334; and Writers' Congress (1934), 139, 166–67, 172, 176, 272; and writers during World War II, 380–92; and Writers Union, 202–8; and Yagoda, 311; and Zoshchenko, 368–69, 414–15, 420, 424, 427

Zhdanovism: and censorship, 351, 364, 398–425; Central Committee Zhdanov resolutions, 349–51; Chukovsky on, 392; and journals, 398–425; and Stalin's involvement with films, 447–58; Zhdanov era versus, 349

Zhelyabov, Andrei, 73, 296, 511

Zhiga, Ivan Fedorovich, 154, 511

Zhivotova, 221

Zhukovsky, G. V., 357, 478n2

Zinger, A. B., 169

Zinoviev, Grigory Yevseevich, 5, 21, 34, 146, 311, 511–12

Zlatogorov, S. I., 19

Zlatogorova, Bronislava Yakovlevna, 227, 512

Zoika's Apartment (Bulgakov), 268

Zonin, A. I., 469, 512

Zorin, O., 78

Zoshchenko, Mikhail Mikhailovich: biographical information on, 512; censorship and criticism of generally, 351, 380, 385, 388, 389, 390, 394, 411; Erlikh on, 387; journals publishing works by, 398; and Orgburo, 421, 423, 424; Popkov on, 416; on post–World War II period, 392; and Saltykov-Shchedrin, 135; on satire, 425–26; and Stalin, 411–12, 420, 425–27; students' approval of, 391; during World War II, 412, 421; Yakovlev on, 36

—works: "Adventures of an Ape," 401–4, 413, 415, 421, 426–27; *Before Sunrise,* 366–75, 381, 421, 426; "Cabbage Soup," 381; "Journey to Olympus," 408–9; "Strategic Assignment," 381; *Under Berlin's Lime Trees,* 426

Zweig, Stefan, 114, 512

BOOKS IN THE ANNALS OF COMMUNISM SERIES

The Diary of Georgi Dimitrov, 1933–1949, introduced and edited by Ivo Banac

Dimitrov and Stalin, 1934–1943: Letters from the Soviet Archives, edited by Alexander Dallin and Fridrikh I. Firsov

Enemies Within the Gates? The Comintern and the Stalinist Repression, 1934–1939, by William J. Chase

The Fall of the Romanovs: Political Dreams and Personal Struggles in a Time of Revolution, by Mark D. Steinberg and Vladimir M. Khrustalëv

The History of the Gulag: From Collectivization to the Great Terror, by Oleg V. Khlevniuk

The KGB File of Andrei Sakharov, edited by Joshua Rubenstein and Alexander Gribanov

The Last Diary of Tsaritsa Alexandra, introduction by Robert K. Massie; edited by Vladimir A. Kozlov and Vladimir M. Khrustalëv

The Road to Terror: Stalin and the Self-Destruction of the Bolsheviks, 1932–1939, by J. Arch Getty and Oleg V. Naumov

The Secret World of American Communism, by Harvey Klehr, John Earl Haynes, and Fridrikh I. Firsov

Soviet Culture and Power, by Katerina Clark and Evgeny Dobrenko, with Andrei Artizov and Oleg Naumov

The Soviet World of American Communism, by Harvey Klehr, John Earl Haynes, and Kyrill M. Anderson

Spain Betrayed: The Soviet Union in the Spanish Civil War, edited by Ronald Radosh, Mary R. Habeck, and G. N. Sevostianov

Stalinism as a Way of Life: A Narrative in Documents, edited by Lewis Siegelbaum and Andrei K. Sokolov

The Stalin-Kaganovich Correspondence, 1931–36, compiled and edited by R. W. Davies, Oleg V. Khlevniuk, E. A. Rees, Liudmila P. Kosheleva, and Larisa A. Rogovaya

Stalin's Letters to Molotov, 1925–1936, edited by Lars T. Lih, Oleg V. Naumov, and Oleg V. Khlevniuk

Stalin's Secret Pogrom: The Postwar Inquisition of the Soviet Jewish Anti-Fascist Committee, edited by Joshua Rubenstein and Vladimir P. Naumov

The Unknown Lenin: From the Secret Archive, edited by Richard Pipes

Voices of Revolution, 1917, by Mark D. Steinberg

The War Against the Peasantry, 1927–1930, edited by Lynne Viola, V. P. Danilov, N. A. Ivnitskii, and Denis Kozlov

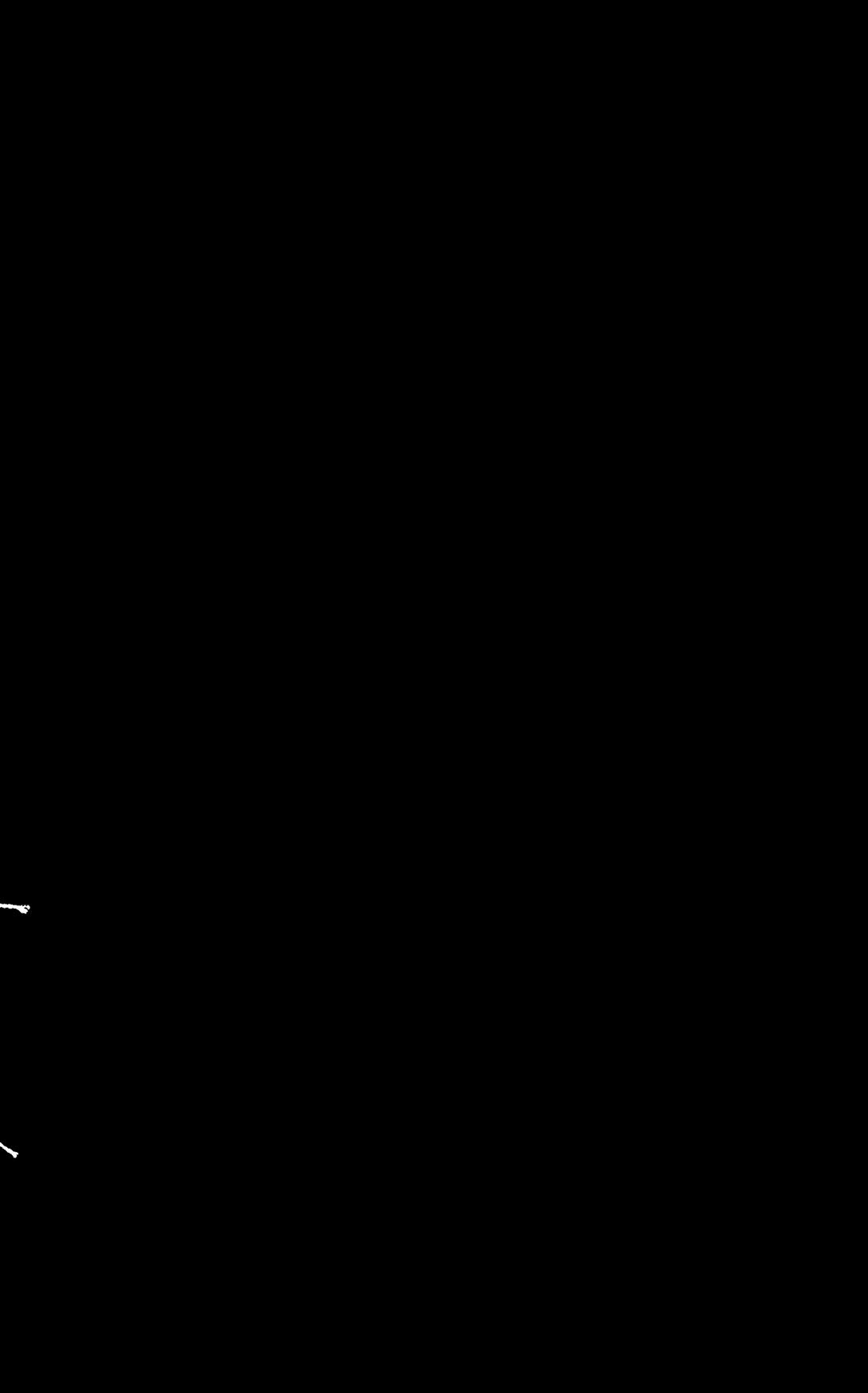

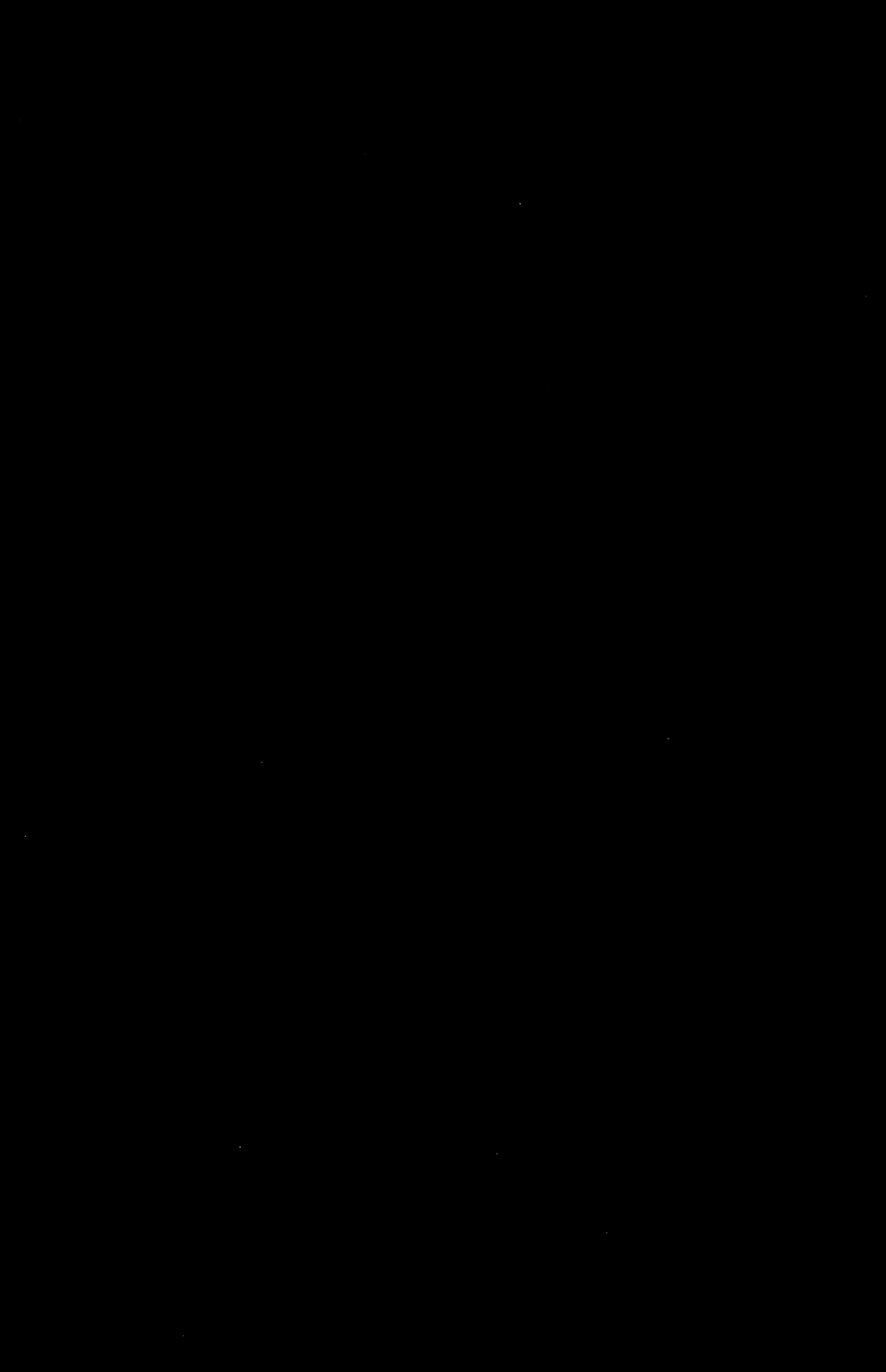